ASVAB® 2015
STRATEGIES, PRACTICE & REVIEW

PUBLISHING

New York

Special thanks to the team that made this book possible: Kim Bowers, Matt Belinkie, Joel Boyce, Matt Burke, Laura Christensen, Elisa Davis, Lola Disparte, Paula Fleming, Joanna Graham, Allison Harm, Craig Harman, Jack Hayes, Kellen Knowles, Brad Labez-Tapang, Catherine Myers, M. Brigid O'Toole-Ryan, Rachel Pearsall, Elijah Schwartz, Bob Verini, Lee Weiss, and many others.

ASVAB® is a registered trademark of the U.S. Department of Defense, which neither sponsors nor endorses this product.

This publication is designed to provide accurate and authoritative information in regard to the subject matter covered. It is sold with the understanding that the publisher is not engaged in rendering legal, accounting, or other professional service. If legal advice or other expert assistance is required, the services of a competent professional should be sought.

Published by Kaplan Publishing, a division of Kaplan, Inc.
395 Hudson Street
New York, NY 10014

Printed in the United States of America

10 9 8 7 6 5 4 3 2 1

ISBN: 978-1-61865-756-5

Kaplan Publishing books are available at special quantity discounts to use for sales promotions, employee premiums, or educational purposes. For more information or to purchase books, please call the Simon & Schuster special sales department at 866-506-1949.

Foreword by Jack Hayes, Former LT., U.S. Navy xiii

Welcome to Your ASVAB Studies xv

   Your Kaplan Resources xv

   Three Levels of Study xvi

   Getting Started xvi

   Managing Stress xviii

   Final Preparations for Test Day xix

   Good Luck! xx

Chapter 1: About the ASVAB 1

   What is the ASVAB? 1

      What does the ASVAB test? 1

   What is the AFQT? 2

      Your AFQT score 3

   AFQT Scores for Different Branches of the Military 3

   ASVAB Logistics 4

      Registering for and taking the ASVAB 4

      How to read your ASVAB Scores 4

      Different versions of the ASVAB 4

      The paper and pencil test vs. the CAT 5

   Kaplan's ASVAB Strategies 6

      CAT-ASVAB strategies 6

      Getting ready for the ASVAB 7

Chapter 2: ASVAB Diagnostic Tests 9

About the Diagnostic Tests 9

ASVAB Diagnostic Test 13

    Part 1: General Science (GS) 13

    Part 2: Arithmetic Reasoning (AR) 16

    Part 3: Word Knowledge (WK) 19

    Part 4: Paragraph Comprehension (PC) 22

    Part 5: Mathematics Knowledge (MK) 25

    Part 6: Electronics Information (EI) 28

    Part 7: Auto and Shop Information (AS) 31

    Part 8: Mechanical Comprehension (MC) 34

    Part 9: Assembling Objects (AO) 38

ASVAB Diagnostic Test Answers and Explanations 44

Chapter 3: Word Knowledge 69

Know What to Expect 69

The Kaplan Method for Word Knowledge Questions 70

Decoding Strategies for Guessing a Word's Meaning 72

    Breaking Words Apart 72

    Prefixes 73

    Suffixes 75

    Greek and Latin Word Roots 77

    Practice with Word Roots 78

    Using Positive or Negative Charge 79

    Using Real-World Context to Guess at a Word's Meaning 80

Making the Most of Context 81

Eliminating Answer Choices Based on Logic 86

Strategies for Building Your Vocabulary 88

Word Knowledge Practice Questions 90

    Answers and Explanations 92

    Review and Reflect 93

Chapter 4: Paragraph Comprehension **95**

Know What to Expect **95**

The Kaplan Method for Paragraph Comprehension Questions **95**

Step 1: Read the Question Stem to Identify Your Task 96

Step 2: Read the Passage Strategically 96

Step 3: Make a Prediction 96

Step 4: Find the Correct Answer 96

Conquering Paragraph Comprehension Questions **97**

Global Questions 97

Detail Questions... 100

Inference Questions.. 102

Vocabulary-in-Context Questions 104

Paragraph Comprehension Practice Questions **107**

Answers and Explanations 110

Review and Reflect... 112

Chapter 5: Math Strategies for the ASVAB **113**

Know What to Expect **113**

The Kaplan Method for ASVAB Math **114**

Strategies for Solving Math Problems **115**

Backsolving 116

Picking Numbers 118

Strategic Guessing Using Logic 122

Combination of Approaches 123

Math Strategies for the ASVAB Practice Questions **125**

Answers and Explanations 126

Review and Reflect... 126

Chapter 6: Arithmetic Reasoning **127**

Know What to Expect **127**

Arithmetic Review **128**

Arithmetic Definitions 128

Number Properties... 129

Absolute Value... 131

Factors, Multiples, and Prime Numbers 132

Divisibility... 135

Fractions and Decimals 136

Decimal Division 139

Exponents and Radicals 141

Factorials 146

Applied Arithmetic Review 147

The Order of Operations 147

Distributive and Commutative Properties 148

Ratios, Proportions, and Rates 150

Combined Work 155

Percent Problems 156

Statistical Terms 159

Sequences 160

Probability 161

Arithmetic Word Problems 163

Translation 164

Word Problems with Formulas 164

Arithmetic Reasoning Practice Questions 166

Answers and Explanations 167

Review and Reflect 168

Chapter 7: Mathematics Knowledge 169

Know What to Expect 169

Algebra Review 169

Terms and Expressions 170

Equations with One Variable 173

Equations with Two Variables 175

Systems of Equations 176

Quadratic Equations with Variables 179

Inequalities 180

Geometry Review 182

Lines and Angles 182

Polygons 185

Circles 191

Solid Geometry 193

Combined Figures 195

Coordinate Geometry 195

Mathematics Knowledge Practice Questions **199**

   Answers and Explanations 200

   Review and Reflect. 201

Chapter 8: Conquering the Technical Subtests **203**

  The Kaplan Method for ASVAB Technical Subtest Questions **203**

   Step 1: Identify What You Are Being Asked for 204

   Step 2: Simplify or Solve 204

   Step 3: Make a Prediction 205

   Step 4: Evaluate the Choices Strategically. 205

   Bringing It All Together. 205

   Final Thought Before You Dive In 206

Chapter 9: General Science **207**

  Know What to Expect **207**

  PART I: LIFE SCIENCE **207**

  Nutrition and Health **207**

  Human Body Systems and Diseases **210**

   The Skeleton and Muscles. 210

   The Respiratory System 211

   Blood and the Circulatory System. 212

   The Digestive and Excretory Systems 214

   The Nervous System. 216

   The Reproductive System 217

   Human Pathogens 218

  Genetics **219**

  Cellular Structures and Functions **221**

  Ecology. **224**

  The Classification of Living Things **226**

  Life Science Practice Questions **229**

   Answers and Explanations 230

  PART II: EARTH AND SPACE SCIENCE **231**

  Geology **231**

   Structure of Earth. 231

   Plate Tectonics 232

Types of Rocks 232

Geologic Time Scale. 233

Cycles in Earth Science. 233

Meteorology 236

Earth's Atmosphere 236

Fronts 237

Clouds. 238

Our Solar System 239

The Sun. 239

The Planets and Other Phenomena 239

Earth and Space Science Practice Questions. 243

Answers and Explanations 244

PART III: PHYSICAL SCIENCE 245

Measurement. 245

Physics. 248

Motion 248

Forces and Energy 250

Newton's Laws 252

Energy. 254

Sound Waves 254

The Electromagnetic Spectrum 254

Optics 255

Heat. 257

Magnetism 258

Chemistry. 259

Elements and the Periodic Table. 259

Compounds 263

Acids and Bases. 263

Physical Change 264

Chemical Change. 265

Physical Science Practice Questions 267

Answers and Explanations 268

Review and Reflect 268

Chapter 10: Electronics Information **269**

Know What to Expect **269**

Electron Flow Theory **269**

    Current 270

    Voltage 271

    Resistance 271

    Exceptions and Additional Notes 272

Circuits **274**

    Ohm's Law 275

    Series Circuits. 276

    Parallel Circuits 277

    Series-Parallel Circuits. 279

    Electrical Power 280

    Standard Electrical Units and the Metric System. 281

Structure of Electrical and Electronic Systems **282**

    AC *vs.* DC. 282

    Ground 283

    Important Electric and Electronic Components 283

    Semiconductors 288

    Diodes. 288

    Transistors 289

Electricity and Magnetism **293**

    Inductors. 293

    Transformers. 294

    Basic Electrical Motors and Generators 294

Electronics Information Practice Questions **296**

    Answers and Explanations 298

    Review and Reflect. 299

Chapter 11: Automotive Information **301**

Know What to Expect **301**

What's in This Chapter **301**

Engine Systems **302**

    Basic Engine Theory. 302

    Cooling System. 308

    Lubrication System 311

Combustion Systems 313

   Fuel System 313

   Ignition System 315

   Exhaust Systems 317

Electrical and Control Systems 320

   Electrical System 320

   Computer System 321

Chassis Systems 323

   Drive Train System 323

   Suspension and Steering System 326

   Brake System 328

Automotive Information Practice Questions 331

   Answers and Explanations 333

   Review and Reflect 334

Chapter 12: Shop Information 335

Know What to Expect 335

Measuring Tools 335

   Tape Measures and Steel Rules 335

   Micrometers 336

   Calipers 337

   Spirit Levels 338

   Steel Squares 339

Striking Tools 340

   Hammers 340

   Nails 342

   Rivets 342

   Chisels, Punches, and Drifts 343

Turning Tools 344

   Screwdrivers 345

   Wrenches 345

   Sockets 346

   Nuts and Bolts 348

Fastening Tools 351

   Ring Fasteners 351

   Soldering Tools 352

   Welding Tools 353

Gripping Tools **355**

   Pliers 355

   Clamps 358

   Vises 358

Cutting Tools **359**

   Manual (Hand) Saws 359

   Powered Saws 361

   Drilling and Boring Tools 362

Finishing Tools **364**

   Planes 364

   Wood Chisels 365

   Files and Rasps 365

Shop Information Practice Questions **367**

   Answers and Explanations 369

   Review and Reflect 370

Chapter 13: Mechanical Comprehension **371**

Know What to Expect **371**

A Review of the Physics of Mechanical Devices **371**

   Mass and Force 372

   Newton's Laws of Motion 372

Common Types of Forces **374**

   Gravity and Weight 374

   Friction 375

   Tension 378

   Hydraulic Pressure 380

   Torque 381

Energy, Work, and Power **383**

   Energy 384

   Work 387

   Power 388

Simple Machines **389**

   Inclined Plane 389

   Wedge 390

Levers 391

Pulleys 392

Block and Tackle. 393

Wheel and Axle 393

Gears and Gear Ratios. 394

Mechanical Comprehension Practice Questions **395**

Answers and Explanations 397

Review and Reflect 398

Chapter 14: Assembling Objects **399**

Know What to Expect **399**

Jigsaw-Puzzle-Type Problems **400**

Connector-Type Problems **403**

Assembling Objects Practice Questions **407**

Answers and Explanations 409

Review and Reflect. 410

Chapter 15: ASVAB Practice Tests **411**

ASVAB Practice Test A **415**

ASVAB Practice Test A Answers and Explanations **442**

ASVAB Practice Test B **463**

ASVAB Practice Test B Answers and Explanations **493**

Appendix: Word Parts. **517**

Part I: Prefixes. **518**

Part II: Suffixes **526**

Part III: Word Roots. **531**

Index **549**

ASVAB Verbal Strategy Sheet

ASVAB Math Strategy Sheet

FOREWORD

Congratulations on taking an important step toward enlisting in one of the United States Armed Services! The Air Force, Army, Coast Guard, Marines, Navy, and National Guard all emphasize the importance of mission preparedness. By obtaining this Kaplan ASVAB book, you are on your way toward being well prepared to take the ASVAB test that is a prerequisite for enlisting in one of the services. The United States Military Entrance Processing Command administers the ASVAB for all the services. That organization calls the enlistment process "Freedom's Front Door."

The Armed Services give our marines, sailors, soldiers, guardsmen and women, and airmen and women the opportunity to grow personally and professionally, to assume major responsibilities, and to work in integrated teams to achieve their goals. We need bright, talented young men and women to serve our country, and the ASVAB is one of the factors used by the military to enlist the most qualified applicants. Being selected for the military is very competitive; not only do you have to meet certain threshold standards, including ASVAB scores, but you are also competing with thousands of other applicants for these coveted openings.

My efforts as a member of the team that prepared this edition of the Kaplan ASVAB book brought back many memories of my four and a half years as a proud member of the U.S. Navy. When I was in the engineering department on a destroyer, an unusual combination of circumstances resulted in our ship being about 40 percent below the proper staffing level just three months before we were scheduled for a major deployment. Our crew had to be augmented quickly but, as the saying goes, it takes three years to get three years' experience. Consequently, sailors just graduating from advanced training ("A School" in Navy parlance) were slotted into positions on our ship normally staffed by third-class petty officers with two or so years under their belts and sometimes even second-class petty officers who might have been in their second term of enlistment.

Fortunately, almost all of our new crew members were well suited for their shipboard duties thanks, in part, to the version of the ASVAB that was being used at that time. Consequently, they learned quickly and assumed their responsibilities well. During their first full year on board, we were deployed 290 days and we never missed a beat. In fact, many of us were awarded the Navy Commendation Medal for re-staffing so successfully that we even covered a couple of operational commitments for other ships.

Needless to say, my experience convinced me that the process of selecting the right people for the right jobs was very well executed. I made many lifetime friendships in the Navy, and I have stayed in touch with some of my shipmates since I left. Some went on to very successful careers in the Navy. Several others used the G.I. Bill to help further their education and went on to civilian careers.

Enough of my reminiscing! I mention my experiences to encourage you to get the most that you can from this Kaplan ASVAB book so that you score up to your maximum potential and are selected for the service and occupational specialty that you want and that will enable you to excel.

Kaplan is the premier test preparation company in the world, and we have applied our expertise and experience to this new edition. Because practice is so important to your preparation, we have included three full-length practice ASVAB tests in this book and scores of practice problems and explanations. Your purchase of this book will also give you access to Kaplan's online resources, including a computer-based ASVAB test. When you complete the online test, your online SmartReports will give you detailed performance breakdowns by skill or concept.

You have chosen the right tool to help you score as highly as possible on the ASVAB; the rest is up to you. Merely reading the book might help some, but the real payoff will come from studying the material, taking the practice assessments, and focusing on the areas where you can demonstrate the most improvement. Remember, your hard work will pay off with rewards on Test Day and beyond! I wish you the best as you begin your journey and hope that you find your time in the military as rewarding as I did.

Jack Hayes

Former LT., USN (and also a former recruiter)

WELCOME TO YOUR ASVAB STUDIES!

Thank you for choosing Kaplan to help you study for the ASVAB! We are honored to be part of your preparation for a military career. Your Kaplan book and Online Center contain all the resources you need to succeed on Test Day and earn your place in a branch of the armed services.

YOUR KAPLAN RESOURCES

Your Kaplan book contains:

- a full-length diagnostic test
- tools to help you plan your studies
- chapters that cover each of the ASVAB subject tests, including:
  - Kaplan Methods for every question type
  - worked examples that display the expert approach
  - practice questions with explanations
- two full-length practice tests

Your Kaplan Online Center offers:

- one online full-length practice test, to prepare you for Test Day
- SmartReports®, our exclusive diagnostic software, which keeps track of your strengths and areas of opportunity

Between the Kaplan book and Online Center, you have over 500 practice items at your disposal, as well as multiple tools to help personalize your studies to your individual needs. In other words, you've already purchased the only resource you'll need to achieve your goals on the ASVAB.

THREE LEVELS OF STUDY

Perhaps you are already pretty good at the ASVAB, but you need to brush up on specific skills or to review all of the skills quickly before Test Day. Or perhaps you feel moderately confident about the ASVAB but you need some significant review on some or all of the topics. Or perhaps, like many people, you have forgotten much of what you learned in high school and you need a comprehensive review.

Kaplan's book and online resources will help you prepare for the ASVAB regardless of which of those groups you fall into. The chart below outlines the different approaches you might take depending on your needs. Of course, your individual situation may vary; these are simply broad guidelines.

If you need a quick brush-up or light overall review ...	If you need a moderate review of some or all of the topics ...	If you need to (re)learn many of the skills from scratch ...
Start by devoting one week to each of the subject tests. During each of those weeks, read the appropriate chapter and do the practice items in the book.	Use the results from your diagnostic to identify your areas of greatest need. Start by devoting two weeks to each of those subject tests. During each of those weeks, read the appropriate chapter and do the practice items in the book.	Give yourself plenty of time to work through this book, chapter by chapter. Periodically review the earlier chapters so that those skills do not rust.
After you've completed your comprehensive review, take a full-length test in the book or online. If you haven't seen significant improvement, continue to work on the areas you find most challenging. Take another full-length test every week or two, depending on your test date.	After you've done so, take a full-length test in the book or online to gauge your progress. Continue to study and take a full-length test every week or two, depending on your Test Day. In the last few weeks before Test Day, give a week or several days to each of the subtests on which you were already strong.	Don't take many full-length tests until you've reviewed most of the subject tests. In the last few weeks before Test Day, take a full-length practice test (either in the book or online) once a week or once every two weeks, depending on your test date.

GETTING STARTED

HOW TO GET STARTED:

1. Register your Kaplan Online Center.
2. Take the diagnostic test in your Kaplan book.
3. Enter your diagnostic test answers online.
4. Contact a recruiter and do some research about your desired military career.
5. Learn, practice, review.
6. Take full-length practice tests in your Kaplan book and in your Online Center.

Register your Kaplan Online Center

To obtain access to your Kaplan Online Center, visit **http://kaptest.com/booksonline**. Create your account by choosing "ASVAB" and answering the question or questions that appear.

Once you have created your username and password, log into your resources at **www.kaptest.com**. Click "log in" at the top of the page and enter your username and password. Click on your ASVAB Online Center to see your resources.

Take the diagnostic test in your Kaplan book

Chapter 2 of this book offers a full-length diagnostic test. As a first step in your studies, set aside about three uninterrupted hours when you can take the diagnostic test. Work through the subject tests in the order they're presented, with one break at most.

Enter your diagnostic test answers online

After you've taken the complete diagnostic test, check your answers using the explanations that appear immediately after the tests. Then go to the "Diagnostic Test" portion of your online resources in order to enter your answers. You'll receive detailed feedback about your diagnostic test, broken down not just by subject test but also by topic and/or question type within each subtest.

Also, as you're checking your answers, don't just check to see if you got the question right or not. Rather, read the explanations for all the questions. That's because you can learn a great deal from reviewing questions you've already done, even if you got those questions right. As you review your performance on the diagnostic, really think about why the right answers are right, why the wrong answers are wrong, and what drew you to the answer you chose.

Contact a recruiter and do some research

You're going to want to set some goals regarding your ASVAB score, but different enlistees will have different priorities in studying for the ASVAB, depending on their career aspirations. For example, a test taker who wants to go into a technical career (such as equipment or computer technician) will likely need high scores in Word Knowledge, Paragraph Comprehension, Mathematics Knowledge, Arithmetic Reasoning, General Science, and Mechanical Comprehension. However, a test-taker who wants to go into a career repairing structures or vehicles should likely emphasize Auto Information and Shop Information over General Science.

Your recruiter is the best source of information about careers in the military and the scores you will need to earn to be competitive for those careers. Use information from your recruiter as well as information available on the various branches' websites to inform your ASVAB score goals.

Learn, practice, review

Once you have taken your diagnostic and established some goals regarding your ASVAB score, you're ready to get down to serious studying. Effective studying has three phases: learn, practice, review.

Learn: Each subject test on the ASVAB has its own chapter in this book. Read these chapters carefully, and pay particular attention to these features:

- Concepts are introduced with **learning objectives**. Use these learning objectives as a checklist of skills, to keep track of which you have mastered and which you need to work on more.
- **Key terms** you'll need to understand are introduced in bold type.
- Important strategies, takeaways, and shortcuts are highlighted in **gray boxes** sprinkled throughout the book.
- **Worked examples** appear throughout the book: each one shows, step-by-step, how an expert test taker would approach ASVAB questions.

Practice: Practice items are sprinkled throughout each chapter. Do each one as you come to it, and then carefully review the explanation that follows. Moreover, each chapter ends with a practice set. Don't time yourself on these practice questions. It's more important to really understand how the questions work; you can work on timing later.

When you do these practice sets, don't just tally up how many you got right. Rather ...

Review: Always review the explanation for every practice problem. Think about why the right answer is right and why the wrong answer is wrong. If you answered the question incorrectly, think carefully about where your thinking went astray and use that to inform your next steps. (For example, in an algebra problem, perhaps you understood the underlying concept but you made a simple addition error. In that case, the remedy would not be to study more algebra; rather, the remedy would be to practice adding and subtracting quickly while avoiding errors.) If you answered the question correctly, ask yourself if you got it right for the right reasons, and if you could have arrived at the same answer more efficiently.

Repeat this process every time you take a full-length test. Review all the answers and explanations for every item in the test, as well as thinking about how you performed overall.

Take full-length practice tests

Once you have learned, practiced, and reviewed all of the test concepts, use the full-length tests available in your book and Online Center. Taking a full-length test helps you in four ways:

- It reinforces the skills and strategies you've learned.
- It helps you work on timing.
- It gives you a sense of how you're doing on the various topics and what you need to work on more.
- It helps you learn to cope with test fatigue.

Now, you'll notice that one item *not* on that list is "helping you learn concepts." You don't learn how to approach questions correctly by taking a full-length test: that learning should be done in an untimed fashion and accompanied by deep thinking, as described above. That's why we don't recommend that you start your studies by taking a bunch of full-length tests. However, the last few weeks before Test Day are a perfect time to take full-length tests.

Your Kaplan book has two full-length practice tests in the back. These follow the ASVAB's paper and pencil format. You also have an additional practice test in your Online Center. This is a computer-based test that will help you get used to testing using a computer under the time constraints used by the CAT-ASVAB. While the computer-based test in your online account is not adaptive, its structure does allow you to prepare for the CAT-ASVAB's format and content.

MANAGING STRESS

You have a lot riding on the ASVAB. However, you're also doing the work you need to do to reach your goals. Unfortunately, though, simply knowing that you're working hard won't make your test anxiety go away. Thus, here are some stress-management tips from our long experience of helping students prepare for standardized tests.

Clock in and out: Once you've set up a study schedule for yourself, treat it like a job. That is, imagine clocking yourself in and out of ASVAB studies according to that schedule. Do your best to stick to stick to your schedule, and when you're not "clocked in," don't let yourself think about the ASVAB. That will help you release your stress about the test in between study sessions.

Don't punish yourself: If you get tired or overwhelmed or discouraged when studying, don't respond by pushing yourself harder. Rather, step away and engage in a relaxing activity like going for a walk, watching a movie, or playing with your cat or dog. Then, when you're ready, return to your studies with fresh eyes.

Breathe: Remember to breathe into your stomach. That forces some of the muscles that tense up when you're stressed to relax.

Set small, manageable goals: Each week, set manageable goals related to your ASVAB progress, and reward yourself when you've achieved them. Examples of small goals might be:

- This week, memorize and practice Kaplan Method for Assembling Objects questions until I no longer have to think about what the steps of the method are.
- This week, use 40 math questions, and practice choosing a strategy for solving each (such as Backsolving, Picking Numbers [covered in chapter 5], estimating, straight-up math).
- This week, review all Paragraph Comprehension question types until I can identify each question's type and the appropriate strategy.

Keep yourself healthy: Poor health, fatigue, and isolation make it harder to cope with stress and anxiety. Get on a regular sleep schedule as much as possible during your studies, eat well, continue to exercise, and spend time with those you care about. Also, don't fuel your studies with caffeine and sugar. Those substances may make you feel alert, but they can also damage focus.

Keep the right mindset: Most importantly, keep telling yourself that you *can* do this. Don't fall into the trap of thinking that you're not "allowed" to feel confident yet. That's a self-punishing attitude that will only hurt you. Rather, remember that confidence breeds success. So let yourself be confident about your abilities. You're obviously ambitious and intelligent, so walk into the ASVAB knowing that about yourself.

If you get discouraged, make a list: If you ever start to wonder if you'll ever reach your ASVAB goals, stop what you're doing and make a list of everything you're good at. List *every specific skill* that you are bringing to the ASVAB. Examples of specific skills might include:

- finding the main point of a paragraph
- using suffixes to tell whether a vocabulary word is a noun, verb, or adjective
- identifying what a math question is asking for
- factoring a quadratic equation
- identifying whether a circuit is built in series or in parallel
- identifying types of hammers

Post that list of things you're good at somewhere you'll see it every day, and add to it as you continue to study. We at Kaplan recommend this because many people focus too heavily on their weaknesses while preparing for a standardized test. But if you only focus on your weaknesses, you aren't seeing an objective picture. There *are* ASVAB skills you're good at. Keep that in mind and focus on building on those strengths.

FINAL PREPARATIONS FOR TEST DAY

In the last few weeks before Test Day, do a comprehensive review of all ASVAB topics. Pay particular attention to the subject tests that are most important to your preferred career(s) and to the four subject tests that are most important for enlistment. (Those are Mathematics Knowledge, Arithmetic Reasoning, Paragraph Comprehension, and Word Knowledge; see chapter 1 for more information.) Take a full-length test once or twice a week, and use the results of those full-lengths to inform your review.

Be sure to contact your recruiter to find out more about what to expect from Test Day—what you should bring with you, when you can expect your scores (if you're taking the paper version of the ASVAB), and other specifics.

In the Week Before Test Day

Your activities in the last week before Test Day should include:

Rest: Make sure you're on a regular sleep schedule.

Rehearse: Find out where your testing center is located and consider doing a "dry run." That is, drive or commute to the testing center around the same time of day as your testing appointment. You don't want to be surprised by traffic or road construction on Test Day.

Review: Do a very brief, high-level review. In other words, flip through the lessons and rework a few practice problems here and there to reinforce all of the good habits you've developed in your preparation. (Redoing practice problems you've already done is fine: you can actually learn a lot that way about how to approach those types of questions more efficiently in the future.)

Stop: Two days before the test, stop studying. No studying at all: you're not likely to learn anything new in those two days, and you'll get a lot more out of walking into the test feeling rested.

Relax: The evening before the test, do something fun but not crazy or tiring. Maybe you could have a nice dinner (without alcohol), watch a movie, or do something else relaxing.

Go to bed at your usual time the night before the exam.

On Test Day Itself

On the day of the test, be sure to follow the guidance below:

Warm up: Before you take the test, do an ASVAB warm-up. This can help your brain get ready to function at its best. You probably can't take any practice materials into the testing center, but you can do a few easy practice problems at home or in the car before you go into the testing center.

Don't let nerves derail you: If you feel nervous while taking the test, remember to breathe deeply into your stomach. Take a few deep breaths and focus your eyes on something other than the computer screen or test booklet for a moment.

Keep moving: Don't let yourself get bogged down on any one question. If you're taking the paper version, you can come back to questions that you weren't sure about, so skip questions whenever they threaten to slow you down or to steal time from the other questions. If you're taking the CAT-ASVAB, you can't return to previous questions, so you will have to decide to make a guess whenever a question is threatening to take too much time.

Don't assess yourself: This is very important. As you're testing, don't let yourself stop and think about how you *feel* you're doing. Taking a standardized test hardly ever *feels* good. Your own impressions of how it's going are totally unreliable. So, instead of focusing on that, remind yourself that you're prepared and that you are going to succeed, even if you feel discouraged as the test is underway.

After the test, celebrate!

You've prepared, practiced, and performed like a champion. Now that the test is over, it's time to congratulate yourself on a job well done. Celebrate responsibly with friends and family, and enjoy the rest of your day, knowing you just took an important step toward reaching your goals.

GOOD LUCK!

Everyone at Kaplan wishes you the very best in your studies, on the ASVAB, and in your military career. We're rooting for you!

ABOUT THE ASVAB

WHAT IS THE ASVAB?

The ASVAB (Armed Services Vocational Aptitude Battery) is the most widely used multiple-aptitude test battery in the world. It measures a test taker's suitability to enlist in the Unites States Armed Forces and assesses his or her abilities to be trained in specific civilian or military jobs.

When you take the ASVAB officially, you will be given either a paper and pencil version of the test or a computer version (also referred to as a Computer Adaptive Test ASVAB, or CAT-ASVAB). Almost 90 percent of prospective recruits take the CAT-ASVAB, so that's likely to be the version you'll encounter.

In this book, you'll learn how the ASVAB is structured and what it tests. You'll also learn strategies and methods that will help you improve your score significantly in each section.

What Does the ASVAB Test?

In addition to evaluating math and reading skills, the ASVAB also assesses performance in categories such as science, electronics, auto repair, and the ability to assemble objects. While the section topics and question types are the same on both the paper and pencil and CAT-ASVAB versions of the test, the amount of time and number of questions will differ slightly on each version. In the table below, you'll see the order in which the ASVAB subtests are ordered, the material tested in each section, and the differences between the paper and pencil and CAT-ASVAB versions. Additionally, note the sections that are highlighted in gray. These subtests make up the AFQT, which is discussed in more depth in the following table. In this table, the subtests are listed in the order in which you'll take them on Test Day.

Subtest	Questions / Time Limit in Minutes (CAT-ASVAB)	Questions / Time Limit in Minutes (Paper & Pencil)	What's Tested
General Science (GS)	16 questions / 8 minutes	25 questions / 11 minutes	Knowledge of general concepts from life, earth and space, and physical sciences
Arithmetic Reasoning (AR)	16 questions / 39 minutes	30 questions / 36 minutes	Ability to answer word problems that involve basic arithmetic calculations
Word Knowledge (WK)	16 questions / 8 minutes	35 questions / 11 minutes	Ability to recognize synonyms of words
Paragraph Comprehension (PC)	11 questions / 22 minutes	15 questions / 13 minutes	Ability to answer questions based on short passages (of 30–120 words)
Mathematics Knowledge (MK)	16 questions / 20 minutes	25 questions / 24 minutes	Knowledge of math concepts, including applied arithmetic, algebra, and geometry
Electronics Information (EI)	16 questions / 8 minutes	20 questions / 9 minutes	Knowledge of electronic principles and terminology, and basic electronic circuitry
Auto and Shop Information (AS)*	11 questions / 7 minutes; and 11 questions / 6 minutes	25 questions / 11 minutes	Knowledge of automobiles, and of tool and shop practices and terminology
Mechanical Comprehension (MC)	16 questions / 20 minutes	25 questions / 19 minutes	Knowledge of basic mechanical and physical principles
Assembling Objects (AO)	16 questions / 16 minutes	25 questions / 15 minutes	Ability to determine how a disassembled object will look when it is put back together
Totals	145 questions / 154 minutes	225 questions / 149 minutes	

*On the CAT-ASVAB, Auto and Shop Information is split into two parts (Auto Information [AI] and Shop Information [SI]), but one score is reported.

WHAT IS THE AFQT?

While the ASVAB is designed to determine a potential recruit's occupational fit in the military, there is no actual "overall" ASVAB score. When people talk about getting a score of, say, a 75 or 80 on the ASVAB, they are really talking about something called the AFQT (Armed Forces Qualification Test) score. A candidate's score on the AFQT determines that candidate's eligibility for all branches of the Armed Services. The AFQT score is derived from your performance on just the verbal and math subtests of the ASVAB, as explained below.

Your AFQT Score

The military determines your AFQT score by first adding your Word Knowledge and Paragraph Comprehension scores together to get your "Verbal Expression" or "VE" score. The formula to derive the AFQT "raw score" is 2VE + AR (Arithmetic Reasoning) + MK (Mathematics Knowledge) = AFQT score.

2 × [Word Knowledge + Paragraph Comprehension]

+

[Arithmetic Reasoning + Mathematical Knowledge]

= AFQT RAW SCORE

The AFQT raw score you receive is then translated into a percentile score that tells you how well you did on the AFQT compared to a base group of approximately 6000 other test takers ages 18–23. For instance, if your percentile score is 63, you scored as well as or better than 63 percent of the base group. This AFQT percentile score is used to determine your eligibility for the armed forces.

AFQT QUALIFYING SCORES FOR DIFFERENT BRANCHES OF THE MILITARY

The requirements listed below are **minimum** standards and are subject to change. They are primarily oriented toward high school graduates. The requirements may be more stringent for those who have earned their high school equivalency diplomas by taking the GED® test, the TASC™, or the HiSET™ exam. Any applicant without a high school degree or equivalent can only be accepted into military service in special circumstances. You should refer to the services' websites or publications for more specific information or contact a military recruiter. Applicants who possess special skills or experience (for example, fluency in a certain language or computer programming experience) **may** be eligible for waivers of AFQT current minimums. Also, if you score well on any subtest(s) that relate to particular occupations that are recruiting targets, you **may** be able to get a waiver.

Air Force—minimum AFQT score of 36. Those who have earned their high school equivalency degree by taking the GED® test or another equivalent test should have a minimum score of 65 to join or complete 15 hours of college credit.

Army—minimum AFQT score of 31. Those who have earned their high school equivalency degree by taking the GED® test or another equivalent test should score a 50 or better.

Marine Corps—minimum AFQT score of 32. Those who have earned their high school equivalency degree by taking the GED® test or another equivalent test should score at least 50.

Navy—minimum AFQT score of 35. Those who have earned their high school equivalency degree by taking the GED® test or another equivalent test should score at least 50 and complete 15 hours of college credit.

Coast Guard—minimum AFQT score of 36. Those who have earned their high school equivalency degree by taking the GED® test or another equivalent test should score at least 50, and complete 15 hours of college credit.

ASVAB LOGISTICS

Registering for and Taking the ASVAB

Unless you are taking the ASVAB at your high school as part of the Department of Defense Career Exploration Program, your first step towards registering to take the ASVAB is to visit the local recruiter for the service branch that you wish to join. The recruiter will help you complete your enlistment application and you will also need to provide necessary documentation. Once you have met the basic qualifications for enlistment, the recruiter will schedule your ASVAB test.

ASVAB results are valid for two years. After taking an initial ASVAB test, you may retake it after 30 days. After the first retest, you may take another retest 30 or more days later. If you have had two retests, you must wait at least six months before taking the test again.

How to Read Your ASVAB Scores

Your official ASVAB scores will come in a variety of styles and will be fully explained to you by your guidance counselor or recruiter. All of the scores matter, though some may matter more than others. Here's a quick breakdown of what you will find.

AFQT Score—You will receive a single numerical score for the AFQT.

Standard Scores—You will receive a "Standard Score" for each of the subtests. These scores are calculated using a comparison of your raw scores to the raw scores of a standard national sample. According to the Department of Defense, roughly half the population achieves a Standard Score of 50 or above but only about 16 percent scores higher than 59.

Service Composite Scores—These score combinations, sometimes called Line Scores, are used to determine whether a test taker has the necessary vocational aptitude to be trained for different job assignments in all the military branches. For example, a Navy "General Technician" composite score (abbreviated "GT") is twice the sum of the Paragraph Comprehension and Word Knowledge scores plus the Arithmetic Reasoning score. An enlistee must achieve a minimum composite score for the vocation of interest to be able to qualify to be trained for the job. To cite another example, to qualify for electronics training and occupations in the Army, you must attain a certain score that combines your results on the General Science, Arithmetic Reasoning, Mathematics Knowledge, and Electronics Information tests. For more detailed information, contact your local recruiter or visit the website for your service branch of interest.

Career Exploration Scores—In addition to the Standard Scores, students who take the ASVAB in their high schools as part of the Career Exploration Program also receive three Career Exploration Scores in the composite areas of Verbal Skills, Math Skills, and Science and Technical Skills, which are all reported as percentiles.

Different Versions of the ASVAB

Depending upon your reasons for taking the ASVAB and your stage in the career decision-making process, you will take on one of the following three versions of the test battery:

Enlistment Testing Program ASVAB

This version of the ASVAB, sometimes referred to as the *Production Version*, is used for enlistment purposes only and is administered to potential enlistees in all branches of the military. A potential recruit's performance on the ASVAB subtests is used to determine whether the candidate has the necessary aptitudes to enlist in a desired branch of service, and for which military jobs the candidate is best suited.

Career Exploration Program ASVAB

This is a paper and pencil, eight-subtest version of the ASVAB that is administered, along with an interest inventory, to high school and postsecondary students as part of the Department of Defense's Career Exploration Program. The content and format of this ASVAB are the same as the enlistment paper and pencil version, with two exceptions: the Assembling Objects subtest is not given, and the Auto and Shop Information subtests are combined into one subtest.

Armed Forces Classification Test (AFCT)

Also known as the "In-Service" ASVAB, the AFCT is identical to the paper and pencil version and is administered to those already in the military who are looking to switch jobs within the military.

The Paper and Pencil Test vs. the CAT

Computer-adaptive testing, or CAT for short, has recently become a staple among test makers. Computer-adaptive testing is really just a fancy way of saying that the difficulty of the questions you get on the test adapts based on your performance up to that point.

The diagram below models how a computer adaptive test works. In the diagram, each dot represents a question. Each question is labeled with whether the test taker got the questions correct (C) or incorrect (I). Moreover, questions are aligned with different scoring levels based on difficulty.

The first question you will see will be of medium difficulty—that is, it will be aligned to the average ability of test-takers. Notice that each time you answer a question correctly, you "earn" a more difficult question, which is aligned to a higher scoring level. Each time you give a wrong answer, your next question will be easier, and thus aligned to a lower scoring level. The CAT continues to adapt until you are getting roughly half of the questions you see correct. Once your performance has stabilized in this way, the CAT determines your score based on the difficulty level around which your answers are hovering.

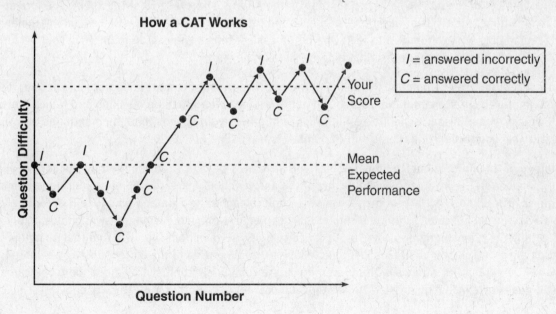

How a CAT Works

I = answered incorrectly
C = answered correctly

Your Score

Mean Expected Performance

Question Difficulty

Question Number

Studies have shown that, overall, people perform the same on the ASVAB whether they take the paper or CAT version of the test. There are, however, some individuals who will tend to do better on one version of the test than the other. Now, you may not have a choice regarding which version of the ASVAB you take. If you do have a choice as to which version of the test you will take, here are some of the advantages and disadvantages of taking the CAT versus the paper test:

Advantages of Taking the CAT-ASVAB

- The length of time of many of the subtests has been reduced from the paper and pencil ASVAB, and the number of questions that you are required to answer has been reduced even more.
- The test can be scored immediately. You will know how well you did as soon as you finish the test.
- The test administration is very flexible, so you don't have to wait for the next scheduled test date to take the test.
- There's no chance of losing points by filling out your answer sheet incorrectly.
- The CAT format gives you the chance to work methodically on one question at a time with no other questions there to distract you.

Disadvantages of Taking the CAT-ASVAB

- You cannot skip around on this test; you must answer the questions one at a time in the order the computer gives them to you.
- If you realize later that you answered a question incorrectly, you cannot go back and change your answer.
- You can't cross off an answer choice, so you'll have to use your scrap paper to keep track of the answers you've eliminated.

KAPLAN'S ASVAB STRATEGIES

Always answer every question—There is no guessing penalty on the ASVAB. This means that it is absolutely in your interest to guess on every question on every subtest of the ASVAB! Even if you have to make a completely blind guess, you have a 25 percent chance of picking the correct answer.

Familiarize yourself with the test—One key to success on the ASVAB is knowing what to expect. The format—which includes the directions, the types of questions, and even the traps that the test maker places among the answer choices—is remarkably similar from test to test. One of the easiest things you can do to improve your performance on the ASVAB is to understand the test format before you take the test.

Practice, practice, practice—Completing the sample problems and practice tests that Kaplan puts at your disposal will help you improve your scores for three reasons. First, it will help you brush up on skills and topics that you have not used since you finished school. Second, practice improves your speed. Third, as mentioned above, practicing will help you recognize patterns and trap answers.

Take advantage of the multiple-choice format—Since you have a 25 percent chance of getting the correct answer just by guessing blindly, being able to eliminate any of the answer choices greatly improves your odds of making a correct guess. If you know that one of the four answer choices cannot be right and eliminate it accordingly, you now have a 33 percent chance of getting the correct answer. Remove one more wrong answer choice, and your chance of getting the question right is now 50-50. On certain ASVAB questions, you will find that using the process of elimination on wrong answer choices is just as effective a way of getting to the correct answer as spotting the correct answer the straightforward way. Often, even if you are completely confused by a question, you can still make a solid guess by eliminating answer choices that run counter to the other three answer choices.

CAT-ASVAB Strategies

If you are taking the CAT-ASVAB, applying certain CAT-specific strategies will have a direct, positive impact on your score:

- At the beginning of the section, each question you get right or wrong will rapidly move the computer's estimate of your score up or down. Thus it pays to spend enough time on each question so that you can work your way up to the more difficult questions. Getting to the hard questions as soon as possible can only help your final score—as long as you don't run out of time at the end of the section. If you answer several questions wrong at the end of the section (because, for example, you are rushing), or if you do not finish the section, you will undo your earlier gains. Thus, you must manage your time so that you are using just enough time to answer early questions correctly without taking time away from the later questions.

- As you progress through the middle part of a section, try to avoid getting several questions in a row wrong, as this can sink your score on the CAT. If you know that the previous question you answered was a blind guess, spend a little extra time trying to get the next one right.

- The CAT does not allow you to skip questions. So if you are given a question you cannot answer, you'll have to guess. Guess intelligently and strategically by eliminating any answer choices that you know are wrong and choosing from those remaining.

- Don't get rattled if you see difficult questions. Because the CAT increases difficulty when you get correct answers, earning difficult questions just means that you are doing well. Moreover, keep in mind that the CAT will continue to adapt until you are answering roughly half of the questions you see correctly. Thus, toward the end of the test, you likely will feel that you are getting about half the questions you see wrong. That means the test is working the way it should. So don't get discouraged—just keep doing your best and keep your confidence up!

Getting Ready for the ASVAB

This book is divided into chapters that offer specific test-taking strategies for dealing with each of the subtests, with emphasis on those subtests that constitute the AFQT. Kaplan recommends that you take the first practice test, in chapter 2, before you work through this book. By doing so you can pay special attention to the areas that were difficult for you as you progress through the book. You've made the right move in deciding to prepare for the ASVAB. It is a highly coachable test, and we will give you the tools you need to score high on the ASVAB and qualify for the military career you desire.

ASVAB DIAGNOSTIC TESTS

ABOUT THE DIAGNOSTIC TESTS

These diagnostic tests are intended to help guide you in your ASVAB preparation. You'll learn several things at once by taking these diagnostic tests:

What's on the ASVAB: This diagnostic test will help you become familiar with the topics and question types that will appear on the ASVAB. After taking the diagnostic test, review your answers carefully, and make mental notes about the question types or topics that seem least familiar.

What your strengths and areas of opportunity are: After you take this diagnostic test, enter your answers into your online resources under the "Diagnostic Test" heading. Doing so will allow you to receive detailed feedback about your strengths and areas of opportunity, not just by subject test but also by question type and/or topic within each subject test.

The diagnostic mimics the paper and pencil ASVAB, rather than the CAT-ASVAB, which means it has more questions than you'll see on the CAT-ASVAB. There's a good reason for that: the greater number of questions on this diagnostic test will allow you to see more clearly which topics you need more work on.

How you react to test fatigue: Find a quiet space where you won't be interrupted for about three hours. Take this test under timed conditions, one subject after another in the order they appear here. You can take a five minute bathroom break if needed, but don't let yourself take a long break. This experience will help you assess how ready you are to focus on test material for an extended time period. If you find that fatigue interferes with your performance, be sure to take a full-length test (either in the book or online) each week in the last few weeks before your test date.

Hint: If you run out of time before you finish any given section, be sure to fill in all the blanks on your answer sheet, as there's no wrong answer penalty on the paper and pencil ASVAB, and some of your guesses could turn out to be correct! Good luck!

ANSWER SHEET

Part 1: General Science (GS)

1 Ⓐ Ⓑ Ⓒ Ⓓ	6 Ⓐ Ⓑ Ⓒ Ⓓ	11 Ⓐ Ⓑ Ⓒ Ⓓ	16 Ⓐ Ⓑ Ⓒ Ⓓ	21 Ⓐ Ⓑ Ⓒ Ⓓ
2 Ⓐ Ⓑ Ⓒ Ⓓ	7 Ⓐ Ⓑ Ⓒ Ⓓ	12 Ⓐ Ⓑ Ⓒ Ⓓ	17 Ⓐ Ⓑ Ⓒ Ⓓ	22 Ⓐ Ⓑ Ⓒ Ⓓ
3 Ⓐ Ⓑ Ⓒ Ⓓ	8 Ⓐ Ⓑ Ⓒ Ⓓ	13 Ⓐ Ⓑ Ⓒ Ⓓ	18 Ⓐ Ⓑ Ⓒ Ⓓ	23 Ⓐ Ⓑ Ⓒ Ⓓ
4 Ⓐ Ⓑ Ⓒ Ⓓ	9 Ⓐ Ⓑ Ⓒ Ⓓ	14 Ⓐ Ⓑ Ⓒ Ⓓ	19 Ⓐ Ⓑ Ⓒ Ⓓ	24 Ⓐ Ⓑ Ⓒ Ⓓ
5 Ⓐ Ⓑ Ⓒ Ⓓ	10 Ⓐ Ⓑ Ⓒ Ⓓ	15 Ⓐ Ⓑ Ⓒ Ⓓ	20 Ⓐ Ⓑ Ⓒ Ⓓ	25 Ⓐ Ⓑ Ⓒ Ⓓ

Part 2: Arithmetic Reasoning (AR)

1 Ⓐ Ⓑ Ⓒ Ⓓ	7 Ⓐ Ⓑ Ⓒ Ⓓ	13 Ⓐ Ⓑ Ⓒ Ⓓ	19 Ⓐ Ⓑ Ⓒ Ⓓ	25 Ⓐ Ⓑ Ⓒ Ⓓ
2 Ⓐ Ⓑ Ⓒ Ⓓ	8 Ⓐ Ⓑ Ⓒ Ⓓ	14 Ⓐ Ⓑ Ⓒ Ⓓ	20 Ⓐ Ⓑ Ⓒ Ⓓ	26 Ⓐ Ⓑ Ⓒ Ⓓ
3 Ⓐ Ⓑ Ⓒ Ⓓ	9 Ⓐ Ⓑ Ⓒ Ⓓ	15 Ⓐ Ⓑ Ⓒ Ⓓ	21 Ⓐ Ⓑ Ⓒ Ⓓ	27 Ⓐ Ⓑ Ⓒ Ⓓ
4 Ⓐ Ⓑ Ⓒ Ⓓ	10 Ⓐ Ⓑ Ⓒ Ⓓ	16 Ⓐ Ⓑ Ⓒ Ⓓ	22 Ⓐ Ⓑ Ⓒ Ⓓ	28 Ⓐ Ⓑ Ⓒ Ⓓ
5 Ⓐ Ⓑ Ⓒ Ⓓ	11 Ⓐ Ⓑ Ⓒ Ⓓ	17 Ⓐ Ⓑ Ⓒ Ⓓ	23 Ⓐ Ⓑ Ⓒ Ⓓ	29 Ⓐ Ⓑ Ⓒ Ⓓ
6 Ⓐ Ⓑ Ⓒ Ⓓ	12 Ⓐ Ⓑ Ⓒ Ⓓ	18 Ⓐ Ⓑ Ⓒ Ⓓ	24 Ⓐ Ⓑ Ⓒ Ⓓ	30 Ⓐ Ⓑ Ⓒ Ⓓ

Part 3: Word Knowledge (WK)

1 Ⓐ Ⓑ Ⓒ Ⓓ	8 Ⓐ Ⓑ Ⓒ Ⓓ	15 Ⓐ Ⓑ Ⓒ Ⓓ	22 Ⓐ Ⓑ Ⓒ Ⓓ	29 Ⓐ Ⓑ Ⓒ Ⓓ
2 Ⓐ Ⓑ Ⓒ Ⓓ	9 Ⓐ Ⓑ Ⓒ Ⓓ	16 Ⓐ Ⓑ Ⓒ Ⓓ	23 Ⓐ Ⓑ Ⓒ Ⓓ	30 Ⓐ Ⓑ Ⓒ Ⓓ
3 Ⓐ Ⓑ Ⓒ Ⓓ	10 Ⓐ Ⓑ Ⓒ Ⓓ	17 Ⓐ Ⓑ Ⓒ Ⓓ	24 Ⓐ Ⓑ Ⓒ Ⓓ	31 Ⓐ Ⓑ Ⓒ Ⓓ
4 Ⓐ Ⓑ Ⓒ Ⓓ	11 Ⓐ Ⓑ Ⓒ Ⓓ	18 Ⓐ Ⓑ Ⓒ Ⓓ	25 Ⓐ Ⓑ Ⓒ Ⓓ	32 Ⓐ Ⓑ Ⓒ Ⓓ
5 Ⓐ Ⓑ Ⓒ Ⓓ	12 Ⓐ Ⓑ Ⓒ Ⓓ	19 Ⓐ Ⓑ Ⓒ Ⓓ	26 Ⓐ Ⓑ Ⓒ Ⓓ	33 Ⓐ Ⓑ Ⓒ Ⓓ
6 Ⓐ Ⓑ Ⓒ Ⓓ	13 Ⓐ Ⓑ Ⓒ Ⓓ	20 Ⓐ Ⓑ Ⓒ Ⓓ	27 Ⓐ Ⓑ Ⓒ Ⓓ	34 Ⓐ Ⓑ Ⓒ Ⓓ
7 Ⓐ Ⓑ Ⓒ Ⓓ	14 Ⓐ Ⓑ Ⓒ Ⓓ	21 Ⓐ Ⓑ Ⓒ Ⓓ	28 Ⓐ Ⓑ Ⓒ Ⓓ	35 Ⓐ Ⓑ Ⓒ Ⓓ

Part 4: Paragraph Comprehension (PC)

1 Ⓐ Ⓑ Ⓒ Ⓓ	4 Ⓐ Ⓑ Ⓒ Ⓓ	7 Ⓐ Ⓑ Ⓒ Ⓓ	10 Ⓐ Ⓑ Ⓒ Ⓓ	13 Ⓐ Ⓑ Ⓒ Ⓓ
2 Ⓐ Ⓑ Ⓒ Ⓓ	5 Ⓐ Ⓑ Ⓒ Ⓓ	8 Ⓐ Ⓑ Ⓒ Ⓓ	11 Ⓐ Ⓑ Ⓒ Ⓓ	14 Ⓐ Ⓑ Ⓒ Ⓓ
3 Ⓐ Ⓑ Ⓒ Ⓓ	6 Ⓐ Ⓑ Ⓒ Ⓓ	9 Ⓐ Ⓑ Ⓒ Ⓓ	12 Ⓐ Ⓑ Ⓒ Ⓓ	15 Ⓐ Ⓑ Ⓒ Ⓓ

Part 5: Mathematics Knowledge (MK)

1 Ⓐ Ⓑ Ⓒ Ⓓ	6 Ⓐ Ⓑ Ⓒ Ⓓ	11 Ⓐ Ⓑ Ⓒ Ⓓ	16 Ⓐ Ⓑ Ⓒ Ⓓ	21 Ⓐ Ⓑ Ⓒ Ⓓ
2 Ⓐ Ⓑ Ⓒ Ⓓ	7 Ⓐ Ⓑ Ⓒ Ⓓ	12 Ⓐ Ⓑ Ⓒ Ⓓ	17 Ⓐ Ⓑ Ⓒ Ⓓ	22 Ⓐ Ⓑ Ⓒ Ⓓ
3 Ⓐ Ⓑ Ⓒ Ⓓ	8 Ⓐ Ⓑ Ⓒ Ⓓ	13 Ⓐ Ⓑ Ⓒ Ⓓ	18 Ⓐ Ⓑ Ⓒ Ⓓ	23 Ⓐ Ⓑ Ⓒ Ⓓ
4 Ⓐ Ⓑ Ⓒ Ⓓ	9 Ⓐ Ⓑ Ⓒ Ⓓ	14 Ⓐ Ⓑ Ⓒ Ⓓ	19 Ⓐ Ⓑ Ⓒ Ⓓ	24 Ⓐ Ⓑ Ⓒ Ⓓ
5 Ⓐ Ⓑ Ⓒ Ⓓ	10 Ⓐ Ⓑ Ⓒ Ⓓ	15 Ⓐ Ⓑ Ⓒ Ⓓ	20 Ⓐ Ⓑ Ⓒ Ⓓ	25 Ⓐ Ⓑ Ⓒ Ⓓ

ANSWER SHEET

Part 6: Electronics Information (EI)

1 Ⓐ Ⓑ Ⓒ Ⓓ	5 Ⓐ Ⓑ Ⓒ Ⓓ	9 Ⓐ Ⓑ Ⓒ Ⓓ	13 Ⓐ Ⓑ Ⓒ Ⓓ	17 Ⓐ Ⓑ Ⓒ Ⓓ
2 Ⓐ Ⓑ Ⓒ Ⓓ	6 Ⓐ Ⓑ Ⓒ Ⓓ	10 Ⓐ Ⓑ Ⓒ Ⓓ	14 Ⓐ Ⓑ Ⓒ Ⓓ	18 Ⓐ Ⓑ Ⓒ Ⓓ
3 Ⓐ Ⓑ Ⓒ Ⓓ	7 Ⓐ Ⓑ Ⓒ Ⓓ	11 Ⓐ Ⓑ Ⓒ Ⓓ	15 Ⓐ Ⓑ Ⓒ Ⓓ	19 Ⓐ Ⓑ Ⓒ Ⓓ
4 Ⓐ Ⓑ Ⓒ Ⓓ	8 Ⓐ Ⓑ Ⓒ Ⓓ	12 Ⓐ Ⓑ Ⓒ Ⓓ	16 Ⓐ Ⓑ Ⓒ Ⓓ	20 Ⓐ Ⓑ Ⓒ Ⓓ

Part 7: Automotive and Shop Information (AS)

1 Ⓐ Ⓑ Ⓒ Ⓓ	6 Ⓐ Ⓑ Ⓒ Ⓓ	11 Ⓐ Ⓑ Ⓒ Ⓓ	16 Ⓐ Ⓑ Ⓒ Ⓓ	21 Ⓐ Ⓑ Ⓒ Ⓓ
2 Ⓐ Ⓑ Ⓒ Ⓓ	7 Ⓐ Ⓑ Ⓒ Ⓓ	12 Ⓐ Ⓑ Ⓒ Ⓓ	17 Ⓐ Ⓑ Ⓒ Ⓓ	22 Ⓐ Ⓑ Ⓒ Ⓓ
3 Ⓐ Ⓑ Ⓒ Ⓓ	8 Ⓐ Ⓑ Ⓒ Ⓓ	13 Ⓐ Ⓑ Ⓒ Ⓓ	18 Ⓐ Ⓑ Ⓒ Ⓓ	23 Ⓐ Ⓑ Ⓒ Ⓓ
4 Ⓐ Ⓑ Ⓒ Ⓓ	9 Ⓐ Ⓑ Ⓒ Ⓓ	14 Ⓐ Ⓑ Ⓒ Ⓓ	19 Ⓐ Ⓑ Ⓒ Ⓓ	24 Ⓐ Ⓑ Ⓒ Ⓓ
5 Ⓐ Ⓑ Ⓒ Ⓓ	10 Ⓐ Ⓑ Ⓒ Ⓓ	15 Ⓐ Ⓑ Ⓒ Ⓓ	20 Ⓐ Ⓑ Ⓒ Ⓓ	25 Ⓐ Ⓑ Ⓒ Ⓓ

Part 8: Mechanical Comprehension (MC)

1 Ⓐ Ⓑ Ⓒ Ⓓ	6 Ⓐ Ⓑ Ⓒ Ⓓ	11 Ⓐ Ⓑ Ⓒ Ⓓ	16 Ⓐ Ⓑ Ⓒ Ⓓ	21 Ⓐ Ⓑ Ⓒ Ⓓ
2 Ⓐ Ⓑ Ⓒ Ⓓ	7 Ⓐ Ⓑ Ⓒ Ⓓ	12 Ⓐ Ⓑ Ⓒ Ⓓ	17 Ⓐ Ⓑ Ⓒ Ⓓ	22 Ⓐ Ⓑ Ⓒ Ⓓ
3 Ⓐ Ⓑ Ⓒ Ⓓ	8 Ⓐ Ⓑ Ⓒ Ⓓ	13 Ⓐ Ⓑ Ⓒ Ⓓ	18 Ⓐ Ⓑ Ⓒ Ⓓ	23 Ⓐ Ⓑ Ⓒ Ⓓ
4 Ⓐ Ⓑ Ⓒ Ⓓ	9 Ⓐ Ⓑ Ⓒ Ⓓ	14 Ⓐ Ⓑ Ⓒ Ⓓ	19 Ⓐ Ⓑ Ⓒ Ⓓ	24 Ⓐ Ⓑ Ⓒ Ⓓ
5 Ⓐ Ⓑ Ⓒ Ⓓ	10 Ⓐ Ⓑ Ⓒ Ⓓ	15 Ⓐ Ⓑ Ⓒ Ⓓ	20 Ⓐ Ⓑ Ⓒ Ⓓ	25 Ⓐ Ⓑ Ⓒ Ⓓ

Part 9: Assembling Objects (AO)

1 Ⓐ Ⓑ Ⓒ Ⓓ	6 Ⓐ Ⓑ Ⓒ Ⓓ	11 Ⓐ Ⓑ Ⓒ Ⓓ	16 Ⓐ Ⓑ Ⓒ Ⓓ	21 Ⓐ Ⓑ Ⓒ Ⓓ
2 Ⓐ Ⓑ Ⓒ Ⓓ	7 Ⓐ Ⓑ Ⓒ Ⓓ	12 Ⓐ Ⓑ Ⓖ Ⓓ	17 Ⓐ Ⓑ Ⓒ Ⓓ	22 Ⓐ Ⓑ Ⓒ Ⓓ
3 Ⓐ Ⓑ Ⓒ Ⓓ	8 Ⓐ Ⓑ Ⓒ Ⓓ	13 Ⓐ Ⓑ Ⓒ Ⓓ	18 Ⓐ Ⓑ Ⓒ Ⓓ	23 Ⓐ Ⓑ Ⓒ Ⓓ
4 Ⓐ Ⓑ Ⓒ Ⓓ	9 Ⓐ Ⓑ Ⓒ Ⓓ	14 Ⓐ Ⓑ Ⓒ Ⓓ	19 Ⓐ Ⓑ Ⓒ Ⓓ	24 Ⓐ Ⓑ Ⓒ Ⓓ
5 Ⓐ Ⓑ Ⓒ Ⓓ	10 Ⓐ Ⓑ Ⓒ Ⓓ	15 Ⓐ Ⓑ Ⓒ Ⓓ	20 Ⓐ Ⓑ Ⓒ Ⓓ	25 Ⓐ Ⓑ Ⓒ Ⓓ

ASVAB DIAGNOSTIC TEST

Part 1: General Science (GS)

Time: 11 minutes; 25 questions

<u>Directions</u>: In this section, you will be tested on your knowledge of concepts in science generally reviewed in high school. For each question, select the best answer and mark the corresponding oval on your answer sheet.

1. _____ are necessary for the body's maintenance, growth, and repair.

   (A) Proteins
   (B) Carbohydrates
   (C) Fats
   (D) Vitamins

2. On a Fahrenheit thermometer the boiling point of water at sea level is

   (A) 100°
   (B) 180°
   (C) 212°
   (D) 373°

3. The process by which the body's cells use oxygen and glucose to produce energy, while releasing carbon dioxide and water vapor as waste products, is known as

   (A) decomposition
   (B) photosynthesis
   (C) oxidation
   (D) respiration

4. _____ carry blood back to the heart from the capillaries.

   (A) Arteries
   (B) Veins
   (C) Ventricles
   (D) Red blood cells

5. Which of the following is an example of a chemical process?

   (A) Helium mixes with neon.
   (B) Iron forms rust.
   (C) Sugar dissolves in water.
   (D) Ice melts.

6. A universal donor is a person with which of the following blood types?

   (A) O negative
   (B) A positive
   (C) AB positive
   (D) B negative

7. Blood enters the right atrium of the heart from the

   (A) aorta
   (B) left ventricle
   (C) pulmonary vein
   (D) vena cava

8. Which of the following substances has the highest pH?

   (A) ammonia
   (B) battery acid
   (C) isopropyl alcohol
   (D) water

9. Which of the following organs does the most work to break down food using enzymes?

   (A) pancreas
   (B) stomach
   (C) small intestine
   (D) large intestine

10. Which of the following is NOT part of the female reproductive system?

    (A) oviduct
    (B) uterus
    (C) ovary
    (D) testes

11. The most basic unit of inheritance is known as a

   (A)   phenotype
   (B)   genotype
   (C)   chromosome
   (D)   gene

12. Which of the following is a sedimentary rock?

   (A)   granite
   (B)   marble
   (C)   shale
   (D)   slate

13. A producer is also known as a(n):

   (A)   heterotroph
   (B)   saprotroph
   (C)   autotroph
   (D)   scavenger

14. A vulture would be considered a

   (A)   producer
   (B)   decomposer
   (C)   scavenger
   (D)   parasite

15. What type of rock is obsidian?

   (A)   sedimentary
   (B)   igneous
   (C)   metamorphic
   (D)   sandstone

16. During a lunar eclipse

   (A)   the Moon lies between the Earth and Sun
   (B)   the Sun lies between the Moon and Earth
   (C)   the Earth lies between the Moon and Sun
   (D)   the Sun lies outside the Moon's umbra

17. A centimeter is

   (A)   one hundredth of a meter
   (B)   one tenth of a meter
   (C)   ten meters
   (D)   one hundred meters

18. Momentum is

   (A)   the push or pull that forces an object to change its speed or direction
   (B)   the rate of change of velocity
   (C)   the rate at which an object changes position
   (D)   the tendency of an object to continue moving in the same direction

19. Which color's light waves have the highest frequency?

   (A)   yellow
   (B)   green
   (C)   red
   (D)   violet

20. The major portion of an atom's mass consists of

   (A)   neutrons and protons
   (B)   electrons and protons
   (C)   electrons and neutrons
   (D)   neutrons and positrons

21. Which of the following is NOT an example of an arthropod?

   (A)   crab
   (B)   centipede
   (C)   sea urchin
   (D)   spider

22. Table salt is considered a(n)

   (A)   ionic compound
   (B)   semi-ionic compound
   (C)   covalent compound
   (D)   element

23. Over the course of 24 hours

   (A)   the Earth rotates 360 degrees around the sun
   (B)   the Moon rotates 360 degrees around the Earth
   (C)   the Earth rotates 360 degrees about its axis
   (D)   the Moon rotates 360 degrees about its axis

24. Which of the following kingdoms is composed of prokaryotic life forms such as bacteria, and as such is considered the most primitive?

   (A)   Fungi
   (B)   Protista
   (C)   Monera
   (D)   Plantae

25. Human beings belong to the phylum

   (A)   Animalia
   (B)   Chordata
   (C)   Mammalia
   (D)   Primata

STOP. IF YOU FINISH BEFORE THE TIME IS UP, YOU MAY CHECK OVER YOUR WORK ON THIS PART ONLY.

Part 2: Arithmetic Reasoning (AR)

Time: 36 minutes; 30 questions

<u>Directions</u>: In this section, you are tested on your ability to use arithmetic. For each question, select the best answer and mark the corresponding oval on your answer sheet.

1. John bought a camera on sale that normally costs $160. If the price was reduced 20% during the sale, what was the sale price of the camera?

   (A) $120
   (B) $124
   (C) $128
   (D) $140

2. A subway car passes 3 stations every 10 minutes. At this rate, how many stations will it pass in one hour?

   (A) 15
   (B) 18
   (C) 20
   (D) 30

3. On a certain map, $\frac{3}{4}$ inch represents one mile. What distance, in miles, is represented by $1\frac{3}{4}$ inches?

   (A) $1\frac{1}{2}$

   (B) $2\frac{1}{3}$

   (C) $2\frac{1}{2}$

   (D) $5\frac{1}{4}$

4. A certain box contains baseballs and golf balls. If the ratio of baseballs to golf balls is 2:3 and there are 30 baseballs in the box, how many golf balls are in the box?

   (A) 18
   (B) 20
   (C) 36
   (D) 45

5. Four people shared a taxi to the airport. The fare was $36.00, and they gave the driver a tip equal to 25% of the fare. If they equally shared the cost of the fare and tip, how much did each person pay?

   (A) $9.75
   (B) $10.25
   (C) $10.75
   (D) $11.25

6. If a car travels $\frac{1}{100}$ of a kilometer each second, how many kilometers does it travel in an hour?

   (A) 36
   (B) 60
   (C) 72
   (D) 100

7. $20 - (-5) =$

   (A) −25
   (B) 25
   (C) 15
   (D) −15

8. Ms. Smith drove a total of 700 miles on a business trip. If her car averaged 35 miles per gallon of gasoline and gasoline cost $1.25 per gallon, what was the cost in dollars of the gasoline for the trip?

   (A) $20.00
   (B) $24.00
   (C) $25.00
   (D) $40.00

9. After eating 25% of the jelly beans, Brett had 72 left. How many jelly beans did Brett have originally?

   (A) 90
   (B) 94
   (C) 95
   (D) 96

10. A student finishes the first half of an exam in $\frac{2}{3}$ the time it takes him to finish the second half. If the entire exam takes him an hour, how many minutes does he spend on the first half of the exam?

    (A) 20
    (B) 24
    (C) 27
    (D) 36

11. A 25 ounce solution is 20% alcohol. If 50 ounces of water are added to it, what percent of the new solution is alcohol?

    (A) $6\frac{2}{3}\%$

    (B) $7\frac{1}{2}\%$

    (C) 10%

    (D) $13\frac{1}{3}\%$

12. Marty has exactly 5 blue pens, 6 black pens, and 4 red pens in his backpack. If he pulls out one pen at random from his backpack, what is the probability that the pen is either red or black?

    (A) $\frac{2}{3}$

    (B) $\frac{3}{5}$

    (C) $\frac{2}{5}$

    (D) $\frac{1}{3}$

13. From 1980 through 1990, the population of Country X increased by 100%. From 1990 to 2000, the population increased by 50%. What was the combined increase for the period 1980–2000?

    (A) 150%
    (B) $166\frac{2}{3}\%$
    (C) 175%
    (D) 200%

14. If a man earns $200 for his first 40 hours of work in a week and then is paid one-and-one-half times his regular rate for any additional hours, how many hours must he work to make $230 in a week?

    (A) 43
    (B) 44
    (C) 45
    (D) 46

15. If 50% of x is 150, what is 75% of x?

    (A) 225
    (B) 250
    (C) 275
    (D) 300

16. The total fare for two adults and three children on an excursion boat is $14. If each child's fare is one half of each adult's fare, what is the adult fare?

    (A) $2.00
    (B) $3.00
    (C) $3.50
    (D) $4.00

17. What is the prime factorization of 140?

    (A) 2×70
    (B) $2 \times 3 \times 5 \times 7$
    (C) $2 \times 2 \times 5 \times 7$
    (D) $2 \times 2 \times 2 \times 5 \times 7$

18. A painter charges $12 an hour while his son charges $6 an hour. If the father and son worked the same amount of time together on a job, how many hours did each of them work if their combined charge for their labor was $108?

    (A) 6
    (B) 9
    (C) 12
    (D) 18

19. $4! =$

    (A) 4
    (B) 16
    (C) 24
    (D) 256

20. At garage A, it costs $8.75 to park a car for the first hour and $1.25 for each additional hour. At garage B, it costs $5.50 to park a car for the first hour and $2.50 for each additional hour. What is the difference between the cost of parking a car for 5 hours at garage A and parking it for the same length of time at garage B?

    (A) $2.25
    (B) $1.75
    (C) $1.50
    (D) $1.25

21. Jan types at an average rate of 12 pages per hour. At that rate, how long will it take Jan to type 100 pages?

    (A) 8 hours and 10 minutes
    (B) 8 hours and 15 minutes
    (C) 8 hours and 20 minutes
    (D) 8 hours and 30 minutes

22. Two large sodas contain the same amount as three medium sodas. Two medium sodas contain the same amount as three small sodas. How many small sodas contain the same amount as eight large sodas?

    (A) 24
    (B) 18
    (C) 16
    (D) 12

23. If each digit 5 in the number 258,546 is replaced with the digit 7, by how much will the number be increased?

    (A) 2,020
    (B) 2,200
    (C) 20,020
    (D) 20,200

24. Michael bought $2\frac{1}{4}$ pounds of lumber at $4.00 per pound. If a 7% sales tax was added, how much did Michael pay?

    (A) $9.63
    (B) $9.98
    (C) $10.70
    (D) $11.77

25. The ratio of $3\frac{1}{4}$ to $5\frac{1}{4}$ is equivalent to the ratio of

    (A) 3 to 5
    (B) 4 to 7
    (C) 8 to 13
    (D) 13 to 21

26. A cat is fed $\frac{3}{8}$ of a pound of cat food every day. For how many days will 72 pounds of this cat food feed the cat?

    (A) 160
    (B) 172
    (C) 180
    (D) 192

27. After spending $\frac{5}{12}$ of his salary, a man has $420 left. What is his salary?

    (A) $175
    (B) $245
    (C) $720
    (D) $1,008

28. A stock decreases in value by 20%. By what percent must the stock price increase to reach its former value?

    (A) 15%
    (B) 20%
    (C) 25%
    (D) 40%

29. Joan can shovel a certain driveway in 50 minutes. If Mary can shovel the same driveway in 20 minutes, how long will it take them, to the nearest minute, to shovel the driveway if they work together?

    (A) 12
    (B) 13
    (C) 14
    (D) 15

30. June's weekly salary is $70 less than Kelly's, which is $50 more than Eileen's. If Eileen earns $280 per week, how much does June earn per week?

    (A) $160
    (B) $260
    (C) $280
    (D) $300

STOP. IF YOU FINISH BEFORE THE TIME IS UP, YOU MAY CHECK OVER YOUR WORK ON THIS PART ONLY.

Part 3: Word Knowledge (WK)

Time: 11 minutes; 35 questions

<u>Directions</u>: In this section, you are tested on the meaning of words. Each of the following questions has an underlined word. Select the answer that most nearly means the same as the underlined word and mark the corresponding oval on your answer sheet.

1. <u>Noble</u> most nearly means

   (A)   comely
   (B)   loose
   (C)   aristocratic
   (D)   lackadaisical

2. John initially disagreed with Megan, but then he had to <u>concede</u> her point about the budget.

   (A) argue
   (B) understand
   (C) counter
   (D) admit

3. <u>Goad</u> most nearly means

   (A)   listen
   (B)   provoke
   (C)   pacify
   (D)   ignore

4. Teenagers at the mall love to roam in a <u>herd</u>.

   (A)   jacket
   (B)   line
   (C)   pack
   (D)   ratio

5. Panicking in an emergency is not a <u>viable</u> response for an EMT.

   (A)   total
   (B)   collective
   (C)   lucid
   (D)   workable

6. <u>Judicious</u> most nearly means

   (A)   accessible
   (B)   cold
   (C)   wise
   (D)   talkative

7. <u>Hesitating</u> in a time of crisis can often lead to failure.

   (A)   broadening
   (B)   creating
   (C)   leaving
   (D)   pausing

8. Applicants who insist on <u>falsifying</u> information ruin the process for everyone.

   (A)   fabricating
   (B)   listing
   (C)   furthering
   (D)   taking on

9. <u>Hollow</u> most nearly means

   (A)   dangerous
   (B)   potent
   (C)   empty
   (D)   superb

10. <u>Coax</u> most nearly means

   (A)   advise
   (B)   trade
   (C)   plead
   (D)   grace

11. The <u>monotonous</u> speech left them all feeling sleepy.

   (A)   telling
   (B)   boring
   (C)   caustic
   (D)   hilarious

12. As Mrs. Higgins attempted to teach the difficult material, she sensed growing <u>consternation</u> among her students.

   (A)   desires
   (B)   inability
   (C)   frustration
   (D)   behavior

13. With the holidays approaching, Dave looked forward to a savory feast or two.

    (A) tasty
    (B) guilty
    (C) heroic
    (D) skimpy

14. A man of some renown, the mayor walked with his chest puffed out.

    (A) size
    (B) fame
    (C) confusion
    (D) toil

15. Raconteur most nearly means

    (A) believer
    (B) storyteller
    (C) standout
    (D) pedant

16. She felt that nothing could really quench her curiosity.

    (A) justify
    (B) break
    (C) illuminate
    (D) satisfy

17. The committee was polarized on the issue.

    (A) split
    (B) disgusted
    (C) grateful
    (D) cold

18. The need to be precise was clear to everyone.

    (A) after the fact
    (B) cautious
    (C) exact
    (D) barren

19. Drucker surveyed the terrain before him for water.

    (A) oversight
    (B) landscape
    (C) river
    (D) goal

20. Terminal most nearly means

    (A) easy
    (B) glittering
    (C) busy
    (D) final

21. Augment most nearly means

    (A) craft
    (B) end
    (C) throw away
    (D) enhance

22. Her involuntary spasm knocked over a lamp.

    (A) unintentional
    (B) painful
    (C) listless
    (D) binary

23. The other owners accused the brothers of collusion.

    (A) coalition
    (B) secret agreement
    (C) hoping
    (D) pretending

24. The mongoose shows great tenacity in the face of danger.

    (A) fear
    (B) candor
    (C) determination
    (D) speed

25. Tactile most nearly means

    (A) ghastly
    (B) easy
    (C) patient
    (D) tangible

26. The dark clouds seemed to portend a gloomy weekend ahead.

    (A) fake
    (B) lose
    (C) predict
    (D) edit

27. <u>Germinate</u> most nearly means

   (A) sprout
   (B) oppress
   (C) adulate
   (D) foster

28. <u>Restore</u> most nearly means

   (A) trip up
   (B) invigorate
   (C) care for
   (D) toughen

29. <u>Filament</u> most nearly means

   (A) horse
   (B) triage
   (C) nightmare
   (D) thread

30. Whatever the original intent, the focus has clearly <u>mutated</u> at this point.

   (A) disappeared
   (B) reiterated
   (C) altered
   (D) intensified

31. To be elected president, one must be a calm yet still <u>dynamic</u> figure.

   (A) reassuring
   (B) exciting
   (C) manic
   (D) terrible

32. <u>Congeal</u> most nearly means

   (A) fade
   (B) swirl
   (C) harden
   (D) undulate

33. <u>Reconnoiter</u> most nearly means

   (A) advance
   (B) posit
   (C) grade
   (D) scout

34. Whether one can <u>accrue</u> enough money to live on is always the question.

   (A) accumulate
   (B) acquiesce
   (C) trap
   (D) magnify

35. His <u>innate</u> ability to make the correct turn was amazing.

   (A) unsure
   (B) discussed
   (C) creative
   (D) natural

STOP. IF YOU FINISH BEFORE THE TIME IS UP, YOU MAY CHECK OVER YOUR WORK ON THIS PART ONLY.

Part 4: Paragraph Comprehension (PC)

Time: 13 minutes; 15 questions

Directions: This section contains paragraphs followed by incomplete statements or questions. For each question, read the paragraph and select the answer that best completes the statements or answers the question that follows. Mark the corresponding oval on your answer sheet.

The first detective stories, written by Edgar Allan Poe and Arthur Conan Doyle, emerged in the mid-nineteenth century, at a time when there was enormous public interest in science. The newspapers of the day continually publicized the latest scientific discoveries, and scientists were acclaimed as the heroes of the age. Poe and Conan Doyle shared this fascination with the methodical, logical approach used by scientists in their experiments, and instilled their detective heroes with outstanding powers of scientific reasoning.

1. The main idea of this passage is

    (A) science fiction was not popular among nineteenth-century readers
    (B) scientific progress made its way into the fiction of the time
    (C) newspapers detailed detective work each day
    (D) the first detective stories were written by scientists

Children have an amazing talent for learning vocabulary. Between the ages of one and seventeen, the average child learns the meaning of about 80,000 words—about 14 per day. Dictionaries and traditional classroom vocabulary lessons only account for part of this knowledge growth. More important are individuals' reading habits and their dialogues with people whose vocabularies are larger than their own. Reading shows students how words are used in sentences. Conversation offers students the chance to ask questions about the language.

2. According to the passage, reading is valuable to students because

    (A) children learn differently than adults
    (B) words used in stories are generally harder
    (C) reading provides vocabulary clues within sentences
    (D) vocabulary is learned mostly through conversation

The first truly American art movement was formed by a group of landscape painters that emerged in the early nineteenth century called the Hudson River School. The first works in this style were created by Thomas Cole, Thomas Doughty, and Asher Durand, a trio of painters who worked during the 1820s in the Hudson River Valley and surrounding locations. Heavily influenced by European artists, these painters set out to convey the remoteness and splendor of the American wilderness. The strongly patriotic tone of their paintings caught the spirit of the times, and within a generation the movement had grown to include landscape painters from all over the United States.

3. The passage is primarily concerned with which of the following?

    (A) the history of the Hudson River School of painters
    (B) American art movements of the nineteenth century
    (C) how American landscape painters were influenced by European painters
    (D) the artistic origins of nationalism in the United States

Different people have different approaches to choosing a personal computer. Some people pick a new computer at random, falling victim to the latest trend or advertisement. These people often regret their decisions in the long run. On the other hand, people who do thorough research before purchasing a computer are much happier with their decisions in the long run. When you are shopping for a new computer, conducting research is an important step.

4. Which of the following statements best expresses the main idea of the passage?

    (A) People should base computer purchase decisions on advertisements.
    (B) People should not base computer purchase decisions on advertisements.
    (C) People should conduct research to be happy in life.
    (D) People should conduct research before purchasing a computer.

Questions 5 and 6 refer to the following passage.

The painter Georgia O'Keeffe was born in Wisconsin in 1887 and grew up on her family's farm. At seventeen she decided she wanted to be an artist and left the farm for schools in Chicago and New York, but she never lost her bond with the land. Like most painters, O'Keeffe painted the things that were most important to her, and nearly all her works are portrayals of nature. O'Keeffe became famous when her paintings were discovered in New York by the photographer Alfred Stieglitz, whom she married in 1924. During a visit to New Mexico in 1929, O'Keeffe was so moved by the bleak landscape and broad skies of the Western desert that she began to paint its images.

5. In this context, the word *bleak* most nearly means

   (A) empty
   (B) moody
   (C) cold
   (D) vivid

6. Georgia O'Keeffe's work generally shows

   (A) an ability to paint something complex accurately
   (B) her love for Alfred Stieglitz
   (C) her desire for fame
   (D) her love of the land

The four brightest moons of Jupiter were the first objects in the solar system discovered with the use of the telescope. This proof played a central role in Galileo's famous argument in support of the Copernican model of the solar system, in which the planets are described as revolving around the Sun. For several hundred years, scientific understanding of these moons was slow to develop. But spectacular close-up photographs sent back by the 1979 Voyager missions forever changed our perception of these moons.

7. Which best describes the Copernican model of the solar system?

   (A) Planets move counterclockwise as they rotate.
   (B) The Sun and other planets revolve around the Earth.
   (C) The planets move in orbit around the Sun.
   (D) The four brightest moons of Jupiter used to be planets.

As the sky opened up and sun at last rushed into the room, Toby smiled knowing that the game would proceed as planned. It had to, if only because his father would be there and it might be the last opportunity he would have to see Toby play. Now the birds began to appear here and there. Toby got out his baseball glove and ball and waited for his dad to arrive to take him to the game.

8. The mood of the character in the passage is

   (A) sad
   (B) careless
   (C) uneasy
   (D) eager

A human body can survive without water for several days and without food for as many as several weeks. If breathing stops for as little as three to six minutes, however, death is likely. All animals require a constant supply of oxygen to the body tissues, and especially to the heart or brain. In the human body, the respiratory and circulatory systems perform this function by delivering oxygen to the blood, which then transports it to tissues throughout the body. Respiration in large animals involves more than just breathing in oxygen. It is a complex process that delivers oxygen while eliminating carbon dioxide produced by cells.

9. Which bodily function, according to the passage, is least essential to the immediate survival of a human being?

   (A) eating
   (B) drinking
   (C) breathing
   (D) excretion

The media are really out of control. When the press gets a story, it seems that within minutes it have produced flashy moving graphics and sound effects to entice viewers and garner ratings. Real facts and unbiased coverage of an issue are totally abandoned in exchange for an overly sentimental or one-sided story that too often distorts the truth. Viewers need to learn to recognize real reporting from the junk on nearly every television channel these days.

10. The author would be most likely to agree with which of the following?

   (A) Newspapers should have more editorials.
   (B) Flashy graphics add substance to television news reporting.
   (C) Objective news reporting is a dying art.
   (D) Television news anchors are valuable sources of information.

The poems of the earliest Greeks, like those of other ancient societies, consisted of magical charms, mysterious predictions, prayers, and traditional songs of work and war. These poems were intended to be sung or recited, not written down, since they were created before the Greeks began to use writing for literary purposes. The different forms of early Greek poetry all had something in common: They described the way of life of the Greek people. Poetry expressed ideas and feelings that were shared by everyone in a community—their folktales, their memories of historical events, and their religious speculation.

11. Early Greek poetry was which of the following?

   (A) mainly an oral form
   (B) a departure from poetic traditions in other societies
   (C) widely thought to be an act of the gods
   (D) usually about lost love and sadness

In computer design, the effectiveness of a program generally depends on the ability of the programmer. Still, remarkable progress has been made in the development of artificial intelligence. This progress has scientists wondering whether it will eventually be possible to develop a computer capable of intelligent thought. When a computer defeated Garry Kasparov, considered by many the greatest chess player of all time, it was taken to be a vindication of the claims of the strongest supporters of artificial intelligence. Despite this accomplishment, others argue that while computers may imitate the human mind, they will never possess the capacity for true intelligence.

12. The main idea of this passage is

   (A) computers can never learn to think
   (B) chess is a game in which computers are superior
   (C) great strides have been made in artificial intelligence
   (D) artificial intelligence is a scientific miracle

Questions 13 and 14 refer to the following passage.

Coral reefs are created over the course of hundreds or even thousands of years. The main architect in coral reef formation is the stony coral, a relative of the sea anemone that lives in tropical climates and secretes a skeleton of almost pure calcium carbonate. Its partner is the green alga, a tiny unicellular plant that lives within the tissues of the coral. The two organisms form a mutually beneficial relationship, with the algae consuming carbon dioxide given off by the corals, and the corals thriving on the abundant oxygen produced photosynthetically by the algae. When the coral dies, its skeleton is left, and other organisms grow on top of it. Over the years the mass of coral skeletons together with those of associated organisms combines to form the petrified underwater forest that divers find so fascinating.

13. Which of the following best describes what this passage is about?

   (A) the varieties of animal life that live in coral reefs
   (B) the formation of coral reefs
   (C) the life and death cycles of coral reefs
   (D) the physical beauty of coral reefs

14. The relationship between the coral and the algae is best described as

   (A) parasitic
   (B) competitive
   (C) predatory
   (D) cooperative

For do-it-yourself types, the cost of getting regular oil changes seems unnecessary. After all, the steps are fairly easy as long as you are safe. First, make sure that the car is stationary and on a level surface. Always use the emergency brake to ensure that the car does not roll on top of you. Next, locate the drain plug for the oil under the engine. Remember to place the oil drain pan under the plug before you start. When it is drained fully, wipe off the drain plug and the plug opening and then replace the drain plug. Next, simply place your funnel in the engine and pour in new oil. Be sure to return the oil cap when you're done. Finally, run the engine for a minute, and then check the dipstick to see if you need more oil in your engine.

15. After draining the old oil from the engine, you should

   (A) replace the oil cap
   (B) run the engine for a moment and check the dipstick
   (C) wipe off and replace the drain plug
   (D) engage the emergency brake

STOP. IF YOU FINISH BEFORE THE TIME IS UP, YOU MAY CHECK OVER YOUR WORK ON THIS PART ONLY.

Part 5: Mathematics Knowledge (MK)

Time: 24 minutes; 25 questions

Directions: In this section, you will be tested on your knowledge of basic mathematics. For each question, select the best answer and mark the corresponding oval on your answer sheet.

1. If 48 is divided by 0.08, the result is
   - (A) 0.06
   - (B) 0.6
   - (C) 60
   - (D) 600

2. If the number 9,899,399 is increased by 2,082, the result will be
   - (A) 9,901,481
   - (B) 9,901,471
   - (C) 9,902,481
   - (D) 9,902,471

3. The cube of 9 is
   - (A) 27
   - (B) 81
   - (C) 243
   - (D) 729

4. What is the value of $(-ab)(a)$ when $a = -2$ and $b = 3$?
   - (A) −12
   - (B) −6
   - (C) 6
   - (D) 12

5. $(x - 4)(x - 4) =$
   - (A) $x^2 + 8x - 16$
   - (B) $x^2 - 8x - 16$
   - (C) $x^2 - 8x + 16$
   - (D) $x^2 - 16x + 8$

6. $0.123 \times 10^4 =$
   - (A) .0000123
   - (B) .00123
   - (C) 1.23
   - (D) 1,230

7. $\sqrt{100} - \sqrt{64} =$
   - (A) 2
   - (B) 4
   - (C) 6
   - (D) 8

8. A circle has a diameter of 6, an area of b square units, and a circumference of c units. What is the value of $b + c$?
   - (A) 9π
   - (B) 15π
   - (C) 18π
   - (D) 42π

9. A bag contains 8 white, 4 red, 7 green, and 5 blue marbles. Eight marbles are withdrawn at random. How many of the withdrawn marbles are white if the chance of drawing a white marble is now 1 in 4?
   - (A) 3
   - (B) 4
   - (C) 5
   - (D) 6

10. Liza has 40 fewer than 3 times the number of books that Janice has. If B is equal to the number of books that Janice has, which of the following expressions shows the number of books that Liza and Janice have together?
    - (A) $3B - 40$
    - (B) $3B + 40$
    - (C) $4B - 40$
    - (D) $4B + 40$

11. If the perimeter of a square is 32 meters, then what is the area of the square, in square meters?
    - (A) 16
    - (B) 32
    - (C) 48
    - (D) 64

12. If $x \neq 0$, then $\dfrac{6x^6}{2x^2} =$

    (A) $4x^4$
    (B) $4x^3$
    (C) $3x^4$
    (D) $3x^3$

13. A number is considered "blue" if the sum of its digits is equal to the product of its digits. Which of the following is "blue"?

    (A) 111
    (B) 220
    (C) 321
    (D) 422

14. If $x = \dfrac{1}{8}$, what is the value of y when $\dfrac{2}{x} = \dfrac{y}{4}$?

    (A) $\dfrac{1}{4}$
    (B) 4
    (C) 16
    (D) 64

15. If line p above is parallel to line q, what is the value of $x + y$?

    (A) 90
    (B) 110
    (C) 125
    (D) 180

16. If $3ab = 6$, what is the value of a in terms of b?

    (A) $\dfrac{2}{b}$
    (B) $\dfrac{2}{b^2}$
    (C) $2b$
    (D) $2b^2$

17. For what value of y is $4(y - 1) = 2(y + 2)$?

    (A) 0
    (B) 2
    (C) 4
    (D) 6

18. In triangle RST above, if $RS = RT$, what is the degree measure of angle S?

    (A) 40
    (B) 55
    (C) 70
    (D) cannot be determined from the information given

19. When D is divided by 15, the result is 6 with a remainder of 2. What is the remainder when D is divided by 6?

    (A) 0
    (B) 2
    (C) 3
    (D) 4

20. If the average of 7 consecutive even numbers is 24, then the largest number is

    (A) 26
    (B) 28
    (C) 30
    (D) 34

21. A box that has dimensions of 2 inches by 3 inches by 4 inches has a total surface area of

    (A) 24 square inches.
    (B) 26 square inches.
    (C) 48 square inches.
    (D) 52 square inches.

22. If $100 \div x = 10n$, then which of the following is equal to nx?

    (A)   10
    (B) $10x$
    (C)   100
    (D) $10xn$

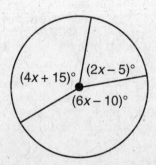

23. In the figure above, what is the value of x?

    (A)   15
    (B)   30
    (C)   55
    (D)   70

24. If $7! = 7 \times 6 \times 5 \times 4 \times 3 \times 2 \times 1$, then $5! =$

    (A)   15
    (B)   75
    (C)   120
    (D)   125

25. Melissa took $5n$ photographs on a certain trip. If she gives n photographs to each of her 3 friends, how many photographs will she have left?

    (A) $2n$
    (B) $3n$
    (C) $4n - 3$
    (D) $4n + 3$

STOP. IF YOU FINISH BEFORE THE TIME IS UP, YOU MAY CHECK OVER YOUR WORK ON THIS PART ONLY.

Part 6: Electronics Information (EI)

Time: 9 minutes; 20 questions

<u>Directions</u>: In this section, you will be tested on your knowledge of electronics basics. For each question, select the best answer and mark the corresponding oval on your answer sheet.

1. A load

    (A)   has very low resistance and conducts current throughout the circuit
    (B)   is a device that converts electrical energy into heat, light, or motion
    (C)   is a voltage source
    (D)   switches electrical current off and on

2. Which of the following symbols represents a photosensitive diode?

    (A)

    (B)

    (C)

    (D)

3. *One* hertz is equivalent to

    (A)   one cycle per second of any continuous process
    (B)   an acceleration of 1 m/s^2
    (C)   a change in frequency of one cycle per second per second
    (D)   the negative of the period

4. A(n) _____ is an element that freely conducts electricity.

    (A)   insulator
    (B)   conductor
    (C)   semiconductor
    (D)   molecule

5. Which of the following CANNOT describe an "earth ground" in home electricity?

    (A)   a buried conduit
    (B)   a copper rod driven into the ground
    (C)   a device made to protect occupants from electrical shock
    (D)   a device for measuring electrical resistance

6. Electron flow theory states that

    (A)   electrons flow best through liquids
    (B)   electrons flow from areas of excess negative charge to areas of less negative charge
    (C)   electrons flow from areas of excess positive charge to areas of less positive charge
    (D)   electrons can only flow from one area to another if there is no resistance

7. The "electrical pressure" that causes electrons to flow in one direction through a conducting path is a result of

    (A)   a voltage
    (B)   a difference in resistance
    (C)   parallel paths
    (D)   a wire moving downhill

8. This is the symbol for which type of meter?

    (A)   voltmeter
    (B)   ammeter
    (C)   ohmmeter
    (D)   galvanometer

9. What type of circuit does this symbol represent?

(A) parallel circuit
(B) series-parallel circuit
(C) series circuit
(D) short circuit

10. Under a constant voltage, increasing resistance results in current flow

(A) dropping
(B) rising
(C) staying the same
(D) changing direction

11. Increasing the voltage in a circuit and keeping resistance the same will result in

(A) increased current flow
(B) decreased current flow
(C) current flow staying the same
(D) zero current flow

12. Several loads in series have different resistances. Given that the same current flows through each of them, what relationship does Ohm's law predict between resistance and voltage drop?

(A) Larger voltage drops occur across loads with greater resistances.
(B) Smaller voltage drops occur across loads with greater resistances.
(C) Larger voltage drops occur across loads with lesser resistances.
(D) An equal voltage drop occurs across each load in series, independent of resistance.

13. Capacitive reactance decreases as electrical frequency

(A) decreases
(B) increases
(C) varies
(D) gets closer to DC

14. Which is the emitter in the transistor symbol below?

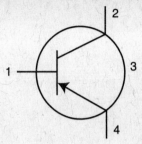

(A) 1
(B) 2
(C) 3
(D) 4

15. Which of the following CANNOT be used to make the magnetic field in a coil of wire stronger?

(A) increasing the number of turns of wire in the coil
(B) increasing the current flowing through the coil
(C) inserting an iron core into the middle of the coil
(D) inserting a dielectric between each coil

16. Whenever current passes through a resistance, _____ is most often generated.

(A) voltage
(B) capacitance
(C) heat
(D) light

17. The formula for Ohm's Law is

(A) $V = I \times R$
(B) $V = I - R$
(C) $V = I + R$
(D) $V = I \div R$

18. If current is able to pass through a diode, the diode must be

(A) reverse-biased
(B) forward-biased
(C) open
(D) grounded

19. Transistors are turned on and off by voltages applied to their

    (A) collector
    (B) emitter
    (C) base
    (D) cathode

20. If each resistor in this circuit equals 1,000 ohms, what is the total resistance in this circuit?

    (A) 250 ohms
    (B) 500 ohms
    (C) 1,000 ohms
    (D) 4,000 ohms

STOP. IF YOU FINISH BEFORE THE TIME IS UP, YOU MAY CHECK OVER YOUR WORK ON THIS PART ONLY.

Part 7: Auto and Shop Information (AS)

Time: 11 minutes; 25 questions

<u>Directions</u>: In this section, you will be tested on your knowledge of automotive and shop basics. For each question, select the best answer and mark the corresponding oval on your answer sheet.

1. High-intensity ultraviolet light is generated during _____.

   (A) welding
   (B) sawing
   (C) soldering
   (D) drilling

2. Most drill bits are made to cut when

   (A) rotating to the right when viewed from the top
   (B) rotating to the left when viewed from the top
   (C) rotating to the right when viewed from the bottom
   (D) oscillating

3. A motor oil with a ____ prefix for its quality rating would be suited for a diesel engine.

   (A) CD
   (B) SA
   (C) SJ
   (D) DM

4. Coil-on-plug ignition systems eliminate the need for

   (A) secondary coil winding
   (B) spark plug wires
   (C) spark plugs
   (D) primary coil winding

5. A DOHC V-8 engine would have a total of _____ camshafts.

   (A) two
   (B) three
   (C) four
   (D) eight

6. What type of file is depicted below?

   (A) smoothing file
   (B) bastard file
   (C) round rasp
   (D) flat rasp

7. Cutting torches use a mixture of _____ and _____ to produce a high-temperature flame.

   (A) nitrogen ; acetylene
   (B) nitrogen ; oxygen
   (C) acetylene ; helium
   (D) acetylene ; oxygen

8. All cars are currently being built with _____ electrical systems.

   (A) direct current
   (B) alternating current
   (C) negative ground
   (D) both direct and alternating current

9. As lead-acid batteries discharge, their electrolyte gradually turns to

   (A) sulphuric acid
   (B) water
   (C) lead peroxide
   (D) none of the above

10. The camshaft turns at _____ the speed of the engine's crankshaft.

    (A) one-half
    (B) one-fourth
    (C) twice
    (D) triple

11. An outside micrometer can be used to measure all of the following EXCEPT

   (A)   the distance between two wooden posts
   (B)   the thickness of flat objects
   (C)   the outside diameter of small cylindrically shaped objects
   (D)   the outside diameter of small spherical objects

12. Which of the following is the most common type of pliers?

   (A)

   (B)

   (C)

   (D)

13. What type of saw is depicted below?

   (A)   rip saw
   (B)   crosscut saw
   (C)   coping saw
   (D)   back saw

14. Engine temperature is controlled by the

   (A)   electrical system
   (B)   water pump
   (C)   radiator
   (D)   thermostat

15. This image depicts what stroke in the four-stroke cycle?

   (A)   intake stroke
   (B)   compression stroke
   (C)   power stroke
   (D)   exhaust stroke

16. The three elements needed to initiate combustion are

   (A)   air, light, and fuel
   (B)   air, fuel, and an ignition source
   (C)   air, compression, and an ignition source
   (D)   air, heat, and compression

17. A four-cylinder engine's firing order always starts with cylinder number

   (A)   1
   (B)   2
   (C)   4
   (D)   8

18. _____ cylinders will fire in one revolution of a six-cylinder engine.

   (A)   Two
   (B)   Three
   (C)   Four
   (D)   Eight

19. Which of the following is the LEAST likely to be found in an auto mechanic's toolbox?

(A)

(B)

(C)

(D)

20. Most solders are an alloy of _____ and _____.

(A) tin ; copper
(B) tin ; lead
(C) copper ; lead
(D) brass ; copper

21. A lead-acid battery has lead plates immersed in electrolyte composed of _____ and water.

(A) citric acid
(B) hydrochloric acid
(C) carbolic acid
(D) sulphuric acid

22. The starter motor's drive gear engages with the engine's

(A) flywheel ring gear
(B) crankshaft
(C) vibration damper
(D) timing chain

23. Sockets come in both _____ and _____ point designs

(A) 6 and 12
(B) 7 and 13
(C) 5 and 10
(D) 1 and 2

24. The stoichiometric, or ideal, air-fuel ratio is

(A) 10:1
(B) 17:1
(C) 14.7:1
(D) 17:4.2

25. With disc brakes, the _____ rotates with the vehicle's wheels.

(A) brake rotor
(B) brake caliper
(C) brake drum
(D) wheel cylinder

STOP. IF YOU FINISH BEFORE THE TIME IS UP, YOU MAY CHECK OVER YOUR WORK ON THIS PART ONLY.

Part 8: Mechanical Comprehension (MC)

Time: 19 minutes; 25 questions

<u>Directions</u>: In this section, you will be tested on your knowledge of mechanics and basic physics. Select the best answer for each question and mark the corresponding oval on your answer sheet.

1. Torque is

   (A)   the degree to which a force causes an object to rotate
   (B)   the same as horsepower
   (C)   a push or pull
   (D)   a force that travels in a circle

2. Speed is different from velocity because

   (A)   speed is measured in metric units while velocity is measured in English units
   (B)   velocity involves both speed and direction
   (C)   speed involves both velocity and direction
   (D)   velocity is a scalar quantity

3. Compared to a smaller mass, a larger mass requires _____ force to achieve the same acceleration rate.

   (A)   less
   (B)   more
   (C)   the same
   (D)   varying

4. Which of the following statements about force is NOT true?

   (A)   Force is a scalar quantity
   (B)   Force is a push or pull
   (C)   Greater force results in greater acceleration
   (D)   Smaller masses require less force to achieve the same acceleration as larger masses

5. Mechanical advantage is the advantage gained by the use of _____ in transmitting force.

   (A)   power
   (B)   a transformer
   (C)   a mechanism
   (D)   an engine

6. A hockey puck sliding on the ice

   (A)   has no net force acting on it
   (B)   would slide forever if the rink was long enough
   (C)   has speed, but not velocity
   (D)   experiences kinetic friction

7. If gear A turns in a counterclockwise direction, how does gear B turn?

   (A)   in a counterclockwise direction
   (B)   in a clockwise direction
   (C)   remains stationary
   (D)   turns more slowly than gear A

8. Which of the following statements about weight is NOT true?

   (A) Weight increases closer to earth's surface.
   (B) Weight is not totally dependent on mass.
   (C) Weight is greater on planets with greater mass.
   (D) Weight varies from location to location.

9. While attempting to push a heavy box across the floor

   (A) the amount of force required to start the box sliding is less than that required to keep it sliding
   (B) the amount of work being done is not dependent on how far the box moves
   (C) the coefficient of static friction is dependent on the nature of the surface the box is resting on
   (D) the mass of the box does not affect the amount of force required

10. Which of the following represents the mechanical advantage of a wheel and axle system where the driven wheel has a radius of 10" and the drive wheel has a diameter of 5"?

    (A) 4:1
    (B) 2:1
    (C) 1:2
    (D) 1:4

11. If it takes a force of 20 pounds to stretch the spring one inch, how much force must be applied to stretch the spring three inches?

    (A) 180 pounds
    (B) 60 pounds
    (C) 20 pounds
    (D) 6.67 pounds

12. In order to apply more torque to a bolt, a mechanic could

    (A) use a longer wrench
    (B) apply less force to the wrench
    (C) use a shorter wrench
    (D) move the wrench more quickly

13. A vehicle travels at a constant speed on the highway. It can be said that

    (A) its acceleration rate is less than zero
    (B) the net force acting on the vehicle are zero
    (C) the force applied by the vehicle's drive wheels is greater than the forces that act to slow the vehicle
    (D) it is accelerating at a constant rate

14. The two water towers below are of equal size and height above the ground. If both towers are completely full and their valves are opened, which of the following statements is true?

    (A) The two towers will release the same amount of water.
    (B) Tower B will release more water than tower A.
    (C) Tower A will release water three times as fast as tower B.
    (D) Tower A will release more water than tower B.

15. Two signs of equal weight are attached to a beam, using cords of equal length. Which of the following statements is true?

30 lbs   30 lbs

A   B

(A) All cords have the same amount of tension because the signs are of equal weight
(B) The cord holding sign A is under twice the tension of the cords holding sign B
(C) The cords holding sign B are under $\frac{1}{3}$ the tension of the cord holding sign A
(D) The cords holding sign B are under $\frac{1}{9}$ the tension of the cord holding sign A

16. The illustration below is an example of which kind of lever?

Object

Effort

Fulcrum

(A) first-class lever
(B) second-class lever
(C) third-class lever
(D) this is not a lever

17. If a vehicle accelerates from a standstill at a rate of $1\frac{m}{s^2}$, its velocity after 10 seconds will be

(A) $0.10\frac{m}{s}$

(B) $0.10\frac{m}{s^2}$

(C) $10\frac{m}{s}$

(D) $10\frac{m}{s^2}$

18. A wheelbarrow, as pictured below, is an example of

(A) a second-class lever
(B) a pulley system
(C) a third-class lever
(D) a crank

19. The gears in the illustration all have the same number of teeth. If gear X moves clockwise, which statement about gear Y is true?

(A) Gear Y moves counterclockwise.
(B) Gear Y moves twice as fast as gear X.
(C) Gear Y moves $\frac{1}{3}$ more slowly than gear X.
(D) Gear Y moves clockwise.

20. One pound of force is applied to move an object a distance of one foot. How much work has been done?

(A) 1 foot-pound
(B) 1 watt
(C) 2 foot-pounds
(D) 1 hertz

21. Which of the following statements about energy is NOT true?

(A) Energy cannot be created.
(B) The amount of energy in the universe is slowly diminishing.
(C) Energy cannot be destroyed.
(D) Energy can be converted from one form into another.

22. The two pulleys shown have equal weight to move. Which of the following statements is true?

    A   B

(A) The pulleys require the same force to counteract the weight of the object.

(B) Pulley B will not move the weight.

(C) Pulley A requires less force to counteract the weight of the object.

(D) Pulley B requires less force to counteract the weight of the object.

23. Which of the following is NOT a true statement about the principles that underlie hydraulics?

(A) Liquids conform to the shape of their container.

(B) A liquid can be dramatically compressed in order to increase the amount of force the liquid can transfer.

(C) A liquid is effectively incompressible.

(D) When pressure is applied to a completely enclosed fluid, this pressure is transmitted to all parts of the fluid and the enclosing walls.

24. Efficiency of a machine is determined by

(A) how much horsepower it can produce

(B) how much energy it consumes

(C) how much of the source energy is converted into usable energy

(D) how long the machine can operate at full output

25. In order to hit a baseball so that the ball has greater velocity, the player must

(A) hit the ball with less force

(B) make contact with the ball for a longer period of time

(C) apply more torque to the ball

(D) hit the ball so that it travels at roughly a 45° angle relative to the ground

STOP. IF YOU FINISH BEFORE THE TIME IS UP, YOU MAY CHECK OVER YOUR WORK ON THIS PART ONLY.

Part 9: Assembling Objects (AO)

Time: 15 minutes; 25 questions

Directions: In this section, you will be tested on your ability to determine how an object will look when its parts are put together. For each question, select the best answer and mark the corresponding oval on your answer sheet.

For questions 1–12:
Which figure best shows how the objects in the left box will appear if they are fit together?

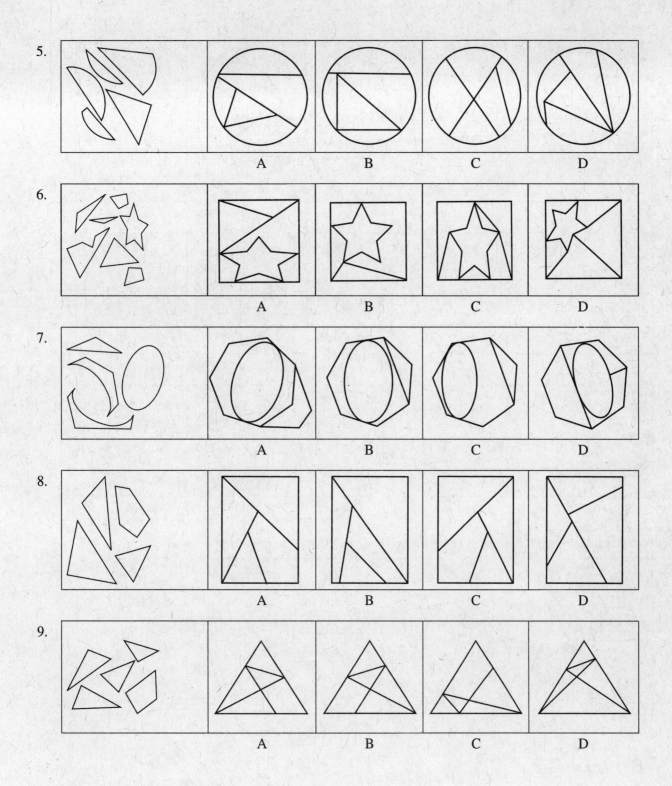

5. A   B   C   D

6. A   B   C   D

7. A   B   C   D

8. A   B   C   D

9. A   B   C   D

10.

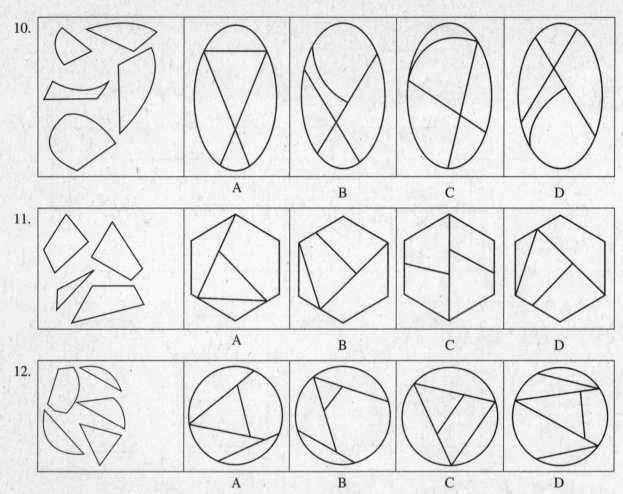

For questions 13–25:

Which figure best shows how the objects in the left box will touch if the letters for each object are matched?

13.

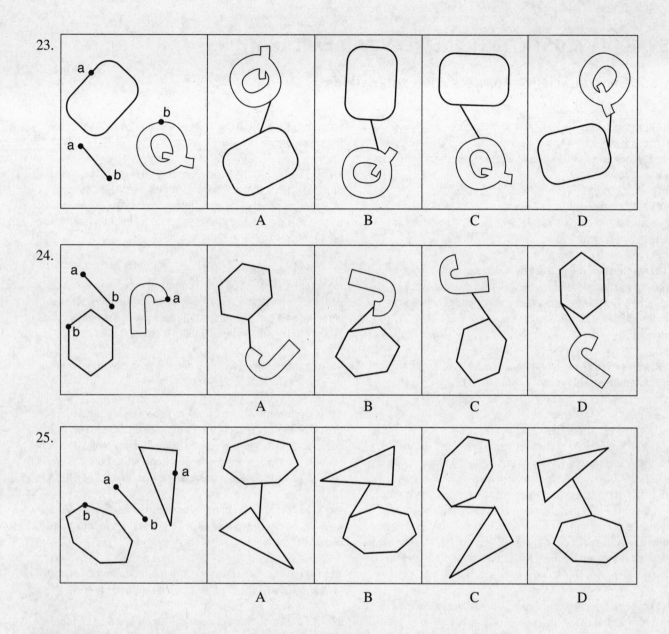

23.

A   B   C   D

24.

A   B   C   D

25.

A   B   C   D

STOP. IF YOU FINISH BEFORE THE TIME IS UP, YOU MAY CHECK OVER YOUR WORK ON THIS PART ONLY.

CONGRATULATIONS! YOU HAVE COMPLETED THE DIAGNOSTIC TEST.

ASVAB DIAGNOSTIC TEST ANSWERS AND EXPLANATIONS

Part 1: General Science Answers and Explanations

1. **(A) Proteins** Proteins are necessary for the body's maintenance, growth, and repair. Carbohydrates and fats are used primarily for energy. Vitamins are necessary for the functioning of various enzymes.

2. **(C) 212°** Water boils at 212 degrees on the Fahrenheit scale at sea level. On the Celsius scale, it boils at 100 degrees and on the Kelvin scale at 373 K.

3. **(D) respiration** The process by which animals convert oxygen (and sugars) into carbon dioxide and water is called respiration. The reverse process, by which plants convert carbon dioxide and water into sugar and oxygen, is called photosynthesis.

4. **(B) Veins** Veins carry blood from capillaries toward the heart. Arteries carry blood away from the heart. Ventricles are the lower chamber of the heart. Red blood cells are the component of blood that carries oxygen.

5. **(B) Iron forms rust.** Iron forms rust when water (or an even better electrolyte) turns iron and oxygen into iron oxide (Fe_2O_3); this is a chemical process. Helium and neon are both inert noble gases, so they do not react chemically. When sugar dissolves in water, the sugar particles become evenly distributed throughout the water forming a solution. However, neither are changed chemically. The sugar can be restored by boiling off the water. Ice melting does not alter the chemistry of H_2O.

6. **(A) O negative** Type O negative is the universal donor, which means that type O negative blood can be given to anybody without an adverse reaction.

7. **(D) vena cava.** Blood enters the right atrium of the heart from the vena cava.

8. **(A) ammonia.** The more basic (that is, alkaline) a substance is, the higher the pH. A substance with a pH of 7 is neutral, like pure water. A substance with a pH of less than 7 is acidic, and a substance with a pH of greater than 7 is basic/alkaline. Look in the answer choices for a base. Of the substances listed, ammonia is the most basic or alkaline.

9. **(C) small intestine** Of the various digestive organs, the small intestine does the most work in breaking the food down into usable nutrients. Food is broken down completely by

enzymes produced in the walls of the small intestine, in the pancreas, and in the liver.

10. **(D) testes.** In the male reproductive system, the testes produce sperm. In the female reproductive system during ovulation, an egg, or ovum, is released from the ovary and begins to travel through the oviduct (fallopian tube) and into the uterus.

11. **(D) gene.** A gene is defined as the most basic unit of inheritance. A genotype is the combination of alleles that codes for a particular trait. A phenotype is the physical expression of a particular genotype. Chromosomes are tightly coiled strands of DNA that contain multiple genes.

12. **(C) shale** Shale, which is derived from clay sediments, is an example of sedimentary rock.

13. **(C) autotroph.** An autotroph is known as a producer or self-feeder because it can produce its own food. This is generally done through photosynthesis or chemosynthesis. A saprotroph is a decomposer, a hetereotroph relies on other organisms to be its food and a scavenger feeds on decaying flesh.

14. **(C) scavenger** A vulture is considered a scavenger. These animals mostly consume refuse and decaying organic matter, especially carrion, which is decaying flesh.

15. **(B) igneous** Igneous rocks are formed from the cooling of lava and include obsidian, granite, basalt, and others.

16. **(C) the Earth lies between the Moon and Sun.** A lunar eclipse happens when the Moon passes through the Earth's shadow. During a lunar eclipse, the Earth lies between the Moon and Sun.

17. **(A) one hundredth of a meter.** The prefix *centi–* indicates *hundredth*. One thousandth of a meter is called a millimeter. 10 meters is a decameter and 100 meters is a hectometer.

18. **(D) the tendency of an object to continue moving in the same direction.** Momentum is the tendency of an object to continue moving in the same direction. Velocity is the rate at which an object changes position. Acceleration is the rate of change of velocity. Force is the push or pull that forces an object to change its speed or direction.

19. **(D) violet** Visible light is composed of different colors each with a different frequency. Red has the lowest frequency, and violet has the highest frequency.

20. **(A) neutrons and protons.** The major portion of an atom's mass consists of neutrons and protons. Electrons, positrons, neutrinos, and other subatomic particles have negligible masses.

21. **(C) sea urchin** Arthropods represent a large phylum of the animal kingdom characterized by chitinous exoskeletons, segmented bodies, and jointed legs. Examples include crabs, centipedes, and spiders, but not the sea urchin, which belongs to the phylum Echinodermata.

22. **(A) ionic compound.** Table salt (NaCl) is an ionic compound because each chlorine atom borrows an electron from each sodium atom. This results in very strong ionic bonds that enable salt to form a tightly bound crystalline structure when in the solid form. When salt is placed in water, however, the crystalline structure breaks down, and the individual sodium and chlorine ions are both able to dissociate into the water.

23. **(C) the Earth rotates 360 degrees about its axis.** Over the course of 24 hours the Earth rotates 360 degrees, or one complete rotation, about its axis.

24. **(C) Monera** The Monera kingdom is considered the most primitive kingdom because its organisms are prokaryotic—that is, their cells lack nuclei.

25. **(B) Chordata.** The phylum Chordata contains animals with vertebrae. (In human beings, the vertebrae are the bones that make up the spine.) Animalia is the Kingdom that includes humans. Mammalia is the Class that includes humans. Primata is an order that includes primates (such as humans).

Part 2: Arithmetic Reasoning Answers and Explanations

1. **(C) $128** This question asks you to determine the sale price of a camera that normally sells at $160 and is discounted 20%. To solve, determine what 20% of $160 equals. Rewrite 20% as a decimal. 20% = 0.20. So 20% of $160 = 0.20 × $160 = $32 The sale price of the camera would be $160 − $32 = $128, choice (C).

2. **(B) 18** First, set up the rate as a proportion, where x is the number of stations.

$$\frac{3 \text{ stations}}{10 \text{ minutes}} = \frac{x \text{ stations}}{1 \text{ hour}}$$

Then, convert the units.

$$\frac{3 \text{ stations}}{10 \text{ minutes}} = \frac{x \text{ stations}}{60 \text{ minutes}}$$

Cross multiply and solve for x.

$$180 = 10x$$

$$18 = x$$

3. **(B) $2\frac{1}{3}$** In this question, the ratio is implied: for every $\frac{3}{4}$ inch of map there is 1 real mile, so the ratio of inches to the miles they represent is always $\frac{3}{4}$ to 1. Therefore, you can set up the proportion:

$$\frac{\text{Number of inches}}{\text{Number of miles}} = \frac{\frac{3}{4}}{1} = \frac{3}{4}$$

Now $1\frac{3}{4}$ inches $= \frac{7}{4}$ inches.

Set up a proportion:

$$\frac{7}{4} \text{ inches}$$

$$\frac{\frac{7}{4} \text{ inches}}{\text{Number of miles}} = \frac{3}{4}$$

Cross-multiply:

$$\frac{7}{4}(4) = 3 \text{ (Number of miles)}$$

$$7 = 3 \text{ (Number of miles)}$$

$$\frac{7}{3} = \text{Number of miles}$$

or $2\frac{1}{3} = \text{Number of miles}$

4. **(D) 45** You can express the ratio of baseballs to golf balls as $\frac{2}{3}$. Since you know the number of baseballs, you can set up a proportion: $\frac{2}{3} = \frac{30}{x}$ where x is the number of golf balls. To solve, cross-multiply to get $2x = 90$, or $x = 45$.

5. **(D) $11.25** The total cost of the taxi ride equals $36 + (25\% \text{ of } \$36)$, or $36 + (.25 × \$36) = \$36 + \$9 = \$45$. If four people split the cost equally, then each person paid $\frac{\$45}{4}$, or $11.25 each.

6. **(A) 36** Find the number of seconds in an hour and then multiply this by the distance the car is traveling each second. There are 60 seconds in a minute and 60 minutes in one hour; therefore, there are 60 × 60, or 3,600, seconds in an hour. In one second the car travels $\frac{1}{100}$ kilometers; in one hour the car will travel $3,600 × \frac{1}{100}$ or 36 kilometers.

7. **(B) 25** Subtracting a negative number is the same as addition, so $20 − (−5)$ is really $20 + 5 = 25$.

8. **(C) $25.00** If Ms. Smith's car averages 35 miles per gallon, she can go 35 miles on 1 gallon. To go 700 miles she will need $\frac{700}{35}$, or 20 gallons of gasoline. The price of gasoline was $1.25 per gallon, so she spent 20 × $1.25, or $25, for her trip.

9. **(D) 96** Be careful with a question like this one. You're given the percent decrease (25%) and the *new* number (72), and you're asked to reconstruct the original number. Don't just take 25% of 72 and add it on. That 25% is based not on the new number, 72, but on the original number—the number you're looking for. The best way to do a problem like this is to set up an equation:

$$(\text{Original number}) − (25\% \text{ of Original number}) = \text{New number}$$
$$x − 0.25x = 72$$
$$0.75x = 72$$
$$x = 96$$

Alternatively, you can use the answer choices to determine the correct answer. The original number of jelly beans has to be reducible by 25%, or $\frac{1}{4}$. That means the original number of jelly beans has to be a multiple of 4 (or else you'd be reducing by pieces of jelly beans). Only the correct answer, 96, is a multiple of 4.

10. **(B) 24** The time it takes to complete the entire exam is the sum of the time spent on the first half of the exam and the time spent on the second half. The time spent on the first half is $\frac{2}{3}$ of the time spent on the second half. If S represents the time spent on the second half, then the total time spent is $\frac{2}{3}S + S$ or $\frac{5}{3}S$. You know this total time is one hour, or 60 minutes. Set up a simple equation and solve for S.

$$\frac{5}{3}S = 60$$
$$\frac{3}{5} \times \frac{5}{3}S = \frac{3}{5} \times 60$$
$$S = 36$$

So the second half takes 36 minutes. The first half takes $\frac{2}{3}$ of this, or 24 minutes. You could also find the first half by subtracting 36 minutes from the total time, 60 minutes.

11. **(A)** $6\frac{2}{3}$ **%** You're asked what percent of the new solution is alcohol. The *part* is the number of ounces of alcohol; the *whole* is the total number of ounces of the new solution. There were 25 ounces originally. Then 50 ounces were added, so there are 75 ounces of new solution. How many ounces are alcohol? 20% of the original 25-ounce solution was alcohol. 20% is $\frac{1}{5}$, so $\frac{1}{5}$ of 25, or 5 ounces are alcohol. Now you can find the percent of alcohol in the new solution:

$$\% \text{ alcohol} = \frac{\text{alcohol}}{\text{total solution}} \times 100\%$$
$$= \frac{5}{75} \times 100\%$$
$$= \frac{20}{3}\% = 6\frac{2}{3}\%$$

12. **(A)** $\frac{2}{3}$ To find probability, determine the number of desired outcomes and divide that by the number of possible outcomes. The probability formula looks like this:

$$\text{Probability} = \frac{\# \text{ of desired outcomes}}{\# \text{ of possible outcomes}}$$

In this case, Marty is pulling one pen at random from his knapsack, and you want to determine the probability that the pen is either red or black. There are 5 blue pens, 6 black pens, and 4 red pens in the knapsack. Let's return to the probability formula:

$$\text{Probability} = \frac{\# \text{ of desired outcomes}}{\# \text{ of possible outcomes}}$$
$$= \frac{\text{Number of red } + \text{ black pens}}{\text{Number of red } + \text{ black } + \text{ blue pens}}$$
$$= \frac{4 + 6}{4 + 6 + 5} = \frac{10}{15} = \frac{2}{3}$$

13. **(D) 200%** Be careful with combined percent increase. You cannot just add the two percents, because they're percents of different bases. In this instance, the 100% increase is based on the 1980 population, but the 50% increase is based on the larger 1990 population. If you just added 100% and 50% to get 150%, you would have chosen a wrong answer.

The best way to do a problem like this one is to pick a number for the original whole and just see what happens. The best number to pick here is 100. (That may be a small number for the population of a country, but reality is not important—all that matters is the math.)

If the 1980 population was 100, then a 100% increase would put the 1990 population at 200. And a 50% increase over 200 would be $200 + 100 = 300$.

Since the population went from 100 to 300, that's a percent increase of 200%.

$$\frac{300 - 100}{100} \times 100\% = \frac{200}{100} \times 100\% = 200\%$$

14. **(B) 44** To learn the man's overtime rate of pay, first figure out his regular rate of pay. Divide the amount of money made, $200, by the time it took to make it, 40 hours.
$200 \div 40$ hours $= \$5$ per hour. That is the normal rate. The man is paid $1\frac{1}{2}$ times his regular rate during overtime, so when working more than 40 hours he makes $\frac{3}{2} \times \$5$ per hour $= \$7.50$ per hour. Now figure out how long it takes the man to make $230. It takes him 40 hours to make the first $200. The last $30 are made at the overtime rate. Since it takes the man one hour to make $7.50 at this rate, you can figure out the number of extra hours by dividing $30 by $7.50 per hour. $30 \div \$7.50$ per hour $= 4$ hours. The total time needed is 40 hours plus 4 hours, or 44 hours.

15. **(A) 225** The calculations aren't too bad on this one. The most important thing to keep in mind is that you're solving for 75% of x and not for x *itself*. First, you are told that 50% of x is 150. That means that half of x is 150, and that x is 300. So 75% of $x = 0.75 \times 300 = 225$.

16. **(D) $4.00** This is a question where Backsolving (plugging in an answer choice to see if it's correct) can save you a lot of time. Let's start with choice (B) and see if it works. If (B) is correct, an adult's ticket would cost $3.00, and a child's ticket would cost $1.50. The total fare you're asked for is for two adults and three children. If an adult's fare was $3.00, that total fare would be $2(\$3.00) + 3(\$1.50) = \$6.00 + \$4.50 = \$10.50$. That's too low since the question states that the total fare is $14.00.

Now see what happens if an adult fare was more expensive. If (D) was correct, an adult's ticket would cost $4.00 and a child's ticket would cost $2.00. The total fare would equal $2(\$4.00) + 3(\$2.00) = \$8.00 + \$6.00 = \$14.00$. That's the total fare you're looking for, so (D) is correct.

17. **(C) 2 × 2 × 5 × 7** To find the prime factorization of a number, find one prime that will go into the number (here 2 is a good place to start). Express the number as that prime multiplied by some other number.

$$140 = 2 \times 70$$

Then keep breaking down the larger factor until you are left with only prime numbers.

$$140 = 2 \times 2 \times 35$$

$$140 = 2 \times 2 \times 5 \times 7$$

18. **(A) 6** When the painter and his son work together, they charge the sum of their hourly rates, $12 + $6, or $18 per hour. Their bill equals the product of this combined rate and the number of hours they worked. Therefore $108 must equal $18 per hour times the number of hours they worked. Divide $108 by $18 per hour to find the number of hours. $108 ÷ $18 = 6.

19. **(C) 24** The exclamation mark indicates a factorial. A factorial is an integer multiplied by every smaller integer, down to the number 1, like this: 4! = 4 × 3 × 2 × 1 = 24

20. **(B) $1.75** Compute the cost of parking a car for 5 hours at each garage. Since the two garages have a split-rate system of charging, the cost for the first hour is different from the cost of each remaining hour.

The first hour at garage *A* costs $8.75

The next 4 hours cost 4 × $1.25 = $5.00

The total cost for parking at garage *A* = $8.75 + 5.00 = $13.75

The first hour at garage *B* costs $5.50

The next 4 hours cost 4 × $2.50 = $10.00

The total cost for parking at garage *B* = $5.50 + $10.00 = $15.50

So the difference in cost = $15.50 − $13.75 = $1.75, (B).

21. **(C) 8 hours and 20 minutes** Set up a proportion:

$$\frac{12 \, pages}{1 \, hour} = \frac{100 \, pages}{x \, hours}$$
$$12x = 100$$
$$x = \frac{100}{12} = 8\frac{1}{3}$$

An hour is 60 minutes; one third of that is 20 minutes. So $8\frac{1}{3}$ hours is 8 hours and 20 minutes.

22. **(B) 18** This problem sets up relationships among large, medium, and small sodas—2 large sodas are equal to 3 medium sodas, and 2 medium sodas are equal to 3 small sodas. How many small sodas equal 8 large sodas? Well, 2 larges equal 3 mediums, so 12 mediums must equal 4 × 2 or 8 large sodas. You now can find how many small sodas represent 12 mediums. Since 2 mediums are the same as 3 small sodas, 12 mediums must equal 6 × 3 or 18 small sodas.

23. **(D) 20,200** If you change each digit 5 into a 7 in the number 258,546, the new number would be 278,746. The difference between these two numbers would be 278,746 − 258,546 = 20,200.

24. **(A) $9.63** Since 1 pound of lumber costs $4.00, $2\frac{1}{4}$ pounds of lumber cost 2.25 × $4.00 = $9.00. Then add 7% sales tax to $9.00. Find 7% of $9.00 by multiplying 0.07 × $9.00 = $0.63. Add $0.63 to $9.00 to get $9.63, choice (A).

25. **(D) 13 to 21** The question asks which of five ratios is equivalent to the ratio of $3\frac{1}{4}$ to $5\frac{1}{4}$. Since the ratios in the answer choices are expressed in whole numbers, turn this ratio into whole numbers. Start by turning the ratio into improper fractions:

$$3\frac{1}{4} : 2\frac{1}{4}$$
$$= \frac{13}{4} : \frac{21}{4}$$

Multiply both sides of the ratio by 4.

$$= 13 : 21$$

26. **(D) 192** Set up the proportion.

$$\frac{\frac{3}{8} \, lb}{1 \, day} = \frac{72 \, lbs}{x \, days}$$

Cross multiply.
$$\frac{3}{8}x = 72$$
$$x = 72 \times \frac{8}{3}$$
$$x = 192$$

27. **(C) $720** You can save valuable time by estimating on this one. Pay special attention to how much you have left and how much you've already spent. If a man spent $\frac{5}{12}$ of his salary and was left with $420, that means that he had $\frac{7}{12}$ left, and if the man's salary is *x* dollars, then $\frac{7}{12}x = $420 That means that $420 is a little more than half of his salary. So his salary would be a little less than 2($420) = $840. Choice (C), $720 is a little less than $840. So (C) works perfectly, and it's the correct answer here.

28. **(C) 25%** The key to this question is that while the value of the stock decreases and increases by the same *amount*, it doesn't decrease and increase by the same *percent*. When the stock first decreases, that amount of change is part of a larger whole. If the stock were to increase to its former value, that same amount of change would be a larger percent of a smaller whole.

Pick a number for the original value of the stock, such as $100. (Since it's easy to take percents of 100, it's usually best to choose 100.) The 20% decrease represents $20, so the stock decreases to a value of $80. Now in order for the stock to reach the value of $100 again, there must be a $20 increase. What percent of $80 is $20? It's $\frac{\$20}{\$80} \times 100\%$, or $\frac{1}{4} \times 100\%$, or 25%.

29. **(C) 14** This is a combined work problem. Joan can shovel the whole driveway in 50 minutes, so each minute she does $\frac{1}{50}$ of the driveway. Mary can shovel the whole driveway in 20 minutes; in each minute she does $\frac{1}{20}$ of the driveway. In one minute they do:

$$\frac{1}{50} + \frac{1}{20} = \frac{2}{100} + \frac{5}{100} = \frac{7}{100}$$

If they do $\frac{7}{100}$ of the driveway in one minute, they do the entire driveway in $\frac{100}{7}$ minutes. (If you do $\frac{1}{2}$ of a job in 1 minute, you do the whole job in the reciprocal of $\frac{1}{2}$, or 2 minutes.) So all that remains is to round $\frac{100}{7}$ off to the nearest integer. Since $\frac{100}{7} = 14\frac{2}{7}$, $\frac{100}{7}$ is approximately 14. It takes about 14 minutes for both of them to shovel the driveway.

30. **(B) $260** You're told that Eileen earns $280 per week. Kelly earns $50 more than Eileen, so Kelly earns $280 + $50 = $330 per week. June's salary is $70 less than Kelly's, so June earns $330 − $70 = $260 per week, and (B) is correct.

CHAPTER 2

Part 3: Word Knowledge Answers and Explanations

1. **(C) aristocratic** *Noble* means *related to high rank or social class*. The *aristocracy* is composed of the highest classes in society, so therefore, choice (C) is correct.

2. **(D) admit** The sentence draws a contrast between John initially disagreeing with Megan and then conceding her point. That context suggests that *concede* likely means the opposite of *disagree*. *Admit* is the best match: to admit a point is to agree with it.

3. **(B) provoke** The verb form of *goad* means to *prod into action or coerce*. Of the answer choices, only *provoke* approximates this meaning.

4. **(C) pack** The word *herd* refers to a group of people or animals. Similarly, a *pack* is a group of people or animals, like a wolf pack or a scout pack.

5. **(D) workable** If you know that an EMT is a rescue technician, then you may grasp the idea that panic is not allowed. *Viable* then can mean *capable of survival or success*. Only (D), *workable*, which means *able to produce the desired result*, suggests that meaning.

6. **(C) wise** *Judicious* means *possessing or displaying good judgment*, or in other words, being *wise*.

7. **(D) pausing** *Hesitating* can mean *pausing before doing something*, or sometimes *reluctant* or *indecisive*. Among the answer choices available, the only possible correct answer is (D), *pausing*.

8. **(A) fabricating** You probably know the root word *false* as meaning *wrong*, or in reference to a lie. The textbook definition is to *misrepresent*. Looking at the possible answer choices, choice (A), *fabricating*, which means *making up*, is the best possible answer.

9. **(C) empty** The word *hollow* means *lacking a center* or *empty*.

10. **(C) plead** The verb *to coax* means *to try to persuade*. Of the answer choices, only (C), *plead*, approaches being correct.

11. **(B) boring** The root of the word *monotonous* is *mono* meaning *one*. Something *monotone* is in one flat tone and is completely lacking in variety. *Boring* would be another way to say this.

12. **(C) frustration** The word *consternation* means *anxiety or dismay*. Of the answer choices, *frustration* is the closest match. The context of the sentence hints at this meaning, because the material the students are learning is difficult.

13. **(A) tasty** *Savory* in reference to food means *appetizing to taste*. Choice (A), *tasty*, is the best answer.

14. **(B) fame** *Renown* means *fame or reputation*.

15. **(B) storyteller** A *raconteur* is someone who tells stories. The word even sounds a little like "recount."

16. **(D) satisfy** To *quench* something is to *sate* or *satisfy* it.

17. **(A) split** The word *polarized* has the same root as *polar*. Think of "polar opposites" and you will be on the right track. In this case, choice (A), *split*, is closest in meaning to *polarized*.

18. **(C) exact** *Precise* means *exact* or *specific*.

19. **(B) landscape** *Terrain* comes from the root *terra* or *earth*. So of the answer choices, only *landscape* would be appropriate. *Landscape* is the ground in view.

20. **(D) final** *Terminal* means *relating to an end, limit, or boundary*. Choice (D), *final*, is most similar in meaning.

21. **(D) enhance** *Augment* means to *enhance something already developed*.

22. **(A) unintentional** Something *involuntary* is something done *without plan or accidentally*–in other words, *unintentionally*.

23. **(B) secret agreement** The noun *collusion* refers to *an agreement of an illicit or secret nature*. The prefix *con*– (which here appears as *col*–) is a useful hint here, since it means *together*: people who *collude* agree to act together.

24. **(C) determination** *Tenacity* means showing *persistence and determination*. The word root *ten* relates to holding, so you could guess that *tenacity* might mean something like *holding on*.

25. **(D) tangible** *Tactile* means *relating to the sense of touch*. Of the answer choices, (D), *tangible*, is the most similar in meaning to the original word. In fact, *tactile* and *tangible* come from the same root: in Latin, *tangere* means *to touch*.

26. **(C) predict** To *portend* is to *foreshadow* or *foretell*, as an omen or advance warning sign. Here, *predict* is the closest match.

27. **(A) sprout** To *germinate* means to *sprout or bud, as a plant*.

28. **(B) invigorate** *Restore* has the prefix *re–*, meaning *again*. Thus, *restore* means *bring back something that had been lost*. Of the choices given, both (B) and (D) refer to affecting change on something. But of the two, only (B), *invigorate*, means to renew.

29. **(D) thread** A *filament* is a *thread or string that is very thin*.

30. **(C) altered** *Mutate* is a word you've probably seen before. Comic books often have mutated characters (like the Hulk or Godzilla). The word means *something that has changed from its original state*. Of the choices given, (C), *altered*, is the best choice.

31. **(B) exciting** The adjective *dynamic* means *constantly changing* or *exciting*. The word *yet* in the sentence is a clue that you are looking for a word that contrasts with *calm*, making *exciting* a good choice.

32. **(C) harden** *Congeal* means to *solidify, coagulate, or harden*.

33. **(D) scout** To *reconnoiter* means to *make a preliminary inspection*, or *see before others*. Of the answer choices, only (D), *scout*, means the same thing as the given word.

34. **(A) accumulate** The verb *accrue* means to *accumulate over time as a result of growth*.

35. **(D) natural** An *innate* trait is one that is *inherent* or *natural*.

Part 4: Paragraph Comprehension Answers and Explanations

1. **(B) scientific progress made its way into the fiction of the time.** The main idea of a passage is the most important idea conveyed by the author. Choice (B) pinpoints the author's main point. Choice (C) distorts a detail from the passage. Choice (A) is not mentioned in the passage. The author states that science was extremely popular in the nineteenth century, which implies that science fiction was as well, but no direct information is given about the popularity of science fiction. Choice (D) is incorrect because there is no mention of Poe and Doyle being scientists.

2. **(C) reading provides vocabulary clues within sentences.** The answer to a detail question such as this will be a paraphrase of what you find in the passage. You are told that reading shows students how words are used in sentences, so (C) is correct. (A) is incorrect because adults are never mentioned. (B) also was not stated in the passage. (D) does not answer the question and is not necessarily true based on the information given.

3. **(A) the history of the Hudson River School of painters** Wrong answer choices on global questions (that is, questions that ask about the passage's topic or main idea) are often too broad or too specific. (B) is too broad because the passage is not about all American art movements, only the Hudson River School movement. (C) is too specific because the influence of European painters is just one detail mentioned, while (A), the history of the Hudson River School painters, is being described. (D) is incorrect because nationalism is not the focus of the passage.

4. **(D) People should conduct research before purchasing a computer.** This is the central idea of the passage. (If a passage begins or ends with a recommendation, that recommendation will often be the main idea.) The author does imply that people should not base their decisions on advertisements (B) but that is a detail rather than the main idea. Choice (A) is the opposite of the detail stated in the passage. Choice (C) is too broad. The passage is primarily concerned with computer purchase decisions, not life in general.

5. **(A) empty.** It is important on Vocabulary-in-Context questions not to rely on your vocabulary knowledge alone for the word in question, but instead to choose an answer that best represents how the word is being used in the paragraph. *Bleak* can be used to mean *cold*, choice (C), or *depressing*, which might make choice (B) seem appealing. But only choice (A) does not alter the meaning of the sentence when plugged in: "the empty landscape and broad skies."

6. **(D) her love of the land.** Since the answer to a detail question can be found in the text, the clause "nearly all her works are portrayals of nature" would direct you to choice (D). Choices (A), (B), and (C) all state things that were never mentioned in the passage, a characteristic typical of wrong answer choices to detail questions.

7. **(C) The planets move in orbit around the sun.** The text states that the Copernican model of the solar system describes that planets are revolving around the Sun, choice (C). This is contradicted by choice (B). (A) and (D) are not mentioned.

8. **(D) eager.** Toby is smiling while he waits for his father, already holding his baseball glove and ball. He is *eager*, choice (D), to get to the game. Choice (A) is distracting since it is sad that it might be the last game that Toby's father will be able to attend, but the descriptive language of the passage supports eagerness and not sadness: the sun rushes into the room, now the birds are appearing. Toby is smiling, so there is no evidence of him being *uneasy*, choice (C). He is anxiously waiting for his father, which contradicts his being *careless*, choice (B).

9. **(A) eating** Since the body can survive without food longer than it can survive without *drinking* (B) or *breathing* (C), *eating* is the least essential to survival. Choice (A) is correct. (D) is incorrect because excretion is not mentioned in the passage.

10. **(C) Objective news reporting is a dying art.** For Inference questions you should read the entire passage, and it is often best to attack each answer choice and eliminate those that do not follow from the passage. (B) clearly contradicts the author's words. You have no information about how the author feels about television anchors, so (D) is unsupported. (A) goes beyond the scope of the passage, and may or may not be true based on what you have read. The correct answer will be something that must be true based on what's given, like choice (C).

11. **(A) mainly an oral form** This is a Detail question, which means that you can look up the answer in the text. The poems "were intended to be sung or recited, not written down," so they were mainly an oral form, choice (A). (B), which states that Greek poetry was unlike those of other societies, contradicts the passage. (C) and (D) are not mentioned.

12. **(C) great strides have been made in artificial intelligence.** The correct choice for a main idea question will express what the author believes. The passage states that remarkable progress has been made in artificial intelligence, so choice (C) is correct. While the author discusses the difference of opinion between those who believe that there will eventually be a computer capable of intelligent thought and those who do not, she does not assert the truth of either statement, so choice (A) is incorrect. Be wary of answer choices such as (D) that use extreme language. Chess is not the main focus of the passage, so choice (B) is incorrect.

13. **(B) the formation of coral reefs** This is a main idea question, so either the correct answer will make so much sense you will want to pick it, or you can eliminate wrong answer choices because they are too broad, too specific, or otherwise don't properly describe the passage. Here the correct answer choice does make a lot of sense. The passage describes how coral reefs are created, so choice (B), the formation of coral reefs, describes the passage well. Choice (A) is out because "varieties" of animal life are nowhere described. (C) is wrong because "death cycles" of coral reefs are never touched upon. And (D) is far too narrow; there's only the barest reference in the passage to "the physical beauty" of coral reefs.

14. **(D) cooperative.** For this detail question, you just want to pick the answer choice that best paraphrases the relationship between the coral and algae as described in the passage. The passage states that the "two organisms form a mutually beneficial relationship"; in other words, the relationship is cooperative, choice (D).

15. **(C) wipe off and replace the drain plug.** For correct sequence questions, look up the answer in the text. According to the passage, when the engine is fully drained, you should wipe off the drain plug and replace it, choice (C).

Part 5: Mathematics Knowledge Answers and Explanations

1. **(D) 600.** A question like this one tests your ability to work with decimals. $\frac{48}{0.08}$ is the same as $\frac{4,800}{8} = 600$. (D) is correct. When dividing by a decimal, be sure to move the decimal place the same number of spaces for both numbers.

2. **(A) 9,901,471.** Be careful with your number crunching here. $9,899,399 + 2,082 = 9,901,481$, choice (A).

3. **(D) 729.** The cube of a number is that number multiplied by itself three times. So the cube of 9 would be $9 \times 9 \times 9 = 729$, choice (D).

4. **(A) −12** Plug in the values for a and b and remember your order of operations when working through your calculations. When $a = -2$ and $b = 3$,

$$(-ab)(a) = [-(-2) \times 3](-2)$$
$$= (-[-6])(-2)$$
$$= (6) \times (-2) = -12, \text{ choice (A).}$$

5. **(C) $x^2 - 8x + 16$** This is a classic product of two binomials. Remember to FOIL, and you're good to go.

$$(x - 4)(x - 4)$$
$$= (x)(x) + (x)(-4) + (-4)(x) + (-4)(-4)$$
$$= x^2 - 4x - 4x + 16$$
$$= x^2 - 8x + 16.$$

Choice (C) is correct. If you recognized this as one of the classic quadratics, a binomial squared, you could have answered this correctly without using FOIL.

6. **(D) 1,230** $10^4 = 10,000$, indicating that you should move the decimal four places to the right.
So $0.123 \times 10^4 = 0.123 \times 10,000 = 1,230$, choice (D).

7. **(A) 2** Know your perfect squares. $\sqrt{100} = 10$ and $\sqrt{64} = 8$. So $\sqrt{100} - \sqrt{64} = 10 - 8$, choice (A).

8. **(B) 15π** Given a diameter of 6, the radius must equal $\frac{1}{2}$ of 6, or 3. Next, the circumference $(c) = 2\pi r = 2\pi(3) = 6\pi$. The area $(b) = \pi r^2 = \pi(3^2) = 9\pi$. Add those two: $9\pi + 6\pi = 15\pi$.

9. **(B) 4** To find the probability of something occurring, divide the number of desired outcomes by the number of total outcomes. In the example of the bag of marbles, you begin with $8 + 4 + 7 + 5 = 24$ marbles, and draw out 8, leaving you with 16 marbles. Out of those 16 marbles, 4 must be white since the chance of drawing a white marble is now $\frac{4}{16}$ or $\frac{1}{4}$. If you are left with 4 white marbles, you must have already withdrawn 4 white marbles. (B) is correct.

10. **(C) $4B - 40$** If B is equal to the number of books that Janice has, and you know that Liza has 40 fewer than 3 times the number of books that Janice has, Liza has $3B - 40$ books, and Janice has B books. Together they have $4B - 40$ books, choice (C).

11. **(D) 64** The perimeter of a square is $4s$ where s is the length of a side. If a square has a perimeter of 32, then it has a side length of 8. The area of the square is $s^2 = 8^2 = 64$, choice (D).

12. **(C) $3x^4$** You can simplify this expression as follows:

$$\frac{6x^2}{2x^2} = \frac{6}{2}\left(\frac{x^6}{x^2}\right) = 3x^4$$

Remember to subtract exponents when dividing.

13. **(C) 321** Go through the answer choices one at a time, and select the choice whose digits have a sum and product that are equal.

(A) 111. Product = $(1)(1)(1) = 1$. Sum $= 1 + 1 + 1 = 3$. Eliminate.

(B) 220. Product = $(2)(2)(0) = 0$. Sum $= 2 + 2 + 0 = 4$. Eliminate.

(C) 321. Product = $(3)(2)(1) = 6$. Sum $= 3 + 2 + 1 = 6$.

Choice (C) is correct.

14. **(D) 64** If $x = \frac{1}{8}$, and we are asked to solve for y when $\frac{2}{x} = \frac{y}{4}$, begin by plugging in $\frac{1}{8}$ for x. $\frac{2}{\frac{1}{8}} = \frac{y}{4}$. Cross-multiply and solve. $\frac{1}{8}y = 8$, so $y = 64$, (D).

15. **(D) 180** When parallel lines are crossed by a transversal, all acute angles formed are equal, and all acute angles are supplementary to all obtuse angles. So in this diagram, obtuse angle y is supplementary to the acute angle of 55°. Angle x is an acute angle, so it is equal to 55°. Therefore, angle x is supplementary to angle y, and the two must sum to 180°.

16. **(A) $\frac{2}{b}$** If you're looking for a in terms of b, isolate the a on one side of the equation.

$$3ab = 6$$
$$ab = 2$$
$$a = \frac{2}{b}$$

17. **(C) 4** Distribute the numbers outside the parentheses and solve for y.

$$4(y - 1) = 2(y + 2)$$
$$4y - 4 = 2y + 4$$
$$2y = 8$$
$$y = 4$$

18. **(B) 55** Since RS and RT are equal, the angles opposite them must be equal. Therefore, angle $T =$ angle S. Since the degree measures of the three interior angles of a triangle sum to 180, $70 +$ angle measure $S +$ angle measure $T = 180$, and angle measure $S +$ angle measure $T = 110$. Since the two angles, S and T, are equal, each must have angle measures half of 110, or 55.

19. **(B) 2** When D is divided by 15, the result is 6 with a remainder of 2. That means that $D = 6(15) + 2$ or 92. When 92 is divided by 6, the remainder is 2. (B) is correct.

20. **(C) 30** The average of 7 consecutive even numbers is 24. In a set of evenly spaced numbers, the median is the same as the average. That means that 24 must be the middle number the set of numbers. So the set must be {18, 20, 22, 24, 26, 28, 30}. The largest number is 30, choice (C).

21. **(D) 52 square inches.** The surface area of a rectangular solid is $2lw + 2lh + 2wh$. In this case that would be $(2 \times 2 \times 3) + (2 \times 2 \times 4) + (2 \times 3 \times 4) = 12 + 16 + 24 = 52$ square inches, choice (D).

22. **(A) 10** If $100 \div x = 10n$, that can be rewritten as $\frac{100}{x} = 10n$. Cross-multiply and you get $100 = 10nx$. Divide both sides by 10 to solve for nx.

$$nx = \frac{100}{10} = 10.$$ (A) is correct.

23. **(B) 30** A circle contains 360°, so:

$$(4x + 15) + (2x - 5) + (6x - 10) = 360$$
$$4x + 2x + 6x + 15 - 5 - 10 = 360$$
$$12x = 360$$
$$x = 30$$

24. **(C) 120** $5! = 5 \times 4 \times 3 \times 2 \times 1 = 120$.

25. **(A) 2n** If Melissa has $5n$ photographs, and she gives n photographs to each of three friends, she would have given away $3n$ photographs. $5n - 3n = 2n$. (A) is correct.

Part 6: Electronics Information Answers and Explanations

1. **(B) is a device that converts electrical energy into heat, light, or motion** Loads convert electrical energy into some other form of energy. Examples of loads include heating elements (heat), light bulbs (light), and solenoids (motion).

2. **(C)**

Anode — Cathode

The choices represent four different diode symbols: a zener diode (A), tunnel diode (B), photosensitive diode (C), and light-emitting diode (LED) (D).

3. **(A) one cycle per second of any continuous process** A hertz is a unit of measurement used to express the frequency (cycles per second) of alternating current. One hertz (Hz) is the same as one cycle per second. Choice (C) is incorrect because it indicates the rate of change in frequency rather than the frequency itself.

4. **(B) conductor** A conductor is an element that freely conducts electricity, whereas an insulator does not conduct electricity at all. A semiconductor is neither a good conductor nor insulator, but has some remarkable properties that make it very useful for making electronic components.

5. **(D) a device for measuring electrical resistance** An earth ground is found outside a building, and normally utilizes conductors such as conduit or pipe that is already in the ground. All of the ground connectors in a residential wiring system will be attached to an earth ground, which is used to "funnel" away stray electricity in appliances and prevent it from causing electrical shock. A ground does not measure resistance.

6. **(B) Electrons flow from areas of excess negative charge to areas of less negative charge.** In electron flow theory, electrons flow away from areas of excess negative charge, to those with a deficiency of negative charge. When a conductor is connected across the terminals of a battery, the electrons in the conductor will be forced away from the negative terminal of the battery and toward the positive terminal. Therefore (C) is clearly wrong. Electrons can flow through solids and gases as well as liquids, so (A) is incorrect. While resistance can reduce the flow of electrons it does not necessarily stop the flow completely, so (D) is incorrect.

7. **(A) voltage** Electrical pressure is known as voltage, and it is measured in volts (symbolized by the letter V).

8. **(C) ohmmeter** This is the circuit symbol for an ohmmeter (C), which is used to measure resistance.

9. **(B) series-parallel circuit** This symbol represents a series-parallel circuit, which would have some components, such as an on/off switch, wired in series with a number of loads that are connected in parallel.

10. **(A) dropping** Ohm's law tells us that $V = I \times R$. If voltage stays constant, and resistance R rises, current I would have to drop.

11. **(A) increased current flow** Ohm's law tells us that $R = V \div I$. If resistance R stays constant, and voltage V rises, current I will also have to increase.

12. **(A) Larger voltage drops occur across loads with greater resistances.** Since $V = I \times R$, and the current is the same across all the resistors, an increase in resistance must result in an increase in the voltage drop.

13. **(B) increases** A capacitor is made to block DC (direct current), but allow AC (alternating current) to flow. Capacitive reactance is a capacitor's "opposition" to the flow of current, and this tends to diminish as the frequency of alternating current increases.

14. **(D) 4** The symbol for the transistor has an arrow that identifies the emitter. The direction of the arrow tells us what type of transistor it is; this is a PNP transistor.

15. **(D) inserting a dielectric between each coil** An electromagnet's magnetic field becomes stronger when more turns of wire are added to it, more current is passed through the coil, or an iron core is placed in the middle of the coil.

16. **(C) heat** When current passes through a resistance, a voltage drop will take place. This represents an energy loss, and this energy is normally dissipated in the form of heat.

17. **(A) $V = I \times R$** Ohm's law states that voltage in volts is equal to the current in amperes multiplied by the resistance in ohms, or $V = I \times R$. V represents voltage, and I represents current. Current is the rate of flow of electrons, or the *intensity* of the flow. (Specifically, I is the rate of charge flow.) Finally, R represents *resistance*.

18. **(B) forward-biased** When current flows freely through a diode, this is known as "forward bias." If the orientation of the diode is such that it blocks current flow, that would be reverse bias. *Open* and *grounded* are irrelevant to the question that was asked.

19. **(C) base.** A transistor has three connections: the base, the emitter, and the collector. The transistor is switched off and on by voltages applied to their base. When a voltage appears across the base-emitter junction, the transistor switches on and allows current to flow between the collector and emitter.

20. **(A) 250 ohms** For a simple parallel circuit with four resistors of equal value, divide the resistance of a single component by the total number of components. For this parallel circuit, you have four 1,000 ohm resistors, so 1,000 ohms ÷ 4 = 250 ohms.

Part 7: Auto and Shop Information Answers and Explanations

1. **(A) welding** Soldering does not produce the electric arc that welding does. Welders must cover all exposed skin with protective clothing and wear face shields with light filters for protection.

2. **(A) rotating to the right when viewed from the top** The vast majority of drill bits are made to cut while rotating in a clockwise direction (as viewed from above). These are known as *right hand* drill bits. (Notice that choices (B) and (C) are logically equivalent and therefore must be incorrect, as each question has only one correct answer.)

3. **(A) CD** A motor oil with a "C" prefix for its quality rating would be suited for diesel engine use (i.e., a CD rating). Motor oil that had both an "S" and a "C" rating would be suited for either gasoline or diesel engine use. An example of this would be motor oil with a rating of SJ/CD.

4. **(B) spark plug wires** Coil-on-plug ignition systems eliminate the need for spark plug wires because the ignition coil is mounted directly over the spark plugs. Secondary coil winding (A), spark plugs (C), and primary coil winding (D) are still necessary components in a coil-on-plug ignition system.

5. **(C) four** A double overhead cam arrangement puts two camshafts into each cylinder head, and makes it so one cam operates the exhaust valves in that head, and the other operates all the intake valves. Since the configuration of a V-8 engine has two heads, there would be a total of four camshafts.

6. **(C) round rasp** This is a round rasp. Carpenters would use a round rasp for cleaning out holes in wood. Round rasps are useful for cleaning up holes, whereas a flat rasp would be used to smooth flat surfaces.

7. **(D) acetylene ; oxygen** Using an oxyacetylene cutting torch involves the burning of oxygen and acetylene to produce a flame that is hot enough to melt steel.

8. **(A) direct current** All automotive electrical systems are designed to utilize direct current (DC). Some vehicles may use a negative ground as part of their electrical systems, but not all cars do, so (C) is incorrect.

9. **(B) water** As the lead-acid battery discharges, the sulphuric acid in the electrolyte is reduced to water. The lead plates then become lead sulphate. Charging the battery restores the chemical composition of the lead plates and the electrolyte.

10. **(A) one-half** The camshaft is responsible for the opening and closing of the engine's intake and exhaust valves. The camshaft turns at one-half the speed of the engine's crankshaft.

11. **(A) the distance between two wooden posts.** An outside micrometer is used to measure the outside dimensions of small things, such as cylinders, spheres, or relatively flat, thin objects.

12. **(D)**

The most common type of pliers is the combination slip-joint. These are adjustable at the joint of the two handles of the pliers. With two different positions to choose from, these pliers can grip objects in a wide range of sizes.

13. **(C) coping saw** A coping saw is used to make fine, curving cuts. This saw uses a thin, flexible blade that is held tight on a wide frame.

14. **(D) thermostat** The thermostat controls engine temperature by allowing coolant to flow into the radiator when the coolant temperature rises above a certain level.

15. **(A) intake stroke** Since the piston is moving downward and the intake valve is open, this image depicts the intake stroke, which is the first stroke in the four-stroke cycle.

16. **(B) air, fuel, and an ignition source** A specific mixture of air and fuel plus an ignition source to get the whole thing going is required for combustion.

17. **(A) 1** The firing order for four-cylinder engines is 1-3-4-2. Therefore, (A) is the answer.

18. **(B) Three** It takes two full revolutions of the crankshaft to complete one cycle of events in a four-stroke cycle engine. This means that all of the cylinders in the engine must complete a power stroke in two revolutions of the crankshaft. So in *one* revolution, only three cylinders will fire. Thus, the correct answer is (B).

19. **(C)**

Claw hammers are a more specialized tool often preferred by carpenters. Their purpose is two-fold. The hammer head has two ends: One drives nails and the other removes them. This is the tool least likely to be found in a mechanic's tool box.

20. **(B) tin; lead** Most solders are an alloy of lead and tin. The percentages of each metal in the solder will vary depending on the desired properties of the solder, i.e., melting point.

21. **(D) sulphuric acid** An automobile battery, or lead-acid battery, is made up of lead plates immersed in an electrolyte made up of sulphuric acid and water.

22. **(A) flywheel ring gear** Moving the ignition switch to the "start" position sends an electrical current to the starter solenoid. This engages the starter drive gear onto the engine's ring gear, which is located on the flywheel.

23. **(A) 6 and 12** Sockets come in both 6- and 12-point designs. Six-point is a stronger design, and is usually the mechanic's first choice in the smaller socket drive sizes. However, 12-point is definitely the most popular in large drive sizes.

24. **(C) 14.7:1** The stoichiometric, or ideal, air-fuel ratio is 14.7:1. This means that 14.7 pounds of air is combined with 1 pound of fuel to create an ideal air-fuel mix.

25. **(A) brake rotor** It is the brake rotor attached to the wheel that rotates. Then the brake caliper clamps to slow the car wheels down. While a brake drum does rotate with the wheel, it is not a component of a disc brake system.

Part 8: Mechanical Comprehension Answers and Explanations

1. **(A) the degree to which a force causes an object to rotate** Torque results in a twisting motion in an object. This is very different from horsepower (the rate that work is done), or force (either a (C) push/pull force or (D) a force traveling in a circle).

2. **(B) velocity involves both speed and direction** Speed is different from velocity, in that velocity (which is a vector quantity) implies both speed (a scalar quantity) and direction.

3. **(B) more** The relationship between force, mass, and acceleration is described using the formula $F = ma$. If mass increases, more force is required to achieve the same acceleration rate.

4. **(A) force is a scalar quality** Force is a vector quantity. This means that it expresses both magnitude and direction.

5. **(C) a mechanism** The definition of *mechanical advantage* is the advantage gained by the use of a mechanism in transmitting force. For example, a lever and fulcrum can be used to multiply the force applied to an object.

6. **(D) experiences kinetic friction** A hockey puck experiences kinetic friction (however small) that causes it to lose velocity.

7. **(B) in a clockwise direction** This is an example of meshed gears. Meshed gears always revolve in opposite directions.

8. **(B) Weight is not totally dependent on mass.** Weight is dependent on mass and acceleration due to gravity ($W = mg$).

9. **(C) the coefficient of static friction is dependent on the nature of the surface the box is resting on** The coefficient of static friction is always greater than the coefficient of kinetic friction. If a force is applied, but the box does not move, no work has been done ($W = Fd$). The nature of the surface the box rests on will define the coefficient of friction between the box and that surface.

10. **(A) 4:1** The mechanical advantage of a wheel and axle system is determined by the ratio of the radius of the wheel where the force is applied to the radius of the wheel where the force is transferred. In this case, the ratio of the radii is 10:2.5 or 4:1.

11. **(B) 60 pounds** Three inches of movement multiplied by 20 pounds per inch is 60 pounds of force.

12. **(A) use a longer wrench** Torque (twisting force) can be increased by increasing the length of the wrench, or by increasing the force applied to the wrench.

13. **(B) the net force acting on the vehicle are zero** In accordance with Newton's first law of motion, vehicle traveling at a constant speed has no net forces acting on it.

14. **(B) Tower B will release more water than tower A.** The outlet pipe on tower B is nearer to the bottom of the cistern than the outlet pipe for tower A. Therefore, it will release more water than tower A. While Tower B will release water faster due to increased pressure lower in the cistern, there is no way of knowing how much faster from the information that is provided.

15. **(C) The cords holding sign B are under $\frac{1}{3}$ the tension of the cord holding sign A.** Because there are three cords holding sign B, they are under $\frac{1}{3}$ the tension of the cord holding sign A.

16. **(A) first-class lever** The illustration shows a first-class lever because the fulcrum is between the load and the effort (force).

17. **(C) $10\frac{m}{s}$** Accelerating at the rate of $1\frac{m}{s^2}$ will result in a velocity of $10\frac{m}{s}$ at the end of ten seconds.

$$10\frac{m}{s^2} \times 10s = 10\frac{m}{s}$$

18. **(A) a second-class lever** A wheelbarrow is an example of a second-class lever because the fulcrum is at one end, the effort is at the other, and the load is in between.

19. **(A) Gear Y moves counterclockwise.** Gears an odd number away from the indicated gear move in the opposite direction, while gears an even number away move in the same direction as the indicated gear. In this case, gear Y is three gears away from gear X, which means it will move in the opposite direction as gear X. Gear X is moving clockwise, so gear Y must move counterclockwise.

20. **(A) 1 foot-pound** Using the formula $W = Fd$, it can be seen that 1 pound of force applied through a distance of 1 foot will result in 1 foot-pound of work being done.

21. **(B) The amount of energy in the universe is slowly diminishing.** The principle of conservation of energy tells us that the amount of energy in the universe is constant.

22. **(A) The pulleys require the same force to counteract the weight of the object.** Regardless of the two configurations, both are simple pulleys with no mechanical advantage. Since the objects both exert the same downward force (weight), the force required to counteract that weight will be the same for both pulleys.

23. **(B) A liquid can be dramatically compressed in order to increase the amount of force the liquid can transfer.** Choice (B) is not a true statement; the use of hydraulic force relies on the fact that liquids are effectively incompressible.

24. **(C) how much of the source energy is converted into usable energy** A machine's efficiency is expressed as the percentage of the source energy that it converts into usable energy.

25. **(B) make contact with the ball for a longer period of time** The velocity at which the ball travels will depend upon the impulse that was applied to it. Impulse is determined by multiplying the force by the amount of time that the force was applied. To increase the impulse, the player should hit the ball with greater force and make contact with the ball for a longer period of time.

Part 9: Assembling Objects Answers and Explanations

Time: 15 minutes; 25 questions

For answers 1–12:
In the answers below, we have numbered the pieces, in order to help you see how the correct answer relates to the instructions box.

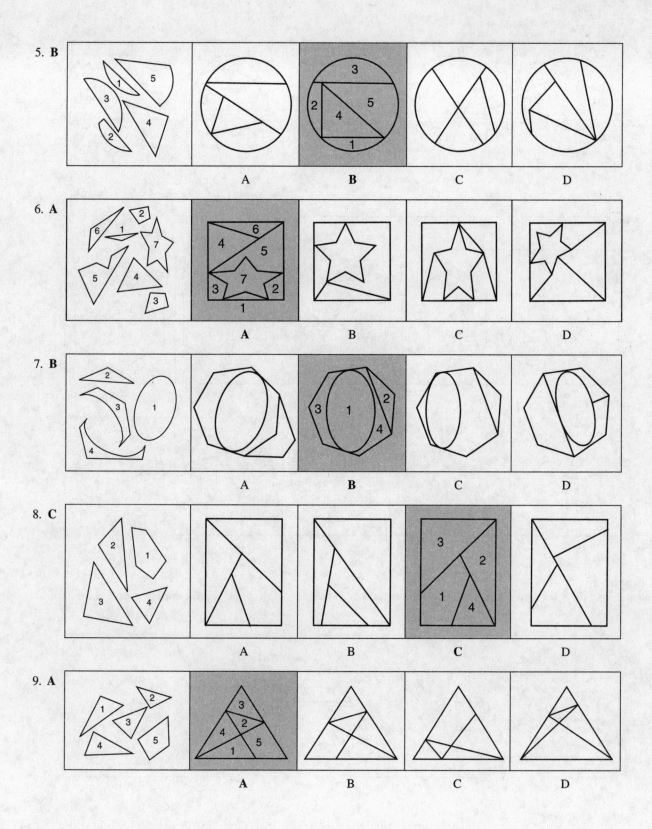

5. **B**

A **B** C D

6. **A**

A B C D

7. **B**

A **B** C D

8. **C**

A B **C** D

9. **A**

A B C D

10. **D**

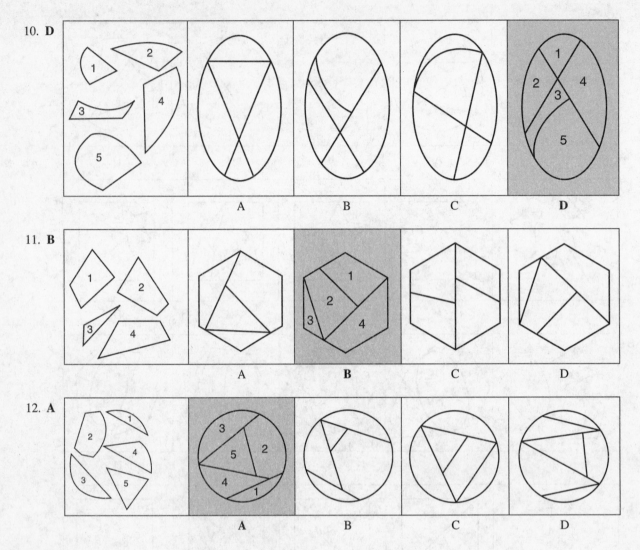

11. **B**

12. **A**

For questions 13–25:
In the answers below, we have placed dots in the answer choices, in order to help you see how the correct answer relates to the instructions box.

13. **C**

14. **C**

15. **B**

16. **D**

17. **B**

18. **A**

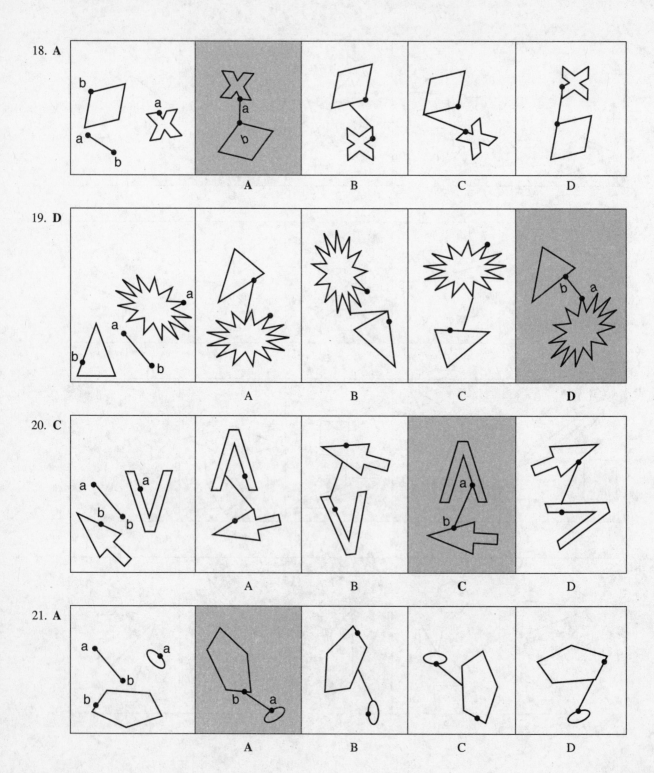

| | A | B | C | D |

19. **D**

20. **C**

21. **A**

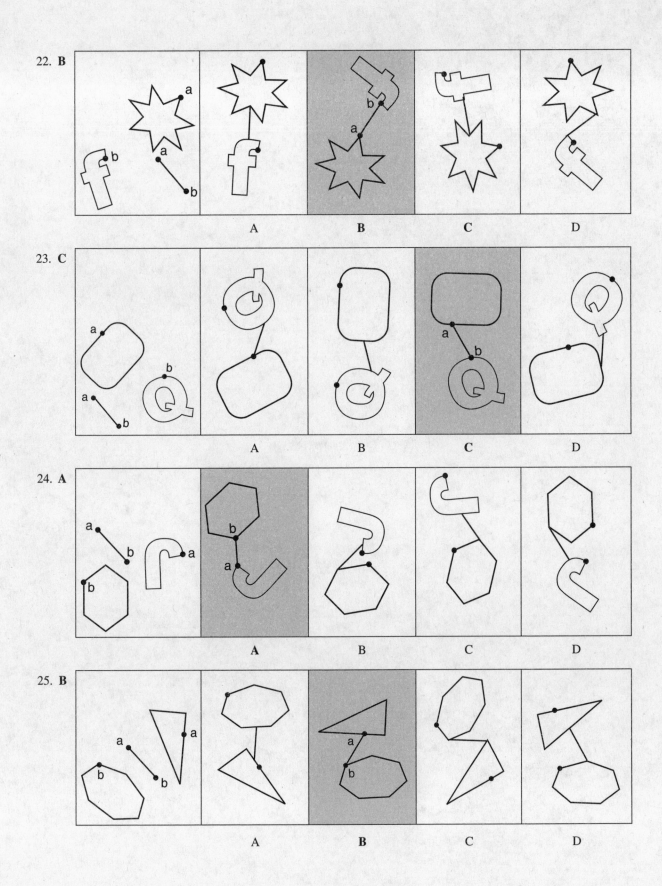

22. **B**

    A   B   C   D

23. **C**

    A   B   C   D

24. **A**

    A   B   C   D

25. **B**

    A   B   C   D

CHAPTER 3

WORD KNOWLEDGE

KNOW WHAT TO EXPECT

One of the subsections of the ASVAB evaluates your ability to identify the meanings of words. This section, called the **Word Knowledge** (WK) section, is essentially a test of your vocabulary. However, that's not the entire story. While knowing the definitions of many words will certainly help you in this section, there are other ways to identify the correct answer and eliminate the wrong answers in WK questions. This chapter will not only focus on helping you improve your vocabulary, it will also help you develop strategies to guess effectively when you may not know the meanings of the words in the question.

On the WK section of the CAT-ASVAB, you will have 8 minutes to answer 16 vocabulary questions. If you are taking the paper and pencil ASVAB, you will be given 11 minutes to complete a total of 35 questions. Whichever version of the test you're taking, your goal is the same: find the synonym for a given word in a fraction of a minute.

A little more than half of the questions in the WK section will ask you to define words with no context. We'll call these **No-Context** WK questions. Here's an example of this type of question.

Gregarious most nearly means

(A) conspicuous
(B) twisting
(C) outgoing
(D) deep

If you happen to know the meaning of the underlined word, fantastic. If not, don't get discouraged. Although questions of this type do not provide you with context clues, there are **decoding strategies,** or ways of guessing a word's meaning, that can help you answer these questions correctly. Decoding strategies that involve understanding words' prefixes, suffixes, and roots will be a major emphasis of this chapter.

The other type of question you're likely to see in this section will ask you to define a word that appears in the context of a sentence. We'll call these **In-Context** WK questions. Take a look at an example of this type of question:

Nomadic tribes often move their villages when the
seasons change.

(A) warlike
(B) wandering
(C) exclusive
(D) hasty

Notice that in this type of WK question, you can use clues in the sentence to help you find the word's meaning. Later in this chapter, we'll discuss ways to get the most out of each sentence's context to help you more effectively predict the underlined word's meaning. Oh, and don't worry—we'll be sure to revisit the two questions above later in this chapter.

This chapter includes:
- the Kaplan Method for Word Knowledge Questions
- paraphrasing a word's meaning
- decoding strategies for guessing a word's meaning, including:
  - prefixes, suffixes, and word roots
  - loose meaning associations
  - positive and negative charge
  - remembered context
- using context to guess a word's meaning
- eliminating answer choices based on logic
- strategies for building your vocabulary
- practice questions

Regardless of the type of WK question you're facing, having a consistent and repeatable method will help you tremendously in this section. Use Kaplan's 3-Step Method for WK to attack every question you see in your practice; by Test Day, it will be second nature.

THE KAPLAN METHOD FOR WORD KNOWLEDGE QUESTIONS

LEARNING OBJECTIVES

In this section, you'll learn to:

- apply the Kaplan Method to Word Knowledge questions
- paraphrase the meaning of a word you are already familiar with

The sooner you learn and apply this method to your studies, the sooner it can help you conquer the WK subtest.

THE KAPLAN METHOD FOR WORD KNOWLEDGE QUESTIONS

Step 1: Identify the word's meaning, or apply decoding strategies to guess its meaning.

Step 2: Make a prediction.

Step 3: Look for your prediction among the answer choices, or strategically eliminate wrong answers.

Let's see how you'd apply that to a question in which you know the meaning of the underlined word.

Question	Analysis
The unusually cold weather was an <u>anomaly</u>.	**Step 1:** *Anomaly* means something unusual, or something that doesn't seem to fit expectations.
	Step 2: Make a prediction before looking at the choices: the answer choice will mean *out of the ordinary* or *unexpected*.
(A) oddity	**Step 3:** Correct. *Oddity* closely matches that prediction.
(B) ally	An *ally* is a friend. Incorrect.
(C) anonymity	*Anonymity* is the state of not being known. Incorrect.
(D) heat wave	A *heat wave* is not, by definition, out of the ordinary. Also, in the context of the sentence, a heat wave does not make sense. Incorrect.

Try one now on your own. Follow the method and try to make a prediction if you can.

Bob shows excellent <u>judgment</u> in his choice of friends.

(A) dispensation
(B) wisdom
(C) jurist
(D) ability

Explanation

Your prediction may have differed but should have resembled the following:

Step 1: *Judgment*, the way it's used in this sentence, means the ability to make good decisions.

Step 2: The answer choice will mean something like *discernment*, or *good decision-making*.

Step 3: Only choice (B) matches that meaning: *wisdom* also means the ability to make good decisions.

You'll notice that Step 2 requires coming up with your own paraphrase of what the answer choice will say. That can take some practice. So here's a chance to try it on your own. Use the following list of common words to practice paraphrasing their meaning. If you don't know what any of these words mean, first look them up in a dictionary and then write down a paraphrase in your own words. You can use casual language to describe them if you like; you don't have to sound like a dictionary when you're paraphrasing.

Word	Your Paraphrase
decision	_____
anxiety	_____
platform	_____
invention	_____
disgusting	_____

How easy did you find it to paraphrase the words' meanings? It can take a while to get the hang of paraphrasing, even when you know what a word means, but it's well worth it. Knowing what you're looking for in the answer choices will help you zero in on the answer much more efficiently and accurately.

Your paraphrases may have varied; the following are sample answers using casual, everyday language:

Word	Paraphrase
decision	*choice*
anxiety	*nervousness, fear*
platform	*basis, thing that something is built on*
invention	*something new, or a lie*
disgusting	*nauseating, stomach-turning*

Of course, there will be times when you will not know the underlined word's meaning. In those cases you'll have to use decoding strategies or context to make a guess about it. Let's begin with decoding strategies.

DECODING STRATEGIES FOR GUESSING A WORD'S MEANING

LEARNING OBJECTIVES

In this section, you will learn to:

- break apart words into prefix, suffix, and root
- learn common prefixes, suffixes, and Greek and Latin word roots
- guess at a word's meaning using the word's positive or negative charge

You have many tools at your disposal for guessing a word's meaning, and this section will cover them each in turn.

Breaking Words Apart

One of the most effective decoding strategies is to break a word into parts. We can do this because many long words in English are composed of a **prefix** (a first syllable that affects the word's meaning) and/or a **suffix** (a final syllable that can also affect the word's meaning), plus a **word root** (a middle part that often derives from a Greek or Latin word).

For example, consider the word *convolution*. It breaks into parts like this:

con	+	*volu*	+	*tion*
prefix	+	word root	+	suffix

Suppose that you didn't know what the word *convolution* means, but you did know that the prefix *con–* means *together* and that the word root *volu* means *turning* or *rolling*. The suffix *–tion* indicates that the word is a noun. So you could guess that a *convolution* is something rolled up together. And that's a pretty good guess: In fact, *convolution* means a *coil* or *twist*, or *the act of coiling*. It can also refer to a complicated thought process that might be described as "twisty."

As a first step, get some practice breaking words apart into prefix, suffix, and root. Be aware that not all the words below will have all of those parts. The first one has been done for you.

Word	Prefix	Root	Suffix
dejection	de	ject	ion
paraphrase	_____	_____	_____
multilingual	_____	_____	_____
regenerate	_____	_____	_____
ossify	_____	_____	_____

Check your work against the answers below.

Word	Prefix	Root	Suffix
dejection	*de*	*ject*	*ion*
paraphrase	*para*	*phrase*	*(none)*
multilingual	*multi*	*lingu*	*al*
regenerate	*re*	*gener*	*ate*
ossify	*(none)*	*oss*	*ify*

So far so good, but what do all those word parts *mean*? Let's start with the meanings of common prefixes.

Prefixes

There are many prefixes you might see on Test Day. **We offer a comprehensive list of prefixes in the Appendix of this book.** If you are struggling to raise your Word Knowledge score, we would encourage you to make flashcards out of the word parts in the Appendix.

For our purposes here, we're going to present a few prefixes to enable you to get some practice working with them. Here are some extremely common prefixes with examples:

Prefix	Meaning	Examples
a, an	not, without	amoral: not related to morality; lacking regard for morality atypical: not typical
co, col, con, com	together, completely	collaborate: to work with another, cooperate compatible: able to exist together with someone or something else; capable of harmonious co-existence
de	away, off, down, reversal	defame: to slander; to publicly speak ill of descend: to move from a higher to a lower place

Prefix	Meaning	Examples
e, ex	out of, from, former	efface: to rub or wipe out; surpass, eclipse exclude: to shut out; to leave out
i, in, im	not, without	immoral: not moral; evil impartial: unbiased; fair
pre	before, in front	premonition: a feeling that an unwanted event may happen in the future presentiment: foreboding
pro	in front, before, much, for	proceed: to go forward propound: to set forth for consideration
re	back, again	recline: to lean back; to lie down regain: to gain again; to take back
sub, sup	below, under	subliminal: existing beneath consciousness substandard: inadequate, below expectations or requirements

Try your hand at working with prefixes. Use the list above to predict the meaning of the following words:

Word	Your Prediction
preset	_____
subset	_____
reset	_____

The word root *gno* relates to knowing or discerning. Use that information and the list of prefixes above to predict the meanings of the following words.

Word	Your Prediction
agnostic	_____
prognosis	_____
ignoramus	_____

The word root *ject* relates to throwing or throwing downward. Use that information and the list of prefixes above to predict the meanings of the following words.

Word	Your Prediction
eject	_____
dejected	_____
conjecture	_____

How did you do? Your answers may vary somewhat, but they should resemble the definitions below.

Word	Your Prediction
preset	set before: that is, arranged beforehand
subset	something set under: that is, a small group within a larger group

Word	Your Prediction
reset	set again
agnostic	a without-knower: that is, a person that believes that the nature of God or the universe is unknowable
prognosis	the act of knowing before: that is, a prediction about how a problem will progress
ignoramus	a not-knower: that is, a very ignorant person, an idiot (formed by combining *in* + *gno* and then dropping the first *n*)
eject	throw out
dejected	thrown off or down: that is, sad, depressed
conjecture	something thrown together: that is, the formation of an opinion or guess without enough information

Great work! The next step in decoding a long word involves looking at the end of the word. That brings us to suffixes.

Suffixes

Unlike prefixes, suffixes usually do two jobs at once. They affect the meaning of a word, and they *also* typically tell you what part of speech the word is. Here's a reminder about parts of speech:

PARTS OF SPEECH INDICATED BY SUFFIXES

Noun: a word that names a person, place, thing, or idea. For example, the underlined words below are all nouns:

Hegel, a famous philosopher who lived in Germany, believed in an idea called *dialectic*.

Verb: a word that expresses an action or state of being. Examples:

Julius constructed his own bookshelves.

I am normally a cheerful person.

Adjective: a word that modifies a noun. For example, the underlined words below are all adjectives:

The quick brown fox jumps over the lazy dog.

Adverb: a word that modifies a verb, adjective, or another adverb. For example, the underlined words below are all adverbs:

The second time he played poker, his skills were greatly improved and he played his cards very carefully.

The other parts of speech are **pronouns** (*he, she, it*), **interjections** (*wow, ouch*), **prepositions** (*of, to, in, on*), and **conjunctions** (*but, nor, for*). However, long words that end in suffixes don't usually belong to those parts of speech.

There are many prefixes you might see on Test Day. **We offer a comprehensive list of suffixes in the Appendix of this book.** If you are struggling to raise your Word Knowledge score, we would encourage you to make flashcards out of the word parts in the Appendix.

For our purposes here, we're going to present a few suffixes to enable you to get some practice working with them. Below is a list of some extremely common suffixes with examples.

Suffix	Part of Speech It Usually Indicates	Meaning	Examples
able, ible	adjective	capable of, worthy of	changeable: able to be changed combustible: capable of catching fire easily
ic	adjective	having the quality of, related to	robotic: like a robot or having to do with robots melodic: having to do with melody, sweetly musical
ion, tion, sion	noun	act of doing, act of being, result of action	notation: act or process of making notes sensation: act of feeling or perceiving
ist	noun	one who does an action or has a trait	pianist: one who plays the piano anesthetist: a medical professional who administers anesthesia (that is, drugs that lessen pain or cause unconsciousness)
ity	noun	state or quality of	novelty: state of being new, a new thing solemnity: state of being solemn or serious
logy	noun	study of	geology: study of earth's structure zoology: study of animals
oid	adjective or noun	resembling or almost	ovoid: resembling an egg, having an oval or egg-like shape asteroid: a small body orbiting the Sun (literally, an almost-star)
ous	adjective	having the quality of, having to do with	bulbous: having a bulb-like shape venous: related to the veins

The word root *am* or *amo* relates to love or liking. Use that information and your knowledge of suffixes to predict the parts of speech and the meanings of the following words:

Word	Your Prediction: Part of Speech	Your Prediction: Meaning
amiable	_____	_____
amorous	_____	_____
amity	_____	_____

The word root *anthro* or *andro* means *man* or *human*. Use that information and your knowledge of suffixes to predict the parts of speech and the meanings of the following words:

Word	Your Prediction: Part of Speech	Your Prediction: Meaning
anthropology	_____	_____
anthropologist	_____	_____
anthropomorphize	_____	_____
android	_____	_____
misanthropic	_____	_____

How did you do? Your answers may have varied, but they should resemble the definitions below.

Word	Your Prediction: Part of Speech	Your Prediction: Meaning
amiable	adjective	capable of being liked or loved; likable
amorous	adjective	displaying love or attraction
amity	noun	liking, friendship
anthropology	noun	study of human beings
anthropologist	noun	one who studies human beings
anthropomorphize	verb	to make into something that resembles humans
android	noun	something (such as a robot) that resembles humans
misanthropic	adjective	having a hatred of people (remember, *mis* means bad, wrong, or hateful)

Of course, prefixes and suffixes are only part of the story. You'll also need to be able to decode what's in the middle of a word.

Greek and Latin Word Roots

Many, though not all, of the long words in English derive from Greek or Latin, which means that learning some Greek and Latin word roots can help you decode English words. In your practice with prefixes and suffixes, above, you have already seen that a single word root can produce many words in English.

This section will examine a selection of word roots and how they form the basis for English words. This discussion will be followed by in-format exercises designed to help you put your decoding strategies to work.

There are many word roots you might see on Test Day. **We offer a comprehensive list of word roots in the Appendix of this book.** If you are struggling to raise your Word Knowledge score, we would encourage you to make flashcards out of the word parts in the Appendix.

For our purposes here, we're going to present a few word roots to enable you to get some practice working with them. Below is a list of some extremely common roots with examples.

Root	Meaning	Examples
centr	center	central: in the center, important concentrate: to bring to the center, to direct to one point
pat, path	feeling, suffering	empathy: identification with the feelings of another impassive: showing no feeling or emotion
vi, viv	life, living	vital: concerned with or necessary to life
ced, ceed, cess	yield, stop	cessation: stoppage incessant: continuous, without stopping

Practice with Word Roots

Use your knowledge of prefixes and suffixes, along with the word root list above, to predict the part of speech and meaning of the following words:

Word	Your Prediction: Part of Speech	Your Prediction: Meaning
concentric	_____	_____
viable	_____	_____
concession	_____	_____
procession	_____	_____
apathetic	_____	_____
pathology	_____	_____
vitality	_____	_____
eccentricity	_____	_____

How did you do? Your answers may have varied, but they should resemble the definitions below.

Word	Your Prediction: Part of Speech	Your Prediction: Meaning
concentric	adjective	together with the center: that is, having a common center
viable	adjective	able to live: possible or workable
concession	noun	act of yielding
procession	noun	act of moving forward
apathetic	adjective	without feeling or emotion
pathology	noun	study of suffering; study of diseases
vitality	noun	capacity for life or survival; state of being strong or full of life
eccentricity	noun	state of being out of the center: that is, oddity, state of being odd or unusual

Full lists of word parts are in the back of this book, in the Appendix. Be sure to get more practice with word parts before Test Day. The best way to do this might be to read a variety of sources and, when you come across a long, unfamiliar word, see if you can break it into parts and analyze the parts.

Using Positive or Negative Charge

One of the secrets to success in the WK section of the ASVAB is knowing that you don't actually need precise definitions of the words that are being tested. As long as you can confidently eliminate three answer choices as being incorrect, you'll find your way to the correct answer. That means that many times, just knowing if a word is positive, negative, or neutral will be enough to answer the question correctly. For example, let's return to a question you've seen previously:

Gregarious most nearly means

(A)   conspicuous
(B)   twisting
(C)   outgoing
(D)   dark

Do you know what the word *gregarious* means? If so, then great, this is an easy question for you. But let's say you don't know what it means. What do you do then? Well, you can start by breaking the word down into parts, as you've seen demonstrated earlier in the chapter.

But let's imagine that you aren't familiar with the root *greg*. While you may be tempted to throw in the towel and give up, try something else: do you think *gregarious* has a positive, negative, or neutral charge? If you've ever heard the word *gregarious* used in conversation, then you probably heard it used to describe a person. And was the person using the word *gregarious* delivering a compliment or an insult?

Now, you may be thinking to yourself, "hmm, okay, I don't really know what *gregarious* means, but I'm pretty sure I've heard it used to compliment someone, so this is a positive word." Now look through the answer choices. Which of those, if applied to a person, would be considered positive? Three answer choices are either negative or neutral. Only (C), *outgoing*, is positive when applied to a person. Select it and move on.

Of course, using a word's positive or negative charge should never be your first strategy when tackling a WK question. Use this approach only when you have a general but not specific understanding of the word.

(For the record, the root *greg* means to flock to, and the suffix *-ious* means to be full of. Therefore, *gregarious* means "living with others, like a flock of animals," and the closest choice is (C) *outgoing*.)

Try this method out on a few words below. For each word you see, rate it as positive, negative, or neutral.

Word	Positive, negative, or neutral?
diabolic	_____
harmony	_____
fanfare	_____
destitute	_____
burdensome	_____
zestful	_____
decision	_____
swampy	_____
currently	_____

Think about how you made the predictions you listed above. How did you come to that determination? Was it because you recognized word parts or remembered situations in which you've heard the word? Or was it more that the word simply "sounded" positive or negative? Either one can work, depending on how reliable your memory is. Now, take a look below. We've included each word's meaning, simply to confirm why it has a positive or negative charge.

Word	Positive, negative, or neutral?	Meaning
diabolic	negative	devilish or evil
harmony	positive	agreement, or a pleasing combination of tones in music
fanfare	positive	song played in celebration, or advertisement
destitute	negative	poverty-stricken
burdensome	negative	very heavy, tiresome, troublesome
zestful	positive	full of enjoyment
decision	neutral	choice
swampy	negative	unpleasantly humid, resembling a swamp
currently	neutral	at the present time, now

Using Real-World Context to Guess at a Word's Meaning

One of the most common—and effective—ways of guessing a word's meaning is to place the word in context. Even if you may not know a textbook definition of the word, perhaps you remember it being used in a specific phrase. Ask yourself, "where have I heard this word before?" Sometimes, you will realize that you did know the meaning of the word.

Take this question, for example:

3. Broach most nearly means

    (A)   poke
    (B)   introduce
    (C)   sermonize
    (D)   cook

Unfortunately, *broach* is one of those words that comes from Middle English, so knowing Latin and Greek roots won't be very helpful. And if you can't rattle off a specific definition of the word right away, you may think that this is a lost point. But ask yourself if you have heard this word used in a common phrase before. Does "broaching the subject" ring a bell? Perhaps you've heard a parent, teacher, or television character use this phrase. Something along the lines of: "Well, I didn't want to talk about it, but Donny broached the subject anyway." Using the context of how the word is used in a phrase you've heard before is a remarkable way to understand the "fuzzy definition" of a word. In this example, *broach* would mean something like "bring up" or "started to discuss." The only word that is a close fit is answer choice (B), *introduce*.

Try this approach yourself. For each of the words below, try to place the word in a common phrase that you may have heard before. How does the context of the phrase help you determine the meaning of the word?

Word	Think of a phrase you've heard the word used in, and then use that to guess at the meaning of the word:
vicarious	_____
jiffy	_____
guzzle	_____
hybrid	_____

Did those words sounds familiar? When you tried to place them in phrases or a real-world context, what did you come up with? Below, take a look at how a person might have used common usage to help them determine the right definition. Your answers, of course, may vary.

Word	Think of a phrase you've heard the word used in, and then use that to guess at the meaning of the word (sample answers):
vicarious	"I've heard the phrase 'So and so lived vicariously through someone else.' I guess that means vicariously is like experiencing something through someone else's eyes."
jiffy	"My dad used to say 'I'll be back in a jiffy.' I guess a jiffy is really fast."
guzzle	"I have a friend who is always talking about his truck being a real gas guzzler. He's always filling it up, so I guess being a guzzler means you consume a lot."
hybrid	"There are a bunch of new cars out there that are considered to be hybrids because they use a little bit of gas and a little bit of electric. Maybe hybrid means doing two things at the same time."

Notice that the predictions are not specific definitions or predictions that point to the word's meaning. Instead, the phrases allow you to form a fuzzy definition of the word in your mind; that fuzzy definition will often be more than enough to select the right answer.

MAKING THE MOST OF CONTEXT

LEARNING OBJECTIVES

In this section, you will learn to:

- use the meaning of a sentence to predict an answer on In-Context WK questions
- use the meaning of a sentence to eliminate answer choices on In-Context WK questions

In addition to the decoding strategies discussed above, you can also use the sentence itself to help you answer In-Context WK questions. **Context** simply means the words or phrases surrounding an underlined word, and using context involves looking for clues in those other words in order to help you guess at the underlined word's meaning.

There are several ways context can be helpful. Sometimes the sentence signals that the underlined word *resembles* another idea in the sentence. Consider the following:

Question	Analysis
The children <u>thronged</u> around the table like moths around a flame.	The word *like* signals that, whatever the children were doing, they resembled moths swarming around a flame. So *thronged* must convey that same sense.

Sure enough, *thronged* means *swarmed* or *gathered in a crowd*.

In each of the examples below, identify the word that tells you that the underlined word is similar to some other idea in the sentence, and then predict the meaning of the underlined word.

Sentence	What word or words signal similarity?	Predict the underlined word's meaning
The crowd greeted the famous chef with an eagerness amounting to <u>fervor</u>.	_____	_____
The budget meeting was a difficult conversation; indeed, it was almost a <u>quagmire</u>.	_____	_____
Today's creative child may be tomorrow's <u>virtuoso</u>.	_____	_____

Explanation

Your paraphrases may differ somewhat but should resemble the following:

Sentence	What word or words signal similarity?	Predict the underlined word's meaning
The crowd greeted the famous chef with an eagerness amounting to <u>fervor</u>.	*amounting to*	*tremendous enthusiasm*
The budget meeting was a difficult conversation; indeed, it was almost a <u>quagmire</u>.	*indeed*	*extremely difficult or awkward situation*
Today's creative child may be tomorrow's <u>virtuoso</u>.	parallel drawn between *today* and *tomorrow*	*someone very skilled at a creative activity like art or music*

In other cases, sentences may contain words that signal that the underlined word *contrasts with* or *forms an unexpected combination with* another idea in the sentence. Consider the following example:

Question	Analysis
The best coaches are supportive but <u>exacting</u>.	The word *but* tells you that *exacting* either contrasts with *supportive* or else that you would not expect to see *supportive* and *exacting* linked together. It is unlikely that *exacting* is the direct opposite of *supportive*, since the writer of this sentence thinks good coaches display both traits. So it must be the case that *supportive* and *exacting* are somehow a surprising pair.

In fact, *exacting* means *making large demands*. Thus, the prediction above is correct: while *exacting* does not mean the opposite of *supportive*, it is perhaps a surprising idea to find linked with *supportive*.

In each of the examples below, identify the word that tells you that the underlined word contrasts with or forms a surprising combination with some other idea in the sentence, and then predict the meaning of the underlined word.

Sentence	What word signals contrast or an unexpected combination of ideas?	Predict the underlined word's meaning
Some human behavior is learned, while other human behavior is <u>instinctive</u>.	_____	_____
Trisha found the task to be enjoyable rather than <u>onerous</u>.	_____	_____
I prefer action films but had to sit through a <u>cloying</u> love story last Friday night.	_____	_____

Explanation

Your paraphrases may differ somewhat but should resemble the following:

Sentence	What word signals contrast or an unexpected combination of ideas?	Predict the underlined word's meaning
Some human behavior is learned, while other human behavior is <u>instinctive</u>.	*while*	contrasts with *learned*, so *innate* or *inborn*
Trisha found the task to be enjoyable rather than <u>onerous</u>.	*rather*	contrasts with *enjoyable*, so *tiresome* or *burdensome*
I prefer action films but had to sit through a <u>cloying</u> love story last Friday night.	*but*	contrasts with *action films* and has a negative charge, so *too sentimental* or *sugary*

Sometimes context merely tells you whether an underlined word has a negative or positive connotation. In many cases, this deduction may be enough to answer the WK question. Consider the following example:

Question	Analysis
Jalisa was looking forward to a well-earned <u>respite</u>.	**Step 1.** A *respite* must be a good thing, because Jalisa is *looking forward* to it. Also, the adjective *well-earned* has a positive connotation.
	Step 2. *Respite* must be something enjoyable or beneficial.
(A) deadline (B) incarceration (C) rest (D) prediction	**Step 3.** Of the answer choices, only (C) *rest* is likely to be enjoyable or beneficial. Choose (C).

In fact, a *respite* is a period of rest or relief from work or from something unpleasant.

Try it on your own. For each of the sentences below, identify the word or words that signal whether the underlined word has a positive or negative connotation. Then try, if possible, to predict the underlined word's meaning.

Sentence	What word or words signal that the underlined word has a positive or negative connotation?	Predict the underlined word's meaning
I struggled to stay awake as the presentation <u>droned</u> into evening.	_____	_____
Your <u>injudicious</u> proposal would have serious consequences for our town's future.	_____	_____
Wasting more money on the machine would only <u>exacerbate</u> our difficulties.	_____	_____

Explanation

Your paraphrases may have differed but should have resembled the following:

Sentence	What word or words signal that the underlined word has a positive or negative connotation?	Predict the underlined word's meaning
I struggled to stay awake as the presentation <u>droned</u> into evening.	*struggled*	*continued in a boring or monotonous way*
Your <u>injudicious</u> proposal would have serious consequences for our town's future.	*serious consequences*	*unwise*
Wasting more money on the machine would only <u>exacerbate</u> our difficulties.	*wasting*	*worsen*

Finally, sometimes the context surrounding an underlined word's meaning simply defines that word or hints at its meaning. Remember this example from the beginning of the chapter?

Question	Analysis
<u>Nomadic</u> tribes often move their villages when the seasons change.	**Step 1.** Whatever *nomadic* tribes may be, they move around a good deal.
	Step 2. Check the answer choices for a word that means *moving around*.
(A) warlike (B) wandering (C) exclusive (D) hasty	**Step 3.** (B) *wandering* matches the prediction best.

In fact, the sentence in the question above simply defines *nomadic*, which means *moving from place to place, having no fixed dwelling-place.*

Try your hand at the following examples:

Sentence	Predict the meaning of the underlined word
As Lydia struggled to understand the difficult material, her <u>bewilderment</u> became obvious to the teacher.	_____
The thieves took pains to cover their tracks on the way to their <u>clandestine</u> meeting.	_____
The incoming freshman found the Advanced Econometrics course material to be <u>opaque</u>.	_____

Explanations

Your paraphrases may differ somewhat but should resemble the following.

Sentence	Predict the meaning of the underlined word
As Lydia struggled to understand the difficult material, her <u>bewilderment</u> became obvious to the teacher.	She *struggled to understand*, so *bewilderment* likely means *confusion* or *lack of understanding*.
The thieves took pains to cover their tracks on the way to their <u>clandestine</u> meeting.	The thieves were clearly trying to keep their meeting a secret, so *clandestine* likely means *secret*.
The incoming freshman found the Advanced Econometrics course material to be <u>opaque</u>.	Whatever *Advanced Econometrics* is, it sounds too hard for a freshman. So the freshman likely found it to be *very difficult to understand*.

Of course, sometimes you will struggle to glean clues from the context of a sentence. You may, in these cases, be able to eliminate some answer choices by mentally replacing the underlined word with each of the answer choices to try to "hear" which choices sound wrong. Study the following example to learn how a test taker might go about this:

Question	Analysis
Everyone on the committee agreed that acting with <u>circumspection</u> was important.	**Steps 1 and 2.** The sentence doesn't give many hints aside from suggesting that *circumspection* is probably a good thing.
(A) wisdom (B) voting (C) caution (D) individuality	**Step 3.** More than one of the answer choices has a positive connotation. Try each in the original sentence: (A) *Everyone on the committee agreed that acting with wisdom was important.* That seems like an odd thing to say. Isn't wisdom always important? Try the others. (B) *Everyone on the committee agreed that acting with voting was important.* That doesn't seem to make much sense. (C) *Everyone on the committee agreed that acting with caution was important.* That makes a great deal of sense. (D) *Everyone on the committee agreed that acting with individuality was important.* That seems to go against the idea of a committee, especially one where everyone agrees. Choice (C) is the best fit.

Not surprisingly, *circumspection* means *caution* or *the act of carefully considering*.

Try your hand at the example below. If you are having trouble predicting what the underlined word means, mentally reread the sentence, substituting each answer choice, to find the one that sounds most sensible.

Joanna <u>feigned</u> happiness at the wedding.

(A)   created
(B)   passed out
(C)   pretended
(D)   concealed

Explanation

Steps 1 and 2. Perhaps you had trouble applying decoding strategies or using context here. If so, go directly to the choices.

Step 3. Try the answer choices one by one in the sentence:

(A) *Joanna created happiness at the wedding.* That doesn't make a lot of sense. Weddings might make people happy, but people don't typically say that one individual *creates* happiness.

(B) *Joanna passed out happiness at the wedding.* Unless happiness is a new kind of party favor, this makes no sense. (This answer choice was probably intended to tempt test takers who think *feign* looks like *faint*.)

(C) *Joanna pretended happiness at the wedding.* This makes sense: if Joanna had some reason to be unhappy that day, she may have had to pretend to be happy.

(D) *Joanna concealed happiness at the wedding.* Although it's possible that someone might have a reason to conceal, or hide, their happiness at a wedding, that seems far less likely than choice (C).

ELIMINATING ANSWER CHOICES BASED ON LOGIC

If you really can't come up with a prediction, or if context is proving to be no help, then you may in some cases be able to eliminate answer choices by thinking logically about them. For example, if two answer choices mean nearly the same thing, they must be wrong, since the ASVAB has only one right answer for each question. Consider the following example:

Question	Analysis
<u>Legerdemain</u> most nearly means	**Steps 1 and 2.** Hard to see recognizable prefixes, suffixes, or word parts in this word. Also, there's no context. Difficult to predict. Look at the choices.
(A) monster (B) massive amount (C) magic trick (D) ogre	**Step 3.** Now, *monster* and *ogre* are not exactly synonyms, but they both mean creatures that are frightening and dangerous. Therefore it's unlikely that either of them are correct. Eliminate (A) and (D). At this point, either make a guess between (B) and (C) or try to remember situations in which you've heard the word *legerdemain*.

In fact, *legerdemain* means *sleight of hand*, so *magic trick* is the best fit.

If two answer choices have opposite meanings, it may be likely that one of them is correct. That's because test makers often include an answer choice that means the opposite of the correct answer. Study the following example:

Question	Analysis
<u>Hauteur</u> most nearly means	**Steps 1 and 2.** Hard to see recognizable prefixes, suffixes, or word parts in this word. Also, there's no context. Difficult to predict. Look at the choices.
(A) author (B) arrogance (C) moisture (D) humility	**Step 3.** Choices (B) and (D) have opposite meanings, so it may be the case that one of them is correct.

Once you have eliminated (A) and (C), you may have to simply guess between the other two. Alternatively, if you happen to have a sense that *hauteur* has a negative charge, you could use that to guess that it probably means *arrogance*. You could also think about the fact that *hauteur* sounds like *haughty*, which means arrogant. So (B) is indeed correct.

In conclusion, eliminating choices based on logic usually helps you to narrow choices down to two. You may need to use another strategy or simply guess in order to select from the remaining two choices.

Try to eliminate wrong answer choices using logic in the following questions.

1. <u>Demur</u> most nearly means

    (A)   trust
    (B)   investigate
    (C)   believe
    (D)   disagree

2. <u>Logy</u> most nearly means

    (A) oblong
    (B) lively
    (C) sluggish
    (D) chubby

Explanation

1. Steps 1 and 2. Perhaps you don't know the meaning of *demur* and are having trouble applying decoding strategies to the word.

Step 3. Scan the choices. (A) *trust* and (C) *believe* are very similar in meaning, and therefore it's unlikely that one of them is correct. Eliminate them.

Either guess between (B) and (D) or apply another strategy. It may be helpful to note that the prefix *de* can mean *away from*, and the prefix *dis* can mean *not* or *opposed to*. That may signal that these words are similar. Choose (D) *disagree*. (In fact, to *demur* means *to raise objections, disagree, or hesitate*.)

2. Steps 1 and 2. Perhaps you don't know the meaning of *logy* and are having trouble applying decoding strategies to the word.

Step 3. Scan the choices. (B) *lively* and (C) *sluggish* are opposites, so it may be that one of them is correct. Either hazard a guess or try to remember if you've heard *logy* anywhere. You may remember that it has a slightly negative charge, which makes (C) is a better fit. (In fact, *logy* means *sluggish*.)

STRATEGIES FOR BUILDING YOUR VOCABULARY

You now have a variety of strategies for conquering the WK section of the ASVAB. But those tips aren't helpful if your vocabulary remains poor. To learn more words between now and your ASVAB Test Day, make this commitment: **learn seven new words a day.** If that sounds like too few, rest assured, it's plenty—in fact, that's nearly 50 words a week.

The best and most efficient way to improve your vocabulary is to consume as many books, magazines, and newspapers that you can get your hands on. The reason for this is pretty straightforward: learning words in context, as you read, helps you retain those words longer and with greater precision than learning those words by themselves, with no context. If you have a smartphone, download a dictionary app and look up any words that you don't know. If you're at your computer, simply use a search engine. Always look up unfamiliar words that you encounter in your reading of books and magazines, as well as words you see on the Internet, hear in movies, or encounter in daily conversation.

Another tried and true method for improving your vocabulary is to **make and use vocabulary flashcards**. While the "making" part of flashcards is often overlooked, its value is significant—the act of writing a word and its definition on an index card will help you remember that word's definition both as a visual image and as an action. So, here's your task: as you encounter and learn new words, write them down on index cards and, as soon as you're able, write the definitions of those words on the backs of the cards. Then, when you have some spare time, browse through your pile. Once you feel like you've really "got" a word, and that you won't lose its definition, remove it from the pile. If you follow through with this method, you'll find that you're constantly adding and removing words from your pile of vocabulary cards.

Some folks find that **creating a vocabulary notebook** is more convenient than flashcards. The idea is similar: jot down words you don't know as you find them in your readings and daily interactions, and look up their definitions. List words in the left-hand column and their meanings in the right-hand column. Cover up or fold over the page to test yourself. See how many words you can define from memory.

Finally, there are a number of **apps and websites** you might use to improve your vocabulary. To find out about Kaplan vocabulary apps, call 1-800-KAPTEST or visit your virtual app store.

After you learn new words, try to use them in conversation. This is an excellent way to confirm that you truly understand a word's meaning and the proper context in which to use it. If you have an ASVAB study partner, try to have a conversation in which each person must use an ASVAB vocabulary word in a sentence. You'll be surprised by how well the words' definitions "stick" once you've correctly used them in conversation.

ASVAB TIPS

Improve your vocabulary by:

- reading books, magazines, newspapers, and articles on the Internet
- look up words you don't know and jot down their definitions either:
    - on flashcards or
    - in a vocabulary notebook
- make use of vocabulary-building websites or apps
- commit to learning seven words per day
- use recently-learned words in daily conversation

WORD KNOWLEDGE PRACTICE QUESTIONS

For each question, select the answer choice that most closely matches the meaning of the underlined word.

1. Ghastly most nearly means

   (A) fun
   (B) lazy
   (C) torrid
   (D) awful

2. The brothers ran away in cowardice.

   (A) pain
   (B) fear
   (C) hopelessness
   (D) temperance

3. Resignation most nearly means

   (A) losing
   (B) waste
   (C) acceptance
   (D) pride

4. He promised to cooperate with the authorities.

   (A) fight
   (B) talk
   (C) work with
   (D) placate

5. It is imperative that you pursue training or education beyond high school in order to get a good job.

   (A) sad
   (B) timely
   (C) open
   (D) crucial

6. Everyone says he lost the election due to lack of initiative.

   (A) satisfaction
   (B) irritation
   (C) money
   (D) ambition

7. The city council sought reparations for the oil spill.

   (A) compensation
   (B) sadness
   (C) thanks
   (D) antipathy

8. Many times, the older sibling holds dominion over his younger siblings.

   (A) authority
   (B) safety
   (C) ability
   (D) guilt

9. His professors made a point of acting erudite.

   (A) civil
   (B) progressive
   (C) scholarly
   (D) amoral

10. Tangible most nearly means

    (A) real
    (B) open
    (C) graphic
    (D) costly

11. Alleviate most nearly means

    (A) elevate
    (B) improve
    (C) encompass
    (D) make foreign

12. Trite most nearly means

    (A) snug
    (B) correct
    (C) modern
    (D) stale

13. Imitating a marching band, the children used pots and pans to make a loud clamor.

    (A) noise
    (B) protest
    (C) music
    (D) harmony

14. Candid most nearly means

    (A) able
    (B) whimsical
    (C) valid
    (D) honest

15. After careful study, she was able to <u>discern</u> which model would be the best car for her needs.

    (A) avoid
    (B) spoil
    (C) perceive
    (D) savor

16. <u>Dupe</u> most nearly means

    (A) double
    (B) delay
    (C) deceive
    (D) delight

17. The athlete trained for the competition with <u>vigor</u>.

    (A) stiffness
    (B) intensity
    (C) swelling
    (D) concern

18. <u>Enigma</u> most nearly means

    (A) puzzle
    (B) motor
    (C) energy
    (D) clarity

19. She displayed <u>fortitude</u> in finishing the race despite the pain in her foot.

    (A) speed
    (B) cheerfulness
    (C) courage
    (D) vulnerability

20. The <u>frugal</u> man was always reluctant to spend money.

    (A) fearful
    (B) thrifty
    (C) imprudent
    (D) lavish

Answers and Explanations

1. **(D) awful** Even if you didn't know that *ghastly* means "awful," if you had a sense that *ghastly* has a negative charge, you could have gotten the correct answer that way. *Torrid*, by the way, means hot or passionate, as in a "torrid love affair."

2. **(B) fear** Context is useful here: the brothers *ran away*, so ask yourself what might make someone run away. While *pain* and *hopelessness* are both bad things, *fear* is far more likely to produce the response of running away.

3. **(C) acceptance** The suffix *–ation* tells you that this is a noun made out of a verb. The verb here is *resign*. A good strategy at this point might be to remember the contexts in which you've heard the word *resign* in life: people *resign* from their jobs, but none of the answer choices convey that sense. You may also have heard people say that someone was *resigned* to his fate. That means the person had accepted his fate. So the noun form, *resignation*, means *acceptance*.

4. **(C) work with** This is a good candidate for using word roots: *co–* means *with* and *operate* means *work*.

5. **(D) crucial** Here's another case where you could get the correct answer just by the context of the sentence. The writer of this sentence seems to consider getting a good job to be something desirable, and so you can guess that *imperative* means *very important* or *crucial* for meeting that goal.

6. **(D) ambition** A good strategy here might be to mentally reread the sentence, substituting each of the choices in turn. Choices (A) and (B) make no sense in the context of this sentence. So now you're left with (C) and (D). Think about what words *initiative* sounds like: *initial* and *initiate* might come to mind. They both have to do with starting things. That doesn't seem to have much to do with money, so eliminate (C). In fact, *initiative* means *resourcefulness* or *drive*, so *ambition* is the best match. (You could say that someone who has *initiative* or *ambition* is a self-starter; hence the link with *initial*.)

7. **(A) compensation** Try decoding this one using word parts: *Re–* means back or again. The root *par* means *equal*, and the suffix *–ation* tells you that the word a noun that describes the act of doing something. So *reparation* means something like *the act of making something equal again* or perhaps *the act of making something right*. Thus, choice (A) *compensation* is the best match. In fact, *reparations* means *repayment for loss suffered*.

8. **(A) authority** An excellent strategy here would be to predict a meaning based on the context of the sentence. What might an older sibling do to younger siblings? Perhaps he would influence them or even boss them around. Indeed, *dominion* means *control*, *sway*, or *authority*. (You could also have used word parts here: *dom* relates to ruling or authority.)

9. **(C) scholarly** You could have made a prediction based on context by asking yourself how professors would likely want to appear. You could also have mentally reread the sentence, substituting each answer choice for the underlined word. Choice (C) makes the most sense in the context of the sentence. *Civil* might make sense, but being civil isn't particular to professors. *Progressive*? That describes some professors, but certainly not all of them. *Scholarly*? That's the best match. Professors are expected to act like scholars. Choice (D) *amoral* means lacking in moral standards; it's highly unlikely anyone would make a point of acting amoral.

10. **(A) real** You might be able to remember other circumstances in which you've heard the word *tangible*. And from those, you might have a sense that something *tangible* can be felt or seen. From that, you should be able to pick *real* (A) as the closest match. You could also use word roots here: the root *tang* or *tac* relates to touch: something *tangible* is *touchable* or *real*.

11. **(B) improve** You may have heard the word *alleviate* in the context of "alleviating pain," meaning to make the pain less and help someone feel better. *Alleviate* is a positive word that means to ease or allay a bad situation, so the correct answer here is *improve* (B). *Elevate* means to raise (think *elevator*), and *encompass* means to surround.

12. **(D) stale** If something is *trite*, it has been used or done so many times that it is no longer fresh or original. For example, you might say that your friend's story about being stuck in an elevator was funny the first hundred times he told it but is now *trite*. The correct answer is *stale* (D).

13. **(A) noise** Use context to predict an answer: what are children likely to make with pots and pans? Probably a loud, unpleasant noise. (B) *protest* is not supported by the context of the sentence. And choices (C) and (D) both have far too positive a connotation. It is unlikely the children produced pleasant *music* or *harmony*.

14. **(D) honest** This question is a good candidate for loose meaning associations. *Candid* comes from the noun *candor*, which means *honesty*. Candid means *sincere* or *honest* (D). Although *candid* might sound a little like "can do," it does not mean *able*. *Valid* is another positive word that relates to truth, so it might have been tempting here, but *valid* relates to facts or logic whereas *candid* and *honest* refer to people. *Whimsical* means playful or not serious; if you buy a new phone on a *whim*, you purchase it impulsively.

15. **(C) perceive** Use the context to make a prediction: *study* gives a person more information, and more information allows that person to make better choices. So after study, she was able to see or decide which car to choose. You could also mentally reread the sentence, substituting each answer choice.

She is unlikely to want to *avoid* or *spoil* the best car. She might *savor*, or enjoy, her car after picking it out, but this sentence does not concern what happens after she finds a good vehicle.

16. **(C) deceive** You may have a sense that *dupe* has a negative charge. If so, you can eliminate (A) *double*, which is neither negative nor positive, and (D) *delight,* which has a strong positive charge. In fact, to *dupe* someone is to cheat or lie to that person, and *deceive* (A) matches that meaning. Related words are *betray*, *delude*, and *dissimulate*. *Dupe* can also be a noun, meaning someone who is easily taken advantage of. You don't want to be someone's *dupe*!

17. **(B) intensity** Use context to predict the meaning of this word. An athlete will work hard to prepare for a competition, and *vigor* means strength, force, or intensity (B). The athlete may feel concerned about the competition, but the underlined word here deals with the athlete's training, not his feelings. If you thought the underlined word was *rigor*, you might have picked *stiffness*: be sure to read carefully.

18. **(A) puzzle** An *enigma* is a mystery or puzzle (A). You may have heard of the Enigma machine, which was a famous encryption device used by the Germans in World War II.

19. **(C) courage** Because she finished the race even though she was in pain, you know she was pretty tough. This aligns with her showing (C) *courage*. If anything, a sore foot implies that she ran more slowly than usual, so *speed* doesn't fit. You don't know whether she showed *cheerfulness* or was gritting her teeth with every step. *Vulnerability*, or weakness, is the opposite of what you need here.

20. **(B) thrifty** On this question, the sentence actually defines the word for you. Someone who is frugal avoids spending money; in other words, he's *thrifty*. *Fearful* is too strong; you don't know that he is actually afraid to spend money, just that he's not eager to do so. *Imprudent* means not careful, and is the opposite of the correct answer. *Lavish* means very generous or abundant and is also the opposite of *frugal*.

Review and Reflect

As you review your work on these practice questions, ask yourself some questions:

- Did you remember to apply strategies, such as using word parts or using real-life remembered context?
- How often were you able to sense whether a word had a positive or negative charge?
- How well did you use context on the In-Context questions?
- Use your thoughts about these questions to guide your review of this chapter.

PARAGRAPH COMPREHENSION

KNOW WHAT TO EXPECT

The ASVAB includes a reading section among its several subtests. This section, called the Paragraph Comprehension (PC) section, presents short passages for you to read and then asks questions based on those passages. While the subject matter of each passage will vary, no outside knowledge is required to answer the questions correctly. For each question in this section, everything you need to answer the question will be contained in the passage above it.

On the paper and pencil version of the ASVAB, the PC section will ask 15 questions about 13 or 14 short passages. Timing is extremely important in this version of the test, as you are only given 13 minutes to answer these 15 questions. On the CAT-ASVAB, you are given 22 minutes to answer 11 questions. The extra time allows for the fact that question difficulty can increase as you accumulate correct answers.

THE KAPLAN METHOD FOR PARAGRAPH COMPREHENSION QUESTIONS

LEARNING OBJECTIVE

In this section, you'll learn to:

- apply the Kaplan Method to PC Questions

To be successful in both the paper and pencil and CAT versions of the PC subtest, you will need to read the passages in an effective and efficient manner. Keep in mind that your goal in this section is not to learn the subject matter of the passages but simply to answer the questions correctly. Therefore, your focus should be on understanding each question's task rather than absorbing every detail in the passage. In this chapter, you'll learn how to use Kaplan's approach to PC questions to help you answer each type of question you'll see on the PC subtest.

Having a consistent and repeatable method will help you quickly and confidently answer questions in this section. Use Kaplan's 4-Step Method for PC to attack every question you see in your practice and on Test Day.

KAPLAN METHOD FOR PARAGRAPH COMPREHENSION

Step 1: Read the question stem to identify your task.

Step 2: Read the passage strategically.

Step 3: Make a prediction.

Step 4: Find the correct answer.

Step 1: Read the question stem to identify your task.

How you read and analyze a passage will vary depending upon the task defined by the question stem, so it's important to always read the question before you look at the passage. After you read the question stem and identify the specific type of question you're being asked, it's time to read the passage strategically. In this chapter, we will cover all the different types of questions you might see on Test Day.

Step 2: Read the passage strategically.

Once you know your task, read as much of the passage as necessary to answer the question. In a question that asks you to identify the main idea of a passage, separate supporting details from opinions and recommendations to determine the author's overall point. Other PC questions may ask you to identify specific details, or to determine the meaning of a word. The key in this step is to read the passage in the way that is appropriate to answer the specific question that is being asked.

Step 3: Make a prediction.

As mentioned earlier, every question in this section can be answered by the information in the passage that precedes it; no outside information is necessary. For each question, spend a few seconds to predict what the correct answer will look like. Sometimes you'll know the answer without even looking at the answer choices. Other times, you'll have only a general idea of the phrasing of the correct answer. Either way, spending the time to predict will make it easier to find the correct answer.

Step 4: Find the correct answer.

Once you come up with a prediction of the correct answer, simply find the answer choice that is the closest match. If you are unable to make a prediction, you'll still have an opportunity to find the correct answer by eliminating answer choices that you know are incorrect. Many will be incorrect because they stray beyond the scope of the subject matter in the passage. Other answer choices are incorrect because they are too extreme, or they distort details in the passage. After you've eliminated the wrong answer choices, select the one that remains and move on to the next question.

CONQUERING PARAGRAPH COMPREHENSION QUESTIONS

LEARNING OBJECTIVES

In this section, you'll learn to:

- identify PC question types
- read PC passages strategically
- make accurate predictions
- match your prediction to the correct answer

Global Questions

A common question type in the PC section is one that asks you to identify a passage's main idea or theme, the author's purpose, or the tone of the passage. Here's what a Global question stem might look like:

Which of the following is the main idea of the passage?

The author's tone in the passage above can be characterized as

The purpose of the passage above is to

The passage above is primarily concerned with

In order to find the main idea in a passage, you must be able to distinguish the values an author assigns to different statements. In each passage that asks you to determine a main idea, the author will use supporting details to establish a main idea. Things like simple facts, other people's opinions, and background information can all operate as supporting details in a passage. Those details are then used to support an author's claim, which often comes in the form of a strong opinion, a recommendation, a prediction, or a rebuttal to another person's position.

As an example, imagine a passage with the following main idea: "Purchasing gold is a wise investment." This claim is not a fact but rather a recommendation. In turn, the author needs to support this claim by offering reasons why gold is such a good investment. Perhaps it's because "the amount of gold available worldwide is set to plateau," or maybe it's because "gold is the worldwide monetary standard." Those two statements, alone or together, help to explain why gold would make a wise investment. But the fact that gold is a good investment does not explain why gold is the worldwide monetary standard.

So, one method for separating the main idea from the rest of the passage is to realize that the supporting details and the main idea answer two different types of questions, as you can see:

This:	*Answers the question:*
Main idea	What does the author believe?
Supporting details	Why does the author believe what he or she believes?

Sometimes, like when the author expresses a strong opinion, the main idea will be clear. Words and phrases like *thus, therefore, I suggest,* and *I believe* all indicate that the author is providing a strong conclusion. Other times, a passage's main idea will be more difficult to identify. In those passages, be prepared to work a little harder to separate supporting ideas from the main idea. Often, one of the tricks to zeroing in on the main idea of a passage is to pay attention to structural clues that indicate a contrast. Words such as *but, though, however, although,* and *yet* provide subtle clues into an author's point of view: the statement after the contrast word is frequently a reflection of the author's opinion, especially in passages where the author disagrees with someone else's opinion.

Finally, on Global questions it is often easy to eliminate a few answer choices immediately. Wrong answer choices for Global questions usually do one of the following:

- They're too specific, dealing with just one small detail of the passage.
- They're too general, going beyond the scope of the passage.
- They're contradictory to the information presented in the passage.
- They're too extreme; that is, they distort the author's opinion by overstating it.

Below, take a look at how a Kaplan-trained test taker approaches a typical Paragraph Comprehension Global question. Remember to start with the question stem, labeled with "Step 1" below.

Question	Analysis
Many countries around the world have instituted laws that mandate phasing out the use of incandescent light bulbs and replacing them with alternative light sources that consume less energy. However, many incandescent bulbs have been replaced with fluorescent lights containing the extremely toxic element, mercury. Similarly, some governments have required gasoline for automobiles to contain ethanol, a fuel that generates less pollutants than gasoline when burned. However, ethanol is produced from crops such as corn. Cultivating the crops and converting them to ethanol require large amounts of energy, and the former also increases the use of fertilizers, which can leach into streams and rivers.	**Step 2:** The passage starts with background information that describes what countries are doing about light bulbs. Then a possible conflict is introduced: the new type of bulb contains mercury, which is toxic. More background information is provided: some governments are pushing to add ethanol to gasoline. The fourth and fifth sentences introduce a possible drawback to the proposed change: using corn for fuel uses a lot of energy.
The main theme of the passage is that	**Step 1:** This is a Global question. Read the passage to determine the author's main point.
	Step 3: The author discusses two things governments are trying to do to reduce energy and pollutants. After each example, she uses the contrast keyword "however" to highlight the fact that *there are drawbacks to these plans*. That's a solid prediction.
(A) environmental regulations can have negative consequences.	**Step 4:** Correct. This matches the prediction.
(B) light bulbs and ethanol regulations are misguided.	Just because the regulations have some drawbacks does not mean they are necessarily misguided. Incorrect.
(C) environmental concerns should take precedence over economic issues.	This is an irrelevant comparison between two considerations that are not explicitly discussed in the passage.
(D) fluorescent lights contain more mercury than incandescent lights.	While this is a valid inference that can be made from the passage, this detail is not the main theme of the passage.

Notice that the well-trained test taker follows a specific method. She is not in a rush and takes his time in Step 3. She knows that a well-phrased prediction will help her answer the question efficiently and confidently.

Now it's your turn. Follow the Kaplan Method for PC by working through each step deliberately. Focus on reading the passage strategically and making a strong prediction. When you're finished, check your work against the explanation below.

> Alchemy is the name given to the attempt to change lead, copper, and other metals into silver or gold. Today alchemy is regarded as a pseudoscience. It is associated with astrology and the occult in the modern mind, and the alchemist is viewed in retrospect as a charlatan obsessed with dreams of impossible wealth. But for many centuries, alchemy was a respected art. In the search for the elusive secret to making gold, alchemists helped to develop many of the apparatuses and procedures used in laboratories today, and the results of their experiments laid the basic conceptual basis for the modern science of chemistry.

The central point of the passage is that

(A) alchemy is a pseudoscience.
(B) alchemists tried, but failed, to make gold from other metals.
(C) many alchemists dreamt of becoming rich.
(D) modern chemistry evolved out of alchemy.

Explanation

Step 1: This Global question asks for the passage's central point, or main idea.

Step 2: The first sentence defines the topic of the passage: alchemy. The second and third sentences state that alchemy is no longer recognized as a real science; an analogy is drawn to astrology and the occult. The author then uses the keyword "but" to draw a contrast: for a long time, alchemy was a respected art. The passage then finishes by describing all of the things that alchemists did that helped pave the way for modern chemists.

Step 3: There is no clear opinion from the author, but she does indicate contrast in the middle of the passage. Focus on what the author discusses after the contrast: alchemy used to be a respected art, and the work of alchemists laid the foundation for modern chemistry.

Step 4: Answer choice **(D)** matches the prediction that "the work of alchemists laid the foundation for modern chemistry." The other answer choices don't match the prediction, so eliminate them.

ASVAB STRATEGY

To correctly answer Global questions:

- Identify any opinions, recommendations, suggestions, or predictions made by the author.
- Look to contrast words to help separate supporting details from the author's view.
- Always make a prediction before looking at the answer choices.

Detail Questions

Detail questions ask you to find specific information that is explicitly stated within the passage. Here are some examples of Detail question stems:

According to the author, which of the following is a type of rug found in French castles?

The second step in constructing a picket fence is to

Which of the following is cited in the passage as an advantage of a retirement account?

Notice how these questions are very different from Global questions. In these types of questions, you do not have to read for the author's main idea. In fact, it is crucial in Detail questions not to overanalyze or read too much into the question. The correct answer to these questions will almost always be a paraphrase of something found directly in the passage.

Beware of the difference between simply recognizing text from the passage and recognizing text from the passage that answers the question. Wrong answer choices will sometimes be pulled from irrelevant areas of the given text. For Detail questions, always research the text, make a prediction, and then find a match for that prediction among the answer choices.

Below, take a look at how a Kaplan-trained test taker approaches a typical Paragraph Comprehension Detail question. Remember to start with the question stem, labeled with "Step 1" below.

Question	Analysis
The dancer and choreographer Martha Graham is regarded as one of the outstanding innovators in the history of dance. In a career that lasted over 50 years, Graham created more than 170 works ranging from solos to large-scale pieces, and danced in most of them herself. Trained in a variety of different international styles of dance, she began in the early 1920s to break away from the rigid traditions of classical ballet. She wanted to create a new dance form that would reflect the transformed atmosphere of the postwar period.	**Step 2:** Read the passage, looking for *why* Graham introduced new techniques. The passage starts with background information regarding Martha Graham and her accomplishments. Then, her dancing background and training are discussed. The final sentence discusses *why* she created a new dance style.
Martha Graham introduced new dance techniques in order to:	**Step 1:** This is a Detail question. You are looking for a reason why Martha Graham introduced new dance techniques.
	Step 3: Rephrase the last sentence of the passage: Graham introduced new dance techniques because she wanted to come up with a new, original dance form that expressed the way the world felt after the war.
(A) break away from the traditions of classical ballet.	**Step 4:** This choice describes *what* Martha did, but is incorrect because it does not answer the given question of *why* she did it.
(B) attract attention to her dance troupe	This is a distortion of what the passage said. While attracting attention may have been a nice side effect, it's not the reason *why* Graham introduced new dance techniques. Incorrect.

Question	Analysis
(C) express the changed mood of her time	Correct. This matches the prediction.
(D) emphasize the rigidity of conventional dance movement	This is incorrect because it distorts Martha's intention. She was not commenting on conventional dance movement. She was updating dance to reflect the current times.

Now, you take a shot! Use the example above to help you through the following practice item. Make sure to follow the Kaplan Method to secure great habits for Test Day.

Golden retrievers, one of the most popular dog breeds in the United States, have earned their wide acceptance for a variety of reasons. As hunting dogs, they will retrieve game carefully and willingly bring it back to the hunter without damage. As family pets, goldens are gentle and patient additions to the household, willingly abiding unintentional abuse by toddlers. Goldens are intelligent and can be readily trained to respond to a wide variety of commands. For this reason, they are among the favorite breeds chosen to be trained as assistance dogs for disabled persons. Also, their friendly nature has made them perfect visitors to communities for the elderly. A golden retriever will do its utmost to please its human master.

The author states that golden retrievers are excellent assistance dogs because they are

(A) friendly
(B) intelligent
(C) gentle
(D) available

Explanation

Step 1: The question asks for what the passage states is the reason why golden retrievers are excellent assistance dogs. This is a Detail question.

Step 2: The passage discusses various reasons for why golden retrievers are so popular. Sentences four and five describe the attributes that make golden retrievers excellent assistance dogs.

Step 3: Combine sentences four and five to formulate your prediction: *goldens are excellent assistance dogs because they are intelligent and easily trained.*

Step 4: Answer choice **(B)** matches the prediction that goldens make great assistance dogs because they are smart and easily trained. Because the other answer choices don't match the prediction, we can eliminate them.

> ## ASVAB STRATEGY
>
> To correctly answer Detail questions:
>
> - Identify specific information in the passage that answers the question.
> - Don't fall for answer choices that rephrase statements in the passage but that don't answer the question.

Inference Questions

Sometimes the ASVAB will ask you questions about the passage to which the answers are not directly stated in the text, but are instead implied by the passage. Here are just a few of the ways an Inference question might be worded:

Which of the following is implied by the passage?

The author apparently feels that

It can be inferred from the passage that

As you can see, the wording in Inference questions rarely points you to a specific part of the passage, as Detail questions do. And Inference questions won't necessarily ask you about the ideas that are most important to the author, as Global questions do. Instead, Inference questions require you to consider multiple statements in a passage and, from them, determine what else the author must believe. Because there are many inferences that can be made from a given piece of text, it's not necessary to predict before considering the answer choices. Rather, paraphrase the passage and move through the answer choices, selecting the one that is supported by the given text.

Because the correct answer to an Inference question is simply the one answer choice that is strongly supported by what is stated in the passage, you can also eliminate wrong answer choices because they commit one of the following errors:

- They contradict information in the passage.
- They bring in outside information that is not discussed in the passage.
- They distort the information presented in the passage.
- They make an extreme claim that is not completely supported by the passage.

Let's see how a Kaplan-trained test taker handles a Paragraph Comprehension Inference question. Remember to start with the question stem, labeled with "Step 1" below.

Question	Analysis
Dan and Sonya are married and have exactly three children—Betty, George, and Tara—and exactly three grandchildren. George usually babysits Betty's twin daughters, while Tara usually babysits George's child.	**Step 2:** The passage starts with background on Dan and Sonya, who are married and have three children: Betty, George, and Tara. They also have three grandchildren. The passage states that Betty has twin daughters, and that George has a child.
If these statements are true, which of the following must be true?	**Step 1:** This questions asks what must be true based on what the passage stated, so it's an Inference question. Because there are no clues in the question stem pointing to a single area of the text, read and paraphrase the entire passage.
	Step 3: Mentally or on scratch paper, create a "family tree" to visualize the relationships: Dan & Sonya Betty George Tara 2 Daughters 1 Child This is a summary of the given information. Since there are only three grandchildren, this means that Tara must not have any children.
(A) All of Dan's grandchildren are female.	**Step 4:** Though Betty has two daughters, the sex of George's child is not known. Therefore, it's not necessarily true that all of the grandchildren are female. Eliminate.
(B) Tara has no children.	Correct. This must be true according to the statements in the passage.
(C) Tara sometimes babysits for Betty's children.	Though the passage states that Tara usually babysits George's child, it does not mention whether she ever babysits for Betty or not.
(D) Sonya has at least one grandson.	From the statements given in the passage, all that is known for sure is that Sonya has two granddaughters and another grandchild, whose sex is unknown.

Now, you try it. Follow the steps used in the example above to help you master your technique for tackling Inference questions on Test Day.

> In each of the last three years, a court in this country has awarded a settlement in excess of $300 million. This is a travesty of justice, and it unfairly burdens the court system. To alleviate the strain on the nation's court system, _____.
>
> Which of the following best completes the above passage?
>
> (A) there should be fewer lawsuits
> (B) lawsuits should name more than one defendant
> (C) courts should cease awarding excessive settlements
> (D) settlements should be awarded based solely on need

Explanation

Step 1: The question asks what would complete the passage. Since the correct answer will be based on what was said in the rest of the passage, this is an Inference question.

Step 2: The passage states that, in the past three years, courts have been awarding extremely high settlements. The author feels that these awards are outrageous, saying that they are a "travesty of justice" and they "unfairly burden the court system."

Step 3: The gist of the argument is that awards are too big, so it would seem logical that if courts stopped going overboard in awarding settlements, it would help lessen the burden on the courts.

Step 4: The correct answer here is choice **(C)**, that courts should stop awarding excessive settlements. Answer choices (A) and (B) are not issues discussed in this passage. Choice (D), likewise, is not discussed in the passage, and the use of "solely" makes it too extreme as well. There is nothing in the passage to support that settlements should be awarded only based on need.

ASVAB STRATEGY

To correctly answer Inference questions:

- Remember that the correct answer is supported by statements in the passage.
- Don't read between the lines too much.
- Choose the answer that is most strongly supported by the text.

Vocabulary-in-Context Questions

One final type of question found in the PC section will ask you for the meaning of a word used in the paragraph. These questions, which we call Vocabulary-in-Context questions, are pretty straightforward: the correct answer will be a word that can replace the word in question without altering the meaning of the sentence.

To handle this question type, focus on the word in the question stem while you are reading the passage. Then, predict an answer by defining the word as it is used in context. Finally, attack the answer choices by looking for a word that matches your prediction. Once you have selected an answer choice, reread the initial sentence with the answer choice in place of the vocabulary word to be sure the meaning is the same.

If you feel as though your vocabulary could use some improvement, be sure to utilize the vocabulary-building resources available to you in chapter 3 (Word Knowledge) and in Appendix A.

Below, take a look at how an expert uses the Kaplan Method to efficiently and effectively attack a Vocabulary-in-Context passage. Remember to start with the question stem, labeled with "Step 1" below.

Question	Analysis
When voters choose a candidate in an election, they cast one vote for one candidate. However, there are other ways that votes can be cast in different situations. One of the more common alternatives is rank voting. In this scheme, each voter ranks the choices from first to last. Thus, if there were ten positions to fill, each voter would assign ten points to her favorite choice, nine points to the second favorite, and so on. This system is used by the Associated Press to rank college sports teams and a modified version is used in Australian elections.	**Step 2:** The word *scheme* is used in the fourth sentence of the passage. Leading up to the word, the passage is talking about the process of choosing a candidate in an election.
A word that could be properly substituted for *scheme* in the passage is	**Step 1.** The question asks you to determine the meaning of a word used in the passage. This is a Vocabulary-in-Context question.
	Step 3: There are different approaches to elections listed. This tells us the word is being used to describe a *procedure* or a *process*. One of those words, or a synonym, would be a good prediction for the meaning of the word *scheme* in this passage.
(A) plot	**Step 4:** While a common usage of the word *scheme* is to describe a plot, no one is plotting anything in the passage.
(B) collection	*Collection* does not make sense in the context of the passage. Eliminate.
(C) vision	*Vision* does not make sense in the context of the passage. Eliminate.
(D) method	Correct. *This scheme* refers to rank voting, which is a *method* of voting.

Now it's your turn. Follow the steps used in the example above to correctly and confidently answer the Vocabulary-in-Context question below.

> Who was the first man to discover the North Pole? Soon after the turn of the twentieth century, two men each claimed the honor individually. While Frederick Cook claimed he was the first to discover the North Pole in 1908, Robert Peary disputed Cook's account and set out on his own expedition in 1909. Today, it is unclear which man, if either, actually reached the North Pole. Poring through the written accounts of Cook and Peary's expeditions, researchers believe that while both men came close to the North Pole, neither man actually found it.
>
> As it used in the passage, "poring through" most nearly means
>
> (A) reading carefully
> (B) filtering out
> (C) searching for
> (D) making notes in

Explanation

Step 1: How is the phrase "poring through" being used in the passage in this Vocabulary-in-Context question?

Step 2: The researchers had access to Cook and Peary's written accounts, so they must have evaluated them by reading through them.

Step 3: Anything that expresses the idea of "reading" the accounts will be correct.

Step 4: Only answer choice (A), *reading carefully,* matches. Answer choice (B), *filtering out,* changes the meaning of the sentence: the researchers weren't removing some of the written accounts. Similarly, the researchers weren't *searching for* the accounts, (C), since it's inferred that they already had the documents. Same with answer choice (D): the researchers were not *making notes in* the explorers' accounts.

ASVAB STRATEGY

To correctly answer Vocabulary-in-Context questions:

- Always make a prediction before you look through the answer choices.
- If you are unsure of the correct answer choice based on your prediction, reread the sentence while plugging in the answer choices.
- The correct choice will sound right and will not change the meaning of the sentence.

PARAGRAPH COMPREHENSION PRACTICE QUESTIONS

The presidential election in November 2000 showed once again how important it is for all Americans to take advantage of their right to vote. The election was so close that it took weeks to finalize the tally, and the controversy surrounding chads, voting machines, and the court system only served to reinforce the sentiment that each vote counts.

1. The main idea of the passage is that

    (A) voting machines are not adequate
    (B) the Supreme Court should decide who will be the president
    (C) voting is a right that can be taken away
    (D) every voter should exercise his or her right and vote

Four years ago, the governor came into office seeking to change the way politics were run in this state. Now, it appears he has been the victim of his own ambitious political philosophy. Trying to do too much has given him a reputation as being pushy, and the backlash in the state has let him accomplish little. He may very well lose in his reelection bid.

2. The governor's approach to politics was

    (A) business as usual
    (B) overly idealistic
    (C) careless and sloppy
    (D) influenced by his critics

Since its first official documentation by Sir George Everest in 1865, Mount Everest in Nepal has been the "Holy Grail" of mountaineers. Sir Edmund Hillary was the first man to successfully complete the ascent to the peak in May 1953. His feat won him international acclaim, not to mention knighthood. But much less celebrated is the first successful ascent of Everest by a woman, which did not take place until May 16, 1975. Junko Tabei of Japan was the first woman to reach the summit of the world's most famous single peak. The first American woman to scale its heights successfully was Stacy Allison of Portland in 1988.

3. Mount Everest was first conquered by

    (A) Sir George Everest
    (B) Junko Tabei
    (C) Sir Edmund Hillary
    (D) Stacy Allison

It is without question a travesty that our children are no longer given healthy, nutritious food options for lunch in our public schools. Hamburgers, pizza, and chocolate are not only giving our kids bigger waistlines, but these junk foods are also helping teach them poor eating habits. It is imperative that we change the mindset that any food is good food and start offering students better meals at the same prices. Otherwise, a new generation of obese Americans is a given.

4. According to the passage, over the past few years, school lunches have gotten

    (A) more expensive
    (B) more exotic
    (C) healthier
    (D) less nutritious

Many times families choose to replace old furniture when just a minor amount of maintenance is all that is needed. To fix a wooden chair that is wobbly, follow these easy steps. First, check the joints of the chair to see if the chair is structurally sound. There should be small dowel rods and a corner block to keep the chair together. Next, use a ripping chisel to remove the corner block. Once the block is free from the chair, you should be able to glue the joints back together. Finally, once the glue looks dry, place the corner block back on the chair and gently mallet the block onto the dowels. In no time, you will have saved not only the chair, but also your hard-earned money!

5. After removing the corner block, you should

    (A) mallet the dowels into place
    (B) check the joints for damage
    (C) glue the joints together
    (D) replace the corner block

James felt the pulse of the crowd. There was a low murmur just under the house music. Backstage, his bandmates were tuning or drumming lightly on tabletops. In a few moments, the whole country would watch the band play. What a change from those dingy bars and clubs a few years ago. Maybe all the hard work had finally paid off. Looking down at his callused hands, he wondered if maybe this would be the break they had been working so hard for.

6. The tone of this passage is one of

    (A) sadness
    (B) anticipation
    (C) anger
    (D) ambivalence

Packaging on many popular foods is deceiving to consumers. Too often, the print is small and hard to read. And if you can read it, it's often confusing or intentionally vague. This is especially true on the nutrition label. The government really ought to do something about the nutrition labels on food because the existing laws just don't go far enough.

7. The author would probably support which of the following?

    (A) magazine advertisements for cigarettes
    (B) allergy information prominently listed on food labels
    (C) fine print on a contract
    (D) food ads in the Sunday paper

In an age where we have pills for depression, dysfunction, and aggression, not to mention headaches, it is important that we not forget that many drugs can have serious side effects. These may range from internal bleeding, vomiting, or soreness in the limbs to, in more extreme cases, loss of consciousness or even coma. If you experience unwanted side effects, it is important to get to a hospital immediately and seek treatment. Drinking alcohol or smoking cigarettes may also contribute to violent side effects.

8. According to the passage, one of the possible side effects of drugs is

    (A) drinking alcohol
    (B) dysfunction
    (C) internal bleeding
    (D) aggression

First created at the height of atomic postwar paranoia, the Incredible Hulk stories offer a fascinating look at the dual nature of human beings. On the one hand, he is a mild-mannered, bespectacled scientist. On the other, he is a raging, rampaging beast. More than a statement about nuclear dangers, the Hulk is a reflection of the two sides in each of us—the calm, logical human and the raging animal.

9. According to the author, the comic book character of the Hulk is

    (A) a reflection of humanity
    (B) really an animal
    (C) mild mannered
    (D) a protest about atomic power

Once considered the best high school player in the country, the onetime prodigy now spends his days working as a bricklayer for a local construction company. Asked if he is bitter about the way his life turned out, he replies, "Not at all." In fact, he says, his only regret is that he didn't study hard enough and go to college. He still gets recognized on occasion, but an extra 80 pounds and bad knees keep him from reliving his former glory on the court.

10. The word prodigy in the passage most nearly means

    (A) depressed loner
    (B) shy scientist
    (C) gifted youngster
    (D) bitter malcontent

Celebrated as one of the greatest film directors of the twentieth century, Alfred Hitchcock made his name creating some of the most critically acclaimed suspense films of all time. But while other directors of the genre seemed content telling stories of domestic intrigue, Hitchcock was not afraid to make films centering on unconventional subjects. In fact, one of his most celebrated films, *The Birds,* has no typical antagonist: the suspense comes not from a person who is out to do wrong, but rather from nature itself.

11. The main idea of the passage above is that

    (A) Alfred Hitchcock is one of the greatest film directors ever.
    (B) most suspense films tell stories of domestic intrigue.
    (C) Alfred Hitchcock was not afraid to tell unconventional stories.
    (D) *The Birds* is scarier than traditional suspense films.

Bassoons are double-reeded wood instruments that produce a deep baritone sound. A bassoon's pitch can be altered by adjusting a curved tube called a bocal. The deeper the bocal is inserted into the bassoon, the higher the pitch. Conversely, pulling the bocal out of the instrument lowers the pitch.

12. It can be inferred from the passage that the bassoon

    (A) is a larger instrument than the oboe
    (B) is the deepest-sounding wood instrument
    (C) is the only instrument that utilizes a bocal
    (D) is capable of a range of pitches

Investors who believe that a company's stock price is overvalued can perform an action called a "short sale." To short a stock, an investor sells shares that he does not currently own. If the stock goes down in price, the investor is able to buy the shares at a lower price. Shorting stocks is risky, though; if the stock suddenly rises in price, a broker can force the investor to purchase the shares at the higher price, resulting in a significant loss.

13. According to the passage, an investor who shorts stocks first

   (A) buys shares of a company's stock, then sells those shares for a loss
   (B) sells shares of a company's stock, then buys those shares at a later date
   (C) buys shares of a company's stock, then sells those shares whenever he wishes
   (D) sells shares of a company's stock, then uses that money to buy stock in another company

As rays of sunlight peeked through the tops of the trees, Mark felt at peace. It had been years since he had walked these trails. Everything was quiet and calm. It seemed to him that he finally saw the woods as they truly were: a refuge, a place to be renewed, a respite from the clamor and chaos of the city.

14. In this passage, *respite* most nearly means

   (A) relief
   (B) opposite
   (C) valley
   (D) hope

The bus system in the city is in need of a drastic overhaul. Last week, the Main Street bus line was reduced from one bus every 15 minutes to one bus an hour. The week before that, the Uptown bus was canceled completely. Each change occurred with no notice! If the city expects people to continue to use public transportation, it needs to reduce the bus system issues.

15. Which of the following is mentioned in the passage?

   (A) The city needs to notify customers of bus line interruptions.
   (B) The city should allocate money from other programs to revamp the bus system.
   (C) The Main Street bus line has experienced reduced service in the past.
   (D) The Main Street bus line has been shut down in the past.

Answers and Explanations

1. **(D) every voter should exercise his or her right and vote.** From the first sentence to the very last, the author is clearly in favor of the idea that "each vote counts." Choice (D) most clearly reflects this sentiment. You can also eliminate wrong answer choices (B) and (C) because they are never mentioned in the passage. And "voting machines," (A), are mentioned in the passage, but only to support the conclusion that every vote counts.

2. **(B) overly idealistic** From the information given, you should have seen that the governor was very determined to get things done his way. So his approach could hardly be described as *business as usual,* choice (A). Nowhere in the passage is his approach described as *careless and sloppy,* choice (C). And since the mayor insisted on doing things his way, his approach was not *influenced by his critics,* choice (D). Only (B) is addressed in the paragraph. Seeking to change the way politics are run indicates an *idealistic* approach to politics.

3. **(C) Sir Edmund Hillary** This Detail question asks you for the first person to conquer Mount Everest. Researching the passage, you must be careful not to assume that the mountain is named for its conqueror. While *Sir George Everest,* (A), first documented and recorded the height of Everest in 1865, it was *Sir Edmund Hillary* who completed the first ascent to the peak in 1953. The question does not ask for the first woman, or the first American woman, to reach the summit, so (B), *Junko Tabei,* and (D), *Stacy Allison,* are out. The correct answer is (C).

4. **(D) less nutritious** The author feels strongly that meals in school cafeterias have become more and more similar to junk food. Choice (A) is not applicable, regardless of its validity, because it is not the central point of the passage. Choice (B) is nowhere indicated in the passage, and choice (C) is the opposite of the correct answer. Of the answer choices given, only choice (D), *less nutritious,* correctly answers the question.

5. **(C) glue the joints together** This Detail question asks you to identify a specific step in a process, so your first task is to locate the step that discusses removing the corner block. Removing the corner block is finally mentioned in the fifth sentence. After using a ripping chisel to remove the block from the chair, the worker is free to glue the joints back together to tighten them, choice (C).

6. **(B) anticipation.** To correctly gauge the tone of a passage, you should pay attention not only to the details, but also to the language and description. In this passage, James is clearly waiting to go onstage. Words like *pulse, murmur,* and *maybe* invite the reader to feel excitement and nervousness as James does. Of the answer choices given, (D), *ambivalence,* is clearly wrong, as James definitely cares about what is going to happen. He seems wistful, but never sad, (A), or angry, (C). The only answer that successfully captures James's mood is choice (B), *anticipation.*

7. **(B) allergy information prominently listed on food labels** Judging from the critical tone of the author and the subject matter at hand, one can safely assume that the author is interested in public safety. Clearly small print is not going to be favored by this author, so choice (C) is out. Choice (D) doesn't make sense and choice (A) is not something thought of as good for public safety. Choice (B), *allergy information prominently listed on food labels*, fits the author's passion for consumer labels.

8. **(C) internal bleeding** According to the details of the passage, one possible side effect from prescription drug usage is *internal bleeding,* answer choice (C). *Drinking alcohol,* (A), can exacerbate side effects, but it is not a side effect itself. *Dysfunction,* (B), and *aggression,* (D), are discussed as conditions treated by drugs, not as side effects of drug use.

9. **(A) a reflection of humanity** From the details of the passage, it is clear that the author sees the character of the Hulk as a symbol. The passage states that the Hulk is a reflection of the two sides of each of us, which matches choice (A) a reflection of humanity. The passage states that the Hulk varies between an *animal* mentality (B) and a *mild-mannered* person (C) but it does not claim that he is one over the other. While the passage mentions atomic postwar paranoia, it does not suggest that the Hulk is used as a *protest* of any type as in choice (D).

10. **(C) gifted youngster** According to the passage, the one-time star athlete is now a local bricklayer. There is nothing in the passage to indicate that the person in question was ever a *depressed loner* (A), *shy scientist* (B), or *bitter malcontent* (D), but it only makes sense that he was once a *gifted youngster* (C). The term *prodigy* refers to a person with natural ability, often at a young age.

11. **(C) Alfred Hitchcock was not afraid to tell unconventional stories.** Remember to look to contrast keywords to help determine an author's main point. Here, the passage makes a distinction between the work of typical directors and that of Hitchcock: Hitchcock, unlike the others, dared to make films that were unconventional, which is answer choice (C). While answer choices (A) and (B) are supported by the passage, they are too narrow to encompass the main point. Answer choice (D) is out of scope and is not stated or inferred in the passage.

12. **(D) is capable of a range of pitches** While it may be true that the bassoon is larger than the oboe, that claim is not supported by information in the passage, so (A) is out. The passage does state that the bassoon produces a deep sound, but claiming that it is the deepest-sounding wood instrument is too extreme, so (B) is out. Nothing in the passage supports the claim that the bassoon is the only instrument that utilizes a bocal, which means (C) is incorrect. The passage does state that a bassoon's pitch can be altered by adjusting the bocal, so (D) is correct.

13. **(B) sells shares of a company's stock, then buys those shares at a later date** In this Detail question that asks about a process, refer back to the passage to find the correct answer. You will find the information in the second, third, and fourth sentences. The second sentence states that an investor sells shares he does not currently own, while the third and fourth sentences indicate that he then purchases those shares at a later date. That sequence is described in answer choice (B). Both (A) and (C) are incorrect because a short seller does not first buy shares of stock. (D) is out because although a short seller does first sell shares of stock, nothing in the passage indicates that that money is then used to purchase stock in another company.

14. **(A) relief** Always make a prediction in Vocabulary-in-Context questions. The tone of this passage is one of peacefulness and calm. Therefore, you could infer that Mark's quiet, relaxing walk in the woods is a break, or a period of relief, from the clamor and chaos of the city. While (B) *opposite* might sound appealing, since the passage contrasts the forest with the city, *opposite* doesn't make sense if inserted into the sentence. Mark might be in a (C) *valley*, but that also doesn't make sense if inserted into the sentence. Finally, (D) *hope* doesn't match the idea that Mark has simply found a quiet place away from the city.

15. **(C) The Main Street bus line has experienced reduced service in the past.** This statement is a specific detail taken from the second sentence of the passage, "the Main Street bus line was reduced from one bus every 15 minutes to one bus an hour." There is no evidence that the Main Street bus line has ever been completely shut down (D). The author does mention not being given any notification, but he does not state choice (A), that the city needs to notify customers. Choice (B) might be an idea the author would agree with, but it is not mentioned in the passage.

Review and Reflect

So, how did you do? What was challenging about these problems? Did you notice that you were performing better on some question types than others?

Going back over these problems may be helpful. As you review your performance, ask yourself a few questions:

- Were you able to identify different Paragraph Comprehension question types?
- Do you have a strategy for each of the different question types?
- Are you reading Paragraph Comprehension passages strategically?
- Can you separate background information, supporting details, and main points?
- Do you make accurate predictions?
- Are you able to match my prediction to the correct answer?
- Can you identify and eliminate common wrong answer types?

In future Paragraph Comprehension questions, apply what you've learned in this chapter. Approach each question with Kaplan's 4-step method, and you'll see your performance in this section continue to improve.

MATH STRATEGIES FOR THE ASVAB

KNOW WHAT TO EXPECT

Often the most efficient way to get the correct answer to a math problem is to use a strategy rather than just to "do the math." That's especially true on the ASVAB, since you cannot use a calculator on the exam. On some math tests, if you get the wrong answer but show that you set up at least some of the math correctly, you'll still get partial credit. On the ASVAB, you only get credit for a right answer. One advantage of this is that you will get credit for the correct answer regardless of how you get to it.

The two math sections on the ASVAB are called "Arithmetic Reasoning" and "Mathematics Knowledge." Together they form the quantitative half of the Armed Forces Qualifying Test (AFQT), so you'll want to do well on these sections no matter what your ultimate vocational aim in the military.

The **Arithmetic Reasoning** (AR) section tests your ability to handle arithmetic word problems. The CAT version of this section gives you 39 minutes to answer 16 questions, while the paper and pencil version gives you 36 minutes for 30 questions. This section is designed to measure your ability to apply reasoning to solve problems involving common math concepts. Many of the questions will be in the format of word problems. Typical AR topics involve number properties, rates, percentages, ratios, proportions, averages, and unit conversions.

The **Mathematics Knowledge** (MK) section tests your understanding of a wide range of concepts in applied arithmetic, algebra, and geometry. The CAT version gives you 20 minutes to answer 16 questions; the paper and pencil version gives you 24 minutes to answer 25 questions. This section is designed to measure general mathematical knowledge. You may see the occasional word problem on the MK section of the ASVAB, but in general the questions are more direct than the word problems found on the AR section. For this reason, you are given less time per question on this section than on the AR section.

THE KAPLAN METHOD FOR ASVAB MATH

LEARNING OBJECTIVES

In this section, you will learn to:

- identify your task on math problems
- determine the most efficient strategy for getting the correct answer
- apply the Kaplan Method for ASVAB Math

Working quickly and efficiently is essential to maximizing your score on these sections. To accomplish this, use the **Kaplan Method for ASVAB Math**.

THE KAPLAN METHOD FOR ASVAB MATH

Step 1: Analyze the information given.

Step 2: Identify what you are being asked for.

Step 3: Solve strategically.

Step 4: Confirm your answer.

Step 1. Analyze the information given

Read the entire question carefully *before* you start solving the problem. If you don't read the question carefully, you may make a careless mistake or overlook the simplest approach to answering the question.

Step 2. Identify what you are being asked for

Before you choose your approach, make sure you know what you're solving for. In other words, what does the correct answer choice represent? This is an important step to keep you from falling for tempting wrong answer choices. For example, if you are given an equation with two variables, x and y, identify whether you are solving for x, for y, or for something else. This step is important because the ASVAB may give you wrong answer choices that represent the "right answer to the wrong question." That is, if you are asked to solve for x, one wrong answer choice might represent the value of y.

Step 3. Solve strategically

Once you understand what the question is asking for, it's time to look for the most strategic approach. Use your analysis from Steps 1 and 2 to find the most efficient route to the correct answer. This step might involve performing calculations (that is, "doing the math"), or it might be the case that applying a strategy would get you to the correct answer more quickly. This chapter will discuss these strategic approaches.

Step 4. Confirm your answer

Reread the question as you select your answer. Make sure you are answering the question asked. If you notice that you missed something earlier, rework the problem and change your answer if necessary.

Here's an example of the Kaplan Method for ASVAB Math in action.

Question	Analysis
One bag contains 6 pieces of candy, another bag contains 8 pieces, and a third bag contains 16 pieces. What is the average number of pieces of candy in a single bag?	**Step 1:** The question tells you the number of pieces of candy in three bags.
	Step 2: Your task is to calculate the average number of candies in one bag.
(A) 6 (B) 8 (C) 10 (D) 30	**Step 3:** Use the average formula: $$\frac{\text{Sum of terms}}{\text{Number of terms}} = \text{Average}$$ $$\frac{6+8+16}{3} =$$ $$\frac{30}{3} = 10$$ The average is 10, answer choice **(C)**.
	Step 4: Don't rework the math from scratch; rather, ask yourself whether the answer makes sense given what you were asked for. Does 10 seem like a likely average given the numbers 6, 8, and 16? Yes: Since the average of a set of numbers has a value that's between the smallest and largest numbers in the set, 10 makes sense as an answer.

STRATEGIES FOR SOLVING MATH PROBLEMS

ASVAB MATH STRATEGIES

- Backsolving
- Picking Numbers
- Strategic Guessing Using Logic
- Combination of approaches

Several methods are extremely useful when you don't know—or don't have time to use—the textbook approach to solving the question. In addition, performing all the calculations called for in the question can often be more time consuming than using a strategic approach and can increase the potential for mistakes.

Two problem-solving strategies that may be new to you are **Backsolving** and **Picking Numbers**. These strategies are a great way to make confusing problems more concrete. If you know how to apply these strategies, you'll nail the correct answer every time you use them.

Strategic Guessing Using Logic and using a **combination of approaches** are other useful shortcuts to getting more correct answers, quickly. Remember, you get points for correct answers, not for how you got those answers, so efficiency is key to maximizing your score. This section will discuss each of these strategies in turn.

Backsolving

Sometimes it's easiest to work backward from the answer choices. Since many Arithmetic Reasoning questions are word problems with numbers in the answer choices, you can often use this to your advantage by **Backsolving**. After all, the test gives you the correct answer—it's just mixed in with the wrong answer choices. If you try an answer choice in the question and it fits with the information given, then you've got the right answer.

Here's how it works. When the answer choices are numbers, you can expect them to be arranged from small to large (or occasionally from large to small). Start by trying either choice (B) or (C). If that number works when you plug it into the problem, you've found the correct answer. If it doesn't work, you can usually figure out whether to try a larger or smaller answer choice next. Even better, if you deduce that you need a smaller (or larger) number, and only one such smaller (or larger) number appears among the answer choices, that choice must be correct. You do not have to try that answer choice: simply select it and move on to the next question.

By Backsolving strategically this way, you won't have to try out more than two answer choices before you zero in on the correct answer. To see an example of Backsolving, check out the following problem and explanation.

Question	Analysis
An appliance store reduced the price of a refrigerator by 20% and then raised the price by 10% from the lower price. What was the original price of the refrigerator, if the final price was $70.40? Answer choices:	**Step 1:** The price of a refrigerator is reduced 20% and then that reduced price is raised 10%. The final price is $70.40.
	Step 2: The correct answer represents the original price, before the changes.

Question	Analysis
(A) $50 (B) $70 (C) $80 (D) $100	**Step 3:** To answer this question using algebra would be complex and time-consuming and would afford many opportunities for errors. Instead, since all the answer choices are numbers, Backsolve. Start by trying out (B) $70. $70 reduced by 20%: $\quad$ $70 − $14 = $56 $56 raised by 10%; $\quad$ $56 + $5.60 = $61.60. That's lower than the final price of $70.40, so choice (B) is too low. Eliminate both answer choices (B) and (A). Now try either (C) or (D). (D) is easier for a percent problem. Reduce $100 by 20%: $\quad$ $100 − $20 = $80 Raise that $80 by 10%: $\quad$ $80 + $8 = $88. That final price is far too high, so **(C)** must be the correct answer.
	Step 4: The answer of $80 is the only one that is neither too large nor too small to yield the final price of $70.40 specified in the question. Done.

In Backsolving, when you start with (B) or (C) and that answer doesn't work, you'll usually know which direction to go. For example, if the answer choices are listed smallest to largest and (B) is too large when you plug it in, you will know that (A) is the correct answer. If, on the other hand, (B) had been too small, you would know that the answer was (C) or (D).

Now, try this one on your own. Use Backsolving.

(*Hint:* The hypotenuse (or longest side) of a right triangle is equal to the square root of the sum of the squares of the other two sides. In other words, if the other two sides are *a* and *b* and the hypotenuse is *c*, then $a^2 + b^2 = c^2$.)

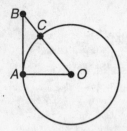

In the figure above, the circle with center O has a radius of 6 (in other words, $AO = 6$). If $AB = 10$ and $\angle OAB$ is a right angle, what is the length of BC?

(A) $2(\sqrt{17} - 3)$

(B) 4

(C) $2(\sqrt{34} - 3)$

(D) 6

Explanation

Step 1: You are told that the length of the circle's radius is 6, and the length of one leg of a right triangle that is partly embedded in the circle. Because the other leg of the triangle, OA, is also a radius of the circle, you know it has a length of 6. Also, a portion of the hypotenuse of the triangle, OC, is also a radius of the circle and, likewise, has a length of 6.

Step 2: Your task is to determine the part of the hypotenuse outside the circle, or the entire hypotenuse minus 6.

Step 3: You could use the Pythagorean theorem here: $a^2 + b^2 = c^2$, where a and b are the lengths of the legs of a right triangle and c is the length of the hypotenuse. However, a look at the answer choices reveals that you might have to do some really burdensome calculations.

Instead, Backsolve. Choosing between answer choices (B) or (C), start with (B) because 4 is much easier to work with than $2(\sqrt{34} - 3)$. If $BC = 4$, the hypotenuse would equal $4 + 6 = 10$. Since one of the legs has that same length, and the hypotenuse is always the longest side of a right triangle, this is too short. Eliminate (A) and (B).

Next, try (D) 6. If $BC = 6$, the hypotenuse would equal $6 + 6 = 12$. Using the Pythagorean theorem, test to see if $6^2 + 10^2$ equals 12^2. In fact, $36 + 100$ does not equal 144, so the correct answer must be **(C)**.

Step 4: Because the other answer choices cannot be correct, choice (C) must represent the length of BC.

Picking Numbers

Another strategy that comes in handy on many Mathematics Knowledge questions and also on some Arithmetic Reasoning questions is **Picking Numbers**. Just because the question contains numbers in the answer choices, that doesn't mean that you can always Backsolve. There may be numbers in the answer choices, but sometimes you won't have enough information in the question to easily match up an answer choice to a specific value in the question stem. For example, a problem might present an equation with many variables, or it might give you information about percentages of some unknown quantity and ask you for another percent. If the test maker hasn't provided you with a quantity that it would be really helpful to have in order to solve the problem, you may be able to simply pick a value to assign to that unknown. The other case in which you can pick numbers is when there are variables in the answer choices.

When you are Picking Numbers, be sure that the numbers you select are permissible (follow the rules of the problem) and manageable (easy to work with). In general, it's a good idea to avoid picking −1, 0, or 1 because they have unique number properties that can skew your results.

Here's a great example showing how Picking Numbers can make an abstract problem concrete.

Question	Analysis
When *n* is divided by 14, the remainder is 9. What is the remainder when *n* is divided by 7?	**Step 1:** An unknown number, *n*, is 9 larger than a multiple of 14.
	Step 2: The correct answer represents the remainder when *n* is divided by 7.
(A) 1 (B) 2 (C) 3 (D) 4	**Step 3:** To make this abstract question concrete, pick a number for *n* that leaves a remainder of 9 when divided by 14. The most manageable number to pick that is also permissible in the problem is *n* = 23 (because 14 + 9 = 23). Now try out your number: 23 ÷ 7 = 3 with a remainder of 2. **(B)** is the correct answer.
	Step 4: Briefly look back over the math to check that you are solving for the correct value. Done.

Now, try this one on your own using the Picking Numbers strategy.

If a bicyclist in motion increases his speed by 30 percent and then increases this speed by 10 percent, what percent of the original speed is the total increase in speed?

(A) 10%
(B) 40%
(C) 43%
(D) 140%

Explanation

Step 1: The question gives information about two increases to the speed of a bicyclist.

Step 2: The question asks for the total percent increase.

Step 3: You are not told how fast the bicyclist is going when he starts his trip, so this is a great opportunity for Picking Numbers. The easiest number to use in percent problems is 100, so start the bicyclist at a speed of 100 miles per hour. Remember, the numbers you pick should be permissible and manageable, but they do not have to be realistic.

The first increase in speed is 30%. Because 30% of 100 is 30, the new speed is 100 + 30 = 130. The second increase in speed is 10%, but not 10% of the original speed--10% of the new speed. Because 10% of 130 is 13, the final speed is 130 + 13 = 143. Subtract the original speed from the final speed, and the increase in speed is 143 − 100 = 43. Since 100 was the initial number, 43 is simply 43% of the original, answer choice **(C)**.

Step 4: When confirming the answer for questions that ask about multiple percent changes, make sure that you calculated the percent changes appropriately and didn't simply add the percentages given in the question, as (B) does. Also, check to make sure that you solved for the correct value, here the *increase* in speed as a percentage of the *original speed*. Answer choice (D) makes the same mistake as (B) but may look tempting to some test takers, because it is close to the final speed of 143.

When there are variables in the problem and in the answer choices, you can Pick Numbers for those variables. Evaluate the expression in the question stem using your chosen numbers and then evaluate each answer choice using the same numbers. Your goal is to find the answer that yields the same numerical result as the one you calculated using your chosen numbers. When you use this method, you must evaluate *all* of the answer choices. If more than one yields the same numerical result, choose a different set of numbers to evaluate only the remaining choices that gave matching solutions with the first set of numbers that you chose.

To solve problems containing variables in the question stem and answer choices using Picking Numbers, start by picking permissible and manageable numbers for the variables. Answer the question using the numbers you've picked. This answer is your target number. Then, substitute the numbers you picked for the variables into the answer choices. You are looking for the answer choice that gives you the target number.

Take a look at this example.

Question	Analysis
Camilla spent d dollars on groceries each week for w weeks, and p percent of the amount she spent on groceries was spent on fresh vegetables. How much money did she spend over the whole time period on groceries other than fresh vegetables?	**Step 1:** The question contains no numbers; only variables: d = the amount Camilla spent on groceries each week w = the number of weeks she shopped p = the percent of that money that went to fresh vegetables.
	Step 2: The correct answer represents the amount of grocery money not spent on fresh vegetables.

Question	Analysis
(A) $dw\left(1 - \dfrac{p}{100}\right)$ (B) $\dfrac{dwp}{100}$ (C) $100p(1 - dw)$ (D) $\dfrac{100p}{dw}$	**Step 3:** Make this problem concrete by replacing all the variables with numbers. Pick manageable numbers: $d = 20$ $w = 5$ $p = 10$ With those numbers, Camilla spent $20 a week on groceries for 5 weeks, for a total of $100. 10% of that, or $10, was on fresh veggies. This means that $100 − $10 = **$90** was on other groceries. $90 is the target number. See what number results from plugging the same values into choice (A): $dw\left(1 - \dfrac{p}{100}\right) = (20 \times 5)\left(1 - \dfrac{10}{100}\right) = 100 \times (1 - \cdot 1)$ $= 100 \times (\cdot 9) = 90.$ That matches! However, because you chose numbers for the variables, more than one answer might match the target number. Keep testing the other answer choices. (B) $\dfrac{dwp}{100} = \dfrac{20 \times 5 \times 10}{100} = \dfrac{1{,}000}{100} = 10.$ Incorrect. (C) $100p(1 - dw) = 100 \times 10(1 - 20 \times 5) = 10.$ This will be negative, which is incorrect. (D) $\dfrac{100p}{dw} = \dfrac{100 \times 10}{20 \times 5} = 10.$ Incorrect. Only one answer choice, **(A)**, matches the target number, so it is correct.
	Step 4: Briefly look back over the math you did when checking choice (A). If you plugged in the numbers correctly, you're done.

Try this one on your own. Use the Picking Numbers strategy.

For all r, s, t, and u, what does $r(t + u) - s(t + u)$ equal?

    (A) $(r + s)(t + u)$
    (B) $(r - s)(t - u)$
    (C) $(r + s)(t - u)$
    (D) $(r - s)(t + u)$

Explanation

Step 1: You are given an algebraic expression and asked to find an equivalent expression.

Step 2: The correct answer simplifies the expression $r(t + u) - s(t + u)$.

Step 3: Since you are given no values for any of the four variables, you can Pick Numbers for each of them. Some good numbers to pick here are $r = 5$, $s = 4$, $t = 3$, and $u = 2$. You can, however, use any permissible and manageable numbers you wish.

Replacing the variables in the expressions with the numbers picked, you get:

$5(3 + 2) - 4(3 + 2) = 25 - 20 = 5$.

Then replace the variables in each answer choice to see which choice gives the target number of 5:

(A)	$(r + s)(t + u)$	$(5 + 4)(3 + 2) = (9)(5) = 45$	Incorrect
(B)	$(r - s)(t - u)$	$(5 - 4)(3 - 2) = (1)(1) = 1$	Incorrect
(C)	$(r + s)(t - u)$	$(5 + 4)(3 - 2) = (9)(1) = 9$	Incorrect
(D)	$(r - s)(t + u)$	$(5 - 4)(3 + 2) = (1)(5) = 5$	Correct!

Step 4: In this example, only choice (D) works. If more than one choice had worked, you would need to pick another set of numbers and try only those answer choices again.

Not only does Picking Numbers make some problems easier to understand, but also, when you solve a problem by Picking Numbers, you can be sure you got the right answer because you've already proven the answer works with real numbers.

Strategic Guessing Using Logic

Sometimes, you can determine the characteristics of a correct answer without doing a lot of calculations. Study the example below.

Question	Analysis
After eating 25 percent of the pretzels, Sonya had 42 left. How many pretzels did Sonya have originally?	**Step 1:** Original # of pretzels $-$ 25% of pretzels $= 42$.
	Step 2: The correct answer represents the original number of pretzels, before Sonya ate any.
(A) 50 (B) 54 (C) 56 (D) 58	**Step 3:** Because 25% is the same as one-quarter, the correct answer must be divisible by 4 with no remainder. If the number of pretzels Sonia started with was not divisible by 4, and she then ate $\frac{1}{4}$ of the pretzels, she'd be left with fractions of pretzels left over. Of the answer choices, only **(C)** 56, is evenly divisible by 4, so it has to be the correct answer.
	Step 4: One-quarter of 56 is 14, and $56 - 14 = 42$, the number of pretzels Sonya had left.

Now, try this one on your own. Try to avoid doing extensive calculations; rather, see if you can eliminate some answer choices based on logic.

Mark can paint a room in 3 hours, and Kevin can paint an identical room in 4 hours. How many hours would it take Mark and Kevin to paint the room if they work together at their respective rates?

(A) $\dfrac{3}{2}$

(B) $\dfrac{12}{7}$

(C) $\dfrac{10}{3}$

(D) 4

Explanation

Step 1: You are told the rates at which two people can paint a room separately.

Step 2: The correct answer represents how long it would take the two people to paint the room together, each working at the same rate at which he works alone.

Step 3: If Mark, the faster painter, works completely on his own, he will complete the task in 3 hours. With help, he will take even less time to complete the job, so you can eliminate answer choices (C) and (D), which are greater than 3. Since Kevin is slower than Mark, working together will take longer than half of 3 hours. Since (A) is half of 3, you can eliminate it. That leaves only answer choice **(B)** which must be correct.

Step 4: Check to make sure that the question asked for how long it took to paint just one room. It did, so (B) is correct.

Combination of Approaches

There is no rule that says you have to use just one approach to get the correct answer. Study the example below.

Question	Analysis
Youssef can either walk from his home to his workplace or ride his bicycle. He walks at a pace of 1 block per minute, but he can travel 1 block in 20 seconds on his bicycle. If it takes Youssef 10 minutes longer to walk to work than to ride his bike, how many blocks away from work does he live?	**Step 1:** The question involves two different units of time. In order to be able to compare the rates, first convert Youssef's biking rate into minutes. Since a minute is 60 seconds, he bikes to work at a rate of $\frac{20}{60}$, or $\frac{1}{3}$, minute per block. He walks to work at 1 minute per block. Time to walk − time to bike = 10 minutes.
	Step 2: The correct answer represents the number of blocks Youssef lives from his workplace.

Question	Analysis
(A) 5 (B) 10 (C) 15 (D) 20	**Step 3:** This problem could be solved with algebra, but using some logic mixed with Backsolving can get the correct answer more quickly. If Youssef walks 1 block per minute and it takes him 10 minutes longer to walk than to ride his bike, the correct answer must be greater than 10 blocks. Otherwise his bike time would be zero or less. That leaves only two choices, 15 or 20, so pick one and see if it works. If Youssef lived 15 blocks from work, walking to work would take him 15 minutes. Riding his bike at the rate of 20 seconds per block, he can travel 3 blocks every minute, so he could ride to work in 15 ÷ 3 = 5 minutes. Then 15 minutes − 5 minutes = 10 minutes longer to walk, so 15 is the correct answer. (Had you chosen to start with 20 instead, you could quickly have determined that 20 is incorrect, leaving 15 as the only possible correct answer.)
	Step 4: You tested the correct answer based on the information given in the question, and it worked. **(C)** is correct.

Now, try this one on your own. A combination of strategies may be helpful on this problem.

Shoshanna bought a new cell phone, cell phone case, and wall charger. The cell phone cost $149.99, the case cost $19.99, and the wall charger cost $29.99. If tax on each of these items was 9.5%, which of the following is closest to the total amount Shoshanna spent?

(A) $180
(B) $200
(C) $205
(D) $220

Explanation

Step 1: You are told the prices of three items that Shoshanna purchased, plus a sales tax rate.

Step 2: You are asked to find the answer that is closest to the total amount Shoshanna paid for her purchases.

Step 3: Because you are asked for the *closest* amount, you do not have to use an exact calculation to find the correct answer. Estimation will work well. Round the prices for each item before tax to the nearest dollar: Shoshanna spent $150 + $20 + $30 = $200 before tax. You can eliminate answer choices (A) and (B) because they are too small. Now round the tax rate to 10%. Because 10% of $200 is $20, Shoshanna spent about $200 + $20 = $220 in total. Answer choice **(D)** is correct.

Step 4: Check that you did the arithmetic correctly and that the answer makes sense. All the other answer choices are too low to be close to what she spent.

Sometimes, you'll find that you have to make a guess, but don't guess at random. Narrow down the answer choices to increase your odds of guessing the correct one. First, eliminate answer choices you know are wrong. Next, avoid answer choices that don't make logical sense. Finally, choose one of the remaining answer choices.

MATH STRATEGIES FOR THE ASVAB PRACTICE QUESTIONS

On the ASVAB, either the question itself or the answer choices will signal which strategy will be most helpful. Look at the partial questions or answer choices below (note that complete problems are not shown). Then determine which strategy (Picking Numbers, Backsolving, Strategic Guessing Using Logic, or a combination of approaches) is likely to be useful.

1. An airplane uses 79% of a tank of fuel to fly 1,496 miles. If a full tank holds 996 gallons of fuel, how many gallons would the plane use to fly 3,016 miles?

    Which strategy is likely to be useful for this question, and why?

    _____

    _____

2. (A) 80

    (B) 100

    (C) 120

    (D) 150

    Which strategy is likely to be useful for this question, and why?

    _____

    _____

3. (A) $\dfrac{p(b + d)}{c}$

    (B) $pb + dc$

    (C) $\dfrac{d + p}{c + b}$

    (D) $\dfrac{c + b}{d + p}$

    Which strategy is likely to be useful for this question, and why?

    _____

    _____

4. (A) $\dfrac{1}{625}$

    (B) $\dfrac{26}{125}$

    (C) $\dfrac{64}{125}$

    (D) $\dfrac{523}{625}$

    Which strategy is likely to be useful for this question, and why?

    _____

    _____

5. If $|4x + 6| = 18$, what is one possible value for x?

    Which strategy is likely to be useful for this question, and why?

    _____

    _____

6. Jim spent 30% of his paycheck on rent, and he spent 40% of the remainder on car repairs. What percent of his paycheck was left after his rent and car repairs?

    Which strategy is likely to be useful for this question, and why?

    _____

    _____

Answers and Explanations

1. **Combination of Approaches** This problem includes some unwieldy numbers, but rounding them for estimation should get you an approximate answer. Find 80% of 1,000 gallons to determine how many gallons are used for the first trip (80% × 1,000 = 800 gallons). Then, round 1,496 to 1,500 and round 3,016 to 3,000. Notice that the question really asks, "How many gallons of fuel would the airplane use to fly about twice as far as the first trip?" Just multiply 800 × 2 = 1,600 gallons and find the answer choice closest to 1,600. In other words, combining a little calculation with some estimation works well here.

2. **Backsolving** Even without a question stem, you can see that all the answer choices are numbers. That makes this an excellent candidate for Backsolving. Start by trying (B) or (C).

3. **Picking Numbers** There are variables in the answer choices. Picking Numbers will make the problem more concrete, and plugging the numbers you picked into the answer choices will allow you to find your target number.

4. **Strategic Guessing Using Logic** Although these fractions might look intimidating at first, closer examination will show that they are quite spread out. (A) is very tiny, (B) is about $\frac{1}{5}$, (C) is about $\frac{1}{2}$, and (D) is close to $\frac{5}{6}$. Depending on the question asked, you can probably get a rough idea of which answer choice is the right answer without doing a lot of complex calculating.

5. **Backsolving** Quickly plug answer choices into the equation to eliminate choices that are too large or too small.

6. **Picking Numbers** A problem with percents and no amount given for Jim's paycheck makes this a perfect opportunity for Picking Numbers. Use $100 for the amount of Jim's paycheck and then apply the percentages in the problem. He spends 30% of $100, or $30, on rent. This leaves him $70, of which he spends 40% on his car, or 40% × $70 = $28. Subtract $30 for rent and $28 for the car repairs from his $100 paycheck, and he has $42 left. Since $100 represents the full paycheck, the dollar amount left is the same as the percent left, 42%.

Review and Reflect

How did you do? If you weren't sure which strategy to apply to some of the partial questions in the practice set, you might want to reread this chapter. Also, return to it from time to time throughout your ASVAB math practice to refresh your memory of the various strategies available to you.

The rest of the math section of this book will deal with math content review. Even if you feel comfortable with a particular subject, make sure to do the practice sets. There's no harm in practicing extra problems. Throughout the math section, you will be given many opportunities to "do the math." However, every time you begin a question, first check if you can use a strategy to minimize your time and effort toward getting the correct answer. This will allow you to move through the section more efficiently.

ARITHMETIC REASONING

KNOW WHAT TO EXPECT

For the Arithmetic Reasoning (AR) section of the paper and pencil ASVAB you will have 36 minutes to complete 30 arithmetic word problems. For the CAT-ASVAB, you will have 39 minutes to complete 16 problems. This chapter will review the concepts you need to understand in order to succeed on the Arithmetic Reasoning test. As you work through this chapter, don't forget that many problems are best solved by using the strategies you read about in chapter 5.

The principles covered in this chapter will also serve you well as the building blocks for Mathematics Knowledge (MK), which will be the focus of chapter 7. Both the AR and MK subtests are particularly important because they are part of the AFQT score. Additionally, high AR and MK scores are required to be eligible to enter many of the specialized occupations in the military.

This chapter will take you through a review of arithmetic concepts including:

- key arithmetic definitions
- number properties
- absolute value
- primes, factors, multiples, and remainders
- divisibility rules
- fractions, decimals, and scientific notation
- exponents and radicals
- factorials

The chapter will then review applied arithmetic concepts, such as:

- order of operations and calculation rules
- ratios, proportions, and rates
- combined work
- percentages
- averages, means, medians, and modes
- sequences and probability

The chapter will also discuss Arithmetic word problems including:

- translation
- word problems with formulas

The chapter concludes with a practice set.

ARITHMETIC REVIEW

LEARNING OBJECTIVES

In this section you will learn to:

- use the same definitions of key concepts as the ASVAB uses
- apply the rules that govern number properties
- identify and utilize factors and prime factorization
- perform arithmetic operations with decimals, fractions, exponents, radicals, and factorials
- convert numbers to and from the scientific notation format

Arithmetic Definitions

It is important that you use certain critical arithmetic terms in exactly the same manner as the ASVAB. Familiarize yourself with these key terms and concepts.

Concept	Definition	Examples
Integers	All whole numbers, including zero, and their negative counterparts.	$-900, -3, 0, 1, 54$
Fractions	A fraction is a number that is written in the form $\frac{A}{B}$, where A is the numerator and B is the denominator.	$-\frac{5}{6}, -\frac{3}{17}, \frac{1}{2}, \frac{899}{901}$
	An improper fraction has a numerator with a greater absolute value than that of the denominator.	$-\frac{65}{64}, \frac{9}{8}, \frac{57}{10}$
	A mixed number consists of a whole number and a fraction	$-1\frac{1}{64}, 1\frac{1}{8}, 5\frac{7}{10}$
	An improper fraction can be converted to a mixed number and vice versa.	$2\frac{3}{5} = \frac{13}{5}$

Concept	Definition	Examples
Positive/Negative	Numbers greater than 0 are positive numbers; numbers less than 0 are negative numbers. 0 is neither positive nor negative.	Positive: $\frac{7}{8}$, 1, 5.6, 900 Negative: -64, -40, -1.11, $-\frac{6}{13}$
Even/Odd	An even number is an integer that is a multiple of 2. An odd number is an integer that is not a multiple of 2. Fractions and mixed numbers are neither even nor odd.	Even numbers: -8, -2, 0, 12, 188 Odd numbers: -17, -1, 3, 9, 457
Factor	A factor is a positive integer that divides evenly into a given number.	The complete list of factors of 12: 1, 2, 3, 4, 6, 12
Prime number	An integer greater than 1 that has no factors other than 1 and itself. 2 is the only even prime number.	2, 3, 5, 7, 11, 59, 83
Consecutive numbers	Numbers that follow one after another, in order, without skipping any. In a series of consecutive numbers, the differences between any consecutive numbers are equal.	Consecutive integers: 3, 4, 5, 6 Consecutive even integers: 2, 4, 6, 8, 10 Consecutive multiples of -9: -9, -18, -27, -36
Multiple	A multiple of a number is the product of that number and an integer.	Some multiples of 12: 0, 12, 24, 60

Number Properties

Certain number properties follow rules that will never vary. Often, you can use these rules as an effective way to help you solve problems on the ASVAB.

There are only a few things to remember about **positive** and **negative** numbers.

Adding a negative number is the same as subtracting a positive number with the same absolute value.

$6 + (-4)$ is equal to $6 - 4$ which equals 2.

$4 + (-6)$ is equal to $4 - 6$ which equals -2.

Subtracting a negative number is the same as adding a positive number with the same absolute value.

$6 - (-4)$ is equal to $6 + 4$ which equals 10.

$-6 - (-4)$ is equal to $-6 + 4$ which equals -2.

Multiplying and dividing positive and negative numbers is the same as all other multiplication and division, with one catch: you need to figure out whether the solution is positive or negative. To do this, count the number of negative numbers. If you had an odd number of negatives, the answer will be negative. If you started with an even number of negative numbers, the answer will be positive.

$$(-6) \times (-4) = 24 \qquad \text{(2 negatives} \rightarrow \text{positive product)}$$

$$(-1) \times (-6) \times (-4) = -24 \qquad \text{(3 negatives} \rightarrow \text{negative product)}$$

Similarly,

$$-24 \div 6 = -4 \qquad \text{(1 negative} \rightarrow \text{negative quotient)}$$

$$-24 \div (-4) = 6 \qquad \text{(2 negatives} \rightarrow \text{positive quotient)}$$

The rules for working with integers are very brief. If you add, subtract, or multiply two integers, the result will always be an integer. However, if you divide two integers, the result *may or may not be* an integer.

$8 \div 4 = 2$ which is an integer, but $8 \div 3 = \frac{8}{3} = 2\frac{2}{3}$ which is *not* an integer.

Working with odd and even numbers can be described with a few rules as well. When you add or subtract two odd numbers or two even numbers, the result will always be an even number.

$$6 + 4 = 10 \qquad \text{(even + even = even)}$$

$$7 - 3 = 4 \qquad \text{(odd - odd = even)}$$

When you add or subtract an even with an odd, the result will be odd.

$$2 + 7 = 9 \qquad \text{(even + odd = odd)}$$

$$5 - 4 = 1 \qquad \text{(odd - even = odd)}$$

When multiplying two numbers, the rule for determining whether the result is even or odd is that any integer times an even integer will result in an even number. The only way the product of two integers will be an odd number is if you multiply two odd numbers.

$$6 \times 4 = 24 \qquad \text{(even} \times \text{even = even)}$$

$$3 \times 4 = 12 \qquad \text{(odd} \times \text{even = even)}$$

$$3 \times 5 = 15 \qquad \text{(odd} \times \text{odd = odd)}$$

There are no rules predicting whether the outcome of division will be even or odd, because division does not always result in an integer. Sometimes dividing produces a fraction, and fractions are neither odd nor even.

Study how a well-prepared test-taker would apply these rules to an AR question.

Question	Analysis
If n is an integer, what is $2(n) + 1$?	**Step 1:** The question tells you that n is an integer.
	Step 2: The question asks for the value of a formula with a variable, n.
(A) an even integer (B) an odd integer (C) an even non-integer (D) possibly either even or odd	**Step 3:** Even though you don't know whether n is odd or even, it is an integer. When any integer is multiplied by an even number the result is also an even number so the term $2(n)$ must be even. If the odd number 1 is added to an even number, then the result is an odd number. Answer choice **(B)** is correct.
	Step 4: Check that you used number properties correctly throughout the problem. Note that (C) is impossible no matter what the result of the equation because only integers can be odd or even.

Absolute Value

When you see a number or expression bracketed by two vertical lines like this $|-3|$, you are seeing the symbol for **absolute value**. The absolute value of what is between the vertical lines is the *positive magnitude* of the number regardless of whether it is positive or negative.

If $|x| = 5$, then $x = ?$

Clearly x can equal 5, but x could also equal -5 since absolute value is the positive magnitude of what is between the vertical lines. Therefore $x = +5$ or -5.

If $|x - 5| = 5$, then $x = ?$

The definition of absolute value says that the expression between the lines can be either 5 or -5. Therefore, in order to find the possible values of x you must write two equations:

$x - 5 = 5$ and $x - 5 = -5$

If $x - 5 = 5$, then $x = 10$, but if $x - 5 = -5$, then $x = 0$. This makes the two possible values of x: 10 and 0.

When you encounter an **absolute value** problem on the ASVAB you must solve for **both** the positive and negative values of whatever is between the vertical lines. Test your understanding of the absolute value concept on the following problem:

Question	Analysis
If $|x - 2| + 3 = 7$ which of the following is a possible value of x?	**Step 1:** The question gives you a formula with variable x.
	Step 2: The question asks for one possible value of x.

Question	Analysis
(A) 6 (B) −6 (C) 2 (D) 4	**Step 3:** First, subtract 3 from both sides. $\|x - 2\| + 3 = 7$ becomes $\|x - 2\| = 4$. Thus, $x - 2$ must equal either $+4$ or -4. If $x - 2 = 4$, then $x = 6$ If $x - 2 = -4$, then $x = -2$. Since -2 is not among the answer choices, **(A) 6** is the only correct choice.
	Step 4: Check your math and check to make sure you solved for the proper variable. In this case, the only variable was x but other problems might contain more than one variable and require you to choose correctly.

Factors, Multiples, and Prime Numbers

In order to determine the **factors** of a number, find the pairs of positive integers which can be multiplied together to produce the number that is being factored. Start with 1 and the number itself which are **always** factors of any integer. Then examine 2, 3, 4 and so on as shown in this example of finding the factors of 36:

1×36

2×18

3×12

4×9

6×6

Examining the two columns shows that the factors of 36 are 1, 2, 3, 4, 6, 9, 12, 18, and 36. When creating the list of factors, as soon as you reach a factor on the left which is equal to or greater than a factor already listed on the right, you can stop, since you're about to start repeating factor pairs. In this table, you need go no higher than 6 because any number greater than 6 that is a factor of 36 is already in the right column.

Multiples are, in a way, the opposite of factors. For instance, in the example above, 1, 2, 3, 4, 6, 9, 12, and 18 are factors of 36. Conversely, 36 is a multiple of 1, 2, 3, 4, 6, 9, 12, and 18.

If you become confused between the terms factor and multiple, you can remember that *multiples* are larger because you can produce them by *multiplying*. There are a finite number of factors of any number, but there are an infinite number of multiples.

Prime numbers, by their very definition, cannot be multiples of any integers other than 1 and the prime number itself. However, prime numbers can be factors of other numbers.

$3 \times 13 = 39$ (3 and 13 are prime numbers, but 39 is not because it is a multiple of 3 and a multiple of 13.)

A number's **prime factors** are factors that are prime. The **prime factorization** of a number is the number expressed using multiplication containing only primes, even if some of those primes repeat.

To determine the prime factorization of a number, keep dividing by prime numbers until you can no longer divide because you are left with only prime numbers.

For example, to find the prime factorization of 168:
Since 168 is an even number, the prime number 2 is a factor of 168.

$168 = 84 \times 2$, so **2** is a prime factor of 168.

84 is still an even number equal to 42×2, so **2** is a prime factor for a second time.

42 is still an even number equal to 21×2, so **2** is a prime factor for the third time.

21 is the product of **3** and **7**.

Since these are both prime numbers the process of finding the prime factors is complete.

An efficient way to determine the prime factors of any number is to use a "tree" as shown below.

Based on the above operations and tree, the prime factorization of 168 is $2 \times 2 \times 2 \times 3 \times 7$. All the prime factors, including repeated numbers, must be listed because the original number is the product of all of these numbers.

Prime factorization can be a very useful tool to help answer some questions on the ASVAB. For instance, if you need to find the **greatest common factor (GCF)** of two integers, break down both integers into their prime factorizations and multiply all prime factors they have in common, as shown in the example below:

Question	Analysis
Find the greatest common factor of 40 and 140.	**Step 1:** You are given two numbers, 40 and 140.
	Step 2: The question asks for the greatest common factor of the two numbers.
	Step 3: The prime factors of 40 are 2, 2, 2, and 5. The prime factors of 140 are 2, 2, 5, and 7. Both numbers share two 2s and a 5 as prime factors, so the GCF is $2 \times 2 \times 5 = 20$.
	Step 4: Double-checking the result, $40 = 20 \times 2$ and $140 = 20 \times 7$.

This can be helpful when you need to reduce a fraction because you can find the GCF and then divide the top and bottom of the fraction by that number.

If you need to find a **common multiple** of two integers, you can just multiply them. However, in other cases you may need to find the **least common multiple (LCM)**. You can use prime factors to efficiently identify LCMs. Take a look at this example to see how that works.

Question	Analysis
Find the least common multiple of 20 and 16.	**Step 1:** You are given two numbers, 20 and 16.
	Step 2: The question asks for the least common multiple of the two numbers.
	Step 3: First, identify the prime factors of each number: $16 = 2 \times 2 \times 2 \times 2$ $20 = 2 \times 2 \times 5$ Any integer that is a multiple of 16 must have four prime factors of 2. Any integer that is a multiple of 20 must have two prime factors of 2 and one prime factor of 5. Therefore, any number that is a multiple of both 16 and 20 must have four prime factors of 2 and one prime factor of 5. The **least common multiple** equals $2 \times 2 \times 2 \times 2 \times 5 = 80$.
	Step 4: Double-check that all of the prime factors for each number were included in the least common multiple.

Practice the technique on this question:

Marcus needs to order some parts for his machine shop. His supplier sometimes fills orders with boxes that contain 15 of these parts and sometimes with boxes of 18, depending upon what he happens to have in stock. The supplier will only ship complete boxes, and will ship only one size of box in a given order. What is the minimum quantity of parts that Marcus can order and be assured that he will receive exactly that many parts regardless of which boxes his supplier uses?

(A) 15
(B) 18
(C) 90
(D) 270

Explanation

Step 1: The question gives you a situation in which Marcus is ordering parts. He wants to receive the exact number of parts he needs. You are told that the company ships parts in boxes of 15 and 18.

Step 2: You are asked to find the smallest number of parts that can be filled with full boxes of 15 parts or full boxes of 18 parts. Thus, you need to find the least common multiple of 15 and 18.

Step 3: The prime factors of 18 are $2 \times 3 \times 3$ and the prime factors 15 are 5×3 Therefore, the least common multiple must have two factors of 3, one factor of 2, and one factor of 5. This is $2 \times 3 \times 3 \times 5 = 90$. Answer choice **(C)** is correct.

Notice that (D), 270, is a common multiple of 15 and 18, but it is not the least common multiple.

Step 4: Confirm that 15 and 18 both divide evenly into 90.

Divisibility

Whether evaluating integers to determine if they are prime numbers, finding factors, or finding prime factors, you can check whether a number is a factor of another number more quickly and effectively if you use the following tips to check for divisibility.

Divisibility Rules

Number	Divisibility Rule
2	All even numbers are divisible by 2.
3	Add up the individual digits of the number. If the total is divisible by 3, then the number itself is divisible by 3; for example, 243 is divisible by 3 because the sum of its digits is $2 + 4 + 3 = 9$, but 367 is not because the sum of its digits is $3 + 6 + 7 = 16$ and 16 is not a multiple of 3.
4	Take the last two digits and divide them by 2. If the result is even, the number is divisible by 4. If the result is odd, then the number is not divisible by 4.
5	All numbers ending in 5 or 0 are divisible by 5.
6	All *even* numbers that meet the test for divisibility by 3 are divisible by 6.
8	Divide the number by 2 twice; if the result is even, then the number is divisible by 8.
9	Add up the digits of the number; if the total is divisible by 9, then the number is divisible by 9.

Practice divisibility rules on this question:

Question	Analysis
What are all the prime numbers between 60 and 70 inclusive?	**Step 1:** You are given a range of numbers.
	Step 2: The question asks for number of primes within a given range.

Question	Analysis
(A) 61, 67 (B) 61, 63, 67 (C) 61, 63, 65, 67 (D) 62, 64, 66, 68	**Step 3:** Use divisibility tests to eliminate numbers that are not prime. Eliminate 60, 62, 64, 66, 68, and 70 because they are all divisible by 2. Eliminate 65 because it is divisible by 5. Checking for divisibility by 3 eliminates 63 (sum of the digits is 9) and 69 (sum of the digits is 15). The only remaining numbers are 61 and 67. Answer choice **(A)**.
	Step 4: All of the other answer choices contain numbers that were eliminated by using divisibility rules.

Fractions and Decimals

Generally, it's a good idea to **reduce fractions** when solving math questions. To do this, use your knowledge of factors to cancel all factors that the numerator and denominator have in common.

$$\frac{28}{36} = \frac{\cancel{4} \times 7}{\cancel{4} \times 9} = \frac{7}{9}$$

When you perform operations on fractions, always remember to perform the same operation on both the numerator and the denominator. For instance, in the example above, both the numerator and denominator were divided by 4.

To **add or subtract fractions,** you must convert all the fractions so that they have a common denominator. Think of the process of converting to a common denominator as finding the least common multiple of all the denominators. Don't forget to multiply the individual numerators by the same number that was used to convert to a common denominator. Once you have converted the individual fractions so that they have common denominators you merely add or subtract the numerators to obtain your result.

$$\frac{1}{4} + \frac{1}{3} = \frac{1 \times 3}{4 \times 3} + \frac{1 \times 4}{3 \times 4} = \frac{3}{12} + \frac{4}{12} = \frac{7}{12}$$

$$\frac{1}{4} - \frac{1}{3} = \frac{3}{12} - \frac{4}{12} = \frac{3-4}{12} = -\frac{1}{12}$$

To **multiply fractions,** multiply the numerators together and then multiply the denominators together.

$$\frac{1}{4} \times \frac{1}{3} = \frac{1 \times 1}{4 \times 3} = \frac{1}{12}$$

To **divide** one fraction by another you invert (flip) the second fraction and multiply. In other words, multiply the first fraction by the reciprocal of the second fraction.

$$\frac{1}{4} \div \frac{1}{3} = \frac{1}{4} \times \frac{3}{1} = \frac{1 \times 3}{4 \times 1} = \frac{3}{4}$$

Occasionally a question may require that you **compare fractions** to determine which has the greater value. The most straightforward way to do this is to convert the fractions being compared to a common denominator and compare their numerators.

Question	Analysis
Compare $\frac{2}{3}$ and $\frac{5}{8}$.	The lowest common denominator is $3 \times 8 = 24$.
	Multiple the first fraction by $\frac{8}{8}$ and the second fraction by $\frac{3}{3}$.
	$\frac{2}{3} = \frac{2 \times 8}{3 \times 8} = \frac{16}{24}$ $\frac{5}{8} = \frac{5 \times 3}{8 \times 3} = \frac{15}{24}$
	16 is greater than 15, so $\frac{2}{3}$ is greater than $\frac{5}{8}$.

Practice the operations for fractions to answer the following question:

$$\frac{\frac{1}{4} + \frac{3}{5}}{\frac{2}{3}} = ?$$

(A) $\frac{2}{15}$

(B) $\frac{17}{30}$

(C) $1\frac{11}{40}$

(D) $2\frac{1}{40}$

Explanation

Step 1: You are given an equation.

Step 2: You need to solve the equation using fraction rules.

Step 3: Dividing by a fraction is the same as multiplying by its reciprocal, so you can get rid of the cumbersome double-stack fraction by rewriting: $\left(\frac{1}{4} + \frac{3}{5}\right) \times \left(\frac{3}{2}\right) = ?$

You need to add the two fractions in the left parentheses before multiplying. In order to add the two fractions, convert them to have a common denominator of 20. $\left(\frac{5}{20} + \frac{12}{20}\right) \times \left(\frac{3}{2}\right) = ?$

Now add the first two fractions. $\left(\frac{17}{20}\right) \times \left(\frac{3}{2}\right) = ?$

Multiplying the numerators and denominators results in an answer of $\frac{51}{40}$. But this answer is not in the answer choices as written. For this problem, you must convert an improper fraction to a mixed number. $\frac{40}{40} + \frac{11}{40} = 1\frac{11}{40}$

Step 4: Check to be sure you used the proper order of operations and check your math.

To **convert a fraction to a decimal,** divide the denominator into the numerator.

To convert $\frac{8}{25}$ to a decimal, divide 25 into 8.

$$\frac{8}{25} = 0.32$$

To **convert a decimal to a fraction,** first set the decimal as the numerator of a fraction with a denominator of 1. Then, move the decimal over as many places as it takes until it is immediately to the right of the units digit. Count the number of places that you moved the decimal. Then add that many 0s to the 1 in the denominator.

$$0.3 = \frac{0.3}{1} = \frac{3.0}{10} = \frac{3}{10}$$

Try this one on your own:

0.0025 = ?
- (A) $\dfrac{1}{4000}$
- (B) $\dfrac{1}{400}$
- (C) $\dfrac{1}{40}$
- (D) $\dfrac{1}{25}$

Explanation

Step 1: The question gives you a number in decimal format.

Step 2: The answer choices show you that you will need to convert to a fraction.

Step 3: First, convert to a fraction with a denominator of 1, $\frac{.0025}{1}$. In order to get rid of the decimal in the numerator, you will need to move it four places to the right and simultaneously add four 0's to the denominator. This results in the fraction $\frac{25}{10000}$.

To reduce this fraction to its simplest terms, divide both the numerator and denominator by 5 you will have $\frac{5}{2000}$. Since both the numerator and denominator are still divisible by 5, repeat the process to get $\frac{1}{400}$. Select answer choice **(B)**.

Step 4: Since many of the answer choices vary by the number of zeros in the denominator, double-check that you added the appropriate number of zeros to the denominator before you started simplifying.

Decimal Division

One common type of arithmetic problem on the ASVAB involves dividing numbers that contain decimals. Keeping track of the decimal places can complicate a division problem, so get rid of the decimal places before you divide. You can accomplish this by multiplying by 10 as many times as necessary. When you multiply a number with decimals by 10, simply move the decimal point one place to the right. When multiplying numbers without decimals by ten, add a zero at the end.

As an example,

$$1.22 \times 10 = 12.2$$
$$12.2 \times 10 = 122$$
$$122 \times 10 = 1220$$

When presented with a decimal division question you should write the division problem as a fraction:

$$7.2 \div 0.004 = \frac{7.2}{0.004}$$

Then you will move the decimal points in the denominator and the numerator the same number of places to the right, adding zeros as necessary, until you have completely gotten rid of any decimal points.

$$\frac{7.2}{0.004} = \frac{7200}{4} = 1800$$

The example below shows how to tackle an ASVAB question about decimal operations.

Question	Analysis
David is drawing a blueprint for a model home. Due to the scale he used, the width of the bathroom floor is 0.18 inches on his paper. He needs to draw 30 tiles across that width. What is the width of each individual tile in his sketch in inches?	**Step 1:** You are told that there are 0.18 inches to draw 30 tiles.
	Step 2: The question asks for the measurement of width in inches of each tile as drawn on the paper.
(A) 0.006 (B) 0.06 (C) 0.6 (D) 6	**Step 3:** You need to divide 30 into 0.18. Write the problem as a fraction: $\frac{0.18}{30}$. Eliminate the decimal point by moving it two places to the right and adding 2 zeros to the denominator: $\frac{18}{3000}$. A quick glance at the answer choices reveals that they are in decimal format rather than fractions, so you need to convert to a decimal. Divide both the numerator and denominator by the common factor of 3 so that the numbers are easier to work with: $\frac{6}{1000}$. You have to get rid of the 3 zeros in the denominator so that the denominator becomes 1. Move the decimal point in the numerator 3 places to the left, inserting zeros after the decimal as needed, resulting in $\frac{.006}{1} = 0.006$. Answer choice **(A)** is correct.
	Step 4: Check your math carefully. Double-check that you inserted the correct number of zeros.

Scientific notation is a method of writing very large and very small numbers that also involves moving decimal points. The first part of a number in scientific notation will be equal to or greater than 1 and less than 10. The second part of the number will be a power of 10. For powers of 10, the exponent is the number of zeroes the number has when written out. For example, $10^4 = 10,000$. For numbers written in scientific notation, where the first number always has exactly one digit to the left of the decimal point, the long version of the number can be written out by moving the decimal to the right by the same number of places as the value in the exponent of the power of 10.

$1.23 \times 10^4 = 12,300$

Scientific notation also uses negative exponents to indicate the proper placement of the decimal point in a very small number. When dividing the power of 10 is negative, move the decimal point to the left. Once the decimal point has been moved as far left as possible, start adding zeros to the right of the decimal.

$4.321 \times 10^{-2} = 0.04321$

Use this problem to practice your understanding of scientific notation:

Question	Analysis
Sam writes for a scientific journal. In her research, she finds a number written as 6,483,000. How can she express that in scientific notation?	**Step 1:** You are given a number.
	Step 2: You are asked to rewrite the number in scientific notation.
(A) 6.483×10^3 (B) 6.483×10^5 (C) 6.483×10^6 (D) 6.483×10^7	**Step 3:** Move the decimal point 6 places to the left so 6,483,000 becomes 6.483000. If you move the decimal 6 places to the left, you must write 10^6. Thus, written in scientific notation the number becomes **(C)** 6.483×10^6
	Step 4: Check to be sure you moved the decimal over the correct number of places.

Exponents and Radicals

Exponents are the small raised numbers written above and to the right of a variable or number (the **base**). They indicate the number of times that the variable or number is multiplied by itself. The rules for performing different operations on terms involving a base and an exponent will require you to pay close attention to the details. There are two important things to remember about exponents. First, any number or variable with an exponent of 1 is equal to the base itself. Second, any number or variable with an exponent of 0 equals 1.

$x^1 = x \qquad 5^1 = 5 \qquad x^0 = 1 \qquad 5^0 = 1$

To **add** or **subtract** terms involving variables and exponents, **both** the variables and the exponents must be the same.

$2x^2 + x^2 = 3x^2$

$3x^4 - 2x^4 = x^4$

$x^2 + x^3$ cannot be combined.

$a^2 + b^2$ cannot be combined.

To **multiply terms** with the *same base*, merely add the exponents. This can be done because exponents represent how many times the base is multiplied by itself.

$2^3 \times 2^2 = (2 \times 2 \times 2) \times (2 \times 2) = 2^{3+2} = 2^5$

Similarly, to **divide terms** with the *same base*, subtract the exponent that is in the denominator from the exponent in the numerator.

$\dfrac{3^4}{3^2} = 3^{4-2} = 3^2$

To **raise a term involving an exponent to another exponent,** multiply the exponents.

$(x^2)^4 = x^{2 \times 4} = x^8$

A **coefficient** is a number multiplied by a variable in a term. For instance, in the term $2x^2$, the coefficient is 2. To multiply terms consisting of coefficients and exponents that have the same variable in the base, multiply the coefficients and add the exponents.

$6x^7 \times 2x^5 = (6 \times 2)\,(x^{7+5}) = 12x^{12}$

To **divide** terms consisting of coefficients and exponents that have the same variable in the base, divide the coefficients and subtract the exponents.

$6x^7 \div 2x^5 = (6 \div 2)\,(x^{7-5}) = 3x^2$

You might see a **negative exponent** in a problem on the ASVAB. Don't panic! Negative exponents are just the reciprocal of their positive counterparts.

$2^{-3} = \dfrac{1}{2^3} = \dfrac{1}{8}$

Practice working with exponents on this problem:

Question	Analysis
$\left(\dfrac{(n^5) \times (n^3)}{n^4}\right)^2 + \dfrac{2}{n^{-8}} = ?$	**Step 1:** You are given an equation.
	Step 2: You need to simplify the equation.
(A) n^8 (B) $2n^8$ (C) $3n^8$ (D) n^{20}	**Step 3:** Since there are variables in the question stem and the answer, you can use Picking Numbers here.
	Pick a number for n and solve for the equation in the question stem. The result is your target number.
	Then plug your initial number for n into all of the answer choices and the one that yields the target number would be correct.
	To solve with straightforward math, apply the exponent rules one at a time.

Question	Analysis
	Using the rule for multiplying two terms with the same base (in this case, n) the numerator of the first expression can be simplified to read: $\left(\frac{n^8}{n^4}\right)^2 + \frac{2}{n^{-8}}$. Next, apply the rule for division of terms with the same base so that the expression on the left becomes: $\left(n^4\right)^2 + \frac{2}{n^{-8}}$. Use the rule for raising an exponent to an exponent and you have $n^8 + \frac{2}{n^{-8}}$. A number to a negative exponent is the same as the reciprocal of that number to a positive exponent. Thus, the expression on the right can be rewritten to: $n^8 + 2n^8$. Since both terms have the same base and the same exponent you can add them together to get the correct answer, $3n^8$ **(C)**.
	Step 4: Briefly confirm that you performed the steps correctly.

Try this problem both by Picking Numbers and by using straightforward math so that you get a sense of which method you will be more comfortable with for this type of problem on Test Day.

Perfect squares are integers that are the result of **squaring** (multiplying by itself) another integer. For instance, 25 is a perfect square because it is 5×5. You can save time and trouble on the ASVAB if you memorize the perfect squares up through $12 \times 12 = 144$.

Hone your skills with the following practice problem:

Question	Analysis
Which of the following numbers is NOT a perfect square?	**Step 1:** The question stem doesn't give much information, but you can infer that three of the answer choices ARE perfect squares.
	Step 2: You are looking for a number that is not equal to an integer times itself.
(A) 1 (B) 16 (C) 27 (D) 36	**Step 3:** $1 = 1 \times 1$, so it is a perfect square. $16 = 4 \times 4$, which is also a perfect square. $27 = 3 \times 3 \times 3$, which is not a perfect square because it is a number multiplied by itself three times rather than twice. Answer choice **(C)** is correct.
	Step 4: Check to see if the remaining answer choice is a perfect square. $36 = 6 \times 6$, so it is a perfect square.

A **square root** is a number that, when multiplied by itself, produces the given quantity. The **radical** sign $\sqrt{}$ is used to represent the positive square root of a number, so $\sqrt{25} = 5$, since $5 \times 5 = 25$. (Even though $(-5) \times (-5)$ is also 25, when you are asked for the square root, the answer will be a positive number.) To **add** or **subtract radicals**, make sure the numbers under the radical sign are the same. If they are, you can add or subtract the coefficients outside the radical signs.

$$2\sqrt{2} + 3\sqrt{2} = 5\sqrt{2}$$

$\sqrt{2} + \sqrt{3}$ cannot be combined.

To **simplify** radicals, factor out the perfect squares under the radical, calculate the square roots of the perfect squares, and put the results in front of the radical sign.

$$\sqrt{32} = \sqrt{16 \times 2} = 4\sqrt{2}$$

Note that when you have simplified to the point where the number under the radical does not contain any perfect squares, your result will be sufficient for the ASVAB.

To **multiply** or **divide** radicals, multiply (or divide) the coefficients outside and inside the radical separately.

$$\sqrt{x} \times \sqrt{y} = \sqrt{xy}$$

$$3\sqrt{2} \times 4\sqrt{5} = 12\sqrt{10}$$

$$\frac{\sqrt{x}}{\sqrt{y}} = \sqrt{\frac{x}{y}}$$

$$\frac{12\sqrt{10}}{3\sqrt{2}} = 4\sqrt{5}$$

To **take the square root of a fraction,** you can break the fraction into two separate roots and take the square root of the numerator and the denominator separately.

$$\sqrt{\frac{16}{25}} = \frac{\sqrt{16}}{\sqrt{25}} = \frac{4}{5}$$

Practice computations with radicals on this problem:

Question	Analysis
Simplify $\sqrt{\frac{(3 \times 27)}{(2 \times 32)}}$	**Step 1:** The question gives an expression in the form of a fraction.
	Step 2: You are asked to simplify the fraction as much as possible.
(A) $\frac{2}{3}$ (B) $\frac{8}{9}$ (C) $1\frac{1}{8}$ (D) $1\frac{1}{3}$	**Step 3:** First, check to see if there is anything you can divide out of the top and bottom to make the fraction easier to work with. In this case, there is not. Since the example contains a radical sign, check to see if any of the numbers (as written) are perfect squares. None of the numbers are perfect squares, so complete the multiplication on the top and on the bottom. $\sqrt{\frac{81}{64}}$ Before performing the division, check to see if any of the numbers are perfect squares. $81 = 9 \times 9$ $64 = 8 \times 8$ Since both numbers are perfect squares, take the square root of the top and bottom independently. $\sqrt{\frac{81}{64}} = \frac{\sqrt{81}}{\sqrt{64}} = \frac{9}{8}$

Question	Analysis
	Scanning the answer choices, $\frac{9}{8}$ is not present as written. However, since the numerator is greater than the denominator, this is an improper fraction that can be converted to a mixed number. $$\frac{9}{8} = \frac{8}{8} + \frac{1}{8} = 1 + \frac{1}{8} = 1\frac{1}{8}$$ Answer choice (C) is correct.
	Step 4: Check your math and check to be sure you solved for the correct question.

Factorials

On the ASVAB math sections, you may see an occasional **factorial** question. You'll know you're dealing with a factorial when you see an integer followed by an exclamation point (!). A factorial is the product of the integer before the factorial sign and all the positive integers below it. For instance, when you see the following:

$7! = ?$

The question is actually asking you what "7 factorial" is, and the answer to that question is:

$7! = 7 \times 6 \times 5 \times 4 \times 3 \times 2 \times 1 = 5,040$

If you're ever given a fraction with factorials, there's often a lot of canceling that you can do before you try to multiply out the factorials.

Look at the following example.

Question	Analysis
Solve for $\frac{6!}{4!}$	**Step 1:** You are given a fraction containing factorials.
	Step 2: You need to perform the calculations.
	Step 3: Write out the factorials $$\frac{6!}{4!} = \frac{6 \times 5 \times 4 \times 3 \times 2 \times 1}{4 \times 3 \times 2 \times 1}$$ Cancel out the numbers that appear on the top and bottom. $$\frac{6 \times 5 \times \cancel{4 \times 3 \times 2 \times 1}}{\cancel{4 \times 3 \times 2 \times 1}} = \frac{6 \times 5}{1} = 6 \times 5 = 30$$ The correct answer is 30.
	Step 4: Double-check your calculations and your elimination.

If you see a problem with factorials in a fraction on Test Day, simplify before attempting to solve.

APPLIED ARITHMETIC REVIEW

LEARNING OBJECTIVES

In this section you will learn to:

- calculate values for complex arithmetic expressions using the proper rules and order of operations
- utilize ratios, percentages, and proportions to solve problems involving comparisons
- solve rate and work problems
- apply the formulas for statistical terms to different situations
- compute numerical probabilities

While the arithmetic concepts you've looked at so far could appear on the Arithmetic Reasoning section of the ASVAB, it's worth noting that, due to the very nature of word problems, most of the questions in this section will involve some form of "applied arithmetic." On the ASVAB you will use arithmetic principles to solve practical problems. Applied arithmetic includes subjects like ratios, percent problems, rates, averages, and probability.

The Order of Operations

You must perform arithmetic operations in the proper order to get the correct answer to complex arithmetic problems. The acronym **PEMDAS** can help you remember that order.

$\underline{P}$ = Parentheses

$\underline{E}$ = Exponents

$\underline{M}\ \underline{D}$ = Multiplication and Division (from left to right)

$\underline{A}\ \underline{S}$ = Addition and Subtraction (from left to right)

For example:

$3^3 - 8(4 - 2) + 60 \div 4$

$= 3^3 - 8(2) + 60 \div 4$ \qquad (P)

$= 27 - 8(2) + 60 \div 4$ \qquad (E)

$= 27 - 16 + 15$ \qquad (MD)

$= 26$ \qquad (AS)

One way to remember PEMDAS is to think of the phrase "**P**lease **E**xcuse **M**y **D**ear **A**unt **S**ally."

Try out PEMDAS on this problem:

Question	Analysis
Solve $3 \times 5 + (6 \times 2) - 3^3$	**Step 1:** You are given an equation.
	Step 2: You are asked to solve that equation.
	Step 3: Use PEMDAS $3 \times 5 + (6 \times 2) - 3^3$ (P) $3 \times 5 + 12 - 3^3$ (E) $3 \times 5 + 12 - 27$ (MD) $15 + 12 - 27$ (AS) 0
	Step 4: Double-check that you performed the operations in the correct order and that your math calculations were performed correctly.

Distributive and Commutative Properties

In addition to being certain to follow the correct order of operations when solving complex arithmetic problems, you may find that you need to utilize the distributive and commutative properties of mathematics to facilitate your computations. It's not important that you remember the specific terms "distributive" and "commutative," but it is important that you know how to *use* these properties.

The **distributive property** says that the result of multiplying one number by the sum or difference of two numbers can be obtained by multiplying each number individually and then totaling the results.

$$5 \times (20 + 2) = 5 \times 20 + 5 \times 2 = 100 + 10 = 110$$

$$5 \times (20 - 2) = 5 \times 20 - 5 \times 2 = 100 - 10 = 90$$

Similarly, a fraction with multiple terms in the numerator and **only one term in the denominator** can be subdivided.

$$\frac{x^3 + 4x^2}{x^2} = \frac{x^3}{x^2} + \frac{4x^2}{x^2} = x + 4$$

Do not attempt to use this property if the denominator has more than one term.

$\dfrac{x^2}{x^3 + 4x^2}$ cannot be split up

Not only is the distributive property useful in solving problems on the ASVAB, it can also help you quickly and accurately multiply in the absence of a calculator.

Question	Analysis
Multiply 6×38 without a calculator.	You can convert that to $6 \times (30 + 8)$
	Then, $6 \times 30 + 6 \times 8 = 180 + 48 = 228$

Try this sample problem:

$$17 \times 8 + \frac{48x - 8}{4} = ?$$

(A) $10x + 34$
(B) $10x + 136$
(C) $12x + 134$
(D) $12x + 136$

Explanation

Step 1: You are given an equation.

Step 2: You are asked to solve that equation.

Step 3: You can simplify multiplying 17×8 by treating that as $(10 + 7) \times 8 = 80 + 56 = 136$.

The fraction is equivalent to $\frac{48x}{4} - \frac{8}{4} = 12x - 2$.

Now the simplified expression is $136 + 12x - 2 = 12x + 134$. Answer choice **(C)**.

Step 4: Check your math and make sure you used the correct order of operations.

The **commutative property** says, in a nutshell, that order does not matter when **adding or multiplying** numbers. For example

$3 \times 4 = 4 \times 3$

$3 + 4 = 4 + 3$

This property does not change PEMDAS; it merely gives you some flexibility when you get to the multiply or add part of the order of operations. The commutative property does **not** apply to subtraction or division.

$4 - 3$ does not equal $3 - 4$

$\frac{4}{3}$ does not equal $\frac{3}{4}$

This flexibility when dealing with addition and, in particular, multiplication can be a handy addition to your arithmetic toolbox as shown in the example below:

Question	Analysis
Solve for $2 \times 19 \times 5$ without a calculator.	**Step 1:** You are given an equation.
	Step 2: You need to solve this equation without a calculator.
	Step 3: You could answer this by first multiplying $2 \times 19 = 38$ then multiplying $38 \times 5 = 190$. However, before jumping straight into the math, use strategic logic. Note that $2 \times 5 = 10$. This is helpful because 10 is an easy number to multiply. If you rearrange the equation $2 \times 5 \times 19$ before solving, the math becomes more manageable. $2 \times 5 \times 19 = 10 \times 19 = 190$
	Step 4: Double-check your math.

Ratios, Proportions, and Rates

Ratios represent the relationship of one quantity to another. Ratios can be presented in three different ways. They can be verbal, such as "the ratio of cats to dogs is 3 to 4." Another way of describing a ratio is to use a colon, as in "3 : 4." In order to use ratios in calculations, however, you will use the fractional form, $\frac{3}{4}$. Ratios do not necessarily represent the actual number of two different things. In this example, you don't know if there are actually 3 dogs and 4 cats, or 6 cats and 8 dogs, or 600 cats and 800 dogs.

Ratios are either **part to part** or **part to whole** relationships, depending upon what quantities are being compared:

A class contains 12 male students and 21 female students.

The **part to part** ratio of male students to female students is

$$\frac{12}{21} = \frac{4}{7}$$

The **part to whole** ratio of male students to all the students in the class is

$$\frac{12}{12 + 21} = \frac{12}{33} = \frac{4}{11}$$

Always simplify ratios to their lowest terms, as was done in the above example.

Here's how an expert test taker would apply these basic rules for ratios to an AR question:

Question	Analysis
Alicia is an avid video game player. She has a total of 21 video games. Her ratio of sports games to action games to mystery games is 4:2:1. How many action games does she have?	**Step 1:** The question gives the total number of video games and the ratio of different types of games in the collection.
	Step 2: The question asks for the number of action games in the collection.
(A) 2 (B) 6 (C) 8 (D) 12	**Step 3:** The part to whole ratio of action games to total video games can be represented as $\frac{2}{4+2+1} = \frac{2}{7}$. But Alicia has a total of 21 games, not 7. In order to determine how many action games Alicia has, multiply the part to whole ratio by the total number of games: $21 \times \left(\frac{2}{7}\right) = 6$. Answer choice **(B)**.
	Step 4: You can double-check that $\frac{6}{21}$ does, in fact, equal the part to whole ratio of $\frac{2}{7}$ by dividing the numerator and denominator by their Lowest Common Multiple, which is 3.

A **proportion** is an equation of two ratios that shows the comparative relationship between parts, things, or elements with respect to size, amount, or degree.

When working with proportions, you can use a helpful technique called **cross-multiplying** to help solve the equation. To cross-multiply an equation that consists of two fractions you multiply the numerator of the first fraction by the denominator of the second and vice versa. Here is an example of cross-multiplying.

$$\frac{2x}{5} = \frac{3}{4}$$

$$2x(4) = 3(5)$$

Here's an example of a proportion question in which you can use cross-multiplying:

Question	Analysis
A picture that is 4 inches wide and 6 inches long is enlarged so that it is $7\frac{1}{2}$ inches long. What is the width of the enlarged picture?	**Step 1:** The question gives you the dimensions of a picture and says that the picture was then enlarged.
	Step 2: The question asks for the new width of the picture.
	Step 3: Set the given information up as a proportion. The ratio of width to length in the original picture is 4:6 and the ratio of width to length of the enlargement will be the same. The length of the enlargement will be $7\frac{1}{2}$ inches, but the width is some unknown value (w). Since the width/length ratio of the two pictures must be the same, you can set the proportions equal to each other: $$\frac{4}{6}=\frac{w}{7.5}$$ $$4\times 7.5=6w$$ $$30=6w$$ $$5=w$$ So, the enlarged picture is 5 inches wide.
	Step 4: Double-check your math. Also, be sure you put the correct measurements in the correct places in the ratio.

Practice working with ratios on this sample problem:

> Micah can ride his bicycle 42 miles in 3 hours. Assuming that he travels at the same speed, how long would it take Micah to ride 70 miles?
>
> (A) 5.0 hours
> (B) 5.5 hours
> (C) 7.0 hours
> (D) 7.5 hours

Explanation

Step 1: The problem states that Micah rides at the same speed in both instances. You are told how long it takes to ride 42 miles.

Step 2: You are asked how long it will take him to ride 70 miles.

Step 3: Micah's distance to time relationship can be set up using a proportion.

$$\frac{3}{42} = \frac{t}{70}$$

Using the cross-multiplication technique, $3 \times 70 = 42t$.

Before multiplying large numbers together and then dividing by 42, check to see if you can reduce the equation. Since 42 is a multiple of 3, you can divide both sides of the equation by 3.

$70 = 14t$

$5 = t$

Answer choice **(A)** is correct.

Step 4: You can double-check your math by inserting your answer into the proportion and cross-multiplying.

$$\frac{3}{42} = \frac{5}{70}$$

$3(70) = 5(42)$

$210 = 210$

A **rate** is simply a ratio that compares two different but related quantities, such as distance divided by time (speed), or amount divided by time, or cost per unit.

In other words: $\text{Rate} = \dfrac{\text{Distance}}{\text{Time}}$ or $\text{Rate} = \dfrac{\text{Amount}}{\text{Time}}$ or $\text{Rate} = \dfrac{\text{Cost}}{\text{Units}}$

Another way to look at rates is to think of them as changes in the numerator per changes in the denominator. For instance, if your rate of pay is \$15/hour, you know that if you work one more hour you will earn an additional \$15.

The key to solving rate problems is to set them up as proportions. Convert the units if necessary and solve for the unknown value.

Take a look at the following rate question:

Question	Analysis
A waitress serves 3 diners every 5 minutes. At this rate, how many customers will she serve in one hour?	**Step 1:** The question gives the rate at which a waitress can serve people. The rate is given in minutes.
	Step 2: The question asks for the number of customers that will be served in one hour.

Question	Analysis
	Step 3:
	Set the rate up as a proportion.
	$$\frac{3 \text{ diners}}{5 \text{ minutes}} = \frac{x \text{ diners}}{1 \text{ hour}}$$
	Convert units
	$$\frac{3 \text{ diners}}{5 \text{ minutes}} = \frac{x \text{ diners}}{60 \text{ minutes}}$$
	Cross-multiply and solve.
	$5x = 180$
	$x = 36$
	Step 4: Double-check your math and that the units were converted correctly.

Pay close attention to units in ratios and proportions. Had hours not been converted to minutes in the example, the answer would have been wrong.

Try this sample problem to practice rates and units:

> The volume of a certain substance is directly proportional to its weight. If 48 cubic inches of the substance weigh 112 ounces, what is the volume, in cubic inches, of 63 ounces of the substance?
>
> (A) 27
> (B) 36
> (C) 42
> (D) 64

Explanation

Step 1: The problem gives the ratio of volume to weight of a certain substance.

Step 2: The problem asks for the volume of a different amount of the substance.

Step 3: Start by setting up the proportion $\frac{48}{112} = \frac{v}{63}$.

You might notice that cross-multiplying this proportion looks difficult without a calculator and wonder if there is a more efficient way to answer the question. There is, by using logic.

In the given ratio, 48 is less than half of 112, so the correct answer will be less than half of 63. Looking at the answer choices, only 27 is less than half of 63.

Answer choice **(A)** is correct.

Step 4: You can double-check your work by reducing the proportions to their lowest form and checking that they equal each other.

$$\frac{48}{112} \div \frac{2}{2} = \frac{24}{56} \qquad\qquad \frac{27}{63} \div \frac{3}{3} = \frac{9}{21}$$

$$\frac{24}{56} \div \frac{2}{2} = \frac{12}{28} \qquad\qquad \frac{9}{21} \div \frac{3}{3} = \frac{3}{7}$$

$$\frac{12}{28} \div \frac{4}{4} = \frac{3}{7}$$

Both proportions reduce to $\frac{3}{7}$, which means that the two proportions are equal and the answer choice is confirmed.

Combined Work

You may see a problem on the ASVAB that asks you to determine how long it takes the combined effort of two people or machines to complete a task, or something similar such as how long it takes for two pipes to fill a tank. These are just a different form of rate problem.

For instance, if it takes Joe 3 hours to paint a room, then his rate of painting is $\frac{1\ room}{3\ hours}$. The tasks to be completed that are on the ASVAB are additive; the **combined work** of the people (or machines or pipes) can be added together to obtain a combined rate. This approach also works for more than two entities working on the same task.

Question	Analysis
Jose can paint a room in 3 hours. Jill can paint the same room in 2 hours. How long will it take them to paint the room working together?	**Step 1:** The question gives the amount of time it takes two different people to paint a room.
	Step 2: The question asks for the length of time it will take them to paint the room together.
	Step 3: Express the individual times as rates. $\frac{1}{3} + \frac{1}{2} = ?$ Convert to a common denominator and add the rates. $\frac{2}{6} + \frac{3}{6} = \frac{5}{6}\ \frac{rooms}{hours}$ Invert the fraction. $\frac{5\ rooms}{6\ hours} = \frac{6\ hours}{5\ rooms}$ If it takes 6 hours to paint 5 rooms, it would take $\frac{6}{5}$ hours to paint 1 room. $\frac{6}{5} = \frac{5}{5} + \frac{1}{5} = 1\frac{1}{5} = 1.2\ \text{hours}$

Question	Analysis
	Step 4: Double-check your math. Also double-check that you are solving for the correct number of rooms, in this case, 1 room.

Try this problem (which does not have answer choices) on your own:

> There are three pipes that can be used to fill a tank. One of them can fill the tank in 2 hours, another can fill it in 3 hours, and the third can fill the tank in 6 hours. If all three pipes are used to fill the tank simultaneously, how long will it take?

Explanation

Step 1: The three times needed for each pipe to fill the tank individually are given.

Step 2: You are asked to calculate the rate at which they would be able to fill the tank together.

Step 3: The rates can be converted to $\frac{tanks}{hour}$, specifically $\frac{1}{2}$, $\frac{1}{3}$, and $\frac{1}{6}$. Convert their rates to a common denominator and add: $\frac{3}{6} + \frac{2}{6} + \frac{1}{6} = \frac{6}{6} = 1\frac{tank}{hour}$. Therefore to fill the one tank, the three pipes working together can accomplish the task in **1 hour.**

Percent Problems

Percents are ratios of an amount to 100, so the techniques used to work with ratios and proportions are valuable tools when you work with percents.

Question	Analysis
A bag contains 8 marbles and 6 of them are green. What percent of the marbles in the bag are green?	**Step 1:** The question gives the total amount of marbles and the amount of green marbles.
	Step 2: The question asks for the percent of total marbles that are green.
	Step 3: To solve this you can set up a proportion equating the numbers of marbles to the unknown percentage: $\frac{6}{8} = \frac{g}{100}$ $600 = 8g$ $75 = g$ So 75% of the marbles are green.
	Step 4: Double-check to confirm your math is correct.

To convert the English into math on a percent problem, use the following conversion table.

English	Math Translation
% or percent	÷ 100 (or use decimal or fractional equivalent)
of	× (times)
what	x (or n, or any variable you like)
is	= (equals)

Using these translations, you can see, for instance, that 40% of 25 = 0.40 × 25 = 10.

Some ASVAB questions require you to **increase or decrease a number by a given percent.** To calculate such increases or decrease, take that percent of the original number and add it to or subtract it from the original number.

To increase 25 by 60%, first find 60% of 25.

25 × 0.6 = 15

Then add the result to the original number.

25 + 15 = 40

To decrease 25 by the same percent, subtract the 15.

25 − 15 = 10

Other ASVAB questions, rather than giving you the percent increase or decrease, will ask you to calculate the percentage change between an original value and a new value. In order to calculate that change, always use this formula:

$$\text{Percent Change} = 100\% \times \frac{\text{New Value} - \text{Original Value}}{\text{Original Value}}$$

If the percent change is an **increase**, the result will be **positive**. If the change is a **decrease**, the result will be **negative.** ASVAB percentage change problems ask for the change relative to the original value; using the new value in the denominator will produce an incorrect answer.

Question	Analysis
A camera that originally cost $125 was sold on sale for $100. The sale price was what percent less than the original price?	**Step 1:** The question gives the original price and the sale price of a camera.
	Step 2: The question asks for the percentage decrease between the sale price and the original price.
	Step 3: Percent Change = $100\% \times \frac{100 - 125}{125} =$ $100\% \times \frac{-25}{125} = 100\% \times \frac{-1}{5} = -20\%$ Since the result is negative, you know that there was a price decrease. The answer is −20%.
	Step 4: Briefly confirm that the answer makes sense. 20% of 125 is 25, so your answer is correct.

Practice using the formula on this sample problem:

> Ryan weighed 40 pounds when he finished kindergarten
> and 44 pounds when he started first grade. What was the
> percentage change in his weight between kindergarten and
> first grade?
>
> (A) 10% decrease
> (B) 4% increase
> (C) 10% increase
> (D) 40% increase

Explanation

Step 1: The problem gives Ryan's weight at various ages.

Step 2: The question asks for his percent change in weight.

Step 3:

$$\text{Percent Change} = 100\% \times \frac{44 - 40}{40} = 100\% \times \frac{4}{40} = 100\% \times \frac{1}{10} = 10\%$$

Since the result is positive, the answer is a 10% increase, choice **(C)**.

Step 4: Check your calculations and check that you solved for the percent asked for.

Now practice this skill on another problem.

> Rachel made a certain investment in the stock market but
> the value of her investment declined by 20%. However,
> the value of that investment then increased by 50%. What
> was the overall percentage change in the value of the
> investment from the original purchase price?
>
> (A) 30% decrease
> (B) No change
> (C) 20% increase
> (D) 30% increase

Explanation

Step 1: The question gives information about the decrease and increase in the value of a stock.

Step 2: The question asks for the overall change.

Step 3: Notice that the question does not mention any specific prices. That makes this problem an excellent candidate for the Picking Numbers technique. Since the problem deals with percentages, start with an original value equal to 100.

If the investment lost 20% of its value, that would have been a loss of 20, so the value after the decrease would have been 80. Fortunately for Rachel, the value then increased 50%. Since the 50% increase was based upon a value of 80, that would be a gain of 40. This results in a final value of 80 + 40 = 120, which is a 20% increase from the original assigned value of 100, answer choice **(C)**.

Step 4: Confirm that your math is correct and that you are solving for the correct piece of information.

Statistical Terms

Averages, like ratios, proportions, and rates, use fractions to find the answer to a problem. Here is the average formula:

$$\text{Average} = \frac{\text{Sum of the terms}}{\text{Number of terms}}$$

What is the average of 3, 4, and 8?

$$\text{Average} = \frac{\text{Sum of the terms}}{\text{Number of terms}} = \frac{3+4+8}{3} = \frac{15}{3} = 5$$

Sometimes the ASVAB may not present the information in such simple terms. The formula for averages, like other three-part formulas, can be rearranged as needed.

Question	Analysis
Six people went fishing and caught an average of 7 fish each. How many total fish did they catch?	**Step 1:** You are given the average amount of fish caught by 7 people.
	Step 2: You are asked for the total number of fish.
	Step 3: Plug the values that you are given into the formula and solve for the value needed. $$7 = \frac{\text{Total}}{6}$$ Multiply both sides of the equation by 6. $$6 \times 7 = \text{Total} = 42 \text{ fish}$$
	Step 4: Check to be sure you used the numbers given in the problem and that you performed the calculations correctly.

Here is a practice problem for you:

Lola was pleased to learn that her final grade in her history course, which was based upon her average for 4 tests, was 90. She knew that she had scored 93, 80, and 90 on her first three tests, but she could not remember her score on the last test. What was Lola's score on the fourth test?

(A) 87
(B) 90
(C) 93
(D) 97

Explanation

Step 1: You are given the score on 3 tests and the average score of 4 tests.

Step 2: The question asks for the score of the fourth test that would give the average listed.

Step 3: Use the average formula to write the equation $90 = \frac{93+80+90+t}{4}$ with t representing the unknown score. The denominator is 4 because the final grade of 90 was based on 4 tests even though Lola only knew the results of 3 tests.

Solving the average equation for t, add all the numbers in the numerator. $90 = \frac{263+t}{4}$

Multiply both sides of the equation by 4 to get $360 = 263 + t$. Then t is $360 - 263$ which equals 97, choice **(D)**.

Step 4: Check your math. Make sure you plugged the correct values into the average formula in the beginning.

The ASVAB will not require you to make complex statistical calculations, but there are a few basic statistical terms with which you should be familiar. **Mean** is the same as average and is calculated the same way. The **Range** is how "wide" the group of numbers is and can be calculated by subtracting the smallest number from the largest. The **Mode** is the number that appears most frequently. Finally, **Median** is the middle value of a group of numbers.

Practice by identifying these terms using the number set: 1, 2, 7, −3, 0, 5, 2

In order to apply the statistical terms to a group of numbers, the very first thing you must do is arrange the numbers in ascending order: −3, 0, 1, 2, 2, 5, 7.

The **mean** of these numbers is $\frac{-3+0+1+2+2+5+7}{7} = 2$.

The **mode** of the group is **2** since it is the only number that appears twice.

The **range** is $7 - (-3) = $ **10**.

The **median** is **2**, since three numbers are smaller than that and three are larger.

Should you encounter a situation whereby there are two numbers in the middle, the average of those two middle numbers is the median.

For instance, the median of −3, 0, 1, 2, 2, 5 is $\frac{1+2}{2} = $ **1.5**

Sequences

A **sequence** is merely a group of numbers placed in order, as in the example above. You are most likely to encounter a special type of sequence on the ASVAB called an **arithmetic sequence**. The property that creates an arithmetic sequence is that each number is equal to the number before it plus a constant number. The sequence 1, 3, 5, 7 is an arithmetic sequence because each number is 2 more than the previous number in the sequence. One property that makes arithmetic sequences special is that the mean equals the median.

Here's an example of the type of sequence problem that may be on the ASVAB:

Question	Analysis
What is the mean of a sequence of multiples of 3 that begins with −3 and ends with 15?	**Step 1:** The question gives you the rules of a sequence as well as the beginning and ending terms of that sequence.
	Step 2: The question asks for the mean.

Question	Analysis
	Step 3: Since the numbers are multiples of 3, the numbers will all be 3 apart. This is an arithmetic sequence. You can write down the sequence: $-3, 0, 3, 6, 9, 12, 15$. Because this is an arithmetic sequence, the median is equal to the mean, **6**.
	Step 4: Check that you defined the sequence properly and solved for the correct statistical term.

Probability

Probability is the numerical likelihood that a particular outcome will occur. To find the probability that something is going to happen, use this formula:

$$\text{Probability} = \frac{\text{Number of Outcomes of Interest}}{\text{Number of Possible Outcomes}}$$

Probability can be expressed as a fraction, a decimal, or a percent.

Question	Analysis
If there are 12 books on a shelf and 9 of them are mysteries, what is the probability of picking a mystery at random?	**Step 1:** The question gives the total number of books and the number of mystery books.
	Step 2: The question asks for the probability of picking a mystery book. In other words, the proportion of mystery books to total books.
	Step 3: Probability $= \frac{9}{12} = \frac{3}{4}$ This probability can also be expressed as 0.75 or 75%.
	Step 4: Check that you set up and simplified the fraction appropriately.

Probabilities are always between 0 and 1 (or between 0% and 100%). A probability of 0 means that there are no outcomes of interest and a probability of 1 means that all the possible outcomes result in the outcome of interest occurring.

To find the probability that both of **two events** will occur, find the probability that the first event occurs and **multiply** this by the probability that the second event occurs. The probability of two independent events both occurring will be less than the probability of either occurring by itself. When you see a probability question that deals with one event **and** another event both occurring you will **multiply** the probabilities.

Study the following example.

Question	Analysis
If there are 12 books on a shelf and 9 of them are mysteries, what is the probability of picking a mystery first AND a non-mystery book second if exactly two books are selected and neither of them is replaced on the shelf?	**Step 1:** You are given the same information about the number of mystery books compared to the number of books overall.
	Step 2: This time, the question asks for the probability that two different events will both occur.
	Step 3: The probability of picking a mystery book first: $\frac{9}{12} = \frac{3}{4}$ Probability of picking a non-mystery book second (If a mystery is picked first): $\frac{3}{11}$ (Originally there were 9 mysteries and 3 non-mysteries. After the mystery is selected first, there are 8 mysteries and 3 non-mysteries, i.e., 11 books remaining.) Probability of picking a mystery book first and then a non-mystery book second: $\frac{3}{4} \times \frac{3}{11} = \frac{9}{44}$
	Step 4: Check to be sure you set up the second proportion to incorporate the missing book that was already picked. Double-check your math and be sure you solved for the probability that was asked for.

A question might ask you to determine the probability of one **or** another event occurring. In this case, you **add** the individual probabilities. The probability of one **or** another event occurring will be greater than the probability of either event occurring alone.

Question	Analysis
What is the probability of rolling a 1 OR a 2 on one roll of a fair six-sided die?	**Step 1:** The question gives you background information that you are dealing with a die that has 6 faces and isn't weighted.
	Step 2: The question asks for the probability of either of two scenarios happening.
	Step 3: Probability of rolling a 1 $= \frac{1}{6}$. Probability of rolling a 2 $= \frac{1}{6}$. Probability of rolling a 1 **or** a 2 $= \frac{1}{6} + \frac{1}{6} = \frac{2}{6} = \frac{1}{3}$
	Step 4: Briefly check your math before moving on to the next question.

Practice the principles of probability on the following problem:

If a fair coin is flipped 3 times, what is the probability
that none of the occurrences will result in a head?

(A) 0

(B) $\frac{1}{8}$

(C) $\frac{1}{6}$

(D) $\frac{1}{3}$

Explanation

Step 1: The question sets up a scenario of flipping coins.

Step 2: The question asks for the probability of landing on tails three times in a row.

Step 3: In order to flip a coin 3 times with no heads, the first flip must be a tail **and** the second flip must also be a tail **and** the third flip must be a tail, too.

Therefore, the equation to determine the probability of no heads on three flips is $\left(\frac{1}{2}\right)\times\left(\frac{1}{2}\right)\times\left(\frac{1}{2}\right)=\frac{1}{8}$.
Answer choice **(B)**.

Step 4: Double-check that you solved for the correct probability and you performed the calculations correctly.

ARITHMETIC WORD PROBLEMS

LEARNING OBJECTIVES

In this section you will learn to:

- convert word problems to equations
- use common predefined formulas to answer word problems

As you may have noticed, we already started sneaking word problems into the arithmetic review section you just completed. Word problems are simply math problems with another step added. Generally, all you have to do is translate the text into math and solve. In some questions, the translation will be embedded within a "story." Don't be put off by the details of the scenario—it's the numbers that matter. Focus on the math and translate.

Translation

Often, word problems seem tricky because it's hard to figure out precisely what they're asking. The following table lists some common words and phrases that turn up in word problems, along with their mathematical translations.

When you see:	Think:
sum, plus, more than, added to, combined, total	+
minus, less than, difference between, decreased by	−
is, was, equals, is equivalent to, is the same as, adds up to	=
times, product, multiplied by, of	×
divided by, over, quotient, per, out of, into	÷
what, how much, how many, a number	x, n, etc.

Word Problems with Formulas

Some of the more difficult word problems may involve translations with mathematical formulas. The most common ones that you should know are $Rate = \frac{Distance}{Time}$, $Average = \frac{Sum\ of\ the\ Terms}{Number\ of\ Terms}$, and $Probability = \frac{Number\ of\ Outcomes\ of\ Interest}{Number\ of\ Possible\ Outcomes}$, all of which were discussed earlier in this chapter.

Question	Analysis
If a truck travels at 50 miles per hour for $6\frac{1}{2}$ hours, how far will the truck travel?	**Step 1:** The question gives you the rate of the truck and how long that truck will be travelling.
	Step 2: The question asks how far the truck will go in that time.
	Step 3: To answer this question, you need to use the Time-Rate-Distance Formula: $Rate = \frac{Distance}{Time}$ multiplying both sides of the equation by time gives you: $Distance = Rate \times Time$ Now, plug in the numbers. $D = 50 \times 6.5$ $D = 325$ miles
	Step 4: Check that you performed the math correctly.

Try this rate problem:

> Elisa rode her motorcycle for an hour and traveled
> 60.0 miles. Unfortunately she then encountered heavy
> traffic, and it took her 2 hours to travel an additional
> 45.0 miles. What was her overall speed for the entire trip?

(A) 35.0 miles/hour
(B) 45.0 miles/hour
(C) 52.5 miles/hour
(D) 60.0 miles/hour

Explanation

Step 1: The question gives you the time and distance of one portion of a trip and then the time and distance of another portion of the same trip.

Step 2: You are asked to come up with the average speed for both portions of the trip together.

Step 3: The total distance traveled was $60 + 45 = 105$ miles.

The total time was $1 + 2 = 3$ hours.

$Rate = \dfrac{Distance}{Time} = \dfrac{105}{3} = 35$ miles per hour. Answer choice **(A)** is correct.

Step 4: It is important to remember that you cannot simply take the average of the two speeds. This is because Elisa travels at each speed for a different length of time. Make sure you use the rate formula correctly.

ARITHMETIC REASONING PRACTICE QUESTIONS

1. If $|y - 3| = 3$, what is the greatest possible value of y?

   (A) 2
   (B) 4
   (C) 6
   (D) 8

2. Two teams are having a contest in which the prize is a box of candy that the members of the winning team will divide evenly. If team A wins, each player will get exactly 3 pieces of candy, and if team B wins, each player will get exactly 5 pieces of candy. Which of the following could be the number of pieces of candy in the box?

   (A) 325
   (B) 353
   (C) 425
   (D) 555

3. What is the least common multiple of 7, 9, and 21?

   (A) 21
   (B) 63
   (C) 147
   (D) 189

4. What is the value of $\dfrac{\frac{1}{4} + \frac{1}{3} + \frac{1}{8}}{\frac{1}{2}}$?

   (A) $\dfrac{17}{48}$

   (B) $\dfrac{17}{24}$

   (C) $1\dfrac{5}{12}$

   (D) $2\dfrac{1}{24}$

5. What is the value of $\sqrt{\dfrac{5 \times 35 \times 7 \times 16}{50 \times 8}} = ?$

   (A) 5
   (B) 7
   (C) 14
   (D) 35

6. A copier can make 150 copies per minute. At this rate, how many minutes would it take to make 4,500 copies?

   (A) 20
   (B) 25
   (C) 30
   (D) 35

7. The average (arithmetic mean) age of the members in a five-person choir is 34. If the ages of four of the members are 47, 31, 27, and 36, what is the fifth member's age?

   (A) 29
   (B) 32
   (C) 34
   (D) 37

8. In the past year XYZ Corporation reported sales of 1.17×10^6. The year before the company's sales were 9.00×10^5. What was the percentage change in sales?

   (A) 30% decrease
   (B) 27% decrease
   (C) 27% increase
   (D) 30% increase

9. What is the value of $30 - 5 \times 4 + (7 - 3)^2 \div 8$?

   (A) 4
   (B) 12
   (C) 36
   (D) 102

10. A group of five workers want to have a fair way of deciding who has to perform a difficult task so they place 4 green balls and 1 red ball into an opaque box from which each worker will draw a ball at random. The person who draws the red ball will have to perform the task. What is the probability that the last (5th) person will get the red ball?

   (A) 0.10
   (B) 0.15
   (C) 0.20
   (D) 0.25

Answers and Explanations

1. (C) 6 To simplify an absolute value problem by eliminating the absolute value function, write two equations, one of which sets whatever is inside the vertical lines to its positive value, and the other of which sets that equal to its negative value. So, either $y - 3 = 3$ or $y - 3 = -3$. Clearly, y has a greater value in the first equation. By adding 3 to both sides of the equation $y = 6$.

2. (D) 555 This problem tells you that the number of pieces of candy in the box can be divided evenly by 5 and 3. So the correct answer is the choice that has a 0 or 5 as its last digit, and the sum of whose digits is divisible by 3. Eliminate (B) because it doesn't end in either 0 or 5. Of the remaining choices, only 555 (D) is also divisible by 3, since $5 + 5 + 5 = 15$.

3. (B) 63 To find the least common multiple, you should identify the prime factors of each number. The prime factor of 7 is 7 since it is a prime number. The prime factors of 9 are 3×3. The prime factors of 21 are 7 and 3. Therefore the LCM must have two factors of 3 and one factor of 7; $3 \times 3 \times 7 = 63$. To check your work, you can confirm that 7, 9 and 21 all divide evenly into 63.

4. (C) $1\frac{5}{12}$ When given a complex expression such as the one in this problem, simplify it one step at a time. Dividing by a fraction is the same as multiplying by its reciprocal so

$$\frac{\frac{1}{4} + \frac{1}{3} + \frac{1}{8}}{\frac{1}{2}} = \left(\frac{1}{4} + \frac{1}{3} + \frac{1}{8}\right) \times 2$$

In order to add these fractions, you'll have to use a common denominator. Since 4, 3, and 8 are all factors of 24:

$$\left(\frac{1 \times 6}{4 \times 6} + \frac{1 \times 8}{3 \times 8} + \frac{1 \times 3}{8 \times 3}\right) \times 2 = \left(\frac{6 + 8 + 3}{24}\right) \times 2 = \frac{17}{12}.$$

Because this is an improper fraction and the answer choices are written as mixed numbers, convert it to $1\frac{5}{12}$.

5. (B) 7 While this problem may look formidable at first glance, it can be solved by reducing the fraction to simpler terms before attempting to identify the square root. When you see a complex calculation that makes you wonder how you are going to do the math without a calculator, that is often a hint to use prime factorization. If you restate the problem as

$$\sqrt{\frac{(5 \times 5 \times 7 \times 7 \times 2 \times 2 \times 2 \times 2)}{5 \times 5 \times 2 \times 2 \times 2 \times 2}}$$ you can see that many terms in

the numerator and denominator of the radical cancel out

$$\sqrt{\frac{(\cancel{5 \times 5} \times 7 \times 7 \times \cancel{2 \times 2 \times 2 \times 2})}{\cancel{5 \times 5} \times \cancel{2 \times 2 \times 2 \times 2}}}$$ so that you are left with

$\sqrt{7 \times 7} = 7$.

6. (C) 30 Set up a proportion: $\dfrac{150\,\text{copies}}{1\,\text{minute}} = \dfrac{4{,}500}{x\,\text{minutes}}$
Now cross-multiply and solve: $150x = 4{,}500$. So

$$x = \frac{4{,}500}{150} = 30.$$

7. (A) 29 Average $= \dfrac{\text{Sum of the terms}}{\text{Number of terms}}$, so here the average is

$$\frac{47 + 31 + 27 + 36 + n}{5} = 34. \text{ Thus } 34 = \frac{141 + n}{5}, \text{ multiply}$$

both sides by 5 to get $170 = 141 + n$.

Subtract 141 from both sides and $n = 29$.

8. (D) 30% increase This is a percent change problem so you will need to identify the original and new values that are being compared and use the formula for calculating percent change. $\dfrac{(1.17 \times 10^6) - (9.00 \times 10^5)}{9.00 \times 10^5}$. In order to subtract powers, they must have the same base and exponent, so you'll have to convert one of the terms $\dfrac{(11.7 \times 10^5) - (9.00 \times 10^5)}{9.00 \times 10^5} = \dfrac{2.7 \times 10^5}{9.00 \times 10^5}$

This can be simplified to $\dfrac{2.7}{9} = \dfrac{27}{90} = \dfrac{3}{10} = 30\%$.

9. **(B) 12** Follow PEMDAS to get the answer. Since there is a set of **P**arentheses, start there and change the expression to $30 - 5 \times 4 + 4^2 \div 8$. There is an **E**xponent, so calculate the value of the exponent term next: $30 - 5 \times 4 + 16 \div 8$. Now you can calculate the **M**ultiplication and **D**ivision parts of the expression from left to right to get $30 - 20 + 2$. Finish up with the **A**ddition and **S**ubtraction from left to right to get the answer, 12.

10. **(C) 0.20** This is a probability question with multiple events. In order for the last person to get stuck with the red ball, the first person must draw a green ball **and** so must the 2nd, 3rd, and 4th persons. The number of green balls will decrease with each successive pick, so the probability is

$$\frac{4}{5} \times \frac{3}{4} \times \frac{2}{3} \times \frac{1}{2} = \frac{4 \times 3 \times 2 \times 1}{5 \times 4 \times 3 \times 2} = \frac{1}{5} = 0.2$$

Review and Reflect

After completing this chapter, think about the areas that you fully understand. Are there any areas still giving you trouble? Pay close attention to the themes that help you on multiple types of questions, such as finding the least common multiple and determining factors. Also, be sure that you practice simplifying fractions and performing basic calculations without a calculator.

MATHEMATICS KNOWLEDGE

KNOW WHAT TO EXPECT

The Mathematics Knowledge subtest gives you 20 minutes to answer 16 questions, if you take the computer adaptive test. If you take the paper and pencil version, then you have 24 minutes to answer 25 questions. Thus, the pace on the Mathematics Knowledge section is quicker than on the Arithmetic Reasoning section, giving you about a minute per problem.

You may see applied arithmetic problems on the MK subtest. Review these topics in chapter 6: Arithmetic Reasoning. Additionally, expect to see algebra and geometry on the MK subtest.

Much of what you learned in the previous chapter about arithmetic applies to algebra as well. The main difference between arithmetic and algebra is that algebra involves variables as well as numbers. In this chapter, you will learn how to work with

- algebraic expressions
- monomials and binomials
- quadratic equations
- solving for variables
- inequalities

You will also learn in this chapter about geometry on the ASVAB. You will learn the rules that apply to lines and angles and two- and three-dimensional shapes, including

- lines and angles
- triangles
- quadrilaterals
- circles
- solid geometry
- coordinate geometry

ALGEBRA REVIEW

The difference between algebra and arithmetic is that algebra uses symbols called **variables**, such as *x* and *y*, to generalize arithmetic relationships.

Algebra problems on the ASVAB can appear in two forms: as straightforward math problems or as word problems. You will find that algebra problems on the Mathematics Knowledge section are often good candidates for a strategic approach, such as Picking Numbers or Backsolving. Nonetheless, if you are comfortable with algebra, using straightforward math may be faster than using a strategy on some problems. You want to have all these tools—Picking Numbers, Backsolving, Strategic Guessing Using Logic, a combination of approaches, and straightforward math—in your toolkit on Test Day.

Terms and Expressions

LEARNING OBJECTIVES

In this section, you will learn how to:

- recognize whether terms can be combined
- add, subtract, multiply, and divide terms
- multiply binomials and factor quadratic expressions

A **term** is a number, a variable, or one or more numbers multiplied by one or more variables. Here are some examples:

$$4 \qquad 3x \qquad 7ab^2 \qquad \frac{6z}{4}$$

An algebraic **expression** on the ASVAB test could look like this:

$$(11 + 3x) - (5 - 2y)$$

If an expression consists of one term, it is a **monomial**. If it consists of two terms, it is a **binomial**. If it consists of more than two terms, like the one above, then it is a **polynomial**.

You can only add or subtract "like terms." **Like terms** have the same variables and the same exponents. The following pairs of terms are like terms:

$$3a + 7a \qquad 10z^2 - 5z^2$$

To combine like terms, add or subtract the coefficients (the numbers that come before the variables) of terms that have the same variable raised to the same exponent as explained in chapter 6. Do not change the variables. Here are some examples:

$$6a + 5a = 11a$$
$$8b^2 - 2b^2 = 6b^2$$
$$3a + 2b - 8a = 3a - 8a + 2b = -5a + 2b \text{ or } 2b - 5a$$

Remember, you cannot combine unlike terms such as these:

$$6a + 5a^2$$
$$3a + 2b$$

Study this example:

Question	Analysis
Simplify: $(11 + 3x) - (5 - 2x)$	
$= 11 + 3x - 5 + 2x$	Distribute the minus sign across the parentheses.
$= 3x + 2x + 11 - 5$	Group like terms together.
$= 5x + 6$	Combine like terms.

Multiplying and dividing monomials is different from adding and subtracting them. In addition and subtraction, you can combine only like terms. With multiplication and division, however, you can multiply and divide terms that are different. When you multiply monomials, multiply the coefficients of each term, add the exponents of like variables, and multiply different variables together. Study this example:

Question	Analysis
Simplify: $(6a)(4b)$	
$= (6 \times 4)(a \times b)$ $= 24ab$	Multiply the coefficients by each other and the variables by each other.

Now try one on your own.

Simplify: $(6a)(4ab) + (3a^2)(8b) = ?$

Explanation

Step 1: The question presents an expression.

Step 2: You need to simplify the expression.

Step 3: Multiply the coefficients together, and multiply the variables together. Remember not to add or subtract unless you're dealing with like terms.

$(6a)(4ab) + (3a^2)(8b) =$
$(6 \times 4)(a \times a \times b) + (3 \times 8)(a^2 \times b) =$
$(6 \times 4)(a^{1+1} \times b) + (3 \times 8)(a^2 \times b) =$
$24a^2b + 24a^2b =$
$48a^2b$

The answer is **$48a^2b$**.

Step 4: Review your work to ensure you multiplied correctly.

To multiply binomials, use the FOIL method. FOIL stands for **F**irst, **O**uter, **I**nner, **L**ast and refers to the position of each term in the parentheses. Here's an example:

Question	Analysis
Simplify: $(y + 1)(y + 2)$	
First terms: $(y \times y)$ Outer terms: $(y \times 2)$ Inner terms: $(1 \times y)$ Last terms: (1×2) $= y^2 + 2y + y + 2$	Use FOIL to multiply each term in the binomials.
$= y^2 + 3y + 2$	Combine like terms.

The final expression above, $y^2 + 3y + 2$, is known as a **quadratic expression**. A quadratic expression contains variables raised to the exponent of 2, in other words, variables that are squared. An expression without an exponent is a linear expression.

You may occasionally be called upon to **factor** a quadratic expression or equation on the ASVAB. Do this with "reverse-FOIL." Take a look:

Question		Analysis
Factor: $x^2 - 4x - 21$		
$(x \quad)(x \quad)$		To begin, build parentheses with the **First** terms that multiply to x^2.
1	−21	What **Last** terms will multiply to produce **−21**?
3	−7	
7	−3	
21	−1	
3	−7	Which of these pairs will add to produce **−4**?
$(x + 3)(x - 7)$		Plug these into the parentheses.

Classic Quadratics

If you learn to recognize the following three common quadratics, you can multiply them and factor them without needing to FOIL or reverse-FOIL:

Classic Quadratic	Example
$(x + y)(x - y) = x^2 - y^2$	$(x + 3)(x - 3) = x^2 - 9$
$(x + y)^2 = x^2 + 2xy + y^2$	$(a + 4)^2 = a^2 + 8a + 16$
$(x - y)^2 = x^2 - 2xy + y^2$	$(y - 6)^2 = y^2 - 12y + 36$

If you see a perfect square, such as x^2 or 16, on each end of a quadratic, it is probably one of these classic quadratics.

Study this example.

Question	Analysis
Which of the following is equivalent to the expression $a^2 - b^2$?	**Step 1:** The question gives a quadratic expression.
	Step 2: You are asked to find the answer that is the same expression, expressed in a different form.
	Step 3: Use math knowledge to recognize that this is a classic quadratic.
	$a^2 - b^2 = (a + b)(a - b)$.
(A) $(a - b)^2$ (B) $(a + b)^2$ (C) $(a + b)(a - b)$ (D) $a^2 - 2ab + b^2$	The answer is (C). **Step 4:** Briefly check your calculations.

Equations with One Variable

LEARNING OBJECTIVE

In this section, you will learn how to:

· find the value of a variable in an equation

An equation is two expressions separated by an equal sign. The key to **solving equations** is to do the same thing to both sides of the equation until you have your variable isolated on one side of the equal sign and everything else on the other side.

Question	Analysis
Solve for a: $12a + 8 = 23 - 3a$	**Step 1:** The question presents an equation with one variable, a. **Step 2:** The task is to find the value of a. **Step 3:** (B) is a fraction, which makes Backsolving potentially awkward. Use straightforward math to isolate the variable. $12a + 8 = 23 - 3a$ $12a = 15 - 3a$ $15a = 15$ $\dfrac{15a}{15} = \dfrac{15}{15}$ $a = 1$
(A) 1 (B) $\dfrac{5}{3}$ (C) 2 (D) 11	**Step 4:** Plug 1 in for a in the equation: $(12)(1) + 8 = 23 - (3)(1)$ $12 + 8 = 23 - 3$ $20 = 20$ Answer choice (A), $a = 1$, works.

Try it on your own.

Solve for x: $2x + 7 = \dfrac{x}{4}$.

Explanation

Step 1: This is a linear equation with one variable.

Step 2: You need to find the value of that variable.

Step 3: Multiply each side by 4 to eliminate the fraction:

$4 \times (2x + 7) = \dfrac{x}{4} \times 4$

$8x + 28 = x$

Subtract x from both sides:
$7x + 28 = 0$

Subtract 28 from both sides:
$7x = -28$

Divide both sides by 7:
$x = -4$

Step 4: To confirm, plug -4 into the original equation for x:

$$2(-4) + 7 = \frac{-4}{4}$$

$$-8 + 7 = -1$$

$$-1 = -1$$

The answer **–4** works and is correct.

Equations with Two Variables

LEARNING OBJECTIVES
In this section, you will learn how to:
· find the value of an expression when given the values of the variables
· solve for one variable in terms of another
· find the values of two different variables when given two equations

Sometimes a problem will give you the numerical value of the variables and ask you for the value of an expression with those variables in it. To solve, just plug the values into the equation. Then make sure to follow the rules of PEMDAS (see chapter 6 on arithmetic) and be careful with your calculations.

Question	Analysis
If $x = 15$ and $y = 10$, what is the value of $4x(x - y)$?	
$4(15)(15 - 10)$	Plug 15 in for x and 10 in for y.
$= 4(15)(5)$ $= (60)(5)$ $= 300$	Use PEMDAS and solve.

Sometimes you are given an equation with two variables and asked to **solve for one variable in terms of the other.** This means that you must isolate the variable for which you are solving on one side of the equation and put everything else on the other side. In other words, when you're done, you'll have x (or whatever the variable is) on one side of the equation and an expression on the other side.

Question	Analysis
Solve $7x + 2y = 3x + 10y - 16$ for x in terms of y.	
$7x + 2y = 3x + 10y - 16$ $7x = 3x + 8y - 16$	Subtract $2y$ from both sides to get all the y's on one side of the equation.
$4x = 8y - 16$ $\dfrac{4x}{4} = \dfrac{8y - 16}{4}$	Subtract $3x$ from both sides to get all the x's on the other side of the equation.
$x = 2y - 4$	Divide both sides by 4 to isolate x. The solution for x in terms of y is $2y - 4$.

Try the next one on your own.

Solve $16t + 6u(3) + 8 = -4t - 2u - 6$ for t in terms of u.

Explanation

Step 1: You are given an equation with two variables.

Step 2: You need to solve for the variable t, but you will not end up with one numerical value. The variable t will be equal to an expression that contains u.

Step 3: First, use PEMDAS to simplify the left side of the equation.

$16t + 18u + 8 = -4t - 2u - 6$

Then, add $4t$ to both sides to get all of the t's on one side of the equation.

$20t + 18u + 8 = -2u - 6$

Subtract $18u$ from both sides.

$20t + 8 = -20u - 6$

Subtract 8 from both sides.

$20t = -20u - 14$

Divide both sides by 20.

$$t = -u - \frac{14}{20} = -u - \frac{7}{10}$$

Step 4: Check that you performed all of your calculations correctly.

Systems of Equations

On the ASVAB, you may be presented with two equations with two variables and be asked to solve for the value of one of the variables. There are two ways to do this: substitution and combination.

Substitution

Using the substitution technique, you will use one equation to express one variable in terms of the other. Then you'll substitute that expression for that variable into the other equation.

Question	Analysis
Find the value of x: $6x + y = 15$ $2x - 3y = -5$	**Step 1:** The question gives you two linear equations with two variables. **Step 2:** You need to solve for one variable, x. **Step 3:** It is easy to isolate y in the first equation, so use substitution to do so: $y = -6x + 15$. Plug in $-6x + 15$ for y in the second equation: $\quad\quad 2x - 3y = -5$ $2x - 3(15 - 6x) = -5$ Solve for x: $2x - 45 + 18x = -5$ $\quad\quad\quad 20x = 40$ $\quad\quad\quad\quad x = 2$

Question	Analysis
(A) $-2\frac{1}{2}$ (B) $\frac{5}{4}$ (C) 2 (D) 3	Choice **(C)** is correct. **Step 4:** Briefly confirm that you followed PEMDAS and performed the calculations correctly.

Alternatively, you could use Backsolving on that problem. Here's how that might work: answer choice (C) is probably the easiest one to start with, since it's a whole number. Plug 2 in for x in $6x + y = 15$ and solve for y:

$$(6)(2) + y = 15$$
$$12 + y = 15$$
$$y = 3$$

Then check $x = 2$ and $y = 3$ in the other equation:

$$2x - 3y = -5$$
$$(2)(2) - (3)(3) = -5$$
$$4 - 9 = -5$$
$$-5 = -5$$

The answer, $x = 2$, works in both equations and is correct.

Combination

The other way to solve for the value of a variable when you have two variables and two equations is to combine the two equations by adding or subtracting them in such a way that you eliminate one of the variables. Then you can solve for the remaining variable.

Question	Analysis
Find the value of a: $4a + 2b = 44$ $6a - 2b = 46$	**Step 1:** The question gives you two linear equations with two variables. **Step 2:** You need to solve for one variable, a. **Step 3:** If you add the two equations together, you will eliminate b. This can be done by using combination. $\begin{array}{r} 4a + 2b = 44 \\ + [6a - 2b = 46] \\ \hline 10a \qquad = 90 \\ a = 9 \end{array}$

Question	Analysis
(A) 4 (B) 9 (C) 10 (D) 12	Choice (B) is correct. **Step 4:** Briefly confirm that you performed the calculations correctly.

Alternatively, you could use Backsolving on that problem. Here's how that might work: if you decided to start with choice (B), you would plug 9 in for a in $4a + 2b = 44$ and solve for b:

$$(4)(9) + 2b = 44$$

$$36 + 2b = 44$$

$$2b = 8$$

$$b = 4$$

Then check $a = 9$ and $b = 4$ in the other equation:

$$6a - 2b = 46$$

$$(6)(9) - (2)(4) = 46$$

$$54 - 8 = 46$$

$$46 = 46$$

The answer, $a = 9$, works in both equations and is correct.

Try it on your own.

Solve for x:
$$5y + 17x = 90$$
$$-2x - 5y = -30$$

Explanation

Step 1: You are given two linear equations with two variables.

Step 2: You need to find the value of one of the variables, x.

Step 3: The term $5y$ appears in both equations, so combination will allow you to get rid of the y term efficiently. Rearrange the terms of the first equation to make them easier to add together.

$$17x + 5y = 90$$
$$+[-2x - 5y = 30]$$
$$\overline{15x = 60}$$
$$x = 4$$

The correct answer is $x = $ **4**.

Step 4: To confirm your answer, check that you performed all of the calculations correctly.

Quadratic Equations with Variables

> ### LEARNING OBJECTIVE
>
> In this section, you will learn how to:
>
> · solve for the value or values of a variable in a quadratic equation

When an equation has a quadratic expression on one side and zero on the other side, you can use factoring to solve for the value or values of the variable.

Question	Analysis
Solve for y: $y^2 + 4y + 3 = 0$	
$(y + 3)(y + 1) = 0$	Factor the left side of the equation.
If $y + 3 = 0$, then $y = -3$. If $y + 1 = 0$, then $y = -1$. Therefore, $y = -3$ or -1.	Whenever multiplication results in zero, at least one of the factors must equal zero. Use this fact to solve for y.

Note that the solution to a quadratic equation often has two values. The only time you will get a single value for the variable is when the factors are the same, as in this example that uses one of the classic quadratics you learned about above:

Question	Analysis
Solve for x: $x^2 - 6x + 9 = 0$.	
$(x - 3)(x - 3) = 0$	Either factor the left side of the equation using reverse-FOIL or use your knowledge of classic quadratics to factor.
If $x - 3 = 0$, then $x = 3$.	Whenever multiplication results in zero, at least one of the factors must equal zero. Since both of the factors are the same, you will only get one result for x.

If you see a quadratic expression set equal to a quantity other than zero, simply manipulate the equation so that the expression is set equal to zero. Similarly, if you see a quadratic expression presented in a different order, simply move the terms around in order to put it in the form $ax^2 + bx + c = 0$. Study this example:

Question	Analysis
Solve for x: $-4 + 2x = 31 - x^2$	This equation appears to have all the parts of a quadratic equation, but it will require some manipulation before you can use reverse-FOIL.

$-4 + 2x - 31 = -x^2$ $-4 + 2x - 31 + x^2 = 0$	First, subtract 31 from both sides, and add x^2 to both sides, so that the expression is set equal to zero.
$x^2 + 2x - 4 - 31 = 0$ $x^2 + 2x - 35 = 0$	Now rearrange and combine the terms, so that the equation has the form $ax^2 + bx + c = 0$.
	Now you're ready to perform reverse-FOIL. What are the factors of 35? 1 35 5 7 One of those factors will be negative, since the third term is negative. If so, which two numbers listed above can have the product of −35 and a difference of +2? −5 +7
$x^2 + 2x - 35 = 0$ $(x - 5)(x + 7) = 0$ $x = 5$ or -7	Therefore, $x = 5$ or -7.

Inequalities

LEARNING OBJECTIVE

In this section, you will learn how to:

- solve for the range of values of a variable in an inequality

PLOTTING INEQUALITIES ON THE NUMBER LINE

An **inequality** is represented by one of the following four signs:

$x > 2$	x is greater than 2.	
$x < -1$	x is less than −1.	
$x \geq 2$	x is greater than or equal to 2.	
$x \leq -1$	x is less than or equal to −1.	

Solve inequalities in the same way you have solved equations. Isolate the variable that you are solving for on one side of the equation and put everything else on the other side of the equation. However, when you have solved an inequality, your solution will typically be a range of values rather than a single value. Study the example below.

Question	Analysis
Solve for a: $4a + 6 > 2a + 10$	
$4a - 2a + 6 > 10$	Subtract $2a$ from both sides.
$4a - 2a > 10 - 6$	Subtract 6 from both sides.
$2a > 4$	Combine like terms.
$a > 2$	Divide both sides by 2.

In this example, the range of possible values of a are all numbers larger than 2. That is, a can be any value greater than 2 but cannot equal 2. Most of the math for inequalities is the same as if you were solving an equation. There is, however, one crucial difference between solving equations and inequalities. When you multiply or divide an inequality by a *negative* number, you must change the direction of the inequality sign. So for example, when you divide both sides of the inequality $-5a > 10$ by -5 to isolate a, you change the direction of the sign: $a < -2$. Because of this rule, you *cannot* multiply or divide both sides of an inequality by a variable, since you do not know whether the variable has a positive or negative value.

To understand why this is so, consider this example, which uses integers:

$1 < 2$

If you multiply both sides by -1:

$-1 \ ? \ -2$

Which is greater? The number -1 is greater than -2, so you need to use a greater than sign:

$-1 > -2$

The inequality sign has flipped. You can test the previous example, in which a is less than -2, by plugging in a couple of numbers. Plug in -3 for a, and you'll find that $(-5)(-3) > 10$ becomes $15 > 10$, a true statement. Plug in a number greater than -2, say 0, and you'll find that $(-5)(0) > 10$ becomes $0 > 10$, which is not a true statement. Only by flipping the inequality sign do you get the correct answer.

Try an inequality question on your own. This question does not have answer choices. Express your answer as an inequality.

Solve for z:
$$-\frac{4z}{2} - 3 > 4z$$

Explanation

Step 1: You are given an inequality.

Step 2: You are asked to solve for the variable, z.

Step 3: First, simplify the fraction:

$-\frac{4z}{2} - 3 > 4z$

$-2z - 3 > 4z$

Isolate z on one side of the inequality by adding $2z$ to both sides:

$-3 > 6z$

Divide both sides by 6:

$$\frac{-3}{6} > \frac{6}{6}z$$

$$-\frac{1}{2} > z$$

If this were Test Day, you might see the correct answer stated that way, or it might be reversed, like this:

$z < -\dfrac{1}{2}$

Step 4: Double check your math. Be sure to check that you used all of the appropriate signs.

GEOMETRY REVIEW

Throughout the geometry on the ASVAB, you will be presented with shapes and diagrams. Unless otherwise noted, you cannot assume the drawings are drawn to scale. Thus, work using the information given in a diagram; don't rely on how it looks.

Lines and Angles

LEARNING OBJECTIVES

In this section, you will learn how to:

- find the length of a line segment
- use the properties of straight lines, intersecting lines, and parallel lines to solve for the value of angles

Line Segments

A **line segment** is a piece of a line, and it has an exact measurable length. Questions may give you a segment divided into several pieces, give you the measurements of some of these pieces, and ask you for the length of another piece.

Question	Analysis
If $PR = 12$ and $QR = 4$, $PQ = ?$	
$PQ = PR - QR$	Subtract QR from the whole segment to find the remaining piece, PQ.
$PQ = 12 - 4$ $PQ = 8$	Plug in the lengths given and solve.

The point exactly in the middle of a line segment, halfway between the endpoints, is called the **midpoint** of the line segment. To **bisect** means to cut in half, so the midpoint of a line segment bisects that line segment.

M is the midpoint of AB, so $AM = MB$.

Angles

right angle

A **right angle** measures 90 degrees and is usually indicated in a diagram by a little box. The figure above is a right angle. Lines that intersect to form right angles are said to be **perpendicular**.

acute angle   obtuse angle

An **acute angle** measures less than 90 degrees. An **obtuse angle** measures more than 90 degrees.

Angles that form a straight line add up to 180 degrees. In the figure above, $a + b = 180$.

Angles around a point add up to 360 degrees. In the figure above, $a + b + c + d + e = 360$.

When two lines intersect, adjacent angles are **supplementary**, meaning they add up to 180 degrees. In the figure above, $a + b = 180$.

When lines intersect, angles across the vertex from each other are called **vertical angles** and are equal to each other. Above, $a = c$ and $b = d$.

Question	Analysis
What is the value of $x + y + z$?	**Step 1:** The figure shows three intersecting lines that form six angles, which all together equal 360°. An unlabeled angle is 90°. Three labeled angles are x, y, and z.
	Step 2: The question asks for the sum of the three labeled angles.
	Step 3: Because the angle labeled y is a vertical angle to the right angle, y must equal 90°.
	Because the angles labeled x and z form a straight line with the right angle, together they equal $180° - 90° = 90°$.
	$y + (x + z) =$
	$90° + 90° = 180°$
(A) 90 (B) 120 (C) 180 (D) 270	**Step 4:** Choose option (C). Confirm that the answer includes the correct three angles and that your arithmetic is correct.

Parallel Lines

Parallel lines are lines that have the same slope as one another. The **slope** represents the steepness of the line and the direction it goes. Therefore, lines that are parallel never intersect each other. You can imagine them as being like railroad tracks. When parallel lines are crossed by another line, this line is called a **transversal**, and angles are formed. All of these angles are said to be **interior angles**. Angles with the same relationship to the transversal are called **corresponding angles**. In the gray box below, variables refer to the diagram above.

PROPERTIES OF ANGLES MADE BY A TRANSVERSAL CROSSING PARALLEL LINES

- Corresponding angles are equal (for example, $a = e$).
- Alternate interior angles are equal ($d = f$).
- Same-side interior angles are supplementary ($c + f = 180$).
- All four acute angles are equal, as are all four obtuse angles (for example, $c = e$ and $b = h$).

Question	Analysis
$m \parallel n$ What is the value of $a + b + c + d$?	**Step 1:** The figure shows two parallel lines, *m* and *n*, crossed by transversal *p*. **Step 2:** Find the sum of the four labeled angles. **Step 3:** Two of the labeled angles are acute, and two are obtuse. Every pair of acute + obtuse angles formed by a transversal crossing parallel lines equals 180°. Two acute + obtuse angle pairs = 2 × 180° = 360°.
(A) 120 (B) 180 (C) 200 (D) 360	Choice (D) is correct. **Step 4:** Confirm that the answer includes the correct four angles and that your arithmetic is correct.

Polygons

LEARNING OBJECTIVES

In this section, you will learn how to:

- find the perimeter and area of a triangle and a quadrilateral
- solve for the length of one side of a right triangle if given the other two sides

Triangles

The three **interior angles** of any triangle add up to 180°. In the figure above, **$x + 50 + 100 = 180$, so $x = 30$.**

An **exterior angle** of a triangle is equal to the sum of the two interior angles that are not adjacent to that exterior angle. In this figure, the exterior angle labeled *y* is equal to the sum of the remote angles: **$y = 40 + 95 = 135$.**

The **perimeter** of a polygon is the sum of the lengths of its sides. The perimeter of a triangle is the sum of the lengths of its three sides. The perimeter of the triangle in the figure above is **3 + 4 + 6 = 13**.

The area of a triangle is equal to the base (that is, the length of one leg) multiplied by the height.

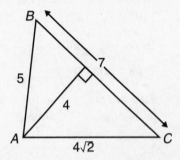

Area of triangle $= \frac{1}{2}$ (base)(height)

The **height** is the perpendicular distance between the side that's chosen as the **base** and the opposite **vertex** (opposite corner). In this triangle, 4 is the height when the side with measure 7 (*BC*) is chosen as the base. In the triangle above:

Area $= \frac{1}{2}bh = \frac{1}{2}(7)(4) = 14$

Similar triangles have the same shape, but they may be different sizes. Their corresponding angles are equal, and their corresponding sides are proportional. The triangles shown above are similar because they have the same angles.

Question	Analysis
Find the value of *s* in the diagram above.	
$\dfrac{3}{4} = \dfrac{6}{s}$	Because the triangles have the same angle measures, their sides are proportional. Set up a proportion.
$3s = (4)(6)$ $3s = 24$ $s = 8$	Cross-multiply to solve for *s*.

isosceles triangles

An **isosceles triangle** is a triangle that has two equal sides. Not only are two sides equal, but the angles opposite the equal sides, called **base angles**, are also equal.

equilateral triangles

Equilateral triangles are triangles in which all three sides are equal. Since all the sides are equal, all three angles are also equal. All angles in an equilateral triangle measure 60 degrees, regardless of the length of the sides.

right triangles

A **right triangle** is a triangle with a right angle. Every right triangle has exactly two acute angles. The sides opposite the acute angles are called the **legs.** The side opposite the right angle is called the **hypotenuse.** Since it's opposite the largest angle, the hypotenuse is the longest side of a right triangle.

If you know two sides of a right triangle, you can solve for the third side using the **Pythagorean theorem**:

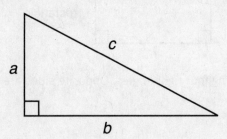

$$a^2 + b^2 = c^2$$

In this equation, a and b are the perpendicular sides, or legs, of a right triangle, and c is the longest side, or hypotenuse, of the triangle.

Question	Analysis
One leg of a right triangle is 2 and the other leg is 3. What is the length of the hypotenuse?	
$a^2 + b^2 = c^2$	Use the Pythagorean theorem.

Question	Analysis
$2^2 + 3^2 = c^2$ $4 + 9 = c^2$ $13 = c^2$ $c = \sqrt{13}$	Plug in the lengths given for the legs and solve for the hypotenuse.

Quadrilaterals

A **quadrilateral** is a figure with four sides.

The perimeter of a quadrilateral is the sum of the measures of all four sides. The perimeter of the quadrilateral in the figure above is $5 + 8 + 3 + 7 = 23$.

A **parallelogram** is a quadrilateral with two sets of parallel sides. Opposite sides are equal, as are opposite angles. The formula for the area of a parallelogram is

Area = (base)(height)

In the diagram above, the base is 2 and the height is 4, so area = $2 \times 4 = 8$.

A **rectangle** is a parallelogram containing four right angles. Opposite sides are equal. The formula for the area of a rectangle is

Area = (length)(width)

In the above diagram above, the length is 7 and the width is 3, so area = $7 \times 3 = 21$.

As with any other polygon, the perimeter of a rectangle is all the sides added together. Because a rectangle has two pairs of equal sides, the formula for the perimeter of a rectangle is

Perimeter = $2(l + w)$

The perimeter of the above rectangle is $2(7 + 3) = 2 \times 10 = 20$.

A **rhombus** has four equal sides, with the opposite sides parallel to one another.

The formula for the perimeter of a rhombus is

Perimeter = 4s

The perimeter of the above rhombus is 4(4) = 16.

A **square** is a rectangle with four equal sides. Here is the formula for the area of a square:

Area = (side)^2

In the diagram above, the length of each side is 6, so area = 6^2 = 36.

The formula for the perimeter of a square is

Perimeter = 4s

The perimeter of the above square is 4(6) = 24.

A **trapezoid** is a quadrilateral with one pair of parallel sides. The two parallel sides of a trapezoid are called the **bases**.

The formula for the area of a trapezoid is

Area = $\frac{1}{2}$ (sum of the lengths of the bases)(height)

In the diagram above, the area of the trapezoid is $\frac{1}{2}$ (4 + 9)(6) = 39.

Study the example below.

Question	Analysis
The trapezoid below has an area that is equal to greater than twice the area of the square below. Which of the following could be the value of *x*?	**Step 1:** You're given two shapes, a square and a trapezoid. Area of the square = 9 Area of trapezoid > 2 × Area of square Area of trapezoid > 18 **Step 2:** You're asked for the value of *x*.
(A) 2 (B) 3 (C) 4 (D) 5	**Step 3:** There's one unknown in the question and numbers in the choices, so use Backsolving. Try choice (B): if $x = 3$, then Area of the trapezoid = $\frac{1}{2}(4 + 5)3 = 13.5$ That's too small. Eliminate (A) and (B). Try choice (C): if $x = 4$, then Area of the trapezoid = $\frac{1}{2}(4 + 5)4 = 18$ That's also too small, since the area of the trapezoid is supposed to be *greater than* 18. Eliminate (C); (D) must be correct.
	Step 4: Briefly check that your answer makes sense and move on to the next question.

Now try one on your own.

The value of the area of the trapezoid below is divisible by 5 with no remainder. Which of the following is a possible value of *y*?

(A) 11
(B) 12
(C) 14
(D) 18

Explanation

Step 1: The area of the trapezoid is a multiple of five. So,

$\frac{1}{2}(y + 11)2 = (y + 11)$ is a multiple of five.

Step 2: You're asked for a possible value of *y*.

Step 3: Start by using Strategic Guessing Using Logic. Multiples of 5 always end in 5 or 0. To produce a number that ends in 5 or 0, *y* would have to end with 4 or 9. Only choice (C) fits.

Step 4: Briefly confirm: $\frac{1}{2}(14+11)\,2 = (14+11) = 25$, which is a multiple of 5.

Circles

LEARNING OBJECTIVE

In this section, you will learn how to:

· determine the circumference and area of a circle

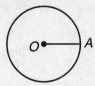

A **circle** is a figure in which each point is an equal distance from its center. In the diagrams in this section, *O* is the center of the circle.

The **radius** of a circle is the straight-line distance from its center to any point on the circle. All radii of a given circle have equal lengths. In the figure above, *OA* is a radius of circle *O*.

A **chord** is a line segment that connects any two points on a circle. Segments *AB* and *AC* are both chords. The largest chord that can be drawn in a circle is a diameter of that circle.

A **diameter** of a circle is a chord that passes through the circle's center. All diameters are the same length and are equal to twice the radius. In the figure below, *AC* is a diameter of circle *O*.

The **circumference** of a circle is the distance around it. It is equal to **π*d*** or **2π*r*.** In this example,

Circumference $= \pi d = 6\pi$

The **area** of a circle equals π times the square of the radius, or **π*r*²**. In this example, since *AC* is the diameter, $r = \frac{6}{2} = 3$, and

Area $= \pi r^2 = \pi(3^2) = 9\pi$

Study the following example.

Question	Analysis
In the figure below, the radius of circle A has length of 1 unit, and the radius of circle B has length of 2 units. What is the ratio of the area of A to the area of B?	**Step 1:** The question gives you two circles and their radius measures. **Step 2:** You need the ratio of the area of A to the area of B. The answer choices are all expressed as fractions, so it will look like this: $\frac{\text{area of A}}{\text{area of B}}$ **Step 3:** Calculate the area of each. Area of A $= \pi 1^2 = \pi$ Area of B $= \pi 2^2 = 4\pi$ $\frac{\text{area of A}}{\text{area of B}} = \frac{\pi}{4\pi} = \frac{1}{4}$
(A) $\frac{1}{4}$ (B) $\frac{1}{2}$ (C) $\frac{1}{\pi}$ (D) $\frac{\pi}{2}$	**Step 4:** Choice (A) is correct. Briefly double-check your calculations and confirm.

Now, try this one on your own.

The diameter of the circle below has measure x. The area of the circle is 64π. What is the value of x?

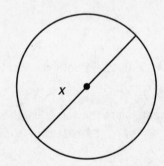

(A) 4
(B) 2π
(C) 8
(D) 16

Explanation

Step 1: The question supplies this information:

$A = 64\pi$

$d = x$

Step 2: You're asked for the measure of the diameter, or x.

Step 3: Work backwards from what you know.

$A = 64\pi = r^2\pi$

$r^2 = 64$

$r = 8$

$x = \text{diameter} = 2r = 16$

Step 4: Choice **(D)** is correct. Briefly double-check your math and confirm.

Solid Geometry

These formulas pertain to a rectangular solid box. Length is ℓ, width is w, and height is h.

Volume of a rectangular solid or box $= \ell \times w \times h$

Surface area of a rectangular solid or box $= 2\ell w + 2wh + 2\ell h$

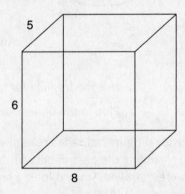

Question	Analysis
Find the volume of the box in the figure above.	
$V = \ell \times w \times h$	Use the formula for the volume of a rectangular solid.
$V = 8 \times 5 \times 6 = 240$	Plug in the dimensions given and solve.

Now try a problem on your own.

Find the surface area of the box above.

Explanation

Step 1: The question provides a diagram of a box.

Step 2: The question asks for the surface area of that box.

Step 3: Use the formula for surface area of a rectangular solid, plug in the values given, and solve:

$$SA = 2\ell w + 2wh + 2\ell h$$

$$SA = (2 \times 8 \times 5) + (2 \times 5 \times 6) + (2 \times 8 \times 6)$$

$$SA = 80 + 60 + 96 = 236$$

Step 4: Confirm that you plugged the correct values in for the correct variables.

To find the volume of a **cylinder**, you find the area of its base (which is a circle) and multiply it by the height.

Volume of a cylinder $= \pi r^2 h$

Question	Analysis
Find the volume of the cylinder in the figure above.	
$V = \pi r^2 h$	Use the formula for the volume of a cylinder.
$V = \pi \times 2^2 \times 5 = \pi \times 4 \times 5 = 20\pi$	Plug in the dimensions given and solve.

To find the surface area of any three-dimensional figure, add the areas of each side of the figure. Accordingly, finding the surface area of a cylinder involves adding the area of both of the circular ends to the area of the curved sides. Note that, if the sides of a cylinder were "unrolled," they'd form a rectangle like this:

circumference of circle

height

Thus, the area for the surface area of a cylinder is:

$$SA = 2(\pi r^2 h) + h2\pi r$$

Combined Figures

When you are presented with a diagram that looks like two shapes put together, consider splitting the shapes to make calculations easier. For example, take a look at the next question:

Question	Analysis
Find the area of the figure above.	Note that the figure is half of a circle sitting on top of a rectangle. Split the figure up and work with the two shapes independently.
$area = l \times w = 7 \times 4 = 28$	Plug the values from the diagram into the area formula for a rectangle.
$area = \pi r^2 = \pi(2)^2 = 4\pi$	Since 4 is the diameter of the circle, 2 is the radius. Use that information in the area formula for a circle.
$4\pi \div 2 = 2\pi$	Since it is only half of a circle, you need to divide the area by two.
$28 + 2\pi$	Add the area for the rectangle and the area of the half circle together to get your answer.

If you see a complicated figure on the test, try to break it down into more manageable components and solve for each individually.

Coordinate Geometry

LEARNING OBJECTIVES

In this section, you will learn how to:

· choose the equation that correctly represents a given line
· calculate the slope and *y*-intercept of a line if given two points on the line
· find the distance between two given points on a coordinate plane

The **coordinate grid** is composed of a horizontal x-axis and a vertical y-axis. The place where the axes meet is called the **origin**. Every point on the coordinate grid has a pair of **coordinates**, with the first being the x-coordinate and the second being the y-coordinate. In the figure above, points A, B, and C are at (3, 2), (–2, 3), and (–3, –5), respectively.

A line on the coordinate grid can be represented by the **slope-intercept form of a linear equation**. In this equation, x and y are the coordinates of a point on the line, b is the y-intercept, and m is the slope. Study the examples below.

Slope-intercept form of a linear equation: $\boldsymbol{y = mx + b}$

The **y-intercept** is the point where the line crosses the y-axis. The x-coordinate is always zero at the y-intercept.

The **slope** defines if a line goes down to the right or up to the right. Slope can be thought of as "rise over run" or "change in y over change in x."

$$\text{Slope} = \frac{\text{Change in } y}{\text{Change in } x}$$

If a line has a positive slope, then y gets larger as x gets larger. If a line has a negative slope, then y gets smaller as x gets larger. The steeper the line, the greater the absolute value of the slope. For example, lines with slopes of –3 or 3 are steeper than lines with slopes of –1 or 1, which in turn are steeper than lines with slopes of $-\frac{1}{3}$ or $\frac{1}{3}$.

Study this example about the coordinate plane.

Question	Analysis
A line on the coordinate grid has a slope of 2 and a y-intercept of –8. What is the correct equation of this line?	
$y = mx + b$	Use the slope-intercept equation for a line.
$y = 2x - 8$	Plug in 2 for m and –8 for b.

Now try this coordinate geometry problem on your own.

> The following points lie on a line on the coordinate grid: $(0, 2)$ and $(6, 5)$. What is the slope of this line?

Explanation

Step 1: You are given two points on a coordinate grid.

Step 2: You need to find the slope of the line that contains these two points.

Step 3: Use the formula for the slope of a line:

$$\text{Slope} = \frac{\text{Change in } y}{\text{Change in } x}$$

Plug in the y-coordinates from the second point and the first point, respectively, and the x-coordinates in the same order.

$$\text{Slope} = \frac{5 - 2}{6 - 0} = \frac{3}{6} = \frac{1}{2}$$

Step 4: Check your math and your fraction reduction. The line has a slope of $\frac{1}{2}$.

If you know the slope of a line and one point on that line, you can calculate the y-intercept. Continuing the example above, plug the information into the slope-intercept formula and solve for the y-intercept.

Question	Analysis
Find the y-intercept of the line that includes points $(0, 2)$ and $(6, 5)$.	
$y = mx + b$	Use the slope-intercept formula.
$y = \frac{1}{2}x + b$	Plug in the slope, which was calculated above to be $\frac{1}{2}$, for m in the equation.
$2 = \frac{1}{2} \times 0 + b$	Plug in the x- and y-values from one pair of coordinates.
$2 = 0 + b$ $2 = b$	Solve for the variable b.

If you are given two points on a grid and asked to find the distance between them, you can do so using the Pythagorean theorem. Continuing to use the points above, find the distance between the two points on the x-axis and the difference between the two points on the y-axis. Then, using those two values as the legs of the right triangle, calculate the hypotenuse, which is the distance between the points.

Question	Analysis
What is the distance between the two points (0, 2) and (6, 5)?	
	Draw the points on a coordinate plane. Then, draw a third dot that makes a right triangle when all points are connected. The third point will be drawn where the *y*-axis of one point crosses the *x*-axis of the other. The distance along the *x*-axis is 6 and the distance along the *y*-axis is 3.
$\sqrt{6^2 + 3^2} = \sqrt{36 + 9} = \sqrt{45}$	Use Pythagorean theorem to solve for the distance between the two points. The distance between the two points is $\sqrt{45}$.
	Note: The triangle also could have been drawn with the third point opposite, with the *y*-axis of the lower point intersecting the *x*-axis of the higher point. Either way, the result is the same.

If you are asked to find the distance between two points on the coordinate plane, draw a right triangle to help you use the Pythagorean theorem to solve.

Now you can try out your math knowledge—and practice the Kaplan Method for math—on the following practice set.

MATHEMATICS KNOWLEDGE PRACTICE QUESTIONS

1. What is the height of a rectangular box with volume of 140, length of 10, and width of 7?

    (A) 2
    (B) 17
    (C) 70
    (D) 9,800

2. If $x = \sqrt{3}$, $y = 2$, and $z = \frac{1}{2}$, then $x^2 - 5yz + y^2 =$

    (A) 1
    (B) 2
    (C) 4
    (D) 7

3. Solve for a: $\frac{a}{-2} + 20 < -100$

    (A) $a < -240$
    (B) $a > 240$
    (C) $a > 180$
    (D) $a > 40$

4. $(3d - 7) - (5 - 2d) =$

    (A) $d - 12$
    (B) $5d - 2$
    (C) $5d + 12$
    (D) $5d - 12$

5. Which of the following are possible values of x, if $x^2 - x - 20 = 0$?

    (A) $-5, 4$
    (B) $-4, 5$
    (C) $-2, 10$
    (D) $5, 4$

6. The following two points lie on a line on the coordinate grid: $(-2, 0)$ and $(4, 6)$. Which of the following is the equation of the line?

    (A) $x = y + 2$
    (B) $y = 3x + 6$
    (C) $y = 2x + 1$
    (D) $y = x + 2$

7. If the perimeter of the above square is 36, what is the circumference of the circle?

    (A) 6π
    (B) 9π
    (C) 12π
    (D) 18π

8. What is the area of the frame in the above diagram if the picture inside has a length of 8 and a width of 4?

    (A) 16
    (B) 24
    (C) 48
    (D) 56

9. In the figure above, what is the distance from the midpoint of $\overline{PQ}$ to the midpoint of $\overline{RS}$?

    (A) 12
    (B) 14
    (C) 16
    (D) 18

10. If $s - t = 5$, what is the value of $3s - 3t + 3$?

    (A) 11
    (B) 12
    (C) 15
    (D) 18

Answers and Explanations

1. (A) 2 This question involves a rectangular box, so you are working with a geometric solid. You are given the box's volume and two of its dimensions, and you're asked for the third dimension. The volume of a rectangular solid is found by multiplying the figure's three dimensions, $\ell \times w \times h$. Each of those dimensions has to be smaller than the volume. Therefore, you can rule out (D) right away—it's way too big.

Now you can choose to Backsolve or use straightforward math. If you Backsolve, start with (C) 70, because it's easier to work with than (B) 17. Does $10 \times 7 \times 70$ equal 140? Just $10 \times 7 = 70$, and you're already halfway there. 70 is way too big for the third dimension. Skip (B) 17, and try (A) 2, because it is easier to work with. Does $10 \times 7 \times 2$ equal 140? Yes, it does, and (A) is the correct answer. If (A) had been too small, you would have known (B) is the correct answer without performing the tricky math with the number 17.

The straightforward math looks like this:

$$\ell \times w \times h = V$$
$$10 \times 7 \times h = 140$$
$$70h = 140$$
$$h = \frac{140}{70}$$
$$h = 2$$

2. (B) 2 You're given values for three variables and asked to solve an equation with those three variables. Plug the values into the equation and solve with arithmetic:

$$x^2 - 5yz + y^2 = (\sqrt{3})^2 - 5(2)\left(\frac{1}{2}\right) + 2^2 = 3 - 5 + 4 = 2$$

3. (B) a > 240 This question gives you an inequality and asks you to solve for a variable, a. First, get the only term with an a in it by itself on one side of the inequality by subtracting 20 from both sides: $\frac{a}{-2} < -120$. Now multiply each side by -2, remembering to switch the inequality sign because you are multiplying by a negative number: $a > 240$.

4. (D) 5d − 12 This question involves an equation with one variable, and the answer choices are simplified forms of the equation. You can use Picking Numbers or straightforward math to solve.

Try picking 2 for d. Then $(3d - 7) - (5 - 2d) = (3 \times 2 - 7) - (5 - 2 \times 2)$. Use PEMDAS to solve: $(6 - 7) - (5 - 4) = -1 - (1) = -2$. -2 is your target number.

Now plug 2 in for d in each of the answer choices to see which gives you the target number -2: (A) $d - 12 = -10$; (B) $5d - 2 = 8$; (C) $5d + 12 = 22$; (D) $5d - 12 = -2$. (D) is the correct answer.

If you use algebra to solve, start by eliminating the parentheses by distributing the minus sign over the second set of parentheses: $(3d - 7) - (5 - 2d) = 3d - 7 - 5 - (-2d) = 3d - 7 - 5 + 2d$. Now combine like terms and perform the addition and subtraction: $3d + 2d - 7 - 5 = 5d - 12$.

5. (B) −4, 5 A quadratic expression is set equal to zero and you are asked to find a pair of values that x could equal. Factor the equation by finding a pair of numbers that multiply to -20 and add to -1. Those numbers are -5 and 4, so the equation becomes $(x + 4)(x - 5) = 0$. When multiplication results in zero, at least one factor must be zero. If $x + 4 = 0$, then $x = -4$; if $x - 5 = 0$, then $x = 5$.

You could also use Backsolving here. Because 4 appears in two answer choices, try it first: $4^2 - 4 - 20 = -8 \neq 0$. So x cannot be 4, and you can eliminate (A) and (D). Now try 5: $5^2 - 5 - 20 = 0$. That works! Of the two remaining choices, only (B) has 5 as a value of x, so that is the correct answer.

6. (D) y = x + 2 The question gives two points on a line and asks for the equation of the line. Three of the equations in the answer choices are in slope-intercept form: $y = mx + b$. Choice (A) starts with x, which you might recognize as not being the correct form of an equation of a line. Therefore, in order to evaluate (A), you should convert it to the format $y = x - 2$. Slope is $\frac{y_2 - y_1}{x_2 - x_1} = \frac{6 - 0}{4 - (-2)} = \frac{6}{6} = 1$. The coefficient of x is 1. Find the y-intercept by plugging one of the coordinate pairs and the slope into the $y = mx + b$ equation: $6 = (1)(4) + b$; $b = 2$.

Plug 1 in for m and 2 in for b in the slope-intercept equation to get the answer. $y = 1x + 2$, which can also be written $y = x + 2$. Choice (D) is the correct answer.

7. (B) 9π This question shows a circle inscribed inside a square. It says that the square's perimeter is 36 and asks for the circle's circumference. A square has four equal sides, and the formula for the circumference of a circle requires knowing either the radius or the diameter of the circle. Your task is to take the information you're given about the square and apply it to the circle.

If the perimeter of the square is 36, then each of the four sides equals $\frac{36}{4} = 9$. The side of the square is the same length as the diameter of the circle, so the diameter of the circle is also 9. Finally, the circumference is $\pi d = 9\pi$.

If it's more efficient for you, you can Backsolve this question. Start with (B). If the circle's circumference is 9π, then its diameter is 9. That makes the side of the square also 9, and the square's perimeter is $4 \times 9 = 36$. That matches the information in the question, and you know that (B) is correct.

8. (C) 48 The diagram shows one rectangle inside another and the dimensions of the larger rectangle. The question says this is a picture in a frame and gives the dimensions of the smaller rectangle (the picture). You need to find the area of the frame. The area of the frame is the area of the larger rectangle minus the area of the smaller rectangle,
$(8 \times 10) - (4 \times 8) = 80 - 32 = 48$.

9. (A) 12 The diagram gives a number line with four points labeled. The question names two line segments and asks for the distance between their midpoints. First, find the midpoints and then calculate the distance between them. To find the midpoint of a segment on the number line, add the endpoints and divide the sum by 2. The midpoint of PQ is $\frac{(-12)+(-2)}{2} = \frac{-14}{2} = -7$. The midpoint of RS is $\frac{1+9}{2} = \frac{10}{2} = 5$. Finally, the distance between the two points is the positive difference between their coordinates, $5 - (-7) = 12$.

10. (D) 18 You're given an equation with two variables and asked for the value of an expression with the same two variables. You might notice that the variables in the second expression contain the variables in the first expression multiplied by 3. If $s - t = 5$, then if you multiply both sides by 3, you get $3s - 3t = 15$. Thus, $3s - 3t + 3 = 15 + 3 = 18$.

Alternatively, you could Pick Numbers. Pick Numbers for s and t so that $s - t = 5$, say $s = 7$ and $t = 2$. Now plug those values into the expression and solve:
$3s - 3t + 3 = 21 - 6 + 3 = 18$.

Review and Reflect

After this chapter and practice question set, how comfortable do you feel with algebra? Which concepts do you need to review? How often were you able to spot the opportunity to use a strategy like Backsolving or Picking Numbers?

Also, how do you do on the items related to geometry—which formulas do you know, and which do you need to brush up on?

Use your thoughts about these questions to guide your review of this chapter.

CHAPTER 8

CONQUERING THE TECHNICAL SUBTESTS

Congratulations! If you've been working through this book in order, then you've reviewed all of the portions of the AFQT, which is crucial for your eligibility to enlist in the armed forces. However, perhaps you don't just want to enlist—you may want to enlist *and* to qualify for a specific job. There are many varieties of specialized job opportunities in the armed forces, which could form the foundation for a lifelong military career or could prepare you for a successful career in civilian life after you've completed your military service. Doing well on the ASVAB's technical subtests, in addition to the AFQT, is important for qualifying for many of those specialized jobs.

The next six chapters will prepare you for the ASVAB technical subtests: General Science, Electronics Information, Automotive Information, Shop Information, Mechanical Comprehension, and Assembling Objects. The amount of emphasis you should give to each of these chapters will depend on which job or jobs you desire. Be sure to speak with a recruiter, do your research, and form a sense of which subtests are most important for your goals. That knowledge, combined with your performance on the Diagnostic Test which forms chapter 2 of this book, will tell you which topics you need to study most.

If you aren't sure which career path you are interested in, pay attention to your strengths and the parts of the ASVAB you enjoy. If there is a particular topic that is of interest to you and you would like to learn more about it, you can use that passion to help you decide a potential career path. Conducting online research and speaking to a recruiter can help you determine which paths would help you pursue your interests in the best way. This information can help focus your study time on the most beneficial sections of the test for your ideal path.

THE KAPLAN METHOD FOR ASVAB TECHNICAL SUBTEST QUESTIONS

LEARNING OBJECTIVE

In this section, you will learn to:

- apply the Kaplan Method for the Technical Subtests to ASVAB questions

Step 1: Identify What You Are Being Asked for.

Just as with math questions, it's very important to figure out what your task is. Does the right answer represent the value of a variable? The name of a planet? The definition of a unit of measure? The name of a type of tool? How much force is required to move an object? and so on.

Often, a quick glance at the answer choices can help point you in the right direction. Don't read them all in depth; simply use them to get a sense of what your task is. If all the answer choices are numbers followed by "mHz," you will be calculating the frequency of a wave and expressing that frequency in megahertz. If all the answer choices are the names of planets, your job is to identify a planet. If it's an Auto Information question and all of the answer choices start with verbs, it's likely you'll be describing how to go about some type of auto repair.

Step 2: Simplify or Solve.

This step varies quite a bit depending on the subject matter. Therefore, this section will discuss a variety of approaches depending on the information you are given.

Diagrams

Some technical subtest question may include a diagram. On those questions, ask yourself:

- What does the diagram represent?
- Are there any important relationships depicted in the diagram?
- How does the diagram help me to answer the question?

Numbers, variables, or formulas

Some technical subtest questions resemble math questions. You may be asked to perform calculations, manipulate variables, or apply a formula (especially on Mechanical Comprehension, but on other tests as well). You can often approach these questions using the same tactics you use for the math subtests. Review chapter 5 to remind yourself of these approaches. For each technical subtest question involving math, ask yourself:

- How can I simplify the information I'm given?
- Am I given a formula or expected to recall one out of my own knowledge?
- Can I Backsolve, Pick Numbers, or guess strategically using logic, or should I simply do the math?

Charts, graphs, or tables

Some technical subtest questions may include a graphical representation of data. If you see a chart, graph, table, or other visual arrangement of data, ask yourself:

- How does the graph relate to the information in the question?
- What are the units?
- What do the axes represent?
- Is there a trend or pattern in the data?

Written information

If a technical subtest question includes a few sentences of introductory text, take a moment to paraphrase them to ensure that you understand before you move on to Step 3.

Step 3: Make a Prediction.

Just as on Paragraph Comprehension and Word Knowledge, having a prediction is a great strategy for finding the right answer efficiently and not being distracted by tempting wrong answer choices. In your practice, try putting a sticky note or your hand over the answer choices as you're working through Step 2, above, to force yourself to practice predicting. (Try to predict unless you're using a strategic math approach like Backsolving or Strategic Guessing. Those strategies do not require making a prediction.) Practice not looking at the answer choices until it becomes natural. On Test Day, it will be a waste of time to literally cover the answer choices in any way. By practicing the skill now, you will understand the benefit of predicting and increase your ability to do so.

Step 4: Evaluate the Choices Strategically.

Got a solid prediction? Look for it among the choices.

If you don't have a solid prediction, seek to discard wrong answer choices that do not make sense. You might be able to eliminate choices that:

- contain numbers that are obviously too large or too small
- are expressed using the wrong units
- belong to a different category than that you were asked for. For example, if you are asked to name a planet, "Sirius" would be a wrong answer, since it is a star rather than a planet.
- are synonyms: each ASVAB question has only one right answer, so two answer choices that mean the same thing cannot be correct. For example, if you are working on a shop information question and two of the answer choices are "Vise Grips" and "locking pliers," cross both those choices off. They both refer to the same tool, so it cannot be the case that one of those answer choices is right and the other is wrong.

Bringing It All Together

Memorize the method below as soon as possible. You don't want to put off learning it. You'll have lots of content review to do in the coming chapters, and you will want the method in place so that you can use what you learn about the subject matter to your advantage on ASVAB questions.

THE KAPLAN METHOD FOR THE ASVAB TECHNICAL SUBTESTS

Step 1: Identify what you are being asked for.

Step 2: Simplify or solve.

Step 3: Make a prediction.

Step 4: Evaluate the choices strategically.

Note: The method above should form your approach to General Science, Electronics Information, Automotive Information, Shop Information, and Mechanical Comprehension questions. However, since the Assembling Objects test requires a somewhat different skill set, we will present a different method for the Assembling Objects test in chapter 14.

Final Thought Before You Dive In

As you study the technical subtest material in the second half of this book, don't forget to periodically review the math and verbal topics in the first half of this book. Good luck with your preparations for the technical subtests!

GENERAL SCIENCE

KNOW WHAT TO EXPECT

The General Science section of the ASVAB covers a grab bag of topics that you may or may not have studied in high school or elsewhere. This subtest covers a wide variety of material, but you'll never be expected to know too much about a single topic. As you study this chapter, seek first to develop a broad overview of the subject matter, learning the broad outlines of anything that's completely unfamiliar and refreshing your memory about topics that seem familiar. Then, if you have time before Test Day, you can dig deeper into these topics.

ASVAB science topics fall into three broad categories: life science, earth and space science, and physical science. This chapter is divided into three parts—one for each of those categories—each with its own set of practice questions. As usual, we've included worked examples and practice questions throughout. Also, key terms you may want to memorize are listed in **bold type**.

You'll be answering 25 questions in 11 minutes on the paper and pencil version, and you are given 8 minutes for 16 questions on the CAT-ASVAB. That means you need to be able to answer ASVAB science questions in roughly half a minute. To help you work efficiently, use the Kaplan Method covered in chapter 8 on every science question you encounter.

PART I: LIFE SCIENCE

NUTRITION AND HEALTH

LEARNING OBJECTIVES

In this section you will learn to:

- describe the role of important micro- and macronutrients in the human body and to identify where these nutrients come from
- identify some diseases that can be caused by nutrient deficiencies

Although nutritionists themselves don't always agree about what constitutes a healthy diet, certain facts are clear. The human body requires a combination of protein, carbohydrates, fat, minerals, vitamins, and fiber. Proteins, carbohydrates, and fats (macronutrients) are necessary to provide energy. Minerals and vitamins (micronutrients), along with fiber, are necessary to maintain proper bodily functions.

Proteins are necessary for the body's maintenance, growth, and repair. Animal proteins are contained in meat, fish, eggs, and cheese. Vegetable proteins are found in peas, beans, nuts, and some grains.

Carbohydrates include both starches and sugars. They are major sources of energy for the body. Starches are found in bread, cereal, rice, potatoes, and pasta. Sugars are found in fruits, cane sugar, and beets, as well as processed foods.

Fats also provide energy for the body. There are three types of fats: saturated, monounsaturated, and polyunsaturated. Saturated fats can raise bad cholesterol (LDL), but mono- and polyunsaturated fats can actually decrease levels of bad cholesterol. Diets high in saturated fat can lead to high cholesterol, which can cause heart disease or stroke. Sources of saturated fats include meats, shellfish, eggs, milk, and milk products. Sources of monounsaturated fats include olives and olive oil, almonds, cashews, Brazil nuts, and avocados. Sources of polyunsaturated fats include corn oil, flaxseed oil, pumpkin seed oil, safflower oil, soybean oil, and sunflower oil.

Fiber is an important part of a healthy diet that provides bulk to help the large intestine carry away waste matter. Good sources of dietary fiber include leafy green vegetables, carrots, turnips, peas, beans, and potatoes, as well as raw and cooked fruits, cereals, and whole-grain foods.

Water is also essential for survival. The body loses approximately four pints of water each day, which must be replenished. Most foods contain water, facilitating proper water maintenance, although it is still necessary to drink water as well! Insufficient water consumption leads to dehydration, which can cause muscle cramps, dizziness, and, if not remedied, even death.

Minerals in small quantities are needed for a balanced diet. Some necessary minerals are iron, zinc, calcium, magnesium, and sodium chloride (salt). Calcium is important for building strong teeth and bones. Iron, on the other hand, is necessary for red blood cell development. Minerals play many different roles in the development and maintenance of a healthy body.

Vitamins, such as vitamins C and D, are organic compounds that are necessary for a wide variety of physiological processes from bone hardness to healthy gums. Fruits and vegetables are rich sources of vitamins. Vitamin D is unique in that one of the best sources comes not from your diet, but from the sun. Exposure to sunlight allows your body to synthesize its own vitamin D.

A lack of the proper amount of certain necessary nutrients in the diet can lead to **deficiency diseases**. One such disease is iron-deficiency anemia, which may cause weakness, dizziness, and headaches. It is especially common among children, young adults, and pregnant women who do not get enough iron in their diets. Another example of a deficiency disease is scurvy, which is caused by a lack of vitamin C. Though at one time very common among pirates and sailors who did not have access to fresh fruits and vegetables, scurvy is now relatively rare.

The following table lists a selection of nutrients and their sources.

Vitamin/Mineral	Sources	Benefits
Iron	Meat (especially liver), beans, whole grains	Allows red blood cells to transfer oxygen to body tissues
Calcium	Dairy products like milk, yogurt, and cheese; spinach	Bone growth, muscle function
Magnesium	Nuts, whole grains, green leafy vegetables, fortified foods	Bone development, muscle and nerve function, enzyme function
Potassium	Bananas, sweet potatoes, nuts and seeds	Balances fluid levels in the body
Vitamin A	Liver, milk, eggs, carrots, spinach	Vision, immune system, cell growth
Vitamin C	Red and green peppers, citrus, broccoli	Collagen formation, immune system function, antioxidant (helps protect cells from damage)
Vitamin D	Fortified milk, juice, or cereal; body makes majority of vitamin D when exposed to sunlight	Bone strength (by helping the body absorb calcium), muscle and nerve function, immune system

Take a look at how an expert test taker might approach an ASVAB question about health and nutrition.

Question	Analysis
A pregnant woman feels dizzy and has a headache. Which of the following would be the most likely diagnosis? (A) iron-deficiency anemia (B) scurvy (C) cancer (D) diabetes	**Step 1:** You're given three important facts: the woman is pregnant, has a headache, and is feeling dizzy. **Step 2:** What condition that causes headache and dizziness is common in pregnant women? **Step 3:** Those symptoms match iron-deficient anemia, which is especially common among pregnant women. **Step 4:** Select choice **(A)**.

Now try one on your own.

If a person has high cholesterol, which one of the following foods might his doctor suggest that he avoid?

(A) olive oil
(B) red meat
(C) almonds
(D) avocados

Explanation

A person with high cholesterol should limit their intake of saturated fat. The only choice here that is high in saturated fat is **(B)** red meat. The others are filled with healthier fats (mono- and polyunsaturated fats) that could possibly help lower high cholesterol.

HUMAN BODY SYSTEMS AND DISEASES

LEARNING OBJECTIVES

In this section you will learn to:

- identify the general components and processes of major human body systems, including the musculoskeletal, respiratory, circulatory, nervous, digestive, and reproductive
- differentiate between blood types and how they influence blood donation
- describe the roles of the main components of the brain
- describe the causes and effects of common health problems
- differentiate between bacteria and viruses and describe several common illnesses caused by each

The Skeleton and Muscles

The skeleton and muscles are responsible for holding the body together as well as for movement. Without a skeleton you would be just an immobile mass of organs, veins, and skin. Some organisms, namely **arthropods** (including insects, spiders, and crustaceans), have **exoskeletons**, or external skeletons. However, **vertebrate** animals, including humans, have internal skeletons, or **endoskeletons**.

The human skeleton contains both **bone** and **cartilage**. Bones provide the primary support, while cartilage, which is more flexible, is found at the end of all bones, at the joints, in the nose, and in the ears. Bones not only provide structural support for the body and protect vital organs, but also produce blood cells and store minerals such as calcium. **Tendons**, tough fibrous cords of connective tissue, connect muscles to the skeleton. **Ligaments**, another type of connective tissue, connect bones to other bones at joints such as the elbow, knee, fingers, and vertebral column.

Selected Bones

Cranium
Humerus (upper arm)
Radius
Ulna
Femur (thigh)
Fibula
Ribs
Spine (26 vertebrae)
Pelvis
Tibia

Here's how an expert test taker would approach an ASVAB question about the skeletal system.

Question	Analysis
What type of tissue would connect the humerus to the ulna? (A) bone (B) muscle (C) tendon (D) ligament	**Step 1:** The question asks what type of tissue connects two bones to each other. **Step 2:** There is nothing to simplify. **Step 3:** Make a prediction: ligaments are connected to bone. **Step 4:** (D) is the correct answer.

The Respiratory System

Respiration—the process by which blood cells absorb **oxygen** and eliminate **carbon dioxide** and **water vapor**—is performed by the **respiratory system**.

The Respiratory System

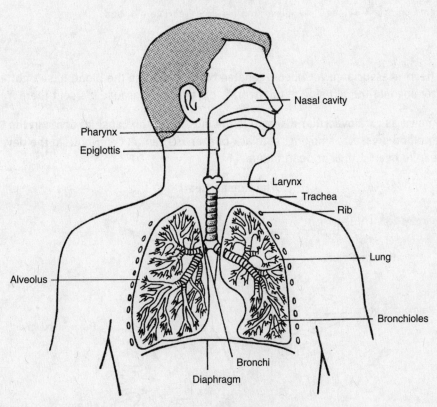

When air enters through the **nose**, it passes through the **nasal cavity**, which filters, moistens, and warms air, and then through the **pharynx**, which further filters the air and aids in protection against infection. The air then passes through the open **epiglottis**, which closes when swallowing to prevent food from going down the airway, and into the **trachea**, which further cleanses the air. The trachea branches into the **left and right bronchi**, which are two tubes that lead to the **lungs**. There the bronchi further subdivide into smaller tubes called **bronchioles**. Each bronchiole ends in a small sac called an **alveolus**. It is in the alveolus that oxygen from the air enters into the bloodstream via tiny blood vessels called **capillaries**. The **diaphragm** is a system of muscles that allows breathing. When the diaphragm causes the lungs to expand, air rushes in to fill the space, in a process called inhalation. When the diaphragm causes the lungs to contract, air is pushed out in an exhalation.

Blood and the Circulatory System

In conjunction with the respiratory system, the **circulatory system** functions to transport oxygen throughout the body while removing carbon dioxide. Additionally, the circulatory system transports nutrients provided by the digestive system and clears away waste by transporting it to the excretory system. The organ that drives the circulatory system is the **heart**. The human heart is a four-chambered pump, with two collecting chambers called **atria** (singular: atrium), and two pumping chambers called **ventricles**. The **right atrium** receives deoxygenated blood from the **venae cavae** (plural of **vena cava**), the two largest veins in the body, and passes it to the **right ventricle**, which pumps the blood to the lungs through the **pulmonary artery**. Blood picks up oxygen in the lungs and returns to the **left atrium** via the **pulmonary vein**. From there it passes to the **left ventricle** and is pumped through the **aorta**, the body's largest artery, into several smaller branching **arteries** that take it through the rest of the body. The heart's **valves** are essential to efficient pumping of the heart. When blood is pumped out of the ventricles, valves close to prevent the blood from flowing backward into the heart after the contraction of the ventricles is complete.

How blood flows from the heart to the body:

right atrium ⟶ right ventricle ⟶ lungs ⟶ left atrium ⟶ left ventricle ⟶ body

---

The right side of the heart is associated with deoxygenated blood (because the blood hasn't gotten to the lungs yet), whereas blood coming into the left side of the heart is oxygenated because it's sent there from the lungs.

Heart disease (also known as **cardiovascular disease**) is the most common cause of death in the United States. High cholesterol, high blood pressure, smoking, and lack of exercise can all contribute to the development of heart disease, which can lead to heart attack or heart failure.

The Human Heart

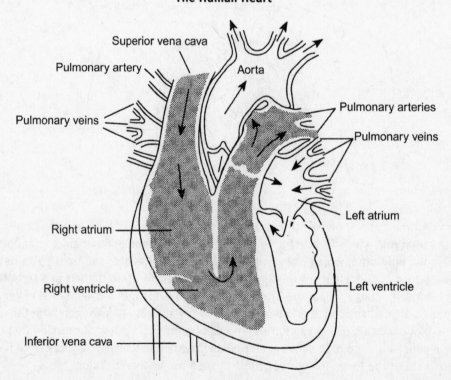

The **arteries** carry blood from the heart to the tissues of the body. They repeatedly branch into smaller arteries (**arterioles**), which supply blood to bodily tissues via the capillaries. Arteries carry blood away from the heart and thus must be thick-walled because they carry oxygenated blood at high blood pressure. Only the pulmonary artery, which carries blood from the heart into the lungs, does not contain oxygenated blood.

Veins, on the other hand, carry blood back to the heart from other parts of the body. Veins are relatively thin-walled, conduct blood at low pressure, and contain many valves to prevent backflow. Veins have no pulse and carry dark red, deoxygenated blood. The lone exception is the pulmonary vein, which carries freshly oxygenated blood from the lungs back into the heart.

Finally, **capillaries** are thin-walled vessels that are very small in diameter. Capillaries, rather than arteries or veins, permit exchange of materials such as oxygen, carbon dioxide, nutrients, and waste between the blood and the body's cells through **diffusion**.

The Capillary System

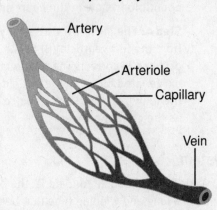

Artery

Arteriole

Capillary

Vein

Hypertension, also known as high blood pressure, can cause damage to blood vessels as well as other parts of the body like the kidneys. Limiting salt intake, maintaining a healthy weight, and exercising can help prevent or manage hypertension.

Blood consists of **cells** suspended in **plasma**, the liquid component of blood. There are three types of cells found in blood: **red blood cells**, which are the oxygen-carrying cells; **white blood cells**, which fight infection by destroying foreign organisms; and **platelets**, which are cell fragments that allow blood to clot. All blood cells are created in the **bone marrow**, which is located in the center of bones.

Each of these blood cell types can be measured in the blood as an indicator of overall health. When white blood cell levels are higher than normal, that indicates that the body is fighting off some sort of infection by either bacteria or a virus.

It is also important to note that blood comes in four different types: A, B, AB, and O, which can be further designated as either "negative" or "positive." One combination may be written as "A+" or "A positive," for example. The letter designation is determined by the type of molecules (**antigens**) found on the outside of the red blood cells. The positive or negative designation is assigned based on whether or not cells have a third type of antigen called the **Rh factor**. A person who has blood that is Rh-factor negative cannot receive blood with a positive type; however, a person with positive type blood can receive donor blood that is Rh-negative. Type O negative is the **universal donor**, which means that type O negative blood can be given to anybody. Type AB positive is the **universal recipient**, which means that someone with this type of blood can receive any other type of blood.

Here's how an expert test taker would think through an ASVAB question about the circulatory system.

Question	Analysis
Which of the following does not contain oxygen-rich blood?	**Step 1:** The question asks which listed item does not contain oxygen-rich blood.
	Step 2: Possible answer choices will contain three choices that *do* contain oxygen-rich blood and one (the correct answer) that *does not*.
	Step 3: A vague question like this can be hard to predict, because it doesn't tell you if you are looking for a blood vessel or a part of the heart. Either way, you should start thinking about what you know about blood flow in the heart and to the body.
(A) aorta (B) left ventricle (C) pulmonary vein (D) right atrium	**Step 4:** The aorta (A) carries oxygenated blood away from the left ventricle (B) of the heart, so neither of those is correct. The pulmonary vein (C) carries oxygenated blood to the left side of the heart from the lungs, so that leaves choice (D), right atrium, as the correct answer.

The Digestive and Excretory Systems

The digestive system is responsible for breaking down foods into material the body can use for energy and building body tissues. The digestive tract is essentially a long and winding tube that begins at the mouth and ends at the anus.

The process of digestion progresses as follows:

- In the mouth, the teeth and the tongue aid in mechanical digestion (chewing), while the enzyme **salivary amylase**, contained in the saliva, begins to break down starch.
- From the mouth, the chewed food moves into the **esophagus**. Contractions push the food down through the esophagus and into the stomach.
- In the **stomach**, food is mixed with **gastric acids** and **pepsin**, which help break down **protein**.
- Most digestion takes place in the **small intestine**. The small intestine is very long, about 23 feet on average. Food is broken down completely by enzymes produced in the walls of the small intestine, in the pancreas, and in the liver. The acids produced by the **pancreas** contain **lipase**, which converts fat to glycerol and fatty acids; **pancreatic amylase**, which breaks down complex carbohydrates into simple sugars; and **trypsin**, which converts polypeptides (the molecules that compose proteins) into amino acids. **Bile**, which is produced by the **liver**, aids in digestion by emulsifying fat (physically separating it into individual molecules). All these digested substances, except for the fatty acids and glycerol, are then absorbed in the small intestine through capillaries that carry the blood into the liver and then throughout the rest of the body.
- In the **large intestine**, also known as the **colon**, water and minerals remaining in the waste matter are absorbed back into the body.
- Chemical waste, such as urea, excess salts, minerals, and water, are filtered from the blood by the **kidneys** and secreted into the urine. Urine is transported to the bladder from the kidneys through the **ureters**.
- In the **rectum**, solid waste matter is stored. Liquid waste (urine) is stored in the **bladder**.
- Solid waste matter is periodically released through the **anus**, and urine is released through the **urethra**.

The Digestive System

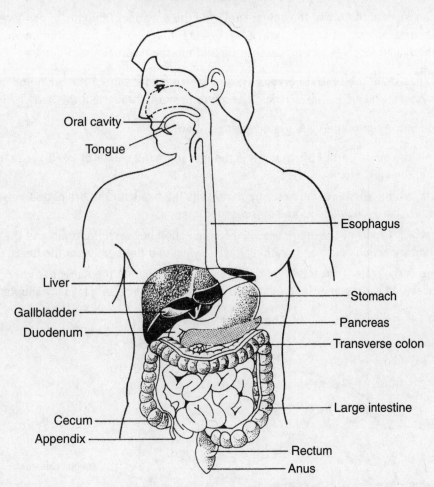

Oral cavity
Tongue
Esophagus
Liver
Gallbladder
Duodenum
Stomach
Pancreas
Transverse colon
Large intestine
Cecum
Appendix
Rectum
Anus

Study the example below to see how an expert test taker might approach a question about the digestive system.

Question	Analysis
Where does food go after the step where proteins begin to be digested?	**Step 1:** The question is asking about the next step in digestion after digestion of proteins begins.
	Step 2: This is essentially two questions in one. First, identify where proteins are digested. Second, recall where food goes after that step.
	Step 3: Recall that protein digestion begins in the stomach with the help of stomach acid and pepsin. Predict where food goes after being in the stomach: the small intestine.
(A) esophagus (B) stomach (C) small intestine (D) large intestine	**Step 4:** Choice (C) is correct.

The Nervous System

The nervous system consists of the **brain**, the **spinal cord**, and the network of billions of nerve cells called **neurons,** which behave like electrical wires that send and receive signals throughout the body. The nervous system controls the functions of the body and receives and processes stimuli from the environment.

The nervous system consists of the **central nervous system**, which is made up of the brain and spinal cord, and the **peripheral nervous system**, which contains all the other neurons found throughout the body.

The main components of the central nervous system are as follows:

- The **cerebrum** is the major part of the brain. It is thought to be the **center of intelligence**, responsible for hearing, seeing, thinking, etc.
- The **cerebellum** is a big cluster of nerve tissue that forms the basis for the brain. It is most closely associated with balance, movement, and muscle coordination.
- The **medulla**, which is part of the brainstem, is the connection between the brain and the spinal cord. It controls **involuntary actions** such as breathing, swallowing, and the beating of the heart.
- The **spinal cord** is the major connecting center between the brain and the network of nerves. It **carries impulses** between all organs and the brain and is also the control center for many **simple reflexes**.

The Human Brain

The peripheral nervous system can be subdivided into:

- The **somatic nervous system**, which consists of nerve fibers that send sensory information to the central nervous system and control **voluntary actions**.
- The **autonomic nervous system**, which regulates **involuntary activity** in the heart, stomach, and intestines.

The example below walks you through the expert approach to an ASVAB question about the nervous system.

Question	Analysis
Which of the following parts of the brain, if damaged, would likely cause a person to have poor balance?	**Step 1:** The question asks for a part of the brain that would affect balance if it were damaged. **Step 2:** There's nothing to simplify. **Step 3:** Make a prediction based on what you know about the brain: the cerebellum is closely related to balance.
(A) medulla (B) spinal cord (C) cerebellum (D) cerebrum	**Step 4:** Choose (C). The medulla and spinal cord are associated with more basic, involuntary functions like breathing and reflexes, whereas the cerebrum handles higher functions like our intelligence, so none of these choices fit.

The Reproductive System

Human reproduction occurs when a female's egg is fertilized by a male's sperm. During female **ovulation**, which occurs approximately every 28 days, an egg (**ovum**) is released from one of the ovaries and begins to travel through the **oviduct (fallopian tube)** and into the **uterus**. At the same time, the **endometrial lining** of the uterus becomes prepared for implantation.

Male and Female Reproductive Systems

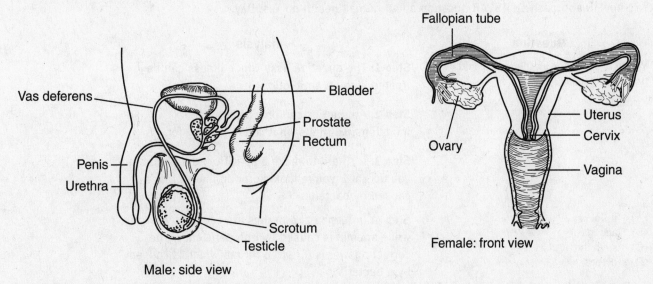

Male: side view

Female: front view

During intercourse, the **penis** ejaculates more than 250 million **sperm**, produced in the **testes**, into the **vagina**. Some of the sperm make their way to the uterus, where they may encounter an egg to fertilize. If the sperm unites with the ovum, a fertilized egg (**zygote**) is formed, which may implant in the uterus and eventually develop into a **fetus**. During pregnancy and after childbirth, **prolactin**, a hormone secreted by the pituitary, activates the production of breast milk (**lactation**).

If the ovum fails to become fertilized, the uterine lining sloughs off during **menstruation**. From puberty to menopause, this **menstrual cycle** repeats monthly except during pregnancy.

Human Pathogens

Some diseases, such as deficiency disorders, hypertension, and heart disease, are caused by diet and/or lifestyle factors. Another major cause of human disease are **pathogens**—disease-causing agents—such as bacteria and viruses. **Bacteria**, which are single-celled organisms, are responsible for diseases such as strep throat, staph infections, and pneumonia; these illnesses may be treated with antibiotic medications.

On the other hand, **viruses** are not technically living things because they are only able to replicate inside a host's cells. Viral illnesses in humans include the common cold and flu, AIDS (acquired immunodeficiency syndrome), and herpes. These illnesses cannot be treated with antibiotics, but may be treated with specially-designed antiviral drugs.

Both bacteria and viruses may be spread from person to person in several different ways. Some bacteria and viruses (including the cold and flu) may be passed through the air, wherein an infected person coughs or sneezes and another individual inhales the pathogen. Some viruses, like HIV (human immunodeficiency virus), can only be transmitted through contact with infected body fluids, as in during sexual intercourse or intravenous drug use. Others, like herpes, can be spread by skin-to-skin contact. Every type of virus and bacteria has a unique profile when it comes to how it is transmitted and what type of cells it infects.

Luckily, many diseases caused by viruses (and a few caused by bacteria) can be prevented through **vaccination**. Vaccination, also called **immunization**, prevents many diseases that, not long ago, would have been very severe if not fatal, including smallpox, polio, and the measles. When a person receives a vaccine, a small amount of deactivated pathogen is injected in the body, causing the immune system to react; if the body is ever exposed to that pathogen in the future, the immune system will have a quick response to it, protecting the person from infection.

Here's how to approach an ASVAB question about human health on Test Day.

Question	Analysis
Which of the following illnesses could be treated with an antibiotic?	**Step 1:** The question asks which illness can be treated with an antibiotic.
	Step 2: Antibiotics can only treat bacterial infections, so that's what you're looking for.
	Step 3: It's hard to make a specific prediction, but you do know you're looking for an illness that's caused by bacteria.
(A) influenza (B) anemia (C) strep throat (D) herpes	**Step 4:** Influenza and herpes are caused by a virus, while anemia is caused by iron deficiency. The correct answer is (C) strep throat, which is caused by a bacteria.

Now that you've gotten an overview of the human body systems and causes of disease, try your hand at a few questions:

1. Blood pressure is generally highest in which of the following?

    (A)   veins
    (B)   capillaries
    (C)   arteries
    (D)   lungs

2. White blood cells are produced in

    (A)   the heart
    (B)   the superior vena cava
    (C)   the lymph nodes
    (D)   the bones

3. Processing of signals from the heart and regulation of cardiac rhythm occurs in

    (A)   the cerebrum
    (B)   the medulla, or brain stem
    (C)   the cerebellum
    (D)   the spinal cord

Explanations

1. **(C) arteries.** Arteries pump blood away from the heart to the rest of the body, so the blood pressure is highest in those vessels. Some veins (A) have such low blood pressure that they need valves to keep the blood from flowing the wrong way! Capillaries (B) are tiny vessels located far from the heart, so their blood pressure is relatively low as well.

2. **(D) the bones.** Reading the question stem carefully, home in on the key word, "produced." Try to make a prediction before looking at your answer choices, if possible. Although white blood cells are found in the blood, and thus pass through the vena cava and heart, they are produced in the center of bones, the marrow, so look for an answer like "marrow" or "bone."

3. **(B) the medulla, or brain stem.** Make a prediction. Regulation of the heart is an autonomic (involuntary) process. It occurs in the brain stem (medulla).

GENETICS

LEARNING OBJECTIVES

In this section you will learn to:

- describe how genetics determine the physical characteristics of an organism
- distinguish between genotype and phenotype
- recognize several health problems that are genetically inherited

Genetics is the study of heredity, the process by which characteristics are passed from parents to offspring. The basic laws of genetics have been understood since the late eighteenth century, when they were first discovered by Gregor Mendel. What Mendel discovered was that in sexual reproduction, individual heredity traits separate in the reproductive cells, so that reproductive cells, known as **gametes**, have half as many **chromosomes** (large strings of hereditary units) as normal cells. Normal body cells are called **diploid**, and gametes are called **haploid**. (Think *DIploid = Double* and *HAploid = HAlf* to help you remember it.)

In human reproduction, the female gamete (ovum) combines with the male gamete (sperm), each of which contains 23 unpaired chromosomes (haploid), to produce a zygote, which contains 23 pairs of chromosomes, or a total of 46 (diploid). **Meiosis** is the process by which gametes are created. Sexual reproduction by meiosis and fertilization results in a great deal of variation among offspring.

DNA (deoxyribonucleic acid) is the molecule that contains genetic information. It is "written" with the **genetic code**, a combination of **nucleotides** that bind together in a specific pattern that can be "read" by the cell to instruct it how to grow and behave. DNA is shaped in a **double helix**, which looks like a ladder that is twisted along its axis.

DNA Molecule

A **gene** is defined as the unit of inheritance contained within the DNA of an individual. A gene may come in several varieties, known as **alleles**. For example, in the gene that determines eye color, a person may have the allele for brown eyes or green eyes. Each of us has two **alleles** for every gene, one inherited from each parent. These alleles may or may not be alike. If the alleles are alike, that person is **homozygous** for that particular gene. If the alleles are different, the person is **heterozygous** for that particular gene. The sex of babies is determined by the genes contained on the sex chromosome. In females, the two sex chromosomes are alike and are designated as XX. In males, the sex chromosomes are heterozygous and designated as XY.

Genetic traits are inherited independently of one another, and when different traits are paired up during the fertilization of an egg, often one trait is **dominant** and the other is **recessive**. A recessive trait is only expressed if the offspring has two copies of that trait. A dominant trait, on the other hand, will be expressed even if only one copy (paired with a recessive trait) is present. For example, Huntington's disease, which causes degeneration of nerve cells and loss of muscle control, is passed from parent to offspring as a dominant trait, so only one copy is necessary for the offspring to inherit the disorder. On the other hand, cystic fibrosis, which affects the lungs, is caused by a recessive trait which must be inherited from both parents in order to cause the disease. Other disorders, such as some types of cancer, Down syndrome, and color blindness, are also caused by genetic traits.

A person's **genotype** is her genetic makeup, including both dominant and recessive alleles. A person's **phenotype** is simply how her genes express themselves in physical characteristics. Take eye color, for example. If a woman has brown eyes, then brown eyes are part of her phenotype.

Study the following example.

Question	Analysis
Suppose that black fur in rabbits is a dominant trait and that white fur in rabbits is a recessive trait. A black rabbit and a white rabbit mate and produce a white kit (that is, baby rabbit). Which of the following inferences is supported by this information?	**Step 1:** You're being asked for a deduction based on a set of facts. Two rabbits—one black and one white—have a white kit. **Step 2:** If white is a recessive trait, the white kit must have inherited a white-fur allele from each of its parents. The white rabbit parent must have two white-fur alleles, and one of those alleles was passed on to the kit. The black rabbit parent must have a black-fur allele and a white-fur allele, if it passed a white-fur allele along to the kit. **Step 3:** One of those insights will show up in the answer choices.
(A) The parents' next kit will be black. (B) The white rabbit has a recessive black-fur allele. (C) The black rabbit has a recessive white-fur allele. (D) The kit is an albino.	**Step 4:** Choice (C) matches one of the deductions made earlier and is correct. You do not have enough information to infer anything about other kits the parents might have, so choice (A) is wrong. Choice (B) contradicts the information in the question stem: you're told that black is dominant. There is no support for the claim (D) that the kit displays albinism.

CELLULAR STRUCTURES AND FUNCTIONS

LEARNING OBJECTIVES

In this section you will learn to:

- describe the broad outlines of cell theory
- identify different types of cells
- identify the structures of eukaryotic cells
- understand cell growth and cell processes

Cell theory states that (1) all living things are composed of cells, (2) cells are the basic units and structure of living things, and (3) new cells are produced from existing cells.

Cells are classified into two categories based on the absence or presence of a nucleus: **prokaryotic** and **eukaryotic**. Prokaryotic cells are characterized by not having a nucleus; bacteria are one example.

Structure of a Prokaryotic Cell

Plants, animals, fungi, and protists are made up of eukaryotic cells and characterized by having a nucleus and a more complex structure than a prokaryotic cell. The **nucleus** of a eukaryotic cell contains the genetic material of the cell. Outside the nucleus lies the **cytoplasm**, a substance which surrounds the other cell structures. The cytoplasm contains many other **organelles** (cell parts with specific functions). These include:

- **ribosomes**, which produce proteins
- **mitochondria** (singular: *mitochondrion*), which produce energy
- **endoplasmic reticulum**, which is involved in the synthesis of proteins and fats
- **Golgi apparatus**, which "packages" proteins for use
- **lyosomes**, which help the cell manage waste
- **centrosomes**, which can be important in guiding the cell's reproduction

Structure of a Eukaryotic Cell

Plant cells also have a somewhat rigid **cell wall** surrounding the membrane. The cell wall provides structure and support for cells.

Some plant cells produce their own energy through the process of photosynthesis. **Photosynthesis** is the process by which sunlight, carbon dioxide, and water react to make sugar and oxygen. It serves as a source of energy for the cells and takes place in plant cells.

Animal cells are surrounded by a semipermeable membrane which allows for the diffusion of water and oxygen from inside the cell to the outside of the cell and vice versa. These cells cannot produce their own energy and rely on consuming outside sources to provide them with the tools to make energy through cellular respiration. **Cellular respiration** is the process by which the mitochondria process sugar and oxygen to produce energy, water and carbon dioxide. Cellular respiration serves as the energy source for animal cells. If no oxygen is present, cellular respiration will result in fermentation, where either lactic acid or alcohol is produced instead of sugar.

Cell division is the process where genetic material is replicated in the nucleus. Cell division begins in interphase, where DNA replication occurs. This results in the replication of the chromosomes in the nucleus. **Chromosomes** are tightly coiled threads of DNA composed of twin strands called **chromatids**. Interphase is the longest part of cell division and is divided into periods of cell growth and DNA replication. The cell grows in size to accommodate the increase in chromosomes. Following interphase is prophase. During prophase, chromatids begin to pair up with their sister chromatids. This leads into metaphase, where the sister chromatids move to opposite poles of the cell. During the next phase, anaphase, the chromatids begin to pull apart into two separate poles. The cell becomes elongated during this phase, which makes it very easy to identify. During telophase, the two new nuclei become completely separated. The final phase in cell division is cytokinesis, where the cytoplasm and cell membranes complete their separation and two daughter cells are formed.

Normally, cell reproduction is closely regulated by genetic signals in the cell that tell it when to stop reproducing; **cancer** occurs when the signals are mutated and cells can grow without limit. Factors such as smoking, sun exposure, and genetic mutations can cause damage to cells and may lead to cancer. The most common type of cancer is skin cancer, caused by exposure to UV rays in sunlight.

Study the example below to see how an expert test taker would approach an ASVAB question about cellular functions.

Question	Analysis
Cellular fermentation takes place when	**Step 1:** The question is asking the circumstances during which cellular fermentation takes place.
	Step 2: There is notthing to simplify here.
	Step 3: Cellular fermentation occurs when no oxygen is present. When oxygen is not present, the cell is in anaerobic respiration and produces either alcohol or lactic acid instead of ATP.
(A) no oxygen is present during cellular respiration (B) oxygen is present during cellular respiration (C) lactic acid is present during cellular respiration (D) yeast is present during cellular respiration	**Step 4:** Based on the prediction above, select answer choice (A).

Try your hand at the problem below:

In which organelle does DNA replication take place?

(A) mitochondria
(B) ribosome
(C) nucleus
(D) endoplasmic reticulum

Explanation

Answer choice (C) is correct. The nucleus contains all genetic material. DNA replication takes place in the nucleus during interphase. Interphase is the longest phase of mitosis.

ECOLOGY

LEARNING OBJECTIVES

In this section you will learn to:

- understand the relationship between organisms and their physical environment
- understand the relationships between living organisms

Ecology is the study of the interrelationships between organisms and their physical surroundings. Just as biologists classify organisms according to terminology that goes from the general to the specific, ecologists employ a similar set of terminology:

Biosphere: The zone of planet Earth where life naturally occurs, including land, water, and air, extending from the deep crust to the lower atmosphere.

Biome: A major life zone of interrelated species bound together by similar climate, vegetation, and animal life.

Ecosystem: A system made up of a community of animals, plants, and other organisms as well as the abiotic (non-living) aspects of its environment.

Community: The collection of all ecologically connected species in an area.

Population: A group of organisms of the same species living in the same region.

An ecosystem can be large or small, and can include both pristine and highly developed areas. An ecosystem contains a community, and this community may contain many populations of organisms. The various populations within a community fall into one of several roles in the food chain.

Producers (mainly plant life): Also known as **autotrophs**, they make their own food via photosynthesis.

Decomposers (bacteria and fungi): Also known as **saprotrophs**, they break down organic matter and release minerals back into the soil.

Scavengers (many insects and certain vertebrates, such as vultures and jackals): These animals exhibit characteristics of decomposers by consuming refuse and decaying organic matter, especially **carrion**, or decaying flesh. Similar organisms called **detritivores** consume the small pieces of decaying organic matter called detritus that are too small for most scavengers to want.

Consumers (most animals): Also known as **heterotrophs**, refers to animals that consume other organisms to survive. Consumers are divided into three types:

Primary consumers: Also known as **herbivores**, they subsist on producers, such as plants. Examples include grasshoppers, deer, cows, squirrels, and rabbits.

Secondary consumers: Also known as **carnivores** or predators, they subsist mainly on primary consumers. Examples of secondary consumers include birds of prey (such as owls and falcons), foxes, and snakes. Some secondary consumers are also **omnivores**, meaning they consume producers and consumers as well. Examples include chickens, rats, some lizards, and sea otters.

Tertiary consumers: Also known as **top carnivores**, they are capable of eating secondary consumers. Many tertiary consumers are also **omnivores**. Examples include lions, wolves, and sharks, as well as human beings.

The diagram below shows roughly the relationships between these groups in an ecosystem:

Hierarchy of Consumers

Food chains are a basic way to see the levels in an ecosystem. However, food webs can show more complex relationships that exist amongst the levels. In the example below, the organism to which an arrow points might eat the organism on the other end of that arrow.

A Food Web

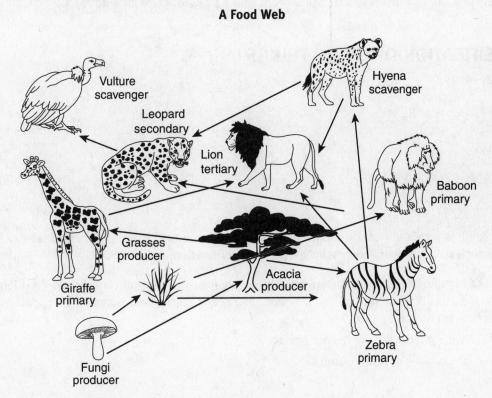

Study this example of a solid approach to an ecology question.

Question	Analysis
Which of the following is the term for the zone that extends from the Earth's crust through the lower atmosphere and which encompasses all life on Earth?	**Step 1:** The question is asking for the name of the zone containing all life on Earth.
	Step 2: Not much to simplify here.
	Step 3: The question describes the biosphere.
(A) biome (B) biosphere (C) ecosystem (D) stratosphere	**Step 4:** Based on the prediction above, select answer choice (B). The biosphere begins in the deep crust of the Earth and includes all areas where life can exist – land, water and air. An ecosystem and a biome are smaller areas. The stratosphere is higher than the lower atmosphere.

Try your hand at the problem below:

Which of the following is a decomposer?

(A) vulture
(B) fly
(C) oak tree
(D) bacteria

Explanation

Choose (D). Bacteria are considered a decomposer because they break down dead matter and release it back to the soil as minerals. Flies and vultures would be scavengers, and a tree would be an autotroph.

THE CLASSIFICATION OF LIVING THINGS

LEARNING OBJECTIVES

In this section you will learn to:

- describe the major classifications of life and how they differ

All living things fall into a careful classification scheme that goes from the broadest level of similarity (**domain**) to the narrowest (**species**). The classification scheme has seven different levels. They are:

Domain: the broadest category; there are only three domains. This level of classification is a fairly recent change to the classification system. You may not have been taught about domains in school, and you may or may not see them on the ASVAB.

Kingdom: which contains several related *phyla*.

Phylum: which contains several related *classes*.

Class: which contains several related *orders*.

Order: which contains several related *families*.

Family: which contains several related *genera*.

Genus: which contains several related *species*.

Species: which contains organisms so similar that they can only reproduce with one another to create viable fertile offspring.

For example, this is the classification of human beings:

Domain - Eukaryota
    Kingdom - Animalia
        Phylum - Chordata
            Class - Mammalia
                Order - Primates
                    Family - Hominidae
                        Genus - Homo
                            Species - Sapiens

> Remember: **Domain Kingdom Phylum Class Order Family Genus Species.**
> Here's a mnemonic to help you: **Dear King Philip Come Over For Good Soup.**
> (Remember, Domain is a fairly recent addition to the classification system, so you may or may not see it on the ASVAB.)

The three domains are:

Eukaryota: All living things whose cells have nuclei are in this domain. Almost all multi-celled organisms (including plants, animals, and fungi) are in this domain.

Bacteria and **Archaea:** Both of these domains contain single-celled organisms whose cells do not have nuclei. Living things in the two domains are distinguishable by metabolic and chemical differences.

The five or six kingdoms are:

Kingdom	Description
Monera (sometimes broken into two kingdoms, one of which belongs to domain Bacteria and one of which belongs to domain Archaea)	Includes bacteria, cyanobacteria (blue green algae), and primitive pathogens. Considered the most primitive kingdom, it represents prokaryotic (as opposed to eukaryotic) life forms—that is, the cells of Moneran organisms do not have distinct nuclei.
Protista	Protista are the simplest eukaryotes (that is, their cells have nuclei). Includes protozoa, unicellular and multicellular algae, and slime and water slime molds. Ancestor organisms to plants, animals, and fungi; many can move around by means of flagella. Some are also photosynthetic.

Kingdom	Description
Fungi	Includes mushrooms, bread molds, and yeasts. Fungi lack the ability to photosynthesize; they are called decomposers, breaking down and feeding on dead protoplasm (extracellular digestion).
Plantae	Have the ability to photosynthesize, so they are called producers. There are four major phyla, Bryophyta, or mosses, and Tracheophyta, which have vascular systems, gymnosperms, and angiosperms.
Animalia	Produce energy by consuming other organisms, so they are called consumers. Can be either vertebrates (which belong to phylum Chordata) or invertebrates such as mollusks, arthropods, sponges, coelenterates, worms, etc. Human beings belong to the kingdom Animalia.

There are many, many phyla (the plural of *phylum*), classes, orders, genera (the plural of *genus*), and species. *If* you have additional time before Test Day *and* you have mastered all of the other subject tests *and* maximizing your General Science score is crucial to your career goals, you may choose to use Internet sources to learn more about some of the largest phyla, classes, etc. Otherwise, that study is unlikely to be the best use of your time.

Study how an expert test taker would approach a general science question about the classification of living things:

Question	Analysis
Mammals are part of the kingdom	**Step 1:** The question is asking you to determine which kingdom mammals belong to.
	Step 2: There is nothing to simplify here.
	Step 3: Mammals are animals; they belong to kingdom Animalia.
(A) Animalia (B) Mammalia (C) Protista (D) Monera	**Step 4:** Based on the prediction above, you would select answer choice (A).

Try one on your own.

5. Not including domains, the correct order of the categories of taxonomy, from most specific to most general, is:

   (A) Species, Genus, Family, Order, Class, Phylum, Kingdom
   (B) Kingdom, Phylum, Class, Order, Family, Genus, Species
   (C) Kingdom, Phylum, Order, Class, Family, Genus, Species
   (D) Species, Genus, Order, Family, Class, Phylum, Kingdom

Explanation

"Species" is the most specific category in taxonomy and "Kingdom" is the most general (not including domains), so choice (A) is correct. Choice (B) lists the categories from largest to smallest. Choice (C) almost does the same but confuses Order and Class. Choice (D) is incorrect because it switches the places of "Order" and "Family."

LIFE SCIENCE PRACTICE QUESTIONS

1. Which of the following describes the proper pathway of blood through the heart?

   (A) vena cava → right atrium → right ventricle → pulmonary artery → pulmonary vein → left atrium → left ventricle → aorta

   (B) vena cava → right atrium → right ventricle → pulmonary vein → pulmonary artery → left atrium → left ventricle → aorta

   (C) vena cava → right atrium → left atrium → pulmonary artery → pulmonary vein → left atrium → left ventricle → aorta

   (D) vena cava → right atrium → left atrium → pulmonary vein → pulmonary artery → left atrium → left ventricle → aorta

2. Most human digestion takes place in the

   (A) esophagus
   (B) stomach
   (C) small intestine
   (D) large intestine

3. Which blood type can be donated to anyone?

   (A) A positive
   (B) B negative
   (C) O negative
   (D) AB positive

4. A typical human gamete contains

   (A) 2 chromosomes
   (B) 23 chromosomes
   (C) 46 chromosomes
   (D) 92 chromosomes

5. Which of the following is an example of a primary consumer?

   (A) moss
   (B) mushroom
   (C) jackal
   (D) deer

6. How many domains are recognized in taxonomy?

   (A) 3
   (B) 5
   (C) 7
   (D) 9

7. Which of the following best describes the difference between eukaryotic cells and prokaryotic cells?

   (A) Prokaryotic cells do not have nuclei.
   (B) Prokaryotic cells are only found in plants.
   (C) Eukaryotic cells are only found in plants.
   (D) Eukaryotic cells do not have nuclei.

8. The cell membrane that surrounds an animal cell is a

   (A) non-permeable structure
   (B) semi-permeable structure
   (C) fully permeable structure
   (D) cell wall

Answers and Explanations

1. **(A)** **vena cava → right atrium → right ventricle → pulmonary artery → pulmonary vein → left atrium → left ventricle → aorta**
To make a prediction on this question, think about what kind of blood flows into and out of the heart.

2. **(C)** **small intestine** The small intestine is the largest digestive organ and does the most work in breaking down food into materials the body can use.

3. **(C)** **O negative** Type O negative blood, also known as the "universal donor" type, can be donated to anyone.

4. **(B)** **23 chromosomes.** A typical human gamete contains half the number of chromosomes as a normal cell, or 23.

5. **(D)** **deer** A deer is an example of a primary consumer; that is, an animal that consumes only vegetation.

6. **(A)** **3** There are three domains in taxonomy: Eukaryota, Bacteria, and Archaea.

7. **(A)** **Prokaryotic cells do not have nuclei.** Prokaryotic cells, such as bacteria, do not have nuclei. Their genetic material is contained within main part of the cell body. Eukaryotic cells do contain nuclei where all genetic material is contained. Eukaryotic cells are plant, animal, fungi and protist cells.

8. **(B)** **semi-permeable structure** Animal cells have semi-permeable membranes which allow for osmosis. Osmosis is essential for maintaining homeostasis within the cell and preventing it from shrinking or bursting.

PART II: EARTH AND SPACE SCIENCE

Earth and space science is the study of the Earth and the universe around it. For purposes of the ASVAB, it's helpful to know a few facts about our planet and the solar system in which it travels.

GEOLOGY

LEARNING OBJECTIVES

In this section you will learn to:

- identify the layers of the Earth and types of rocks
- describe the general principles of plate tectonics
- describe the composition of the Earth

Geology is the science that deals with the history and composition of the Earth and its life, especially as recorded in rocks.

Structure of Earth

In part by studying rocks, scientists have been able to determine that the Earth is made up of three layers. The outermost layer, or **crust**, comprises roughly one percent of the total Earth's volume. It varies in thickness from 10 kilometers to as much as 80 kilometers. Beneath the crust lies the **mantle**, which comprises more than 75 percent of the Earth's volume. Roughly 3,500 kilometers thick, the mantle contains mostly iron, magnesium, and calcium, and is much hotter and denser than the Earth's surface because temperature and pressure inside the Earth increase with depth.

At the center of the Earth lies the **core**, which is nearly twice as dense as the mantle because its composition is metallic (iron-nickel alloy) rather than stony. The Earth's core contains two distinct parts: a 2,300-kilometer-thick liquid **outer core** and a 1,200-kilometer-radius solid **inner core**.

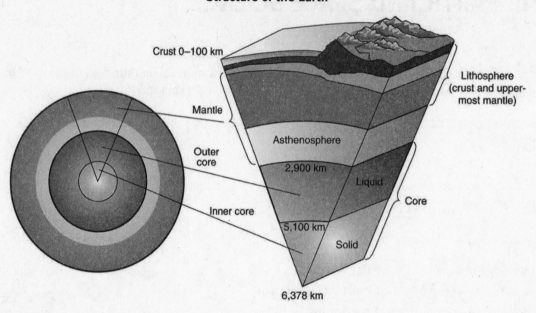

Structure of the Earth

Crust 0–100 km

Mantle

Outer core

Inner core

Lithosphere (crust and upper-most mantle)

Asthenosphere

2,900 km

Liquid

Core

5,100 km

Solid

6,378 km

Plate Tectonics

As noted, the interior of the Earth is quite hot, somewhere between 3,000 and 4,000°C. This heat is generally prevented from escaping thanks to the solid rock in the Earth's upper mantle and crust. The crust and the rigid upper part of the mantle (the **lithosphere**) consist of approximately 30 separate pieces called **plates**. These plates move very slowly upon the more movable mantle beneath (the **asthenosphere**), and this has caused the continental landmasses to drift slowly apart over the course of hundreds of millions of years.

Along the edges of these plates are **fault lines**. (Fault lines are simply places where the plates slide relative to each other.) When plates slide relative to each other along fault lines earthquakes can occur. When an earthquake occurs, scientists use the **Richter scale** or the **moment magnitude scale** to measure its intensity. The Richter scale is perhaps more familiar to most people. The Richter scale begins at 1, with each larger integer representing a magnitude that is about 10 times greater than the preceding step.

Types of Rocks

The Earth's rocks fall into three categories, based upon how they are formed.

Rock type	How it's formed	Examples
Igneous	formed from the hardening of molten rock, or magma, which is called lava when it reaches the surface of the Earth	granite, pumice, basalt, obsidian
Sedimentary	formed by the sedimentation, or gradual depositing, of small bits of rock, clay, and other materials. Over time this deposited material becomes cemented together. Most fossils are found in sedimentary rocks.	shale, sandstone, gypsum, dolomite, coal
Metamorphic	formed when existing rock material is altered through temperature, pressure, or chemical processes	marble, slate, gneiss, quartzite

Geologic Time Scale

Most of what is known about the history of our planet has been learned by studying the fossil record found in sedimentary rock. By studying rocks, we now know that the Earth is approximately 4.6 billion years old, and that for most of that time, very few fossil traces were left. This is why the period from 4.6 billion years to 570 million years ago is called the **Precambrian eon**, meaning the period before the fossil record began. It turns out, however, that early geologists who studied the Precambrian eon were unable to recognize early, primitive fossils, and in fact life first appeared on Earth as early as 3.5 billion years ago!

Here's how a well-prepared test taker would approach a question about geology on Test Day.

Question	Analysis
Studies of the Precambrian eon have shown that life first appeared on Earth approximately	**Step 1:** The Precambrian eon allowed scientists to narrow down the time frame for life formation.
	Step 2: The Precambrian eon ranges from 4.6 billion to 570 million years ago.
	Step 3: The correct number should be within the range of the Precambrian eon.
(A) 570 million years ago. (B) 3.5 billion years ago. (C) 4.6 billion years ago. (D) 5 billion years ago.	**Step 4:** Based on the prediction above, select answer choice (B).

Now try your hand at the problem below.

Which of the following is an igneous rock?

(A) marble
(B) gypsum
(C) pumice
(D) coal

Explanation

Choice **(C)** is correct. Pumice comes from volcanic rock when it cools very quickly on the surface. The small air bubbles formed in it are visible to the naked eye. The bubbles give it its lightweight feel and increase its usefulness in many everyday products.

CYCLES IN EARTH SCIENCE

LEARNING OBJECTIVES

In this section, you will learn to:

- identify the stages of the water cycle
- identify the stages of the carbon cycle

There are several biogeochemical cycles. They all work in similar fashion in that the element or compound is released in the air and returned to the ground. The two basic cycles this section will focus on are the water cycle and the carbon cycle.

The **water cycle** is also known as the **hydrologic cycle**. It involves the movement of water in all states of matter (solid, liquid and gas) through the atmosphere and back to the Earth. As water from the surface of the ocean and other bodies of water **evaporates** (becomes a gas), it rises into the atmosphere. Water also evaporates into the atmosphere from the leaves of plants; this process is known as **transpiration**. This water vapor **condenses** to form clouds. When the clouds become too heavy, they release **precipitation** in the form of a solid (snow and ice). As the precipitation falls to the surface of the Earth, it will either stay in solid form or warm up and become a liquid (rain). Some of the water that accumulates on the surface will travel down in the form of snowmelt or surface **runoff** and return to the ocean via rivers and streams. The rest of the water is absorbed into the Earth's surface and travels to the water table (a process known as **infiltration**). The water table serves as a reservoir and can be drawn upon through the digging of wells.

The Water Cycle

Carbon is one of the most common elements on our planet. The **carbon cycle** helps maintain Earth's ecosystem. Carbon gas exchange is important in maintaining a breathable atmosphere. Carbon is released through human **emissions** (manufacturing) and **respiration.** Respiration results in the release of carbon dioxide waste products into the atmosphere; an animal's breathing is one example. Respiration release is due to human release as well as release from decomposing plant and animal life. Carbon gathers in the atmosphere and is reabsorbed through plants (land and ocean) and soil.

The Carbon Cycle

Study this example of an ideal Test Day approach to this question about the carbon cycle.

Question	Analysis
Which of the following is a way in which carbon is released into the atmosphere?	**Step 1:** Think of the ways that carbon is released into the atmosphere.
	Step 2: It is released through respiration, decomposition, and manufacturing.
	Step 3: The correct answer should discuss one of those possibilities.
(A) pine trees engaging in photosynthesis (B) sediment settling in the ocean (C) dead algae decomposing (D) new plants growing in a forest	**Step 4:** Based on the prediction above, select answer choice (C).

Now try one on your own.

During the water cycle, water enters the atmosphere as a gas through

(A)   transpiration
(B)   condensation
(C)   precipitation
(D)   seepage

The correct answer is **(A)**. Water enters the atmosphere through the process of transpiration and evaporation. *Transpiration* specifically refers to water movement through plants. *Condensation* happens when water vapor condenses together to form *precipitation*, which then falls back the Earth as rain or snow. *Seepage* is the movement of water through soil.

METEOROLOGY

LEARNING OBJECTIVES

In this section you will learn to:

- identify layers of the Earth's atmosphere
- describe different types of fronts and clouds

Meteorology is not just the study of weather, but of the atmosphere and atmospheric phenomena in general.

Earth's Atmosphere

The first thing you should know is that there are several layers to the atmosphere, beginning here on the surface of the Earth and continuing up several thousand kilometers above us. The layers are:

Troposphere: The troposphere is the lowest level of the atmosphere, where all weather takes place; it is a region of rising and falling packets of air. Depending on the latitude and the season, it can range from 6 to 17 kilometers thick. Most of the air surrounding the Earth, which is roughly 79 percent nitrogen and 21 percent oxygen, is found in the troposphere.

Stratosphere: Above the troposphere is the stratosphere, where airflow is mostly horizontal. The thin **ozone layer** in the upper stratosphere has a high concentration of ozone, a particularly reactive form of oxygen. This layer is primarily responsible for absorbing the ultraviolet radiation from the Sun. As you enter the stratosphere, the temperature is about −60°C.

Mesosphere: Above the stratosphere is the mesosphere, which extends to about 90 kilometers above the Earth. As you enter the mesosphere, the temperature starts to drop again, to as low as −90°C. This is where we see "falling stars," meteoroids that fall to the Earth and burn up in the atmosphere.

Thermosphere: Beyond the mesosphere, temperatures actually increase with altitude in the thermosphere because there is little matter to deflect solar radiation. Temperatures as high as 2000° Celsius have been recorded in the thermosphere.

Earth's Atmosphere

Fronts

Differences in air pressure cause wind and the movement of air masses of different temperatures toward each other. When a warm air mass overtakes a cold air mass, you have a **warm front**. As the warm air advances, it rides over the cold air ahead of it, which is heavier. As the warm air rises, the water vapor in it condenses into clouds that can produce rain, snow, sleet, or freezing rain—often all four.

When a cold air mass overtakes a warm air mass, you have a **cold front**. Most cold fronts are preceded by a line of precipitation as they roar across an area. However, some cold fronts produce very little or no precipitation as they move. The only sign that a front has moved through your area is a sudden change in winds and temperature.

Sometimes two air masses meet and neither is displaced. Instead, the two fronts push against each other in a stalemate. This is called a **stationary front**. Stationary fronts often cause cloudy, wet weather that can last a week or more.

Clouds

Clouds come in different varieties based on their shape, size, and altitude. The three main types are:

Stratus clouds are low-hanging, broad, flat clouds that blanket the sky. The lowest of low clouds, when they occur on the ground, are called fog. Dark stratus clouds indicate that rain will soon occur.

Cumulus clouds are massive clouds that are puffy, like popcorn, with relatively flat bottoms and rounded tops. When cumulus clouds darken, you can expect heavy rain.

Cirrus clouds are the thin, wispy clouds that occur much higher in the atmosphere, at elevations of 20,000 feet or more.

Study the following example, which illustrates an expert approach to a meteorology question.

Question	Analysis
The weather report indicates a warm air front is moving in. Which of the following is most likely to occur as a result of that warm air front?	**Step 1:** Think of what happens when a warm front comes in.
	Step 2: A warm front forms when warm air overtakes a cold air mass. Warm air is heavier than cold air and rises.
	Step 3: When warm, heavy air rises, clouds will form. Clouds mean precipitation, so the answer choice will involve precipitation.
(A) a sudden change in temperature (B) freezing rain (C) hurricanes (D) weather stalemate	**Step 4:** Based on the prediction above, select answer choice (B). Warm air fronts generally result in some form of precipitation, though not a full blown storm like a hurricane (which is a specialized storm that develops over warm ocean water). A sudden change in temperature is the result of a cold air front and a stalemate is caused by a stationary front.

Try one on your own.

The sky is filled with dark, puffy clouds, and there is a thunderstorm approaching. What type of clouds are you seeing?

(A) cirrus
(B) stratus
(C) cumulus
(D) stratocumulus

Explanation

The correct answer is **(C)**. Cumulus clouds are often referred to as thunderheads. They have high fluffy peaks that are perfect for generating static electricity and producing thunderstorms. A few scattered cumulus clouds are usually not a threat of a storm, but if several groups of them converge, they could produce heavy rain, thunder and lightning.

OUR SOLAR SYSTEM

LEARNING OBJECTIVES

In this section you will learn to:

- understand the structure of the solar system
- understand the relationship of the Earth to other planets and solar bodies
- understand how Earth's position relative to the Sun produces Earth's seasons

Our solar system consists of one star, which we call the Sun, eight planets and all their moons, several thousand minor planets called asteroids, and an equally large number of comets.

The Sun

Our **Sun** is classified as a **G2V** star, or **yellow dwarf**. G2 stars are approximately 6,000° C at the surface, are yellow, and contain many neutrally charged metals such as iron, magnesium, and calcium. The "V" indicates that the Sun is a dwarf star, or fairly small by the standards of stars. The Sun's age is calculated to be around 4.7 billion years, which is only slightly older than the Earth itself.

Although a dwarf in comparison to other stars, the Sun contains almost 99.9 percent of the mass of our solar system. Like all stars, the Sun is a gigantic ball of superheated plasma, kept hot by atomic reactions emanating from its center. The temperature at the core of our Sun is thought to be about 15,000,000° C; temperatures at the surface range between 4,000° and 15,000° C. The diameter of the Sun is about 1.4 million kilometers, or more than 100 times that of Earth, and its surface area is approximately 12,000 times that of Earth.

The Planets and Other Phenomena

The four planets closest to the Sun—**Mercury**, **Venus**, **Earth**, and **Mars**—are called **terrestrial planets**, meaning they are similar to our own planet in composition, with inner metal cores and surfaces of rock. Earth and Mars are the only terrestrial planets that have moons of their own, although the moons of Mars are much smaller than our own Moon. Earth is the largest of the terrestrial planets.

The four planets beyond Mars—**Jupiter**, **Saturn**, **Uranus**, and **Neptune**—are referred to as the **outer planets**. They also all have rings, most notably so on Saturn. The rings of Saturn, and most likely the other planets as well, are composed mostly of ice crystals. **Pluto**, once considered the ninth planet, is no longer categorized by scientists as a true planet. You may have learned a mnemonic (or memory trick) for the planets in school; here's one that allows for the omission of Pluto: *My Very Educated Mother Just Served Us Nachos.* (In the diagram below, Pluto is included, but remember that it is no longer considered a planet. Also, note that the diagram below is not drawn to scale.)

The Solar System

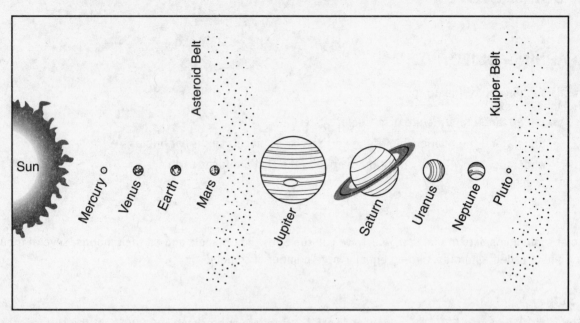

In addition, the solar system contains thousands of small bodies such as **asteroids** and **comets**. Smaller fragments of asteroids and particles shed by comets are known as **meteoroids**, and when they fall into the Earth's gravitational field, they are seen as "falling stars," called **meteors**, as they burn up in the Earth's mesosphere. Those meteoroids that make it to the Earth's surface are called **meteorites**. A belt of asteroids lies between Mars and Jupiter. The **Kuiper Belt**, a much larger collection of asteroids and other objects left over from the formation of the solar system, lies beyond the known planets.

Comets are sometimes called "dirty snowballs" or "icy mudballs." They are a mixture of ices (both water and frozen gases) and dust that for some reason didn't get incorporated into planets when the solar system was formed. Comets are invisible except when they are near the Sun. When they are near the Sun and active, comets have highly visible **tails**, up to several hundred million kilometers long, composed of plasma and laced with rays and streamers caused by interactions with the solar wind.

By far the most important body in the solar system aside from the Sun, as it relates to life on Earth, is our own **Moon**. Because of the gravitational pull that exists between the Moon and Earth, we have **tides**. High tides occur twice a day, when the Moon is at the points closest to and farthest from the affected mass of water. It is suspected that life would never have evolved on land without the constant ebbing and flowing of the oceanic tides on coastal areas.

Earth orbits the Sun once per year. Because the Earth is somewhat tilted on its axis, the northern pole is tilted toward the Sun and the southern pole is tilted away from it for part of the year. That portion of the year is summer in the northern hemisphere and winter in the southern hemisphere. For part of the year that situation is reversed: that period is summer in the northern hemisphere and winter in the southern hemisphere. In between summer and winter, the Earth is tilted so that neither the northern pole nor the southern pole is pointing toward the Sun. These periods are spring and fall. Study the diagram below.

Earth's Seasons

Imagine how terrified ancient humans must have been when their view of the sun or the moon became partially or completely obscured during an eclipse. Today we understand how eclipses occur and can predict them well in advance.

A solar eclipse occurs when the moon passes directly between the Earth and the sun during daylight hours. The relatively small shadow cast by the moon onto the surface of the Earth can either partially or totally obscure the sun. Because the moon is moving in its orbit around the earth and the earth is rotating on its axis, solar eclipses are brief and move across the face of the Earth rapidly.

A lunar eclipse occurs when the Earth passes directly between the sun and the moon and casts a shadow on the moon. Therefore, a lunar eclipse can be seen from any place on Earth where the moon is above the horizon. Like solar eclipses, lunar eclipses can be either partial or total. Because the Earth has a much larger shadow than does the moon, lunar eclipses last much longer than their solar counterparts.

Study this example of how an expert test taker would approach an ASVAB question about the solar system.

Question	Analysis
Which of the following is a characteristic of terrestrial planets?	**Step 1:** The Earth is a terrestrial planet. What are its major characteristics?
	Step 2: The Earth has a solid, rocky surface. There are many layers to it that include a solid inner core.
	Step 3: The answer choice will list one of those characteristics.
(A) an inner core made of ice crystals (B) a surface temperature similar to that of Earth (C) an inner core of metal (D) a surface composed of gasses	**Step 4:** Based on the prediction above, select answer choice (C). Terrestrial planets have an inner core of metal and a rocky surface. Outer planets have inner cores of ice crystals.

Try this one on your own.

A "falling star" is also known as a

(A)   meteor
(B)   asteroid
(C)   comet
(D)   meteorite

The correct answer is **(A)**. A "falling star" is a meteor seen when a meteoroid is burning up in the Earth's atmosphere. If the meteoroid reaches the surface of the Earth, it is then called a meteorite.

EARTH AND SPACE SCIENCE PRACTICE QUESTIONS

1. The ozone layer is found in the

   (A) troposphere
   (B) stratosphere
   (C) mesosphere
   (D) thermosphere

2. What is the layer that is located immediately beneath the Earth's crust?

   (A) inner core
   (B) plates
   (C) mantle
   (D) outer core

3. The clouds that occur at the highest altitudes are called

   (A) cirrus
   (B) cumulus
   (C) nimbus
   (D) stratus

4. Life on Earth has existed for approximately

   (A) 4.6 billion years
   (B) 3.5 billion years
   (C) 2.5 billion years
   (D) 544 million years

5. Which of the following is most responsible for the oceanic tides?

   (A) the gravitational pull of the Sun on the Earth
   (B) the gravitational pull of the Moon on the Earth
   (C) the heat of the Sun
   (D) the magnetic pull of the poles

6. The most common element in the Earth's atmosphere is

   (A) helium
   (B) hydrogen
   (C) nitrogen
   (D) oxygen

7. Which of the following is a terrestrial planet?

   (A) Mars
   (B) Jupiter
   (C) Saturn
   (D) Neptune

8. The air in the troposphere is made up primarily of

   (A) oxygen
   (B) helium
   (C) carbon dioxide
   (D) nitrogen

9. In which level of the atmosphere does all weather take place?

   (A) troposphere
   (B) stratosphere
   (C) mesosphere
   (D) thermosphere

10. Air flow in the stratosphere is primarily

    (A) horizontal
    (B) vertical
    (C) clockwise
    (D) counterclockwise

Answers and Explanations

1. **(B) stratosphere** The ozone layer is found in the upper stratosphere.

2. **(C) mantle** The mantle lies beneath the Earth's crust.

3. **(A) cirrus.** Cirrus clouds are found at the highest altitudes of all clouds.

4. **(B) 3.5 billion years** Life on Earth has existed for approximately 3.5 billion years.

5. **(B) the gravitational pull of the Moon on Earth.** The oceanic tides are caused by the gravitational pull of the Moon on the Earth.

6. **(C) nitrogen** Nitrogen accounts for about 77 percent of the composition of the atmosphere.

7. **(A) Mars** Terrestrial planets are those closest in composition to the Earth. Not surprisingly, they are also the inner planets and those closest in proximity to the Earth. Terrestrial planets have an inner core of metal and rocky surfaces similar to the Earth, though their atmospheric characteristics can be vastly different from the Earth.

8. **(D) nitrogen** The air in the troposphere is approximately 79% nitrogen and 21% oxygen. This is the layer of air closest to the Earth's surface.

9. **(A) troposphere** The troposphere is the lowest level of the atmosphere and where all weather affecting Earth takes place. This is where clouds form and from where precipitation falls.

10. **(A) horizontal** Air flow in the stratosphere is primarily horizontal. This allows for optimal air circulation at that level.

PART III: PHYSICAL SCIENCE

Scientists would know very little about our solar system without an understanding of physics and chemistry, collectively known as the physical sciences. This section will cover those two disciplines as well as the system of measurement used in both.

MEASUREMENT

LEARNING OBJECTIVES

In this section you will learn to:

- employ the common units and basic conventions of the metric system
- relate the major temperature scales (Fahrenheit, Celsius, and Kelvin)

Scientists don't use British measurement units such as ounces, miles, and gallons; instead, they use the **metric system.** The metric system has been used throughout most of this chapter, but it's time for a more detailed examination. The key idea of the metric system is to designate one base unit for every kind of measurement, and then make bigger or smaller units by adding prefixes to it (groups of letters added to the beginnings of words, like *anti-* or *pro-*). For example, the base unit for **length** in metric is called the **meter (m)**, which is just over a yard (about 39.4 inches).

To measure small things like firearm ammunition or large things like the distance between cities, a prefix is added. Milli- means $\frac{1}{1,000}$, so a **millimeter (mm)** is $\frac{1}{1,000}$ the size of a meter. A 9 mm handgun like the Beretta M9 (the US military's standard sidearm) fires rounds that are .009 m in bullet diameter. A **centimeter (cm)** is 10 times as big as a millimeter, and there are about 2.54 cm in one inch. A **kilometer (km)** is 1000 meters. Metric measurements typically have two- or three-letter symbols (like mm, cm, and km), which are usually the first letter of the prefix followed by the first letter of the base unit.

Prefix	Symbol	Value relative to base unit
mega	M	10^6 or 1,000,000
kilo	k	10^3 or 1,000
hecto	h	10^2 or 100
deka	da	10^1 or 10
base (no prefix)	—	1
deci	d	10^{-1} or $\frac{1}{10}$ or 0.1
centi	c	10^{-2} or $\frac{1}{100}$ or 0.01
milli	m	10^{-3} or $\frac{1}{1,000}$ or 0.001
micro	μ (the Greek letter mu, to avoid confusion with "mega")	10^{-6} or $\frac{1}{1,000,000}$ or 0.000001

The most common prefixes (and the most likely to come up on the ASVAB) are milli-, centi-, kilo-, and sometimes mega-. The other prefixes on the table are included for the sake of completion, but it's not important to memorize them, nor other prefixes beyond those listed here. Know both the prefix names as well as their symbols, as the symbol (for example, **km** for **kilometer**) is more likely to come up in a calculation question than the name.

Applying the prefix scheme to other measurements, **mass** is measured in a base unit of **grams (g)**. Therefore, large objects can be measured in **kilograms (kg)**, and very small things can be measured in **milligrams (mg)**; for example, the amount of certain minerals and nutrients per serving as listed on a food package's nutritional information tend to be in milligrams. There are approximately 28.3 grams in an ounce, and a mass of one kilogram will have a weight of approximately 2.2 pounds (at the surface of the Earth).

Volume is the measurement of three-dimensional space. A cube (square box) which is one centimeter on a side can be called just that: a **cubic centimeter (cc)**; but it can also be called a **milliliter (mL)**. The definition of the milliliter automatically implies the **liter (L)**: the prefix means a milliliter is one-thousandth of a liter, which is the same as saying a liter is equal to one thousand milliliters. A liter is equal to slightly more than a quart in liquid measure, or about 33.8 ounces, with about 3.79 liters in a gallon.

Time is measured in **seconds (s)** and metric prefixes are used when smaller units are required (as in milliseconds). However, **minutes (min)** and **hours (h)** are also common.

Finally, the metric system equivalent of temperature is the **Celsius scale**, also known as **degrees centigrade**. According to the **Fahrenheit scale**, which is more familiar to most people in the United States, water freezes at 32°F and boils at 212°F. On the Celsius scale, water freezes at 0°C and boils at 100°C. The general equations for converting from the Fahrenheit scale to the Celsius scale, or vice versa, are as follows:

$$F° = \frac{9}{5}C° + 32$$

$$C° = \frac{5}{9}(F° - 32)$$

Finally, there is one other temperature scale commonly used by scientists, known as the **Kelvin scale**, or the **absolute zero scale**. Absolute zero is the temperature at which matter has no heat and its molecules are completely still; in theory, absolute zero is the lowest temperature possible. On the Kelvin scale, absolute zero is set at 0 K, which is equal to −273°C. Otherwise, the Kelvin scale uses the same increments as degrees Celsius, so that water freezes at 273 K and boils at 373 K. Note that there is no degree symbol when writing out temperatures in the Kelvin scale.

The unit types discussed here are not exhaustive. Different base units come up in different areas of science, but the beauty of metric standards is that the value of each prefix is a constant. Metric prefixes will be applied in new contexts elsewhere in this chapter, and again in chapter 10: Electronics Information.

Question	Analysis
In a chemistry lab, the experimental procedure says to add 50 mL of room temperature water to a beaker. How many liters are in 50 mL?	**Step 1:** The question asks for the value of 50 mL converted to L units.
	Step 2: The prefix milli- has a value of 0.001 of the base unit. Since L are 1,000 times larger than mL, the equivalent number in L will be 1,000 times smaller than the number in mL. The decimal will move by three steps. $$50 \text{ mL} = \frac{50}{1,000} \text{ L}$$ 0.05 L is equivalent to 50 mL.
	Step 3: The solution is 0.05 L.
(A) 50000 L (B) 5 L (C) 0.5 L (D) 0.05 L	**Step 4:** Answer choice (D) is correct.

Now you try one:

In an experiment, you must measure out 0.13 kg of sodium chloride. However, your instruments are only set to work with gram units. Convert 0.13 kg into grams.

(A)   1.3 g
(B)   13 g
(C)   100 g
(D)   130 g

Explanation

Choice **(D)** is correct. Since there are 1,000 g in 1 kg, and this is a conversion to the smaller unit value, simply move the decimal place three places to the right (once for every 0 in 1,000).

PHYSICS

Physics is the science dealing with the properties, changes, and interactions of matter and energy. There are many branches of physics, including mechanics, thermodynamics, magnetism, optics, and electricity. This review will cover only the physics that might appear on the General Science section of the ASVAB.

MASS *vs.* WEIGHT

In physics, words that are often used imprecisely in everyday speech have very strict definitions. For example, the words **mass** and **weight** are often used interchangeably, when in fact they have very different meanings. Mass is defined as the amount of matter that something has, whereas weight is defined as the force exerted on an object's mass by gravity. A person can become nearly weightless in deep space, far from the nearest gravity-producing objects, but that person still has all her mass.

Motion

Velocity is the rate at which an object changes position. Change in position is called **displacement** and velocity is defined as the total displacement per unit time. It can be calculated as **velocity = displacement of an object ÷ time**.

$$\vec{v} = \frac{\vec{d}}{t}$$

In physics, velocity is called a **vector quantity**, meaning it is fully described by both a magnitude *and* a direction. For example, a car traveling west that covers fifteen meters in two seconds would be described as having a velocity of 7.5 m/s (that is, miles per second) west. Displacement is also a vector, and both symbols often have a little arrow above them to signify this. Time is not a vector.

Momentum is a measure of the quantity of motion of an object. It corresponds to how difficult it is for a moving object to stop. The formula definition of momentum is **Momentum = mass × velocity**. In the symbolic version, momentum is represented by the letter *p*, since *m* is already in use for mass.

$$\vec{p} = m\vec{v}$$

This relationship means, for example, that a semitrailer truck moving at 5 km/h has more momentum than a person walking at the same speed, and also that you have more momentum when running than when walking. Momentum is also a vector quantity, so that two objects moving towards each other have opposite directions of momentum which will partially or completely cancel out if they collide.

Acceleration is the rate of change of velocity. **Acceleration = change in velocity ÷ change in time**. The Δ (delta) **symbol** represents change.

$$\vec{a} = \frac{\Delta \vec{v}}{t}$$

You can see acceleration in a stopped vehicle when the light turns green and the driver depresses the gas pedal. The movement of the speedometer needle shows acceleration, as the car's velocity is increasing moment by moment until it plateaus at cruising speed. Acceleration is also a vector quantity.

Question	Analysis
A sports car hits the brakes and changes its velocity from 65 m/s to 40 m/s in five seconds. What is its average rate of acceleration?	**Step 1:** The question asks for the acceleration of the car. The change in velocity and time of acceleration are required.
	Step 2: Change in velocity is the difference between the final and initial velocity. This goes into the acceleration formula. Velocity has decreased so acceleration should be negative. $\Delta \vec{v} = 40 - 65 = -25$ m/s $a = -\frac{25}{5} = -5$ m/s^2
	Step 3: The acceleration is -5 m/s^2, or the car decelerates at a rate of 5 m/s^2. The prediction has a negative value to denote a direction opposite motion.
(A) −5 m/s (B) 5 m/s (C) 8 m/s (D) 13 m/s	**Step 4:** Select choice (A).

Now try one on your own.

A bicycle initially at rest at the top of a hill accelerates as its rider coasts down. An accelerometer (which measures acceleration) records a fairly constant acceleration of 6.5 m/s². If the rider reaches the halfway point 5.2 s into the trip, what was the velocity of the bicycle and rider at this time?

(A)   33.8 m/s, uphill
(B)   1.25 m/s, uphill
(C)   33.8 m/s, downhill
(D)   1.25 m/s, downhill

Explanation

Answer choice **(C)** is correct. The change in velocity can be calculated by rearranging the acceleration equation, then written as $\Delta v = at$. Since the bicycle and rider are initially at rest, the change in velocity is equivalent to the final velocity (after 5.2 s). This also means that both acceleration and the velocity any time after movement has begun are in the downhill direction. Thus, $v2 = (6.5$ m/s2$)(5.2$ s$) = 33.8$ m/s, downhill.

Forces and Energy

Force is the push or pull that causes an object to change its speed or direction of motion.

Weight is just one example of a force; in this case, the force is due to gravity. A unit of force is called a **newton (N)**, which is the force required to impart an acceleration of one meter per second squared to a mass of one kilogram.

Work is performed on an object when there is an applied force that is along the same line of movement. **Work = force × displacement**, where the directions of force and movement are parallel.

$$W = \vec{F}\vec{d}$$

A unit of work is called a **newton-meter** or **joule (J)**. Performing work uses up **energy**, also measured in joules, which is equal to the amount of work performed. The reason we have to regularly consume food is that we are constantly using up energy: when we move, when our heart pumps blood, when our lungs inhale and exhale, when we generate warmth to maintain our body temperature, and so on. The nutritional information on food packages sometimes lists the food energy per serving in **kilojoules (kJ)** in addition to the traditional British unit of kilocalories (usually referred to, confusingly, as "calories" in everyday speech).

Power is the rate at which work is performed, or energy is converted. It's defined as the amount of work done or energy converted per unit of time and can be calculated as **Power = work ÷ time**, or **Power = (force × distance) ÷ time**.

$$P = \frac{W}{t}$$

The main unit of power is the **watt (W)**, where one watt is defined as one joule per second. Be sure not to mix up the symbol for the Watt unit with the symbol for work in the formula, nor the formula symbol for mass with the symbol for the meter unit. Units go with a number. The letter symbols in each formula stand for an unknown measurement value which will be replaced by a number during calculation.

Study this example of an expert approach to an ASVAB question about measurement in science.

Question	Analysis
Once outside the Earth's atmosphere, a space shuttle's propulsion system effects a net force of 10,000 N over a distance of 50 m. The potential energy of the craft is unchanged during this time. What increase in kinetic energy will result?	**Step 1:** The question asks for the increase in energy. Because energy and work are both measured in joules, the answer will be in joules.
	Step 2: Since work performed results in a conversion of energy from one form to another, the amount of increased kinetic energy (energy of movement) has to be the same as the amount of work done. The formula for work is known. $$W = F \times d$$ $$= (10{,}000 \text{ N}) \times (50 \text{ m})$$ $$= 500{,}000 \text{ J}$$
	Step 3: The increase in kinetic energy will be equal to the amount of work done, or 500,000 J.
(A) 0 J (B) 0.005 J (C) 200 J (D) 500,000 J	**Step 4:** Select choice (D).

Now you try your hand at a question.

A hydroelectric dam captures the energy of falling water in order to provide electrical power to the grid. The water turns a turbine a total distance of 2.5 m every 10 s. The average force the water applies to the turbine is 10,000 N. What is the average rate of hydroelectric power generation of that turbine?

(A)   25 W
(B)   2,500 W
(C)   25,000 W
(D)   250,000 W

Explanation

Choice (B) is correct. The work done by the falling water is equal to

$$W = 10{,}000 \text{ N} \times 2.5 \text{ m} = 25{,}000 \text{ J}$$

Power is the rate at which work is done, or at which energy is used, converted, or delivered.

$$P = 25{,}000 \text{ J} / 10 \text{ s} = 2{,}500 \text{ W}$$

Newton's Laws

Sir Isaac Newton was an English mathematician and physicist. In the seventeenth century, he came up with some of our most important formulas for understanding the properties of motion and gravity.

Newton's first law of motion. *An object at rest tends to stay at rest, and an object in motion tends to stay in motion at a constant speed in a straight line (constant velocity), unless acted upon by an unbalanced force.* An example of an unbalanced force—one that keeps objects in motion from staying in motion on Earth—is friction, the force that resists relative motion between two bodies in contact. This law is also known as the **law of inertia**, with **inertia** referring to the tendency of all matter to resist changes in its motion.

Newton's second law of motion. *When dealing with an object for which all existing forces are not balanced, the acceleration of that object, as produced by the net force, is in the same direction as the net force and directly proportional to the magnitude of the net force, and is inversely proportional to the object's mass.* Expressed mathematically, **acceleration = net force ÷ mass**. When using this formula, the units for each of these measures must be m/s^2, N, and kg, respectively.

$$\vec{a} = \frac{\vec{F}}{m}$$

The greater the mass of an object, the greater the force needed to overcome its inertia. This law actually encompasses the first law, as the special case of zero net force results in zero acceleration, i.e., no change in motion. Sometimes this law is written in the equivalent form, **net force = mass × acceleration**.

$$\vec{F} = m\vec{a}$$

Newton's third law of motion. *For every action, there is an equal and opposite reaction.* In other words, when an object exerts a force on another object, the second object exerts a force of the same magnitude but in the opposite direction on the first object. For example, consider what happens when a gun is fired. A bullet fires and the gun recoils. The recoil is the result of action-reaction force pairs. As the gases from the gunpowder explosion expand, the gun pushes the bullet forward and the bullet pushes the gun backward. The acceleration of the recoiling gun is, however, smaller than the acceleration of the bullet, because acceleration is inversely proportional to mass, and the bullet, as a rule, has a smaller mass than the gun, and is more easily accelerated.

In addition to those three laws of motion, Newton also developed **Newton's law of universal gravitation.** *All objects in the universe attract each other with an equal force that varies directly as a product of their masses, and inversely as a square of their distance from each other. This force is known as **gravity**.* Newton's law of universal gravitation is expressed by the following equation (where G is a constant with a value of 6.67×10^{-11} and r is the distance between the two objects' centers of mass):

$$\vec{F_g} = \frac{Gm_1m_2}{r^2}$$

Take, for example, the gravitational force between the Sun and the Earth. The following consequences follow from the law of universal gravitation:

- If the mass of the Earth were doubled, the force on the Earth would double.
- If the mass of the Sun were doubled, the force on the Earth would double.
- If the Earth were twice as far away from the Sun, the force on the Earth would be a factor of four smaller.
- The force exerted on the Earth by the Sun is equal and opposite to the force exerted on the Sun by the Earth (Newton's third law).

At the surface of the Earth, the acceleration due to gravity is 9.8 m/s^2. This bears remembering, and can be applied to the formula for Newton's second law to determine the weight (gravitational force) of any object given its mass.

Question	Analysis
A 600 g squid propels itself by firing a jet of water with a force of 21 N. The water jet is pointed in an easterly direction. What will be the acceleration of the squid?	**Step 1:** The question asks for acceleration and provides mass and force, which means Newton's laws are being used.
	Step 2: The squid is firing a jet towards the east, however the question asks about the acceleration of the squid, not the water jet. From Newton's third law, the water being pushed out in a jet to the east is simultaneously pushing on the squid to the west with the same force, which means acceleration will be westward.
	The mass of the squid must be converted to kg, and then, along with the given force, used to find magnitude of acceleration.
	Force on squid (equal and opposite) = 21 N, west
	Mass of squid = $\frac{600}{1,000}$ = 0.6 kg
	$a = \frac{21}{0.6}$ = 35 m/s^2, west
	Step 3: Acceleration is 35 m/s^2, west. Both the calculated magnitude and the reasoned direction must be included in the prediction.
(A) 0.035 m/s^2, west (B) 35 m/s^2, east (C) 35 m/s^2, west (D) 28.6 m/s^2, east	**Step 4:** Choice (C) matches the prediction.

Now try one on your own:

A man pushes a 15 kg shopping cart across a rough surface, applying a force of 15 N in the direction of motion. A friction force resists the movement of the wheels across the surface with a magnitude of 15 N opposite to the direction of motion. What will be the effect on the motion of the shopping cart?

(A) The cart will slow down at a rate of 1 m/s^2.
(B) The cart will continue its uniform velocity.
(C) The cart will speed up at a rate of 1 m/s^2.
(D) The cart will speed up at a rate of 2 m/s^2.

Explanation

The correct answer is **(B)**. Since the two forces acting on the cart are equal in magnitude but opposite in sign (direction), the net force will be equal to zero. Net force = +15 N − 15 N = 0 N. By Newton's second law, with no net force there can be no acceleration, which means, by definition, the velocity will not change.

Energy

As mentioned earlier in this chapter, **energy** can be defined as the **capacity to do work**. Many ASVAB energy questions deal with **mechanical energy**, which may be either **kinetic** or **potential**. **Kinetic energy** is the energy possessed by a moving object. **Potential energy** is the energy stored in an object as a result of its position, shape, or state.

According to the law of conservation of energy, energy can neither be created nor destroyed. Instead, it changes from one form to another. For example, if a rock is poised right at the edge of a cliff, the rock has potential energy relative to the ground at the bottom of the cliff. If the rock is dislodged and falls freely, that potential energy is converted completely to kinetic energy at the instant just before the rock hits the ground.

Sound and light energy travel in waves (although it gets complicated in the case of light). So let's take a look at the properties of waves.

Sound Waves

Sound waves are produced when an object vibrates, disturbing the medium around it, creating an outward ripple in all directions. These ripples (waves) can travel through air, liquids, and solids, but they cannot be transmitted through a **vacuum**, or empty space. Sound waves transmitted through air do not travel as fast as those transmitted through water, and those transmitted through water do not travel as fast as those transmitted through metal or wood.

The pitch of sound is directly related to the **frequency** (rate of vibration) of the sound waves. Sound waves with a high frequency (high rate of vibration) produce a high pitch. Frequency is usually measured in **hertz (Hz)**, defined as the number of repetitions per second. Sound waves with a very high pitch (high number of vibrations per second) are inaudible to humans, although they can be heard by dogs and other creatures. The typical audible hearing range for a human is from about 20 Hz to 20 kHz. Sometimes, a human (or a dog, for that matter) will perceive a sound as being a different frequency than the actual frequency of the sound. This is due to the **Doppler effect**. The Doppler effect occurs when either the source of the sound waves, the listener, or both, are moving closer together (pitch frequency sounds higher than it is) or farther apart (pitch frequency sounds lower than it is). A perfect example of the Doppler effect is the way the sound of a police or ambulance siren seems to change when it zooms by.

The Electromagnetic Spectrum

It's important to realize that visible light makes up only one small part—the visible part—of the electromagnetic spectrum. The **electromagnetic spectrum** covers all the different wavelengths and frequencies of radiation. Visible light waves fall in the middle of the electromagnetic spectrum. Starting with lowest frequency (which corresponds to the longest wavelength), the electromagnetic spectrum goes from **radio waves** to **microwaves** to **infrared waves** to **visible light** to **ultraviolet light** to **X-rays** and finally to **gamma rays**, the most active radiant energy known to exist.

Visible light breaks down into different colors as well, based upon the frequency of the waves. Red has the lowest frequency, which is why wavelengths just below the frequency of visible light are called infrared; likewise, violet has the highest frequency, so wavelengths just above the frequency of visible light are called ultraviolet.

Optics

As noted above, light, as well as the entire electromagnetic spectrum, possesses properties of waves. However, unlike sound waves, which are mechanical, light waves are electromagnetic and can travel through empty space. They also travel at much higher speeds than do sound waves. The speed of light in vacuum is 299,792,458 meters per second (or roughly 300 million meters per second or 186,000 miles per second).

Refraction

It should be noted, however, that the effective speed of light can vary depending on the material the light waves are passing through; for example, light passes more slowly through water or glass than through a vacuum. The ratio by which light is slowed down is called the **refractive index** of that medium. For instance, the refractive index of a diamond is 2.4, which means that light travels 2.4 times faster when passing through a vacuum than when traveling through a diamond.

The change in speeds causes light to bend when passing from one medium to another (like a vehicle changing direction when hitting a slick patch of road). This bending is what's called **refraction**, and light bends at a greater angle when the change in the index of refraction is greater.

Reflection

Any wave, including light, that bounces off a flat, smooth barrier follows the **law of reflection**, which states that the **angle of incidence** is equal to the **angle of reflection** as measured from a line normal (at a 90° angle) to the barrier. In the case of light, this barrier is often a mirror.

The Law of Reflection

Concave and Convex Mirrors and Lenses

Mirrors and lenses either can be flat, or they can be concave (curved in, like a cave) or convex (curved out, like a swelling). Because of the law of reflection, a **concave mirror** is also called a **converging mirror**, because the angles of incidence of rays of light parallel to the normal all converge upon a point.

Converging Mirror

If you draw the mirror away from the source of the image, the image falls out of focus as the image source nears the mirror's **focal point**, the point where the mirror's angles of incidence converge. As the image source keeps moving beyond the focal point, the image reappears in the mirror, only upside down.

A **convex mirror**, on the other hand, is known as a **diverging mirror** because it diverges the light waves that strike it.

Lenses, unlike mirrors, operate on the principle of refraction. A **convex lens**—one that is thicker in the middle than on the edges—is also called a **converging lens** because it converges parallel waves that pass through it. This type of lens is used in reading glasses to correct farsightedness, as well as in magnifying glasses, cameras, telescopes, and microscopes.

A **concave lens**—one that is thicker on the edges than it is in the middle—is also known as a **diverging lens** because it diverges the light waves that pass through it. In nearsightedness, light waves converge before they meet the retina. A nearsighted person sees objects close up but not far away. A concave lens placed before the eye bends light so that it converges further back in the eye, reaching the retina and correcting nearsightedness.

Converging Lens (a) and Diverging Lens (b)

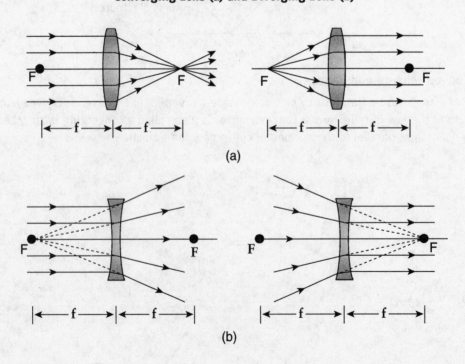

Study the approach an expert test taker would use on an ASVAB question about optics.

Question	Analysis
Through which medium will light travel the fastest?	**Step 1:** The question asks for the fastest medium for light to travel through.
	Step 2: Light is slowed down by different materials. Materials with high indices of refraction tend to be denser, and slow down light the most. The least dense material should provide light the greatest speed.
	Step 3: The answer choice with the least dense material will be correct.
(A) a vacuum (B) air (C) diamond (D) pure hydrogen	**Step 4:** Of the available choices, empty space, or (A) a vacuum, is the least dense material (or lack of material) possible. Light should travel fastest through a vacuum. In fact, the "speed of light" is defined for vacuum.

Try your hand at the question below.

"Waves" of heat can be seen above a hot stove element or flame, as the background appears to be distorted or out of focus just at that spot. This is an example of

(A)   diffraction.
(B)   refraction.
(C)   reflection.
(D)   convergence.

Explanation

Choice (B) is correct. The background can only appear distorted if the light rays are following a different path through the heated area than other light rays moving through the room. Since the light is still traveling through the space, rather than being bounced away, this is refraction, not reflection. It occurs because the air near the heat source is of a different density, resulting in different indices of refraction in different patches of air.

Heat

There are three means by which heat energy may be transferred from one object to another: **conduction**, **convection**, and **radiation.** Heat energy is always transferred from warmer to cooler environments.

Conduction is the simplest method of heat transfer. It is accomplished by direct contact, such as placing your finger on a hot iron, which we recommend that you not try at home. Metals are generally good **conductors** of heat. Other materials, such as wood, Styrofoam, and plastic, are poor conductors of heat, which makes them good **insulators**.

Convection transfers heat by the actual movement of hot particles of a fluid. The hot air rising from a bonfire is an example of convection. Ocean currents and wind are caused by convection movements caused by temperature differences.

Radiation occurs when electromagnetic waves transmit heat. The heat we get from the Sun travels through space as radiation.

Magnetism

Simple magnets have two poles: a **north pole** and a **south pole**. Much as it happens in a Hollywood romance, opposites attract. If you try to bring together two north poles of a magnet—or two south poles, for that matter— they will repel one another, and you can feel their repulsive force. If, on the other hand, you move the north pole of one magnet toward the south pole of another magnet, they will attract each other.

Because the Earth itself is magnetized and has a North Pole and a South Pole, a **magnetic compass**, which contains a small, lightweight magnet balanced on a nearly frictionless, nonmagnetic surface, can be used to tell direction. The magnet, which is generally called a **needle**, has one end marked with an arrow and often the letter "N." This end of the needle is the magnet's south pole, which constantly orients itself to point toward the Earth's North Pole, allowing the person reading the compass to gain bearings from that direction.

Study the example below.

Question	Analysis
The arrival of a warm front, a mass of hot air moving into an area, is an example of	**Step 1:** The question asks for a phenomenon to be identified as one of three methods of heat transfer or as a magnetic effect.
	Step 2: The methods of heat transfer are identified by how heat energy physically travels. If actual hot physical molecules bring heat with them, it's convection.
	Step 3: The question stem specifies that the warm air itself is moving into the area. By definition, that makes this an example of convection.
(A) conduction (B) convection (C) radiation (D) the Earth's magnetic field at work	**Step 4:** Choice (B) matches the prediction.

Now you try one:

Wooden spoons are sometimes used in kitchens instead of metal ones when stirring hot pots of soup. What's a reasonable explanation for this?

(A) Wood does not conduct heat as well as metal, so the person stirring won't get burned.
(B) Wood draws in convection heat so that it does not flow into the pot.
(C) Wood is magnetic, and diverts heat.
(D) Wood is a good conductor of radiation.

Explanation

Choice **(A)** is correct. Of the methods of heat transfer, only conduction would allow heat to move from a hot liquid into a solid spoon. It makes sense that a less conductive material would be purposely chosen to minimize the amount of heat that is able to travel from the soup, through the spoon, to the cook's fingers. The other choices, on the other hand, suggest a misunderstanding of how the methods of heat transfer work.

CHEMISTRY

Elements and the Periodic Table

LEARNING OBJECTIVES

In this section you will learn to:

- understand what differentiates one element from another
- find information using the Periodic Table
- differentiate compound substances from pure elements, and understand the ways in which they are built up from simpler elements and/or compounds
- understand the basic definitions of acids and bases and their relation to the pH scale
- describe phase transitions and the defining features of the solid, liquid, and gaseous states of matter
- understand the basic definition and process of a chemical reaction, and differentiate this from physical change

Chemistry is the science dealing with the composition and properties of **matter,** and with the reactions by which matter is produced from or converted into other types of matter. Matter is anything that has mass and occupies space, and any form of matter has certain chemical properties based upon its molecular composition. To start, here are some basic terms.

Element: A pure type of matter that cannot be separated into different types of matter by ordinary chemical methods. All matter is composed of elements, and all the known elements are listed on the Periodic Table of Elements (see the figure below).

Atom: The smallest component of an element that still retains the properties of the element. An atom may combine with similar particles of other elements to produce compounds. Atoms consist of a complex arrangement of electrons in motion about a positively charged nucleus containing protons and (except for hydrogen) neutrons.

Proton: A subatomic particle found in the atom's nucleus that carries a positive electric charge.

Neutron: A subatomic particle found in the atom's nucleus that does not have an electric charge and is therefore neutral.

Electron: A subatomic particle that orbits the nucleus of an atom. An electron carries a negative charge and has a miniscule mass compared to the other sub-atomic particles (both neutrons and protons are more than 1,800 times as massive as an electron). Ordinarily, an atom has the same number of negative electrons around the nucleus as the number of positive protons in the nucleus.

Structure of an Atom

Nucleus

N = Neutron
P = Proton
e = Electron

Electron
"Cloud Orbit"

Molecule: The smallest multi-atom particle of an element or compound that can exist in the free state and still retain the characteristics of the element or compound. The molecules of elements consist of two or more similar atoms; the molecules of compounds consist of two or more different atoms.

Through decades of research, scientists have organized all the known elements into a structure called the Periodic Table, which conveys multiple pieces of information about each element.

Periodic Table of the Elements

1 IA																	18 VIIIA
1 **H** 1.0	2 IIA											13 IIIA	14 IVA	15 VA	16 VIA	17 VIIA	2 **He** 4.0
3 **Li** 6.9	4 **Be** 9.0											5 **B** 10.8	6 **C** 12.0	7 **N** 14.0	8 **O** 16.0	9 **F** 19.0	10 **Ne** 20.2
11 **Na** 23.0	12 **Mg** 24.3	3 IIIB	4 IVB	5 VB	6 VIB	7 VIIB	8	9 VIIIB	10	11 IB	12 IIB	13 **Al** 27.0	14 **Si** 28.1	15 **P** 31.0	16 **S** 32.1	17 **Cl** 35.5	18 **Ar** 39.9
19 **K** 39.1	20 **Ca** 40.1	21 **Sc** 45.0	22 **Ti** 47.9	23 **V** 50.9	24 **Cr** 52.0	25 **Mn** 54.9	26 **Fe** 55.8	27 **Co** 58.9	28 **Ni** 58.7	29 **Cu** 63.5	30 **Zn** 65.4	31 **Ga** 69.7	32 **Ge** 72.6	33 **As** 74.9	34 **Se** 79.0	35 **Br** 79.9	36 **Kr** 83.8
37 **Rb** 85.5	38 **Sr** 87.6	39 **Y** 88.9	40 **Zr** 91.2	41 **Nb** 92.9	42 **Mo** 96.0	43 **Tc** (98)	44 **Ru** 101.0	45 **Rh** 102.9	46 **Pd** 106.4	47 **Ag** 107.9	48 **Cd** 112.4	49 **In** 114.8	50 **Sn** 118.7	51 **Sb** 121.8	52 **Te** 127.6	53 **I** 126.9	54 **Xe** 131.3
55 **Cs** 132.9	56 **Ba** 137.3	*	72 **Hf** 178.5	73 **Ta** 180.9	74 **W** 183.8	75 **Re** 186.2	76 **Os** 190.2	77 **Ir** 192.2	78 **Pt** 195.1	79 **Au** 197.0	80 **Hg** 200.6	81 **Tl** 204.4	82 **Pb** 207.2	83 **Bi** 209.0	84 **Po** (209)	85 **At** (210)	86 **Rn** (222)
87 **Fr** (223)	88 **Ra** (226)	†	104 **Rf** (267)	105 **Db** (268)	106 **Sg** (269)	107 **Bh** (270)	108 **Hs** (269)	109 **Mt** (278)	110 **Ds** (281)	111 **Rg** (281)	112 **Cn** (285)	113 **Uut** (286)	114 **Fl** (289)	115 **Uup** (288)	116 **Lv** (293)	117 **Uus** (294)	118 **Uuo** (294)

	57 **La** 138.9	58 **Ce** 140.1	59 **Pr** 140.9	60 **Nd** 144.2	61 **Pm** (145)	62 **Sm** 150.4	63 **Eu** 152.0	64 **Gd** 157.3	65 **Tb** 158.9	66 **Dy** 162.5	67 **Ho** 164.9	68 **Er** 167.3	69 **Tm** 168.9	70 **Yb** 173.1	71 **Lu** 175.0
*															
†	89 **Ac** (227)	90 **Th** 232.0	91 **Pa** 231.0	92 **U** 238.0	93 **Np** (237)	94 **Pu** (244)	95 **Am** (243)	96 **Cm** (247)	97 **Bk** (247)	98 **Cf** (251)	99 **Es** (252)	100 **Fm** (257)	101 **Md** (258)	102 **No** (259)	103 **Lr** (262)

In order to be able to read the Periodic Table of the Elements, there are a few things you need to understand. For starters, elements are arranged in order of increasing **atomic number**, from left to right and from top to bottom. An element's atomic number represents the number of its protons (and also the number of its electrons, since those two numbers are the same). The different **rows** of elements are called **periods**. The periods correspond to the **shells**, or the different orbits that electrons occupy around atoms. As a rule, electrons will occupy the lowest shell they can, and move on to higher shells only after lower shells are occupied (although this rule is sometimes violated) so as to minimize the energy of the atom. Every element in the top row (the first period) has one shell for its electrons. Every element in the second row (the second period) has two shells for its electrons, and so on. At this time, the maximum number of shells is seven.

The Periodic Table has a special name for its columns, too. The elements in a column are called a **group**. The elements in a group have the same number of electrons in their outer shell. It is the group that an element occupies, much more than the period, that determines its chemical properties. This is because the number of electrons needed to complete an element's outer shell shapes the way in which it reacts with other elements to form molecules. For instance, every element in the first column (Group I) has one electron in its outer shell. The elements in this group are called **alkali metals**, which describe soft, silvery metals that react strongly with water. The further down the group you go, the more violent this reaction is.

By the same token, every element on the second column (Group II) has two electrons in the outer shell. As you keep counting the columns, you'll know how many electrons are in the outer shell. Note that the far right-hand column is composed of a group called the **noble gases**, sometimes referred to as inert gases, because these elements generally don't react with other elements since their outer shell is completely filled.

Atomic Structure of Lithium and Sodium

Notice that Li has two electron shells so it is in the second row of the periodic table; Na has three shells so it is in the third row. Both elements have one electron in their outer shell and are, therefore, in Group I.

Besides these important chemical properties, an element's **atomic mass** is also related to its position on the Periodic Table. The atomic mass listed in an element box represents the average mass of a single atom. Why average? Because some elements can vary in their number of neutrons, so individual atoms of an element may be found in a couple of slightly different sizes. These different sizes are referred to as **isotopes**.

A pretty good estimate of atomic mass comes from adding the total number of neutrons and protons together. Each proton and neutron has a mass very close to what's called an **atomic mass unit (amu)**. The majority of hydrogen atoms have only one proton, so its atomic mass should be very close to one, and is, at 1.007 amu.

Now take a look at an individual element box within the Periodic Table. Here's chlorine.

Chlorine

17
Cl
35.5

Chlorine's **atomic number** is **17**, which is the number of protons in the nucleus of a chlorine atom and also the number of electrons orbiting its shells. Its **atomic symbol**, **Cl**, is fairly close to its name, unlike the symbols of some other common elements, such as **Fe** (iron), **Au** (gold), **Ag** (silver), **W** (tungsten), or **Na** (sodium), symbols that derive from the elements' Latin names, rather than their familiar English names.

Finally, the atomic mass of chlorine is listed as **35.5**, due to about half of chlorine atoms being close to 35 amu and the other half closer to 36 amu. Since all chlorine atoms have 17 protons, this means chlorine atoms are almost as likely to have either 18 or 19 neutrons.

Question	Analysis
How many neutrons does a single sulfur (S) atom have?	**Step 1:** The question asks for the number of neutrons in sulfur, which are found in the nucleus of an atom with the protons.
	Step 2: Since the atomic mass is about equal to the total number of protons and neutrons, and the atomic number is defined by the number of protons, the difference in these values (available on the Periodic Table earlier in this section) should be about equal to the number of neutrons. Round the atomic mass to the nearest whole number as necessary. For sulfur: Atomic # (protons) = 16 Atomic mass = 32.1 Number of protons and neutrons = 32 Number of neutrons = 32 − 16 = 16
	Step 3: It isn't possible for an atom to have something other than a whole number of neutrons, so round to the nearest whole number. There are exactly 16 neutrons.
(A) 16 (B) 16.1 (C) 32 (D) 48	**Step 4:** Select choice (A).

Now try one on your own:

How many protons, neutrons, and electrons do argon (Ar)
atoms have?

(A) 18, 18, 18
(B) 18, 22, 18
(C) 18, 21.9, 18
(D) 18, 22, 22

Explanation

Answer choice **(B)** is correct. Argon's atomic mass is about 40, so there are 18 protons and 22 neutrons, and, in neutral atoms, there are always the same number of electrons as protons.

Compounds

Unstable elements readily form into **compounds** with properties very distinct from the elements from which they are composed. For instance, sodium and chlorine, both of which are extremely unstable and noxious as elements, combine to form the stable and edible compound sodium chloride (NaCl), more commonly known as **table salt.** Table salt is called an **ionic compound** because each chlorine atom borrows an electron from each sodium atom and the atoms stick closely together to form a very tightly bound crystalline structure when salt is in solid form. When it is placed in solution, however, such as when table salt is poured in water, the atoms dissociate into sodium ions and chloride ions. An **ion** is an electrically charged atom; in this case each of the sodium atoms is positively charged because it has lent an electron to its corresponding chloride atom, and each of the chloride atoms is negatively charged for the same reason.

Table sugar is an example of a **covalent compound**, which means, among other things, that it does not ionize when dissolved in water. In a covalent compound, the atoms in the molecule have covalent bonds; that is, they share electrons in pairs, so that each atom provides half the electrons, and the pair is held tightly by both atoms. For this reason, they will not separate as ions do.

Acids and Bases

An **acid** is a substance that gives up positively charged hydrogen ions (H^+) when dissolved in water. Acids corrode metals and generally have a sour taste (though not all acids are safe to drink). Some common acidic solutions are vinegar (which has acetic acid) and lemon juice (which has citric acid). More potent acids include hydrochloric acid, nitric acid, and sulfuric acid (commonly used in lead batteries), all of which are extremely corrosive and must be handled with the utmost care.

A **base** is a substance that gives up negatively charged hydroxyl ions (OH^-) when dissolved in water. Basic substances are also referred to as **alkaline**. Bases typically taste bitter.

Some common basic substances found in a kitchen include baking soda (sodium bicarbonate) and liquid soap (which often includes potassium hydroxide). More potent bases include sodium hydroxide (also known as lye) and sodium hypochlorite (the most common active ingredient in bleach), and these are just as corrosive and dangerous as comparable acids. When acids and bases react (and they react together rather powerfully), the substances neutralize each other and turn into water and a salt.

The **pH** of a solution is a number from 0 to 14 that indicates how basic or acidic that solution is. According to the pH scale, solutions with a pH less than 7 are acidic, with the degree of acidity increasing tenfold with each declining number. For instance, black coffee has a pH of 5; vinegar, which is 100 times as acidic as coffee, has a pH of 3; and battery acid, which is 100 times as acidic as vinegar, has a pH of 1. A solution with a pH of 7 is neutral. Pure water has a pH of 7.

Common Substances on the pH Scale

Battery acid	Vinegar	Pure water	Borax	Bleach

1   7   14

Solutions with a pH greater than 7 are basic, with the degree of alkalinity once again increasing tenfold with each increasing number. Baking soda has a pH that is a little over 8. Borax, commonly used in cleaning solutions and detergents, is about 10 times as basic, at just over 9 on the pH scale, while household bleach, over 12 pH, is 1,000 times as basic as Borax, and 10,000 times as basic as baking soda. Human blood, just above pH 7, is just slightly basic, with about one-tenth the alkalinity of baking soda.

Study this example of an expert test taker's approach to a question about acids and bases.

Question	Analysis
In a chemistry lab, you are given four solutions and measure their pH values. Which solution contains the greatest number of hydrogen ions?	**Step 1:** The question asks for the highest concentration of hydrogen ions.
	Step 2: Acids produce hydrogen ions, and more acidic substances produce them in greater concentrations. Lower pH values indicate more acidic substances, which means the most hydrogen ions.
(A) the pH 2.5 solution (B) the pH 3.7 solution (C) the pH 7.1 solution (D) the pH 9 solution	**Step 4:** Answer choice (A) has the lowest pH.

Now try your hand at a question about acids and bases.

You find a mystery substance in the lab and note the following qualities: it's bitter to the taste, it releases OH^- ions in solution, and it reacts with an acid to form a salt and water. Which of the following could the mystery substance be?

(A) vinegar
(B) soap
(C) lemon juice
(D) water

Explanation

Choice **(B)** is correct. The properties of the mystery substance match those of a base. Of the choices given, the only basic substance is soap.

Physical Change

Matter may undergo either a **physical change** or a **chemical change**. The form, size, and shape of matter may be altered in a physical change, but the molecules remain unchanged. Building a sand castle or bending a piece of plastic into a new shape are both physical changes. The matter has been rearranged, but it is still made of up of the same kinds of atoms and molecules. In other words, its chemical identity has remained intact.

One of the most important kinds of physical change is what's known as a **phase transition**. A phase transition is when matter switches from one **state of matter**, like solid, liquid, or gas, to another.

The **solid state** exists at lower temperatures relative to the liquid and gaseous states (although the specific temperature ranges depend on the element or compound). In the solid state, atoms or molecules are packed very close together and do not move freely. Solids maintain a constant volume and shape. A good example is an ice cube, consisting of solid-state water molecules.

The **liquid state** exists at a higher temperature range relative to the solid state equivalent of the same element or compound. In the liquid state, molecules flow freely around each other. Liquids have a constant volume, but do not maintain their shape. They will either take on the shape of their container or, let free, will spread out into a puddle. Water from a faucet comes out in the liquid state.

The **gaseous state** occurs at a higher temperature range relative to the previous two states of matter. In the gaseous state, molecules flow even more freely from each other, and will also spread out as far as they can. Gases do not maintain either a constant volume or shape. A small amount of gas will spread to fill a large volume if space is available, or can be highly compressed into smaller spaces (oxygen tanks include a large amount of compressed oxygen gas). Steam or vapor are the common terms for water in a gas state.

Under certain circumstances, it's possible for solids and gases to transition between each other directly, without transforming to the liquid state first. The specific terms for each type of phase transition are summarized below.

Phase Changes

Chemical Change

In a chemical change, molecules of new matter are formed that are different from the original molecules of matter. When elements and compounds undergo a chemical change, the process is called a **chemical reaction**. During a chemical reaction, atoms are rearranged into new combinations, resulting in different kinds of molecules. The molecules and atoms that enter the reaction are called **reactants** and the molecules and atoms that result from the reaction are called **products**.

For example, water is also known as H_2O because a single water molecule is made of two hydrogen atoms and one oxygen atom. One kind of chemical reaction will cause many water molecules to break apart and the atoms to rearrange into hydrogen molecules (H_2) and oxygen molecules (O_2). This is how the reactant, water, is turned into the products, pure hydrogen gas and oxygen gas. Other common examples of chemical reactions include the formation of rust on iron, and the conversion of wood into charcoal, carbon dioxide, and steam in a fire.

To illustrate the profound effects of chemical change, consider one more example: the reaction of chlorine gas and sodium metal. Both substances, in their pure forms, are extremely hazardous to humans. Sodium metal cannot be touched with bare hands; it reacts with any moisture, giving off heat and sparks. It's stored in oil when not in use. Chlorine gas was used as a devastating chemical weapon in the First World War. Yet, these two dangerous substances can undergo a chemical reaction that results in a product of sodium chloride: common table salt, found in any kitchen. That's the power of chemical change.

Here's how the well-prepared test taker would approach a question about states of matter.

Question	Analysis
A sample of matter with an amorphous shape but constant volume has to be	**Step 1:** The question asks for the type or phase of matter with a constant volume but non-fixed shape.
	Step 2: A solid has a fixed shape. A liquid will take the shape of its container, or more exactly, find the lowest possible level.
	Step 3: The only thing that logically *must be* true of the matter sample based on the qualities described in the question is that the substance must in the liquid phase.
(A) in the solid phase (B) in the liquid phase (C) a pure element (D) a compound	**Step 4:** Select choice (B). (Note that the sample *could be* either an element or a compound, since both elements and compounds are capable of being solid, liquid, or gas. Thus, neither (C) nor (D) has to be true.)

Now try one on your own.

Energy is needed for which of the following changes of state?

(A) solid to liquid
(B) gas to liquid
(C) liquid to solid
(D) gas to solid

Explanation

Choice **(A)** is correct. Liquids occur at higher temperatures than solids, and gases occur at higher temperatures still. The evaporation of a solid into a liquid is the only answer choice listed that involves movement to a phase that occurs at higher temperatures, requiring a net input of energy to allow the molecules the freer movement that occurs in the gaseous phase.

PHYSICAL SCIENCE PRACTICE QUESTIONS

1. What is 77°F in degrees Celsius?

   (A) 25°
   (B) 32°
   (C) 37°
   (D) 5°

2. Which of the following best explains the recoil action of a shooting gun?

   (A) Newton's first law of motion
   (B) Newton's second law of motion
   (C) Newton's third law of motion
   (D) Newton's law of universal gravitation

3. The weight of a pendulum clock transforms potential energy to usable mechanical work. Assuming no energy loss, approximately how much work will be done if a 200 g weight descends 0.5 m?

   (A) 0.1 J
   (B) 1 J
   (C) 100 J
   (D) 1000 J

4. Which of the following waves on the electromagnetic spectrum has the highest frequency?

   (A) microwaves
   (B) X-rays
   (C) visible light
   (D) radio waves

5. Pure water has a pH of

   (A) 1
   (B) 7
   (C) 0
   (D) 14

6. During a game of baseball, two players both attempt to catch the same ball. The 50 kg Player A is traveling west at 12 m/s, while the 60 kg Player B is traveling east along the same line at 10 m/s. What will happen when they collide?

   (A) Player A will continue forward at reduced velocity, knocking back Player B.
   (B) Player B will continue forward at reduced velocity, knocking back Player A.
   (C) Player B will continue forward without any decrease in velocity, knocking back Player B.
   (D) Player A and Player B will both come to a complete stop.

7. When a skydiver jumps from a plane, she eventually reaches a maximum falling velocity of −56 m/s. After opening up her parachute, her falling velocity decreases to about −11 m/s. What effect on her motion does the skydiver's parachute have?

   (A) The parachute does not change the skydiver's velocity.
   (B) The parachute applies a negative acceleration on the skydiver.
   (C) The parachute applies a positive acceleration on the skydiver.
   (D) The parachute applies first a negative acceleration, then a positive acceleration on the skydiver.

8. A freight elevator is used to lift loads of 12,000 N a vertical distance of 250 m. The elevator takes 10 s to make this trip. Assuming no energy loss, what is the average power expenditure of the elevator, when working?

   (A) 300,000 W
   (B) 3,000,000 W
   (C) 12,000,000 W
   (D) 30,000,000 W

9. Which of the following is NOT true about the element hydrogen (H)?

   (A) It is the only element with no neutrons.
   (B) It is the lightest element.
   (C) It is a noble (inert) gas and rarely reacts.
   (D) It sometimes behaves like an alkali metal.

10. Which of the following activities results in a chemical change?

   (A) mixing salt and sugar
   (B) drying wet clothes
   (C) boiling a pot of water
   (D) burning pieces of wood

Answers and Explanations

1. (A) 25° To convert the temperature from degrees Fahrenheit to degrees Celsius, first subtract 32, and then multiply by $\frac{5}{9}$.

$$77 - 32 = 45$$

$$45 \times \frac{5}{9} = 25$$

2. (C) Newton's third law of motion The recoil action of a shooting gun is explained by Newton's third law of motion: for every action, there is an equal and opposite reaction.

3. (B) 1 J Using Newton's second law, and the fact that acceleration near the surface of the Earth is 9.8 m/s^2, the force of gravity can be calculated. The mass must be converted to kg units first: m = 200 g = 0.2 kg. Then the force is (0.2 kg) $\times$ (9.8 m/s^2) = 1.96 N. This force acts over a distance of 0.5 m, so W = (1.96 N) $\times$ (0.5 m) = .98 J. Answer choice (B) is the closest match.

4. (B) X-rays Of the wave states listed, X-rays have the highest frequency in the electromagnetic spectrum (gamma rays have an even higher frequency).

5. (B) 7 Pure water has a pH of 7, making it a neutral solution.

6. (D) Player A and Player B will both come to a complete stop. Determine the momenta of each player. Player A has a momentum of 50 kg $\times$ 12 m/s = 600 kg· m/s in a westward direction. Player B has a momentum of 60 kg $\times$ 10 m/s = 600 kg·m/s in an eastward direction. Since the two players' momenta are equal in magnitude but opposite in direction, the total momentum is zero (P_{total} = (+600) + (−600) = 0 kg·m/s). To put it another way, since neither player has a greater quantity of motion than the other, neither one can "win" in a collision. If neither is able to overcome the other, both coming to a stop is the only option that makes sense.

7. (C) The parachute applies a positive acceleration on the skydiver. The direction of velocity of the skydiver is negative for the entire time period discussed in the question, but due to the release of the parachute, the later velocity is smaller in magnitude. Since the parachute acts against the direction of motion of the skydiver (as established by the fact the magnitude of the velocity is decreased instead of increased),

the acceleration must be positive, opposite in sign to the negative velocity. Alternately, this question can be reasoned out as follows: the skydiver is falling and has a negative velocity, therefore down is negative; parachutes slow down skydivers by pulling them in an upwards direction, therefore the parachute provides a positive acceleration.

8. (A) 300,000 W The applied force of the elevator has to counteract the weight of the load in order to ensure a safe, uniform velocity up. So the work done can be calculated as W = (12,000 N) $\times$ (250 m) = 3,000,000 J. Power is energy expended per unit time, so P = (3,000,000 J)/(10 s) = 300,000 W.

9. (C) It is a noble (inert) gas and rarely reacts. The question asks for the statement about hydrogen which is not true. Both answer choices (A) and (B) are true statements (since the atomic number of one means there is one proton, and if there were any neutrons, the mass would be greater than one). The question can now be answered by identifying just one of the remaining statements as definitely true or false. Since hydrogen is definitely not a noble gas (helium is the lightest noble gas, with atomic number two), (C) is the correct answer choice. Alternately, (D) can be identified as the last true statement (hydrogen has a single electron in its outer shell, like alkali metals), which again means (C) is the correct answer choice (by process of elimination). If neither statement is known for certain, the best strategy is to take a best guess as to which is most likely to be true (or most likely to be false).

10. (D) burning pieces of wood Mixing salt and sugar is a physical change. When mixed together, the salt and sugar retain their molecular make-up. Drying wet clothes is also a physical change. When clothes are dried, water molecules evaporate, becoming a gas. The clothes and water molecules remain chemically unchanged. When boiling a pot of water, once again, liquid water molecules move into the gas phase, but there is no change in the chemical makeup of the molecules. Finally, burning wood is a chemical change, because the molecules in the wood are converted into new molecules that are different than the original.

Review and Reflect

As you look back over your work in this chapter, think about these questions:

- Which concepts are you more comfortable with, and which seem less familiar?
- As you worked practice questions in this chapter, were you careful to make predictions whenever possible?
- If you missed practice questions that called for calculations, was it because you didn't understand or remember the concept being tested or because you made a misstep while doing the math?
- Did you pay careful attention to the units required by a problem?
- Which science topics should you review again before Test Day?

ELECTRONICS INFORMATION

KNOW WHAT TO EXPECT

The discovery of electricity and its use in transferring energy has been the foundation of modern technology. It's hard to imagine a world without automobiles, computers, or even flashlights. Though they have vastly different functions, all electrical and electronic devices operate due to the movement of subatomic particles called *electrons* (hence the word *electronics*).

In this chapter, you will learn the basic principles of electricity and electronic components. By the end of the chapter, you will be able to identify some major circuit components and their functions, perform calculations to determine circuit properties, and understand some of the safety devices used in modern household wiring.

On the CAT-ASVAB, you will have 8 minutes to complete 16 EI questions. If you take the paper and pencil ASVAB, you will have 9 minutes to complete 20 Electronics Information questions.

ELECTRON FLOW THEORY

LEARNING OBJECTIVES

In this section you will learn to:

- understand electricity as the flow of electrons through conducting materials
- understand the meaning of voltage, current, and resistance, and how they relate to different aspects of electrical flow

A solid understanding of electricity begins at the atomic level. Matter is composed of **atoms,** which are the smallest particles that elements can be broken into and still retain the properties of that element. An atom is itself broken into even smaller components, called subatomic particles.

Two subatomic particles are found within the nucleus: **protons** and **neutrons**. Protons have a positive charge, and neutrons are neutrally charged. The nucleus is the heaviest part of the atom and accounts for the majority of the atom's mass. **Electrons**, the third type of subatomic particle, are in motion around the nucleus and have a negative charge. For a neutral atom, there is one electron for each proton that resides in the nucleus. From static shock to a lightning strike, all electricity is the movement of electrons.

The electrons occupy various energy levels around the nucleus, known as **shells,** and each time one becomes full, a new one is begun. The outer shell of an atom is known as its **valence shell,** and the number of electrons that reside in the valence shell are what determines whether an element is a **conductor**, a **semiconductor**, or an **insulator**. In many elements, the valence shell holds a maximum of eight electrons.

Boron, a Conductor; Silicon, a Semiconductor; and Phosphorus, an Insulator

Boron: 5p 6n 5e
3 valence electrons

Silicon: 14p 14n 14e
4 valence electrons

Phosphorus: 15p 15n 15e
5 valence electrons

A **conductor** is an element that allows electrons to flow freely. What all conductors have in common is one or more mobile valence electrons per atom that are free to move from one atom to another, as each valence shell has more empty spots than electrons. An **insulator** has a valence shell that is more than half full, or is completely full. It does not conduct electricity much at all, because its electrons are all tightly bound and will not leave their packed valence shells. A **semiconductor**, with a valence shell that is exactly half full, is neither a good conductor nor a good insulator, but it has some remarkable properties that make it very useful for making electronic components.

A convenient way of visualizing how electricity works is to imagine the electrons as drops of water flowing through a pipe. Such a flow is due to applied pressure on one end, forcing the water the opposite way. Likewise, when a conductor is connected across the terminals of the battery, the negative terminal of the battery applies a repulsive pressure on the electrons and pushes them towards the positive terminal. (A basic rule of electricity is that like charges repel each other, while opposite charges attract each other.) The resulting flow of electrons through a conductor is an electric current.

Current

The rate of flow of electrons through a conductor is known as **current**. Just as the gush of water through a pipe has a current, so does the flow of electricity. When you turn on a faucet, it's easy to distinguish between a trickle and a roaring flood by the very different amounts of water flowing out each moment. Electrical current, similarly, is measured by the amount of **charge** flowing past per unit of time. Current is measured in **amperes**, or amps for short, and an ampere is defined as one **coulomb (C)**, the basic unit of electrical charge, flowing past a given point in one second. The symbol used for amperes is **A**. If five coulombs of charge were to pass by a point every second, this would be a current of five amps (5 A).

Try your hand at this EI question.

What would be the current if 18 coulombs passed by in three seconds?

(A)   3 A
(B)   6 A
(C)   18 A
(D)   54 A

Explanation

The correct answer is **(B)**. Since 18 C of charge pass by in 3 s (that is, seconds), there must be 6 C passing by per 1 s. By definition, that's a current of 6 A.

One coulomb, incidentally, is the amount of negative charge in 6.25×10^{18} or 6,250,000,000,000,000,000 electrons. It takes this many electrons flowing past a point in a conductor every second for a modest one ampere of current to be flowing. Current can be measured using a device called an **ammeter**.

Voltage

In order to make electrons move through a conductor, there must be a force that causes them to move. Water will move from a high-pressure area in a pipe toward a lower-pressure area, but if the pressure is equal at both ends, no movement takes place. Electricity is no different. There must be electrical "pressure" applied to a conductor to cause electrons to move.

For an electron, the "pressure" is caused by electromagnetic repulsion from a large negative charge, like that found at the negative terminal of a battery. This negative terminal has a huge excess of electrons, all pushing at each other. When a piece of conducting wire connects the positive and negative terminals of a battery (known as "completing the circuit"), electrons are pushed from the negative terminal into the wire, themselves pushing along the conducting electrons already there, and so on down the line, so that every electron will eventually reach the positive terminal, where there is a shortage of electrons and an excess of attractive protons pulling the electrons in. This will continue until the excess of electrons at the negative terminal is exhausted, and the battery is dead.

Electrical pressure is known as **voltage**, and it is measured in volts (symbolized by the letter **V**). The higher the voltage that is applied to a conductor, the greater the electrical pressure the electrons will experience, and the higher the current (rate of flow of electrons) will tend to be. Voltage and current are therefore **directly proportional**.

To be more exact, voltage is really the difference in electric pressure between two points, such that electrons will tend to be pushed from areas of greater **electric potential** (the proper term for this pressure-like quantity) to areas of lesser electric potential (lower pressure). For this reason, voltage is also known as **electrical potential difference**. It's also referred sometimes as **electromotive force**. A technician would measure voltage using a **voltmeter**.

Resistance

Opposition to the flow of current is known as **resistance**. Resistance is measured in **ohms**, and one ohm is defined as the amount of resistance that will allow one ampere of current to flow if one volt of electrical pressure is placed on a conductor. The symbol for the ohm is Ω (the Greek letter omega), and resistance can be measured using an **ohmmeter**.

As resistance in a conductor increases, current flow decreases. This means that current and resistance are **inversely proportional**. The smaller the resistance a material has, the better a conductor it is. But voltage and current, remember, are **directly proportional**. Any time voltage increases, current will also increase. So in materials with high resistance (that is, in poorer conductors), a higher voltage must be used to get the same current.

All conductors have a certain amount of resistance, with some having more than others. Three materials that are most often used as conductors are silver, copper, and aluminum. Of these three, silver is the best conductor as it exhibits the lowest resistance. Unfortunately, silver is relatively expensive, so the next best choice is copper. Copper has only a slightly higher resistance than silver, but is much less expensive. Most electrical cable and wire is currently made from copper. Aluminum has a higher resistance than copper, and exhibits some other characteristics that make it even less than desirable for use in electrical applications. While aluminum was used extensively in residential wiring at one time, it is now used only in a few select applications.

Exceptions and Additional Notes

The analogy of electron flow to the flow of water through a pipe is helpful, but like all analogies, there are places where it breaks down. For example, when a pipe is broken, water will spray out, but when a conducting wire in an electronic device is broken, current flow simply stops along that path. That's because electricity travels *through* the conducting metal of a wire, not inside a hollow pipe like water does. With no conducting material, electrons cannot move forward, and air molecules are very poor conductors. Except when the gap is very small (spark plugs are designed this way) or the amount of voltage extremely large (as occurs with lightning), an electric current will not flow through air.

Another interesting quirk in the study of electricity is what's known as **conventional current**, which is defined by the (imaginary) flow of positive charge and is opposite in direction to actual electron flow. This strange concept came about because of the difficulty in actually observing electricity at a microscopic level.

Seeing and feeling the direction that water is moving in is easy enough, but electricity is another story. When scientists first started studying electricity seriously, not enough was known about atoms yet, and they realized that either a flow of negative electrons in one direction or a flow of positive protons in the opposite direction could explain the movement of charges discovered to be at the heart of electricity.

Scientists took a guess that it was the protons that moved, and defined the direction of current based on that. Later they discovered that protons stay in the nucleus and don't move, but current direction had already been defined this way. As a result, if a circuit has a conventional current that is moving in a clockwise direction, this means that, in reality, electrons are moving around the circuit in a counter-clockwise direction. Nowadays, we can refer to either conventional current or electron flow, but it's necessary to remember to switch the direction when going from one to the other.

It is straightforward to think of electrical current as a flow of electrons, but an individual electron does not necessarily traverse an entire circuit. Often this is more like a relay race as subsequent electrons carry the charge onward. Some references may, therefore, refer to the flow of a charge.

This chapter hasn't discussed circuits yet, but you still have enough information to understand the worked example below. In the diagram, V stands for a source of voltage, such as a battery cell, and L1 and L2 are lamps connected to that voltage source. An unbroken line means an unbroken connection, and a broken line means a broken connection.

Question	Analysis
In the wiring diagram pictured, which of the lamps will be lit up?	**Step 1:** The question asks which lamp will light up—that is, which will receive a flow of current.
	Step 2: The open switch (the break in the middle line) prevents current from flowing across the path containing lamp L1. That's because current cannot flow into a dead end. However the path from the battery cell, through L2, and back to the opposite terminal of the battery does make a complete circuit. L1 should not have a current passing through it, so will not be lit up. L2 should have a current passing through it, so will be expected to light up.
	Step 3: Since there are no gaps in its path, L2 should be lit up, but L1 should not.
(A) L1 only will be lit. (B) L2 only will be lit. (C) L1 and L2 will both be lit. (D) Neither lamp will be lit.	**Step 4:** Choose option (B).

Now try one on your own.

Certain conducting materials decrease in resistance as the wires heat up. As resistance decreases, which of the following would be expected to happen?

(A) The amount of current should increase.
(B) The amount of current should decrease.
(C) The direction of current should switch.
(D) The current should remain constant.

Explanation

The answer is **(A)**. Resistance and current are inversely proportional, so when resistance decreases, current increases. Remember that resistance is so called because it resists current. If the resistance is less, it makes sense that the amount of current is able to increase, similar to how the rate of traffic flow is greater on the highway where there are fewer traffic lights.

CIRCUITS

LEARNING OBJECTIVES

In this section you will learn to:

- effectively use Ohm's law to perform circuit calculations
- effectively use the power formula in an electrical context
- recognize the features of a basic circuit and give definitions of each
- simplify complex circuits

In order for electric current to flow, there must be a **circuit** for it to follow. A circuit is a complete loop or path that electricity can follow. There are three essential components of an electrical circuit: a **voltage source**, a **load**, and **conductors** to connect the load to the voltage source. When these three components are connected so that current can flow, we have a **closed (completed) circuit**.

Simple Closed Circuit

A **load** is basically a source of resistance that converts electrical energy into some other energy form. For instance, a light bulb is a load. It has resistance and converts electrical energy into light energy and heat. Other examples of loads are electric motors, heating elements, and solenoids.

If a load's resistance were to decrease, the current flowing in the circuit would increase. However, if the circuit were broken, as in a wire (conductor) being disconnected, no current would flow. This would be called an **open circuit**.

When current is flowing, each electron is carrying the voltage the length of the conductor: pushing the electrons ahead of them to keep moving forward, while being pushed themselves by those behind. When the line stops, it stops everywhere, thus when there is no clear path to their destination, as in the gap that occurs in an open circuit, electron flow stops entirely and the current is zero.

Ohm's Law

The relationship between voltage, current, and resistance through a wire is summed up in **Ohm's law**. Ohm's law states that voltage (potential difference) in volts is equal to the current in amperes multiplied by the resistance in ohms. This is represented by the formula:

$V = IR$

V represents *voltage*, also known as potential difference, while **I** represents *current*, and **R** represents *resistance*. If the *I* symbol seems odd, think of current (defined as the amount of charge flowing past a point per unit time) as the *intensity* of charge flow. The other two are easier to remember.

The voltage source is the beginning and end of the circuit. The negative side repels electrons, forcing them to move through the circuit. The positive side helps by attracting electrons, and an electron emitted from the negative side will eventually traverse the complete circuit before arriving at the positive side. Remember that voltage is essentially electric pressure on a charged object, so the voltage source is ultimately responsible for electric flow in a circuit by pushing the electrons forward.

To put it another way, a non-zero voltage will produce a certain amount of current in a closed circuit for a given resistance, as shown by Ohm's law above. Batteries, which have positive and negative terminals, are voltage sources (for example, a 12 V battery). A household electrical socket also provides voltage, which ultimately comes from the power plant. They are also referred to as power sources, because the electric current they create carries energy.

The conductor is just the wire that connects the load(s) and voltage source. For the sake of simplicity, the wire is often considered to have zero resistance. Although this is not true, the resistance in a conducting wire is often small enough compared to any given load that it can be ignored for most calculations. At zero resistance, Ohm's law requires the voltage across such a conducting wire to also be zero, meaning the electrical pressure does not change from one side to another.

Remember, a load is any component with resistance that converts electrical energy into some other energy form. In accordance with Ohm's law, were a load's resistance to decrease, the current flowing in the circuit would increase. However, if the circuit were broken, as in a wire (conductor) being disconnected, no current would flow. This would be called an open circuit. This, too, can be explained by Ohm's law, as the break or gap in the circuit is like a load with infinite resistance (recall from the previous section that air is a terrible conductor).

Series Circuits

An electrical circuit that has only one path for current to flow is known as a **series circuit**. A break (opening) at any point in the circuit will cause current to stop flowing in all parts of the circuit. The simplest possible circuit, one voltage source connected to one load by conductors, is an example of a series circuit.

Series Circuit

Since there is only one path for current to follow in a series circuit, the current flow will be the same in all parts of the circuit. It wouldn't make sense, for example, if one million electrons were leaving the negative terminal of a battery each second, but two million were arriving at the positive terminal at the other end. It would be like a plane taking off from New York and then landing in Miami with twice as many passengers. Thus, the current passing through any single load in a series circuit is the same.

$$I_1 = I_2 = I_3 = \dots$$

On the other hand, what happens if multiple loads were found in a series circuit? If two or more loads are added to a series circuit, their resistances add together, creating what's called the total or effective resistance across the circuit.

$$R_{tot} = R_1 + R_2 + R_3 \dots$$

Voltage, which refers specifically to a *difference* in electric potential ("electric pressure") at two different points (like from the negative to the positive terminals of a voltage source), can also be calculated across a single load. This is also known as the voltage drop across a load, and the total of all voltage drops across each load in a series circuit is equal to the total voltage of the complete circuit, which is equal to the voltage of the voltage source itself.

$$V_{tot} = V_1 + V_2 + V_3 \dots$$

Try applying these ideas to solve the following problem.

> Three different loads with different rated resistances are wired in series.
> Which of the following will be the same through all of them?

(A)   the voltage drop
(B)   the resistance
(C)   the current passing through
(D)   the heat given off

Explanation

Choice **(C)** is correct. The current passing through one point in a series circuit has to be the same in other parts of the circuit, as there is nowhere else for the current to go.

Parallel Circuits

It is much more common for loads to be wired in parallel. With this arrangement, each load is wired in a separate path. If any one of these paths were to have a break or gap, current flow would still continue through the other paths, so there would still remain a closed circuit.

Parallel Circuit

Parallel circuits are the exact opposite of series circuits in that *voltage is the same throughout each parallel branch of the circuit*, while current flow varies. Since voltage is a measure of the difference in electric potential between two points, the voltage across alternate paths connecting the same two points in a circuit must also be equal.

$$V_1 = V_2 = V_3 = \ldots$$

On the other hand, current flow becomes divided when there are parallel paths. It's commonly misstated that electricity follows the path of least resistance. This is not actually true. Electricity actually follows every possible path, though a larger proportion of electrons will take a path of low resistance while a smaller proportion will take a path with higher resistance. For a parallel circuit, therefore, the total current through the circuit is equal to the sum of currents through each closed path.

$$I_{tot} = I_1 + I_2 + I_3 \ldots$$

What about the effective resistance of a circuit when multiple loads are wired in parallel? It's natural to instinctively think that adding more loads is bound to add more resistance, but this is not the case. This is a little less intuitive at first glance, so consider an analogy.

There's a big sale on at a popular retail store. One of the aisles is choked with customers trying to grab the best deal. The jostling customers, abandoned shopping carts, and crates of items waiting to be shelved all create resistance, making it difficult to move forward and slowing the rate at which people move through the aisle. In this analogy, the people are electrons, and the rate at which they move is the current value.

Suddenly, a store clerk clears away a pile of merchandise that was blocking an adjacent aisle. This aisle, too, has a lot of junk in the way. It may even have higher resistance than the original aisle, as it has more stuff. Even so, some shoppers opt for that cramped but less crowded aisle. The total number of shoppers passing through the store each moment is now greater, with the addition of that parallel path.

Likewise, adding a load in parallel, even if that load's resistance is high, decreases the total or effective resistance of a circuit, because even though it has resistance, it provides an additional path while doing nothing to constrain the existing one. The formula for adding resistances in parallel is a slightly more complicated one, but it's very useful.

$$\frac{1}{R_{tot}} = \frac{1}{R_1} + \frac{1}{R_2} + \frac{1}{R_3} + \dots$$

Study the example below.

Question	Analysis
What is the approximate amount of current passing through switch S when it is closed?	**Step 1:** The question asks for current through the whole circuit. Effective resistance of the circuit and total voltage are needed to calculate this.
	Step 2: There are two loads in parallel, so the parallel resistances formula is needed. Given the effective resistance (R_{eff}), Ohm's law can be used to determine the current drawn. The reciprocals of the resistance values are $R_1 = \frac{1}{10}$ and $R_2 = \frac{1}{20}$. Find the least common denominator and add: $R_1 + R_2 = \frac{2}{20} + \frac{1}{20} = \frac{3}{20}$ $R_{eff} = \frac{20}{3}\ \Omega$ or $6.67\ \Omega$ $I = \frac{40}{6.67} \approx 6\ A$
	Step 3: The predicted value is 6 A.
(A) 0 A (B) 2 A (C) 4 A (D) 6 A	**Step 4:** Select answer choice (D).

Now try one on your own.

Which of the following would not increase the rate of direct current flow, I, through a conductor?

(A) decreasing effective resistance via a variable resistor
(B) increasing voltage
(C) adding a resistor to the circuit in parallel
(D) adding a resistor to the circuit in series

Explanation

Answer choice **(D)** is correct. Using process of elimination, (A) would decrease the overall resistance of the circuit, which, according to Ohm's law, would increase current given a constant voltage source. Choice (B) would also increase current flow if resistance remained constant. Choice (C) would also decrease the overall resistance of the circuit and increase current. However, adding a resistor in series would increase effective resistance, which means a decrease in current drawn.

Series-Parallel Circuits

The most popular arrangement is the series-parallel circuit. A series-parallel circuit has some components, such as an on/off switch, wired in series with a number of loads that are connected in parallel.

Series-Parallel Circuit

-\/\/\- = Resistor (Load)

-|||||- = Battery

= Fuse

= Switch

Most residential wiring circuits are series-parallel. Wall outlets are wired in parallel, but are all fed from a circuit breaker (shown in the diagram as a fuse) that is wired in series. Switching off the circuit breaker will turn off power to all of the outlets. However, if the circuit breaker is on, voltage is provided to all of the outlets whether there are loads plugged into them or not.

Determining the total effective resistance across a series-parallel circuit is a step-by-step process. Use the appropriate formula for each group of resistors, either in series or parallel, to simplify the circuit to fewer and fewer calculated effective resistances until a single value for resistance has been found.

To determine the voltage drop or amount of current flowing through any particular load, combine Ohm's law with the rules for current and voltage in series and parallel wiring to solve for a given variable of any particular load.

Question	Analysis
In the diagram shown, all three resistors have a resistance of 4 Ω. What is the effective resistance of the circuit?	**Step 1:** The question asks for the effective resistance of a series-parallel circuit.
	Step 2: The two parallel loads can be combined into a single effective resistance.
	The effective resistance of the last two loads can be added to the first load's resistance since they're in series with the first load.
	$$\frac{1}{R_{23}} = \frac{1}{4} + \frac{1}{4} = \frac{2}{4} = \frac{1}{2}$$
	$$R_{23} = 2\ \Omega$$
	$$R_{\text{tot}} = 4 + 2 = 6\ \Omega$$
	Step 3: The prediction is 6 Ω.
(A) $\frac{4}{3}$ Ω (B) 4 Ω (C) 6 Ω (D) 12 Ω	**Step 4:** Select choice (C).

Now try the question below on your own.

What is the amount of current passing through the 3 Ω resistor in the circuit pictured?

3Ω

(A)   3 A
(B)   4 A
(C)   6 A
(D)   12 A

Explanation

The answer is **(B)**. Since a switch is open on the branch of one of the parallel 6 Ω resistors, it can be ignored. That means this circuit will behave like a simple series circuit. The two connected resistors sum to an equivalent resistance of 3 + 6 = 9 Ω. Using Ohm's law, the current flowing through the 3 Ω resistor (and one of the two 6 Ω resistors) can be calculated as $I = \dfrac{V}{R} = \dfrac{36}{9} = 4$ A.

Electrical Power

Electrical power is a term that refers to the actual rate at which energy is provided to and consumed by an electric circuit. Power is expressed in watts (joules per second) and can be calculated by multiplying the voltage (in volts) applied to the circuit by the current (in amperes) that flows in the circuit. This is represented by the formula:

$P = IV$

Each electron flowing through a circuit or wire has energy. How much energy depends on the voltage applied. Electrons moving through a large voltage have more energy. On the other hand, a higher current means more electrons passing by each moment. So an equivalent rate of energy delivery can be achieved by a smaller number of electrons each moment (lower current) with a larger amount of energy per electron (higher voltage), or a larger number of electrons each moment (higher current) with a smaller amount of energy per electron (lower voltage).

This formula applies not only to the rate of energy delivery (power found in long-distance power lines) but to the rate of energy production (power provided by a generating plant) and to the rate of energy consumption (power usage of an appliance or load). The word *consumption* is actually a little bit misleading, as energy is never used up but just changes form. A forty-watt (40 W) light bulb doesn't really *use up* 40 joules every second. It transforms 40 joules of electrical energy to 40 joules of light and heat energy each second.

Question	Analysis
An electric generator provides a power supply to a cabin at the North American household standard of 120 V. If the effective resistance of the cabin's wiring is 30 Ω, what is the power usage of the generator?	**Step 1:** The question asks for the power of the generator.
	Step 2: Both current and voltage provided by the generator are needed, but only voltage and resistance are given. However, these can be used to find current using Ohm's law. Now, power can be calculated. $I = \frac{120\,V}{30\,\Omega} = 4A$ $P = (4\ A) \times (120\ V) = 480\ W$
	Step 3: The predicted answer is 480 W.
(A) 4 W (B) 150 W (C) 480 W (D) 3600 W	**Step 4:** Select choice (C).

Now try a question on your own.

The power usage of a coffee pot is 1200 W while running, and is powered by a standard North American 120 V electrical supply. What is the resistance of the coffee pot?

(A) 10 Ω
(B) 12 Ω
(C) 120 Ω
(D) 1200 Ω

Explanation

Answer choice **(B)** is correct. Using the power law and solving for current, $I = \frac{1200}{120} = 10$ A. Then using the current and voltage values in Ohm's law and solving for resistance, $R = \frac{120}{10} = 12\ \Omega$.

Standard Electrical Units and the Metric System

When using Ohm's law and other electrical formulas, it is important to keep in mind that the quantities used must be expressed in ohms, amperes, volts, and watts. If any of these quantities are given in other units, these should be converted before making calculations with them.

Any of these base units can be modified with metric prefixes. For example, smaller generating plants typically measure their power output in megawatts (MW), while cardiac doctors may measure tiny electrical signals in the human heart on the scale of milliamps (mA).

For more detail on metric system prefix values, please refer to the measurement information at the beginning of the Physical Science section of chapter 9: General Science.

STRUCTURE OF ELECTRICAL AND ELECTRONIC SYSTEMS

LEARNING OBJECTIVES

In this section, you will learn to:

- explain the safety mechanisms that are used in modern household electric systems
- recognize the basic electrical components in a circuit via their symbols
- explain the basic functions of several electrical components and their uses and benefits

Thus far, you've learned the basic operational and mathematical concepts behind an electric circuit. In this next section, you will continue to build on these skills. The section will include a discussion of different types of current, some safety considerations, and components that give circuits special qualities and enable them to perform specific tasks.

AC vs. DC

There are two types of current. They are **direct current** (DC) and **alternating current** (AC). DC is current that flows in only one direction in a conductor. This is the type of current that is delivered by a battery. Many electronic devices, like cell phones and laptops, work on DC. AC is current that changes direction (moves back and forth) many times in a second as it moves in a conductor. Household electrical outlets deliver alternating current. AC provides a more efficient way to transport electricity from the power stations to your home or business.

Here in North America, AC is always delivered at 60 cycles per second (hertz). One cycle would be voltage starting at zero, increasing to a maximum level in one direction, then decreasing to zero, increasing to a maximum level in the reverse direction, then returning to zero again. The unit hertz (Hz) describes the frequency of the signal and is a measure of how many complete cycles occur in 1 second. The figure below shows a 60 Hz AC signal.

60 Hz AC signal

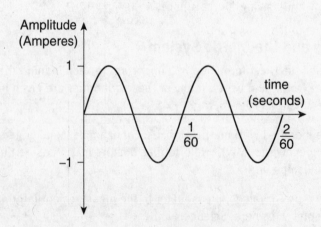

This is the frequency equation:

$$f = \frac{1}{T}$$

In the equation above, f = frequency in Hz and T = the amount of time for one cycle in seconds. You can use that equation to solve for either frequency or period when given one of them. Thus, with a frequency of 60 Hz, it can be determined that one complete cycle occurs in $\frac{1}{60}$ of a second, since:

$$T = \frac{1}{f}$$

So, if power stations deliver AC and most electronic devices work on DC, where and how does the conversion take place? Most electric devices come with built-in AC to DC conversion systems. Later in this section, we will introduce an electric component, the diode, that makes this conversion possible.

Ground

Grounding electrical devices and residential wiring is an important safety factor. **Ground** represents a place of lowest potential in a circuit. Since the potential difference (voltage) is largest between any point in the circuit and the ground point, any "stray" electricity will follow this path since resistance is low here. This is important to prevent shock due to external influences such as lightning, or due to internal circuit failure where conducting wires are compromised.

In residential wiring, ground is a common connection throughout the wiring system that protects against electrical shock. All of the wiring grounds are connected to an earth ground (such as a copper rod driven into the ground or buried conduit) and this is used to guide electrical current away from panels and equipment, should an internal short circuit take place.

Ground Symbol

Important Electric and Electronic Components

The properties of a particular electrical circuit will change depending on the types of components present. In this section, several of the major ones are introduced and discussed.

Resistors

Not all components within an electrical circuit require the same voltage. There are also times when it is useful to be able to raise or limit current in a circuit in order to control certain functions (e.g., volume in a stereo). A component that can be used to limit current and/or voltage is a resistor. A resistor does what its name suggests: it creates a specific amount of resistance that generates a voltage drop when current passes through it.

As you learned previously, resistance can influence current, via Ohm's law. An increase in R will therefore cause a decrease in the current.

Resistor Symbols

Fixed Resistor   Rheostat   Variable   Potentiometer

There are two major types of resistors used today: the **fixed resistor** and the **variable resistor**. Fixed resistors, as their name implies, have a fixed resistance. Variable resistors (**rheostats** or **potentiometers**), have resistances that can be changed. Potentiometers are useful in changing the voltage drop across a component in a circuit. In electronic applications, they can be used to help adjust the volume on a TV, radio or stereo. Rheostats are useful in changing the current in a circuit and can be used as light dimmers or to control the speed of small motorized devices.

Fixed resistors used a color band system to enable us to determine their resistance in ohms. The first color gives the first number. The second color gives the second number, and the third number gives the multiplier or the number of 0's behind the numbers.

Fixed Resistor Color Bands

Color Name	1st digit 1st stripe	2nd digit 2nd stripe	Multiplier 3rd stripe
Black	0	0	×1
Brown	1	1	×10
Red	2	2	×100
Orange	3	3	×1,000
Yellow	4	4	×10,000
Green	5	5	×100,000
Blue	6	6	×1,000,000
Violet	7	7	-
Grey	8	8	-
White	9	9	-

So, given a resistor with a red, violet and yellow band, what is the value of the resistance? According to the chart, the red represents the number 2, the white represents the number 7 and the yellow represents 4 zeros. Putting it all together, the indicated resistance is 270,000 ohms.

red

violet   yellow

Given a simple series circuit with unknown resistance, how could you go about determining the value of resistance in the circuit? This can be done experimentally in one of two ways: first, by measuring resistance directly using an ohmmeter. To use an ohmmeter correctly, remove the device with unknown resistance from the circuit or disconnect the power source from the circuit (an ohmmeter has its own power source). The resistance can then be measured by attaching the ohmmeter leads across both ends of the device.

Alternatively, if no ohmmeter is available, an ammeter connected in series with the resistor and a voltmeter connected in parallel with the resistor as shown below will give I and V. Via Ohm's law, resistance is equal to V divided by I.

Using an Ammeter and Voltmeter to Measure Resistance

Fuses and Circuit Breakers

An electric ground is one essential safety component in a circuit. It helps prevent shock by providing an alternate path for electricity to flow, away from the device. Fuses and circuit breakers are also important safety components in a circuit. When current in a circuit increases too much, wires can overheat, leading to fires.

A **short circuit** occurs when a load is bypassed with a conductor for some reason. Since current and resistance are inversely proportional, the flow of current will increase. This could be caused by something as simple as the insulation on the wires leading to and from the load becoming frayed and allowing the wires to come into direct contact with each other. If a short circuit occurs in part of a series circuit, the net effect is merely to remove the load that was bypassed as a result of the short circuit. If, however, the short circuit occurs at *any* load in parallel circuits or bypasses *all* the loads in series circuits, the resistance of the circuit as a whole is reduced to near zero and a dangerous surge in current could occur. For this reason, it is a good safety precaution to protect circuits with fuses or circuit breakers.

Fuses are thin wires that melt when current exceeds a prescribed amount, thereby preventing any further electricity flow. This prevents any potential damage to the electric device. One disadvantage of using a fuse is that when it has melted, or "blown," it has to be replaced before the circuit will work again. Fuses with different current ratings can be used depending on the device specifications.

Fuse Symbol

Circuit breakers serve the same function as fuses, but have the advantage of being able to be reused multiple times. However, they respond more slowly to increases in current than fuses do, and are more expensive to install. There are several types of circuit breakers, but the underlying principle behind their function remains the same. One class of circuit breakers consists of a bimetallic strip that bends away from its contact in a circuit when too much current is flowing. This makes a break in the circuit and prevents further current flow. Another class of circuit breakers uses an electromagnet to cause a breach in the circuit. When the current rises to a certain value, the ferrous material is sufficiently magnetized to cause the circuit to open, thereby inhibiting further current flow. Later in this chapter we will explore the relationship between electricity and magnetism.

Circuit Breaker Symbol

Capacitors

Capacitors (also known as **condensers**) are electrical storage units. They are constructed using two metal conducting plates with a very thin insulator (known as a **dielectric**) between them. Air can also serve as a dielectric.

Simple Condenser

DC source   Negative plate   Positive plate

A capacitor can store an electrical charge because the DC source creates an excess of electrons on the negative plate and a shortage of electrons on the positive plate. The electrostatic attraction between the positive and negative charges keeps the charge intact in the capacitor, even when the voltage source is removed. The capacitor will discharge itself if a conductor is connected across it, as a path is then created for electrons to flow from the negative plate to the positive plate. A capacitor will allow AC to flow across it, but will block DC. This is why DC is most useful for "charging up" a capacitor.

A capacitor's opposition to the flow of current is known as **capacitive reactance**, and this is measured in ohms. Capacitive reactance is inversely proportional to the frequency of the AC signal. In other words, the higher the frequency, the less opposition there is to the flow of AC across the capacitor.

General Capacitor Symbol

Capacitance, or the ability of the capacitor to store charge, is represented by the symbol **C**, and its unit of measurement is the **farad**. A farad is sufficient capacitance to store one coulomb of electrons with an electrical potential of one volt applied.

Question	Analysis
In the wiring diagram pictured, the fuse is rated for 0.1 A. When the switch is closed, what will happen to the lamp in the circuit?	**Step 1:** The question asks what will happen to the lamp in the circuit when the switch is closed; i.e., will it light or not?
	Step 2: Normally, when the switch is closed, current will flow and the lamp will come on. However, this circuit has a fuse, so its impact on the circuit needs to be considered. The fuse is rated at 0.1 A. This means that it will only allow currents to pass that are 0.1 A or less. The current flowing in the current needs to be determined. Via Ohm's law, $I = \dfrac{V}{R}$. Based on the circuit, which is a simple series, $V = 30\text{V}$, and $R_{tot} = 25\ \Omega + 35\ \Omega = 60\ \Omega$. Thus, $I = \dfrac{30\,V}{60\ \Omega} = 0.5$ A.
	Step 3: Since the current in the circuit is larger than the fuse's 0.1 A rating, the light may come on briefly, but the fuse will blow, breaking the circuit and thus the light will go off.
(A) The lamp will stay lit. (B) The fuse will blow, preventing the lamp from staying lit. (C) The fuse will stay intact, but the lamp will go off. (D) The lamp will blink continually.	**Step 4:** Choose option (B).

Now try a question on your own.

A fuse rated at 0.5A blows in a circuit when the switch is closed.

If the total resistance in the circuit is 100 Ω, which of the following represents the smallest the voltage could have been?

(A) 10 V
(B) 25 V
(C) 60 V
(D) 120 Ω

Explanation

Answer choice **(C)** is correct. If the fuse is rated at 0.5 A, it will blow when current exceeds this amount. Via Ohm's law, current must be greater than 0.5 A. This matches with choice (C), which gives a current of 0.6A. Choice (D) would lead to a blown fuse as well, but the question asks for the smallest the voltage could have been.

Semiconductors

The term **semiconductor** refers to an element that has four electrons in its valence shell. Since the bonds between these four electrons and the nucleus are somewhat strong, these elements are neither good conductors nor good insulators. Elements that are widely recognized as semiconductors are silicon and germanium.

In their pure form, silicon and germanium are not particularly useful. However, when impurities are added to their crystalline structure in a process called **doping**, a whole new world of possibilities springs forth. The crystalline structure of pure silicon is very stable. The four valence electrons in each silicon atom bond with all the valence electrons in the atoms around it, so no free electrons exist to allow current flow. This can be changed by "doping" the silicon's crystal structure with phosphorus, arsenic, or antimony. Since these elements all have five electrons in their valence shell, they will bond themselves to the other silicon atoms, but leave one free electron that is able to migrate throughout the crystal. This changes the silicon crystal into an **N-type material**. This new material is still electrically neutral, but is able to conduct electricity due to the presence of free electrons.

If silicon is doped with elements that have three electrons in their valence shells (such as boron or indium), the result is a "hole" being left where an electron would normally reside in the crystalline structure. This creates repeating regions with an overall positive charge. As the free electrons move into these spaces, they create "holes" in the spots they previously occupied. With such doping, the silicon is now known as **P-type material**.

Diodes

P-type and N-type materials can do little by themselves; however, when the two are joined, a **diode** is formed. A diode is an electrical one-way valve that results from interactions at the junction of P-type and N-type material. Current can pass easily in one direction, but is blocked in the opposite direction.

Since current can only flow in one direction, the orientation of the battery in a circuit is important. If current is able to flow, this is called **forward-biased**. In order for the circuit to be forward-biased, the P-type material (also known as the **anode**) should be connected to the battery's positive terminal and the N-type material (also known as the **cathode**) should be connected to the battery's negative terminal.

The excess of electrons at the battery's negative terminal repels the free electrons in the N-type material and sends them toward the junction. The electrons in the N-type material then cross over the junction to fill the "holes" in the P-type material, and current flows through the diode. Reversing the diode's connection to the battery creates a new set of conditions. The N-type material's free electrons move away from the junction, since they are attracted to the opposite charge on the battery's positive terminal. Since the electrons have moved away from the junction, no electron transfer takes place there and current flow stops. The diode is now in a **reverse-biased** condition.

The most common application for diodes is **rectification**. Rectification is the conversion of AC into DC. Since a diode only allows current to flow in one direction, it will only pass either the upper or lower half of the AC waves. This is known as half-wave rectification. Four diodes can be connected in a diamond configuration to create a full-wave rectifier, which is the foundation for most DC power supplies. Diodes are also used for rectification in automotive alternators, where generated AC is converted into DC to be used in the vehicle electrical system.

Half Wave Rectification (Single Diode)

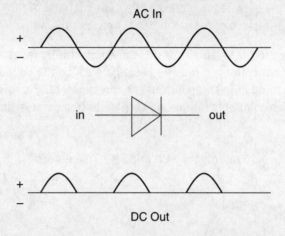

Full Wave Rectification (4 Diodes in Diamond Formation)

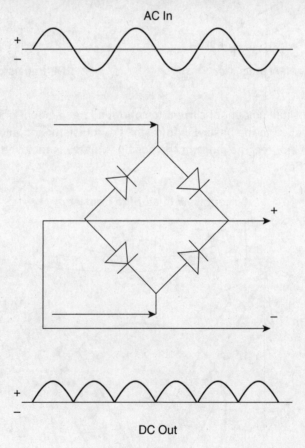

Transistors

The **transistor** is a component that has revolutionized the construction of electronic devices such as computers, calculators and radios. A transistor is versatile, as it can be used as an electrical switch, an amplifier, or a current regulator. Since there are no moving parts in a transistor and it is made from solid silicon, it is known as a **solid-state device**, which makes it very reliable. It is also very compact in its design, as thousands of transistors can fit into a single integrated circuit. An integrated circuit is one that contains all necessary circuit components in one single silicon chip. Transistors are the bedrock of logic operations that a computer uses to process information.

There are two types of transistors: an **NPN transistor** and a **PNP transistor**. An NPN transistor is made up of a thin piece of P-type material sandwiched between two pieces of N-type material. A PNP transistor is the opposite: two pieces of P-type material that have a piece of N-type material between them.

Inside the transistor, wires connect to the three pieces of semi-conductor material. Each piece is given a name. The middle piece is always called the **base**; the two outside pieces are called the **collector** and the **emitter**. The symbol for the transistor has an arrow that identifies the emitter. The direction of the arrow tells us what type of transistor it is. The key to remembering which symbol identifies which type of transistor is that the arrow always points in the direction of the N-type material.

Symbols for NPN and PNP Transistors

NPN transistor　　　　　**PNP transistor**

The transistor works by using a small amount of current to control a large amount of current. In the case of an NPN transistor, a positive voltage applied to the base will "turn on" the transistor and allow a relatively large current to flow from the collector to the emitter. The moment the positive voltage is removed from the base, the transistor turns off and stops the current flow.

Current Flow in an NPN Transistor

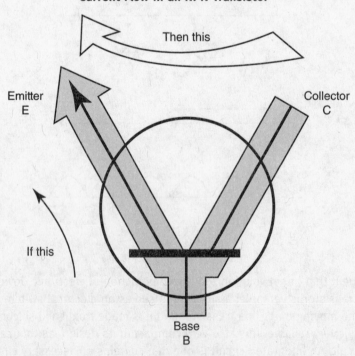

PNP transistors work opposite to NPN transistors. A PNP transistor requires a negative voltage at the base to turn it on, and the current then flows from the emitter to the collector.

Here are additional electronic component symbols that you may come across when you take the ASVAB. Some of them, including transformers, inductors, motors, and generators, will be discussed in the next section.

Wires and Connection Symbols

Wire   Wires Joined   Wires Not Joined

Power Supply Symbols

Cell   Battery   DC Supply   AC Supply   Transformer

Switch Symbols

Push Switch   Push-to-Break Switch   On/Off Switch   Two-Switch

Output Device Symbols

Lamp (lighting)   Lamp (indicator)   Heater   Motor

Diode Symbol

Diode

Meters and Oscilloscope Symbols

Voltmeter   Ammeter   Ohmmeter   Galvanometer   Oscilloscope

Question	Analysis
Which of the following electrical components can be used to convert the given input into the output shown?	**Step 1:** The question asks what circuit component is capable of receiving the input signal and producing the output shown.
Input Electrical Component Output ∿ → [?] → ‿‿	**Step 2:** The image shows AC as the input being converted into DC as the output.
	Step 3: A diode outputs only DC current. Any AC current that is passed through a diode will be converted to DC. Thus, only the positive or negative values of the AC signal will be output. None of the other electrical components listed converts AC into DC.
(A) capacitor (B) fuse (C) resistor (D) diode	**Step 4:** Choose option (D).

Now try a question on your own.

A capacitor is used to store charge. When a given capacitor is "charged up" and then discharged, it will output which of the following:

(A)   direct current
(B)   alternating current
(C)   capacitance
(D)   reactance

Explanation

Answer choice **(A)** is correct. A capacitor stores charge when a DC signal is applied across it. When the capacitor is discharged, it can only output DC.

ELECTRICITY AND MAGNETISM

Electricity and **magnetism** are closely linked. Moving charges produces **magnetic fields**, and the moving electrons in a circuit are no exception. From circuit breakers to transformers; from motors to generators; from microphones to door bells; the interplay between electricity and magnetism has proven useful in a range of applications.

A current-carrying wire generates its own magnetic field. The strength of the field depends on the amount of current flowing in the wires. When the wires are wrapped around a ferrous material and a current is passed through the wires, the resulting magnetic field magnetizes the iron core, producing an electromagnet. This induced magnetism is the basic principle behind many of the aforementioned electrical devices.

Inductors

The magnetic field formed by a current carrying wire can be made stronger by winding the wire into a coil. If the coil is wound onto a ferrous (iron) core, the magnetic field around the coil becomes even stronger, since magnetic lines of force travel more easily through iron than through air. When current first flows through a coil, the magnetic field builds relatively slowly. This is because the expanding magnetic field generates a voltage in the coil that opposes the original current flow, known as **counter-emf.** When the current is cut off, the magnetic field then collapses, and this collapsing magnetic field generates a voltage in the coil that keeps the current flowing. This resistance to the change in current flow in a circuit is known as self-induction and is a property exhibited by electrical components known as **inductors.** Inductors resist change in current flow. If current is increasing, the inductor opposes the increase by generating a voltage that moves against the applied current. If current decreases, the inductor uses the magnetic energy in the coil to oppose the decrease and to keep the current flowing.

Inductor Symbol

Induction is measured in a unit known as **henries,** and the symbol used to represent induction is **L**. Inductors work exactly opposite to capacitors, in the sense that they allow DC to pass easily, but resist the flow of AC. This resistance to current flow is known as inductive reactance and is measured in ohms. It increases with increasing frequency of the AC signal.

Transformers

A transformer is used to increase or decrease the voltage in a circuit. A transformer uses the properties of an inductor to accomplish this. Alternating current flowing in wires wrapped around an iron core magnetize the core, and in turn produce a changing magnetic field in the core. This changing magnetic field generates a voltage in a neighboring coil of wire. Depending on the number of turns of the wire in the primary versus the secondary coil, and the proximity of the coils, a smaller or larger voltage can be induced in the secondary coil. The primary coil is the one that is connected to the source. The secondary coil is the one in which an electric current is induced. A larger number of secondary coils means a larger voltage. The closer the secondary coils are to the primary coils, the more efficient the transformer is in producing a voltage in the secondary coils.

Transformers are especially useful to transmit electricity from power plants to residences and businesses. It is more energy efficient to transmit low current, high voltage electricity. However, by the time it arrives at homes, it must be reduced or "stepped down" to the standard 120–240 volts that most appliances in our homes use.

Basic Electrical Motors and Generators

A current-carrying wire positioned in a permanent magnetic field will experience a force (push or pull). This force can be harnessed to produce useful mechanical energy. This is the principle by which a simple motor works. The mechanical energy can be used to move the tires on a car, spin the blades of a fan, or lift heavy objects, just to name a few examples. The generated force on the current carrying wire is directly proportional to the amount of current flowing, the length of the wire, and the strength of the magnetic field. Increasing any of these will increase the force on the wire and thus the capacity to do work. Motors today are more complex than this, and many use electromagnets in place of the current carrying wire alone, but the underlying principle remains the same. A generator, on the other hand, is simply a motor in reverse. Moving a wire in a permanent magnetic field induces a current in the wire if it is connected in a complete circuit. Thus, a generator takes mechanical energy and converts it into electrical energy.

Here's how an expert test-taker would approach a question about the structure of electrical systems.

Question	Analysis
Given the following circuit, with a switch that has been closed for a long time, what will happen to the lamp immediately after the switch is opened?	**Step 1:** The question asks what will happen to the lamp in the circuit when the switch is opened. Will it stay on or turn off? Burn less brightly or more brightly?
(Inductor) (Closed Switch)	**Step 2:** Normally, in a simple series circuit, when the switch is opened, the lamp will turn off immediately. However, the presence of an inductor in the circuit must be accounted for. An inductor allows DC to pass easily with little resistance, and so most of the current will pass through the inductor and less through the lamp. Thus initially, the lamp will not be glowing very brightly. Once the switch is opened, the current generated by the voltage source will stop, but since the inductor resists this change, it will briefly produce a voltage that keeps current flowing in the circuit.
	Step 3: Therefore, immediately after the switch is opened, the lamp will still stay lit briefly and will burn more brightly, since all the voltage generated by the inductor will be dropped across it.
(A)　The lamp will stay lit for a long time. (B)　The lamp will burn more dimly. (C)　The lamp will immediately turn off. (D)　The lamp will briefly burn more brightly and then turn off.	**Step 4:** Choose option (D).

Now try a question on your own.

Which of the following circuit components, used when electricity travels from power plants to residences, can change the value of the input voltage, in a process known as "stepping-up" or "stepping-down"?

(A)　generator
(B)　motor
(C)　transformer
(D)　inductor

Explanation

Answer choice **(C)** is correct. A transformer can take low current, high voltage electricity from a power plant and reduce the voltage or step it down, before it enters a home. In general, a transformer can increase or decrease the source voltage depending on the application.

ELECTRONICS INFORMATION PRACTICE QUESTIONS

1. How much current will flow in a circuit that has 60 mV applied to a 15 KΩ resistance?

   (A) 0.004 mA
   (B) 0.9 A
   (C) 4.0 A
   (D) 900 A

2. What voltage is required for 30 A to flow through a 60 Ω resistance?

   (A) 1,800 V
   (B) 1.8 KV
   (C) 18 KV
   (D) 1.8 MV

3. What is the current in the 20-ohm resistor?

   20 ohms
   60 volts   40 ohms

   (A) $\frac{1}{2}$ amp
   (B) 1 amp
   (C) 30 amps
   (D) 100 amps

4. Given the image below, which shell is the valence shell in a copper atom?

   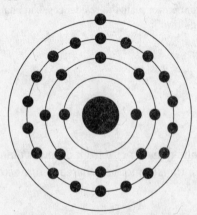

   Copper atom (29 electrons)

   (A) the first
   (B) the second
   (C) the third
   (D) the fourth

5. Which is the collector in the transistor symbol below?

   (A) 1
   (B) 2
   (C) 3
   (D) 4

6. Current can be expressed in

   (A) kilohms
   (B) kilovolts
   (C) milliamperes
   (D) millivolts

7. A circuit with flowing current in it can be assumed to be

   (A) open
   (B) closed
   (C) short
   (D) dead

8. Which of the following symbols represents a polarized capacitor?

   (A)

   (B)

   (C)

   (D)

9. When a P-type material is joined with an N-type material, what is created?

   (A) a resistor
   (B) a diode
   (C) an inductor
   (D) a capacitor

10. How does direct current (DC) flow in a conductor?

    (A)   two ways
    (B)   conductors allow zero current flow
    (C)   one way
    (D)   in the opposite direction as alternating current (AC)

11. Which switch, if flipped, would not close the circuit in the diagram shown?

    (A)   S1
    (B)   S2
    (C)   S3
    (D)   S4

12. Given a circuit with a single resistor, adding two more resistors to the circuit, both with the same resistance value as the original resistor, one in parallel with the original resistor, and one in series with them both, will cause the overall resistance to

    (A)   definitely increase
    (B)   definitely decrease
    (C)   stay the same
    (D)   either increase or decrease depending on wiring order

13. Which of the following would not increase the rate of direct current flow, I, through a conductor?

    (A)   decreasing effective resistance via a variable resistor
    (B)   increasing voltage
    (C)   adding an inductor to the circuit (in series)
    (D)   adding a resistor to the circuit (in parallel)

14. A circuit includes three $2\ \Omega$ resistors wired in parallel. What is their effective resistance?

    (A) $\frac{1}{2}\ \Omega$

    (B) $\frac{2}{3}\ \Omega$

    (C) $\frac{3}{2}\ \Omega$

    (D) $6\ \Omega$

15. Why is copper favored over other conducting materials like aluminum and silver?

    (A)   Copper has the lowest resistance.
    (B)   Copper has the highest resistance.
    (C)   Copper is inexpensive.
    (D)   Copper has low resistance relative to its cost.

16. A 6 V battery is used to provide power to a flashlight whose 10 W light bulb is the only load in the circuit. What is the amount of current flow through the flashlight?

    (A)   0.6 A
    (B)   1.67 A
    (C)   6 A
    (D)   60 A

Answers and Explanations

1. **(A) 0.004 mA** To solve this problem, the first step is to convert 60 mV to V. You can quickly make this conversion by moving the decimal point three places to the left, which yields 0.060 V. Next, convert 15 KΩ to Ω by moving the decimal point three places to the right, which yields 15,000. Since current is the unknown, the formula needed to finish the calculation is $I = E \div R$. Dividing 0.060 by 15,000 gives 0.000004 amperes. This can be converted to 0.004 mA.

2. **(D) 1.8 MV** Like the last problem, this one requires you to first convert the given measurements. Take the resistance and move the decimal. 60 KΩ becomes 60,000 Ω. Using our formula for calculating voltage, $E = I \times R$, we get $30\,A \times 60,000 = 1,800,000\,V$, or 1.8 MV.

3. **(B) 1 amp** The resistors in a series circuit add up, so one 40-ohm resistor in series with a 20-ohm resistor is equal to a 60-ohm resistor. To find current flow through a circuit, divide the total circuit resistance (60 ohms) by the voltage across the circuit (60 volts) to get 1 amp.

4. **(D) the fourth** The valence shell is the outer shell of an atom, which in a copper atom is the fourth shell. A copper atom has 29 electrons, so it would fill the first three shells completely and have one electron left to begin a fourth shell.

5. **(B) 2** In the symbol, the number 2 indicates the collector.

6. **(C) milliamperes** The ampere is the basic unit of current, so current can be expressed in milliamperes.

7. **(B) closed.** A closed circuit has continuity, and will allow current to flow in it.

8. **(C)** ─)|‾⁺

The choices represent four different capacitor symbols: a fixed capacitor (A), variable capacitor (B), polarized capacitor (C), and trimmer capacitor (D).

9. **(B) a diode** When a P-type material is joined with an N-type material, a diode is created.

10. **(C) one way** Direct current (DC) means that current only flows one way in a conductor. This is the type of current in circuits powered by batteries.

11. **(D) S4** The circuit pictured is currently open. The S1 and S3 two-switches connect to the same parallel paths, but presently, each is connected to a different branch. If either of these switches were to flip, a complete circuit would be made, passing through one or the other of these paths. S2 is a simple on/off switch, and if closed, it too would close the circuit. However, S4, a two-switch, cannot affect the current break in the circuit.

12. **(A) definitely increase** This question has no numbers, which can make it tougher to grasp. It can be reasoned out if your understanding of parallel and series resistors is very strong. Otherwise, your best bet in a situation like this might be to just choose some simple numbers and do the math. The question has three identical resistors in a series-parallel circuit. Choose an easy number, three 1 Ω resistors would work just fine, and we can determine the correct answer choice by seeing if the effective resistance is greater than, less than, or equal to 1 Ω. The effective resistance of two 1 Ω resistors in parallel is $\frac{1}{2}$ Ω. Add to this an additional 1 Ω resistor in series, and the final effective resistance is $1\frac{1}{2}$ Ω, an increase. Time permitting, the calculation can be repeated with a different resistance value for the three resistors, just to ensure that the resistance still increases.

13. **(C) adding an inductor to the circuit (in series)** Each answer choice would increase the rate of current flow, except one. Answer choices (A) and (D) would both decrease the overall resistance of the circuit, which, according to Ohm's law, would increase current. Answer choice (B) would also increase current flow if resistance was not changed. However, for a direct current, an inductor in the circuit has little effect. It will resist changes in current flow, but not tend to either decrease or increase it.

14. **(B) $\frac{2}{3}$ Ω** The effective resistance of several resistors wired in parallel can be determined by taking the reciprocal of the sum of the reciprocals of each individual resistance value. Since each resistor has a resistance of 2 Ω, you get $\frac{1}{2} + \frac{1}{2} + \frac{1}{2} = \frac{3}{2}$. Since the reciprocal of this sum is needed, in parallel resistor calculations, it's best to stick with fractions at least until the end. The reciprocal of $\frac{3}{2}$ is simply the fraction created by switching the numerator and denominator values, that is, $\frac{2}{3}$ Ω.

15. **(D) Copper has low resistance relative to its cost.** Copper isn't the best conductor. Silver has a lower resistance and is thus better at conducting electricity than copper is. But though silver is a somewhat better conductor, it is far, far more expensive. Copper is a very good (but not the best) conductor, while also being very affordable. Aluminum is inexpensive, but is a worse conductor than copper. Copper is also safer than aluminum, which, due to some of its heating and expanding properties, is more likely to cause electrical fires in household wiring set-ups.

16. **(B) 1.67 A** Rearranging the power formula, $I = P \div V = 10 \div 6 = 1.67\,A$ (rounded to the nearest hundredth).

Review and Reflect

Look back over your work on this practice set. If you struggled with some of the questions, ask yourself why.

Did you misunderstand a formula or simply make errors in calculations? If it's the latter, be sure to slow down and double-check your math when you do EI questions. If you need to review the formulas discussed in this chapter, consider making flash cards to help you remember them.

Did you have trouble remembering some of the technical terms introduced in this chapter? If so, consider making flash cards to help you memorize the meaning of those terms.

Which areas do you most need to review?

AUTOMOTIVE INFORMATION

KNOW WHAT TO EXPECT

On the CAT-ASVAB, you are given 7 minutes to answer 11 Automotive Information (AI) questions. On the paper and pencil test, the Automotive Information and Shop Information subtests are combined into one, with 11 minutes to answer 25 questions about both topics.

The required pace can be daunting. However, we're confident that by the time you finish this section, you will have a solid understanding of all of the automotive systems and will be able to use Kaplan's proven methods to conquer AI questions. Take your time with this chapter, and remember that you can't possibly know everything after one read-through. Review this chapter multiple times if a high AI score is important to your career goals.

Also remember that there are many, many minute details involved in the makeup of automotive systems. The test maker cannot possibly ask about all of them. Your best approach to studying is to develop a thorough understanding of automotive systems, their major parts, and how those systems work together. This high-level understanding will likely equip you to make solid inferences about details when you need to.

WHAT'S IN THIS CHAPTER

The modern automobile is a technological marvel. Thousands of parts are assembled to form the means that many of us use for our daily transportation. Space-age materials and advanced computer control systems are used extensively in its construction, but in spite of all this, the basic systems within the automobile still function the same as they always have.

Despite its size, any automobile is still only made up of many smaller **parts**. Parts are the smallest pieces that are used in the construction of the automobile. Parts include such items as bolts, screws, spark plugs, or belts. The parts of the vehicle cannot be disassembled any further, so they form the foundation for the construction of the vehicle. **Systems** are combinations of parts that work together to perform a particular function.

This chapter will be organized around four major types of systems:

- **Engine systems** generate power to drive the vehicle's wheels and various accessories. The foundation of engine systems is engine theory, which defines the mechanics and components involved in making the engine run. Engine systems also include the cooling system, which acts to remove excess heat from the engine. Finally, engine systems include the lubrication system, which circulates motor oil through the engine to reduce friction and make the engine run smoothly.

- **Combustion systems** comprise the fuel system, which ensures that correct amounts of air and fuel are available for efficient combustion in the engine; the ignition system, which generates and times the spark that initiates combustion; and the exhaust system, which forms a "pipeline" for waste gases to be removed from the engine and then dissipated to the open atmosphere.

- **Electrical and control systems** are becoming more and more significant in modern vehicles. These include the electrical system, which includes starting, charging, lighting, and accessory systems, as well as the computer system, which controls all aspects of vehicle operation, including engine, drive train, brakes, and suspension.

- **Chassis systems** are made up of the drive train system, which transmits power from the engine to the vehicle's drive wheels, the suspension and steering systems, which control the vehicle's ride quality and handling, and the brake system, which stops the vehicle safely and predictably.

This chapter will conclude with a set of practice questions.

ENGINE SYSTEMS

LEARNING OBJECTIVES

In this section, you will learn to:

- identify the basic function and the major components of the internal combustion engine
- differentiate between the different types and configurations of internal combustion engines
- identify the basic function and the major components of the cooling system
- identify the basic function and the major components of the lubrication system

Basic Engine Theory

The type of engine used in automobiles is known as an **internal combustion engine**. Combustion is the rapid burning of an air-fuel mixture. Internal combustion means exactly that: fuel is burned *internally* and the resulting heat is used directly to power an engine.

Typical fuels used with internal combustion engines are gasoline, diesel fuel, propane, natural gas, and alcohol. Gasoline and diesel fuel are by far the most common.

Three things must be present before combustion can take place: air, fuel, and a heat source that can be used to ignite the air-fuel mixture. If any one of those three elements is missing, combustion stops and the engine will not run. Internal combustion engines convert the **chemical energy** in the fuel and air into **heat energy,** and this heat energy is then converted into **mechanical energy.** (See chapter 9: General Science and chapter 13: Mechanical Comprehension for more information about types of energy.)

Components

There are common components in all internal combustion engines. These components include:

- **Engine block**: forms the framework for the engine cylinders and reciprocating assembly.
- **Piston**: a cylindrically shaped object with a solid crown (top) that moves up and down in the engine's cylinders. Hot gases produced from the combustion of the air-fuel mixture push on the piston to do the actual work.

- **Cylinder**: forms a guide for the piston to move in; allows the piston to move up and down as the engine completes its cycle.
- **Piston rings**: seal the piston to the cylinder and prevent combustion gases from leaking past. Oil rings prevent oil from the engine crankcase from making its way into the combustion chamber.
- **Wrist pin**: connects the piston to the connecting rod, and forms a pivot point for the small end of the connecting rod to move on.
- **Connecting rod**: connects the piston/wrist pin assembly to the engine's crankshaft. The large end of the connecting rod attaches to the crankshaft on the connecting rod journal.
- **Crankshaft**: converts the linear (straight line) motion of the piston into rotary motion, which can then be used to power a vehicle or drive an accessory.
- **Cylinder head**: located above the piston, it houses the combustion chamber, the intake and exhaust valves, and the intake and exhaust ports.
- **Combustion chamber**: located in the cylinder head directly above the piston, it is where the actual combustion of the air-fuel mixture takes place.
- **Intake valve**: allows the air-fuel mixture to be drawn into the combustion chamber. When closed, it must seal the combustion chamber from the intake port.
- **Exhaust valve**: allows waste gases to be removed from the combustion chamber. When closed, it must seal the combustion chamber from the exhaust port.
- **Camshaft**: responsible for the opening and closing of the engine's intake and exhaust valves. The camshaft turns at one-half the speed of the engine's crankshaft.

Basic Engine Components

The conversion of linear (straight line) motion into rotary motion as achieved by the piston-connecting rod-crankshaft combination is very similar to the leg of a bicycle rider. As the rider's upper leg moves up and down (piston), her lower leg (connecting rod), the bicycle pedals, and the sprocket (crankshaft) convert that straight line motion into rotary motion that then can be used to drive the wheels of the bicycle.

Most internal combustion engines are built to utilize a **four-stroke cycle**. This means that it takes four strokes of the piston to complete one cycle of events. A stroke of the piston is defined as the piston movement from the top of its travel in the cylinder (**top dead center or TDC**) to the bottom of its travel (**bottom dead center or BDC**) and back again to TDC.

The four-stroke cycle begins with the **intake stroke**. With the piston at TDC, the intake valve begins to open. As the piston moves downward in the cylinder, it forms a low-pressure area (or vacuum). Because the intake valve is open to the atmosphere, air is sucked into the combustion chamber due to the vacuum in the cylinder during the intake stroke. As the air is traveling through the intake system, fuel is injected into the air stream before it enters the combustion chamber. This allows the cylinder to fill with a fresh mixture of air and fuel. Once the piston reaches BDC, the intake valve is almost closed again and the engine is ready to begin the second stroke of the cycle, the compression stroke.

During the **compression stroke,** the piston starts moving upward in the cylinder while both of the engine's valves are closed. With the combustion chamber then sealed, the continued upward motion of the piston toward TDC compresses the air-fuel mixture in the cylinder, as the air-fuel mixture is forced into a progressively smaller and smaller space. The air-fuel mixture in the combustion chamber becomes progressively hotter as the particles of fuel get closer together due to the compression, making the air-fuel mixture easier to ignite and ultimately increasing the power of the next stroke, the power stroke.

Just before the piston reaches TDC of the compression stroke, the spark plug fires and ignites the air-fuel mixture, starting a flame that then travels across the combustion chamber. This flame further heats the gases in the combustion chamber and the resulting rapid expansion of these gases pushes on the piston as it passes TDC and then continues downward on the third stroke of the cycle, the **power stroke**. During the power stroke, both the intake and exhaust valves remain closed to ensure that the pressure generated from the combustion of the air-fuel mixture is not blown out past the valves but extracted by the motion of the piston toward BDC.

Four-Stroke Cycle

Intake   Compression   Power   Exhaust

Before the piston reaches BDC, combustion of the air-fuel mixture should be completed. Just before the piston reaches BDC, the exhaust valve starts to open and the engine begins its fourth and final stroke, the **exhaust stroke**.

The gases in the combustion chamber are now spent and must be purged from the engine before the next cycle can begin. As the piston begins its upward movement, it pushes exhaust gases past the open exhaust valve and into the engine's exhaust system, where the exhaust gases are eventually sent out to the open atmosphere. The piston continues its travel toward TDC, and at that point will have completed one complete cycle of events. This cycle then starts over as the intake stroke begins again.

Cylinder Arrangement

Automotive engines can be built in a number of different configurations, and these can most easily be classified in terms of the engine's **cylinder arrangement,** which is the position of the various cylinders relative to each other. The most common numbers of cylinders used in automobile engines are four, six, and eight, but there are also designs that utilize three, five, ten, twelve, and even sixteen cylinders.

The simplest cylinder arrangement is known as the **inline** design, in which all of the engine's cylinders are lined up in a row. This is a practical design for four- and six-cylinder engines. Inline four-cylinder engines are very popular in front-wheel drive cars with transverse (sideways) mounted engines. Inline engines are most often found in small- to medium-sized vehicles. Another arrangement that has been utilized by engine designers is the **horizontally opposed** or **flat** design. This arrangement has all of the cylinders lying in a horizontal plane, with half of the cylinders facing away from the other half and the crankshaft located between them. Some refer to this design as a "boxer" engine because the pistons move back and forth like a boxer throwing punches. The one major advantage to this design is that the engine's center of gravity is much lower so it is easier to build a more stable, better-handling vehicle.

The last and most popular design for 6- and 8-cylinder engines is the V-type engine. These engines have one crankshaft connected to pistons on both sides of the V-shaped engine. The two rows of cylinders are located 60 to 90 degrees away from each other, and each row has one cylinder head, for a total of two heads for the engine. A primary advantage of this configuration is the inherent physical balance of the engine's moving components, resulting in a smooth-running engine. Another advantage is the decrease in height and length relative to the in-line engine. The V-type engine improves the aerodynamic flow outside the vehicle; because the engine is smaller, the front of the vehicle can be lower. If an 8-cylinder engine is needed, this configuration creates the power required while also making the engine more compact.

Camshaft Location

Another classification used to describe automotive engines is **camshaft location**. The camshaft is responsible for the opening and closing of the engine's valves, and is driven by the crankshaft through a **timing chain** or **timing belt**. Some modern engines have the camshaft located in the engine block and the intake and exhaust valves located in the cylinder head. Engines built in this manner would be known as **overhead valve** or **OHV** engines because the valves are arranged above the piston and the combustion chamber. In OHV engines, a lever called a rocker arm, which is actuated by the camshaft through a pushrod, operates each valve. The OHV arrangement can be used with either V or flat configuration engines.

Engine designers often locate the camshaft above the valves and are then able to eliminate the pushrods that are necessary for the OHV configuration. The valve operating mechanism itself becomes simpler and lighter. Less mass in the valve train means that higher engine speeds can be attained. This design is known as the **overhead cam** or **OHC**. If only one overhead camshaft is used to operate the intake and exhaust valves of a cylinder for an OHC engine, that arrangement is known as **single overhead cam** or SOHC. In a V-type engine with two cylinder heads, there would be two camshafts, with one installed above each cylinder head.

One final step to make even higher engine speeds possible is to go to a **double overhead cam** or **DOHC** arrangement. This puts two camshafts into each cylinder head, and makes it so one cam operates the exhaust valves in that head, and the other operates all the intake valves. With this arrangement, it is possible to eliminate the rocker arms that are often used in SOHC engines and have the camshafts operate the valves directly through a follower.

Multiple-Valve Cylinder Heads

Engines may also be classified according to the number of valves used for each cylinder. The least expensive and most common arrangement is to use a **two-valve cylinder head**, with one intake valve and one exhaust valve per cylinder. To improve airflow through the engine and, thus, engine performance, it is possible to design a multiple (more than two) valve cylinder head. Manufacturers have designed engines that use three valves per cylinder, but now it is much more common to use a **four-valve** cylinder head. This arrangement has two intake valves and two exhaust valves for each cylinder. The four-valve cylinder head design has several advantages over the two or three valve designs. The four-valve design allows higher engine operating speeds and more complete combustion of the air-fuel mixture, which helps improve engine power and efficiency.

Firing Order

The order that the cylinders fire in is known as the **firing order**. A common firing order for four-cylinder engines is 1-3-4-2. This means that once the first cylinder fires, the crankshaft will make one-half turn, and then the third will fire and so on. Cylinders 1 and 3 will fire on the first turn of the crankshaft, and cylinders 4 and 2 will fire on the second turn of the crankshaft. In the case of a V-8 engine with a firing order of 1-8-4-3-6-5-7-2, cylinders 1, 8, 4, and 3 will fire on the first turn of the crankshaft, and 6, 5, 7, and 2 will fire during the second turn.

Many engines have their firing order cast directly into the intake manifold for easy reference. For those that don't, it is necessary to refer to the engine's service information.

Diesel Engines

Another variation of the internal combustion engine is the diesel. **Diesel engines**—also known as compression ignition engines—are much simpler and more reliable than gasoline engines, mostly because they do not incorporate a spark-ignition system. Instead of using a spark to initiate combustion, diesel engines use a much higher compression ratio to generate sufficient **heat of compression** to ignite the air-fuel mixture. The compression ratio for a diesel engine can range anywhere from 16:1 to 22:1.

Another major difference between a diesel engine and most gasoline engines is that all diesel engines must inject their fuel directly into the combustion chamber or into a portion of the combustion chamber called the pre-combustion chamber in order for combustion to take place. The diesel engine must inject its fuel into the combustion chamber because it needs the heat of the highly compressed air in the combustion chamber to ignite the fuel, whereas all gasoline engines, including direct injected ones, must rely upon the spark-ignition system to initiate combustion.

Diesel Engine

Mechanical injection nozzle sprays fuel into combustion chamber

Injection line

Air enters

Fuel ignites as it touches hot air

High-pressure mechanical pump

No throttle used

Only air flows past intake valve and into combustion chamber

Air compressed so tight it becomes red hot

Diesel fuel from tank

Engine Operating Conditions

Air-fuel mixture

For an engine to run efficiently, it is necessary to mix air and fuel in the correct amounts. Combustion suffers if there is too much fuel and not enough air, or if there is too much air and not enough fuel. The ideal ratio of air to fuel is known as the **stoichiometric ratio**, and it is the responsibility of the engine's fuel system to maintain that balance.

Air-fuel ratio is a comparison of the mass of the air relative to the mass of the fuel that has been mixed with it. The stoichiometric air-fuel ratio for a gasoline engine is 14.7:1. This means that 14.7 pounds of air is combined with 1 pound of fuel to create an ideal air-fuel mix. When fuel is mixed with air by the fuel system, particles of fuel are **atomized** and directed into the air stream that is entering the engine.

Too much air and not enough fuel would be described as a **lean** mixture. Lean mixtures burn relatively slowly because there is greater space between the fuel molecules and it takes more time for a flame to jump from particle to particle. Lean mixtures also burn much hotter, and thus can cause serious engine damage. A typical lean air-fuel ratio might be 17:1.

In contrast, a **rich** air-fuel mixture has too much fuel and not enough air. Rich mixtures burn quicker because of the small distances between fuel particles, and they also burn much cooler. A rich air-fuel mixture can cause spark plug fouling and black exhaust smoke, but is certainly less threatening to an engine than lean mixtures. A typical rich air-fuel mixture might be 10:1.

Ignition timing

Another major factor in making an engine run efficiently is **ignition timing**. Ignition timing is the point in time during the combustion cycle that a spark is generated at the spark plug. This is described relative to the position of the engine's crankshaft. For instance, an ignition timing of five degrees **before top dead center** (**BTDC**) would mean that the spark took place when the crankshaft was five degrees of rotation before top dead center.

The spark is most often timed so it will take place before the piston reaches top dead center on the compression stroke, because it takes time for the flame to move across the combustion chamber and burn the air-fuel mixture contained within. By the time the air-fuel mixture is burnt, the piston is on its way down again and is ready to make an effective power stroke. Regardless of how fast the engine is turning, it will take approximately the same amount of time for the flame to travel across the combustion chamber. This means that for higher engine speeds, the flame must be started earlier in order to generate the most effective downward push on the piston. This is known as **advancing the timing**. An example of an advanced timing would be 25 degrees BTDC. In this case, the spark takes place when the crankshaft is 25 degrees of rotation before top dead center.

In contrast, **retarding the timing** means that the spark is adjusted to take place later in the combustion cycle. Certain engine operating conditions might call for a retarded timing as part of normal engine operation. Ignition timing that is unnecessarily retarded, however, will have an adverse effect on engine performance.

Combustion

Gasoline engine combustion is the rapid, thorough burning of a compressed air-fuel mixture, initiated by a spark from the engine's ignition system. It is a flame that starts at the spark plug and then moves rapidly across the combustion chamber, heating the gases and building pressure in an even, controlled manner.

Normal combustion does not involve an explosion, and it is always initiated by an electric arc at the spark plug. If combustion is started by something other than an electric arc at the spark plug, this is an abnormal condition known as **pre-ignition**. Pre-ignition takes place when the air-fuel mixture is ignited prematurely (before the time the spark plug would normally fire), typically by a hot spot in the combustion chamber, such as a glowing spark plug electrode or a hot piece of carbon.

Detonation is when an air-fuel mixture explodes, rather than burns. It can often take place when an engine's air-fuel mixture is lean. This is because lean mixtures burn very slowly, and as the flame moves across the combustion chamber, the unburned gases become heated due to the advancing flame and the increasing compression in the cylinder. If the temperature of these unburned gases rises sufficiently, they will "auto ignite" and the flame front from this explosion collides with the original flame front. The pressure spike from this abnormal combustion results in a brutal shock to the engine assembly, and can be heard as a "knock." Severe engine damage can result from unchecked detonation.

Cooling System

There are two major types of cooling systems in modern automotive engines. The first type is **air-cooling**, where air is circulated over cooling fins on the outside of the engine to remove excess heat. The second type is **water-cooling**. A water-cooled engine uses a liquid coolant to pick up excess heat and then rejects that heat through a radiator. In order to ensure optimized emissions and efficiency, cylinder temperatures need to quickly reach operating temperature and remain consistent throughout a wide range of ambient temperatures. Therefore, virtually all newly designed automotive engines use liquid cooling due to its greater flexibility in coolant circuit design, its heat transfer ability, and its high heat capacity.

Coolant

The most critical component of the cooling system is the coolant itself. Engine coolant is normally made up of a 50/50 mix of **antifreeze** and water. Frozen coolant can lead to serious engine damage (even a possible cracked block and/or cylinder head), so it is important that the coolant be freeze-protected. The most common type of antifreeze is ethylene glycol. A 50/50 mix of ethylene glycol and water will not freeze until its temperature reaches −34° Fahrenheit. This same 50/50 mix will also raise the boiling point of the coolant, which is important in hot weather, because it makes the coolant that much more efficient at transferring heat.

Components

The major components of a water-cooling system include:

- **Water pump**: responsible for moving coolant through the cooling system in order to transfer and control heat.
- **Water jacket**: hollow sections in the engine block and cylinder head that allow coolant to be transferred through them. These are the areas that the coolant must absorb heat from.
- **Thermostat**: controls engine temperature by allowing coolant to flow into the radiator when the coolant temperature rises above a certain level.
- **Bypass tube**: allows coolant to flow back into the water pump from the cylinder head when the thermostat is closed.
- **Radiator hoses**: flexible hoses that allow hot coolant to flow between the engine and the vehicle's radiator.
- **Radiator**: responsible for transferring heat from the coolant to the outside air.
- **Radiator cap**: responsible for maintaining pressure in the system, and allowing coolant to transfer between the coolant reservoir and the radiator.
- **Coolant recovery bottle**: forms a reservoir for coolant to flow in and out of the cooling system as the engine increases and decreases in temperature.

Operation

Coolant is circulated through the engine by a belt- or timing-chain-driven water pump. The engine crankshaft drives the belt, so the water pump actually uses engine power to operate it. The water pump takes coolant in and pushes it into the engine block. The coolant then makes its way upward into the cylinder head, and then returns to the inlet of the water pump through the bypass tube. As long as the thermostat is closed (engine is below operating temperature), the coolant will continue to circulate in this manner.

When the thermostat opens, hot coolant moves past the thermostat into the upper radiator hose, and then the coolant enters the radiator itself. One of the methods used to raise the boiling point of the water has already been mentioned: using coolants made up of a 50/50 mix of ethylene glycol and water. The other method that can be utilized is raising the pressure in the cooling system. The **radiator cap** is responsible for this, and most are designed to maintain anywhere from 9 to 16 pounds per square inch (psi) of pressure in the cooling system. For every 1 psi of pressure that is placed on the cooling system, the boiling point of the coolant is raised approximately 3°F. A 15-psi radiator cap would then raise the boiling point of the coolant to between 212°F and 260°F.

Radiator caps incorporate two separate valves: a pressure valve and a vacuum valve. As the engine warms up, the coolant in the cooling system will tend to expand. This expansion will raise the pressure in the cooling system, but when the pressure reaches the radiator cap's rating, the pressure valve in the radiator cap will lift and allow some coolant to flow from the radiator into the coolant recovery bottle. This flow will continue as the cooling system pressure exceeds the rating of the radiator cap. The coolant level in the recovery bottle will rise until the engine reaches operating temperature.

When the engine is shut down and begins to cool, the coolant will contract and create a low-pressure area inside the cooling system. If left unchecked, this low-pressure area would cause the radiator hoses to collapse and have an adverse effect on the cooling system at engine startup.

Maintenance

Cooling systems require maintenance in order to keep them operating at peak efficiency. Again, the coolant itself is absolutely critical and making sure to have it replaced every two to three years is a good maintenance practice. The strength of the coolant should be kept at a 50/50 mix of antifreeze and water. This will ensure that the coolant has sufficient freeze protection and corrosion resistance.

It is also important to check that the belt driving the water pump is in good condition, and that there are no leaks in the system. Hoses and the radiator should also be inspected for visible signs of damage or wear. Most often, a leak will be external and can be observed as it drips from hose connections or faulty cooling system components.

Comparison of Cold and Warm Engine Conditions on Automotive Cooling Systems

Engine cold, thermostat closed

Coolant circulates through bypass to pump and back to engine but does not go through radiator.

Engine warm, thermostat open

Coolant circulates through radiator

Lubrication System

Another system critical to engine operation is the **lubrication system**. Without lubrication, the internal parts of the engine would very quickly develop enough friction to stop (seize) the engine completely. The lubrication system is responsible for the following functions:

- Lubricates: it puts an oil film between moving parts to reduce friction and smooth engine operation.
- Cools: it puts motor oil in contact with hot engine parts (such as the underside of the piston) and transfers heat to the oil pan, or the engine oil cooler if applicable.
- Seals: motor oil acts as a sealer between the piston, the piston rings, and the engine cylinder walls. This helps seal combustion gases in the combustion chamber and makes the engine run more efficiently.
- Cleans: additives in the motor oil cause contaminants to be suspended in the oil, so they can be filtered out by the engine's oil filter.
- Quiets: motor oil damps engine noise and makes the engine run more quietly.

Engine oil

Engine oil is a major component of the lubrication system. The engine oil is the lubricant to the moving parts of the engine. The oil must be carefully engineered to provide peak performance under the toughest engine operating conditions, so choosing and using high quality engine oil is extremely important for the life of an engine. Engine oil is made up of two main components: **base oil** and an **additive package**.

One of the most important properties of engine oil is **viscosity**. Viscosity is resistance to flow, and is expressed as a number that is directly proportional to the thickness of the oil. The Society of Automotive Engineers (or SAE) is responsible for developing the standards concerning engine oil viscosity. Oil with a viscosity rating of SAE 5 would have a relatively low viscosity (low resistance to flow), whereas SAE 50 oil would have a high viscosity.

Another important engine oil rating system is the API quality rating. API is the American Petroleum Institute, and it is responsible for setting standards for engine oil quality. For a gasoline engine, this rating would have a prefix of "S," and then the next letter would identify the specific quality standard that the engine oil meets. The first gasoline engine oils produced had a quality rating of SA, but greater demands on engine oils led to ratings that currently exist at the SN, SM, SL and SJ levels. Today's engines would not last very long if they were operated with an SA motor oil.

Engine oil with a "C" prefix for its quality rating would be suited for diesel engine use (e.g., a CJ-4, CI-4 plus, CI-4, and CH-4 rating). Engine oil that had both an "S" and a "C" rating would be suited for either gasoline or diesel engine use. An example of this would be engine oil with a rating of SJ/CD.

Components

The primary components of the lubrication system are as follows:

- **Oil pan**: forms the reservoir for the engine oil at the bottom of the engine.
- **Oil pickup tube and screen**: immersed in engine oil, this filters out large solids and directs oil into the oil pump.
- **Oil pump**: responsible for pumping the oil through the engine oil galleries. It is normally driven by the engine's camshaft.
- **Pressure relief valve**: prevents excessive pressure from building in the lubrication system.
- **Oil filter**: filters oil from the oil pump before it is sent to the various parts of the engine.
- **Oil galleries**: passages or "drillings" in the engine assembly that transport oil to critical components.

Operation

There are two main designs for lubrication systems: **dry sump** and **wet sump lubrication**. The dry sump system is very complex and typically only used on racing vehicles and, therefore, is rarely encountered. Virtually all mass-produced commercial and automotive engines use the wet sump lubrication system design. In the wet sump system design, the engine's oil reservoir is located at the bottom of the engine in the oil pan. All oil used in the engine drains to the oil pan due to gravity. There, it has an opportunity to cool. The oil pump draws oil from the oil pan into its inlet through the pickup tube and screen. The engine oil moves through the oil pump, and then is transferred under pressure to the engine's oil filter. The oil filter removes particulates from the oil, and sends the clean oil on to the main oil galleries.

When the engine is cold, the oil has a higher resistance to flow and thus requires a good deal more energy to pump it through the system. This also causes the engine's oil pressure to rise. If the oil pressure rises above the pressure relief valve's setting, the relief valve will open and allow some of the oil to drain back into the oil pan before it is pumped into the oil filter. This prevents engine oil pressure from rising to the point where it can damage components such as the oil filter, bearings, and engine seals.

The most critical area in the engine in terms of lubrication requirements is the engine's reciprocating assembly. The pistons, connecting rods, and crankshaft all require oil to lower friction and to remove heat. The largest oil galleries in the engine are used to move oil to these areas, and galleries are drilled directly through the crankshaft to provide oil under pressure to the connecting rod bearings. Oil that leaks off the connecting rod bearings is thrown onto the cylinder walls, where it helps lubricate and cool the pistons.

Other oil galleries take oil from the main oil gallery and direct it to the engine's valve train. This is where the camshaft, lifters, push rods, rocker arms, and valve stems get their lubrication. Other parts that may receive lubrication from this oil would be the camshaft drive, or timing chain, and associated gear drives for the oil pump, ignition distributor, etc.

Oil that has circulated through the engine eventually drains back into the oil pan. The oil pan is located at the bottom of the engine and thus sits low in the engine compartment, where cooler air typically resides. This cool outside air helps absorbs heat from the oil pan and helps cool the engine oil. For heavy-duty or hot-weather operation, a liquid-to-air heat exchanger (similar to the radiator in the cooling system) can be used to further cool the engine oil. Once cooled, the oil is ready to be picked up by the oil pump and circulated back into the lubrication system.

Maintenance

The key to lubrication system maintenance is to change the engine oil and filter on a regular basis, and to use top-quality engine oil and filters. This is the cheapest and most effective maintenance that can be performed to minimize wear on the engine.

Questions on the ASVAB may ask you to recall or interpret how the various systems of a vehicle operate. Let's take a look at a sample question from the area of engine systems, which encompasses engine theory, the cooling system, and the lubrication system.

Question	Analysis
An internal combustion engine converts chemical energy of a fuel into _____ energy to power a vehicle.	**Step 1:** This question asks about the conversion of energy in an internal combustion engine.
	Step 2: The answer relates to Engine Theory. Otherwise, there isn't much to simplify here.
	Step 3: Recall that an internal combustion engine converts chemical energy of a fuel into heat energy by burning the fuel and then converts the heat energy into mechanical energy that is used to produce useful work.

Question	Analysis
(A) electrical (B) mechanical (C) work (D) sonic	**Step 4:** The correct answer is (B). Answer choice (A) is incorrect because electrical energy is used to release the chemical energy but is not the result of the release of the energy. Choice (C) is incorrect because work is the result of the mechanical energy produced by the engine. And (D) is incorrect because even though sonic energy (sound) is produced in the energy conversion process, sonic energy is not the source of the engine's power.

Now try a question on your own.

Engine coolant is normally made of a 50/50 mixture of

(A) water and soap solution
(B) salt and alcohol
(C) water and ethylene glycol
(D) antifreeze and saltwater

Explanation

Engine coolant is composed of 50% water and 50% ethylene glycol (also known as antifreeze). The correct answer is (C). You would never want to introduce a corrosive material like salt into an automotive engine coolant; therefore, choices (B) and (D) are incorrect. Answer choice (A) is incorrect because water with a small amount of soap solution added as a "wetting agent" could function as an engine coolant, but not in a mixture of 50/50. Soap does not increase the temperature performance of the coolant as needed in automotive applications.

COMBUSTION SYSTEMS

LEARNING OBJECTIVES

In this section, you will learn to:

- understand the fundamentals of combustion within an internal combustion engine
- identify the basic function and the major components of the fuel system
- identify the basic function and the major components of the ignition system
- identify the basic function and the major components of the exhaust system

Fuel System

The **fuel system** is responsible for maintaining the correct air-fuel mixture for efficient engine operation. If the air-fuel mixture is not adjusted correctly, drivability, emission control, fuel economy, and engine service life can suffer.

Up until about 35 years ago, it was most common for the air-fuel mixture to be determined through mechanical means. This was accomplished through the use of a **carburetor**, which was very reliable but incapable of providing the precision required in modern fuel systems. Due mostly to the demands of emission control regulations, the carburetor has been made obsolete in favor of **electronic fuel injection**. This system is controlled by an onboard computer and incorporates a feedback function that gives it flexibility to adjust to changing engine conditions very quickly.

Components

The following are the major components of an electronic fuel-injection system:

- **Electric fuel pump**: located in the vehicle's fuel tank, the fuel pump supplies fuel under pressure to the fuel injectors.
- **Fuel filter**: filters contaminants from the fuel before it reaches the fuel rail.
- **Fuel rail**: a manifold that supplies fuel under pressure to the inlets of all the engine's fuel injectors.
- **Fuel pressure regulator**: regulates pressure in the fuel rail according to intake manifold vacuum. Excess fuel is bled to the fuel return line, where it is sent back to the fuel tank.
- **Fuel injector**: sprays fuel into the intake air stream as it receives electrical signals from the powertrain control module (PCM). The location of the injector will determine the specific type of fuel injection system being used on the engine.
- **Powertrain control module (PCM)**: another name for the vehicle's central computer, it is responsible for control of all functions associated with the engine and transmission.
- **Intake manifold**: distributes air to the intake ports on the cylinder heads.
- **Intake air filter**: all air entering the engine passes through the air filter, which removes airborne contaminants that could damage internal engine parts.
- **Throttle body/throttle plate**: the throttle plate, which is connected to the throttle pedal, controls engine speed and output torque.

Fuel injection system designs

When fuel injection systems first came into common use, they were designed to utilize either one or two injectors mounted in a **throttle body** that took the place of the carburetor. This is known as a **throttle body injection system** or **TBI**. While this system proved to be reliable, it was not capable of providing a high enough level of fuel control to meet emission control requirements. Most engines are now built with either **multiport fuel injection**, which has an injector for each engine cylinder, or **direct injection**, where the fuel is directly injected into the combustion chamber.

With multiport fuel injection, the injectors are located in the intake manifold, with their spray directed toward the intake valves. As air enters the intake manifold, it will flow all the way to the cylinder head before fuel is injected into it. This allows for much better air-fuel mixing and prevents fuel droplets from falling out on the intake manifold runners. With direct injection, a high-pressure fuel injector is located to spray highly pressurized fuel directly into the combustion chamber. Therefore, only air flows over the intake valves and enters the combustion chamber. Fuel can then be sprayed directly into the combustion chamber at an optimized point in the compression stroke. Also, the fuel acts as a coolant to the hot compressed air in the combustion chamber, which allows the engine to be designed with even greater levels of compression, which further improves power and efficiency.

Fuel Injection Types

Air in

Fuel in

Injector

Fuel spray
into throttle
body air stream

Cylinder
head

To
computer

Throttle
body

Intake
manifold

Throttle body injection

Air in

Fuel spray
into intake
port

Injector

Fuel
in

Only air
passes through
throttle body
and inlet
to intake

Intake
manifold

Intake valve

Multiport injection

Maintenance

The fuel-injection system requires very little maintenance. The filters (both air and fuel filters) must be changed periodically, based on the manufacturer's recommendations. Manufacturers may also require periodic cleaning of the injection system. Aside from that, fuel injection systems are built to give reliable service with a minimum of maintenance.

Ignition System

One of the most critical vehicle systems is the **ignition system**. Without it, combustion cannot take place, so the engine will not run. The ignition system must generate high-voltage sparks at the correct time in order to make the engine run smoothly and efficiently.

Components

The ignition system can be divided into two distinct subsystems: the primary ignition system and the secondary ignition system. The primary is the low-voltage part of the system, whereas the secondary is high voltage.

The following are the major components found in the **primary ignition system** of a basic electronic ignition system:

- **Battery**: supplies power to the ignition system for starting the engine.
- **Ignition switch**: turns the engine on and off by switching power to the ignition system.
- **Primary coil winding**: the low-voltage winding in the ignition coil. This is made up of several hundred turns of relatively heavy wire.
- **Ignition module**: a transistorized switch that turns the primary current on and off.
- **Reluctor and pickup coil**: responsible for generating a signal that operates the ignition module. The reluctor is mounted on the distributor shaft, and generates a signal in the stationary pickup coil as it rotates with the distributor.
- **Distributor**: driven by the engine's camshaft, the distributor is responsible for timing the spark and distributing it to the correct cylinder. Like the camshaft, the distributor turns at one-half the speed of the engine.

The following are the major components found in the **secondary ignition system** of a basic electronic ignition system.

- **Secondary coil winding**: the high-voltage winding in the ignition coil. This is made up of several thousand turns of fine wire, wound around the primary coil winding.
- **Coil wire**: transmits high voltage from the secondary coil winding to the distributor cap.
- **Distributor cap and rotor**: directs high voltage from the coil wire to each cylinder in the firing order. This is a switching mechanism that allows one ignition coil to serve all the engine cylinders.
- **Spark plug wires**: transmit high voltage from the distributor cap to each spark plug.
- **Spark plugs**: threaded into the cylinder head, the spark plug protrudes into the combustion chamber and generates the spark to initiate combustion.

Electronic Ignition Systems

Primary ignition operation

When the driver turns the ignition switch to the "run" position, current is sent from the battery, through the ignition switch, and on to the primary coil winding. From the coil winding, that same current flows through the ignition module and back to the battery through the vehicle ground circuit. The low-voltage (primary) section of the ignition system is responsible for the control of the secondary, or high-voltage section. Whatever happens in the secondary system is in response to the events in the primary section.

The ignition system works because of a phenomenon known as **electromagnetic induction**. If a magnetic field moves across a stationary wire, voltage is induced in the wire. Another dimension of this principle is that electric current passing through a wire will produce a magnetic field around that wire. This means that electric current can be used to generate a magnetic field, and a magnetic field can be used to generate electric current.

Secondary ignition operation

The collapse of the magnetic field in the primary coil winding induces a high voltage in the secondary winding. These secondary system voltages typically range from 20,000 to 40,000 volts, and modern systems can go even higher. This huge increase in voltage in the ignition coil is achieved because of the large number of turns of wire in the secondary winding relative to the primary. The magnetic field in the primary winding cuts across a much larger number of turns of wire in the secondary, creating a **step-up** effect in the coil.

The high-voltage current in the secondary winding must be directed to the correct cylinder in the firing order. This current is directed through the **coil wire** to the center tower of the **distributor cap**. From this point, it flows to the **rotor**, which is mounted on top of the distributor shaft and rotates with the distributor. As the engine turns, the rotor will direct the current to the appropriate cylinder and send it through the **spark plug wire** to the **spark plug**. The electric arc at the spark plug is used to initiate combustion.

Current ignition system design

Since engine performance relies heavily on accurate ignition timing, engineers look carefully at how to eliminate more moving parts from the ignition system. This led to the elimination of the distributor in a design named the **distributorless ignition system** or **DIS**. DIS systems use one ignition coil to operate two spark plugs, so a V-8 engine would require four separate coils instead of one. The increase in the number of coils allows each coil more time to build up its electric charge and, therefore, deliver a more powerful spark when the time comes to discharge. However, this system still utilized spark plug wires, which degrade over time and eventually need replacement for the DIS system to function properly.

The most recent ignition system designs have eliminated the spark plug wires all together. These systems are known as **coil-on-plug** ignitions. Individual ignition coils are mounted directly onto the spark plugs, and the discharge of the coils is controlled by the vehicle computer system. While the incorporation of computer control has increased ignition system complexity, the elimination of moving and high-maintenance components has led to very accurate control of spark timing, which is critical for optimum engine efficiency and emissions, as well as increased reliability of the ignition system.

Exhaust Systems

The exhaust system is responsible for removing waste gases from the engine. It must do this in a way that allows these gases to flow freely, muffles the sound of the exhaust, and keeps the gases and heat away from the vehicle cabin and its occupants.

Components

Typical components found in an exhaust system include the following:

- **Exhaust manifolds**: attached directly to the exhaust ports on the cylinder head. The majority of the exhaust heat and noise is focused on the exhaust manifolds. These are often made from cast iron for durability under high heat conditions.
- **Catalytic converter**: responsible for converting the toxic components of engine exhaust into relatively harmless compounds such as carbon dioxide and water.
- **Muffler**: incorporates an expansion chamber and sound absorbing material to diminish loud exhaust noises.
- **Tailpipe**: the exit point for exhaust gases as they enter the open atmosphere. The tailpipe normally exits at the rear of the vehicle.

Exhaust System Components

Operation

As gases flow from the exhaust ports of the engine, the **exhaust manifold** collects them. On a V-type engine there would be two exhaust manifolds, one for each cylinder head. These manifolds feed the gases into steel exhaust pipes, which connect the major components of the exhaust system.

The exhaust gases are then sent into the **catalytic converter**. High heat is developed in the catalytic converter as it reduces the toxic components of the exhaust to gases that are less toxic. Some vehicles use two, and even three, catalytic converters in an effort to meet emission control regulations.

After leaving the catalytic converter, exhaust gases are directed into the **muffler**. The muffler has expansion chambers built into it that absorb the loud sounds generated by the engine's combustion. The muffler is normally located toward the rear of the car, somewhere after the catalytic converter and before the tailpipe.

Even after passing through the catalytic converter, engine exhaust is highly toxic. The most dangerous of the toxic gases emitted by the engine's exhaust is carbon monoxide, an odorless and colorless deadly gas. It is extremely important that these gases be routed in such a way that they do not come into contact with the driver or passengers in the vehicle. This usually involves sending these gases to the rear of the vehicle where they are dissipated to the open air by the **tailpipe**.

To increase engine efficiency and power, the exhaust system can be tuned to match the design of the engine. "Tuned" exhaust manifolds are often known as **header pipes**. The idea is to allow exhaust gases to flow more freely and allow the engine to breathe better. Increased performance is usually gained at the expense of durability, as header pipes are much more fragile than cast-iron exhaust manifolds.

Maintenance

Inspect the system from time to time for physical damage; there should be no restrictions and no leaks. The system should also be tight in terms of its mounting brackets and clamps. Any damage should be repaired immediately.

The catalytic converter will enjoy a long service life if the vehicle's engine is kept in good running order. An engine that burns oil or has ignition or fuel system problems will damage the catalytic converter.

Questions on the ASVAB may ask you to recall the components or functions of the various systems of a vehicle. Questions may be situational, asking you to interpret the situation at hand and to make an assessment based on your foundational knowledge of automotive systems. Let's take a look at a sample question from the area of combustion systems, which covers the fuel system, the ignition system, and the exhaust system.

Question	Analysis
Multiport fuel injection prevents	**Step 1:** This question asks you to recall one of the benefits of multiport fuel injection.
	Step 2: There is nothing to simplify, but remember what you know about multiport fuel injection.
	Step 3: One of the features of multipoint fuel injection is the ability to precisely atomize the fuel into the intake air stream within the intake manifold runners. This fine atomization enables the fuel to be suspended in the intake air stream as fine particles and prevents larger fuel droplets from falling out onto the walls of the intake manifold runners.
(A) fuel droplets from falling out on the exhaust valves (B) fuel droplets from falling out on the intake manifold runners (C) the overheating of the engine (D) engine fires	**Step 4:** The correct answer is (B). Answer choice (A) is incorrect because injected fuel does not flow over the exhaust valve. Choices (C) and (D) are incorrect because, generally, multiport fuel injection does not directly affect engine overheating or engine fires.

Now give this one a try on your own.

A major component of the primary ignition system is the

(A) reluctor and damper coil
(B) inductor
(C) primary resistor
(D) reluctor and pickup coil

Explanation

The correct answer is (D). The reluctor and pickup coil are responsible for generating a trigger signal that operates the ignition module. Answer choices (A), (B), and (C) are not major components of the primary ignition subsystem, and therefore are not correct.

ELECTRICAL AND CONTROL SYSTEMS

LEARNING OBJECTIVES

In this section, you will learn to:

- identify the basic function and the major components of the electrical system
- understand the basic function and the major components of the computer system

Electrical System

The vehicle's electrical system is growing in importance with each new vehicle model year. Many systems that were once driven mechanically are now being redesigned to operate electrically.

Subsystems

The major subsystems of the electrical system include the following:

- **Battery**: stores electrical energy in chemical form. Provides direct current (DC) for engine starting and accessory operation.
- **Starting system**: responsible for cranking the engine to get it started. The battery and starter motor are the major components of the starting system.
- **Charging system**: responsible for supplying electrical current to charge the battery, as well as for vehicle operation. The major component of the charging system is the alternator.
- **Lighting system**: headlights, marker lights, brake lights, tail lights, etc.
- **Accessories**: this includes the rear-window defogger, windshield wipers, stereo, blower motors, and all other electrically powered accessories.

Battery

The battery is the foundation for the entire electrical system. It provides electrical current for starting the engine, provides current to the electrical system when the load exceeds the output of the alternator, and acts as an electrical "shock absorber," preventing voltage spikes when there is excessive current in the electrical system.

An automobile battery is made up of lead plates immersed in an electrolyte made up of sulfuric acid and water. This is why this type of battery is known as a **lead-acid battery**. As the battery discharges, the sulfuric acid in the electrolyte is reduced to water, and the lead plates become lead sulfate. Charging the battery restores the chemical composition of the lead plates and the electrolyte. Care must be taken when working with an automotive battery because of the great amount of electrical energy and the highly corrosive sulfuric acid stored in it.

Starting system

In order to start the engine, an electrically operated starter motor is utilized. When the ignition switch is moved to the "start" position, an electrical current is sent to the starter solenoid, which engages the starter drive gear onto the engine's ring gear (located on the flywheel). When the drive is engaged, the solenoid connects the battery to the starter motor, which then turns the engine at sufficient speed to start it.

Charging system

Once the engine is running, the charging system provides electrical current to recharge the battery and power the vehicle's electrical system. The main component of the charging system is the **alternator**. The alternator is belt-driven by the engine's crankshaft, and converts mechanical energy into electrical energy. The alternator produces alternating current (AC), which is then **rectified** by an internal set of diodes known as the **rectifier bridge**. The rectifier bridge converts AC to direct current (DC), which can be used to power the vehicle's electrical system.

A **voltage regulator** controls the output of the alternator. Normal system voltage during engine operation is around 14.5 volts. Turning on the headlights, heater motor, and other accessories on the vehicle increase the **load** on the electrical system and system voltage drops. The voltage regulator senses this decrease in system voltage and responds by increasing the alternator's output to compensate for it. As long as the alternator's output is able to match the load on the electrical system, the system voltage will remain close to 14.5 volts.

Lighting system

There are many lights built into a vehicle's lighting system. **Headlights** illuminate the road ahead of the car, **taillights** mark the rear of the car for other drivers, and **interior lights** help the driver see the instrument panel and other areas inside the car when necessary. The various lights are controlled by the driver through **switches** that turn the electrical current to the lighting circuits on and off.

Fuses or circuit breakers protect the vehicle's lighting circuits. If, for some reason, the circuit should draw more current than it has been designed for, the fuse will "blow" and cut off current flow. This protects the wires in the circuits from overheating and may even prevent an electrical fire.

Computer System

Computer control systems work much like the human nervous system. **Sensors** provide data to the **computer**, which processes this information and sends signals to **actuators** to control vehicle functions. In the case of the human body, the eyes and ears send signals to the brain, which processes this information and sends signals to the various muscles to control body movement.

Components

The major components of the automotive computer system include the following:

- **Sensors**: these generate signals based on rotational speed, temperature, pressure, and relative position. The sensors are the "eyes and ears" of the computer system. An example of a sensor would be an oxygen sensor, which is responsible for sending data to the computer concerning the oxygen content of the exhaust gases. The computer uses this information to determine whether the engine's air-fuel mixture is rich or lean.

- **Computer**: processes data from the sensors based on a preprogrammed strategy (software) and then generates outputs to control vehicle functions. The computer is the "brain" of the computer system. In today's vehicles, the computer is often referred to as the **powertrain control module (PCM)** or the **engine control unit (ECU)**.

- **Actuators**: these receive output signals from the computer and control vehicle functions. An example of an actuator would be a fuel injector, because it responds to signals from the computer to inject a specific amount of fuel into the intake air stream.

Automotive technicians communicate with the ECU using a **scan tool**, which allows them to get information from the computer concerning the operation of the various vehicle systems. The scan tool is connected to the vehicle's computer system through a **diagnostic data link** that is typically located near the driver's seat.

Now, let's look at how you will use your understanding of electrical and control systems on Test Day.

Question	Analysis
The alternator produces _____ current.	**Step 1:** This question asks you to recall the type of current produced by the alternator.
	Step 2: There is nothing to simplify here.
	Step 3: The rotating magnetic field of the alternator rotor produces an alternating current (AC) in the alternator stator windings. The AC produced by the alternator must be rectified into a direct current (DC) in order to be compatible with the battery and the rest of the vehicle's electrical system. The rectifier bridge is the component that performs the rectification of AC into DC.
(A) fast (B) slow (C) direct (D) alternating	**Step 4:** Only answer choice (D) addresses the nature of the current produced by the alternator. So it is correct.

Now try another question on your own.

The PCM (or ECU) is the _____ of the computer system.

- (A) actuator
- (B) sensor
- (C) data link
- (D) brain

Explanation

The correct answer is (D). The PCM (or ECU) is the processor that performs the analysis of the sensor signals and sends control signals to the actuators which makes the PCM (or ECU) the brains of the computer system. Answer choices (A), (B), and (C) are supporting subcomponents of the computer system that do not perform any analysis. Therefore, they do not answer the question.

CHASSIS SYSTEMS

LEARNING OBJECTIVES

In this section, you will learn to:

- identify the basic function and the major components of the drive train system
- recognize the basic function and the major components of the suspension and steering systems
- understand the basic function and the major components of the brake system

Drive Train System

The engine can produce power to move the vehicle, but this energy must be processed and transmitted effectively in order to accelerate the vehicle smoothly and quickly. Transmitting power from the engine to the wheels is the responsibility of the vehicle's drive train.

An important part of any drive train is the **transmission**. The transmission is the device that matches engine speed to a desired speed of the vehicle. The two main types of transmissions are the **automatic** and the **manual**. Drivers who like to have more control over the operation of the vehicle will often choose a manual transmission, because the driver is responsible for shifting the gears up and down. A car with an automatic transmission is much easier to operate because it does not use a driver-operated clutch and does all of the gear shifting automatically.

While rear-wheel drive was the most common design in years past, front-wheel drive has become very popular, especially in small- to medium-sized cars.

Components

The typical components found in a front-wheel drive vehicle with a manual transmission include the following:

- **Clutch**: transmits torque from the engine to the transmission. The clutch can be released and engaged to allow smooth starts and transmission shifting.
- **Transaxle**: has several "gears" that are selected according to the speed of the vehicle and how fast the driver would like to accelerate. The transaxle is a combination of the **transmission** and the **drive axle**, which are normally two separate components in a rear-wheel drive vehicle.
- **Half shaft**: a short drive shaft that transmits power from the transaxle to the drive wheels. Used mostly in front-wheel drive vehicles, the half shafts must be able to apply power to the drive wheels while allowing them to move up and down and turn the vehicle. There are two half shafts, one for each drive wheel.
- **Constant-velocity (CV) joints**: located at each end of a halfshaft, CV joints can transmit power through very steep angles. The inboard CV joint is located at the transaxle, while the outboard CV joint is located behind the vehicle wheel.

Rear- and Front-Wheel Drive

Rear-wheel drive

Front-wheel drive

Other drive train components that may be found in other vehicle designs include the following:

- **Transmission**: used in rear- and four-wheel drive vehicles, the transmission is responsible for matching engine speed to the desired speed of the vehicle.

- **Drive shaft**: a longer version of the half shaft, the drive shaft transmits torque from the transmission to the drive axle. The drive shaft is also required to allow up and down movement of the vehicle's wheels, but not to the same extent as the half shaft in a front-wheel drive.

- **Universal joints**: located at each end of the drive shaft, the universal joint allows the shaft to operate at an angle with the component that it is driving. Also known as **U-joints**.

- **Drive axle**: transmits engine power through a 90-degree angle, and splits that power between the two drive wheels. The wheels are attached to the ends of the drive axle. The drive axle incorporates a **differential**, which allows the left and right wheels to turn at different speeds as the vehicle goes around a corner.

- **Transfer case**: located between the transmission and the drive axles on a four-wheel drive vehicle. The transfer case splits the engine's power between the front and rear drive axle.

Gear selection

Transmissions are built with several forward ratios that are based on the specific gears that are used. Typical transmissions are therefore said to have "speeds" or "gears." For instance, a four-speed transmission would have four forward gear ratios and one reverse ratio. A driver would typically start from a stop using **low (first) gear**. In this gear, the transmission would increase the **torque** from the engine sufficiently to be able to start the vehicle from a standstill. However, this would limit the vehicle's speed once it did start rolling, so the driver would then select **second gear** and so on as the vehicle continued to accelerate.

High (fourth) gear would be used to allow the vehicle to cruise on the highway. Engine speed would be moderate to low in this gear, allowing for maximum fuel economy and quiet running. To accelerate quickly, however, the driver would **downshift** to a lower gear in order to increase engine speed and power. Proper gear selection is important when operating a vehicle with a manual transmission. Modern transmissions now have as many as eight forward speeds.

Automatic transmissions

Automatic transmissions are much more complex than their manual counterparts, yet are much easier to operate. The reason that many drivers prefer them is that automatic transmissions do not use a driver-operated clutch.

Instead of using a clutch, automatics transmit engine torque from the engine to the transmission through a **torque converter**. The torque converter uses fluid to transmit power, and allows for a certain amount of slippage when the vehicle is stopped.

Automatic transmissions do all of the gear selection for the driver. This is done in the transmission using hydraulic pressure to select the proper **planetary gear sets**. Virtually all modern automatic transmissions are controlled electronically by the vehicle's powertrain control module.

Another modern automatic transmission is the **continuously variable transmission** or CVT. A CVT transmission does not utilize specific gear sets to determine the transmission ratio (or gears). Instead, it relies on two opposing sets of cones, one for input and one for output, with a chain or belt running between the two cones. The effective ratio of the transmission depends on where the chain (or belt) is riding on the two cones. Because the transmission's effective ratio is not limited to specific gears as in a typical transmission, the ratio can be varied continuously between the limits of the diameters of the two cones.

Torque Converter

Suspension and Steering System

The newest suspension and steering systems have incorporated computer control in an effort to improve vehicle performance. While the sophistication of computer control has increased the overall complexity of these systems, the basic principles remain the same.

Components

The major components of the long-short arm suspension system include the following:

- **Springs**: hold the vehicle's chassis up and allow the wheels to move up and down in relation to it.
- **Shock absorbers**: absorb the energy released by the up-and-down movement of the vehicle wheels.
- **Control arms (A-arms)**: the long-short arm suspension system uses an upper and lower control arm to maintain the vertical orientation of the steering knuckle as the wheel moves up and down.
- **Steering knuckle**: connects to the upper and lower control arms through the use of ball-joints. The wheel hub mounts on the spindle, which is part of the steering knuckle.
- **Ball joints**: ball-and-socket assemblies that allow the steering knuckle to turn and move up and down simultaneously.
- **Steering linkage**: connects the steering wheel to the steering knuckle.
- **Wheel hub**: forms the mounting point for the vehicle's tire assembly.
- **Tire**: makes contact with the road and provides a "footprint" to aid in vehicle stability and handling.

Long-Short Arm Suspension

Construction and operation

In order to make a vehicle ride smoothly, the wheels must be able to move up and down while the vehicle chassis stays steady. This is the job of the vehicle **springs**; they must be able to allow this movement of the wheels without transmitting road shock. However, the springs absorb energy as this happens and must release this energy without bouncing the vehicle after encountering a bump.

The **shock absorber** is installed between the chassis and a control arm to help dissipate or absorb the energy stored in the spring as it is either compressed (or **jounced**) or extended (or **rebounded**). Without properly functioning shock absorbers, the vehicle will continue to bounce up and down after the vehicle has hit a bump in the road. The shock absorber uses a piston and hydraulic oil to absorb the excess mechanical energy from the suspension system and then releases that same energy in the form of heat.

The **upper and lower control arms** form the supports for the steering knuckle. The control arms are attached to the chassis through the use of **control arm bushings**. The spring is placed between the chassis and one of the control arms. The spring can be installed on either the upper or lower control arm in a long-short arm suspension. The control arm with the spring on it becomes the load-bearing arm as the vehicle weight is supported through it on the way to the steering knuckle and tire assembly.

An **upper ball joint** and a **lower ball joint** are used to attach the steering knuckle to the control arms. Ball joints are built similar to a human hip joint, with a ball and stud rotating in a socket to allow a wide arc of movement. As the control arms move up and down, the ball joints allow the steering knuckle to move freely with them. They also allow the steering knuckle to turn left and right as it is moved by the steering linkage.

The **steering linkage** forms the connection between the steering wheel and the steering knuckle. There are two main designs in common use, the **linkage steering** and the **rack and pinion**. Long-short arm suspensions most commonly use linkage steering to connect the steering column to the **pitman arm, center link,** and **idler arm. Tie rods** are then used to make the final connection to the steering knuckles. Smaller vehicles most commonly use the rack-and-pinion steering system because it is the most compact of the two major steering systems.

Linkage Steering

Rack and Pinion Steering

Tie rods

Tires

Rack

Tires

Pinion gear

Steering wheel

Tires

Tires are one of the most critical components of the suspension and steering system. They support the weight of the vehicle and make final contact with the road surface. The most common tire design is the **radial tire**, which is known for its stable footprint and low rolling resistance.

Tire construction begins with the **beads**. The bead is a circular piece of high strength material like steel wire that is encased in rubber. The bead forms the mounting point for the tire on the **rim**. **Body plies** form the main body of the tire and run from bead to bead. All other parts of the tire attach to the body plies, including the **liner** (sealed surface inside the tire), the **sidewalls**, and the **tread**.

Belts are used between the plies and the tread to help stabilize the tire's footprint (where the tire makes contact with the road). A stable footprint means better traction under all road conditions, and makes the vehicle handle and brake better.

Maintenance

The primary maintenance that should be performed on suspension and steering systems is lubrication of the ball joints, tie rod ends, and other components. This should be done with a hand-powered grease gun, and the amount of grease should be metered carefully.

The most important part of tire maintenance is proper inflation. Low inflation pressures can be very dangerous as well as increase the rolling resistance of the vehicle, thereby increasing fuel consumption. An underinflated tire can seriously damage the tire, which could lead to a blow out and accident. Too much tire pressure, or over-inflation, can lead to excessive tire wear. An extremely over-inflated tire can also lead to a possible blow out and an accident. Automotive manufacturers label each vehicle with the recommended inflation pressures for the front and rear tires.

Brake Systems

Of all the systems on a car, the most important may well be the brake system. It is one thing to not be able to move forward; it is another thing again to not be able to stop.

Components

The major components found in any brake system include the following:

- **Brake pedal**: the mechanical connection between the driver's foot and the master cylinder.
- **Master cylinder**: located in the engine compartment just in front of the driver, the master cylinder generates the fluid pressure to operate the brake assemblies at the wheels.

- **Fluid reservoir**: provides fluid to the brake circuits. The fluid reservoir is located on top of the master cylinder.
- **Brake lines**: transmit fluid pressure from the master cylinder to the brake assemblies. These can be steel lines that run along the vehicle chassis or flex hoses that are used to connect the steel lines to the brake assemblies.

Assemblies

Brakes work by converting the energy of the vehicle's motion into heat energy through friction. The two major types of brake assemblies are as follows:

- **Drum brakes**: expanding shoes make contact with a rotating drum to create friction.
- **Disc brakes**: brake pads on either side of a rotating disc are "pinched" together to slow the vehicle.

Brake systems are **hydraulically operated**. A pumping piston, located in the **master cylinder**, is operated by the **brake pedal** and puts pressure on the system's **brake fluid**. Since fluids cannot be compressed, the brake fluid travels through the **brake lines** and moves the pistons in the **brake assemblies** to operate the brakes. The harder the driver presses on the brake pedal, the more fluid pressure is developed and more braking power is generated.

Dual Hydraulic Brake Systems

Drum brakes

The parts that develop the friction in a drum brake are the **brake shoes**. There are two brake shoes in any drum brake assembly. As hydraulic pressure is applied to the wheel cylinder, which is located between the brake shoes, the pistons inside it push apart and act against them. The brake shoes then push outward against the inner surface of the brake drum, and the resulting friction between the brake shoes and the brake drum slows the vehicle.

Disc brakes

Disc brakes are much more powerful than drum brakes because of disc brakes' superior ability to reject heat energy. The pistons used to actuate disc brakes are much larger, and can apply more force to the brake pads. Also, brake rotors used in disc brakes are more easily cooled, as they are better exposed to the cool air under the car and are often designed with air passages through them to enhance heat rejection.

The piston that operates a disc brake is housed in a **brake caliper**. This caliper "floats" laterally as the brake is applied and released, and makes it possible for one piston to operate the pads on both sides of the rotor. This makes the caliper operate similar to a C-clamp. As the screw is tightened on one side, the entire assembly is drawn together and "pinches" tightly on the item being clamped; in this case, the brake rotor.

Power brakes

Braking pressure is usually boosted using a **brake booster**. The brake booster is located between the brake pedal and the master cylinder. Engine intake manifold vacuum is utilized to generate greater force on the master cylinder, so higher hydraulic pressures can be generated in the brake system for the same amount of pedal force provided by the driver. Some brake booster systems use fluid pressure from the power steering system to increase braking power.

Antilock brakes

As in every other vehicle system, computer control is being incorporated into the brake system. Most cars now come equipped with **antilock brakes (ABS)**, which prevent wheel lock under hard braking conditions. The ABS system uses speed sensors attached to each wheel to tell a computer (the ABS computer) the relative speeds of each wheel. If the ABS computer detects a difference in wheel speed more than a preset amount, the computer uses pumps and valves in the ABS system to adjust the brake pressure for the affected wheel or wheels. This gives more control to the driver in slippery conditions and allows the vehicle to stop more predictably and safely.

Let's see how the test maker will assess your understanding of the chassis system, and what process you should use to address the question and pick up the points.

Question	Analysis
Virtually all modern automatic transmissions are controlled by	**Step 1:** This question asks you to recall what component controls almost all modern automatic transmissions.
	Step 2: There isn't much information to simplify here.
	Step 3: Virtually all modern automatic transmissions are controlled electronically by the vehicle's powertrain control module (PCM).
(A) the driver (B) oil pressure (C) the PCM (D) the engine	**Step 4:** Answer choice (C) matches the prediction.

Now try a similar question on your own.

Brakes slow a vehicle by converting motion energy into _____ energy.

(A) sound
(B) electrical
(C) fluid
(D) heat

Explanation

The correct answer is **(D)**. Brakes convert a vehicle's motion energy into heat energy through friction.

AUTOMOTIVE INFORMATION PRACTICE QUESTIONS

1. How many revolutions of the crankshaft does it take to complete one cycle of events in a four-stroke cycle engine?

   (A) one-half
   (B) one
   (C) two
   (D) four

2. This image depicts what stroke in the four-stroke cycle?

   (A) intake stroke
   (B) compression stroke
   (C) power stroke
   (D) exhaust stroke

3. The engine's crankshaft is connected to the piston through the

   (A) cylinder
   (B) intake valve
   (C) exhaust valve
   (D) connecting rod

4. A 12:1 air-fuel mixture would be a _____ mixture.

   (A) rich
   (B) lean
   (C) stoichiometric
   (D) none of the above

5. Diesel engines utilize a

   (A) high compression ratio
   (B) spark ignition system
   (C) low compression ratio
   (D) carburetor

6. The antifreeze in the engine's coolant will

   (A) lower the boiling point of the coolant
   (B) raise the boiling point of the coolant
   (C) raise the freezing point of the coolant
   (D) lower the corrosion resistance of the coolant

7. Identify this engine component.

   (A) spark plug
   (B) fuel injector
   (C) wrist pin
   (D) valve spring

8. Electronic fuel injectors are controlled by the

   (A) powertrain control module
   (B) fuel pressure regulator
   (C) electric fuel pump
   (D) ignition switch

9. Where does combustion take place in the engine?

   (A) 1
   (B) 2
   (C) 3
   (D) 4

10. The PCM receives signals from the vehicle's

    (A) sensors
    (B) diagnostic data link
    (C) actuators
    (D) scan tool

11. Oil galleries in the crank shaft provide pressurized oil to

    (A) the pistons
    (B) the push rods
    (C) the valves
    (D) the connecting rod bearings

12. How do shock absorbers dissipate suspension system energy?

    (A) by converting motion energy into electric power
    (B) by converting motion energy into potential energy
    (C) by converting motion energy into heat energy
    (D) by neutralizing chemical energy

13. The water-cooled engine component that rejects heat is the

    (A) water pump
    (B) thermostat
    (C) radiator
    (D) antifreeze

14. Multiport fuel injectors are located in

    (A) the throttle body
    (B) the combustion chamber
    (C) the intake manifold
    (D) the flame front

15. Which of the following is developed in the catalytic converter?

    (A) toxic gas
    (B) high heat
    (C) hydrocarbon gas
    (D) carbon trioxide

16. Coil-on-plug ignition systems eliminate the need for

    (A) secondary coil winding
    (B) spark plug wires
    (C) spark plugs
    (D) primary coil winding

Answers and Explanations

1. **(C) two** It takes two revolutions of the crankshaft to complete each four-stroke cycle.

2. **(C) power stroke** This image depicts the power stroke, which is the third stroke in the four-stroke cycle. The power stroke generates the engine's power.

3. **(D) connecting rod** The connecting rod is what links the crankshaft to the piston and helps provide rotary motion, and therefore, power.

4. **(A) rich** A 12:1 ratio of air to fuel would be a rich mixture, fast-burning and possibly producing black smoke.

5. **(A) high compression ratio** Diesel engines operate with a high compression ratio. The compression ratio for a diesel engine can range anywhere from 16:1 to 22:1.

6. **(B) raise the boiling point of the coolant** Antifreeze raises the boiling point of your coolant, thereby rendering it much more efficient at transferring heat.

7. **(A) spark plug** This is a spark plug. Spark plugs are threaded into the cylinder head, where they protrude into the combustion chamber and generate the spark to initiate combustion.

8. **(A) powertrain control module** Of the items given, only the powertrain control module is in charge of firing and regulating electronic fuel injectors.

9. **(B) 2** The combustion chamber, indicated in the diagram by the number 2, is where the actual combustion of the air-fuel mixture takes place. It is located in the cylinder head directly above the piston (1 in the diagram).

10. **(A) sensors** As the "brain" of the car, it is the job of the PCM to gather signals from the car's sensors and generate outputs to control the vehicle's functions. The diagnostic data link, choice (B), connects a scan tool to the PCM; the scan tool, (D), is what technicians use to read the PCM.

11. **(D) the connecting rod bearings** The oil galleries are drilled directly through the crank shaft in order to provide pressurized oil to the connecting rod bearings. The pistons, push rods, and valves do not receive pressurized oil from the crank shaft oil galleries, so (A), (B), and (C) are incorrect.

12. **(C) by converting motion energy into heat energy** The shock absorber provides damping to the suspension system. The damping effect converts motion energy into heat, which is then dissipated though the shock absorber body into the atmosphere. The shock absorber does not generate electrical power or potential energy, or neutralize chemical energy. Therefore, choices (A), (B), and (D) are incorrect.

13. **(C) radiator** The radiator is the engine component designed to reject heat in a water-cooled engine. The other answer choices are incorrect because antifreeze is a subcomponent of the coolant, the water pump circulates the coolant, and the thermostat regulates the coolant temperature.

14. **(C) the intake manifold** Throttle body fuel injectors are located in the throttle body, so (A) is incorrect. Direct injection fuel injectors are located in the combustion chamber, so (B) is incorrect. The flame front is the burning portion of the fuel air mixture in the combustion chamber, so (D) is incorrect. Multiport fuel injectors are located in the intake manifold, so (C) is correct.

15. **(B) high heat** The function of the catalytic converter is to further reduce unburned hydrocarbon fuel in the exhaust gas by decomposing the unburned hydrocarbon fuel in the exhaust gas into carbon dioxide, water vapor, and heat. As a result, high heat is developed in the catalytic converter. Answer choices (A), (C), and (D) are incorrect because they represent components not developed in the catalytic converter.

16. **(B) spark plug wires** Coil-on-plug ignition systems eliminate the need for spark plug wires because the ignition coil is mounted directly over the spark plugs. Answer choices (A), (C), and (D) are still necessary components in a coil-on-plug ignition system, and therefore are not correct.

Review and Reflect

Look back over your work on the practice questions. If you got some questions wrong, think about why.

- Are there specific systems you need to review? If so, review this chapter, and then try to draw diagrams of those systems on your own.
- Did you get tripped up over the names of parts? If so, review the chapter, focusing on the words in bold. Also, consider making those words into flash cards.
- How did you do overall? Do you need to review this chapter comprehensively?

SHOP INFORMATION

KNOW WHAT TO EXPECT

In order to work effectively in any industrial or technical environment, a technician must be able to identify tools correctly and use them safely. Hand tools are the foundation of industry; very little work would get done without them. Even the largest and most complex piece of equipment would not run for very long if hand tools were not available for its maintenance and repair.

The ASVAB Shop Information (SI) test will assess your familiarity with common tools and their uses. You are given six minutes to answer 11 Shop Information questions on the CAT-ASVAB. On the paper and pencil test, the Automotive Information and Shop Information subtests are combined into one, with 11 minutes to answer 25 questions about both topics.

MEASURING TOOLS

LEARNING OBJECTIVES

In this section you will learn to:

- identify tools used to measure distances
- determine when a micrometer is needed
- understand the use of calipers
- differentiate between types of spirit levels
- determine the use of a steel square

A critical skill for any technician is the ability to make accurate measurements.

Tape Measures and Steel Rules

A **steel rule** or a **tape measure** can be used to determine distances. These measure in fractions of an inch as low as $\frac{1}{32}$, but are ineffective when more accuracy is required. This is because the scale becomes too difficult to read with smaller measurements. Steel rules are also useful for the layout of straight lines.

Steel Rule

Micrometers

When accuracy to the thousandths of an inch is required, a **micrometer** is used. The most common type of micrometer is the **outside micrometer**. The outside micrometer is made to measure the thickness of flat objects or the outside diameter of cylindrically shaped objects. It is built similarly to a C-clamp (see the discussion of C-clamps later in this chapter). The **spindle** of the micrometer is rotated in and out to adjust the distance between it and the **anvil**. All measurements are taken between the opposing faces of the spindle and the anvil.

Outside Micrometer

The **thimble** of the micrometer is attached directly to the spindle. The **sleeve** of the micrometer is stationary, and has markings on it indicating how far the spindle has been moved relative to the anvil. As the thimble moves outward, it uncovers the graduations on the sleeve. The position of the thimble relative to the sleeve is what reveals the micrometer reading.

Forty turns of the thimble will move the spindle exactly 1 inch. This means that each turn of the thimble moves the spindle $\frac{1}{40}$" or 0.025". The graduations on the sleeve are also marked every 0.025" to keep track of how many times the thimble has been turned. Each time the thimble completes one turn, another mark on the sleeve is uncovered. Four complete turns of the thimble move the spindle $\frac{1}{10}$ of an inch or 0.100", so this is marked with a large "1" on the sleeve. The mark at 0.200" is a "2," and so on.

The outside of the thimble has 25 evenly spaced graduations on it. Since a full turn of the thimble moves the spindle 0.025", this means that one of the graduations on the thimble is the equivalent of 0.001". Reading a micrometer is simply a matter of adding the measurement on the sleeve to the number on the thimble that aligns with the longitudinal line on the sleeve.

Example of Reading a Micrometer

1 Number	= .100
3 Sleeve graduations	= .075
3 Thimble graduations	= .003
Total Reading	= .178

Calipers

A **caliper** is a two-legged instrument that is used to measure the distance between two sides of an object. It can also be used to transfer a measurement from one object to another. Calipers that measure the external size of an object are called **outside calipers**, while those that measure the internal size of an object are called **inside calipers**.

Outside Caliper

Inside Caliper

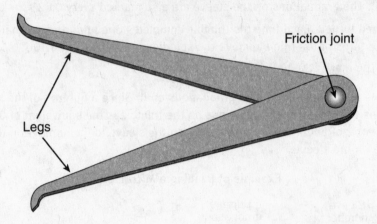

Friction joint

Legs

Spirit Levels

A **spirit level** is used to determine whether a surface is horizontal (level) or vertical (plumb). Spirit levels are also known as **bubble levels** or just **levels**. A **tubular spirit level** is a fluid-filled tube containing a bubble that is centered when level.

Tubular Spirit Level

A **bullseye spirit level** is a fluid-filled circle with a slightly convex face, containing a bubble that is centered when level. While a tubular spirit level only levels in the direction of the tube, a bullseye spirit level can level a surface across a plane.

Bullseye Spirit Level

Steel Squares

A **steel square** is used to measure or lay out angles. A steel square is also known as a **carpenter's square** or **framing square**, because carpenters commonly use it to frame stairs and rafters. Its two arms meet at a 90-degree angle. The long arm is known as the blade (or body) and the short arm is known as the tongue.

Steel Square

Tongue

Blade

Questions on the ASVAB may ask you to choose the most appropriate tool for a job. Look at this example:

Question	Analysis
You need to measure the length of a piece of wood within $\frac{1}{40}$". Which of the following would be the best tool to select for this job?	**Step 1:** This question asks which tool would be best for measuring distance within $\frac{1}{40}$". **Step 2:** There is nothing to simplify. **Step 3:** You can narrow your prediction to tools used for measuring distance. In particular, the tool must be capable of making very accurate measurements of distance.
(A) steel rule (B) measuring tape (C) micrometer (D) spirit level	**Step 4:** Choice (C) matches that prediction. Choice (D) can be eliminated because it is not used to measure distance, and choices (A) and (B) can be eliminated because they cannot perform measurements of distance below $\frac{1}{32}$".

Now give this one a try on your own:

You want to be sure that the joint you are installing is at a flush right angle. Which of the following tools could be used for that?

(A) steel rule
(B) spirit level
(C) steel square
(D) caliper

Explanation

The key term here is "right angle." The only one of these instruments that allows you to measure a right angle is a steel square, choice (C).

STRIKING TOOLS

LEARNING OBJECTIVES

In this section you will learn to:

- differentiate types of hammers and their uses
- understand the use of nails
- understand rivets and the tools used to install them
- identify how punches are used
- determine when a drift is needed

Hammers

Striking objects in order to remove or install them is the job of the **hammer**. Almost every technician uses a hammer of some kind, whether it is used to drive a nail or to loosen pieces of an assembly. Hammers come in many designs and sizes according to their intended use.

The type most often used by metal workers and mechanics is known as a **ball-peen hammer**. This hammer is designed with a regular striking face, like most hammers, but also has a rounded end that can be used for shaping metal and making gaskets.

Ball-Peen Hammer

Mechanics will often use a **rubber mallet** to prevent damage to the parts they are striking. Rubber mallets are not made for maximum impact; they are designed to install or remove delicate parts such as hub caps while preventing damage to their surface. A carpenter would use a **wooden mallet** to achieve the same effect.

Rubber and Wooden Mallets

Rubber mallet

Wooden mallet

Carpenters often will use a **claw hammer,** which serves a dual purpose. The hammer head has two ends; one to drive nails and the other to remove nails. Claw hammers come in a variety of sizes, and these are determined by the weight of the hammer head. A general-purpose claw hammer would have a 13 oz. head, while a rough-framing hammer, typically used for framing wooden houses, might be anywhere from 16 to 20 oz.

Claw Hammer

Heavy jobs, such as driving fence posts or breaking down drywall, require the use of a **sledge hammer**. This is a long-handle hammer with a large steel head that typically requires both hands to operate.

Sledge Hammer

Nails

A **nail** is a pin-shaped fastener made of metal. One end of the nail comes to a sharp point, while the other end usually has a flat head. However, there are also headless nails. The length of the nail body between the head and point is called the shank. Nails are typically driven in to wood by a hammer or **pneumatic nail gun**.

Nail

Rivets

Rivets are metal fasteners that can be used to assemble parts. A rivet is simply a pin with a head at one end. A rivet is installed in a hole (the same diameter as the rivet) that is drilled through two pieces that are to be assembled. With the two pieces tightly clamped, the head of the rivet is placed on a hard surface, while the other end is formed into a head using a hammer or special riveting tool. This creates an assembly that is semipermanent, as the rivet must be drilled out to remove it.

Installation of a Regular Rivet

The rivet is driven through two pieces.

The end is formed into a head with a hammer.

The assembly is complete.

Chisels, Punches, and Drifts

Hammers are often used in conjunction with a chisel, a punch, or a drift. A **chisel** normally has a long, sharp edge and is used for cutting. A **punch** is narrow and is used for driving small fasteners and making layout marks. A **drift** is used for striking an object where it is important that the hammer itself not come in direct contact with the work.

The most common chisel is the **cold chisel**, which has a straight, sharp edge for cutting off bolt heads or separating two pieces of an assembly. Cold chisels get dull from time to time and must be sharpened on a bench grinder.

Punches are made in a number of different designs, but the most common ones are the **pin punch** and the **center punch**. Pin punches are straight and cylindrical in shape. Pin punches come in various sizes, normally starting as small as $\frac{1}{16}$" and going up to $\frac{1}{4}$" in diameter. The pin punch is used to drive pins out of holes, and to follow the pin through the hole as it forces it out.

Pin Punch

Center punches are used to make small indentations that serve as starting marks for drilling operations. Making a small indentation with a center punch can help the drill bit stay on target long enough to get a hole started. Attempting to drill a hole in metal without first marking it with a center punch can allow the drill bit to "walk" across the work and completely miss the original target.

Center Punch

When using a hammer to drive parts in or out of an assembly, it is easy to damage the parts if they are struck directly by the hammer. The head of a ball-peen hammer is made from forged steel, and thus can easily damage parts that are made from softer materials. Placing a **drift** against the object and then striking the drift with a hammer prevents damage to the part that is being driven. Drifts are often made from soft metals such as mild steel, brass, and even aluminum.

Brass Drift

Here is a sample ASVAB question that asks you to differentiate between striking tools:

Question	Analysis
Which of the following hammers would be most appropriate to install a hub cap?	**Step 1:** This question asks which hammer would be most appropriate to install a delicate part. **Step 2:** Not much info to simplify. **Step 3:** You can narrow your prediction to hammers best used for delicate jobs like installing a hubcap.
(A) claw hammer (B) pneumatic hammer (C) ball peen hammer (D) rubber mallet	**Step 4:** Choice (D) matches that prediction. Choices (A) and (C) can be eliminated, because their striking heads are too hard. Choice (B) can be eliminated because it exerts too much force.

Now try one on your own.

You hammered a nail into the wrong part of a board and you want to remove it. With which of the following hammers could you do that?

(A) ball-peen hammer
(B) wooden mallet
(C) rubber mallet
(D) claw hammer

Explanation

Choices (A), (B), and (C) do not contain any device that could remove a nail. However, the claw on a claw hammer (D) is designed especially to remove nails. That is the tool you would need.

TURNING TOOLS

LEARNING OBJECTIVES

In this section you will learn to:

- identify different types of screwdrivers and their coordinating fasteners
- distinguish between different types of wrenches and the benefits of each
- understand how wrenches and sockets are sized
- describe what type of wrench to use for a particular project
- understand the concept of torque as it applies to hand tools
- understand when and why nuts are used
- identify the types of fasteners used with wrenches
- understand the system of labeling common fasteners

Screwdrivers

Screwdrivers, which come in many different sizes and styles, are one of the most common tools used to install and remove fasteners. The oldest screwdriver design is the **flat tip** type, which is basically a flat blade made to turn a screw with a single slot across the top of it.

Flat Tip Screwdriver

The flat tip screwdriver is far less popular now in light of some newer designs, including the **Phillips**, **Robertson**, and **Torx** screwdrivers. A Phillips screwdriver is recognizable by its tip that looks like a plus sign. Robertson screwdrivers have a square tip, and Torx screwdrivers have a characteristic 6-pointed star-shaped tip. All of these newer designs grip the fastener, making the screw easier to remove and install. Since the screwdriver makes better contact with the screw, it is also possible to fasten it more tightly.

Phillips Tip Screwdriver

Robertson Screwdriver

Torx Screwdriver

Screwdrivers are used with only one type of fastener—**screws,** which are **threaded** fasteners that vary in size and shape depending on the project. The threads on screws are designed to tighten when turned clockwise. Read more about how fasteners are classified later in this chapter in the "Nuts and Bolts" section. **Washers**, disk-shaped rings, may be used alongside screws to protect the work surface and distribute the force caused by tightening the screw.

Wrenches

With all wrenches, the longer the wrench, the more leverage and the more twisting force (**torque**) it can apply to tighten or loosen a fastener. There are two basic types of wrenches; the **open-end** and the **box-end**. The open-end wrench is made for speed. Since the end is open, it is easy to slide the wrench on and off a fastener, such as a cap screw. To loosen tight fasteners, it is a good idea to use a box-end wrench. The box end wraps completely around the head of a bolt, and therefore makes greater surface contact, distributing the force more evenly.

Open-End Wrench

Box-End Wrench

The most common wrench arrangement is the **combination wrench**. This design has an open-end and a box-end built into opposite ends of a wrench. Both ends are made to fit the same size fastener, but the technician can loosen the bolt with the box end, and then finish removing the bolt more quickly using the open end.

When the specific size wrench for a fastener is not available, an **adjustable wrench** (sometimes referred to as a **Crescent® wrench**) can be used.

Adjustable Wrench

Sockets

An alternative to using wrenches to loosen fasteners is the use of **sockets**. Like wrenches, sockets come in two designs. **Six-point** is a stronger design because of its greater wall thickness, and is usually the mechanic's first choice in the smaller socket drive sizes. However, **twelve-point** is definitely the most popular in large drive sizes, such as $\frac{3}{4}$" and above.

Six-Point and Twelve-Point Sockets

6-point   12-point

To determine the size of a socket required for a job, simply measure the distance between two parallel sides of the bolt head. If the bolt head measures $\frac{9}{16}$" across two parallel sides, then a $\frac{9}{16}$" socket is required to loosen it.

Sockets come in a variety of **drive sizes**, which are determined by the size of the opening that attaches to the **drive tool**. For instance, if the square end of a socket measures $\frac{3}{8}$" across, then that would be a $\frac{3}{8}$" drive socket. The most popular drive sizes are $\frac{1}{4}$", $\frac{3}{8}$", $\frac{1}{2}$", and $\frac{3}{4}$". Larger drive sizes are available for the very large fasteners used in heavy industry. Take a look at the diagram below.

Common Socket Drive Size Range

$\frac{1}{4}$" $\frac{3}{8}$" $\frac{1}{2}$" $\frac{3}{4}$" 1"

Sockets are very versatile, because they can be used with a variety of drive tools. The most common drive tool for sockets is the **ratchet**, which turns the fastener in only one direction as the handle is moved back and forth through a narrow arc. Ratchets are reversible, so they can be set to tighten or loosen a fastener. They can also be more useful than open end/box end wrenches in tight quarters (especially when paired with an extension bar) because you do not need to replace the tool with each turn—just move the handle back and forth.

Ratchet

Sockets can also be used with **pneumatic** (compressed air) power tools, such as an **air impact wrench**. The air impact wrench can remove fasteners quickly by applying tremendous amounts of **torque** (twisting force) and using a hammering action that vibrates fasteners loose. It is important to remember that only **impact sockets** should be used with an air impact wrench.

Air Wrench

Nuts and Bolts

Some of the most common types of tools to be tested on the ASVAB are fasteners (screws and bolts). It pays to review this wide range of hardware.

Wrenches of all types are used with a variety of **threaded** fasteners called bolts and nuts. A bolt has **external threads**, whereas a nut has **internal threads**. Bolts typically have a hexagonal head, which is held in place with a wrench while the nut is tightened (also with a wrench) to fasten the assembly. A threaded bolt can only be inserted into a nut or hole that has a similar thread.

While there is not a clear-cut distinction between screws and bolts, the most practical way to distinguish between the two is based upon the shape of the head and what tool is used to install or remove the fastener. Bolts typically have a hexagonal (six-sided) or square head and are used with a wrench and nut. On the other hand, screws typically have a round head with an indentation that matches the screwdriver that must be used to install or remove the screw. Both fasteners are threaded on part or all of the shaft.

Nuts thread onto bolts to clamp assemblies together. Nuts usually have either a square head or a hexagonal head, and can be locked into position using several different methods.

> **Wing Nuts** make it possible to disassemble a component by hand. The two "wings" attached to the nut make it easy to tighten and loosen without the aid of hand tools.

Wing Nut

A **castellated nut** uses a **cotter pin** to lock it into place. The cotter pin passes through a hole in the bolt or stud that the nut is threaded on, engaging the cutouts in the nut.

Castellated Nut

Cotter Pin

Lock nuts have a nylon insert incorporated into its threads that provides enough interference to prevent the nut from loosening, thus locking it in place.

Lock Nuts

The type of thread that is placed on a fastener will vary according to the diameter of the fastener and the intended strength of the finished product. Threads are identified by their **pitch,** and this is measured using a **thread pitch gauge**.

Fractional-measurement fasteners (measured in fractions of inches) use threads that are identified by the number of threads per inch. There are two basic thread classifications within this group: **Unified National Coarse (UNC),** and **Unified National Fine (UNF).** A UNC or coarse thread would have relatively few threads per inch, where a UNF or fine thread would have a larger number of threads per inch.

A bolt that is $\frac{3}{8}''$ in diameter could, therefore, have two possible thread pitches. If it were a UNC bolt, it would have 16 threads per inch, whereas if it were a UNF bolt, it would have 24 threads per inch.

Bolt Designation Numbers

Two other important measurements of a fastener include the **diameter** and the **length**. The diameter is the distance across the unthreaded portion of the bolt. This would give an indication of the size of hole that the fastener is made to be installed in. The length of the bolt is the distance between the underside of the bolt head and the end of the bolt. Note that the bolt head does not count toward the length of the bolt.

Fastener Diameter and Length

Let's check out one way fasteners could be tested on the ASVAB:

Question	Analysis
You are assembling a project with bolts that you would like to be able to remove later, even if you do not have a wrench with you. What would be the best type of nut to use in this assembly?	**Step 1:** You're asked to determine the best type of nut to use in the given project.
	Step 2: The key phrase is "even if you do not have a wrench with you." Think about what type of nut can be removed easily with just your hands.
	Step 3: Make a prediction: a wing nut can be removed using only your hands.
(A) lock nut (B) standard nut (C) wing nut (D) castellated nut	**Step 4:** Choose answer (C).

A Test Day question may ask you about the correct size tool to use. Take a look at this question:

You have a bolt that needs to be removed, but an $\frac{11}{16}$" open-end wrench is just slightly too big to fit properly. Which of the following sizes should be tried next?

(A) $\frac{3}{4}$"

(B) $\frac{5}{8}$"

(C) $\frac{3}{8}$"

(D) $\frac{5}{16}$"

Explanation

The key phrase to focus on in this question is that the $\frac{11}{16}$" wrench is just slightly too big. So, you are looking for a wrench that is a bit smaller. It can be tricky to tell which fraction is smaller, but a quick way to do that is to find a common denominator for each fraction. (Review the fraction rules in chapter 6: Arithmetic Reasoning if you need a quick reminder.) Convert all the fractions to have 16 as the denominator so they are easier to compare. Choice (A) is larger than $\frac{11}{16}$", so that can be eliminated right away. Choices (C) and (D) are significantly smaller than $\frac{11}{16}$", so they also do not fit what we are looking for. Choice (B), on the other hand, is the size of a wrench just smaller than an $\frac{11}{16}$" wrench ($\frac{5}{8}$" is equal to $\frac{10}{16}$"), so that is the correct answer.

FASTENING TOOLS

LEARNING OBJECTIVES

In this section you will learn to:

- identify where and why snap rings are used
- differentiate ways to join metals
- determine when and how to solder
- determine when and how to weld

Ring Fasteners

Retaining rings (or **snap rings**) are used to prevent end-movement of cylindrical parts in bores or parts mounted on shafts. **External snap rings** are installed in grooves on shafts, whereas **internal snap rings** install in grooves inside a bore. Snap rings are installed and removed using snap-ring pliers.

Internal Snap Rings and External Snap Rings

Internal prong-type   Internal hole-type   External hole-type   External "E"-type

Soldering Tools

Soldering is a process that joins metals by bonding a metal alloy to their surfaces. It is a low-temperature process that can be performed with simple tools and inexpensive materials.

Most solder is an alloy of lead and tin. The percentages of each metal in the solder will vary depending on the desired properties of the solder; e.g., its melting point. Higher percentages of lead will result in a lower melting point.

The most critical part of soldering is the cleaning of the surfaces to be joined. Any oxides or other contaminants on the surface to be soldered will prevent a solid connection from being made. The best way to prepare a surface for soldering is to use a **flux** that will clean the surfaces with a chemical action. Electrical connections require a **rosin flux**, and solders made for this will have the flux contained in the core of the solder. This is known as **rosin-core solder**.

There are a number of tools that can be used to generate the necessary heat to melt the solder, but in most cases a **soldering iron** is used. Most soldering irons are electrically powered, and can draw anywhere from 25 to 100 watts. Low-power irons would be used to solder electrical connections, whereas higher powered ones would be used in sheet metal work.

Soldering Iron

Tip   Power cord

A tool that is often used for soldering electrical connections is the **soldering gun**. A soldering gun has a two-step trigger that allows the technician to quickly select a low or high heat setting. The main advantage to a soldering gun is the very rapid warm-up cycle. A soldering gun also has a light built into it for illuminating the work.

Soldering Gun

When soldering, start by mechanically cleaning the materials to be joined. This may involve the use of a stainless steel brush or even sandpaper. Heat the surfaces gently while applying flux to them, and then add solder once the flux has thoroughly cleaned the material. **Tin** the surfaces by spreading the solder thinly over the surface, making sure to thoroughly heat any area that is to be tinned.

Before soldering an electrical connection, it is always a good idea to make a solid mechanical connection first. This will involve stripping insulation from wires and twisting them together. Keep in mind that the entire connection needs to be heated before applying solder to it. If only the solder is heated and it then is "melted" onto relatively cool wires, a "cold" solder joint is created that can exhibit unusual electrical properties.

Welding Tools

When joining metals, the best way to achieve a high-strength joint is to use a **welding** process. Welding is very different from soldering in that it involves melting the base metal of the objects to be joined, a process that requires very high temperatures.

There are two major types of welding processes: **oxyacetylene welding** and **electric-arc welding**. Oxyacetylene welding involves the use of a torch that is fueled with oxygen and acetylene. Burning these two gases together creates an extremely hot flame, hot enough to melt steel and other ferrous (iron-based) materials. **Filler rod** is melted along with the base metal to produce a finished weld.

There are many specialized processes that fall under the electric-arc welding classification. The simplest and most easily recognized type is known as **stick welding**. Stick welding involves the use of an electric-arc welding machine and two cables: one that attaches to the work being welded through a ground clamp, and the other going to an electrode that is sometimes referred to as a **stinger**. The stinger is held by the welder and is used to hold the **welding rod**.

Stick Welder

240 Volt Electrical Outlet

ON

Power Switch

OFF

Electrode Holder

Electrode or stinger

Arc

Ground

Cables

Ground Clamp

When the welder touches the welding rod on the work piece, an electric arc is formed. This electric arc generates a tremendous amount of heat and accomplishes three things. First, the heat melts the base metal of the material being welded. Second, the heat melts the electrode and deposits this metal in the weld as filler. Lastly, the **flux** on the outside of the electrodes burns and the generated gases form a "shield" around the weld. This gaseous shield prevents air from reacting with the hot metal and therefore weakening the weld.

As the welder continues the weld, the electrode burns and becomes shorter. The means that the welder must continue moving the stinger closer to the work until the electrode has been consumed. Once the electrode is used up, the welder "breaks off" or stops the arc, and a new electrode is placed in the stinger to continue the weld.

If more heat is needed to perform the weld, the welder can increase the amount of electric current that is supplied by the welding machine. Generally speaking, the larger the pieces that are being welded or the larger the electrode that is being used, the greater the amount of current required to get the weld done.

The electric arc that is generated during this process gives off a very high intensity light. The ultraviolet light is so intense that it can "sunburn" exposed skin and burn the retinas of unprotected eyes. Welders must, therefore, cover all exposed skin with protective clothing (preferably leather) and wear face shields (helmets) with light filters. The filters are usually very dark, so the welder can view the welding process itself but nothing else.

Newer welding helmets have electronic filters that "sense" the ultraviolet light from an electric arc and switch from "clear" to "shaded" in a split second. This allows the welder to leave the helmet down while lining up the next weld, saving the time consumed by flipping the helmet up and down.

Another electric-arc welding process that continues to gain popularity is **MIG (metal inert gas) welding**. MIG welding is also known as **wire-feed welding** because the electrode used for the weld process is a wire that is automatically fed from a spool. MIG uses a bottled inert gas (such as argon) to shield the weld, and requires a relatively sophisticated welding machine.

MIG Gun

Let's look at an example of how the ASVAB might test your knowledge of joining metal:

Question	Analysis
The purpose of flux in metal joining processes is to	**Step 1:** This question asks what function flux serves when joining metal. **Step 2:** There is nothing to simplify. **Step 3:** Predict that flux prevents oxidation by cleaning metal surfaces.
(A) clean metal surfaces to be joined (B) physically bond two metal surfaces (C) transfer electrical current (D) transfer electrical voltage	**Step 4:** Choice (A) matches that prediction. Eliminate choice (B), because although flux is used in the metal joining process, it is not the actual bonding agent. Eliminate choices (C) and (D), because flux is not intended to transfer electricity.

Try out another example about fasteners on your own:

Using which of the following tools absolutely requires the use of a protective face mask?

(A)   electric drill
(B)   stick welder
(C)   ratchet
(D)   hand saw

Explanation

Which tool requires the use of a face mask? That would be the stick welder **(B)**, which produces high-intensity light that could burn the skin and retinas if a protective face mask is not used. While it might be a good idea to wear a protective mask with the other tools, depending on the particular job, it is not always necessary.

GRIPPING TOOLS

LEARNING OBJECTIVES

...on you will learn to:

...fy the different types of pliers
...stand how different types of pliers are used
...be the importance of clamps and vises for carpentry projects

Pliers

Repair operations often call for objects to be gripped, twisted, bent, or turned. Sometimes these objects are irregularly shaped or otherwise difficult to hold. The best tool to use for gripping objects like this is pliers.

The most common type of pliers is the **combination slip-joint**. These are adjustable at the joint of the two handles of the pliers. With two different positions to choose from, these pliers can grip objects in a wide range of sizes. Sometimes, this design also incorporates a wire cutter for increased versatility.

Combination Slip-Joint Pliers

When large diameter objects must be gripped or twisted, a technician would use **adjustable joint pliers** to get the job done. These are adjustable over a large range of sizes, as they have multiple "arc-joints" that the pliers can be set into. The handles are also very long, which gives very good leverage and makes for maximum gripping power. These pliers are also commonly known as **water pump pliers** or **Channellock® pliers**.

Channellock Pliers

Lineman pliers are used for cutting and bending heavy gauge wire. These are not size-adjustable, but are made for maximum leverage at the jaws to make the cutting process easier. This type of pliers would most often be used by electricians, but all trades utilize them at one time or another.

Lineman Pliers

Diagonal cutters are pliers that are made exclusively for cutting. The two jaws are set at an angle (diagonally) to make it easier to cut wires straight across. Diagonal cutters are normally used for cutting wire and small cables.

Diagonal Cutters

For holding small objects in tight places, a pair of **needle nose pliers** could be used. These have very long, pointed jaws for maximum reach. Needle nose pliers are often used for intricate jobs like soldering circuit boards and small components, and they will most often have a wire cutter built into them at the base of the jaws.

Needle Nose Pliers

Locking pliers are used by technicians of all trades. Most people know them as **Vise-Grip**® pliers. They are adjustable, made in a large variety of jaw designs, and will lock tightly in place for holding or clamping objects together. Locking pliers often have wire cutters built into them as well for maximum versatility.

Vise-Grip Pliers

Questions on the ASVAB may give you a hypothetical "job" and ask what tool would be most useful. Look at this example:

Question	Analysis
You are completing a job that requires gripping several different sizes of pipes. Which of the following would be the best tool to select for this job?	**Step 1:** This question asks which tool would be best for gripping a wide range of pipe sizes **Step 2:** There is nothing to simplify. **Step 3:** You can narrow your prediction to types of pliers, since that is the tool of choice for jobs that require gripping. Your prediction can be even more specific if you recall that adjustable joint pliers provide the most versatility because they can be adjusted over a wide range of sizes.
(A) adjustable joint pliers (B) needle nose pliers (C) lineman pliers (D) adjustable wrench	**Step 4:** Choice (A) matches that prediction. Choices (B) and (C) can be eliminated because they are not adjustable, and choice (D) can be eliminated because it is designed for tightening and removing fasteners rather than gripping pipes.

Here is another question, this time dealing with terminology. Try this one on your own:

What type of wrench is commonly known as a Crescent wrench?

(A) open-end wrench
(B) box-end wrench
(C) adjustable wrench
(D) combination wrench

Explanation

Crescent is such a popular brand that it has become practically synonymous with the adjustable wrench; **(C)** is the correct answer. Remember, a combination wrench has an open-end wrench on one end and a box-end wrench on the other.

Clamps

A clamp is a tool that applies pressure to prevent movement between different pieces of a project. For example, a clamp would be useful for holding a project together while glue dries. Consisting of a metal frame (commonly C-shaped) with a flat-edged screw perpendicular to the bottom of the frame, a clamp gets tighter as the screw is turned.

C-Clamp

Vises

Vises are similar to clamps in that they are designed to hold wood or other materials in place. A key difference, however, is that vises are affixed to the workstation and are used to hold a material in place while you saw, sand, drill, or otherwise work on the material. Typically, one side (**jaw**) of the vise is fixed, and the other is moved by turning a handle.

Vise

CUTTING TOOLS

LEARNING OBJECTIVES

In this section you will learn to:

- identify different types of saws
- explain how saw blades differ based on the material they are designed to cut
- select the appropriate hand saw for a particular project
- understand the benefits of using powered saws for certain projects
- understand how power drills and their accessories are used

Manual (Hand) Saws

Cutting a material like wood requires the use of a **saw**. Saws are used in many different trades, but are typically utilized by carpenters.

The **crosscut saw** is designed to do what its name suggests: cut across the grain of the wood. Crosscut saw teeth are unique in that they cut like a knife. This is in contrast to a **rip saw,** which is made to cut with the grain of the wood and whose teeth are shaped like chisels. A rip saw's teeth are also set (bent) alternately from side to side to cut a relatively wide **kerf** (slot). This style of teeth allows the rip saw to cut a straight line even if the grain of the wood is curved.

Crosscut Saw

Rip Saw

A **coping saw** is used to make fine, curving cuts. This saw uses a thin, flexible blade that is held tight on a wide frame. The blade can be rotated in the frame for further flexibility, making it easier to make difficult cuts on larger pieces of material.

Coping Saw

The **back saw** is also made from thin material, but has a rigid strip of steel on its top edge for reinforcement. A back saw is normally used for making fine cuts, so it has 14 to 16 teeth per inch. Back saws can be used with a **miter box** for making even cuts at specific angles.

Miter Box and Back Saw

The one saw that can be found in a mechanic's toolbox is a **hacksaw**. Hacksaws are used for cutting metals such as steel, aluminum, or copper. The blades in a hacksaw are replaceable, and it is important to choose the right blade for the material that is going to be cut.

Hacksaw

When selecting a hacksaw blade, keep in mind that larger numbers of teeth per inch help when cutting thinner materials. Also, remember that when installing a new blade, the blade must be oriented so that the teeth point away from the handle. This makes the hacksaw cut on the forward stroke, so let up on the downward pressure when pulling the hacksaw back to prevent breaking the blade.

Powered Saws

For jobs that require faster cuts or that involve especially strong materials, powered saws may be used in lieu of hand saws. A common type of powered saw is a **circular saw** which, as the name suggests, has a circular blade that rotates quickly to make a cut. There are two very common types of circular saw. A **miter saw** is a self-contained tool that sits atop a tool bench and is useful for making crosscuts in lumber, especially when the cut needs to be at a specific angle. Don't get this confused with a **table saw** which also has a circular blade; a table saw has the blade actually embedded into the table or bench itself. Another key difference lies in how the saws are used. To use a miter saw, clamp or otherwise brace the material to be cut in order to keep it steady, and then lower the rotating circular saw to make the cut. To use a table saw, carefully slide the material to be cut toward the rotating blade.

Miter Saw

Another common type of power saw is a **band saw**, which is so called because its blade is one continuous band of metal that revolves very quickly on two spinning wheels to make a continuous cut in a piece of wood or metal. Band saws are used for creating lumber out of timber and can also be useful for cutting straight or curved lines in a material. When using a saw like this for cutting metal, it is vital to use a coolant wash to keep the material cool and debris-free.

Drilling and Boring Tools

Making small holes in wood or metal is done by **drilling** the material. Large holes can be made in wood or soft metals using a process known as **boring**. The two processes are essentially the same, but they use different tools to get the job done.

Drill bits are used for drilling holes. A carpenter would use drill bits up to $\frac{1}{4}"$ in diameter, but a mechanic would commonly use drill bits as large as $\frac{1}{2}"$. If holes larger than this must be made, special tools would be used to bore the hole.

The vast majority of drill bits are made to cut while rotating in a clockwise direction. These are known as **right-hand** drill bits. **Left-hand** drill bits are made to cut in the opposite direction. The most common practical application for a left-hand drill bit is the removal of broken bolts from threaded holes.

Hole saws can also be used for boring large holes. Hole saws are not adjustable, so each one is only capable of drilling one size of a hole.

Hole Saw

Today, it is rare for anyone to use hand-operated tools to drive drill bits and other boring tools. Instead, it is common practice to perform these operations using an **electric drill**. Electric drills can be identified by chuck size, reversibility, and whether they are designed to operate at a constant or variable speed.

The **chuck** of an electric drill is the part that holds the drill bit. A chuck is identified by the largest diameter bit that will fit in it. Common chuck sizes include $\frac{1}{4}"$, $\frac{3}{8}"$, and $\frac{1}{2}"$ Regular drill chucks can be tightened and loosened using a **chuck key**. Since it is easy to lose a chuck key, **keyless chucks** are becoming more popular. A keyless chuck makes it possible to tighten and loosen the chuck by hand.

Some drills can operate in both the clockwise and counterclockwise directions. These are known as **reversible drills**. **Variable speed drills** are designed to operate over a range of speeds that can be determined by the position of the trigger.

As battery technology advances, it is getting more common for people to use **cordless drills**. Longer times between battery recharges and portability are just two of the reasons why these have become so popular. Many of these cordless drills come with a wide range of attachments (called drivers or bits) and can double as powered screwdrivers and socket wrenches as well.

The most important safety consideration when using a drill is to use a sharp bit. Dull bits require more time and more pressure placed on the drill to get the job done. With smaller bits, this could result in bit breakage and damage to the surface of the material being drilled. Drill bits can be sharpened on a bench grinder using a special attachment.

Question	Analysis
You are attempting to cut a rounded shape from a square piece of wood. What is the best saw to choose?	**Step 1:** This question asks which tool would be best for cutting a round shape from a square.
	Step 2: Not much info to simplify.
	Step 3: You can narrow your prediction by thinking about the type of saw that can cut a round, rather than straight, line.
(A) coping saw (B) crosscut saw (C) hack saw (D) rip saw	**Step 4:** Choice (A) matches that prediction. The remaining saws are designed for straight cuts.

Now try your hand at a question about saws.

Which of these would a mechanic be most likely to use?

(A) coping saw
(B) crosscut saw
(C) hacksaw
(D) rip saw

Explanation

Of these four choices, only choice **(C)**, hacksaw, is commonly used to cut material other than wood, so that is the saw most likely to be in a mechanic's toolbox.

FINISHING TOOLS

Planes

When working with wood, there are many occasions when it is necessary to shave off a small amount of material to make a piece fit properly or to make a surface smooth. One tool that can be used for this purpose is a **plane**.

There are several different types of planes, but the one that would be best-suited for general purpose work is the **jack plane**. The jack plane has a smooth lower surface (plane bottom) and an adjustable-depth blade that protrudes slightly below this surface (through the mouth). This blade is set at an angle, similar to the blade in a disposable razor.

Jack Plane

When using a jack plane, the carpenter grasps the plane with both hands and moves it evenly across the surface of the work, "shaving" a thin layer of wood. If a heavier cut is desired, the blade can be adjusted to protrude farther from the lower surface of the plane.

Wood Chisels

Wood chisels may also be used to shape or smooth a wood surface. Wood chisels come in a variety of widths, which can range from $\frac{1}{8}$" to 2". A wood chisel is normally hand-operated, but when making deep cuts, a soft-faced mallet should be used to lightly tap the chisel through the work.

Wood Chisels

Files and Rasps

Files are used to smooth, polish, and shape materials. Files are made from hardened steel and consist of diagonal rows of teeth. These teeth can be arranged as either a single row of parallel teeth (single-cut) or one row of teeth crisscrossing with another row (double-cut). Files are made in flat, round, half-round, and triangular designs.

Most files do not come with handles. It is important to have a handle ready to attach to a file when it is put to use, as this will prevent the end of the file from being driven into the technician's hand. Remember that a file is made to cut only on the forward stroke, so it should be lifted slightly from the work when it is pulled back.

Flat File, Half-Round File, and Triangular Files

Rasps are basically very coarse files that are used to trim, shape, and smooth materials. While files are used for fine finishes, rasps are used for coarse work. Round rasps are useful for cleaning up holes, whereas a flat rasp would be used to smooth flat surfaces. The cutting teeth on a rasp are coarse enough to clear sawdust easily, so the rasp is always ready for the next stroke.

Rasps

The ASVAB may ask you which tools can be used together on a project. Here is an example:

Question	Analysis
Which of the following finishing tools may be used with a mallet? (A) jack plane (B) wood chisel (C) file (D) rasp	**Step 1:** This question asks which tool would be most appropriate to use with a mallet. **Step 2:** There is nothing to simplify. **Step 3:** Predict the tool that would most likely be struck by a mallet during normal operation. **Step 4:** Only choice (B) is commonly struck by a mallet, to make deep cuts.

Try this example on your own.

What must be used in conjunction with a file for safe operation?

(A) mallet
(B) file
(C) chisel
(D) handle

Explanation

The correct answer here is **(D)** handle. Many files are sold without handles attached, but it is important to use a handle whenever you use a file, to prevent the pointed end of the file from injuring the palm of your hand.

SHOP INFORMATION PRACTICE QUESTIONS

1. In order to make a bolt tighter, a _____ wrench should be used.

   (A) longer
   (B) shorter
   (C) heavier
   (D) shinier

2. A cotter pin is often used in conjunction with a _____.

   (A) lock nut
   (B) lock washer
   (C) castellated nut
   (D) machine screw

3. What is the tool shown below known as?

   (A) water pump pliers only
   (B) retaining ring pliers only
   (C) Channellock pliers only
   (D) both water pump pliers and Channellock pliers

4. A $\frac{3}{8}"$ drill bit will fit into an electric drill with a chuck of size

   (A) $\frac{1}{4}"$ or $\frac{3}{8}"$

   (B) $\frac{3}{8}"$ or $\frac{3}{4}"$

   (C) $\frac{1}{2}"$ or $\frac{2}{3}"$

   (D) $\frac{1}{4}"$ or $\frac{1}{2}"$

5. The blade in a hacksaw should be installed with its teeth pointed

   (A) toward the handle only
   (B) away from the handle only
   (C) either toward or away from the handle
   (D) neither toward nor away from the handle

6. How is the length of a bolt measured?

   (A) by measuring the length from end to end
   (B) by measuring the length of the threaded portion only
   (C) by measuring the length from the underside of the head to the end of the threads
   (D) none of the above

7. A bolt with a hexagonal head could be loosened using all of the following EXCEPT

   (A) an open-end wrench
   (B) a box-end wrench
   (C) a 12-point socket and ratchet
   (D) a Torx screwdriver

8. The tool shown above is used for

   (A) installing pop rivets
   (B) stapling asphalt shingles
   (C) crimping electrical terminals
   (D) soldering electrical connections

9. "Tinning" is a process that is related to

   (A) carpentry
   (B) roofing
   (C) soldering
   (D) welding

10. The following screw head would be used with which type of screwdriver?

    (A) flat tip
    (B) Phillips
    (C) Robertson
    (D) Torx

11. What force is responsible for allowing wrenches to tighten or loosen fasteners?

    (A) acceleration
    (B) torque
    (C) tension
    (D) friction

12. The best choice to loosen a tight fastener is the _____ wrench.

    (A) open-end
    (B) adjustable
    (C) box-end
    (D) allen

13. To determine the correct socket size needed for a given bolt head, measure the distance between two _____ of the bolt head.

    (A) adjacent sides
    (B) parallel threads
    (C) opposite points
    (D) parallel sides

14. What is a chisel?

    (A) a tool designed to install fasteners into wood
    (B) a tool with a sharp cutting edge designed to gouge into a material
    (C) a tool that is made to shear off a large surface of wood
    (D) a tool designed to cut through pieces of wood with a back-and-forth motion

15. What is a benefit of using a ball-peen hammer rather than a claw hammer?

    (A) It is more suitable for hammering on metal because of its generally stronger head.
    (B) It is more delicate and can thus be used on fragile surfaces.
    (C) It can remove nails as well as hammer them in.
    (D) It provides more leverage.

16. You have a bolt that needs to be removed, but a $\frac{5}{16}"$ open-end wrench is just slightly too small to fit properly. Which of the following sizes should be tried next?

    (A) $\frac{3}{4}"$
    (B) $\frac{3}{8}"$
    (C) $\frac{5}{8}"$
    (D) $\frac{11}{16}"$

Answers and Explanations

1. **(A) longer** Fasteners can be tightened best with longer wrenches. Adding an extension or using an adjustable wrench (Crescent) may also improve tightening ability.

2. **(C) castellated nut** A castellated nut uses a cotter pin to lock it into place, which must pass through a hole in the bolt or stud that the nut is threaded on.

3. **(D) both water pump pliers and Channellock pliers** When large-diameter objects must be gripped or twisted, a technician would use adjustable joint pliers to get the job done. These are adjustable over a large range of sizes, as they have multiple "arc-joints" that the pliers can be set into. The handles are also very long, which gives very good leverage and makes for maximum gripping power. These pliers are also commonly known as *water pump pliers* or *Channellock pliers*. Since choice (D) allows for both choices (A) and (C), it is the correct answer.

4. **(D) $\frac{1}{4}$" or $\frac{1}{2}$"** The chuck of an electric drill is the part that holds the drill bit. A chuck is identified by the largest diameter bit that will fit in it. Common chuck sizes include $\frac{1}{4}$", $\frac{3}{8}$", and $\frac{1}{2}$". A $\frac{3}{8}$" drill bit will fit into a $\frac{3}{8}$" or $\frac{1}{2}$" chuck, answer choices (B) and (C), respectively. The correct answer, therefore, to what a $\frac{3}{8}$" drill bit will fit into is (D).

5. **(B) away from the handle only** When installing a new hacksaw blade, orient it so the teeth point away from the handle. This makes the hacksaw cut on the forward stroke, so let up on the downward pressure when pulling the hacksaw back.

6. **(C) by measuring the length from the underside of the head to the end of the threads** One important measurement of a fastener is the length. The length of the bolt is the distance between the underside of the bolt head and the end of the bolt. Note that the bolt head does not count toward the length of the bolt. Therefore, the best answer is (C).

7. **(D) a Torx screwdriver** The two basic types of wrenches—the open end and the box end—are both acceptable for loosening a hexagonal bolt. The open-end wrench is easy to slide on and off a fastener. The downside to the open-end wrench is that it only makes contact with two sides of a six-sided (hex) bolt head. The box-end wraps completely around the head of a bolt, and therefore makes greater surface contact. Box-end wrenches normally come in a 12-point configuration, but some are made as 6-point. Used with a ratchet, the correct size socket is ideal for loosening fasteners such as hexagonal

bolts. Thus, because all the choices are acceptable, (D) is the best answer.

8. **(D) soldering electrical connections** The tool shown is a soldering gun. It is used for soldering electrical connections.

9. **(C) soldering** If two pieces to be joined by soldering are large, it may pay to tin the surfaces before attempting to join them. Heating the surfaces gently while applying flux to them, and then adding solder once the flux has thoroughly cleaned the material will accomplish this. Since soldering is the process involved, the correct answer is (C).

10. **(C) Robertson** The Robertson screwdriver grips the fastener better than a flat tip screwdriver, so the screw is much easier to remove and install.

11. **(B) torque** Whenever you see the words "force" and "wrench" in the same sentence, you should immediately think about *torque* (B). You can think of torque as twisting motion, which is exactly what allows a fastener to be tightened or loosened. Don't get torque confused with *tension* (C), which instead is a pulling force associated with a weight on a string or wire.

12. **(C) box-end** The box-end wrench is closed, which allows for more surface area contact of the wrench with the fastener, compared to the contact offered by the open-end and adjustable wrenches; therefore, answer choices (A) and (B) are incorrect. Allen wrenches are typically intended for low-torque applications; therefore, answer choice (D) is incorrect.

13. **(D) parallel sides** The size of a socket for a given bolt head is determined by the distance between two parallel sides of the bold head.

14. **(B) a tool with a sharp cutting edge designed to gouge into a material** This is a good question to make a prediction if you know what a chisel is, or otherwise eliminate wrong answer choices that describe some other type of tool. Choice (A) describes a tool like a screwdriver or a hammer that can install fasteners, so that is not the correct answer. Choice (C) describes a plane, which is used to smooth or reduce the thickness of a piece of wood by shaving off a layer. Choice (D) describes a saw, so that is not the correct answer either. Choice (B) perfectly describes a chisel, so that is the correct answer.

15. **(A) It is more suitable for hammering on metal because of its generally stronger head.** A ball-peen hammer has one main benefit: it generally has a stronger head made of steel. This matches choice (A). Choice (B) more closely describes a mallet, certainly not a steel hammer, and choice (C) describes a benefit of a claw hammer, so that is the opposite of what you're looking for. Finally, it makes little sense to talk about (D) leverage when discussing striking materials.

16. **(B)** $\frac{3"}{8}$ If a wrench is just slightly too small, you will want to try the next size larger. In this case, $\frac{3"}{8}$ is the next size up. This is the wrench you would want to try next, so choice (B) is the correct answer.

Review and Reflect

How did you do on this practice set? As you review your work, think about these questions:

- Are there certain categories of tools you should review?
- Do you know the names of tools but need more review about when to use them?
- Would it help you to make flash cards out of the bold words in this chapter?

MECHANICAL COMPREHENSION

KNOW WHAT TO EXPECT

In order to understand how machines work, it is important to have a good grasp of **applied physics**. The study of applied physics is the study of the practical application of the laws of physics. Engineering, architecture, and heavy equipment operation depend upon applied physics. This chapter will build on concepts first discussed in the Physical Science portion of chapter 9: General Science to explain how various common mechanical devices operate.

On the CAT-ASVAB, you will have 20 minutes to answer 16 questions in the Mechanical Comprehension subtest. If you are taking the paper and pencil test, you will have 19 minutes to answer 25 questions.

A REVIEW OF THE PHYSICS OF MECHANICAL DEVICES

LEARNING OBJECTIVES

In this section you will learn to:

- recognize a mechanical device as any machine based on force and motion laws
- define *mass* and *force*
- apply Newton's laws of motion to questions about mechanical devices

Mechanics is the area of physics that encompasses the laws of motion, energy, and forces. Velocity, momentum, and Newton's second law relating force, mass, and acceleration are all mechanical concepts. All mechanical devices, including the simple machines discussed in this chapter, are based on the application of force in order to achieve a movement or change in position of a mass.

Each of the physical quantities reviewed in this section were first introduced in the Physical Science section of chapter 9: General Science. This brief review will focus only on the concepts from that chapter which most directly underlie mechanical operation.

Mass and Force

All matter has **mass**. Mass is a measure of the total quantity of matter in an object. Generally speaking, larger objects tend to have greater mass, but some materials contain more mass than others per unit volume (are denser), so bigger doesn't always mean more massive. Unlike the force of weight, which will be discussed in more detail a little later in the chapter, mass is not a vector quantity, since it has magnitude but no direction.

For the purposes of mechanics, the most important thing to know about mass is that it corresponds to how much force is required to achieve a particular acceleration. In other words, the more mass something has, the more difficult it is to change its motion. The term **inertia** is sometimes used to refer to an object's resistance to changes in its motion, but inertia is just a property of mass.

A **force** is a push or pull. Forces are everywhere in the world. Some are fairly obvious, such as a tractor pulling a plow, a baseball being hit into the stands, or a person shoving his way past others in a crowded store. Other forces are often taken for granted. Earth's gravity applies a force (weight) that always pulls down, and it is what keeps objects and people on the ground instead of floating around in midair. All forces are vector quantities and therefore act in a single direction. The term **net force** refers to the total force acting on an object.

Without a force being applied to them, objects would not move (or, if they were already in motion, they would remain in motion without stopping). Objects with a great deal of mass (such as a freight train) require a large force to alter their motion. The goal of all mechanical technology is to most effectively apply forces to the movement of varying mass quantities.

Newton's Laws of Motion

All mechanical devices take Newton's laws for granted in their operation. Newton's first law describes the unchanging state of motion of an object when it experiences no net force. A heavy crate suspended by a pulley is only able to avoid crashing to the ground because the attached ropes fully counteract the force of gravity pulling the mass downwards.

Newton's second law can be summarized by the formula

$$F = ma$$

where m is measured in kilograms (kg), a is in meters per second squared (m/s^2) and F is in newtons (N). This law expresses the linear relationships between either the mass of the moved object or the desired acceleration, with the force required to achieve that movement.

One of the most important historical roles of machines has been in multiplying the force a human or work animal provides in order to move very massive objects that would be otherwise immobile. Ancient structures including Stonehenge and the Egyptian pyramids are evidence of a long human tradition of mechanical aids to labor.

Newton's third law of motion states that for every action there is an equal and opposite reaction. This law applies to all applications of force, including those mediated by simple machines. It's possible to pull on a rope and pulley to lift a weight, only because the force of tension is carried through a rope by a daisy chain of action-reaction force pairs, from one section of rope to the next.

Question	Analysis
Simple machines and other mechanical devices	**Step 1:** The question asks which statement applies to mechanical devices.
	Step 2: Think about the traits that simple machines and other mechanical devices have in common: they are used to transfer force, and they obey Newton's laws.
	Step 3: That's as close as you can get to a prediction with a general question like this, so start evaluating answer choices.
(A) are technologies used to get around certain laws of physics (B) are exclusively based on momentum (C) operate according to the rules of forces and mass (D) transmit and multiply force in order to increase the amount of energy available	**Step 4:** Mechanical devices use the laws of physics, they don't circumvent them, so (A) is not correct. Momentum is important, but it is not the only basis for any and all machines, so eliminate (B). Choice (C) is true. Select it. Choice (D) sounds *almost* correct, but how does a device increase the energy available? By burning fuel? By creating energy from nothing? Simple machines like levers don't themselves burn up fuel. And although force can be multiplied with mechanical advantage (more on that later), energy cannot be created out of nothing.

Now try one on your own.

According to Newton's laws, an object being lifted by a pulley will accelerate

(A) even if the applied force from the rope to the object is a little less than the object's weight, because mechanical advantage makes up the difference.
(B) only if the net force on the object is zero and the object is already in motion.
(C) if the applied force from the rope to the object is greater than the object's weight.
(D) if the object's mass is greater than the applied force.

Explanation

Choice **(C)** is correct. There must be a non-zero net force for any object to accelerate. Objects in motion where the net force is zero will continue moving at a constant velocity, but will not accelerate. Both (C) and (D) talk about a difference between two values, but answer choice (D) compares the applied force to the object's mass rather than weight. Since these quantities have different physical meanings, it doesn't make sense to say one is greater than another.

COMMON TYPES OF FORCES

LEARNING OBJECTIVES

In this section you will learn to:

- distinguish and understand the related terms of mass, weight, and gravity, and apply a formula to calculate one value given the others
- understand friction as a responsive force and apply the formulas for calculating kinetic and static friction
- understand tension as a force found in a cable that stretches it tight
- understand hydraulic pressure as it relates to an applied force, and as a transmitter or multiplier of force
- apply the formula for torque as a measure of how effectively a force can cause an object to rotate

Gravity and Weight

As seen previously, **weight** is different from mass. Mass is an intrinsic property of matter, whereas weight is the force exerted on an object due to gravity. The downward pull that the Earth exerts on bodies outside of itself is a specific case of gravity at work. Weight can be easily measured using a spring scale like that found in many people's bathrooms, and the direction of weight for all objects on Earth is the same: straight down towards the center of the Earth.

The general formula for **Newton's Law of Universal Gravitation** was given in chapter 9: General Science. It can be used to explain why the same person will weigh less on planets of different sizes and masses (for example, when astronauts walked on the moon, their weight was only $\frac{1}{6}$ of what it was while on Earth). However, unless you are told otherwise, it is safe to assume that for the purposes of everyday mechanical work the location is here on Earth.

For bodies free-falling near the Earth's surface, the **acceleration due to gravity (g)** is calculated to be about 9.8 m/s^2, ignoring air resistance. (Note that "near the Earth's surface" really means anywhere on Earth, including on top of Mount Everest or parachuting from a plane thousands of meters in the air. The value of g doesn't change significantly at the top of a stair ladder.)

Applying Newton's second law, $F = ma$, for the specific case of weight, the more general symbol for force, F, is replaced with the more specific force of weight, W, and acceleration, a, is replaced with the constant value of acceleration due to gravity, g. This results in the modified version of the formula

$W = mg$

where W is weight in newtons (N), m is mass in kilograms (kg), and g is acceleration due to gravity (either m/s^2 or N/kg). To determine an object's weight in N, therefore, simply multiply its mass in kg by 9.8.

Study the example that follows, which does not have answer choices, to help you practice predicting an answer to this type of question.

Question	Analysis
How many newtons of force due to gravity will act on an 80 kg man while in a plane flying over Denver, Colorado?	The question asks for the amount of force due to gravity.
	The man is not an astronaut (or if he is an astronaut, he's not currently in outer space or on the moon), so his weight will be pretty much the same as any other 80 kg man on Earth. This weight will be basically unchanged whether he's at sea level, in the United States' highest-altitude large city, or in a plane flying above that same city.
	The phrase "newtons of force due to gravity" is just another way of saying weight. Weight $W = (80 \text{ kg})(9.8 \text{ m/s}^2) = 784 \text{ N}$. The answer is 784 N.

Friction

There are several responsive forces which act to resist movement. When you move an object across a surface, the rubbing of the two surfaces results in **kinetic friction**, which always acts in a direction opposite to the motion of the object. Because it always opposes motion, kinetic friction will eventually slow any moving object to a stop. Ice is polished to minimize kinetic friction, but unless it is constantly being pushed, a hockey puck will eventually slide to a stop in even the most slippery of rinks.

When an object is not moving, a force that attempts to slide it across a surface will encounter a different type of friction. Attempting to push a stationary box across a concrete floor will require a person to overcome the **static friction** that opposes any attempted movement.

Both kinds of friction are based on two factors: the **coefficient of friction**, μ (the Greek letter mu), which represents how much two materials resist sliding against each other; and the **normal force**, F_N, which represents the equal and opposite force a surface exerts when an object presses against it. The formulas for kinetic and static friction, respectively, are

$$F_f = \mu_k F_N$$

$$F_f = \mu_s F_N$$

where μ_k and μ_s stand for the coefficients of kinetic and static friction. The coefficients of friction are constant for any two surfaces in contact. The coefficients of friction are dimensionless quantities, with no units of their own. Therefore, whatever force unit is used to measure F_N (N or lbs, for example), will also be used to measure F_f.

Slippery surfaces like ice or wet asphalt have low coefficients of both kinetic and static friction with most objects. Friction is directly proportional to these coefficients. That's why it's important for drivers of cars to understand that weather conditions can make braking to a stop (which relies on the friction of the wheels with the road surface) less effective.

Free Body Diagram of Forces Acting on a Sliding Object

For any given surface, the coefficient of static friction is higher than the coefficient of kinetic friction. This means that more force is required to initially get a stationary object moving than to keep it moving afterwards. Once the large static friction force has been overcome and the object is in motion, the smaller coefficient of kinetic friction takes over, and the resistant force of friction decreases. This is why moving heavy objects usually involves one extra big push at the beginning, but then a somewhat smaller force for the rest of the trip.

One more important difference between static and kinetic friction is that static friction only arises in response to an attempt to move an object along a surface. Like the normal force that holds up objects with weight, it responds to an applied force by matching and counteracting it. The formula is actually used to determine the maximum of a variable value for static friction, beyond which it breaks and an object will begin to move.

Both kinds of friction forces are directly proportional to the normal force of the surface. As an experiment, try laying your palm flat and sliding your hand along a nearby surface like a table or desk. Feel the resistance of the movement due to kinetic friction. Now, with your palm still flat, try pushing harder against the same surface, while still trying to slide your hand along it.

Is it more difficult? If you push very hard against the surface, you may find you are not even able to overcome the force of static friction and slide your hand without decreasing the normal force first. When a person leans against a wall, they allow a portion of the weight to push against the wall, which pushes back with an equal and opposite normal force. This normal force contributes to a corresponding static friction force that prevents the person from sliding down the wall to the floor.

Most frequently, the normal force arises on flat horizontal surfaces as a response to the weight of an object pressing it down. As a result, the normal force is equal to an object's weight much of the time, so that the forces of friction are equal to the coefficients of friction multiplied by the object's weight. This assumption is false only on non-horizontal surfaces (for example, slopes), or when additional forces are acting to push an object down or hold it up.

Question	Analysis
A 15 kg object rests on a concrete floor, and the coefficients of static and kinetic friction are 0.3 and 0.2, respectively. If a continuous force of 35 N is applied to the object in a direction parallel with the floor, what will happen?	**Step 1:** The question asks for a prediction as to whether an object will move given an applied force and taking into account friction.

Question	Analysis
	Step 2: Comparing the applied force to the frictional forces should make it obvious whether the object will move or not. The weight of the object will be equal to the normal force holding the object up. Then the force of friction can be determined. $F_N = W = (15 \text{ kg})(9.8 \text{ m/s}^2) = 147 \text{ N}$ $F_f = \mu_k F_N = (147 \text{ N})(0.2) = 29.4 \text{ N}$ $F_f = \mu_s F_N = (147 \text{ N})(0.3) = 44.1 \text{ N}$
	Step 3: The applied force of 35 N is less than the maximum value for the force of static friction. Since the object is already at rest, and the applied force is not enough to "break" the force of static friction, the net force will be zero and the object will stay put. The lesser force of kinetic friction is irrelevant since the object will not slide to begin with.
(A) The object will be bounced back due to friction. (B) The object will remain at rest as the applied force is unable to overcome the static friction. (C) The object will initially move but then stop as kinetic friction overcomes the applied force. (D) The object will accelerate continuously.	**Step 4:** Answer choice (B) is correct. (The key is that an object at rest must experience a large enough applied force to overcome static friction before kinetic friction becomes relevant.)

Now you try one:

Four objects of the same material and dimensions, but different weights, are placed on four different tabletops. When a force is applied that causes the boxes to move, which one generates the greatest amount of kinetic friction?

CHAPTER 13

Explanation

Answer choice **(C)** is correct. According to the formula for kinetic friction, the box with the greater weight will have the greater normal force and thus greater frictional force compared to one of less weight. The oily surface will have a lower coefficient of friction than the dry surface. Therefore, the heaviest box on the driest surface will experience the most friction.

Another responsive force comes from air resistance, sometimes known as air friction but more commonly known as **drag**. Drag opposes movement not across a solid surface but through a fluid, like water or air. The two main variables that affect drag are cross-sectional area and speed. High-performance cars, boats, and aircraft are designed to be sleek and pointy, to minimize the area of the side that is plowing through the air or water. Parachutes work by intentionally increasing area for a skydiver, so that drag is increased and the person can be slowed down to a safe speed before hitting the ground.

Tension

When cables are used to pull an object, an applied force exerted on one end results in the attached object receiving the same pulling force from the other end. When force is transmitted through rope or other pullable materials, the internal stretch force of the material is called **tension**. Tension can be measured in N or lbs, or any other force unit measurement.

As a simplification, tension is often assumed to be equal in all parts of the material. This assumes, however, that the mass of the material under tension is either zero or negligible. In reality, tension is greatest where the force is being applied. To understand why this is, imagine a 100-pound weight suspended from a 10-pound chain. The bottommost link in the chain has an important job. It's holding up the 100-pound weight. The tension at this point in the chain, therefore, is 100 pounds.

But the chain link just above it also has an important job. It's holding up the link that's holding up the 100-pound weight, which means it must have a tension equal to 100 pounds, plus the weight of one chain link. If you continue to the top of the chain, where the applied force is holding it in place, the topmost link is responsible for not only the 100-pound weight, but for another 10 pounds from the chain itself. At this section of the chain, the tension is 110 pounds.

The takeaway from this is that, barring imperfections or weaknesses in the material under tension, the most likely place for a rope or cable to snap is not near the object it is holding or pulling, but near the place where the rope or cable is itself being pulled. When a winch (a mechanical device used to wind a rope) draws in a heavy-duty cable and the tension exceeds the material's tensile strength, it will likely snap very close to the winch, rather than close to the load.

Question	Analysis
A concrete block is suspended by two steel cables, spaced equidistant from the edges. What best describes the value of T1?	**Step 1:** The question asks for the tension of one of two cables from which a weight is suspended.
	Step 2: The system is in static equilibrium. Since the block is remaining in one place without accelerating, the net force is zero and the downward force due to gravity must be exactly balanced by the tension in the two cables. Each cable must contribute half of the upward force (tension). $T1 + T2 = 50$ N $T1 = T2 = 25$ N
	Step 3: The tension in the first cable must be equal to half of the downward force on the block.
(A) 5 N (B) 25 N (C) 50 N (D) 100 N	**Step 4:** Choice (B) is correct.

Now try one on your own.

Using a cable attached at one end, a force is applied to a slab of metal. At which point along the cable is the cable most likely to snap?

(A)   A
(B)   B
(C)   C
(D)   It is equally likely to break at any point along the rope.

Explanation

Choice **(C)** is correct. The force applied to the cable will result in acceleration of the metal slab. However, the metal slab by itself requires less force than the slab and cable combination. Thus, more force is applied at the end of the cable where the force is applied compared to what is actually acting on the metal slab itself. This corresponds to a greater tension near point C compared to points B and A. If the cable were to snap, it would likely happen where there is higher tension.

Hydraulic Pressure

Fluid power can also be used to gain mechanical advantage. **Hydraulics** is the transmission of force through the use of liquids. While the classic simple machines are effective and reliable for many purposes, hydraulics is a little more versatile at redirecting and multiplying forces in complex systems. In order to understand how hydraulics works, it is first necessary to have a grasp of the concept of **pressure**. If force is applied evenly over a certain area, then pressure is applied to that area. Pressure is calculated using the formula

$$P = \frac{F}{A}$$

where F is force in pounds (lb), A is area in square inches (in²), and P is pressure in pounds per square inch (psi). While other applications of pressure in physics and chemistry use standard units of newtons and square meters, the above units are more common in hydraulics. Keep in mind that F is divided by A. A force of 100 pounds applied over an area of 10 square inches results in a pressure of 10 psi being developed.

Using the formula for pressure, you can derive $F = PA$, which is useful for calculating the amount of force that is developed when pressure P is applied to area A.

Even when extremely high pressure is applied to a liquid, the volume of the liquid will decrease only a very small amount. This property of near-incompressibility makes liquids very effective at transmitting force, as no force (or very little) is used up in compressing the liquids into a smaller space. Liquids also tend to take the shape of their container, filling up any available space (given enough of the liquid). According to **Pascal's law** (discovered by French mathematician and physicist Blaise Pascal in the seventeenth century), the pressure in any part of an enclosed fluid is the same and points in all directions.

Putting it all together, applying force to one end of a hydraulic system will increase the pressure everywhere, which, when applied to an area of the same size, produces the same force at a different location and in a different direction. Changing the area over which force acts can also change the magnitude of the force. A smaller force applied over a greater distance produces a greater force over a smaller distance in a hydraulic system.

Hydraulic Lift

Try your hand at a problem about pressure.

Pressure is equal to force acting over

(A) a distance
(B) a period of time
(C) a volume
(D) an area

Explanation

Choice **(D)** is correct. Pressure is equal to force acting over an area.

Torque

Torque measures how much a force is able to cause an object to rotate. Torque, like pressure, cannot be properly called a force itself. The formula for torque is

$$\tau = rF$$

where torque (τ, the Greek letter tau) is the product of an applied force (F) perpendicular to the lever arm of the rotated object, and the length of the lever arm (r), measured from the pivot point (center of rotation) or fulcrum, to the point where the force is being is applied. Force is normally measured in either N or lb and the length of the lever arm in m or ft. Torque may therefore be measured in standard N-m (newton-meters) or the ft-lb (foot-pound) unit.

However, remember this length measurement is perpendicular to the force applied in rotating the object, not parallel, so torque is not equivalent to work, whose N-m units (more often expressed as joules, J) represent a force applied through a distance. (Nor is torque equivalent to energy, also measured in J.)

Torque Applied via a Wrench

Torque is directly proportional to the force applied to rotation, and is also proportional to the distance from the center of rotation where the force acts. Applying a force at the farthest end of a lever arm is advisable in getting the greatest possible torque. When a mechanic applies his maximum force but is unable to turn a difficult bolt, a longer wrench may do the trick. This doesn't increase the force he is able to apply, but the use of a longer lever arm for the same force does result in increased torque and therefore, hopefully, better success in loosening the bolt. Unlike work, an object does not have to be successfully rotated before a torque is said to have been applied.

Question	Analysis
How much force is needed to apply 50 ft-lb of torque to a bolt using a 2 ft long wrench?	**Step 1:** The question asks for the amount of force applied to a lever arm for a certain torque.
	Step 2: The torque formula relates length, force, and torque. To solve this question, isolate force and plug in values.
	Based on the units in this question, force is measured in pounds (since pounds multiplied by feet is the only way to get foot-pound units for torque).
	$\tau = rF$
	$F = \tau/r = (50 \text{ ft-lb})/(2 \text{ ft}) = 25 \text{ lb}$
	Step 3: The force must be 25 lbs, not 25 N.
(A) 100 lb (B) 50 N (C) 25 lb (D) 25 N	**Step 4:** There is only one perfect match: choice (C).

Now try a question about torque on your own.

Which of the following applied forces will result in the greatest torque?

Explanation

Choice **(A)** is correct. The product of the force and the length of the lever arm, where the two quantities are perpendicular to each other, produces torque. For (A), $\tau = (1.5 \text{ m})(50 \text{ N}) = 75$ N·m, compared to 60 N·m in (B) and 70 N·m in (C). (D) provides no torque at all. Although there is a large applied force, it is pushing along the lever arm towards the fulcrum, and cannot result in any rotation.

ENERGY, WORK, AND POWER

LEARNING OBJECTIVES

In this section you will learn to:

- compute values for kinetic and potential energy
- apply the principle of conservation of mechanical energy
- calculate the amount of work performed on an object

Energy

In a broad sense, energy is the capacity to cause a change in the state of something. Energy can take many different forms, but the Mechanical Comprehension portion of the ASVAB deals largely with the type called **mechanical energy**. In order to answer questions on the MC test, you will need to understand the two different types of mechanical energy: kinetic and potential.

Kinetic energy is the energy of movement. Your personal observation likely tells you that a baseball thrown by a major league pitcher at 40 meters per second has more kinetic energy than a pitch that you might throw at 25 meters per second. Similarly, a car travelling at 10 meters per second has more kinetic energy than a bicycle travelling at the same speed. So you could say that kinetic energy must be a function of both mass and velocity and you would be correct.

The formula to calculate kinetic energy (KE) is:

$$KE = \frac{1}{2}mv^2$$

where m is mass in kilograms (kg), v is speed in meters per second $\left(\frac{m}{s}\right)$ and KE is kinetic energy in a standard unit called joules (J), which has the units $\left(\frac{kg \times m^2}{s^2}\right)$. Note that KE is a linear function of mass but the velocity component is squared. Here is how the formula could be applied:

Question	Analysis
Truck A has a mass of 10,000 kg and is travelling at a speed of 30 m/s. Truck B has a mass of 5,000 kg and a speed of 15 m/s. What is the ratio of the kinetic energy of Truck A to that of Truck B?	**Step 1:** The question asks for the **ratio** of the KEs of the two trucks, not the actual values.
	Step 2: The values needed to calculate KE for both trucks are given so no further simplification is necessary.
	Step 3: Use relationships rather than actually calculating. Both the mass and speed of A are 2 times those of B. The masses by themselves cause the KE of A to be greater by a factor of 2. Since KE is a function of v^2, the KE of A is 2^2 times that of B due to speed. In total A's KE is $4 \times 2 = 8$ times that of Truck B.
(A) 1:8 (B) 2:1 (C) 4:1 (D) 8:1	**Step 4:** Select choice (D). Double check that the question asked for the KE ratio of A:B and that calculations are correct.

Try this problem on your own. This question does not have answer choices.

> If an automobile with a mass of 1500 kg is travelling at 72 kilometers per hour, what is its kinetic energy in joules?

Explanation

Note that the units of joules $\left(\frac{kg \times m^2}{s^2}\right)$ are not the same as the units in the problem. To convert, first restate the speed as 72,000 meters per hour. Since there are 60 seconds in a minute and 60 minutes in an hour, there are 3,600 seconds in an hour. Now you can set up the calculations:

$$V = \frac{\left(72,000 \frac{m}{hr}\right)}{\left(3,600 \frac{s}{hr}\right)} = 20 \text{ m/s}$$

$$KE = \frac{1}{2} \times \left(1,500 kg\right) \times \left(20 \frac{m}{s}\right)^2 = \frac{1}{2} \times 1,500 kg \times 400 \frac{m^2}{s^2} = 300,000 \text{ J.}$$

Potential energy (PE), as the name implies, is energy that has the potential to be converted to kinetic energy. Many ASVAB questions use one particular type of *PE*, **gravitational potential energy**. If you hold an object in your hand raised above the floor and then let it fall, its potential energy is fully converted to *KE* by the time it hits the floor. The higher the object is raised (*h*), the greater the potential energy of the object. Since heavy objects and light objects fall at the same rate, a heavier object released from the same height would have greater *KE* when it hits the floor and therefore greater *PE* when held above the floor. The force acting on the dropped object is, of course, gravity. If you were to drop an object from the same height on the moon, the speed when it hit the ground would be less than on Earth because the pull of gravity is much lower. Therefore, the object's *PE* would be less on the moon.

The formula to calculate gravitational potential energy follows the logic above.

$$PE = mgh$$

where *m* is mass in kilograms (kg), *g* is **acceleration due to gravity** $\left(9.8 \frac{m}{s^2}\right)$, *h* is the height of the object in meters (m), and *PE* is gravitational potential energy measured in joules (J).

On the ASVAB, it does not matter whether the object is dropped or rolled down a ramp because minor factors such as friction will be ignored on energy problems; the velocity, KE, and PE will be the same in either case even though it will take longer for the object to reach the ground.

Study the following example problem, which does not have answer choices, to help you practice making a prediction on a question of this type.

Question	Analysis
What is the potential energy of a 0.5 kg ball held at the top of a building 20 meters above the ground?	The question asks you to calculate potential energy.
	The question provides two of the variables you need to calculate PE, mass (*m*) and height (*h*).
	It would be a good idea to memorize that $g = 9.8$ m/s^2 or at least that it is approximately 10.
	$PE = mgh = 0.5 \times 9.8 \times 20 = 98$ joules (J)
	The answer is 98 J.

A falling object has its potential energy (*PE*) converted into kinetic energy (*KE*) as it falls. Since the ASVAB ignores such minor factors as resistance on energy problems, problems in the MC section will adhere to the **principle of conservation of mechanical energy.** This rule states that the total mechanical energy (*PE* + *KE*) remains constant as long as no other forces are applied. After the object is dropped but before it hits the ground it will have some *KE* and some *PE*, totalling up to the initial *PE*. At the instant it hits the ground, all of the initial *PE* will have been converted to *KE*. See how this principle is used to solve the following problem:

Question	Analysis
A 1.63 kg object is dropped from a height of 2.5 meters. What will its velocity be at the moment it hits the ground?	**Step 1:** You are asked to calculate the velocity when the object hits the ground.
	Step 2: You are given the mass and height of the object but nothing about velocity. There is nothing to simplify.
	Step 3: The initial *PE* equals the final *KE*, so $mgh = \left(\frac{1}{2}mv^2\right)$. Notice that *m* appears on both sides of the equation so it cancels out: $gh = \left(\frac{1}{2}\right)v^2$ $9.8 \times 2.5 = \left(\frac{1}{2}\right)v^2$. Multiply both sides by 2 for ease of calculation to get $9.8 \times 5 = 49 = v^2$ $v = 7$
(A) 7 m/s (B) 14 m/s (C) 28 m/s (D) 49 m/s	**Step 4:** Select choice (A). By setting *PE* = *KE* you followed the principle of conservation of mechanical energy and the variable *v* is the answer to the right question.

If an object is thrown straight up into the air rather than being dropped, when the object reaches its highest point just before it begins to descend its *KE* = 0 and the potential energy it has at this point equals the kinetic energy it had when it was first thrown. Apply this concept to the problem below:

Question	Analysis
Joel throws a ball straight up in the air at a velocity of 30 m/s. When he releases the ball it is 2 meters above the ground. What is the ball's approximate maximum height above the ground?	**Step 1:** You are given an initial velocity, the additional fact that the ball is released 2 meters above the ground, and the knowledge that the answer will be an approximation.
	Step 2: The question asks for the maximum height above the ground rather than above the point of release.

Question	Analysis
	Step 3: Set $PE = KE$: $h = \left(\frac{1}{2}\right)mv^2$. Cancel out m and plug in v and $g = 10$ since the question asks for an *approximate* value. $$10h = \left(\frac{1}{2}\right)30^2 = 450$$ $$h = 45$$ Add 2 meters to get the total height, 47. Since you used 10 for g rather than 9.8, the true value will be greater than 47.
(A) 40 meters (B) 45 meters (C) 48 meters (D) 60 meters	**Step 4:** Only (C) and (D) are greater than 47, but (D) is clearly too high. (C) is correct. Check the math and that the question requires the additional 2 meters.

Work

Work is accomplished when force is applied to move an object. Like the formulas for energy, the formula to calculate work coincides with what you can observe in the real world. The more force that has to be exerted to move an object a certain distance, the more work is done. Similarly, the farther an object is moved by exerting force, the more the work. These facts are summarized by the formula:

$$W = Fd$$

where W is work in joules (J), F is force in newtons (N), and d is distance in meters (m).

If a force of 100 N is applied to a car, and the car is moved 10 meters, then a total of $100 \times 10 = 1000$ joules of work has been done.

Force F Pushing a Car over Distance d

Work is done if force *F* is applied over distance *d*

If force is applied to the car, but the car does not move, no work has been done. This can be seen in the formula $W = Fd$, where zero distance (d) results in work (W) being zero as well. No matter how much force is applied, no movement results in zero work being accomplished.

Note that work and kinetic energy are both measured in joules. This is not a coincidence, as any work that is done to accelerate an object at rest to velocity v will be converted into the kinetic energy of that object. This principle is known as the **work-energy theorem**.

Question	Analysis
A force of 10 N is applied to a stationary object with 1 kg mass for a sufficient time to attain a velocity of 4 m/s. How much work was done to accomplish this?	The question has values for F, m, and v and asks how much work was done to attain that velocity.
	Work can't be calculated directly because the distance isn't known. However, $W = KE$, per the work-energy theorem. $W = \left(\frac{1}{2}\right)mv^2$
	Plug the known values into the equation and solve. $W = \left(\frac{1}{2}\right) \times 1 \times 4^2$
	Answer: **8 joules**

Apply the information in this section to answer the problem below.

Jane pushes a 20 kg box 20 m in 20 seconds by pushing with a constant force of 10 N. Kellen pushes a 40 kg box 10 m in 15 seconds by pushing with a constant force of 20 N. Which person did more work?

(A) Jane
(B) Kellen
(C) They both did the same amount of work.
(D) It cannot be determined from the information given.

Explanation

The data regarding the mass of the boxes and the time it took each person to move a box are irrelevant. Jane accomplished 10N × 20m = 200 J of work; Kellen's work was (20N) × 20m = 200 J. Therefore, **(C)** is correct.

Power

Power is the **rate** at which work is done:

$$P = \frac{W}{t}$$

Consider the example of a man pushing a small car over a distance of 100 meters. If the man pushes with a force of 100 N to move the car, then using $W = F \times d$, you can see that 100 N × 100 m = 10,000 J of work has been done. If he accomplishes the task at a constant rate over the course of 500 seconds, then the power applied was $\frac{10,000}{500} = 20\frac{J}{s}$. If another man can do the same amount of work in 250 seconds, then that man has twice as much power, or $40\frac{J}{s}$.

One common unit used to express power is the watt, which equals $1\frac{J}{s}$ or $1\frac{newton \times m}{s}$. The watt is named after James Watt, an engineer who died in 1819 and whose work on the steam engine helped make the Industrial Revolution possible. The unit of power that many people in the United States are more familiar with is **horsepower**, since this is the unit that is used to rate internal combustion engines. Horsepower uses a different system of measurement:

it is defined as 550 foot-pounds per second of work being done. One horsepower is the equivalent of 746 watts. Study the example below, which is presented without answer choices, in order to help you practice predicting on a question of this type.

Question	Analysis
Jane pushes a 20 kg box 20 m in 20 seconds by pushing with a constant force of 10 N. How much power did she exert?	You are asked to calculate how much power Jane exerted.
	You already know that Jane did 200 J of work. Since she accomplished that in 20 seconds, the power she applied was 10 watts.

SIMPLE MACHINES

LEARNING OBJECTIVES

In this section you will learn how to:

- identify simple machines and their uses
- calculate the mechanical advantage of specific simple machines
- determine forces in simple machine problems

Simple machines were invented centuries ago to reduce the force or effort needed to perform a variety of tasks; heavy objects need to be lifted, parts need to be pushed together or pulled apart, and large machines need to be moved. Often, it is difficult or impossible for a human being to apply enough force to get the job done.

In order to increase the available force to a much larger one, **mechanical advantage** is used. Mechanical advantage is defined as "the advantage gained by the use of a mechanism in transmitting force." Using the proper equipment, it is possible to increase the force applied severalfold. However, while mechanical advantage can be used to amplify force, this is accomplished by exerting a force over a greater distance. In other words, the work output can never exceed the work input. The good news, however, is that simple machines can make hard work easier by breaking it down into smaller, more manageable pieces.

The **efficiency** of a machine describes how much of the power inputted into the machine is turned into movement or force. A machine that turned 100% of the power applied to it into outputted force would have 100% efficiency. In the real world, however, no machine is 100% efficient, because all machines are affected by friction and most are affected by worn-down and/or imperfectly-fitted parts.

Inclined Plane

One of the simplest ways of managing lifting tasks is through the use of the **inclined plane**. Lifting a 100 kg (about 220 pound) box is a difficult, if not impossible, task for one person. However, the use of an inclined plane (or ramp) can make this a manageable chore.

Pushing a Box Up a Ramp or Lifting It to Height *h*

Remember that the work that is done to lift the box will be the same as the final gravitational potential energy of the box (*PE = mgh*). Therefore, the same amount of work will be done whether the box is pushed up the ramp (assuming no friction), or if it is lifted directly. The difference with the ramp is that a much smaller force can be applied to raise the box. This force must be applied over a longer distance, but it will give some mechanical advantage to make the task easier. Study the following problem to see how much the mechanical advantage of inclined planes can reduce the force needed to raise a heavy object.

Question	Analysis
Jose has to push an object that weighs 1000 N up an inclined ramp to a height 2 m above its current location. If the ramp is 20 m long (measured up the slope), how much force will Jose have to use if the effects of friction are ignored?	The questions asks you to calculate force and ignore friction.
	When Jose has completed the task, the object will have 2m × 1000N = 2000 J greater potential energy than when he started, so he will have to accomplish 2000 J of work. Since $W = f \times d$ and the ramp is 20 m in length, he will only have to exert $\frac{2000}{2} = 100$ N.
	The answer is 100 N.

Wedge

The **wedge** is a variation of the inclined plane. While the inclined plane stays stationary, the wedge is designed to move. It can be used for many purposes, including lifting, splitting, and tightening. The mechanical advantage that can be gained with a wedge is determined by the ratio of its length to its height.

Wedge

Making the wedge longer relative to its height (that is, with a smaller slope) will decrease the amount of lift that takes place as the wedge is moved horizontally. This increases the amount of force that can be generated by the wedge and makes it easier to lift heavy objects. Remember that if force is increased by the wedge, then the distance it will lift will be less than the distance it moved horizontally.

Common applications of the wedge include knives, chisels, and log splitters.

Levers

Another simple machine that can be used to amplify force or distance, as well as change direction, is the **lever**. There are three basic types of levers, so this machine lends itself to many different applications.

The **first-class lever** is used to increase force or distance, and to change the direction of the force. An example of a first-class lever is a child's teeter-totter.

First-Class Lever

The **fulcrum** is the point upon which the lever pivots. When force is applied to one end of the lever, the movement at the other end is in the opposite direction. The position of the fulcrum will define whether any mechanical advantage is gained. If the fulcrum is closer to the object being lifted, less force is required to do the work. However, the end that the effort is applied to must move farther to get the job done.

The opposite effect takes place when the fulcrum is moved closer to where the effort is applied. Now the distance the object can be moved is amplified, but the force required is diminished.

The mechanical advantage gained by the use of a lever is simply the ratio of the distance of the applied force from the fulcrum to the distance of the object from the fulcrum. Thus, a lever where the force is applied 3 meters from the fulcrum and the object being acted upon is 1 meter from the fulcrum will have a mechanical advantage of 3:1. The force applied will move 3 times as far as the object but the force on the object will be 3 times as great as the force applied.

A **second-class lever** is used to increase force on the object in the same direction as the force applied. This type of lever requires a smaller force to lift a larger load but the force must be exerted over a greater distance. An example of a second-class lever is a wheelbarrow.

Second-Class Lever

The mechanical advantage of the second-class lever increases as the object is moved closer to the fulcrum. This can also be accomplished by increasing the length of the lever. The following example illustrates the mechanical advantage of a second class lever:

Question	Analysis
Which of the following forces would be the least needed to lift a 10 N object placed 0.5 m from the fulcrum of a second-class lever if the lifting force is exerted 2 m from the fulcrum?	**Step 1:** The question asks for the minimum force needed to lift the object given the dimensions of the lever.
	Step 2: The problem provides the weight of an object and the measurements of a second-class lever that is used to lift the object.
	Step 3: The mechanical advantage of the lever is $\frac{2}{0.5} = 4$, so a force of $\frac{1}{4}$ the weight of the object or 2.5 N is needed. However, this amount of force would balance the downward and upward forces, so the correct answer must be > 2.5 N.
(A) 0.5 N (B) 2 N (C) 3 N (D) 10 N	**Step 4:** Choose option (C). Verify that this is the *minimum* force needed from among these choices (that's why (D) is incorrect) and double check the dimensions and calculations.

The **third-class lever** is also used to increase distance travelled by the object in the same direction as the force applied. It is similar to the second-class lever in that the fulcrum is at one end. The object, however, is at the other end of the lever, with the force being applied somewhere in between the fulcrum and the object. Examples of third-class levers would be a fishing pole and a catapult.

Third-Class Lever

Fulcrum   Force   Object

Since the distance moved at the point where the force is applied is less than the distance travelled by the load with a third-class lever, the force needed is increased. This effect magnifies as the force is applied closer to the fulcrum.

Pulleys

Applying force to an object is sometimes accomplished through the use of a **pulley**. A pulley is a system that is used to change the direction, but not the amount, of a force.

Person Pulling a Rope Through a Pulley to Lift an Object

A pulley system consists of a rope, belt, or chain looped over a wheel. It can be useful in certain situations because it is often easier to pull with a downward force than an upward force.

Block and Tackle

It is relatively uncommon for one pulley to be used by itself. Often, two or more pulleys will be used in an arrangement known as a **block and tackle** to increase lifting force.

Block and Tackle

Rope is pulled
to lift object

Object to be lifted

The block and tackle shown here has four pulleys; two are attached to a stationary object (such as the ceiling or wall of a building) and the other two are attached to the lower block (the load). As the rope is pulled, the lower block moves toward the stationary pulleys. Note that in order to lift the load 1 foot, it is necessary to pull the rope a total of 4 feet. This is because each of the four rope links must shorten by 1 foot to get the lower block to move 1 foot. Neglecting friction, this gives a total mechanical advantage of 4:1, so if 4 pounds of force are required to lift a load, only 1 pound needs to be applied to the rope. Note that you can determine the mechanical advantage ratio of a block and tackle system by counting the number of pulleys.

Wheel and Axle

The **wheel and axle** mechanism is not just a simple free-turning wheel such as the front wheel of a typical bicycle. Instead, this type of machine uses two wheels mounted on a shaft, with one wheel having a larger diameter than the other. The wheel and axle can be used to increase mechanical advantage. An example of a wheel and axle is the steering wheel of a car.

Wheel and Axle

Movement at B is smaller than movement at A—force
is increased at B.

The large-diameter wheel will usually be the one that has the effort applied to it. Large movements of the large wheel result in small movements of the small wheel. The larger wheel has a greater circumference, so a point on the edge of it travels further per turn compared to a point on the smaller wheel. Since a large movement (or distance) is being translated into a small movement, the force is then being increased. The amount of mechanical advantage is determined by the ratio of the diameters of the wheels. If the large wheel is 20 inches in diameter, and the small wheel is 10 inches in diameter, the total mechanical advantage is 2:1.

Gears and Gear Ratios

Gears can be used anywhere that force is being transmitted between two points, and are excellent for gaining mechanical advantage.

Meshed Gears

Gears can be used to change rotational speed and torque. The **gear ratio** is determined by comparing the number of teeth on the large gear to the number on the small gear. In the figure, the large gear has 18 teeth and the small gear has 12, so the gear ratio is 3:2.

If a small gear drives a large gear, a **speed reduction** takes place. The large gear will turn slower than the small gear and the speed of the output will be slower in proportion to the gear ratio. However, an associated **torque multiplication** (increase) will take place, and the torque output of the large gear will be greater than what was applied to the small gear, in proportion to the gear ratio. A speed decrease means that torque will increase. A mathematician would describe these two properties as **inversely proportional**.

Check your understanding of gears with this problem:

Question	Analysis
Gear A in the figure above turns counter-clockwise at the rate of 60 revolutions per minute (RPM). In what direction and at what rate will Gear B turn?	**Step 1:** The question asks both the direction and the rotational speed of Gear B.
	Step 2: The relationship of the gears, the number of teeth on each, and the RPM and direction of Gear A are given. No simplification is needed.
	Step 3: The two gears move in opposite directions, so eliminate answer choices (C) and (D). Since Gear B is larger and has more teeth, it must turn more slowly.
(A) clockwise at 40 RPM (B) clockwise at 90 RPM (C) counter-clockwise at 40 RPM (D) counter-clockwise at 90 RPM	**Step 4:** The correct answer is (A). The gear ratio is 3:2 and the ratio of the rate of revolutions is 2:3, so the answer checks correctly.

MECHANICAL COMPREHENSION PRACTICE QUESTIONS

1. The work required to lift an object is the same as

    (A) the final potential energy of the object
    (B) the weight of the object divided by gravity
    (C) the force required to overcome friction
    (D) half of the work required to put the object down

2. A constant force of 2 N is applied to a mass of 6 kg that is initially at rest for 3 seconds. Assuming there is no friction or any other force applied to the mass, what is the velocity of the mass after 3 seconds?

    (A) 0.5 m/s
    (B) 1.0 m/s
    (C) 6.0 m/s
    (D) 12.0 m/s

3. Approximately how much force is needed to lift the weight below?

    24 lbs

    (A) 6 lbs
    (B) 12 lbs
    (C) 24 lbs
    (D) 48 lbs

4. If a ball is dropped from a height of 5 m, what will be its approximate speed when it hits the ground?

    (A) cannot be determined because the mass is unknown.
    (B) cannot be determined because the time it takes to reach the ground is unknown.
    (C) 5 m/s
    (D) 10 m/s

5. Adam's car is stuck in the mud, so he recruits some friends to help push it out. If they apply 2,000 N of force to push the car 5 m, how much work did they accomplish?

    (A) 400 J
    (B) 1,000 J
    (C) 2,000 J
    (D) 10,000 J

6. A machine in an assembly plant lifts parts weighing 10 N each from the floor to a height of 2 m. If this machine must lift batches of 20 parts at a time in 2 seconds, what amount of power is required?

    (A) 20 watts
    (B) 100 watts
    (C) 200 watts
    (D) 400 watts

7. A man who weighs 900 N wants to compress some loose soil in his garden, so he puts a thick plate that is $\frac{1}{2}$ m wide and $\frac{3}{4}$ m long on the ground and stands on the plate. Assuming that the plate distributes his weight evenly, how much pressure is applied to the soil?

    (A) $900 \frac{N}{m^2}$
    (B) $1600 \frac{N}{m^2}$
    (C) $1800 \frac{N}{m^2}$
    (D) $2400 \frac{N}{m^2}$

8. Gear A has 15 teeth and gear B has 10. If gear A makes 14 revolutions, how many will gear B make?

    (A) 7
    (B) 14
    (C) 21
    (D) 28

9. Two wheels are secured to a common axle. If the larger wheel has a radius of $\frac{1}{2}m$ and the smaller wheel has a diameter of $\frac{1}{10}m$ what is the mechanical advantage for a force applied to the larger wheel?

    (A)   5 to 1
    (B)   10 to 1
    (C)   20 to 1
    (D)   40 to 1

10. A basic kitchen knife, like the one below, is based on which of the following simple machines?

    (A)   wedge
    (B)   first-class lever
    (C)   pulley
    (D)   second-class lever

11. In order for Person X pulling a rope to lift an object with a block and tackle at the same rate of speed as Person Y pulling a rope to lift an identical object with a simple pulley, Person X will have to pull the rope _____ as Person Y.

    (A)   at the same rate
    (B)   faster
    (C)   slower
    (D)   at a rate based on the ratio of the diameters of the pulleys

12. How much force is needed to apply 50 ft-lb of torque to a bolt using a 2 ft long wrench?

    (A)   100 pounds
    (B)   50 pounds
    (C)   40 pounds
    (D)   25 pounds

13. If a 10 N force applied to an object produces an acceleration of 10 m/s^2, assuming friction is NOT negligible, what could the mass of the object have been?

    (A)   less than 1 kg
    (B)   equal to 1 kg
    (C)   between 10 kg and 1 kg
    (D)   greater than 10 kg

14. The force of friction between two surfaces moving past each other DOES NOT depend on

    (A)   the normal force.
    (B)   the nature of the surfaces in contact with each other.
    (C)   the area of the surfaces in contact with each other.
    (D)   the speed at which the surfaces are moving past each other.

15. The gravitational acceleration on Earth, g, is 9.8 m/s^2. The gravitational acceleration on a neighboring planet, Xendor, is 3 times as much. What is the approximate weight of a 100 kg person on Xendor? (Hint: you can approximate the gravitational acceleration on Earth as 10 m/s^2 to make calculations easier.)

    (A)   100 N
    (B)   300 N
    (C)   1000 N
    (D)   3000 N

16. Assuming no friction, if 80 J of work was done to move an object 2 m, what was the net force that was applied?

    (A)   4 N
    (B)   16 N
    (C)   40 N
    (D)   160 N

Answers and Explanations

1. **(A) the final potential energy of the object.** The work-energy theorem states that work performed on an object will increase the object's mechanical energy by the amount of work applied to the object. In this case the increase in mechanical energy was the additional potential energy resulting from the object being lifted higher. Therefore the final *PE* equals the work.

2. **(B) 1.0 m/s** Since $F = ma$, then $a = \frac{F}{m} = \frac{2}{6} = \frac{1}{3}\frac{m}{s^2}$. Change in velocity = acceleration × time. Therefore: $\frac{1}{3}\frac{m}{s^2} \times 3\,s = 1\frac{m}{s}$.

3. **(B) 12 lbs** This block and tackle has 2 pulleys, so the mechanical advantage is 2:1, because the weight will only move half the distance that the rope is pulled. As a result, the force applied will be half the weight, or 12 lbs.

4. **(D) 10 m/s** Although the mass and time are unknown, they are not needed to solve the problem. When the ball is 5 *m* above the ground all its energy is *PE*, but when it hits the ground all its energy is *KE*. Since energy is conserved, set $PE = KE$ or $mgh = \frac{1}{2}mv^2$. The mass cancels out and, since the question asks for the approximate speed, $g = 10$ will suffice. $2 \times 10 \times 5 = v^2$ and $100 = v^2$, so $v = 10$.

5. **(D) 10,000 J** Work = Force × Distance or $2000 \times 5 = 10,000$ J.

6. **(C) 200 watts** To calculate power, start by determining the work performed. Since there are 20 parts that weigh (exert a downward force) 10 N each that are lifted 2 m, work = $20 \times 10 \times 2 = 400$ J. The machine accomplishes this work in 2 seconds. Power is $\frac{\text{work}}{\text{time}}$, or 200 watts.

7. **(D) 2400 $\frac{N}{m^2}$** Pressure is force divided by the area over which it is applied, so $P = \frac{900}{\left(\frac{1}{2}\right) \times \left(\frac{3}{4}\right)} = \frac{900}{\frac{3}{8}} = 900 \times \left(\frac{8}{3}\right) = 2400\frac{N}{m^2}$.

8. **(C) 21** This could be solved with two different approaches. Gear A makes 14 revolutions and has 15 teeth, so $14 \times 15 = 210$ teeth would pass any point. Since gear B has 10 teeth, it would need to make 21 revolutions to match the teeth of gear A. Alternatively, the gear ratio is 3:2, so the proportion $\left(\frac{3}{2}\right) = \left(\frac{x}{14}\right)$ could be used to obtain the same answer, 21.

9. **(B) 10 to 1** The mechanical advantage of a wheel and axle is equal to the ratios of the radii of the two wheels. The problem states that the smaller wheel's diameter is $\frac{1}{10}$m, so its radius is $\frac{1}{20}$m and the ratio of the two radii is 10:1.

10. **(A) wedge** The cross-section of a kitchen knife is very small on the cutting side and gets thicker toward the top, just as a wedge does.

11. **(B) faster** Due to the mechanical advantage that is provided by the block and tackle, the distance that the object will move for a given amount of rope pulled is decreased in proportion to the mechanical advantage provided. Therefore, to keep the rate of lifting the object constant between the simple pulley and the block and tackle, Person X will need to pull the rope faster than Person Y but will use less force.

12. **(D) 25 pounds** Torque (T) is determined by multiplying a force (F) by the lever arm length (L) that the force is acting through or $T = F \times L$. In this case, to achieve an applied torque of 50 ft-lb, with a 2 ft lever arm, (where $F = T/L$), 50ft-lb/2ft = 25 lb of force is needed.

13. **(A) less than 1 kg** Based on Newton's second law, $F = ma$, where F = force in newtons, m = mass in kilograms, and a = acceleration in m/s². Therefore, rearranging the equation for mass, you get: $m = \frac{F}{a}$. Since you know that friction is not negligible, you also know that the resultant force will be less than 10 N (see diagram below). Therefore, the maximum mass possible, in a frictionless system is calculated by dividing 10 N by 10 m/s², which gives 1 kg. Knowing that friction will diminish the applied force, the resulting mass has to be less than 1 kg, which matches answer choice (A).

10 N
applied force

? N
opposing frictional force

Resultant Force = 10 N − force of friction
Thus, the resultant force will be less than 10 N.

14. **(D) the speed at which the surfaces are moving past each other** Kinetic friction is exhibited when surfaces/objects move past one another. The normal force, which is a factor of the weight of the object, will affect friction (for example: move your hand across a table lightly and then again with more force; increased force leads to increased friction). The nature and area of the surfaces in contact with each other will also affect the friction that develops between two surfaces (for example: moving your hand across a desk with oil on it is a lot easier than with honey; also, moving one finger across a desk develops less friction than moving your entire hand). The speed at which the surfaces move past each other however, does not impact the frictional forces (though it may generate more heat).

15. **(D) 3000 N** Weight = gm, where g = gravitational acceleration (m/s^2) and m = mass in kg. On Xendor, the gravitational acceleration is 3 times as much as on Earth, giving a new g of approximately 30 m/s^2. To calculate weight on Xendor, multiply the new gravitational acceleration by the person's mass: Weight = 30 m/s^2 × 100 kg = 3000 N.

16. **(C) 40 N** Recall that $W = Fd$, where W is work in joules, F is force in newtons and d is distance in meters. Therefore, rearranging the equation for force, you get: $F = \frac{W}{d}$. Taking 80 J and dividing by 2 m, you get 40 N.

Review and Reflect

How did you do on this practice set? As you review your work, ask yourself some questions:

- Did you remember the equations you learned in the chapter?
- Did you think about how various forces were at work in the practice questions?
- Did you stop to think carefully about what the question is asking for, simplify or solve, and then make a prediction before looking at the choices?

ASSEMBLING OBJECTS

KNOW WHAT TO EXPECT

The ASVAB analyzes your abilities and aptitude to help you discover what military careers would be the best match for you. For example, pilots, mechanics, machine operators, and engineers need to develop good spatial relationship skills—that is, the ability to see how parts will look when assembled into a whole. The **Assembling Objects** (AO) subtest examines your spatial relationship skills, so it gives you an opportunity to show that you are good at putting things together. As always, we recommend checking with your recruiter or career counselor to learn more about which subtests will be important to you in reaching your goals.

The skills required for the AO test are *learnable*. Even test takers who struggle to visualize how shapes fit together can greatly improve their spatial relationship skills by learning strategies and practicing. In this chapter, you'll have the opportunity to do just that.

The CAT-ASVAB test includes 16 AO questions, with a time limit of 16 minutes. Remember, unlike the paper and pencil ASVAB, you will not be able to review or change an answer once you submit it. The paper and pencil ASVAB includes 25 AO questions, with a 15-minute time limit.

The Assembling Objects subtest contains two types of test items. We're going to call these:

- **Jigsaw-Puzzle-Type Problems,** which test your ability to choose how an object will look when its parts are put together into a larger shape.
- **Connector-Type Problems,** which test your ability to correctly connect two objects with a line at the indicated points.

In both types of AO items, you are offered five boxes. The left-most or first box contains drawings of unconnected parts. The four answer-choice boxes hold drawings of shapes, only one of which shows the shape that would result when all the parts are correctly assembled.

JIGSAW-PUZZLE-TYPE PROBLEMS

LEARNING OBJECTIVES

In this section, you will learn to:

- identify what your task is on Jigsaw-Puzzle-Type problems
- apply the Kaplan Method for Assembling Objects questions to Jigsaw-Puzzle-Type problems

Study the question below.

Which figure best shows how the objects in the left box will appear if they are fit together?

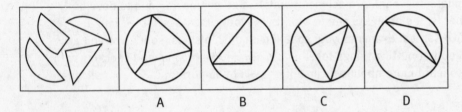

Every AO question has a box on the very left that shows a number of individual parts. Let's call that box on the left the **instructions box**. Each AO question then offers four answer choices. Three of those choices distort the shapes in the instructions box. Only one of them accurately shows how the shapes would fit together into a whole. In this case, (C) is correct.

Having trouble visualizing why (C) is correct? Study the diagram below.

However, you *do not* have to visualize assembling the parts in your head in order to answer AO questions. (That's good news.)

Rather, approach these questions strategically. Did you notice that each of the answer choices in the example above is a circle dominated by a large triangle? That will be helpful. Now, focusing on the circle outline won't be helpful, because it's the same in all four choices. However, the placement and shape of that large triangle varies among the answer choices. Thus, focusing on that prominent triangle will help you eliminate some choices right off the bat. You can call that key shape a **landmark**, in the sense that it helps you find what you're looking for.

What do you notice about the triangle depicted in the instructions box? It's a right triangle, or very close to being a right triangle. How many of the answer choices clearly do *not* have right triangles? (A) and (D). Cross them off. Your landmark just knocked out half the choices.

Only (B) and (C) remain as possible choices. Find another key trait in the instructions box. Here, counting the number of shapes might be helpful. There are four shapes in the instructions box. How many shapes do (B) and (C) have? (B) has only three, so it can't be right. Circle (C) and move on to the next question.

Here's a method you'll use on all Assembling Objects questions. Memorize this method now, so that you can work on mastering it in your practice.

The Kaplan Method for Assembling Objects Questions

Step 1: Identify a landmark in the instructions box.

Step 2: Eliminate any answer choices that don't display the landmark.

Step 3: Compare other shapes to eliminate remaining choices.

Study the example below.

Question

Which figure best shows how the objects in the left box will appear if they are fit together?

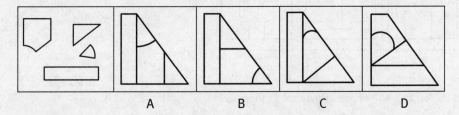

Analysis

Step 1: The easiest landmark here might be the smallest shape, which looks like a small pizza slice.

Step 2: (C) and (D) don't have that small pizza shape, so they're out. (A) has a similar shape, but it's far too big. So (A) is out as well. (B) is correct.

Step 3: No need to compare other shapes here.

In **Step 1**, your landmark shape in Jigsaw-Puzzle-Type AO problems might be:

- the largest shape
- the smallest shape
- the shape that seems to differ the most among the answer choices
- the most oddly-shaped piece
- a shape with a recognizable angle or side (such as a right angle, or a steeply curved side)

With practice, you will learn to efficiently spot a useful landmark in the instructions box.

When you get to **Step 3,** here are strategies you can use to eliminate any remaining wrong answer choices:

- Count the number of parts. If you are taking the paper and pencil test, you can actually assign each part a number and write it in.
- Find a second landmark. If you used the largest shape in Kaplan Method Steps 1 and 2, perhaps you would use the smallest shape as your second landmark.
- Compare the sizes of the shapes in the instructions box to the remaining choices.

And here are some things to watch out for in wrong answer choices on Jigsaw-Puzzle-Type AO questions:

- You can expect one or more of the shapes in the instructions box to be inverted left-to-right or top-to-bottom in one or more of the wrong answer choices. The correct answer might move the parts around or rotate them, but it won't invert any of them.
- An enlarged or shrunken version of a shape in the instructions box might appear in the wrong answer choices. The correct answer will have the same shapes in the same sizes.
- A shape that has all straight edges in the instructions box may have a curved edge in some wrong answer choices.
- A shape from the instructions box may be carved into two or more smaller shapes in some wrong answer choices.

Try these problems on your own, and then read the explanations below.

Which figure best shows how the objects in the left box will appear if they are fit together?

1.

           A   B   C   D

Which figure best shows how the objects in the left box will appear if they are fit together?

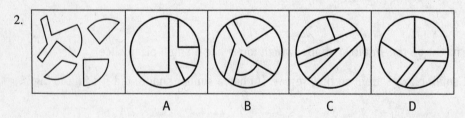

2.

           A   B   C   D

Explanations

Note: It's perfectly fine if you chose different landmarks than the ones below, as long as you were able to work efficiently through the questions.

1.

Step 1: The instructions box has two shapes that look like fat square brackets; those are good landmarks.

Step 2: (B) doesn't have two of those shapes; eliminate. (C) has two but they're too long; eliminate. Only (A) and (D) remain.

Step 3: Count the number of pieces in the instruction box: there are five. (D) has three shapes; eliminate.

(A) is correct.

2.

Step 1: The instructions box has an odd shape that looks like a pie piece with two branches growing out of the narrow end; that's a good landmark.

Step 2: (A) and (C) have no such piece; eliminate. (B) and (D) remain.

Step 3: The instructions box has four shapes; (B) has five. Eliminate (B).

(D) is correct.

CONNECTOR-TYPE PROBLEMS

LEARNING OBJECTIVES

In this section, you will learn to:

- identify what your task is on Connector-Type problems
- apply the Kaplan Method for Assembling Objects questions to Connector-Type problems

---

Study the example below.

Which figure best shows how the objects in the left box will touch if the letters for each object are matched?

The instructions box of a Connector-Type problem displays two geometric shapes. Some problems have familiar shapes such as circles, squares, rectangles, and triangles, while others have more unusual shapes such as letters, clouds, or hearts. The instructions box will also display a **connector line**. You could think of the connector line as being a string you must tie to the two shapes in precisely the places indicated.

The two shapes and the connector line are labeled with dots and small letters to indicate points where you are to connect the shapes. You will see one dot on each shape, each labeled with a letter. Dots on the ends of the connector line will correspond to these letters. Sometimes the dots will be on the edges of shapes, and sometimes they will be inside the shapes.

You are asked to attach the two shapes to the line at the correct points, based on the diagram in the instructions box. The shapes may be rotated in the solution boxes, but the correct solution cannot be flipped. In the example above, choice (D) is correct.

Having trouble seeing it? Study the diagram below.

However, just as with Jigsaw-Puzzle-Type questions, you do *not* need to be able to visualize the solution in your head. The Kaplan Method works on Connector-Type problems just as it does on Jigsaw-Puzzle-Type problems. Study the example below.

Question

Which figure best shows how the objects in the left box will touch if the letters for each object are matched?

Analysis

Step 1: A good landmark here is the fact that dot *a* is in the middle of the straight side of the semicircle in the instructions box.

Step 2: Choices (B) and (D) don't display the correct placement of connection *a*; eliminate. Only (A) and (C) remain.

Step 3: A second landmark could be the placement of connection *b*: it's on a corner of the rectangle. Choice (C) places it wrongly in the middle of one side of the rectangle. **(A)** is correct.

In **Step 1**, your landmark in Connector-Type AO problems might be:

- whether a dot is placed in the middle of a side or on a corner of a shape
- whether a dot is placed on the edge or inside a shape
- a shape itself

With practice, you will learn to efficiently spot a useful landmark in the instructions box. If you are testing on paper and pencil, you could actually add the labels *a* and *b* to the answer choices in order to help you eliminate choices that don't display your landmark.

When you get to **Step 3**, here are strategies you can use to eliminate any remaining wrong answer choices:

- Find a second landmark. If you used dot *a* as your first landmark, you might use dot *b* as your second landmark.
- If a dot is placed on the corner of a shape in the instructions box, check to see *which* corner is attached to the connector line in the answer choices.
- Check to see if any of the shapes have been flipped or inverted in the answer choices.

Here are some things to watch out for in wrong answer choices on Connector-Type AO questions:

- If the connection point is on the edge of a shape in the instructions box, it may appear inside the shape in some wrong answer choices (or vice versa).
- If the connection point is on the corner of a shape, expect it to either appear on other corners in some of the wrong answer choices *or* appear in the middle of an edge in some wrong answer choices.
- One or more of the shapes in the instructions box may be inverted left-to-right or top-to-bottom in one or more of the wrong answer choices.
- An enlarged or shrunken version of a shape in the instructions box might appear in the wrong answer choices. The correct answer will have the same shapes in the same proportions.

Try it on your own, and then review the explanations below.

Which figure best shows how the objects in the left box will touch if the letters for each object are matched?

1.

Which figure best shows how the objects in the left box will touch if the letters for each object are matched?

2.

| | A | B | C | D |

Explanations

Note: your landmarks may differ. That's fine, as long as you were able to work through the problems efficiently and accurately.

1.
Step 1: Dot *b* looks like a good landmark: it's on the narrowest point of the triangle.

Step 2: Choice (C) places the connector on a different corner of the triangle, and choice (D) places it in the middle of the triangle. Eliminate. (A) and (B) remain.

Step 3: A good second landmark would be the placement of dot *a*: it's in the middle of the three-lobed shape. Choice (A) wrongly places it on the edge.

Choice **(B)** is correct.

2.
Step 1: The instructions box includes a shape that looks like a hair dryer, and dot *a* is at the point where the trigger of the hair dryer meets the barrel of the hair dryer. That's a good landmark.

Step 2: Choices (A) and (B) misplace the connection point on the hair dryer; eliminate. (C) and (D) remain.

Step 3: The circle with dot *b* is the same in choices (C) and (D), so a different landmark needs to be used. Instead, compare the hair dryer: turns out it's flipped in choice (C).

Choice **(D)** is correct.

ASSEMBLING OBJECTS PRACTICE QUESTIONS

For questions 1–5:

Which figure best shows how the objects in the left box will appear if they are fit together?

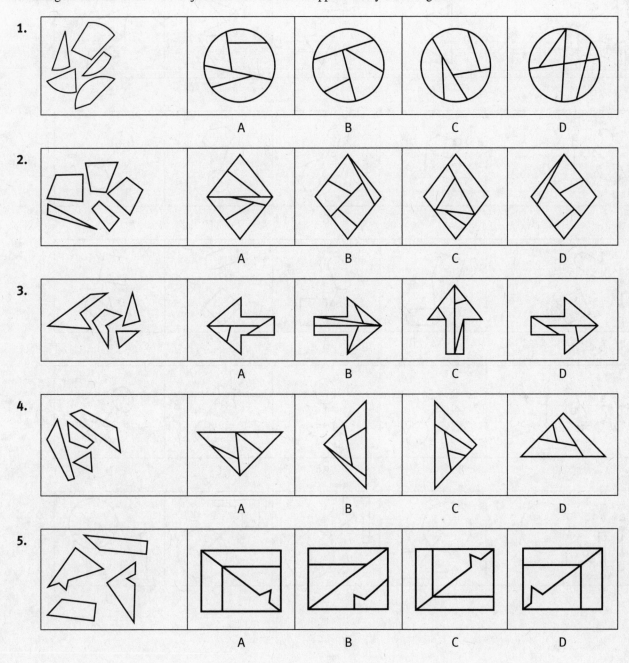

For questions 6–10:

Which figure best shows how the objects in the left box will touch if the letters for each object are matched?

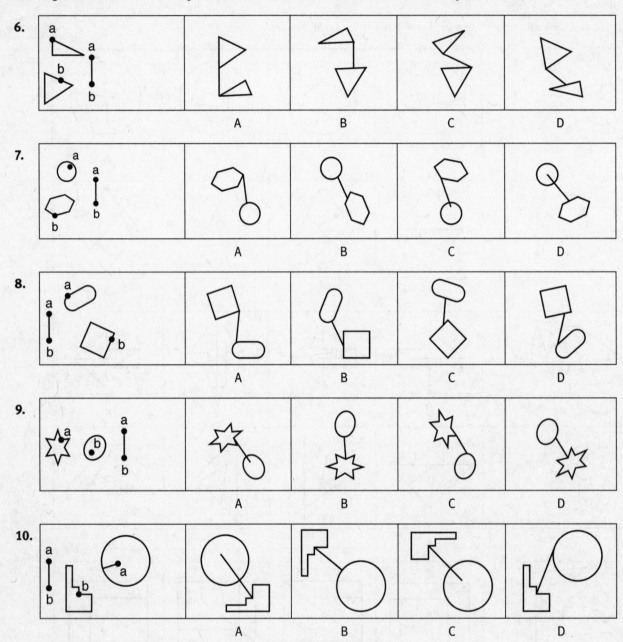

Answers and Explanations

In the answers below, we have numbered the pieces, in order to help you see how the correct answer relates to the instructions box. If you got any of them wrong, go back to the question, identify good landmarks, and try again.

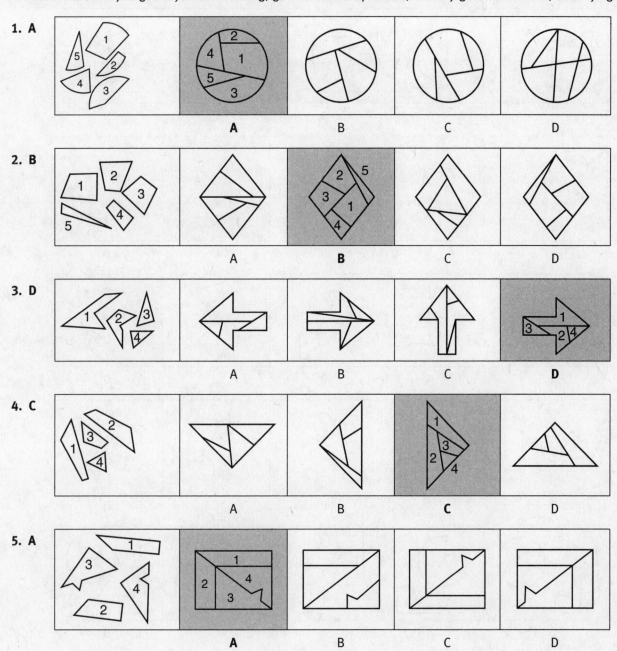

In the answers below, we have placed dots in the answer choices, in order to help you see how the correct answer relates to the instructions box. If you got any of them wrong, go back to the question, identify good landmarks, and try again.

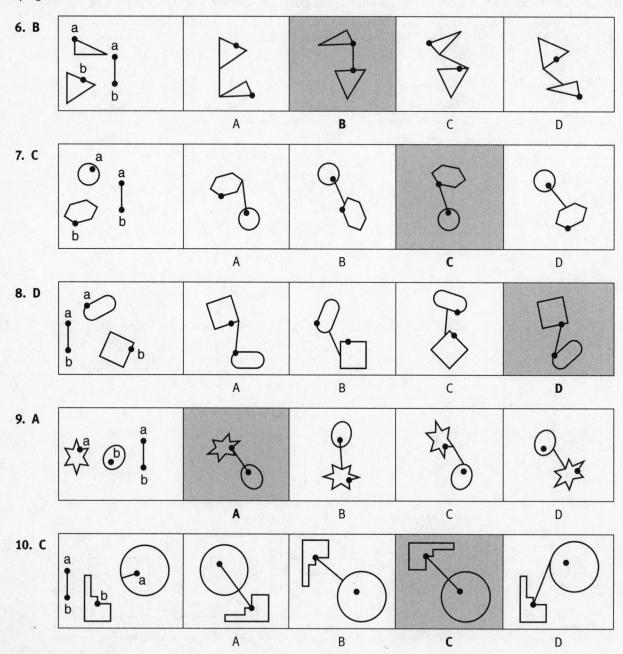

Review and Reflect

How did you do? Which questions were more challenging? How could you improve your choice of landmarks? Going over the questions again may prove helpful.

ASVAB PRACTICE TESTS

Congratulations on finishing your review of the ASVAB subjects! Now that you have completed the chapters, it is time to take a full-length practice test. On the following pages, there are two full-length practice tests with complete answers and explanations. Do your best to mimic the Test Day scenario. Take the test in a quiet location, do not use a calculator, and stick to the time frames allotted for each section.

ANSWER SHEET

Part 1: General Science (GS)

1 A B C D	6 A B C D	11 A B C D	16 A B C D	21 A B C D
2 A B C D	7 A B C D	12 A B C D	17 A B C D	22 A B C D
3 A B C D	8 A B C D	13 A B C D	18 A B C D	23 A B C D
4 A B C D	9 A B C D	14 A B C D	19 A B C D	24 A B C D
5 A B C D	10 A B C D	15 A B C D	20 A B C D	25 A B C D

Part 2: Arithmetic Reasoning (AR)

1 A B C D	7 A B C D	13 A B C D	19 A B C D	25 A B C D
2 A B C D	8 A B C D	14 A B C D	20 A B C D	26 A B C D
3 A B C D	9 A B C D	15 A B C D	21 A B C D	27 A B C D
4 A B C D	10 A B C D	16 A B C D	22 A B C D	28 A B C D
5 A B C D	11 A B C D	17 A B C D	23 A B C D	29 A B C D
6 A B C D	12 A B C D	18 A B C D	24 A B C D	30 A B C D

Part 3: Word Knowledge (WK)

1 A B C D	8 A B C D	15 A B C D	22 A B C D	29 A B C D
2 A B C D	9 A B C D	16 A B C D	23 A B C D	30 A B C D
3 A B C D	10 A B C D	17 A B C D	24 A B C D	31 A B C D
4 A B C D	11 A B C D	18 A B C D	25 A B C D	32 A B C D
5 A B C D	12 A B C D	19 A B C D	26 A B C D	33 A B C D
6 A B C D	13 A B C D	20 A B C D	27 A B C D	34 A B C D
7 A B C D	14 A B C D	21 A B C D	28 A B C D	35 A B C D

Part 4: Paragraph Comprehension (PC)

1 A B C D	4 A B C D	7 A B C D	10 A B C D	13 A B C D
2 A B C D	5 A B C D	8 A B C D	11 A B C D	14 A B C D
3 A B C D	6 A B C D	9 A B C D	12 A B C D	15 A B C D

Part 5: Mathematics Knowledge (MK)

1 A B C D	6 A B C D	11 A B C D	16 A B C D	21 A B C D
2 A B C D	7 A B C D	12 A B C D	17 A B C D	22 A B C D
3 A B C D	8 A B C D	13 A B C D	18 A B C D	23 A B C D
4 A B C D	9 A B C D	14 A B C D	19 A B C D	24 A B C D
5 A B C D	10 A B C D	15 A B C D	20 A B C D	25 A B C D

ANSWER SHEET

Part 6: Electronics Information (EI)

1	Ⓐ Ⓑ Ⓒ Ⓓ	5	Ⓐ Ⓑ Ⓒ Ⓓ	9	Ⓐ Ⓑ Ⓒ Ⓓ	13	Ⓐ Ⓑ Ⓒ Ⓓ	17	Ⓐ Ⓑ Ⓒ Ⓓ
2	Ⓐ Ⓑ Ⓒ Ⓓ	6	Ⓐ Ⓑ Ⓒ Ⓓ	10	Ⓐ Ⓑ Ⓒ Ⓓ	14	Ⓐ Ⓑ Ⓒ Ⓓ	18	Ⓐ Ⓑ Ⓒ Ⓓ
3	Ⓐ Ⓑ Ⓒ Ⓓ	7	Ⓐ Ⓑ Ⓒ Ⓓ	11	Ⓐ Ⓑ Ⓒ Ⓓ	15	Ⓐ Ⓑ Ⓒ Ⓓ	19	Ⓐ Ⓑ Ⓒ Ⓓ
4	Ⓐ Ⓑ Ⓒ Ⓓ	8	Ⓐ Ⓑ Ⓒ Ⓓ	12	Ⓐ Ⓑ Ⓒ Ⓓ	16	Ⓐ Ⓑ Ⓒ Ⓓ	20	Ⓐ Ⓑ Ⓒ Ⓓ

Part 7: Automotive and Shop Information (AS)

1	Ⓐ Ⓑ Ⓒ Ⓓ	6	Ⓐ Ⓑ Ⓒ Ⓓ	11	Ⓐ Ⓑ Ⓒ Ⓓ	16	Ⓐ Ⓑ Ⓒ Ⓓ	21	Ⓐ Ⓑ Ⓒ Ⓓ
2	Ⓐ Ⓑ Ⓒ Ⓓ	7	Ⓐ Ⓑ Ⓒ Ⓓ	12	Ⓐ Ⓑ Ⓒ Ⓓ	17	Ⓐ Ⓑ Ⓒ Ⓓ	22	Ⓐ Ⓑ Ⓒ Ⓓ
3	Ⓐ Ⓑ Ⓒ Ⓓ	8	Ⓐ Ⓑ Ⓒ Ⓓ	13	Ⓐ Ⓑ Ⓒ Ⓓ	18	Ⓐ Ⓑ Ⓒ Ⓓ	23	Ⓐ Ⓑ Ⓒ Ⓓ
4	Ⓐ Ⓑ Ⓒ Ⓓ	9	Ⓐ Ⓑ Ⓒ Ⓓ	14	Ⓐ Ⓑ Ⓒ Ⓓ	19	Ⓐ Ⓑ Ⓒ Ⓓ	24	Ⓐ Ⓑ Ⓒ Ⓓ
5	Ⓐ Ⓑ Ⓒ Ⓓ	10	Ⓐ Ⓑ Ⓒ Ⓓ	15	Ⓐ Ⓑ Ⓒ Ⓓ	20	Ⓐ Ⓑ Ⓒ Ⓓ	25	Ⓐ Ⓑ Ⓒ Ⓓ

Part 8: Mechanical Comprehension (MC)

1	Ⓐ Ⓑ Ⓒ Ⓓ	6	Ⓐ Ⓑ Ⓒ Ⓓ	11	Ⓐ Ⓑ Ⓒ Ⓓ	16	Ⓐ Ⓑ Ⓒ Ⓓ	21	Ⓐ Ⓑ Ⓒ Ⓓ
2	Ⓐ Ⓑ Ⓒ Ⓓ	7	Ⓐ Ⓑ Ⓒ Ⓓ	12	Ⓐ Ⓑ Ⓒ Ⓓ	17	Ⓐ Ⓑ Ⓒ Ⓓ	22	Ⓐ Ⓑ Ⓒ Ⓓ
3	Ⓐ Ⓑ Ⓒ Ⓓ	8	Ⓐ Ⓑ Ⓒ Ⓓ	13	Ⓐ Ⓑ Ⓒ Ⓓ	18	Ⓐ Ⓑ Ⓒ Ⓓ	23	Ⓐ Ⓑ Ⓒ Ⓓ
4	Ⓐ Ⓑ Ⓒ Ⓓ	9	Ⓐ Ⓑ Ⓒ Ⓓ	14	Ⓐ Ⓑ Ⓒ Ⓓ	19	Ⓐ Ⓑ Ⓒ Ⓓ	24	Ⓐ Ⓑ Ⓒ Ⓓ
5	Ⓐ Ⓑ Ⓒ Ⓓ	10	Ⓐ Ⓑ Ⓒ Ⓓ	15	Ⓐ Ⓑ Ⓒ Ⓓ	20	Ⓐ Ⓑ Ⓒ Ⓓ	25	Ⓐ Ⓑ Ⓒ Ⓓ

Part 9: Assembling Objects (AO)

1	Ⓐ Ⓑ Ⓒ Ⓓ	6	Ⓐ Ⓑ Ⓒ Ⓓ	11	Ⓐ Ⓑ Ⓒ Ⓓ	16	Ⓐ Ⓑ Ⓒ Ⓓ	21	Ⓐ Ⓑ Ⓒ Ⓓ
2	Ⓐ Ⓑ Ⓒ Ⓓ	7	Ⓐ Ⓑ Ⓒ Ⓓ	12	Ⓐ Ⓑ Ⓒ Ⓓ	17	Ⓐ Ⓑ Ⓒ Ⓓ	22	Ⓐ Ⓑ Ⓒ Ⓓ
3	Ⓐ Ⓑ Ⓒ Ⓓ	8	Ⓐ Ⓑ Ⓒ Ⓓ	13	Ⓐ Ⓑ Ⓒ Ⓓ	18	Ⓐ Ⓑ Ⓒ Ⓓ	23	Ⓐ Ⓑ Ⓒ Ⓓ
4	Ⓐ Ⓑ Ⓒ Ⓓ	9	Ⓐ Ⓑ Ⓒ Ⓓ	14	Ⓐ Ⓑ Ⓒ Ⓓ	19	Ⓐ Ⓑ Ⓒ Ⓓ	24	Ⓐ Ⓑ Ⓒ Ⓓ
5	Ⓐ Ⓑ Ⓒ Ⓓ	10	Ⓐ Ⓑ Ⓒ Ⓓ	15	Ⓐ Ⓑ Ⓒ Ⓓ	20	Ⓐ Ⓑ Ⓒ Ⓓ	25	Ⓐ Ⓑ Ⓒ Ⓓ

ASVAB PRACTICE TEST A

Part 1: General Science (GS)

Time: 11 minutes; 25 questions

Directions: In this section, you will be tested on your knowledge of concepts in science generally reviewed in high school. For each question, select the best answer and mark the corresponding oval on your answer sheet.

1. A genus classification contains several related

    (A)   species
    (B)   families
    (C)   orders
    (D)   phyla

2. Particles that orbit the nucleus of an atom are

    (A)   anions
    (B)   electrons
    (C)   positrons
    (D)   photons

3. As a human breathes, air is first warmed and filtered in the

    (A)   trachea
    (B)   pharynx
    (C)   oral cavity
    (D)   nasal cavity

4. In the food chain described below, which is the tertiary consumer?

    dandelion → rabbit → fox → coyote

    (A)   dandelion
    (B)   rabbit
    (C)   fox
    (D)   coyote

5. The process by which a solid becomes a gas is known as

    (A)   boiling
    (B)   sublimation
    (C)   melting
    (D)   diffusion

6. The gravitational force the Moon exerts on the Earth is

    (A)   less than one-half as much as that exerted by the Earth on the Moon
    (B)   one-half as much as that exerted by the Earth on the Moon
    (C)   the same as that exerted by the Earth on the Moon
    (D)   more than that exerted by the Earth on the Moon

7. Fungi are organisms that break down dead matter and return the organic material back into the environment for reuse. They are examples of

    (A)   producers
    (B)   decomposers
    (C)   consumers
    (D)   mutualists

8. What is the freezing point of water in Kelvin?

    (A)   −273 K
    (B)   0 K
    (C)   100 K
    (D)   273 K

9. Tough elastic tissues found in the joints that connect bones to bones are called

    (A)   ligaments
    (B)   tendons
    (C)   cartilage
    (D)   muscles

10. Stress, a poor diet, cigarette smoking, and hereditary factors all contribute to individuals developing

    (A)   diarrhea
    (B)   high blood pressure
    (C)   gall stones
    (D)   anemia

11. Which clouds are thin and wispy and occur high in the atmosphere?

    (A)   cirrus
    (B)   cumulus
    (C)   stratus
    (D)   stratocumulus

12. Fossils are most likely to be found in which of the following types of rock?

    (A)   igneous
    (B)   metamorphic
    (C)   sedimentary
    (D)   volcanic

13. Animals that consume only plants are called

    (A) saprophytes
    (B) herbivores
    (C) carnivores
    (D) omnivores

14. What type of star is the Sun?

    (A) red dwarf
    (B) blue giant
    (C) white dwarf
    (D) yellow dwarf

15. Which of the following is a group of organisms of the same species living in the same region?

    (A) biome
    (B) ecosystem
    (C) community
    (D) population

16. Which one of these planets is NOT an outer planet?

    (A) Jupiter
    (B) Saturn
    (C) Uranus
    (D) Earth

17. A boulder that begins to roll down a hill is an example of an energy conversion from

    (A) potential to thermal
    (B) potential to kinetic
    (C) kinetic to thermal
    (D) kinetic to potential

18. The lowest layer of the Earth's atmosphere is called the

    (A) ionosphere
    (B) mesosphere
    (C) stratosphere
    (D) troposphere

19. According to the law of conservation of energy

    (A) energy is the capacity to do work
    (B) energy can neither be created nor destroyed
    (C) energy is possessed by a moving object
    (D) energy is stored in an object as a result of its position, shape, or state

20. As an ambulance passes, its pitch seems to change. This perception is best explained by

    (A) convection
    (B) Newton's third law
    (C) the Doppler effect
    (D) momentum

21. A concave lens is also known as a

    (A) focal point
    (B) converging lens
    (C) convex lens
    (D) diverging lens

22. The smallest particle of a covalent compound that can exist in a free state and still retain the characteristics of that compound is a(n)

    (A) proton
    (B) quark
    (C) atom
    (D) molecule

23. Which of the following is most responsible for oceanic tides?

    (A) the orbit of the Earth around its own axis
    (B) the magnetic polarity of the Earth
    (C) the orbit of the Moon around the Earth
    (D) the orbit of the Earth around the Sun

24. In the Periodic Table of the elements, the elements in a column are referred to as a

    (A) period
    (B) group
    (C) configuration
    (D) unit

25. In a chemical change, the molecules that enter the reaction are called

    (A) reactants
    (B) products
    (C) compounds
    (D) elements

STOP. IF YOU FINISH BEFORE THE TIME IS UP, YOU MAY CHECK OVER YOUR WORK ON THIS PART ONLY.

Part 2: Arithmetic Reasoning (AR)

Time: 36 minutes; 30 questions

Directions: In this section, you are tested on your ability to use arithmetic. For each question, select the best answer and mark the corresponding oval on your answer sheet.

1. Three apples cost as much as 4 pears. Three pears cost as much as 2 oranges. How many apples cost as much as 72 oranges?

    (A)   36
    (B)   48
    (C)   64
    (D)   81

2. If 48 of the 60 seats on a bus were occupied, what percent of the seats were NOT occupied?

    (A)   12%
    (B)   15%
    (C)   20%
    (D)   25%

3. Effin sings for $1,000 an hour. Her rate increases by 50% after midnight. If she sings one night from 8:30 p.m. until 1:00 a.m., how much should she be paid?

    (A) $4,500
    (B) $5,000
    (C) $5,500
    (D) $6,000

4. Fran has a drawer containing 4 black T-shirts, 3 orange T-shirts, and 5 blue T-shirts. If she picks one T-shirt at random from the drawer, what are the chances that it will NOT be orange?

    (A) $\dfrac{1}{4}$

    (B) $\dfrac{1}{3}$

    (C) $\dfrac{2}{3}$

    (D) $\dfrac{3}{4}$

5. After a 5-hour flight from Newark, Harry arrives in Denver at 2:30 p.m. If the time in Newark is 2 hours later than the time in Denver, what was the time in Newark when Harry began the flight?

    (A)   10:30 a.m.
    (B)   11:30 a.m.
    (C)   3:30 p.m.
    (D)   5:30 p.m.

6. A full box of chocolate contains 24 pieces. If Doris starts out with 198 pieces of chocolate, how many pieces will she have left over if she fills as many boxes as she can?

    (A)   3
    (B)   6
    (C)   8
    (D)   10

7. If 75% of x is 150, what is the value of x?

    (A)   150
    (B)   175
    (C)   200
    (D)   250

8. Rachel's average score after 6 tests is 83. If Rachel earns a score of 97 on the 7th test, what is her new average?

    (A)   85
    (B)   86
    (C)   87
    (D)   88

9. A delivery service charges $25.00 per pound for making a delivery. If there is an additional 8% sales tax, what is the cost of delivering an item that weighs $\dfrac{4}{5}$ of a pound?

    (A) $20.00
    (B) $21.60
    (C) $22.60
    (D) $24.00

10. A cake recipe requires $\frac{3}{5}$ of an ounce of vanilla extract. How many cakes can be made using a package containing 60 ounces of vanilla extract?

    (A) 48
    (B) 80
    (C) 96
    (D) 100

11. Ed has 100 more dollars than Robert. After Ed spends 20 dollars on groceries, he now has 5 times as much money as Robert. How much money does Robert have?

    (A) $16
    (B) $20
    (C) $24
    (D) $30

12. 587 people are traveling by bus for a field trip. If each bus seats 48 people and all of the buses but one are filled to capacity, how many people sit in the unfilled bus?

    (A) 37
    (B) 36
    (C) 12
    (D) 11

13. Riley brings 100 cookies to school for her class party. If there are 15 students in the class, including Riley, and there are 25 cookies left after the party, what is the average number of cookies that Riley and her classmates ate?

    (A) 1
    (B) 4
    (C) 5
    (D) 6

14. A person 4 feet tall casts a 9-foot shadow at the same time that a nearby tree casts a 21-foot shadow. What is the height of this tree, in feet?

    (A) 7

    (B) $8\frac{1}{2}$

    (C) $9\frac{1}{3}$

    (D) 10

15. In a group of 25 students, 16 are female. What percent of the group is female?

    (A) 16%
    (B) 40%
    (C) 60%
    (D) 64%

16. Phil is making a 40-kilometer canoe trip. If he travels at 30 kilometers per hour for the first 10 kilometers, and then at 15 kilometers per hour for the rest of the trip, how many more minutes will it take him than if he travels the entire trip at 20 kilometers per hour?

    (A) 20
    (B) 24
    (C) 30
    (D) 40

17. In a certain class, 3 out of 24 students are in student organizations. What is the ratio of students in student organizations to students not in student organizations?

    (A) $\frac{1}{8}$

    (B) $\frac{1}{7}$

    (C) $\frac{1}{6}$

    (D) $\frac{1}{4}$

18. In a certain baseball league, each team plays 160 games. After playing half of their games, team A has won 60 games and team B has won 49 games. If team A wins half of its remaining games, how many of its remaining games must team B win to have the same number of wins as team A at the end of the season?

    (A) 51
    (B) 59
    (C) 60
    (D) 61

19. A vendor bought 10 crates of oranges for a total cost of $80. If he lost 2 of the crates, at what price would he have to sell the remaining crates in order to earn a total profit of 25% of the total cost?

    (A) $8.00
    (B) $10.00
    (C) $12.50
    (D) $15.00

20. A machine labels 150 bottles in 20 minutes. At this rate, how many minutes does it take to label 60 bottles?

    (A) 2
    (B) 4
    (C) 6
    (D) 8

21. $15 \times (-5) =$

    (A) 10
    (B) 75
    (C) −75
    (D) −225

22. Mike has a collection of baseball cards and baseball figurines. If the ratio of cards to figurines is 5:7 and there are 25 cards in his collection, how many figurines does he have?

    (A) 20
    (B) 35
    (C) 40
    (D) 45

23. Two hot dogs and a soda cost $3.25. If three hot dogs and a soda cost $4.50, what is the cost of two sodas?

    (A) $0.75
    (B) $1.25
    (C) $1.50
    (D) $2.50

24. Danielle drives from her home to the store at an average speed of 40 miles per hour. She returns home along the same route at an average speed of 60 miles per hour. What is her average speed, in miles per hour, for the entire trip?

    (A) 48
    (B) 50
    (C) 52
    (D) 55

25. At a certain school the ratio of teachers to students is 1 to 10. Which of the following could be the total number of teachers and students?

    (A) 100
    (B) 121
    (C) 222
    (D) 1,011

26. The average of two numbers is equal to twice the positive difference between the two numbers. If the larger number is 35, what is the smaller number?

    (A) 9
    (B) 15
    (C) 21
    (D) 27

27. Each of seven runners on a relay team must run a distance of 1.27 kilometers. Approximately what is the total combined number of kilometers run by the team in the race?

    (A) 11
    (B) 10
    (C) 9
    (D) 8

28. A scanner can scan 12 photos per minute. At this rate, how many minutes would it take to scan 60 photos?

    (A) 2
    (B) 3
    (C) 5
    (D) 7

29. An employee's net pay is equal to gross pay minus total deductions. A certain employee's gross pay is $1,769.23 and her deductions are as follows: FICA, $218.99; Social Security, $107.05; Medicare, $25.03; state tax, $68.65; municipal tax, $42.75. What is the employee's net pay?

    (A) $1,306.76
    (B) $1,306.66
    (C) $1,305.76
    (D) $1,305.66

30. A student takes four tests. His grades are 94, 72, 84, and 98. What is this student's average test grade?

    (A) 92
    (B) 65
    (C) 87
    (D) 88

STOP. IF YOU FINISH BEFORE THE TIME IS UP, YOU MAY CHECK OVER YOUR WORK ON THIS PART ONLY.

Part 3: Word Knowledge (WK)

Time: 11 minutes; 35 questions

<u>Directions</u>: In this section, you are tested on the meaning of words. Each of the following questions has an underlined word. Select the answer that most nearly means the same as the underlined word and mark the corresponding oval on your answer sheet.

1. <u>Impose</u> most nearly means

   (A) create
   (B) force
   (C) damage
   (D) trade

2. <u>Stunted</u> most nearly means

   (A) halted
   (B) frightened
   (C) aged
   (D) overstated

3. A <u>sturdy</u> home can withstand nearly any disaster.

   (A) huge
   (B) strong
   (C) cold
   (D) cautious

4. He was <u>undeterred</u> in his quest to find her.

   (A) surprised
   (B) persistent
   (C) careless
   (D) brazen

5. <u>Ennui</u> most nearly means

   (A) patient
   (B) gloating
   (C) boredom
   (D) tasteful

6. <u>Mutable</u> most nearly means

   (A) changeable
   (B) silent
   (C) big-hearted
   (D) calm

7. The way they <u>squandered</u> the money was shameful.

   (A) gathered
   (B) stole
   (C) wasted
   (D) owned

8. The handwriting was nearly <u>illegible</u>.

   (A) unreadable
   (B) unethical
   (C) creative
   (D) dangerous

9. <u>Infinite</u> most nearly means

   (A) costly
   (B) unending
   (C) babyish
   (D) daily

10. <u>Longevity</u> most nearly means

    (A) training
    (B) duration
    (C) girth
    (D) lifestyle

11. Tourists always fall for that <u>ruse</u>.

    (A) trick
    (B) display
    (C) itinerary
    (D) backtalk

12. The president <u>proclaimed</u> it a national holiday.

    (A) suggested
    (B) renamed
    (C) announced
    (D) unmade

13. Even the most <u>rudimentary</u> details are crucial to understanding this problem.

    (A) basic
    (B) ecstatic
    (C) illogical
    (D) fancy

14. <u>Rout</u> most nearly means

    (A) careful
    (B) defeat
    (C) blatant
    (D) open

15. His <u>rogue</u> attitude didn't fit the "team" concept.

    (A) aggressive
    (B) sad
    (C) rebellious
    (D) low-brow

16. Her point of view didn't <u>resonate</u> with everyone on the committee.

    (A) create irritation
    (B) display clarity
    (C) evoke agreement
    (D) generate discussion

17. Duplicating steps is far too <u>redundant</u> at this late stage.

    (A) repetitive
    (B) upsetting
    (C) colorful
    (D) wishy-washy

18. Far be it from me to <u>prescribe</u> how to raise one's own children.

    (A) predict
    (B) dictate
    (C) judge
    (D) decide

19. <u>Logical</u> most nearly means

    (A) cognizant
    (B) easy
    (C) rowdy
    (D) sensible

20. <u>Prerequisite</u> most nearly means

    (A) requirement
    (B) evaluation
    (C) glee
    (D) good taste

21. It seems that loud people tend to <u>gravitate</u> toward other loud people.

    (A) be drawn
    (B) be hostile
    (C) be inquisitive
    (D) be competitive

22. The police felt it was best to be <u>cautious</u> when approaching the house.

    (A) excited
    (B) apathetic
    (C) dodgy
    (D) careful

23. <u>Braggart</u> most nearly means

    (A) clown
    (B) leader
    (C) boaster
    (D) deputy

24. Basing his opinions on <u>hearsay</u> doomed the case.

    (A) rumor
    (B) samples
    (C) truth
    (D) belief

25. <u>Taunt</u> most nearly means

    (A) grade
    (B) relate
    (C) ridicule
    (D) party

26. Most of our employees respond well to <u>constructive</u> criticism.

    (A) damaging
    (B) productive
    (C) gentle
    (D) flattering

27. Quantifiable most nearly means

(A) laughable
(B) standard
(C) countable
(D) breakable

28. The least effective way of dealing with children is yelling.

(A) tantalizing
(B) creative
(C) useful
(D) positive

29. Apathy most nearly means

(A) greatness
(B) laziness
(C) disinterest
(D) boredom

30. It left a glaring blemish on his permanent record.

(A) impact
(B) defect
(C) commendation
(D) compliment

31. It will take a consensus to get this measure passed.

(A) agreement
(B) discussion
(C) infighting
(D) reprimand

32. No coach can handle dissent from his players for long.

(A) discussion
(B) laughter
(C) laziness
(D) insubordination

33. Tempo most nearly means

(A) heartbeat
(B) safety
(C) modernity
(D) speed

34. She can take solace in the fact that it couldn't get much worse.

(A) protection
(B) comfort
(C) glee
(D) depth

35. Many pitfalls await the inexperienced climber.

(A) joys
(B) traps
(C) ropes
(D) talents

STOP. IF YOU FINISH BEFORE THE TIME IS UP, YOU MAY CHECK OVER YOUR WORK ON THIS PART ONLY.

Part 4: Paragraph Comprehension (PC)

Time: 13 minutes; 15 questions

<u>Directions</u>: This section contains paragraphs followed by incomplete statements or questions. Read the paragraph and select the answer that best completes the statements or answers the questions that follow, and mark the corresponding oval on your answer sheet.

Questions 1 and 2 refer to the following passage.

In modern society, a form of folktale called the *urban legend* has emerged. These stories persist both for their entertainment value and for the transmission of popular values and beliefs. Urban legends are stories many have heard; they are supposed to have really happened, but they cannot be verified. It turns out that the people involved can never be found. Researchers of urban legends call the elusive participant in these supposedly "real-life" events a "FOAF": friend of a friend.

One classic urban legend involves alligators in the sewer systems of major metropolitan areas. According to the story, before alligators were a protected species, people vacationing in Florida purchased baby alligators to take home as souvenirs. After the novelty of having a pet alligator wore off, people would flush their souvenirs down the toilet. The baby alligators found a perfect growing environment in city sewer systems, where to this day they thrive on an ample supply of rats.

1. The passage suggests that the real-life participants of urban legends

    (A) can be very difficult to track down
    (B) are usually known, but only barely, by the teller
    (C) are friends with a large number of people
    (D) are the original tellers of the stories

2. According to the passage, the successful urban legend contains all of the following characteristics EXCEPT

    (A) the capacity to entertain
    (B) messages that conform to popular values
    (C) qualities of a folktale
    (D) a basis in reality

For most students of biology, Charles Darwin is considered the father of evolution. But few realize that he was but one of many theorists who noticed that the genetics of animals showed progression over time. Henri Bergson, for instance, formulated a theory that today is known more commonly as *theistic evolution,* or evolution from God. However, Darwin's ability to articulate his theories in writing and to account for many diverse examples of evolutionary biology means that other theories are often seen as little more than offshoots of the original idea of Darwinian evolution.

3. According to the passage, Darwin's theory persists because

    (A) Bergson's theory was incorrect
    (B) Darwin's theory accounted for many examples of evolution
    (C) genetics is an inexact science
    (D) evolution is not accepted by the mainstream

Local elementary schools have changed considerably over the past 50 years. Where once we had schools in every small town, now students bus for miles to attend larger, more advanced schools. While most parents see this as a positive step for progress and education, some worry about their children losing touch with the simple things around them. A few have even decided to homeschool their children instead of sending them to nearby towns.

4. The author's tone in this passage is

    (A) embittered
    (B) informative
    (C) biased
    (D) ambivalent

Questions 5 and 6 refer to the following passage.

Most life is fundamentally dependent on photosynthetic organisms that store radiant energy from the Sun. In almost all the world's ecosystems and food chains, photosynthetic organisms such as plants and algae are eaten by other organisms, which are then consumed by still others. The existence of organisms that are not dependent on the Sun's light has long been established, but until recently they were regarded as anomalies.

Over the last 20 years, however, research in deep-sea areas has revealed the existence of entire ecosystems in which the primary producers are chemosynthetic bacteria that are dependent on energy from within the Earth itself. Indeed, the growing evidence suggests that these sub-sea ecosystems model the way in which life first came about on this planet.

5. The passage suggests that most life is ultimately dependent on which of the following?

   (A) photosynthetic algae
   (B) the world's oceans
   (C) bacterial microorganisms
   (D) light from the Sun

6. Which of the following conclusions about photosynthetic and chemosynthetic organisms is supported by this passage?

   (A) Both perform similar functions in different food chains.
   (B) Both are known to support communities of higher organisms at great ocean depths.
   (C) Sunlight is the basic source of energy for both.
   (D) Chemosynthetic organisms are less nourishing than photosynthetic organisms.

Halley's Comet has been known since at least 240 B.C.E. and possibly since 1059 B.C.E. Its most famous appearance was in 1066 C.E. when it appeared right before the Battle of Hastings. It was named after the astronomer Edmund Halley, who calculated its orbit. He determined that the comets seen in 1530 and 1606 were the same object following a 76-year orbit. Unfortunately, Halley died in 1742, never living to see his prediction come true when the comet returned on Christmas Eve 1758.

7. It can be inferred from the passage that the appearance of Halley's Comet in 1758

   (A) presaged catastrophic events in world history
   (B) could not have been foreseen
   (C) shocked the scientific community
   (D) confirmed Halley's calculations

Both alligators and crocodiles can be found in southern Florida, particularly in the Everglades National Park. Alligators and crocodiles look similar but there are several physical characteristics that differentiate the two giant reptiles. The most easily observed difference between alligators and crocodiles is the shape of the head. The crocodile's skull and jaws are longer and narrower than the alligator's. When a crocodile closes its mouth, the long teeth remain visible, protruding outside the upper jaw. When an alligator closes its mouth, those long teeth slip into sockets in the upper jaw and disappear. In general, if you can still see a lot of teeth even when the animal's mouth is closed, you are looking at a crocodile.

8. According to the passage, one can distinguish a crocodile from an alligator

   (A) only when the animal's mouth is closed
   (B) by the location in Florida where the animal is found
   (C) by its thick, heavily armored skin
   (D) by the narrower snout found on a crocodile

A talent agent analyzed her company's records in an attempt to determine why it was placing so few actors in roles. She attributed the company's poor performance to the fact that often the actors sent to an audition were completely inappropriate for the role.

9. It can be inferred from the passage that the agent believes that

   (A) certain actors are inappropriate for certain roles
   (B) the actors her company represents are not very good
   (C) it is difficult to predict how appropriate an actor will be for a role
   (D) her company does not send enough actors to audition for major roles

One of the most commonly used of all poetic meters is iambic pentameter. *Pentameter* refers to the number of feet, or groupings of syllables. The prefix *penta-* means five, so a poem written in pentameter has five feet per line. In iambic pentameter, the type of foot used is an iamb. An *iamb* is a word or words with two syllables with the stress on the second syllable. William Shakespeare is perhaps the most famous writer of iambic pentameter. Shakespeare composed hundreds of poems and plays in this meter and popularized it for the masses.

10. According to the passage, a *foot* is

   (A) a grouping of syllables
   (B) similar to a meter
   (C) an innovation credited to William Shakespeare
   (D) a type of poem

It is often said that American involvement in World War I would not have begun in earnest were it not for the German sinking of the passenger ship the *Lusitania* on February 18, 1915. Preferring prior to then to stay neutral in the war, America was until that time offering only financial and tactical support for Britain and France against Germany and Austria-Hungary. The sinking of the huge passenger ship, however, altered public opinion about U.S. involvement and subsequently led to military escalation, truly making the war a matter for the whole world.

11. The main idea of the passage is that

   (A) the Germans sank the *Lusitania* because of America's financial and tactical support for Britain and France

   (B) Austria-Hungary and Germany were allies in World War I

   (C) American involvement in World War I was minimal

   (D) the sinking of the *Lusitania* prompted increased American involvement in World War I

When a movie criticized by most film critics is a popular success, it is often seen as a sign of poor taste on the part of general audiences. But there is little diversity among film critics, and the critics' preferences are often a product of their backgrounds and class prejudices. Thus, their opinions are no more likely to be an unerring guide to quality than those of the average moviegoer.

12. The passage above best supports which of the following conclusions?

   (A) Judgments of film quality by professional film critics are usually wrong.

   (B) Judgments of quality applied to movies are meaningless.

   (C) Film critics usually consider popular movies to be of poor quality.

   (D) When critics and general audiences disagree about a movie's quality, the critics' opinion is not necessarily more valid.

The tomato originated in the New World. It was first domesticated around 700 C.E. by the Aztec and Incan civilizations. In the sixteenth century, European explorers were so appreciative of the tomato that they introduced it to the rest of Europe. Although the French, Spanish, and Italians quickly began to adapt their recipes to use tomatoes, the English considered tomatoes poisonous. This myth travelled to the colonies, where settlers in America continued to avoid the supposedly deadly tomato. It wasn't until the middle 1800s that the tomato began to gain acceptance in the U.S.

13. According to the passage, Americans did not start using the tomato until the mid-nineteenth century because

   (A) it was unavailable in the new world.

   (B) they lacked recipes for using it.

   (C) they believed it to be poisonous.

   (D) it was viewed as a Mediterranean food.

Daria has been picking up many extra shifts at the local restaurant. Her school work has also been increasing at an alarming rate. The past few weeks have left Daria feeling very drowsy. She looks forward to heading to bed each night and getting as much sleep as possible.

14. What does the word "drowsy" mean in context?

   (A) drunk

   (B) tired

   (C) happy

   (D) satisfied

The sun was relentless as I started my hike through the woods. Sitting under the large branches of the trees was the only way I was able to escape the oppressive heat. Without the leafy canopy sheltering me throughout my journey, I would have had to cut my hike short.

15. The author implies which of the following about the trees in the forest?

   (A) They provide adequate shade.

   (B) They do not provide adequate shade.

   (C) They impair her ability to enjoy the sunshine.

   (D) They provide a home to many animals.

STOP. IF YOU FINISH BEFORE THE TIME IS UP, YOU MAY CHECK OVER YOUR WORK ON THIS PART ONLY.

Part 5: Mathematics Knowledge (MK)

Time: 24 minutes; 25 questions

<u>Directions</u>: In this section, you will be tested on your knowledge of basic mathematics. For each question, select the best answer and mark the corresponding oval on your answer sheet.

1. For all x, $(3x + 4)(4x - 3) =$

   (A) $7x - 12$
   (B) $12x^2 - 12$
   (C) $12x^2 - 25x - 12$
   (D) $12x^2 + 7x - 12$

2. If a tree grew 5 feet in n years, what was the average rate at which the tree grew, in inches per year?

   (A) $\dfrac{60}{n}$

   (B) $\dfrac{5}{12n}$

   (C) $\dfrac{12n}{5}$

   (D) $\dfrac{n}{60}$

3. In the figure above, if the perimeter of rectangle $ABCD$ is 56, and the length of AD is 16, what is the area of $ABCD$?

   (A)   40
   (B)   64
   (C)   160
   (D)   192

4. A square is a rectangle with four _____ sides.

   (A)   equal
   (B)   parallel
   (C)   unequal
   (D)   curvilinear

5. If $a < b$ and $b < c$, which of the following must be true?

   (A) $b + c < 2a$
   (B) $a + b < c$
   (C) $a - b < b - c$
   (D) $a + b < 2c$

6. In the figure above, $x = 2z$ and $y = 3z$. What is the value of z?

   (A)   24
   (B)   30
   (C)   36
   (D)   54

7. If the minute hand of a properly functioning clock has just moved 45 degrees, how many minutes passed while it did so?

   (A)   6
   (B)   7.5
   (C)   12.5
   (D)   27

8. What is the area of the figure below?

   (A)   4
   (B)   6
   (C)   12
   (D)   24

9. In the figure below, if line p is parallel to line q, what is the value of y?

(A) 65
(B) 115
(C) 125
(D) 130

10. 15% of 15% of 200 is

(A) 4.5
(B) 6
(C) 12.5
(D) 45

11. What is the average (arithmetic mean) of $\frac{1}{20}$ and $\frac{1}{30}$?

(A) $\frac{1}{25}$

(B) $\frac{1}{24}$

(C) $\frac{2}{25}$

(D) $\frac{1}{12}$

12. If an angle measures $y°$, what will its supplement measure in terms of y?

(A) $(90 - y)°$
(B) $(90 + y)°$
(C) $(180 - y)°$
(D) $(180 + y)°$

13. Diane painted $\frac{1}{3}$ of her room with $2\frac{1}{2}$ cans of paint. How many more cans of paint will she need to finish painting her room?

(A) $2\frac{1}{2}$

(B) 5

(C) $7\frac{1}{2}$

(D) 10

14. If $13 + a = 25 + b$, then $b - a =$

(A) 12
(B) 8
(C) −8
(D) −12

15. For all x, $3x^2 \times 5x^3 =$

(A) $8x^5$
(B) $8x^6$
(C) $15x^5$
(D) $15x^6$

16. If the sides of a square increase in length by 10%, the area of the square increases by

(A) 10%
(B) 15%
(C) 20%
(D) 21%

17. If $\frac{m}{2} = 15$, then $\frac{m}{3} =$

(A) 7.5
(B) 10
(C) 22.5
(D) 30

18. Which of the following is a factor of $6x^2 - 13x + 6$?

(A) $2x + 2$
(B) $2x + 3$
(C) $3x - 2$
(D) $3x - 3$

19. If the product of 3 and x is equal to 2 less than y, which of the following must be true?

(A) $\frac{3x - 2}{y} = 0$

(B) $3x - y - 2 = 0$
(C) $3x + y - 2 = 0$
(D) $3x - y + 2 = 0$

20. If $x > 1$ and $\dfrac{a}{b} = 1 - \dfrac{1}{x}$, then $\dfrac{b}{a} =$

    (A) $\dfrac{x}{x-1}$

    (B) $\dfrac{x-1}{x}$

    (C) $x - 1$

    (D) $\dfrac{1}{x} - 1$

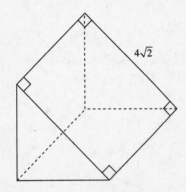

$4\sqrt{2}$

21. If the solid above is half of a cube, then the volume of the solid is

    (A) 16
    (B) $16\sqrt{2}$
    (C) 32
    (D) $32\sqrt{2}$

22. When 7.6 is divided by 0.019, the quotient is

    (A) 4,000
    (B) 400
    (C) 40
    (D) 4

23. What is the area of a circle with a circumference of 8?

    (A) $\dfrac{4}{\pi}$

    (B) $\dfrac{16}{\pi}$

    (C) 4π
    (D) 16π

24. 36% of 18 is 18% of what number?

    (A) 9
    (B) 36
    (C) 72
    (D) 200

25. $\sqrt{104,906}$ is between which two numbers?

    (A) 100 and 200
    (B) 200 and 300
    (C) 300 and 400
    (D) 400 and 500

STOP. IF YOU FINISH BEFORE THE TIME IS UP, YOU MAY CHECK OVER YOUR WORK ON THIS PART ONLY.

Part 6: Electronics Information (EI)

Time: 9 minutes; 20 questions

<u>Directions</u>: In this section, you will be tested on your knowledge of electronics basics. For each question, select the best answer and mark the corresponding oval on your answer sheet.

1. Resistance is measured in

   (A) amperes
   (B) ohms
   (C) V
   (D) W

2. Protons have a _____ charge, and neutrons are _____ charged.

   (A) positive, negatively
   (B) positive, neutrally
   (C) negative, positively
   (D) neutral, negatively

3. What is the term for a current flowing in a conductor which changes direction (moves back and forth) many times in a second?

   (A) alternating current
   (B) direct current
   (C) electromotive force
   (D) variable current

4. What type of circuit does this symbol represent?

   (A) parallel circuit
   (B) series circuit
   (C) series-parallel circuit
   (D) short circuit

5. In the formula for Ohm's Law, $V = I \times R$, the I represents

   (A) voltage
   (B) current
   (C) resistance
   (D) impedance

6. The P-type material in a diode is also known as the

   (A) electrode
   (B) cathode
   (C) base
   (D) anode

7. Introducing impurities into the crystal structure of silicon is also known as

   (A) tinning
   (B) enhancing
   (C) processing
   (D) doping

8. Which of the following causes the least resistance to a high frequency alternating current?

   (A) capacitor
   (B) fixed resistor
   (C) variable resistor
   (D) inductor

9. A circuit contains four resistors of 2 Ω, 4 Ω, 6 Ω, and 8 Ω in series. What is their effective resistance?

   (A) 2 Ω
   (B) 5 Ω
   (C) 8 Ω
   (D) 20 Ω

10. All of the following statements about transistors are true EXCEPT

   (A) N-type material has free electrons
   (B) NPN transistors require a positive voltage at the base to turn them on
   (C) the arrow in the transistor symbol is always placed on the collector
   (D) P-type material conducts current through the movement of holes

11. This is the symbol for which type of meter?

   (A) voltmeter
   (B) ammeter
   (C) ohmmeter
   (D) galvanometer

12. Which of the following is NOT an essential component of an electrical circuit?

   (A) voltage source
   (B) watt
   (C) load
   (D) conductor

13. What type of switch would be utilized by a doorbell?

   (A) —o⌐o—

   (B) —o⌐o—

   (C) —o o—

   (D) —o o—
        o—

14. Which of the following is the symbol for an AC voltage source?

   (A) —⊣|⊦ |⊦—
         +

   (B) ⊘

   (C) —Ⓐ—

   (D) —Ⓟ—

15. Capacitors are also known as

   (A) capacitances
   (B) dielectrics
   (C) condensers
   (D) inductors

16. A material that will not conduct electricity is known as

   (A) a conductor
   (B) a semiconductor
   (C) an insulator
   (D) a voltage source

17. Which of the following materials is NOT a conductor?

   (A) rubber
   (B) silver
   (C) copper
   (D) aluminum

18. A circuit with four 6-ohm resistors wired in series has 12 volts applied to it. What current flows through this circuit?

   (A) 5 mA
   (B) 50 mA
   (C) 500 mA
   (D) 5 A

19. An element that is widely recognized as a semiconductor is

   (A) silicon
   (B) aluminum
   (C) helium
   (D) wood

20. This is the symbol for which type of meter?

   (A) voltmeter
   (B) ammeter
   (C) ohmmeter
   (D) galvanometer

STOP. IF YOU FINISH BEFORE THE TIME IS UP, YOU MAY CHECK OVER YOUR WORK ON THIS PART ONLY.

Part 7: Automotive and Shop Information (AS)

Time: 11 minutes; 25 questions

<u>Directions</u>: In this section, you will be tested on your knowledge of automotive and shop basics. For each question, select the best answer and mark the corresponding oval on your answer sheet.

1. Wood can be shaped using all of the following tools EXCEPT

    (A)   jack plane
    (B)   wood chisel
    (C)   flat rasp
    (D)   miter box

2. Ride quality is the job of the vehicle's _____ system.

    (A)   steering
    (B)   suspension
    (C)   charging
    (D)   brake

3. The cut in the wood left behind by a saw is known as the

    (A)   gap
    (B)   line
    (C)   trace
    (D)   kerf

4. A four-wheel drive vehicle uses a _____ to distribute power to the front and rear drive axles.

    (A)   transmission
    (B)   drive shaft
    (C)   torque converter
    (D)   transfer case

5. What type of cut is this saw made for?

    (A)   a cut with the grain of the wood
    (B)   a cut across the grain of the wood
    (C)   a cut made in plywood only
    (D)   a cut made in steel only

6. This image depicts what stroke in the four-stroke cycle?

    (A)   intake stroke
    (B)   power stroke
    (C)   compression stroke
    (D)   exhaust stroke

7. Thread pitch of a fractional measurement fastener is determined by

    (A)   counting the number of threads per inch
    (B)   measuring the distance in millimeters between threads
    (C)   measuring the distance in inches between threads
    (D)   counting the number of threads per millimeter

8. Which would be best to use to loosen tight fasteners?

    (A) only this tool:

    (B) only this tool:

    (C) only this tool:

    (D) the tools shown in both (B) and (C)

9. All of the following are parts of the vehicle's steering system EXCEPT

    (A)   coil spring
    (B)   steering knuckle
    (C)   tie rod end
    (D)   idler arm

10. Which engine component is responsible for the opening and closing of the engine's intake and exhaust valves?

(A) 1
(B) 2
(C) 3
(D) 4

11. On a fuel-injected engine, the fuel pump is normally located

(A) on the engine
(B) on the vehicle frame
(C) near the rear bumper
(D) in the fuel tank

12. UNC fasteners have _____ threads per inch when compared to UNF fasteners of the same diameter.

(A) the same number of
(B) fewer
(C) twice as many
(D) thrice as many

13. In power brake systems, braking pressures are increased using

(A) only the engine intake manifold vacuum
(B) only the fluid pressure from the power steering system
(C) both the engine intake manifold vacuum and fluid pressure from the power steering system
(D) neither the engine intake manifold vacuum nor the fluid pressure from the power steering system

14. All of the following are parts of the ignition primary system EXCEPT the

(A) battery
(B) ignition switch
(C) reluctor and pickup
(D) rotor

15. "Stoichiometric" is a term that describes

(A) the ideal air-fuel mixture in a gasoline engine
(B) the voltage required to generate a spark
(C) the engine's breathing efficiency
(D) theoretical horsepower

16. An oil's resistance to flow is known as its

(A) quality rating
(B) pumpability
(C) lubricity
(D) viscosity

17. All cars are currently being built with _____ electrical systems.

(A) only direct current
(B) only alternating current
(C) both direct and alternating current
(D) neither direct nor alternating current

18. When arc-welding, the ground clamp should be connected to the

(A) floor
(B) welding rod
(C) electrical outlet
(D) work

19. What cylinder design is referred to as a "boxer" engine?

(A) inline only
(B) flat only
(C) horizontally opposed only
(D) both flat and horizontally opposed

20. What are these tools used for?

(A) securing a rivet in place where a tight rivet is important
(B) striking an object where it is important that the hammer itself not come in direct contact with the work
(C) driving small fasteners and making layout marks in metalwork
(D) guiding a saw when making a cutting across the grain

21. In a V-type engine with two cylinder heads, which of these designs would have two camshafts, with one installed above each cylinder head?

(A) single overhead cam or SOHC
(B) double overhead cam or DOHC
(C) triple overhead cam or TOHC
(D) overhead value or OHV

22. Air entering an engine's combustion chamber must pass through each of the following EXCEPT

(A) the air filter
(B) the intake manifold
(C) the intake port in the cylinder head
(D) the catalytic converter

23. Which tool would be best suited for loosening a very tight nut?

(A) open-end wrench
(B) 12-point socket and breaker bar
(C) 6-point socket and ratchet
(D) 6-point socket and breaker bar

24. What type of retaining ring is depicted here?

(A) internal prong-type
(B) internal hole-type
(C) external "E"-type
(D) external hole-type

25. As a car's battery discharges its energy, which of the following takes place in the battery's lead plates?

(A) They release water.
(B) They are converted to lead sulfate.
(C) They discharge impurities.
(D) They are converted to electrolytes.

STOP. IF YOU FINISH BEFORE THE TIME IS UP, YOU MAY CHECK OVER YOUR WORK ON THIS PART ONLY.

Part 8: Mechanical Comprehension (MC)

Time: 19 minutes; 25 questions

Directions: In this section, you will be tested on your knowledge of mechanics and basic physics. Select the best answer for each question and mark the corresponding oval on your answer sheet.

1. A car rolls down a hill. It travels progressively faster because

    (A) its potential energy is being converted into kinetic energy
    (B) its kinetic energy is being converted to potential energy
    (C) its energy is maximized
    (D) its energy is minimized

2. When a ball is thrown into the air, it has its maximum potential energy when

    (A) it leaves the hand of the person throwing it
    (B) it enters the hand of the person catching it
    (C) its velocity is zero
    (D) its velocity is greatest

3. Objects that require more force to get them moving have greater

    (A) momentum
    (B) inertia
    (C) torque
    (D) pressure

4. Isaac Newton discovered that every particle in the universe is attracted to every other particle. This law is called Newton's

    (A) first law of motion
    (B) third law of motion
    (C) law of universal gravitation
    (D) second law of motion

5. A 30N force is applied to 5 kg box. Assuming no friction, what is the acceleration gained by the box?

    (A) 0.15 m/s^2
    (B) 0.6 m/s^2
    (C) 1.5 m/s^2
    (D) 6 m/s^2

6. Compared to lifting a heavy box directly from ground level up to the top of a ramp, pushing the box up the ramp (neglecting friction) is doing:

    (A) less work
    (B) more work
    (C) the same amount of work
    (D) no work

7. All of the following statements about work are true EXCEPT

    (A) force is a factor of work
    (B) it is possible to get more work out of a machine than what is put in
    (C) to do work, an object must be moved
    (D) work can be measured in foot-pounds

8. A chisel is illustrated below. A chisel is an example of a(n)

   (A) wedge
   (B) first-class lever
   (C) inclined plane
   (D) wheel and axle

9. The difference between a wedge and an inclined plane is

   (A) a wedge has a steeper slope than an inclined plane
   (B) a wedge is made to move, whereas an inclined plane stays stationary
   (C) a wedge stays stationary, whereas an inclined plane is made to move
   (D) a wedge has less friction

10. Which post holds up the greater part of the load?

   (A) post A
   (B) post B
   (C) both hold up the load equally
   (D) answer cannot be determined based on information provided

11. Work and kinetic energy are both measured in

   (A) kilograms
   (B) meters per second
   (C) joules
   (D) newtons

12. The design of a screwdriver is based on which of the following simple machines?

   (A) inclined plane
   (B) wheel and axle
   (C) first-class lever
   (D) pulley

13. An increase in force accomplished through mechanical advantage is always accompanied by _____ in distance moved.

   (A) an increase
   (B) a decrease
   (C) no change
   (D) an increase at times and a decrease at other times

14. The design of a prybar, as illustrated, is based on which of the following simple machines?

   (A) first-class lever
   (B) second-class lever
   (C) third-class lever
   (D) inclined plane

15. One horsepower is equal to how many watts?

   (A) 550
   (B) 746
   (C) 10,000
   (D) 100

16. In order to increase force with a first-class lever, the fulcrum should be

   (A) moved toward where the effort is applied
   (B) kept in the same position
   (C) moved toward where the object is moved
   (D) removed altogether

17. Which of the following statements is correct?

   (A) The work put out by a simple machine can sometimes exceed the work put in.
   (B) The work put out by a simple machine always exceeds the work put in.
   (C) The work put out by a simple machine can never exceed the work put in.
   (D) The work put in by a simple machine is equal and opposite of the work put in.

18. If a small gear drives a large gear, a _____ takes place.

    (A) mechanical advantage
    (B) block and tackle
    (C) torque multiplication
    (D) reduction in rotational speed

19. A block and tackle, as shown below, utilizes

Rope is pulled to lift object

Object to be lifted

    (A) a single pulley
    (B) multiple pulleys
    (C) only moveable pulleys
    (D) only fixed pulleys

20. The force required by a person pulling on a rope using a single pulley to lift an object is equal to

    (A) the weight of the object
    (B) twice the weight of the object
    (C) one half of the weight of the object
    (D) the weight of the object divided by the diameter of the pulley

21. The design of a doorknob is based on which of the following simple machines?

    (A) inclined plane
    (B) wheel and axle
    (C) first-class lever
    (D) pulley

22. An astronaut's mass is 30 kg on Earth. What is his mass on the moon?

    (A) the same
    (B) lower
    (C) higher
    (D) cannot be determined

23. In a gear train, torque and speed can be described as

    (A) exactly the same
    (B) directly proportional
    (C) inversely proportional
    (D) sometimes proportional

24. An object's potential energy can be calculated using the formula

    (A) $PE = \frac{1}{2}m \times v^2$
    (B) $PE = m \times v$
    (C) $PE = m \times g \times h$
    (D) $PE = m \times a$

25. A child applies a 10N force to a large box. The box however, does not move. How much work has the child done?

    (A) 0 J
    (B) 5 J
    (C) 10 J
    (D) 100 J

STOP. IF YOU FINISH BEFORE THE TIME IS UP, YOU MAY CHECK OVER YOUR WORK ON THIS PART ONLY.

Part 9: Assembling Objects (AO)

Time: 15 minutes; 25 questions

<u>Directions</u>: In this section, you will be tested on your ability to determine how an object will look when its parts are put together. For each question, select the best answer and mark the corresponding oval on your answer sheet.

STOP. IF YOU FINISH BEFORE THE TIME IS UP, YOU MAY CHECK OVER YOUR WORK ON THIS PART ONLY.

CONGRATULATIONS! YOU HAVE COMPLETED ASVAB PRACTICE TEST A. CHECK YOUR WORK USING THE EXPLANATIONS THAT BEGIN ON THE NEXT PAGE.

ASVAB PRACTICE TEST A ANSWERS AND EXPLANATIONS

Part 1: General Science Answers and Explanations

1. **(A) species** The levels of classification, from largest to smallest, are: kingdom, phylum, class, order, family, genus, species. Thus, a *genus* is a group that contains related species.

2. **(B) electrons** Electrons orbit around the nucleus of an atom.

3. **(D) nasal cavity** As a human inhales, the incoming air first passes through the nasal cavity, where it is both warmed and filtered.

4. **(D) coyote** A "tertiary consumer" is an animal that consumes secondary consumers, or other carnivores. Coyotes are the tertiary consumer in this food chain. They feed on foxes, which in turn feed on rabbits. Dandelions represent the producers in the food chain.

5. **(B) sublimation** The process by which a solid becomes a gas is *sublimation*. *Boiling* is the process by which a liquid becomes gas. *Melting* is the process by which a solid becomes a liquid. *Diffusion* describes the process by which a gas or liquid intermingles with another.

6. **(C) the same as that exerted by the Earth on the Moon** The gravitational force the Moon exerts on the Earth is the same as the gravitational force the Earth exerts on the Moon. According to Newton's third law, for every force exerted on object A by object B, object B experiences an equal and opposite force from object A. Thus, when the Earth exerts its gravitational force on an object, such as the Moon, the Moon exerts an equal and opposite force on the Earth.

7. **(B) decomposers** Fungi are *decomposers* (also known as saprophytes), returning the organic material from dead matter such as leaves, trees, and animal remains back into the environment. *Producers* make their own food. *Consumers* must eat other organisms in order to gain energy. *Mutualism* is a type of symbiosis whereby both organisms benefit.

8. **(D) 273 K** The freezing point of water on the Kelvin scale occurs at 273 K. Kelvin and Celsius share a similar scale (i.e. a change of one Kelvin is the same as a change of one degree Celsius). However, they differ by 273 units. To convert Celsius to Kelvin, add 273. To convert Kelvin to Celsius, subtract 273. Since water freezes at 0 degrees Celsius, this is equivalent to 0 + 273 = 273 K.

9. **(A) ligaments** Tough elastic tissues found in the joints that connect bones to bones are called ligaments. Tendons are connective tissues that unite a muscle with some other part, such as a bone. Cartilage is a somewhat elastic tissue (unlike bone). In adults it is found in joints (where it helps reduce friction between bones), in respiratory passages, and in the external ear. Although cartilage appears in joints where bones meet, its role is not to hold them together, but to keep them apart, acting as a buffer to prevent rubbing and wear. Finally, muscles are body tissue consisting of long cells that contract when stimulated to produce motion.

10. **(B) high blood pressure** Stress, a poor diet, cigarette smoking, and heredity are all factors that are linked to high blood pressure.

11. **(A) cirrus** Cirrus clouds are the thin, wispy clouds that occur very high in the atmosphere, at elevations of 20,000 feet or more. Stratus and cumulus clouds are both low-forming. Stratocumulus clouds contain clumps of clouds and are not thin or wispy.

12. **(C) sedimentary** Fossils are most likely to be found in sedimentary rock such as shale, which is rock formed by the sedimentation of clay, mud, or silt. Sedimentary rock is composed of minerals and other matter, such as animal remains.

13. **(B) herbivores** Animals that consume only plants are called *herbivores*. *Carnivores* consume meat. *Omnivores* consume both meat and plants. *Saprophytes* gain their nutrients through dead organisms.

14. **(D) yellow dwarf** The Sun is a fairly young star and therefore has lower temperature and luminosity, resulting in its yellow color. The Sun is also fairly small as stars go and falls under the "dwarf" category.

15. **(D) population** A population is a group of organisms of the same species living in the same region. Biomes, ecosystems, and communities all encompass more than one type of species.

16. **(D) Earth** The four planets beyond Mars—Jupiter, Saturn, Uranus, and Neptune, are referred to as the outer planets. Earth is one of the four planets closest to the Sun and is thus considered an inner planet.

17. **(B) potential to kinetic** A boulder that begins to roll down a hill is an example of an energy conversion from potential energy to kinetic energy. The boulder has maximum potential energy at the top of the hill, and this energy is converted into kinetic energy as the boulder rolls down the hill and picks up speed. At the foot of the hill, all potential energy has been converted into kinetic energy.

18. **(D) troposphere** The lowest layer of the Earth's atmosphere is called the troposphere. This layer extends from the surface to the bottom of the stratosphere. Most weather changes occur here and the temperature generally decreases rapidly with altitude.

19. **(B) energy can neither be created nor destroyed** According to the law of conservation of energy, energy can neither be created nor destroyed. Instead, it changes from one form to another.

20. **(C) the Doppler effect** As an ambulance approaches, the sound waves from its siren are compressed toward the observer. The intervals between waves diminish, which translates into an increase in frequency or pitch. As the ambulance recedes, the sound waves are stretched relative to the observer, causing the siren's pitch to decrease. By the change in pitch of the siren, one can determine if the ambulance is coming nearer or speeding away. This perceived change in pitch is known as the Doppler effect.

21. **(D) diverging lens** A concave lens—one that is thicker on the edges than it is in the middle—is also known as a diverging lens because it diverges the light waves that pass through it.

22. **(D) molecule** A *molecule* is the smallest particle of an element or compound that can exist in a free state and still retain the characteristics of the element or compound. The molecules of elements consist of one atom (e.g., Cu) or two or more similar atoms (e.g., N_2). The molecules of covalent compounds consist of two or more different atoms (e.g., H_2O). *Protons* and *quarks* are subatomic particles; *atoms* are the building blocks of molecules.

23. **(C) the orbit of the Moon around the Earth** The orbit of the Moon around the Earth, which exerts a gravitational pull on the ocean's waters, is the phenomenon most responsible for oceanic tides.

24. **(B) group** The elements in a column on the Periodic Table are referred to as a group; each member of a group has the same number of electrons in its outer shell. Each row on the Periodic Table is referred to as a period.

25. **(A) reactants** When molecules undergo a chemical change, the process is called a chemical reaction. The molecules that enter the reaction are called reactants and the molecules that result from the reaction are called products.

Part 2: Arithmetic Reasoning Answers and Explanations

1. **(D) 81** The ratios of apples to pears and pears to oranges for a given cost are provided. What's needed to solve this problem, however, is the ratio of apples to oranges. To merge these into one ratio relating all three fruits, you need to express both ratios using the same number of pears. In one ratio it's 4, and in the other it's 3. Since the least common multiple of 3 and 4 is 12, you can multiply both individual ratios so that the number of pears comes to equal 12:

apples:pears $= 3:4 = 9:12$ (multiply both sides of the ratio by 3)
pears:oranges $= 3:2 = 12:8$ (multiply both sides of the ratio by 4)

Now you can combine the ratios:

apples : pears : oranges
9:12:8

Now you can also state the ratio of apples to oranges:

apples:oranges $= 9:8$

Given a value for the number of oranges as 72, you can now set up a proportion:

$$\frac{\text{apples}}{\text{oranges}} = \frac{9}{8} = \frac{72}{x}$$

Cross-multiply and solve for x:

$\frac{9}{8} = \frac{x}{72}$. Cross-multiply, getting $8x = (9)(72)$. Divide both sides by 8 to get $x = \frac{(9)(72)}{(8)}$. To make the arithmetic easier, divide 72 by 8 first, which equals 9, then multiply this answer by 9, getting $9 \times 9 = 81$.

2. **(C) 20%** If 48 of 60 seats are occupied, then 12 of 60 seats are unoccupied (since $60 - 48 = 12$). What percent of the seats are unoccupied?

$\text{Percent} = \frac{\text{Part}}{\text{Whole}} \times 100\% = \frac{12}{60} \times 100\% =$

$\frac{1}{5} \times 100\% = 20\%$, choice (C).

3. **(B) $5,000** Break this question down into pieces. Before midnight, Effin gets paid $1,000 an hour. If she starts singing at 8:30 p.m., then she sings for $3\frac{1}{2}$ hours before midnight. Her earnings for that time are $3\frac{1}{2} \times \$1,000 = \$3,500$. After midnight, her rate increases 50%, so her hourly rate after becomes $\$1,000 + \$1,000(50\%) = \$1,000 + \$500 = \$1,500$. She works one hour after midnight, earning $1,500. Add the amount she earns before midnight and the amount she earns after midnight, so her total pay is $\$3,500 + \$1,500 = \$5,000$.

4. **(D)** $\frac{3}{4}$ The probability of an event occurring is a fraction: the number of possible outcomes in which the event can occur divided by the total number of possible outcomes. Fran is going to pick one shirt and the question asks for the probability that it will not be orange. In other words, you need to find the probability of picking a black or blue shirt. There are 4 black shirts and 5 blue shirts, so altogether there are 9 possible successful outcomes. The total number of shirts to choose from, including the orange shirts, is 12, so there are 12 possible outcomes. The probability of Fran picking a non-orange shirt is $\frac{9}{12}$. Since $\frac{9}{12}$ is not available in the answer choices, reduce the fraction by dividing the top and bottom by 3 to get $\frac{3}{4}$.

5. **(B) 11:30 a.m.** Newark is two hours later than Denver, so if the time in Denver when Harry arrives is 2:30 p.m., then the time in Newark when he arrives is 4:30 p.m. The flight takes 5 hours, so the time he began in Newark is 5 hours earlier than 4:30 p.m., or 11:30 a.m.

6. **(B) 6** How many times does 24 go into 198? $198 \div 24 = 8$ with a remainder of 6, so Doris will have 6 pieces of chocolate left over.

7. **(C) 200** If 75% of x is 150, then $0.75(x) = 150$ or $\frac{3}{4}(x) = 150$. Multiply both sides by $\frac{4}{3}$ and $x = 200$. You could also Backsolve. Only choice (C), 200, works. If $x = 200$, then $0.75(x) = 150$ since $0.75(200) = 150$.

8. **(A) 85** The formula for finding the average is:

$$\text{Average} = \frac{\text{Sum of the terms}}{\text{Number of terms}}$$

Don't just average the old average and the last test score—that would give the last score as much weight as all the other scores combined. The best way to deal with changing averages is to use the sums. Use the old average to figure out the total of the first 6 scores:

Sum of first 6 scores $= (83)(6) = 498$

Then add the 7th score and divide:

$$\frac{498 + 97}{7} = \frac{595}{7} = 85.$$

9. **(B) $21.60** If the charge for one pound is $25.00, then the charge for $\frac{4}{5}$ of a pound would be $\frac{4}{5} \times \$25.00 = \$20.00$ plus 8% sales tax. 8% of $20.00 = $0.08($20.00) = $1.60. $20.00 + $1.60 = $21.60.

10. **(D) 100** To answer this question, determine how many times $\frac{3}{5}$ goes into 60. It will be more than 60, so right away you can eliminate (A). $60 \div \frac{3}{5} = \frac{60}{1} \times \frac{5}{3}$. This is easier to multiply if you cancel first. 3 goes into 60 twenty times, so replace the 3 with a 1, and replace the 60 with a 20 to get $\frac{20}{1} \times \frac{5}{1} = 20 \times 5 = 100$.

11. **(B) $20** Set up equations based on the information given in the problem. The question asks for the amount of money Robert has.

Ed has 100 more dollars than Robert:

$E = R + 100.$

Ed then spends 20 dollars and has five times as much money as Robert:

$E - 20 = 5R.$

Solve a question like this using algebra if it's a strong area for you. Substitute $R + 100$ for E and solve:

$R + 100 - 20 = 5R$

$R + 80 = 5R$

$80 = 4R$

$R = \$20$

You could also Backsolve, starting with choice (B) or (C) for Robert's money. If you started with (C) 24, you would plug 24 into both equations and see if you got the same value for E.

In the first equation:

$E = R + 100$

$E = 24 + 100$

$E = 124$

In the second equation:

$E - 20 = 5R$

$E - 20 = 5(24)$

$E - 20 = 120$

$E = 140$

The numbers don't match, so eliminate (C) and try (B) 20.

In the first equation:

$E = R + 100$

$E = 20 + 100$

$E = 120$

In the second equation:

$E - 20 = 5R$

$E - 20 = 5(20)$

$E - 20 = 120$

$E = 120$

The value for E is the same in both equations, which tells you that 20 is the correct answer.

12. **(D) 11** This question is actually a remainder question in disguise. If 587 people are to be divided among buses that each seat 48 people, divide 587 by 48 to see how many buses would be filled completely. The remainder is the number of people in the unfilled bus. $587 \div 48 = 12$ with a remainder of 11.

13. **(C) 5** Riley brought 100 cookies, and 25 are left over. That means that Riley and her classmates ate 75 cookies.

$\text{Average} = \dfrac{\text{Sum of the terms}}{\text{Number of terms}} = \dfrac{75 \text{ cookies}}{15 \text{ students}}$

$= 5$ cookies for each student.

14. **(C)** $9\dfrac{1}{3}$ This is a proportion question:

$\dfrac{4 \text{ ft object}}{9 \text{ ft shadow}} = \dfrac{x \text{ ft object}}{21 \text{ ft shadow}}$

Cross-multiply to solve:

$4 \times 21 = 9x$

$\dfrac{84}{9} = \dfrac{9x}{9}$

$x = 9\dfrac{1}{3}$

15. **(D) 64%** *Percent* times *whole* equals *part*:

$\text{Percent} \times 25 = 16$

$\text{Percent} = \dfrac{16}{25} \times 100\% = 64\%$

16. **(A) 20** First find how long the trip takes him at each of the two different rates, using the formula

$\text{Time} = \dfrac{\text{Distance}}{\text{Rate}}$

He travels the first 10 km at 30 km per hour, so he takes $\dfrac{10}{30} = \dfrac{1}{3}$ hour = 20 minutes for this portion of the journey. He travels the remaining 30 km at 15 km per hour, so he takes $\dfrac{30}{15} = 2$ hours for this portion of the journey.
The whole journey takes him

$2 + \dfrac{1}{3} = 2\dfrac{1}{3}$ hours = 2 hours 20 minutes.

Now calculate the amount of time it would take to make the same trip at a constant rate of 20 km per hour. If he traveled the whole 40 km at 20 km per hour, it would take $\dfrac{40}{20} = 2$ hours. Now $2\dfrac{1}{3}$ hours is more than 2 hours by $\dfrac{1}{3}$ hour, or 20 minutes.

17. **(B)** $\dfrac{1}{7}$ Since 3 out of 24 students are in student organizations, the remaining $24 - 3 = 21$, students are not in student organizations. Therefore, the ratio of students in organizations to students not in organizations is: $\dfrac{3}{21} = \dfrac{1}{7}$.

18. **(A) 51** By midseason, team A had won 60 and team B had won 49 games. Over the remaining 80 games, team A won 40 and lost 40. That means that team A wound up with $60 + 40 = 100$ wins. To win 100 games, team B would have to win $100 - 49 = 51$ games over the remainder of the season.

19. **(C) $12.50** A vendor bought 10 crates for a total cost of $80. He wants to make a total profit of 25% over the total cost. So the total sale would have to equal $80 + (0.25)(\$80) = \$80 + \$20 = \$100$. He lost 2 crates, so he would need to sell the remaining $10 - 2 = 8$ crates for $100 to make the required profit. $\dfrac{\$100}{8 \text{ crates}} = \$12.50$ per crate.

20. **(D) 8** Set up a proportion on questions that give rates:

$$\frac{150 \text{ bottles}}{20 \text{ minutes}} = \frac{60 \text{ bottles}}{x \text{ minutes}}$$

Before you cross-multiply, reduce the first fraction as much as possible to make the calculations easier. Divide the numerator and denominator by 10:

$$\frac{15 \text{ bottles}}{2 \text{ minutes}} = \frac{60 \text{ bottles}}{x \text{ minutes}}$$

Cross-multiply:

$15x = 120$

Divide both sides by 15:

$x = 8$

21. **(C) −75** To figure out whether the product is positive or negative, count the number of negatives given. If there are an odd number of negatives, the product is negative. That eliminates (A) and (B). Multiplying the two numbers gives: $15 \times (-5) = -75$.

22. **(B) 35** The ratio of baseball cards to baseball figurines is $\frac{5}{7}$. You are given the number of cards, so you can set up a proportion: $\frac{5 \text{ cards}}{7 \text{ figurines}} = \frac{25 \text{ cards}}{x \text{ figurines}}$. Cross-multiply to get $5x = 175$ and divide both sides by 5 so $x = 35$.

23. **(C) $1.50** Set up equations to represent the relationships given in the problem:

$2h + 1s = \$3.25$

$3h + 1s = \$4.50$

The difference between the two totals is the price of a single hot dog. Thus, a single hot dog costs: $\$4.50 - \$3.25 = \$1.25$.

Plug the price of a single hot dog into the first equation to get the price of a soda:

$2(\$1.25) + 1s = \$3.25$

$\$2.50 + 1s = \$3.25$

$s = \$0.75$

The question asks for the cost of two sodas: $2 \times \$0.75 = \$1.50$. Always double-check to be sure you are solving for the value the question asks for. In this case, choice (A) is a trap answer because it is the price of one soda.

24. **(A) 48** When you are given two rates, you cannot simply take the average of the two. Thus, answer choice (B) 50 is a trap answer here. Because it takes more time to travel at a slower speed, the average for the entire trip will be closer to the slower speed. To solve this problem, pick a number for the distance of the entire trip. Since 40 and 60 are the rates, use the least common multiple, 120 for the number of miles. First, find the time spent travelling at each speed:

120 miles at 40 mph = 3 hours

120 miles at 60 mph = 2 hours

Total distance = 240 miles. Total time = 5 hours.

The average for the entire trip will be the total distance divided by the total time.

$$\text{Average speed} = \frac{\text{Total distance}}{\text{Total time}} = \frac{240 \text{ miles}}{5 \text{ hours}} = 48 \text{ mph.}$$

25. **(B) 121** Call the number of teachers n. Then the number of students is $10n$. The total number of teachers and students is $n + 10n = 11n$.

Since you can't have a fraction of a person, n must be an integer, which means the total number of teachers and students must be a multiple of 11. Scan the answer choices and locate (B), 11×11, as the correct answer. None of the other answer choices are multiples of 11.

26. **(C) 21** Use Backsolving for this one, beginning with choice (C). If the smaller number is 21 (and the larger number is 35), does the math from the question work?

The average of 21 and $35 = \frac{21 + 35}{2} = \frac{56}{2} = 28$.

The positive difference between 21 and 35 is 14. Twice the positive difference would be $2 \times 14 = 28$.

Thus, 21 is the smaller number and the correct answer.

You can also solve this question algebraically. Set the smaller number equal to y. Then, the average of the two numbers is: $\frac{35+y}{2}$. Twice the positive difference of the two numbers is: $2(35 - y)$. The average is equal to twice the positive difference, so $\frac{35+y}{2} = 2(35 - y)$. Solve:

$$\frac{35 + y}{2} = 2(35 - y)$$

$$35 + y = 4(35 - y)$$

$$35 + y = 140 - 4y$$

$$5y = 105$$

$$y = 21$$

27. **(C) 9** If a question uses the word "approximately" you can approximate the answer. If each of seven runners is running a little less than 1.3 kilometers, the total distance run would be a little less than $7 \times 1.3 = 9.1$, which is approximately 9 kilometers.

28. **(C) 5** Set up a proportion:

$$\frac{12 \text{ photos}}{1 \text{ minute}} = \frac{60 \text{ photos}}{x \text{ minutes}}$$

Now cross-multiply and solve: $12x = 60$, so $x = \frac{60}{12} = 5$.

29. **(A) $1,306.76** This is a pure arithmetic computation question. First, add up all of the deductions:

$218.99 + 107.05 + 25.03 + 68.65 + 42.75 = 462.47$

Now subtract total deductions from gross pay:

$1,769.23 - 462.47 = 1,306.76$.

30. **(C) 87** This is a standard average problem. Take the sum of all the terms and divide by the number of terms. $94 + 72 + 84 + 98 = 348$. $348 \div 4 = 87$. If dividing 348 by 4 was time consuming for you, you could have used Backsolving. Once you found the sum was 348, you could multiply the answer choices by 4, starting with (B) or (C), to see which answer choice gives 348. $87 \times 4 = 348$.

Part 3: Word Knowledge Answers and Explanations

1. **(B) force** *Impose* as a verb means to *establish by authority*. Of the answer choices given, only one implies one person dictating to another. *To force* as a verb can be construed as *to establish by authority*. Thus, answer choice (B) is correct. Remembered real-life context might be helpful. If you have ever heard someone described as "an imposing figure," you may remember that person as an authoritative or forceful individual.

2. **(A) halted** *Stunted* means *stopped short* or *cancelled abruptly*. Answer choice (A), *halted*, also means *stopped short*. Remembered real-life context may be helpful here as well. If you have ever heard that someone's "growth was stunted," something prevented that person from growing as much as he or she otherwise might have.

3. **(B) strong** While a *sturdy* home might be huge, it does not by nature have to be. Something sturdy, however, would be considered *strong*. Choice (B) is the most accurate answer.

4. **(B) persistent** *Undeterred* uses the prefix *un–*, meaning *opposite of*, with the root word "deter." To deter something is to stop or hinder it. So something *undeterred* would be something unhindered or *persistent*.

5. **(C) boredom** *Ennui* derives from a French word meaning *boredom* or *listlessness*. Choice (C) is correct.

6. **(A) changeable** *Mutable* means *prone to change*. Consider the word root *mut*, which appears in *mutant* (something or someone changed from the norm). Choice (A), *changeable*, is the best answer.

7. **(C) wasted** To *squander* is to *waste* or *fritter away* something. Of the choices given, only (C), *wasted*, means the same. This is a good question on which to use context to eliminate some of the choices. There's nothing necessarily shameful about (A) *gathering* or (D) *owning money. Stealing*, choice (B), is certainly shameful, so at that point you may have to make a 50-50 guess. Or you could use another tool, like remembered real-life context. It is unlikely you have ever heard "squander" on the news in the context of a story about theft.

8. **(A) unreadable** You could use context on this one: handwriting is more likely to be described as *unreadable* than as *unethical* or *dangerous*. A written work might be *creative*, but *handwriting* refers to the way the letters are made and not to the content of the writing.

9. **(B) unending** The word *infinite* means *lasting forever* or *unending*. Break the word into parts: *in–* means *not*, and the word root *fin* relates to ending. (Think about *final, finite*, or *finish*, all of which relate to ending.)

10. **(B) duration** *Longevity* means the length of time of a life or project, so choice (B), *duration*, is correct. The word part *long* relates to length, so look for an answer choice that also relates to length.

11. **(A) trick** Remember where you have heard "to fall for" used before. One "falls for" a *trick*. Answer choice (A) is correct.

12. **(C) announced** To *proclaim* is to *announce* or *decree*, especially in regards to a prominent figure like a president. Think about word parts: *pro–* means in *front* or *before* and *claim* is an English word meaning *state* or *assert*. To *proclaim* therefore means something like *state in front of*. Answer choice (C), *announced*, is a synonym for the given word.

13. **(A) basic** *Rudimentary* means *simple* or *easy*. Of the answer choices given, only (A), *basic*, applies to something simple or rudimentary. On this question, try rereading the sentence in your mind and substitute each answer choice. When you do so, choice (A) makes the most sense.

14. **(B) defeat** The word *rout* means to *defeat soundly* in battle or competition. You may have heard it in the context of stories about sports on the news. Answer choice (B) is correct.

15. **(C) rebellious** A *rogue* is someone who does not play by the rules. Use context: the sentence draws a contrast between the idea of a *team* and the idea of *rogue*. Answer choice (C) most directly contradicts the idea of teamwork or team spirit.

16. **(C) evoke agreement** *Resonate* has the word root *son*, which relates to sound, and the prefix *re–* which means *again* or *back*. So *resonate* means something like *sound again* or *sound back*. From there, you could think about which answer choice both fits that meaning and fits the context. Irritation (A) and discussion (D) do not seem to fit with the idea of sounding back. Choice (B) doesn't make any sense in the context. (In fact, to *resonate* in music means *to have a full sound that seems to reverberate*. In other contexts, *resonate* has come to mean *sit well* or *generate agreement*.)

17. **(A) repetitive** *Redundant* starts with the prefix *re–*, or *again*. The first choice you have available is *repetitive*, which means again and again. Context is also useful here: the sentence suggests that *redundant* has something to do with *duplicating*.

18. **(B) dictate** *Prescribe* means to *state authoritatively or recommend*. Remembered real-life context may be useful here. Think about when your doctor prescribes a medicine: she is urging you, with some authority, to take the medicine.

19. **(D) sensible** *Logical* means *based on logic* or *sensible.* Answer choice (D) is the only choice that has anything to do with logic. If you weren't sure what *sensible* meant, you could have used remembered real-life context. Think about the phrase "sensible shoes," which are shoes that display good sense or judgement on the part of the wearer.

20. **(A) requirement** Note that choice (A), *requirement,* has the same root as the given word. A *prerequisite* is *something that is required* before a project or course of study begins. Answer choice (A) is correct.

21. **(A) be drawn** *Gravitate* is based on a word it looks like: gravity. Even if you didn't know that *gravitate* means *moving towards,* you might be able to make a guess based on the knowledge that the force of gravity pulls things closer together. Choice (A) is correct.

22. **(D) careful** *Cautious* means *careful.* Mentally re-reading the sentence with each answer choice substituted for the underlined word would likely have been helpful here.

23. **(C) boaster** The meaning of *braggart* is *someone who brags.* While many (B) *leaders* might brag, the correct answer choice here is (C), *boaster* (one who boasts).

24. **(A) rumor** *Hearsay* is a term often used in law. It means *secondhand stories:* literally, what someone has heard someone else say. A *rumor* is a story that has been heard from others without proof. Choice (A) is correct.

25. **(C) ridicule.** To *taunt* is to *ridicule* or *tease.* Even if you didn't remember a context in which you've heard the word *taunt,* you might have a sense that it has a negative charge. Only choice (C) also has a negative charge.

26. **(B) productive** The term *constructive criticism* refers to criticism that constructs or *builds up* the listener rather than destroying her. Think of the word *construction,* which means *building.* While (D) *flattering* words might build some people up, *flattery* contradicts the idea of *criticism.* The correct answer here is choice (B), *productive.*

27. **(C) countable** To *quantify* something is to *be able to count* it. Think about the root *quant,* which relates to numbers and which gives us the word *quantity,* or *amount.*

28. **(C) useful** Remembered real-life context might be helpful here. If you think about where you have heard the word *effective,* advertisements for cosmetics, drugs, and supplements might come to mind. Now ask yourself: what do the companies who sell cosmetics or drugs want to tell us about those products? They're most likely to want to tell us that their products are useful, productive, or successful.

29. **(C) disinterest** *Apathy* means the state of not caring or *disinterest.* Think about word parts: the prefix *a–* means *not,* and the word root *path* relates to feeling. Think about *sympathetic,* which means sharing the feelings of others. Thus, *apathy* means something like the state of not entering into others' feelings, *or disinterest.*

30. **(B) defect** A *blemish* is a *glaring problem or defect.* Try mentally rereading the sentence with each choice substituted. You wouldn't describe an (A) *impact* as *glaring,* so that one is out. Moreover, *glaring* has a negative context that does not fit with (C) *commendation* or (D) *compliment.*

31. **(A) agreement** *Consensus* has a root of *con–* meaning *with* (don't confuse this with *con–* meaning *not*). Only answer choice (A) suggests togetherness. Another way of tackling this question is to read the sentence carefully and glean that to get a measure passed, one would need *agreement,* not (C) *infighting* (that is, fighting within a group). (A) is the correct answer.

32. **(D) insubordination** Think about word parts: *dis–* means *not.* The word root *sent* relates to perceiving or feeing and also appears in the word *consent,* which means agreement. Thus, you can guess that *dissent* is the opposite of agreement. Even if you don't know what *insubordination* means, you can eliminate the other choices because none of them suggest the opposite of agreement.

33. **(D) speed** *Tempo* means *the speed of something.* Remembered real-life context might be helpful here: if you have heard the word *tempo,* it was likely in a discussion about music. And it makes far more sense to say that music has a speed than to say that it has a *heartbeat, safety,* or *modernity.*

34. **(B) comfort** Try to fit some of the words into the sentence given to test their context. *Glee* and *protection* may be tempting at first glance, but neither fit the construction of the sentence if you replace them for the word *solace.* But *comfort,* (B), would make her feel better.

35. **(B) traps** *Pitfalls* are *traps and problems that await.* Try mentally rereading the sentence and substituting each choice. While climbers might experience (A) *joys* and probably do work with (C) *ropes,* neither of those ideas relate specifically to inexperienced climbers.

Part 4: Paragraph Comprehension Answers and Explanations

1. **(A) can be very difficult to track down** This is an Inference question, so the correct answer may be implied but not spelled out directly. The first paragraph talks about the participants of urban legends. It turns out that those participants can never be found.

2. **(D) a basis in reality** This is an EXCEPT question, so the correct answer is the one that does not characterize successful urban legends. If you were able to determine that urban legends are fictional, the correct answer choice (D), *a basis in reality*, is clearly the correct answer. Otherwise, you could use the process of elimination on the wrong answer choices. The passage states that urban legends "persist both for their entertainment value and for the transmission of popular values and beliefs," so choices (A) and (B), which paraphrase this, are wrong. Finally, the very first sentence describes urban legends as a new form of folktale, so (C) is out.

3. **(B) Darwin's theory accounted for many examples of evolution.** The author, while maintaining that there were other scientists with similar evolutionary ideas, notes toward the end that Darwin's eloquence and his ability "to account for many diverse examples" helped him establish his theories as the benchmark by which others stacked up. Thus, choice (B) is correct. None of the other choices are supported by the passage.

4. **(B) informative** In questions that ask about the author's tone, beware of answer choices that exaggerate the author's point of view. Choice (B) is correct because the passage merely conveys relevant facts about an issue. While the author does describe two opposing reactions that parents have had to the changes that have taken place in elementary schools, no preference is implied. Therefore choices (A) and (C) are incorrect. Be cautious with choices such as these that use extreme language.

5. **(D) light from the Sun** Although the wording of this question indicates that this is an Inference question, the correct answer choice (D) can be taken directly from the first sentence. If most life is "dependent on organisms that store radiant energy from the Sun," it is dependent on light from the Sun. Remember that on Inference questions you are looking for the one answer that must be true based on what is stated in the passage.

6. **(A) Both perform similar functions in different food chains** The first paragraph describes ecosystems that are dependent on photosynthetic organisms, while the second paragraph describes ecosystems that are dependent on chemosynthetic organisms. In both cases, the organisms serve similar functions as primary producers within their different food chains, so choice (A) is correct. Choice (B) is wrong because only chemosynthetic organisms are described in the passage as supporting higher organisms "at great ocean depths." (C) is wrong because chemosynthetic organisms do not rely on sunlight for their basic source of energy. Choice (D) is never discussed in the passage.

7. **(D) confirmed Halley's calculations** The last sentence of the passage implies that Halley accurately predicted the 1758 appearance of the comet. Thus, you can infer that that appearance of the comet confirmed Halley's theory and accorded with his calculations.

8. **(D) by the narrower snout found on a crocodile** The passage discusses a few ways to distinguish a crocodile from an alligator. The first and most easily observed of these is the fact that the crocodile's head and jaws are longer and narrower. In other words, it has a narrower snout, choice (D). (A) is out, because the animals' mouths do not necessarily have to be closed to distinguish one from the other. Choice (B) is out because both animals can be found in the Everglades National Park, and (C) is never discussed as one of the ways to distinguish one giant reptile from the other.

9. **(A) certain actors are inappropriate for certain roles** On this question you are asked to infer what the agent believes. She must assume that certain actors are inappropriate for certain parts, because if she didn't believe this her conclusion would make no sense; it wouldn't be possible for an actor to audition for an inappropriate part. The actors' talent (B) isn't questioned by the agent; she focuses on the types of roles. The possibility that an actor's appropriateness for the part may be difficult to predict (C) is never assumed by the agent; in fact, if anything, such a belief would weaken her conclusion. Major roles (D) are never discussed in the passage.

10. **(A) a grouping of syllables** To answer this Detail question, scan the passage for a reference to foot or feet. The first such mention is in the third sentence, which states: "Pentameter refers to the number of feet, or groupings of syllables." So a foot is just that, a grouping of syllables, choice (A).

11. **(D) the sinking of the *Lusitania* prompted increased American involvement in World War I** This is a main idea question, so reading the passage for details is not necessary, although paying attention to the overall effect of those details is. The author notes that public opinion on the war was swayed when the *Lusitania* was attacked, prompting increased military involvement from the United States. Choice (D) is a paraphrase of this main idea. Of the wrong answer choices, (A) distorts a detail found in the passage, implying a causal link between America's support for Britain and France and Germany's sinking of the *Lusitania* that is not supported by the passage. Choice (B) refers to a minor detail in the passage, and choice (C) is simply not true according to the passage, particularly after the sinking of the *Lusitania*.

12. **(D) When critics and general audiences disagree about a movie's quality, the critics' opinion is not necessarily more valid.** In this Inference question, you are asked to supply a conclusion that is best supported by the passage. The author seems to believe that critics' opinions aren't necessarily more significant than those of the average person, so (D), which restates this idea, is a valid inference. Though the author says the critics' opinions aren't more valid than those of average moviegoers, he doesn't imply (A), that the critics' opinions are *usually* incorrect. Choice (B) is out because the author does not say that the critics' judgments are meaningless—merely that critics don't always make the right judgments. And the passage doesn't state how frequently critics dislike popular movies (C).

13. **(C) they believed it to be poisonous** This Detail question asks why Americans did not start using the tomato until the mid-nineteenth century. According to the passage, the English considered the tomato poisonous, and this myth continued to hold sway in America until the mid-nineteenth century. In other words, they, too, believed it to be poisonous, choice (C). None of the other answer choices are supported by the statements in the passage.

14. **(B) tired** The word "drowsy" is used to describe Daria. In the following sentence, you learn that Daria looks forward to going to sleep each night. From this information, you can determine that "drowsy" means *tired* or sleepy. Nothing in the passage suggests that Daria was *drunk* (A). Throughout the passage, Daria is presented as the opposite of (C) *happy* and (D) *satisfied*.

15. **(A) They provide adequate shade.** The author discusses how she enjoys escaping the sun by sitting under the variety of trees in the forest. This implies that the trees provide adequate shade for her enjoyment as stated in choice (A). Choice (B) is the opposite of the meaning the author conveys. The author is thankful for the shade from the trees, so it's not accurate to say they are impairing her enjoyment (C). While it may be true that trees provide a home for many animals, this concept is never discussed or implied in the passage, so choice (D) is incorrect.

Part 5: Mathematics Knowledge Answers and Explanations

1. **(D) $12x^2 + 7x - 12$** Use FOIL to solve:

$(3x + 4)(4x - 3)$
$= (3x)(4x) + (3x)(-3) + (4)(4x) + (4)(-3)$
$= 12x^2 - 9x + 16x - 12$
$= 12x^2 + 7x - 12$

2. **(A) $\frac{60}{n}$** Pick numbers to solve this one. If $n = 2$ the tree grew 5 feet, or 60 inches, in 2 years, which means it grew at a rate of 30 inches per year. Plug in 2 for n into the answer choices, and only (A) gives the target number, 30.

3. **(D) 192** If the perimeter of $ABCD$ is 56, then half that, or 28, is the sum of the length and the width, since the perimeter of a rectangle = 2(length + width). If $AD = 16$, then $AB = 28 - 16 = 12$, and the area of $ABCD$ must be $16 \times 12 = 192$.

4. **(A) equal** A square is a rectangle with four equal sides. Choice (B) may be tempting, but in fact, any two opposing sides of a square are parallel. It would be inaccurate to say that a square has four sides, all of which are parallel. Choice (D), *curvilinear*, means curved and is not correct.

5. **(D) $a + b < 2c$** The question gives two inequalities here: $a < b$ and $b < c$, which can combine into one, $a < b < c$. Go through the answer choices to see which *must* be true. If you add the corresponding sides of these inequalities: $a + b < c + c$, or $a + b < 2c$. This statement is *always* true, so it must be the correct answer.

This question could also be approached by Picking Numbers. That might look like this:

Choose $a = 2$, $b = 3$, and $c = 4$, to conform to the information in the question stem. Now try each choice to see whether it is a true statement about those numbers:

(A) $3 + 4 < 4$ No way! Incorrect.

(B) $2 + 3 < 4$ Also not true. Incorrect.

(C) $2 - 3 < 3 - 4$ Nope. Incorrect.

(D) $2 + 3 < 8$ Definitely true. This choice is correct.

If more than one answer choice had produced a true statement, you would have tried again using different numerical values until you had only one true statement.

6. **(C) 36** Since the angle marked $x°$ and the angle marked $y°$ together form a straight angle, their measures must sum to 180°. Substitute in $2z$ for x and $3z$ for y, and solve for z:

$x + y = 180$
$2z + 3z = 180$
$5z = 180$
$z = 36$

7. **(B) 7.5** There are 360 degrees in a circle and 60 minutes in an hour, so you could solve this question by setting up a proportion in which n is the number of minutes $\frac{45}{360} = \frac{n}{60}$ Then cross-multiply and reduce the fraction:

$n = \dfrac{45 \times 60}{360}$

$n = \dfrac{45 \times 60}{360} \div \dfrac{60}{60} = \dfrac{45}{6}$

$n = \dfrac{45}{6} \div \dfrac{3}{3} = \dfrac{15}{2}$

$n = \dfrac{15}{2} = 7.5$

8. **(C) 12** The area of a triangle is $\frac{1}{2} \times base \times height$:

$\dfrac{1}{2} \times 6 \times 4 = 3 \times 4 = 12$

9. **(B) 115** Since lines p and q are parallel, use the rule about alternate interior angles. The angle marked $y°$ is supplementary to a 65° angle, so $y = 180 - 65 = 115$.

10. **(A) 4.5** You could either turn the percentages into decimals and multiply: $0.15 \times 0.15 \times 200 = 0.15 \times 30 = 4.5$ and get the answer (A), or you could take it one step at a time. 15% of 200 is $\frac{15}{100} \times 200 = 15 \times 2 = 30$. 15% of 30 is

$\dfrac{15}{100} \times 30 = \dfrac{3}{20} \times 30 = \dfrac{3}{2} \times 3 = \dfrac{9}{2} = 4.5$.

11. **(B) $\frac{1}{24}$** Don't fall for the answer choice trap and assume that the average of $\frac{1}{20}$ and $\frac{1}{30}$ is $\frac{1}{25}$. Instead, use the average formula: $Average = \frac{Sum\,of\,the\,terms}{Number\,of\,terms}$ In this case:

$Average = \dfrac{\frac{1}{20} + \frac{1}{30}}{2} = \dfrac{\frac{3}{60} + \frac{2}{60}}{2} = \dfrac{\frac{5}{60}}{2} = \dfrac{5}{120} = \dfrac{1}{24}$.

12. **(C) $180 - y$** This question is testing your knowledge of definitions. The *supplement* of an angle is the angle that when added to the original angle equals 180°. So if an angle measures $y°$, its supplement is $180 - y$.

13. **(B) 5** If Diane has $\frac{2}{3}$ of her room still to paint, she'll need $2 \times 2\frac{1}{2}$ or 5 more cans to do the job.

14. **(D) -12** You can't find the value of either variable alone, but you don't need to. Rearranging the equation, you get:

$13 + a = 25 + b$
$13 = 25 + b - a$
$13 - 25 = b - a$
$-12 = b - a$

15. **(C) $15x^5$** When you multiply terms that have exponents over the same base, you add the exponents and multiply the coefficients:

$3x^2 \times 5x^3 = (3 \times 5)x^{2+3} = 15x^5$

16. **(D) 21%** You can Pick Numbers to make sense of this geometry problem. You are asked to increase the sides of a square by 10%, so you want to pick a number for the original sides of the square of which it's easy to take 10%. For instance, you could say that the original square is 10 by 10. 10% of 10 is 1, so the dimensions of the increased square are 11 by 11. In this case, the area of the original square is 100, and the area of the new square is 121, which represents a 21% increase.

17. **(B) 10** If $\frac{m}{2} = 15$, then $m = 15 \times 2 = 30$

Plug 30 in for m to solve the expression asked for in the question:

$\frac{m}{3} = \frac{30}{3} = 10$

18. **(C) $3x - 2$** To factor $6x^2 - 13x + 6$, you need a pair of binomials whose "first" terms will give you a product of $6x^2$ and whose "last" terms will give you a product of 6. Since the middle term of the result is negative and the last term is positive, the two last terms of the factors must both be negative. One of the factors is among the answer choices, so you can use the answer choices in your trial-and-error effort to factor. You're looking for a factor with a minus sign in it, so the answer's either (C) or (D). Try (C) first: Its first term is $3x$, so the other factor's first term would have to be $2x$ (to get that $6x^2$ in the product). (C)'s last term is -2, so the other factor's last term would have to be -3.

Check to see if $(3x - 2)(2x - 3)$ works:

$(3x - 2)(2x - 3)$

$= (3x)(2x) + 3x(-3) + (-2)(2x) + (-2)(-3)$

$= 6x^2 - 9x - 4x + 6$

$= 6x^2 - 13x + 6$

It works. There's no need to check (D).

19. **(D) $3x - y + 2 = 0$** Just be careful and translate the English into math: "the product of 3 and x is equal to 2 less than y" becomes $3x = y - 2$. But all of the equations in the answer choices set the right side of the equation to zero, so do that to your equation:

$3x = y - 2$

$3x - y = -2$

$3x - y + 2 = 0$

20. **(A) $\frac{x}{x-1}$** Since $\frac{b}{a}$ is the reciprocal of $\frac{a}{b}$, $\frac{b}{a}$ must be the reciprocal of $1 - \frac{1}{x}$ as well. Combine the terms in $1 - \frac{1}{x}$ and then find the reciprocal:

$\frac{a}{b} = 1 - \frac{1}{x} = \frac{x}{x} - \frac{1}{x} = \frac{x-1}{x}$

Therefore, $\frac{b}{a} = \frac{x}{x-1}$

21. **(C) 32** This figure is an unfamiliar solid, so don't try to calculate the volume directly. The question says that the solid in question is half of a cube. Imagine the other half lying on top of the solid, forming a complete cube.

Notice that the diagonal with length $4\sqrt{2}$ and two of the cube's edges form an isosceles right triangle. In an isosceles right triangle, the hypotenuse is $\sqrt{2}$ times the length of a leg. Here the hypotenuse has length $4\sqrt{2}$, so the legs have length 4. Thus, the edges of the cube have a length of 4. The volume of a cube is the length of an edge cubed. So the volume of the whole cube is $4 \times 4 \times 4$, or 64. The volume of the solid in question is $\frac{1}{2}$ of this, or 32.

22. **(B) 400** Begin by writing the division problem as a fraction: $\frac{7.6}{0.019} = x$. Now move the decimal points on the top and the bottom of the fraction the same number of places to the right until you are dealing with whole numbers: $\frac{7.6}{0.019} = \frac{7,600}{19}$. Now divide: $\frac{7,600}{19} = 400$.

23. **(B) $\frac{16}{\pi}$** The circumference of a circle $= 2\pi(\text{radius})$, so radius $= \frac{circumference}{2\pi}$. The circumference is 8: $\frac{8}{2\pi} = \frac{4}{\pi}$. The area of a circle $= \pi(\text{radius})^2$, so the area of a circle with a radius

of $\frac{4}{\pi}$ is: $\pi\left(\frac{4}{\pi}\right)^2 = \pi\left(\frac{16}{\pi^2}\right) = \frac{16}{\pi}$

24. **(B) 36** You could translate the English into math to get:

$.36 \times 18 = .18 \times n$

$n = \frac{.36 \times 18}{.18} = 2 \times 18 = 36$

However, you don't have to go through all that work if you realize that x percent of $y = y$ percent of x.

25. **(C) 300 and 400** Here you're looking for an extremely rough approximation (the answer choices all have a range of 100), so square the upper bounds of the ranges in the answer choices, until you find the range that encompasses 104,906. Start with the upper bound of (A), $(200)^2 = 40,000$, which is less than 104,906. Now try (B): $(300)^2 = 90,000$, which is still too low. Now check (C): $(400)^2 = 160,000$. 104,906 is between 90,000 and 160,000, so (C) is the answer.

Part 6: Electronics Information Answers and Explanations

1. **(B) ohms** Resistance is measured in ohms, and the symbol for an ohm is Ω (omega).

2. **(B) positive, neutrally** Two types of particles are found within the nucleus: protons and neutrons. Protons have a positive charge, and neutrons are neutrally charged.

3. **(A) alternating current** Alternating current (AC) is when the electric current reverses direction many times in a second.

4. **(D) short circuit** This symbol represents a short circuit, which is an accidental path of low resistance that passes an irregularly high amount of current.

5. **(B) current** I represents current. Current is the rate of flow of electrons, or the Intensity of the flow. (Specifically, I is the rate of charge flow.)

6. **(D) anode** The P-type material in a diode is the anode, and the N-type material is known as the cathode.

7. **(D) doping** Pure silicon must be doped in order to generate holes or free electrons. This process creates the P and N materials needed to make diodes and transistors.

8. **(A) capacitor** Capacitors stop direct current flow but not alternating current. The higher the frequency of an alternating current, the less resistant effect a capacitor has. Standard resistors, both fixed and variable, definitely resist AC flow, as do inductors.

9. **(D) 20 Ω** When wired in series, the resistance of several loads can be added together to determine the effective resistance. The sum of the four resistances is 20 Ω.

10. **(C) the arrow in the transistor symbol is always placed on the collector** The arrow in a transistor symbol is always placed on the emitter, and the arrow always points toward the N-type material at that junction.

11. **(A) voltmeter** This is the circuit symbol for a voltmeter, which is used to measure voltage.

12. **(B) watt** There are three essential components of an electrical circuit: a voltage source, a load, and conductors to connect the load to the voltage source. When these three components are connected so that current can flow, it is a closed circuit.

13. **(A)**

A doorbell is typically operated by a push switch, which allows current to flow only when a button is pressed. (A) is the symbol for a push switch.

14. **(B)**

This is the schematic symbol for an alternating current (AC) voltage source.

15. **(C) condensers** Capacitors that are electrical storage units are also known as condensers.

16. **(C) an insulator** An insulator is a material that does not conduct electricity.

17. **(A) rubber** Rubber is an example of an insulator. All of the other examples in this question are conductors.

18. **(C) 500 mA** Four 6-ohm resistors wired in series will have a total resistance of 24 ohms. Using $I = V \div R$, a total of 0.5 A will flow in this circuit. 0.5 A is the same as 500 mA.

19. **(A) silicon** The term *semiconductor* refers to an element that has four electrons in its valence shell. Since the bonds between these four electrons and the nucleus are somewhat strong, these elements are neither good conductors nor good insulators. One element that is widely recognized as a semiconductor is silicon.

20. **(D) galvanometer** This is the circuit symbol for a galvanometer, which is used to measure extremely small currents, usually of 1 mA voltage or less.

Part 7: Auto and Shop Information Answers and Explanations

1. **(D) miter box** While a *miter box* might be used with a backsaw to make even cuts in wood at specific angles, by itself, it is not capable of shaping wood. All of the other choices are tools capable of making cuts or smoothing edges on wood.

2. **(B) suspension** Of all the aspects of vehicle operation, two that are a high priority for most drivers are ride comfort and handling. The suspension system, choice (B), is responsible for the ride quality of the vehicle.

3. **(D) kerf** The cut or slot left by a saw in a piece of wood is also known as a *kerf*.

4. **(D) transfer case** The *transfer case* is located between the transmission and the drive axles on a four-wheel drive vehicle and is the piece that splits the engine's power between the front- and rear-drive axles.

5. **(B) a cut across the grain of the wood** This is a crosscut saw. It is designed to, as its name suggests, cut across the grain of the wood. Crosscut saw teeth are unique in that they cut like a knife, in contrast to a ripsaw, which is made to cut with the grain of wood.

6. **(C) compression stroke** This image depicts the compression stroke, which is the second stroke in the four-stroke cycle.

7. **(A) counting the number of threads per inch** Fractional measurement fasteners (measured in fractions of inches) use threads that are identified by the number of threads per inch.

8. **(D) the tools shown in both (B) and (C)** To loosen tight fasteners, it is good to use a box-end wrench. Choice (B) depicts a combination wrench, which has an open end wrench on one side and a box end on the other. Choice (C) shows a wrench with box ends on both sides. Therefore, both (B) and (C) are suitable for loosening tight fasteners; choice (D) is the correct answer. The box end wraps completely around the head of a bolt, and therefore makes greater surface contact.

9. **(A) coil spring** Of the answer choices given, only (A), *coil spring*, is not a part associated with the steering system. Coil springs are what aid the wheels in moving up and down while the vehicle chassis stays steady. The other pieces listed—steering knuckle, tie rod end, and idler arm—are all parts of the steering system.

10. **(C) 3** The camshaft, indicated in the diagram by the number 3, is responsible for the opening and closing of the engine's intake and exhaust valves. The camshaft turns at one-half the speed of the engine's crankshaft.

11. **(D) in the fuel tank** In fuel-injected engines, the electric fuel pump is located in the vehicle's fuel tank and is what supplies fuel under pressure to the fuel injectors.

12. **(B) fewer** The two basic thread classifications—*Unified National Coarse (UNC)*, and *Unified National Fine (UNF)*—have different numbers of threads per inch. A UNC or coarse thread would have relatively few threads per inch, where a UNF or fine thread would have a larger number of threads per inch.

13. **(C) both the engine intake manifold vacuum and fluid pressure from the power steering system** Power brake systems use both the engine intake manifold vacuum and fluid pressure from the power steering system to increase pressure. Engine intake manifold vacuum is utilized to generate greater force on the master cylinder, so higher hydraulic pressures can be generated in the brake system. Some brake booster systems use fluid pressure from the power steering system to increase braking power.

14. **(D) rotor** The primary is the low-voltage part of the system and contains a battery, an ignition switch, a primary coil winding, an ignition module, a reluctor and pickup coil, and a distributor. A rotor is not a part of the ignition primary system.

15. **(A) the ideal air-fuel mixture in a gasoline engine** *Stoichiometric* is the ideal ratio of air to fuel in the engine and it is the responsibility of the engine's fuel system to maintain this balance.

16. **(D) viscosity** *Viscosity* is resistance to flow, and is expressed as a number that is directly proportional to the thickness of the oil.

17. **(C) both direct and alternating current** Because they serve different purposes within an automobile, both negative ground current and direct current electrical systems are being built. Alternating current is used primarily for household appliances.

18. **(D) work** Stick welding involves the use of an electric arc welding machine and two cables: one that attaches to the work being welded through a *ground clamp*, and the other going to an electrode that is sometimes referred to as a *stinger*. For safety reasons, always clamp to the work.

19. **(D) both flat and horizontally opposed** The last major cylinder arrangement that has been utilized by engine designers is the horizontally opposed or flat design. This has all of the cylinders lying on the horizontal plane, with half of the cylinders facing away from the other half and the crankshaft located between them. Some refer to this design as a "boxer" engine because the pistons move back and forth like a boxer throwing punches.

20. **(B) striking an object where it is important that the hammer itself not come in direct contact with the work** The tool pictured is a drift. It is used for striking an object where it is important that the hammer itself does not come in direct contact with the work. A chisel normally has a long edge and is used for cutting (A), where a punch is narrow and is used for driving small fasteners and making layout marks (C). To guide a saw when cutting across the grain (D), you might use a miter box, but you would certainly not use a drift.

21. **(A) single overhead cam or SOHC** This design is known as single overhead cam or SOHC. In a V-type engine with two cylinder heads, there would be two camshafts, with one installed above each cylinder head.

22. **(D) the catalytic converter** Any air passing through to the car's combustion chamber must naturally pass through the intake port in the cylinder head, the intake manifold, and the air filter. Since the intake valve is open and is allowing atmospheric air to enter the combustion chamber, higher atmospheric air pressure pushes air through the engine's intake system and toward the low-pressure area above the piston. As the air is traveling through the intake system, fuel is injected into the air stream before it enters the combustion chamber. Gases do not pass through the catalytic converter until they are almost ready to be expelled from the car.

23. **(D) 6-point socket and breaker bar** Since most nuts are smaller sized, and because the 6-*point* socket is a stronger design, it is usually the mechanic's first choice in the smaller socket drive sizes. And a *breaker bar* attached to a socket can give enough twisting force to loosen very tight fasteners.

24. **(D) external hole-type** This is an external hole-type retaining ring. Retaining rings (or snap rings) are used to prevent end-movement of cylindrical parts in bores or parts mounted on shafts. External snap rings are installed in grooves on shafts, whereas internal snap rings install in grooves inside a bore. Snap rings are installed and removed using snap ring pliers.

25. **(B) They are converted to lead sulfate.** A car's battery contains lead plates immersed in an electrolyte made up of sulfuric acid and water. When the battery discharges energy, the sulfur binds with the lead plates to make lead sulfate, and the electrolyte is reduced to water. Even though water is a result of this process, it is not true to say that (A) the lead plates release water, because the water is already part of the electrolyte mixture.

Part 8: Mechanical Comprehension Answers and Explanations

1. **(A) its potential energy is being converted into kinetic energy** The principle of conservation of mechanical energy says that the total mechanical energy of an object (*PE* + *KE*) remains constant as an object moves. As the car rolls down the hill, its speed increases because its potential energy (*PE*) is being converted into kinetic energy (*KE*).

2. **(C) its velocity is zero** During the ball's journey upward after being thrown, the ball has its maximum kinetic energy when it leaves the thrower's hand. This kinetic energy is converted into potential energy as it rises. Maximum potential energy (*PE*) occurs when the ball stops rising, and this is where its velocity is zero.

3. **(B) inertia** *Inertia* is a function of an object's mass. A large mass will require a large amount of force to cause it to accelerate. The larger the mass, the greater the inertia of the object. *Momentum* is a quality of an object in motion and describes how difficult it is to change the velocity of a moving object. *Torque* is a rotational force. *Pressure* is force per unit area.

4. **(C) law of universal gravitation** Isaac Newton discovered that every particle in the universe is attracted to every other particle. This concept became a physical law known as Newton's law of universal gravitation. The gravitational force that each body exerts on the other grows stronger as the bodies get closer. The force also increases as the mass of the bodies increase.

5. **(D) 6 m/s²** Based on Newton's second law, $F = ma$. Rearrange that equation to solve for acceleration: $a = \frac{F}{m}$, where units of force are in Newtons and mass is expressed in kg. Here: $a = \frac{30\,N}{5\,kg} = 6\,m/s^2$.

6. **(C) the same amount of work** Work is defined as force times distance. Lifting a box straight up to the top of a ramp will require the same amount of work as pushing the box up the ramp (neglecting friction). The ramp allows a smaller force to be applied over a larger distance. However, the end result or net work done is the same in both cases.

7. **(B) it is possible to get more work out of a machine than what is put in** It is not possible to get more work out of a machine than what is put in. Machines do not reduce work, they simply manage it and make it easier by diminishing the amount of force that is required.

8. **(A) wedge** A chisel is an example of a wedge.

9. **(B) a wedge is made to move, whereas an inclined plane stays stationary** The wedge is a variation of the inclined plane, but is made to move whereas the inclined plane is made to stay in one place.

10. **(A) post A** The distance from post A to the load is less than the distance from post B to the load; therefore, it holds the greater part of the load.

11. **(C) joules** Work and kinetic energy are both measured in joules. This is not a coincidence, as any work that is done to accelerate an object at rest will be converted into the kinetic energy of that object. This principle is known as the work-energy theorem.

12. **(B) wheel and axle** A screwdriver gains mechanical advantage through the use of a large wheel (screwdriver handle) rotating a small wheel (screwdriver tip), much like a wheel and axle. Large movements converted into small movements will amplify the force applied.

13. **(B) a decrease** Any time that force is increased through mechanical advantage, there will always be a proportional decrease in the distance moved.

14. **(A) first-class lever** A prybar can increase mechanical advantage, and can change the direction of motion, so it is a first-class lever.

15. **(B) 746** One horsepower is equal to 550 foot-pounds of work per second or 746 watts.

16. **(C) moved toward where the object is moved** Moving the fulcrum toward the object will increase the force applied to the object, but decrease the distance that the object can be moved.

17. **(C) The work put out by a simple machine can never exceed the work put in.** If a machine were able to produce more work than was put into the machine, there would be a net increase in energy. This would violate the laws of thermodynamics. The work put out by a simple machine can never exceed the work put into it.

18. **(D) reduction in rotational speed** If a small gear drives a large gear, a speed reduction takes place. The large gear will turn more slowly than the small gear and the speed of the output will be slower.

19. **(B) multiple pulleys** A block-and-tackle requires a minimum of two pulleys, with a rope, belt, or chain used to operate them. There is at least one fixed and one moveable pulley in the block and tackle.

20. **(A) the weight of the object** The force exerted to lift an object using a single pulley is the same as the weight of the object itself.

21. **(B) wheel and axle** A doorknob is similar to a wheel and axle in that a large wheel (the doorknob or handle) is used to operate a small wheel (the latch mechanism).

22. **(A) the same** Mass is a measure of the amount of matter in a substance. It does not change from place to place. Weight, however, depends on the gravitational constant, and does change depending on the location.

23. **(C) inversely proportional** Consider "Torque" and "Speed" to be two people on a teeter-totter. Whenever "Torque" goes up, "Speed" goes down, and vice versa. These two quantities can be described as inversely proportional.

24. **(C)** $PE = m \times g \times h$ An object's potential energy (PE) can be calculated using the formula

$$PE = mgh$$

where m is mass in kilograms (kg), g is acceleration due to gravity (9.8 m/s^2), h is the height of the object in meters (m), and PE is gravitational potential energy measured in joules (J).

25. **(A) 0 J** No work is done because the box does not move. $W = Fd$, where F is force (newtons), and d is distance (m). If an object experiences no change in position, then no net work is done.

Part 9: Assembling Objects Answers and Explanations

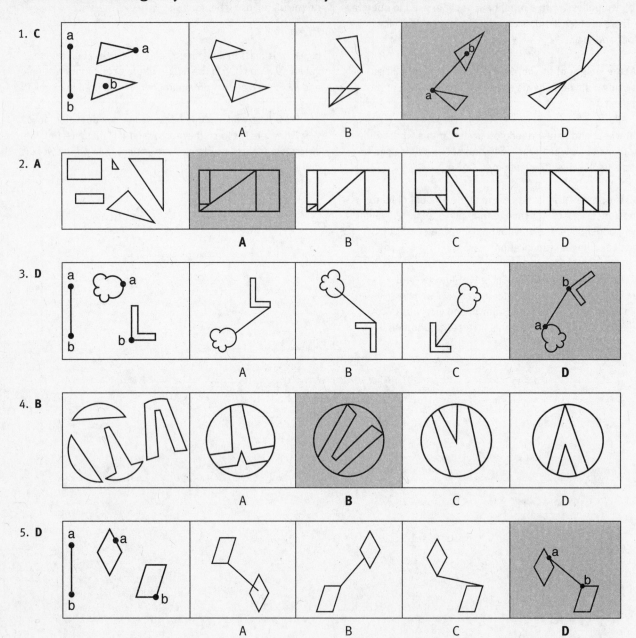

1. **C**

2. **A**

3. **D**

4. **B**

5. **D**

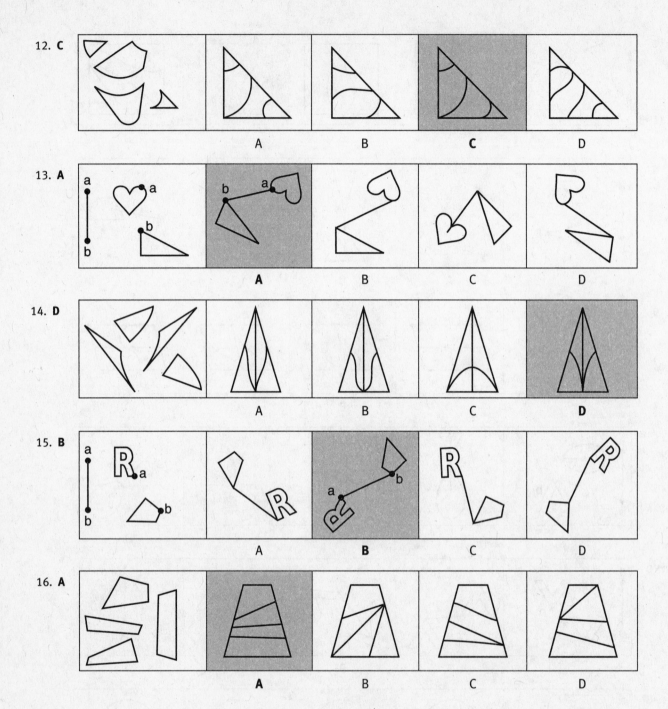

12. **C**

13. **A**

14. **D**

15. **B**

16. **A**

17. **C**

    A   B   **C**   D

18. **D**

    A   B   C   **D**

19. **B**

    A   **B**   C   D

20. **B**

    A   **B**   C   D

21. **C**

    A   B   **C**   D

22. **A**

    A   B   C   D

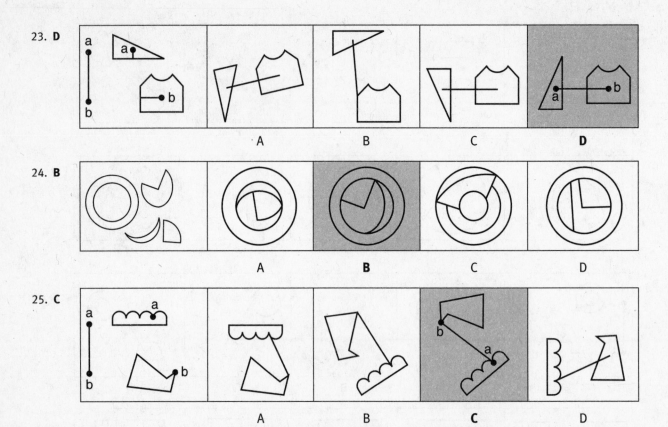

23. **D**

A   B   C   **D**

24. **B**

A   **B**   C   D

25. **C**

A   B   **C**   D

ASVAB PRACTICE TEST B

ANSWER SHEET

Part 1: General Science (GS)

1 (A)(B)(C)(D)	6 (A)(B)(C)(D)	11 (A)(B)(C)(D)	16 (A)(B)(C)(D)	21 (A)(B)(C)(D)
2 (A)(B)(C)(D)	7 (A)(B)(C)(D)	12 (A)(B)(C)(D)	17 (A)(B)(C)(D)	22 (A)(B)(C)(D)
3 (A)(B)(C)(D)	8 (A)(B)(C)(D)	13 (A)(B)(C)(D)	18 (A)(B)(C)(D)	23 (A)(B)(C)(D)
4 (A)(B)(C)(D)	9 (A)(B)(C)(D)	14 (A)(B)(C)(D)	19 (A)(B)(C)(D)	24 (A)(B)(C)(D)
5 (A)(B)(C)(D)	10 (A)(B)(C)(D)	15 (A)(B)(C)(D)	20 (A)(B)(C)(D)	25 (A)(B)(C)(D)

Part 2: Arithmetic Reasoning (AR)

1 (A)(B)(C)(D)	7 (A)(B)(C)(D)	13 (A)(B)(C)(D)	19 (A)(B)(C)(D)	25 (A)(B)(C)(D)
2 (A)(B)(C)(D)	8 (A)(B)(C)(D)	14 (A)(B)(C)(D)	20 (A)(B)(C)(D)	26 (A)(B)(C)(D)
3 (A)(B)(C)(D)	9 (A)(B)(C)(D)	15 (A)(B)(C)(D)	21 (A)(B)(C)(D)	27 (A)(B)(C)(D)
4 (A)(B)(C)(D)	10 (A)(B)(C)(D)	16 (A)(B)(C)(D)	22 (A)(B)(C)(D)	28 (A)(B)(C)(D)
5 (A)(B)(C)(D)	11 (A)(B)(C)(D)	17 (A)(B)(C)(D)	23 (A)(B)(C)(D)	29 (A)(B)(C)(D)
6 (A)(B)(C)(D)	12 (A)(B)(C)(D)	18 (A)(B)(C)(D)	24 (A)(B)(C)(D)	30 (A)(B)(C)(D)

Part 3: Word Knowledge (WK)

1 (A)(B)(C)(D)	8 (A)(B)(C)(D)	15 (A)(B)(C)(D)	22 (A)(B)(C)(D)	29 (A)(B)(C)(D)
2 (A)(B)(C)(D)	9 (A)(B)(C)(D)	16 (A)(B)(C)(D)	23 (A)(B)(C)(D)	30 (A)(B)(C)(D)
3 (A)(B)(C)(D)	10 (A)(B)(C)(D)	17 (A)(B)(C)(D)	24 (A)(B)(C)(D)	31 (A)(B)(C)(D)
4 (A)(B)(C)(D)	11 (A)(B)(C)(D)	18 (A)(B)(C)(D)	25 (A)(B)(C)(D)	32 (A)(B)(C)(D)
5 (A)(B)(C)(D)	12 (A)(B)(C)(D)	19 (A)(B)(C)(D)	26 (A)(B)(C)(D)	33 (A)(B)(C)(D)
6 (A)(B)(C)(D)	13 (A)(B)(C)(D)	20 (A)(B)(C)(D)	27 (A)(B)(C)(D)	34 (A)(B)(C)(D)
7 (A)(B)(C)(D)	14 (A)(B)(C)(D)	21 (A)(B)(C)(D)	28 (A)(B)(C)(D)	35 (A)(B)(C)(D)

Part 4: Paragraph Comprehension (PC)

1 (A)(B)(C)(D)	4 (A)(B)(C)(D)	7 (A)(B)(C)(D)	10 (A)(B)(C)(D)	13 (A)(B)(C)(D)
2 (A)(B)(C)(D)	5 (A)(B)(C)(D)	8 (A)(B)(C)(D)	11 (A)(B)(C)(D)	14 (A)(B)(C)(D)
3 (A)(B)(C)(D)	6 (A)(B)(C)(D)	9 (A)(B)(C)(D)	12 (A)(B)(C)(D)	15 (A)(B)(C)(D)

ANSWER SHEET

Part 5: Mathematics Knowledge (MK)

1 Ⓐ Ⓑ Ⓒ Ⓓ	6 Ⓐ Ⓑ Ⓒ Ⓓ	11 Ⓐ Ⓑ Ⓒ Ⓓ	16 Ⓐ Ⓑ Ⓒ Ⓓ	21 Ⓐ Ⓑ Ⓒ Ⓓ
2 Ⓐ Ⓑ Ⓒ Ⓓ	7 Ⓐ Ⓑ Ⓒ Ⓓ	12 Ⓐ Ⓑ Ⓒ Ⓓ	17 Ⓐ Ⓑ Ⓒ Ⓓ	22 Ⓐ Ⓑ Ⓒ Ⓓ
3 Ⓐ Ⓑ Ⓒ Ⓓ	8 Ⓐ Ⓑ Ⓒ Ⓓ	13 Ⓐ Ⓑ Ⓒ Ⓓ	18 Ⓐ Ⓑ Ⓒ Ⓓ	23 Ⓐ Ⓑ Ⓒ Ⓓ
4 Ⓐ Ⓑ Ⓒ Ⓓ	9 Ⓐ Ⓑ Ⓒ Ⓓ	14 Ⓐ Ⓑ Ⓒ Ⓓ	19 Ⓐ Ⓑ Ⓒ Ⓓ	24 Ⓐ Ⓑ Ⓒ Ⓓ
5 Ⓐ Ⓑ Ⓒ Ⓓ	10 Ⓐ Ⓑ Ⓒ Ⓓ	15 Ⓐ Ⓑ Ⓒ Ⓓ	20 Ⓐ Ⓑ Ⓒ Ⓓ	25 Ⓐ Ⓑ Ⓒ Ⓓ

Part 6: Electronics Information (EI)

1 Ⓐ Ⓑ Ⓒ Ⓓ	5 Ⓐ Ⓑ Ⓒ Ⓓ	9 Ⓐ Ⓑ Ⓒ Ⓓ	13 Ⓐ Ⓑ Ⓒ Ⓓ	17 Ⓐ Ⓑ Ⓒ Ⓓ
2 Ⓐ Ⓑ Ⓒ Ⓓ	6 Ⓐ Ⓑ Ⓒ Ⓓ	10 Ⓐ Ⓑ Ⓒ Ⓓ	14 Ⓐ Ⓑ Ⓒ Ⓓ	18 Ⓐ Ⓑ Ⓒ Ⓓ
3 Ⓐ Ⓑ Ⓒ Ⓓ	7 Ⓐ Ⓑ Ⓒ Ⓓ	11 Ⓐ Ⓑ Ⓒ Ⓓ	15 Ⓐ Ⓑ Ⓒ Ⓓ	19 Ⓐ Ⓑ Ⓒ Ⓓ
4 Ⓐ Ⓑ Ⓒ Ⓓ	8 Ⓐ Ⓑ Ⓒ Ⓓ	12 Ⓐ Ⓑ Ⓒ Ⓓ	16 Ⓐ Ⓑ Ⓒ Ⓓ	20 Ⓐ Ⓑ Ⓒ Ⓓ

Part 7: Automotive and Shop Information (AS)

1 Ⓐ Ⓑ Ⓒ Ⓓ	6 Ⓐ Ⓑ Ⓒ Ⓓ	11 Ⓐ Ⓑ Ⓒ Ⓓ	16 Ⓐ Ⓑ Ⓒ Ⓓ	21 Ⓐ Ⓑ Ⓒ Ⓓ
2 Ⓐ Ⓑ Ⓒ Ⓓ	7 Ⓐ Ⓑ Ⓒ Ⓓ	12 Ⓐ Ⓑ Ⓒ Ⓓ	17 Ⓐ Ⓑ Ⓒ Ⓓ	22 Ⓐ Ⓑ Ⓒ Ⓓ
3 Ⓐ Ⓑ Ⓒ Ⓓ	8 Ⓐ Ⓑ Ⓒ Ⓓ	13 Ⓐ Ⓑ Ⓒ Ⓓ	18 Ⓐ Ⓑ Ⓒ Ⓓ	23 Ⓐ Ⓑ Ⓒ Ⓓ
4 Ⓐ Ⓑ Ⓒ Ⓓ	9 Ⓐ Ⓑ Ⓒ Ⓓ	14 Ⓐ Ⓑ Ⓒ Ⓓ	19 Ⓐ Ⓑ Ⓒ Ⓓ	24 Ⓐ Ⓑ Ⓒ Ⓓ
5 Ⓐ Ⓑ Ⓒ Ⓓ	10 Ⓐ Ⓑ Ⓒ Ⓓ	15 Ⓐ Ⓑ Ⓒ Ⓓ	20 Ⓐ Ⓑ Ⓒ Ⓓ	25 Ⓐ Ⓑ Ⓒ Ⓓ

Part 8: Mechanical Comprehension (MC)

1 Ⓐ Ⓑ Ⓒ Ⓓ	6 Ⓐ Ⓑ Ⓒ Ⓓ	11 Ⓐ Ⓑ Ⓒ Ⓓ	16 Ⓐ Ⓑ Ⓒ Ⓓ	21 Ⓐ Ⓑ Ⓒ Ⓓ
2 Ⓐ Ⓑ Ⓒ Ⓓ	7 Ⓐ Ⓑ Ⓒ Ⓓ	12 Ⓐ Ⓑ Ⓒ Ⓓ	17 Ⓐ Ⓑ Ⓒ Ⓓ	22 Ⓐ Ⓑ Ⓒ Ⓓ
3 Ⓐ Ⓑ Ⓒ Ⓓ	8 Ⓐ Ⓑ Ⓒ Ⓓ	13 Ⓐ Ⓑ Ⓒ Ⓓ	18 Ⓐ Ⓑ Ⓒ Ⓓ	23 Ⓐ Ⓑ Ⓒ Ⓓ
4 Ⓐ Ⓑ Ⓒ Ⓓ	9 Ⓐ Ⓑ Ⓒ Ⓓ	14 Ⓐ Ⓑ Ⓒ Ⓓ	19 Ⓐ Ⓑ Ⓒ Ⓓ	24 Ⓐ Ⓑ Ⓒ Ⓓ
5 Ⓐ Ⓑ Ⓒ Ⓓ	10 Ⓐ Ⓑ Ⓒ Ⓓ	15 Ⓐ Ⓑ Ⓒ Ⓓ	20 Ⓐ Ⓑ Ⓒ Ⓓ	25 Ⓐ Ⓑ Ⓒ Ⓓ

Part 9: Assembling Objects (AO)

1 Ⓐ Ⓑ Ⓒ Ⓓ	6 Ⓐ Ⓑ Ⓒ Ⓓ	11 Ⓐ Ⓑ Ⓒ Ⓓ	16 Ⓐ Ⓑ Ⓒ Ⓓ	21 Ⓐ Ⓑ Ⓒ Ⓓ
2 Ⓐ Ⓑ Ⓒ Ⓓ	7 Ⓐ Ⓑ Ⓒ Ⓓ	12 Ⓐ Ⓑ Ⓒ Ⓓ	17 Ⓐ Ⓑ Ⓒ Ⓓ	22 Ⓐ Ⓑ Ⓒ Ⓓ
3 Ⓐ Ⓑ Ⓒ Ⓓ	8 Ⓐ Ⓑ Ⓒ Ⓓ	13 Ⓐ Ⓑ Ⓒ Ⓓ	18 Ⓐ Ⓑ Ⓒ Ⓓ	23 Ⓐ Ⓑ Ⓒ Ⓓ
4 Ⓐ Ⓑ Ⓒ Ⓓ	9 Ⓐ Ⓑ Ⓒ Ⓓ	14 Ⓐ Ⓑ Ⓒ Ⓓ	19 Ⓐ Ⓑ Ⓒ Ⓓ	24 Ⓐ Ⓑ Ⓒ Ⓓ
5 Ⓐ Ⓑ Ⓒ Ⓓ	10 Ⓐ Ⓑ Ⓒ Ⓓ	15 Ⓐ Ⓑ Ⓒ Ⓓ	20 Ⓐ Ⓑ Ⓒ Ⓓ	25 Ⓐ Ⓑ Ⓒ Ⓓ

Part 1: General Science (GS)

Time: 11 minutes; 25 questions

Directions: In this section, you will be tested on your knowledge of concepts in science generally reviewed in high school. For each question, select the best answer and mark the corresponding oval on your answer sheet.

1. Those wishing to reduce the "bad" cholesterol levels in their blood should avoid

   (A) polyunsaturated fats
   (B) carbohydrates
   (C) monounsaturated fats
   (D) saturated fats

2. Water at sea level freezes at what temperature?

   (A) 373 K
   (B) 0°F
   (C) 100°C
   (D) 32°F

3. Which of the following subatomic particles has the largest mass?

   (A) proton
   (B) electron
   (C) positron
   (D) neutrino

4. Which of the following is an example of an autotroph?

   (A) a vulture
   (B) an apple tree
   (C) a toadstool
   (D) a sea anemone

5. The period from 4.6 billion years to 570 million years ago is called the

   (A) Phanerozoic eon
   (B) Mesozoic era
   (C) Paleozoic era
   (D) Precambrian eon

6. Which of the following planets is larger than Earth?

   (A) Mars
   (B) Mercury
   (C) Uranus
   (D) Venus

7. When these fall into the Earth's gravitational field, they are seen as "falling stars."

   (A) asteroids
   (B) meteoroids
   (C) comets
   (D) craters

8. The study of interactions between organisms and their interrelationships with the physical environment is known as

   (A) cytology
   (B) ecology
   (C) physiology
   (D) embryology

9. Most absorption of nutrients from food happens in the human body's

   (A) stomach
   (B) pylorus
   (C) small intestine
   (D) large intestine

10. High tide occurs

    (A) four times a year
    (B) once a day
    (C) once a year
    (D) twice a day

11. Which is NOT a fact according to Newton's Law of Gravitation?

    (A) If the mass of the Earth were doubled, the gravitational force on the Earth would double.
    (B) The force exerted on the Earth by the Sun is equal and opposite to the force exerted on the Sun by the Earth.
    (C) If the mass of the Earth were doubled, the gravitational force on the Earth would quadruple.
    (D) If the mass of the Sun were doubled, the force it exerts on the Earth would double.

12. Which of the following types of electromagnetic radiation has the longest wavelength and lowest frequency?

    (A) radio waves
    (B) microwaves
    (C) gamma rays
    (D) visible light

13. The ratio by which light is slowed down by a medium is known as the medium's

    (A) electromagnetic spectrum
    (B) angle of incidence
    (C) reflection
    (D) refractive index

14. Which of the following has the highest pH?

    (A) vinegar
    (B) water
    (C) baking soda
    (D) cranberry juice

15. Foods rich in carbohydrates include all of the following except

    (A) potatoes
    (B) pasta
    (C) fruits
    (D) almonds

16. Members of an order are more alike than members of a

    (A) class
    (B) family
    (C) genus
    (D) species

17. The number of protons in the nucleus of an atom is its

    (A) atomic symbol
    (B) atomic weight
    (C) atomic number
    (D) atomic radius

18. The system of muscles that allows the lungs to expand and contract, drawing air in and out is the

    (A) diaphragm
    (B) pharynx
    (C) trachea
    (D) bronchioles

19. The atom of an element with an atomic number of 17 must have

    (A) 17 electrons
    (B) 17 protons
    (C) 17 neutrons
    (D) an atomic mass of 17

20. Because mushrooms absorb nutrients from decaying leaves, they are classified as

    (A) autotrophs
    (B) anaerobes
    (C) saprophytes
    (D) protozoans

21. The blood vessel with the LEAST oxygenated blood is the

    (A) pulmonary artery
    (B) aorta
    (C) pulmonary vein
    (D) arterioles

22. Saliva in the mouth begins the process of breaking down

    (A) starch
    (B) fat
    (C) protein
    (D) vitamins

23. In which of the following kingdoms do cells lack nuclei?

    (A) Fungi
    (B) Monera
    (C) Plantae
    (D) Protista

24. An atom that is not electrically neutral is called a(n)

    (A) isotope
    (B) positron
    (C) ion
    (D) allotrope

25. Which of the following is an example of a metamorphic rock?

    (A) granite
    (B) marble
    (C) limestone
    (D) shale

STOP. IF YOU FINISH BEFORE THE TIME IS UP, YOU MAY CHECK OVER YOUR WORK ON THIS PART ONLY.

Part 2: Arithmetic Reasoning (AR)

Time: 36 minutes; 30 questions

Directions: In this section, you are tested on your ability to use arithmetic. For each question, select the best answer and mark the corresponding oval on your answer sheet.

1. A certain machine caps 5 bottles every 2 seconds. At this rate, how many bottles will be capped in 1 minute?

   (A) 75
   (B) 150
   (C) 225
   (D) 300

2. Jonah travelled 650 miles on his most recent trip and averaged 25 miles to the gallon. If gasoline cost $1.30 per gallon, how much did he spend on his trip?

   (A) $26.00
   (B) $27.30
   (C) $32.50
   (D) $33.80

3. If there are approximately 3.86 liters in a gallon, and gasoline costs $1.54 per gallon, to the nearest penny what is the cost of a liter of gasoline?

   (A) $0.35
   (B) $0.40
   (C) $0.44
   (D) $0.47

4. How many minutes are there in one week?

   (A) 3,600
   (B) 7,200
   (C) 10,080
   (D) 86,400

5. Pat deposited 15% of last week's take-home pay into a savings account. If she deposited $37.50, what was last week's take-home pay?

   (A) $56.25
   (B) $112.50
   (C) $225.00
   (D) $250.00

6. If the ratio of males to females in a group of students is 3:5, which of the following could be the total number of students in the group?

   (A) 148
   (B) 150
   (C) 152
   (D) 154

7. A car travels 288 miles in 6 hours. At that rate, how many miles will it travel in 8 hours?

   (A) 360
   (B) 368
   (C) 376
   (D) 384

8. Martin's average score after 4 tests is 89. What score on the 5th test would bring Martin's average up to exactly 90?

   (A) 91
   (B) 92
   (C) 93
   (D) 94

9. In 2010, the population of town A was 9,400 and the population of town B was 7,600. Since then, each year the population of town A has decreased by 100 and the population of town B has increased by 100. Assuming that in each case the rate continues, in what year will the two populations be equal?

   (A) 2019
   (B) 2020
   (C) 2027
   (D) 2028

10. One number is 5 times another number and their sum is −60. What is the lesser of the two numbers?

   (A) −10
   (B) −12
   (C) −48
   (D) −50

11. John gets paid $6.00 for each of the first 40 toy cars he makes in a week. For any additional toy cars beyond 40 his pay increases by 50%. How much does John get paid in a week in which he makes 48 toy cars?

(A) $288
(B) $300
(C) $312
(D) $321

12. If a bora = 2 fedis, and a fedi = 3 glecks, how many boras are equal to 48 glecks?

(A) 8
(B) 16
(C) 32
(D) 96

13. Nine temperature readings were taken, one reading every four hours, with the first reading taken at 12 p.m. (that is, at noon). What will be the time when the final reading is taken?

(A) 4 p.m.
(B) 8 p.m.
(C) 12 a.m.
(D) 8 a.m.

14. A school raised monthly tuition payments from $225.00 per month to $300.00 per month. The percent of the tuition increase is which of the following?

(A) 25%
(B) $33\frac{1}{3}\%$
(C) $66\frac{1}{2}\%$
(D) 75%

15. A truck going at a rate of 20 miles per hour takes 6 hours to complete a trip. How many fewer hours would the trip have taken if the truck were travelling at a rate of 30 miles per hour?

(A) 4
(B) 3
(C) 2
(D) 1

16. If a barrel has the capacity to hold 75 gallons, how many gallons does it contain when it is $\frac{3}{5}$ full?

(A) 45
(B) 48
(C) 54
(D) 60

17. If a salary of $45,000 is subject to a 40% deduction, the new salary is:

(A) $18,000
(B) $27,000
(C) $30,000
(D) $36,000

18. 8! =

(A) 8
(B) 64
(C) 40,000
(D) 40,320

19. Fifteen people chip in $40 dollars each to throw a birthday bash for a mutual friend. If 35% of the money is spent on a group gift and the rest is spent on the party, how much was spent on the party?

(A) $210
(B) $300
(C) $350
(D) $390

20. If an employee worked a total of $33\frac{1}{2}$ hours over five days, what was the average amount of time that the employee worked each day?

(A) 6 hours, 35 minutes
(B) 6 hours, 40 minutes
(C) 6 hours, 42 minutes
(D) 6 hours, 45 minutes

21. If a train starting out at point A travels 180 miles at a rate of 60 miles per hour and then 150 miles at a rate of 75 miles per hour before arriving at point B, what was the average rate, in miles per hour, for the entire trip?

(A) 66
(B) 67.5
(C) 68.5
(D) 70

22. After being discounted by 20%, a bicycle sells for $140.00. What was the original price of the bicycle?

    (A) $155.00
    (B) $162.00
    (C) $175.00
    (D) $180.00

23. A checking account has a balance of $1,162.76. After a check for $352.68 is deposited into the account and three checks are drawn from the account for the amounts of $152.45, $82.85, and $255.50, what is the new balance for the checking account?

    (A) $1,024.54
    (B) $1,024.64
    (C) $1,025.54
    (D) $1,025.64

24. Harold works 4.5 hours a day, 3 days each week after school. He is paid $4.25 per hour. How much is his weekly pay rounded to the next highest cent?

    (A) $13.50
    (B) $19.13
    (C) $54.00
    (D) $57.38

25. Convert $\frac{6}{24}$ into a decimal.

    (A) 0.2
    (B) 0.25
    (C) 0.4
    (D) 4.0

26. What is the total cost of 4 sheets of 23¢ stamps, 2 sheets of 37¢ stamps, and 3 sheets of 60¢ stamps if each sheet has 100 stamps?

    (A) $336
    (B) $346
    (C) $356
    (D) $366

27. The Pacific standard time (PST) in Los Angeles is 3 hours earlier than the eastern standard time (EST) in New York. A plane leaves Los Angeles at 5:30 p.m. PST and arrives in New York City at 12:45 a.m. EST. How long did the flight take?

    (A) 4 hours, 15 minutes
    (B) 4 hours, 45 minutes
    (C) 6 hours, 45 minutes
    (D) 7 hours, 15 minutes

28. After the price of a digital camera is discounted 25%, the camera sells for $120. What was the original price of the camera?

    (A) $145
    (B) $150
    (C) $160
    (D) $180

29. The square root of 225 is

    (A) 5
    (B) 15
    (C) 25
    (D) 112

30. If it takes 20 minutes to type 5 pages, how long will it take to type a 162-page document?

    (A) 10 hours, 12 minutes
    (B) 10 hours, 36 minutes
    (C) 10 hours, 45 minutes
    (D) 10 hours, 48 minutes

STOP. IF YOU FINISH BEFORE THE TIME IS UP, YOU MAY CHECK OVER YOUR WORK ON THIS PART ONLY.

Part 3: Word Knowledge (WK)

Time: 11 minutes; 35 questions

<u>Directions</u>: In this section, you are tested on the meaning of words. Each of the following questions has an underlined word. Select the answer that most nearly means the same as the underlined word and mark the corresponding oval on your answer sheet.

1. <u>Listless</u> most nearly means

    (A) capable
    (B) lethargic
    (C) talkative
    (D) bungled

2. His ability to <u>comprehend</u> complex ideas made him a great teacher.

    (A) create
    (B) loosen
    (C) understand
    (D) compute

3. Whichever one scores the most points will be the <u>victor</u>.

    (A) singer
    (B) manufacturer
    (C) best
    (D) winner

4. <u>Lackadaisical</u> most nearly means

    (A) talented
    (B) relaxed
    (C) actual
    (D) personable

5. It was his <u>contention</u> that more money should be spent on education.

    (A) celebration
    (B) position
    (C) ideal
    (D) sacrifice

6. The arrest wasn't even <u>newsworthy</u>.

    (A) notable
    (B) defaming
    (C) credible
    (D) safe

7. His attendance in class was, if anything, <u>sporadic</u>.

    (A) latent
    (B) constant
    (C) irregular
    (D) common

8. <u>Potential</u> most nearly means

    (A) scary
    (B) trustable
    (C) telling
    (D) possible

9. <u>Blacklisted</u> most nearly means

    (A) sacred
    (B) barred
    (C) old-fashioned
    (D) barren

10. It is <u>presumptuous</u> to expect a hundred volunteers for such a tough task.

    (A) exciting
    (B) predictable
    (C) satisfying
    (D) overconfident

11. A <u>memento</u> can provide a way to remember your vacation once you are home.

    (A) sacrifice
    (B) emblem
    (C) souvenir
    (D) symbol

12. The school's president is far too concerned with the <u>legacy</u> he will leave.

    (A) memory
    (B) salary
    (C) tension
    (D) grace

13. The economy has some parents worried that their children's future is in jeopardy.

    (A) limbo
    (B) danger
    (C) custody
    (D) paradise

14. Integrity most nearly means

    (A) ability
    (B) coercion
    (C) togetherness
    (D) honesty

15. He was punished too harshly for such a minor infraction.

    (A) aptitude
    (B) belief
    (C) gift
    (D) violation

16. Collective most nearly means

    (A) group
    (B) rare
    (C) soft
    (D) free

17. Hoax most nearly means

    (A) trick
    (B) story
    (C) treat
    (D) complication

18. The genesis of the idea was scribbled on a napkin.

    (A) cancellation
    (B) detail
    (C) origin
    (D) craft

19. The brothers' feud goes back to their childhood days.

    (A) love
    (B) dispute
    (C) sensitivity
    (D) belief

20. Fraudulent most nearly means

    (A) pretty
    (B) fake
    (C) disgusting
    (D) sanitary

21. Adept most nearly means

    (A) older
    (B) talkative
    (C) cautious
    (D) skilled

22. She is an ardent supporter of families' rights.

    (A) passionate
    (B) testy
    (C) unaffiliated
    (D) tired

23. The town suffered from rampant overcrowding and crime.

    (A) overstated
    (B) widespread
    (C) old
    (D) predictable

24. Such a puny fence stands no chance with that big dog.

    (A) satisfying
    (B) colorful
    (C) ghastly
    (D) weak

25. Sinister most nearly means

    (A) brotherhood
    (B) believable
    (C) gaudy
    (D) evil

26. Witty most nearly means

    (A) sulking
    (B) bloody
    (C) clever
    (D) careless

27. The witness's <u>vivid</u> account of the crime certainly opened the jury's eyes.

    (A) clear
    (B) unobstructed
    (C) false
    (D) condescending

28. <u>Relinquish</u> most nearly means

    (A) concede
    (B) color
    (C) trick
    (D) berate

29. I can only hope that these good times <u>recur</u>.

    (A) disappear
    (B) satiate
    (C) return
    (D) let go

30. <u>Incite</u> most nearly means

    (A) induce
    (B) intrigue
    (C) blow
    (D) react

31. It was wise of George to <u>implement</u> such a bold strategy while his critics were distracted.

    (A) enact
    (B) suggest
    (C) trivialize
    (D) investigate

32. <u>Query</u> most nearly means

    (A) telling
    (B) question
    (C) bogus
    (D) captive

33. No one should be in awe of such a <u>timid</u> animal.

    (A) crazy
    (B) cowardly
    (C) dangerous
    (D) salty

34. <u>Colleague</u> most nearly means

    (A) enemy
    (B) savior
    (C) peer
    (D) pedant

35. His opponent proved to have a <u>potent</u> mixture of toughness and intelligence.

    (A) costly
    (B) derelict
    (C) sad
    (D) powerful

STOP. IF YOU FINISH BEFORE THE TIME IS UP, YOU MAY CHECK OVER YOUR WORK ON THIS PART ONLY.

Part 4: Paragraph Comprehension (PC)

Time: 13 minutes; 15 questions

Directions: This section contains paragraphs followed by incomplete statements or questions. Read the paragraph and select the answer that best completes the statements or answers the questions that follow, and mark the corresponding oval on your answer sheet.

The character of Sherlock Holmes illustrates author Arthur Conan Doyle's admiration for the logical mind. In each case that Holmes investigates, he is able to use the most seemingly insignificant evidence to track down his opponent. In fact, Holmes's painstaking attention to detail often reminds the reader of Charles Darwin's *On the Origin of the Species*, published some 20 years earlier.

1. The author compares Sherlock Holmes to Charles Darwin in order to

    (A) show Holmes's educational background
    (B) explain evolution
    (C) show that both were logical and meticulous
    (D) praise Darwin for his research skills

The climate of a major city is often very different from the climate of the surrounding areas. However, the geographic differences between the city and the country do not have to be dramatic to show major climatic differences. Even between the center of a city and its suburbs, there are often differences in air temperature, humidity, wind speed, and direction. Tall buildings, paved streets, and parking lots affect such patterns as wind flow and water runoff.

2. According to the passage, the relationship between cities and climate is

    (A) based on pollution controls
    (B) based on urban structures and the environment
    (C) based on city politics
    (D) based on rural areas

Marianne had seen it all on television—the Cuban Missile Crisis, man's first steps on the Moon, the fall of the Berlin Wall, even the economic boom of the 1990s. So when she won the lottery and the news vans started gathering outside her house, it didn't yet dawn on her just how much her life would be changed. A little attention doesn't hurt you, she thought. But when she stepped outside to an army of eager young reporters, she began to wonder if there weren't bigger events somewhere in need of coverage.

3. The character in the passage would probably do which of the following?

    (A) wear revealing clothing
    (B) watch news on TV
    (C) dye her hair bright colors
    (D) refuse the money publicly

In the "Gunpowder Plot" of 1605, a group of conspirators planned to blow up the English king and Parliament. The conspirators were a group of English Catholics who objected to the government's religious policies and who decided to carry out a daring assassination. They rented a cellar under the Palace of Westminster and hid 20 barrels of gunpowder there, intending to explode the gunpowder when the king and Parliament met. However, the conspirators were unable to keep the plot secret and their infamous plan was foiled.

4. The word *infamous* most nearly means

    (A) heroic
    (B) funny
    (C) secret
    (D) notorious

Just as Johnny hit yet another red light, his cell phone began to ring. He looked at his watch and saw that he was already 20 minutes late to what might be the most important meeting of his career. Reaching for his phone, he knocked over his drink, spilling piping hot coffee all over his lap. He screamed loudly in his car, and though it looked like no one could hear him, a woman nearby ran away from the edge of the car quickly.

5. Johnny's attitude is

    (A) perturbed
    (B) tender
    (C) excited
    (D) snooty

The presence or absence of water can have a dramatic effect on the plants in a given environment. The desert, for example, is a biologically complex area where rain is often violent and unpredictable. Since desert plants are dependent on the occasional rain for survival, they must act quickly to make the most of it when it appears. Many desert plants, as a result, can complete an entire life cycle in a matter of months or even weeks. The more barren a desert is, and thus the less rain, the rarer and more astounding these life cycles and the blooms that accompany them will be.

6. According to the passage, the life cycle of desert plants

    (A) is unrelated to rain levels
    (B) is directly related to their color
    (C) is akin to that of local wildlife
    (D) may be short and dynamic

It is a common belief among writers that great art is born from experience. However, some of the greatest writers in literary history have been people with a very limited knowledge of the world. Novelist Jane Austen, for example, didn't venture far beyond her circle of family and friends. And yet, just by observing the people around her, she was able to write acclaimed comedies about love and marriage. Similarly, Robert Louis Stevenson, the author of classic adventures such as *Treasure Island* and *Kidnapped*, wrote many of his adventures without having similar experiences. Their achievements illustrate that if you have a good imagination, you can write a novel, no matter how unadventurous your life may seem.

7. Based on the information in the passage, some of the greatest writers

(A) always write about people and their social scenes
(B) write only adventure stories
(C) rely on imagination and not just experience
(D) get advice from close family and friends

Tania is an extremely versatile actress. In a recent series of plays, she played a schoolteacher, two divorcees, three best friends, and a stepmother. She played a divorcee throughout the first play, but in subsequent plays she often played more than one part. Who would have suspected her acting prowess a few years ago when she ran crying off the stage with a terrible case of stage fright?

8. The word *prowess* most nearly means

(A) knowledge
(B) disaster
(C) talent
(D) bias

Many people dream about living on a coral island, but probably few of us would be able to describe one with any accuracy. Popular books and films create a romantic image of these islands, but it is not always as nice if seen from the land. Beneath the waves, however, the coral island is a fantastic and very beautiful world, depending entirely upon a complex web of interrelationships between plants and animals. The environment of the coral reef is formed over thousands of years by the life cycle of vast numbers of animals.

9. One logical conclusion to draw from this passage is

(A) coral animals are more colorful than other animals
(B) the true beauty of coral islands is underwater
(C) all coral islands are tropical paradises
(D) coral islands are formed mostly by volcanos

Questions 10 and 11 both refer to the passage below.

Few of the immigrants of the period just before the turn of the century found life in America easy. Many of those who lacked professional skills and did not speak English found themselves living in slum conditions in the busy cities of the Northeast, exploited by their employers and trapped at poverty level. Around the turn of the century, a number of different organizations made efforts to help these newly arrived immigrants adapt to American life. While many groups emerged as leaders in these efforts to aid immigration, one organization preached a much colder answer to adapting to America.

A conservative group called the Daughters of the American Revolution approached immigrants with the expectation that newcomers should completely adopt American customs and culture. Consequently, they supported laws that required immigrants to take oaths of loyalty and to pass English language tests. They also tried to discourage the use of languages other than English in the schools.

10. Which of the following best tells what this passage is about?

(A) how some sought to assimilate immigrants into America
(B) the cultural contributions offered by immigrants
(C) the history of immigration in the United States
(D) how immigrant life affected U.S. cities

11. The author implies that the Daughters of the American Revolution

(A) understood the difficulties facing new immigrants
(B) were ruthless in their intentions toward immigrants
(C) believed that immigrants would not survive in America
(D) preached fitting in, not standing out

Some animals use coloring to safeguard themselves from predators. In certain cases, an animal adapts in color, shape, and behavior in order to blend into its environment. The camouflage of the pale green tree frog is a good example of this. The tree frog blends so perfectly into its surroundings that when it sits motionless it is all but invisible against a background of leaves. Another type of camouflage, shown by zebras and leopards, is a pattern that diverts the eye from the outline of the animal. The chameleon, even more versatile than these, changes color in just a few minutes to match whatever surface it happens to be lying on or clinging to.

12. According to the passage, a reason that animals use camouflage is

   (A)   to divert the eye from the animal's outline
   (B)   to make nesting more safe
   (C)   so that frogs' and chameleons' habitats remain protected
   (D)   to ensure predatory dominance

Perhaps the biggest surprise of the Voyager mission was the discovery on the moons of Jupiter of intense volcanic activity. First seen on the moon Io, the eruptions were recognized as plumes of dust and gas and were immediately noticeable on the Voyager photographs. Further inspection revealed at least seven such events occurring all at once on Io's otherwise frigid surface. At other points, scientists detected three hot spots believed to be ponds of molten lava, sulphur, or sodium. The largest of these hot lakes was estimated to have a greater surface area than the state of Hawaii.

13. What was the most unexpected fact to emerge from the Voyager photographs?

   (A)   the size of Io's molten lakes
   (B)   the discovery of volcanic activity on Io
   (C)   the disappearance of impact sites on Europa
   (D)   the evidence of asteroid bombardment on all four moons

Questions 14 and 15 both refer to the passage below.

Most people think that the Hula Hoop was a fad born in the 1950s, but in fact people were doing much the same thing with circular hoops made from grapevines and stiff grasses all over the ancient world. More than 3,000 years ago, children in Egypt played with large hoops of dried grapevines. The toy was propelled along the ground with a stick or swung around at the waist. During the fourteenth century, a "hooping" craze swept England, and was equally popular among adults and children.

The word *hula* became associated with the toy in the early 1800s when British sailors visited the Hawaiian Islands and noted the similarity between hooping and hula dancing. In 1957, an Australian company began making wood rings for sale in retail stores. The item attracted the attention of Wham-O, a fledgling California toy manufacturer. The plastic Hula Hoop was introduced in 1958 and was an instant hit.

14. According to the passage, all of the following statements are true EXCEPT

   (A)   most people do not appreciate the origins of the Hula Hoop
   (B)   early precursors of the Hula Hoop were made of grape leaves and stiff grasses
   (C)   early precursors to the Hula Hoop were primarily children's toys
   (D)   the Hula Hoop was an early success for the toy maker Wham-O

15. The author's primary purpose in this passage is to

   (A)   describe the way that fads like the Hula Hoop come and go
   (B)   discuss the origins of the Hula Hoop
   (C)   explain how the Hula Hoop got its name
   (D)   question the reasons for the Hula Hoop's popularity

STOP. IF YOU FINISH BEFORE THE TIME IS UP, YOU MAY CHECK OVER YOUR WORK ON THIS PART ONLY.

Part 5: Mathematics Knowledge (MK)

Time: 24 minutes; 25 questions

<u>Directions</u>: In this section, you will be tested on your knowledge of basic mathematics. For each question, select the best answer and mark the corresponding oval on your answer sheet.

1. If $\frac{3}{4} + 1\frac{1}{3} = \frac{5}{6} - x$, then x =

   (A) $-2\frac{11}{12}$

   (B) $-1\frac{1}{4}$

   (C) $\frac{1}{6}$

   (D) $1\frac{1}{4}$

2. For all a, $(3a + 4)(4a - 3) =$

   (A) $3a^2 - 4$
   (B) $9a^2 - 4$
   (C) $12a^2 + 7a - 12$
   (D) $9a^2 - 16$

3. If $2m > 24$ and $3m < 48$, which of the following could NOT be a possible value for m?

   (A) 13
   (B) 14
   (C) 15
   (D) 16

4. $\sqrt{75} + \sqrt{108} =$

   (A) $11\sqrt{3}$

   (B) $6\sqrt{5}$

   (C) $5\sqrt{6}$

   (D) $\sqrt{183}$

5. In the figure above, if *PQRS* is a square, what is the value of *a*?

   (A) $\frac{9}{2}$

   (B) 5

   (C) 7

   (D) 9

6. In triangle *ABC*, the degree measures of the three interior angles are in the ratio of 1:2:3. What is the difference in the degree measures between the largest and the smallest angles?

   (A) 30
   (B) 60
   (C) 90
   (D) 120

7. What is the perimeter of a right triangle with perpendicular sides of lengths 3 and 6?

   (A) $9 + 3\sqrt{5}$

   (B) $9 + 5\sqrt{3}$

   (C) $12 + 3\sqrt{3}$

   (D) 18

8. In the diagram above, if $AD = BE = 6$, $AE = 8$ and $CD = 3BC$, then $BC =$

(A) 4
(B) 3
(C) 2
(D) 1

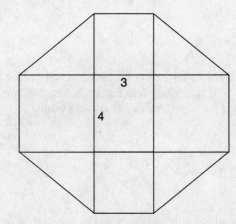

9. The figure above is composed of nine regions: four squares, four triangles, and one rectangle. If the rectangle has sides length 4 and width 3, what is the perimeter of the entire figure?

(A) 30
(B) 34
(C) 40
(D) 48

10. If $\frac{\sqrt{n}}{3}$ is an even integer, which of the following could be the value of n?

(A) 27
(B) 48
(C) 81
(D) 144

11. Gheri is n years old. Carl is 6 years younger than Gheri and 2 years older than Jean. What is the sum of the ages of all three?

(A) $3n + 4$
(B) $3n - 4$
(C) $3n - 8$
(D) $3n - 14$

12. Which of the following is NOT a prime number?

(A) 2
(B) 37
(C) 51
(D) 67

13. What is the area of a circle whose circumference is 2π?

(A) $\frac{\pi}{2}$
(B) π
(C) 2π
(D) 4π

14. A high school band is composed of 13 freshmen, 20 sophomores, 16 juniors, and 15 seniors. What is the probability that a band member chosen at random will be a sophomore?

(A) $\frac{2}{5}$
(B) $\frac{1}{3}$
(C) $\frac{4}{13}$
(D) $\frac{5}{16}$

15. If $k - 3 = -\frac{5}{3}$, then $3 - k =$

(A) $-\frac{5}{3}$
(B) $-\frac{3}{5}$
(C) $\frac{3}{5}$
(D) $\frac{5}{3}$

16. If $x \neq 0$ and $\frac{3x}{5} = 3x^2$, then $x =$

(A) $\frac{1}{5}$
(B) $\frac{3}{5}$
(C) 3
(D) 5

17. If a, b, c, and d are all positive numbers, $a = 2b$, $\frac{1}{2}b = c$, and $4c = 3d$, what is the value of $\frac{d}{a}$?

    (A) $\frac{1}{3}$

    (B) $\frac{3}{4}$

    (C) $\frac{4}{3}$

    (D) 3

18. How many rectangular tiles with dimensions of 3 inches by 4 inches are needed to cover a rectangular area with dimensions of 2 feet and 3 feet?

    (A) 60
    (B) 72
    (C) 120
    (D) 144

19. For how many integer values of x will $\frac{7}{x}$ be greater than $\frac{1}{4}$ and less than $\frac{1}{3}$?

    (A) 6
    (B) 7
    (C) 12
    (D) 28

20. A circular hole is covered by a circular cover that has a diameter of 14 inches. If the hole has a diameter of 12 inches, how much greater than the area of the hole is the area of the cover, in square inches?

    (A) π
    (B) 13π
    (C) 36π
    (D) 52π

21. Which of the following is closest in value to the decimal 0.40?

    (A) $\frac{1}{3}$

    (B) $\frac{3}{8}$

    (C) $\frac{1}{2}$

    (D) $\frac{4}{7}$

22. If x oranges cost the same as y peaches, peaches cost 39 cents each, and the cost of each orange is the same, how many dollars does each orange cost?

    (A) $\frac{39y}{100x}$

    (B) $\frac{39x}{100y}$

    (B) $\frac{3,900}{xy}$

    (D) $\frac{39x}{y}$

23. A class of 40 students is to be divided into smaller groups. If each group is to contain 3, 4, or 5 people, what is the largest number of groups possible?

    (A)   10
    (B)   12
    (C)   13
    (D)   14

24. If the area of a triangle is 36 and its base is 9, what is the length of the altitude to that base?

    (A)   4
    (B)   6
    (C)   8
    (D)   12

25. If $x = -5$, then $2x^2 - 6x + 5 =$

    (A)   15
    (B)   25
    (C)   85
    (D)   135

STOP. IF YOU FINISH BEFORE THE TIME IS UP, YOU MAY CHECK OVER YOUR WORK ON THIS PART ONLY.

Part 6: Electronics Information (EI)

Time: 9 minutes; 20 questions

Directions: In this section, you will be tested on your knowledge of electronics basics. For each question, select the best answer and mark the corresponding oval on your answer sheet.

1. Voltage and current are

   (A) inversely proportional
   (B) directly proportional
   (C) unrelated
   (D) sometimes proportional

2. For a current-carrying wire with a DC source providing a constant 100 amps, which of the following set-ups will produce the largest magnetic field strength at any given point?

   (A) a simple single-loop circuit made of two meters of wire
   (B) a simple single-loop circuit made of five meters of wire
   (C) wrapping the two meters of current-carrying wire in five coiled loops around an iron nail
   (D) wrapping the five meters of current-carrying wire in five coiled loops

3. Which of the following causes the least resistance to a consistent direct current?

   (A) a capacitor
   (B) a fixed resistor
   (C) a variable resistor
   (D) an inductor

4. Which is the base in the transistor symbol below?

   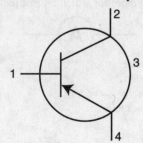

   (A) 1
   (B) 2
   (C) 3
   (D) 4

5. If each resistor in this circuit equals 750 ohms, what is the total resistance in this circuit?

   (A) 250 ohms
   (B) 375 ohms
   (C) 750 ohms
   (D) 1,500 ohms

6. Counter-emf is produced by a process known as

   (A) inductive resistance
   (B) capacitive resistance
   (C) self-induction
   (D) doping

7. In a simple series circuit, what resistance will allow 5 mA to flow when 50 volts is applied to it?

   (A) 0.1 Ω
   (B) 250 Ω
   (C) 10 KΩ
   (D) 250 KΩ

8. What is the proper term for the circuit pictured?

   (A) series circuit
   (B) parallel circuit
   (C) series-parallel circuit
   (D) integrated circuit

9. Adding a resistor in parallel with an existing load

   (A) always increases the effective resistance
   (B) always decreases the effective resistance
   (C) sometimes increases the effective resistance
   (D) sometimes decreases the effective resistance

10. N-type material can conduct electricity because of

    (A) silicon's unique structure
    (B) a free electron outside the valence shell
    (C) a free electron inside the valence shell
    (D) an overall negative charge

11. Which is a type of transistor?

    (A) NPN
    (B) NNP
    (C) PPN
    (D) NNN

12. What is the effective resistance of a 2 Ω resistor and 4 Ω resistor if they are wired in parallel?

    (A) $\frac{3}{4}$ Ω

    (B) $1\frac{1}{3}$ Ω

    (C) 3 Ω
    (D) 6 Ω

13. A circuit contains two 3 Ω resistors in series. What is their effective resistance?

    (A) $\frac{2}{3}$ Ω

    (B) $\frac{3}{2}$ Ω

    (C) 3 Ω
    (D) 6 Ω

14. Adding an additional resistor to a circuit in series with the previous resistor

    (A) always increases the effective resistance
    (B) always decreases the effective resistance
    (C) sometimes increases the effective resistance
    (D) sometimes decreases the effective resistance

15. An element with five electrons in its valence shell is a(n)

    (A) conductor
    (B) semiconductor
    (C) insulator
    (D) metal

16. An ampere is defined as one _____ of electrical charge flowing past a point in one second.

    (A) hertz
    (B) coulomb
    (C) ohm
    (D) voltage

17. Unlike capacitors, inductors

    (A) allow DC current to pass easily
    (B) store charge
    (C) turn DC power around to increase power
    (D) have two parallel plates

18. A circuit initially contains only one load which has a resistance of 5 Ω. Assuming this is the only component of the circuit which provides any resistance initially, which of the following additions would decrease the effective resistance of the circuit by half?

    (A) Adding a resistor of 2.5 Ω in series with the original load
    (B) Adding a resistor of 2.5 Ω in parallel with the original load
    (C) Adding a resistor of 5 Ω in series with the original load
    (D) Adding a resistor of 5 Ω in parallel with the original load

19. This is the symbol for which type of meter?

    (A) voltmeter
    (B) ammeter
    (C) ohmmeter
    (D) galvanometer

20. All of the following statements about series circuits are true, EXCEPT

    (A) current flow is the same throughout
    (B) there is only one path for current to follow
    (C) current flow varies throughout the circuit
    (D) voltage drops across the loads depend on their resistance

Part 7: Automotive and Shop Information (AS)

Time: 11 minutes; 25 questions

<u>Directions</u>: In this section, you will be tested on your knowledge of automotive and shop basics. For each question, select the best answer and mark the corresponding oval on your answer sheet.

1. What is detonation?

   (A) when an air-fuel mixture explodes, rather than burns
   (B) if combustion is started by something other than electricity at the spark plug
   (C) rapid, thorough burning of a compressed air-fuel mixture, initiated by a spark from the engine's ignition system
   (D) slow burning of an air-fuel mixture

2. The ignition _____ coil generates the high voltage for the spark plugs.

   (A) primary
   (B) preliminary
   (C) secondary
   (D) tertiary

3. Engine coolant is normally made up of a _____ mix of antifreeze and water.

   (A) 60/40
   (B) 75/25
   (C) 50/50
   (D) 25/75

4. A socket can be used with which tool?

   (A) a ratchet only
   (B) an impact wrench only
   (C) either a ratchet or an impact wrench
   (D) none of the above

5. An automotive technician who wants to measure the width of an object might use any of the following tools EXCEPT

   (A) an outside micrometer
   (B) a tape measure
   (C) a steel rule
   (D) a Crescent wrench

6. This image depicts what stroke in the four-stroke cycle?

   (A) intake stroke
   (B) exhaust stroke
   (C) power stroke
   (D) compression stroke

7. A fuel injector sprays fuel into the intake air stream as it receives electrical signals from the

   (A) fuel rail
   (B) intake manifold
   (C) fuel pressure regulator
   (D) powertrain control module

8. A general purpose claw hammer would have a _____ oz head.

   (A) 7
   (B) 13
   (C) 40
   (D) 212

9. What would this tool be used to do?

   (A) stop a rotating motor
   (B) start a hole for drilling
   (C) fasten two pieces of metal
   (D) stabilize a car jack

10. Spark plugs are threaded into the

    (A) battery
    (B) distributor
    (C) cylinder head
    (D) coil wire

11. Automatic transmissions use _____ to create speed ratios and transmit torque.

    (A) planetary gear sets
    (B) idler gears
    (C) spur gears
    (D) countershaft gears

12. The brake system is _____ operated.

    (A) hydraulically
    (B) cable
    (C) electrically
    (D) wire

13. Which of the following saws is designed to cut metal?

    (A)

    (B)

    (C)

    (D)

14. MIG welding is also known as

    (A) Russian welding
    (B) coaxle welding
    (C) electric-bit welding
    (D) wire-feed welding

15. What is the name for the tool below?

    (A) carpenter's level
    (B) machinist's level
    (C) line level
    (D) striding level

16. Contact points would be found in _____ ignition systems.

    (A) coil-on-plug
    (B) distributor-less
    (C) electronic
    (D) none of the above

17. To remove a small sliver of wood in order to create a better fit, use

    (A) a plane
    (B) a flat file
    (C) needle-nosed pliers
    (D) Johnson bars

18. The _____ connects the steering box to the steering linkage.

    (A) center link
    (B) idler arm
    (C) tie rod end
    (D) pitman arm

19. The catalytic converter is part of the vehicle's _____ system.

    (A) fuel intake
    (B) braking
    (C) emission control
    (D) steering

20. Which of the following additions often increases the versatility of slip-joint pliers?

    (A) ratchet head
    (B) extension capability
    (C) wire cutter
    (D) variable speeds

21. Advancing the ignition timing means that the spark takes place _____ in the combustion cycle.

    (A) earlier
    (B) later
    (C) at the same time
    (D) none of the above

22. Which of the following hammers is used for forming soft metal?

    (A)

    (B)

    (C)

    (D)

23. Long-short arm suspensions involve all of the following EXCEPT

    (A) ball joints
    (B) upper control arms
    (C) lower control arms
    (D) torque converters

24. To cut off a bolt head, you would most likely use which of the following?

    (A) miter box
    (B) pin punch
    (C) coping saw
    (D) cold chisel

25. A loss of compression in an engine cylinder can be caused by all of the following, EXCEPT

    (A) worn engine bearings
    (B) worn piston rings/cylinder wall
    (C) burned valves
    (D) blown head gasket

STOP. IF YOU FINISH BEFORE THE TIME IS UP, YOU MAY CHECK OVER YOUR WORK ON THIS PART ONLY.

Part 8: Mechanical Comprehension (MC)

Time: 19 minutes; 25 questions

<u>Directions</u>: In this section, you will be tested on your knowledge of mechanics and basic physics. Select the best answer for each question and mark the corresponding oval on your answer sheet.

1. The force of friction between two surfaces moving past each other DOES NOT depend on

    (A) the normal force
    (B) the nature of the surfaces in contact with each other
    (C) the area of the surfaces in contact with each other
    (D) the speed with which the surfaces are moving past each other

2. The formula for work is

    (A) $w = m \times v$
    (B) $w = m \times g \times h$
    (C) $w = m \times a$
    (D) $w = F \times d$

3. A small pulley drives a large pulley with a belt. Which of the following statements about this arrangement are true?

    (A) The pulleys turn in opposite directions.
    (B) The smaller pulley turns faster.
    (C) Speed output is greater than the input.
    (D) The smaller pulley is above the larger pulley.

4. Any work that is done to accelerate an object at rest to speed v will be converted into the kinetic energy of that object. This principle is known as

    (A) the work-energy theorem
    (B) gravitational potential energy
    (C) the principle of conservation of mechanical energy
    (D) Newton's second law

5. Performing work at the rate of 1 joule per second is the same as expending

    (A) 100 foot-pounds
    (B) 10 psi
    (C) 1 meter per second
    (D) 1 watt of power

6. All of the following statements about liquids are true EXCEPT

    (A) liquids are practically incompressible
    (B) liquids can be used to transmit force
    (C) all liquids are good lubricants
    (D) liquids conform to the shape of their container

7. A crate with a weight of 250 N is resting on a rough, horizontal surface with a coefficient of static friction of 0.8. What will happen if an applied horizontal force of 200 N acts on the crate?

    (A) The crate will move and continually accelerate while the force acts.
    (B) The crate will move at a constant speed.
    (C) The crate will not move.
    (D) The crate will move but then decelerate back to rest as friction increases.

8. If 100 pounds of force are applied over an area of 2 square inches, the pressure would be

    (A) 5 psi.
    (B) 50 psi.
    (C) 100 psi.
    (D) 200 psi.

9. The advantage gained by the use of a mechanism in transmitting force is known as

    (A) pressure
    (B) hydraulics
    (C) torque multiplication
    (D) mechanical advantage

10. The point that the lever pivots on is the

    (A) gear
    (B) torque
    (C) fulcrum
    (D) axle

11. A 30N force is applied to 5 kg box. Assuming no friction, what is the acceleration gained by the box?

 (A) 0.17 $\frac{m}{s^2}$

 (B) 6 $\frac{m}{s^2}$

 (C) 15 $\frac{m}{s^2}$

 (D) 150 $\frac{m}{s^2}$

12. When a net force acts on an object,

 (A) the object will slow to a stop
 (B) the force will give the object a cumulative force
 (C) the object will accelerate in the direction of the net force
 (D) constant speed is impossible

13. If pulley X turns in a clockwise direction, in which direction will pulley Y turn?

 (A) clockwise only
 (B) counterclockwise only
 (C) either clockwise or counterclockwise
 (D) the direction cannot be determined based on the information provided

14. The illustration below represents

 (A) a fixed pulley
 (B) a moving pulley
 (C) a rear axle
 (D) a pendulum

15. In order for a piston with a total surface area of 10 square inches to support 100 pounds, how much pressure will have to be applied?

 (A) 1,000 psi
 (B) 50 psi
 (C) 10 psi
 (D) 5 psi

16. Given the following forces acting on a block, what are the net or resultant forces? (Assume that "left" means your left.)

 (A) 80 N to the right and 10 N down
 (B) 80 N to the left and 10 N down
 (C) 20 N to the left and 10 N down
 (D) 20 N to the right and 10 N down

17. Given a block and tackle with four ropes to lift a load one foot, barring friction, what is the mechanical advantage gained?

Rope is pulled to lift object

Object to be lifted

 (A) 24:1
 (B) 10:1
 (C) 8:1
 (D) 4:1

18. A child's teeter-totter, of the sort shown below, is an example of which kind of lever?

    (A) first-class
    (B) second-class
    (C) third-class
    (D) fourth-class

19. A hockey puck slides across frozen ice. The puck will eventually slow to a stop because of

    (A) wind drag
    (B) gravity
    (C) sliding frictional force
    (D) inertia

20. What is being applied to the bolt as it is being tightened?

    (A) torque
    (B) friction
    (C) kinetic energy
    (D) gear ratio

21. When tightening a fastener, if one uses a wrench that is 1 foot long, and applies a force of 100 pounds to the end of the wrench, _____ of torque is being applied.

    (A) 10 foot-pounds
    (B) 100 foot-pounds
    (C) 1,000 foot-pounds
    (D) 10,000 foot-pounds

22. Given the following pulley system, suppose a person is holding the other end of the rope, so that the box is stationary and the system is in equilibrium. What is the Tension force T that develops in the rope?

50N

    (A) 10 N
    (B) 25 N
    (C) 50 N
    (D) 100 N

23. Neglecting friction, the mechanical advantage provided by a block and tackle is equal to

    (A) the number of pulleys used in the block and tackle
    (B) half of the number of pulleys used in the block and tackle
    (C) twice the number of pulleys used in the block and tackle
    (D) the diameter of the pulleys divided by the number of pulleys used in the block and tackle

24. The symbol g, according to Newtonian laws, refers to

    (A) acceleration due to gravity
    (B) mass, in grams
    (C) the Earth's surface
    (D) the ground

25. The fulcrum is

    (A) the location that the force is applied to a lever
    (B) the location that the object is applied to a lever
    (C) the pivot point of a lever
    (D) the distance from the pivot point of a lever to the location the force is applied to the lever

STOP. IF YOU FINISH BEFORE THE TIME IS UP, YOU MAY CHECK OVER YOUR WORK ON THIS PART ONLY.

Part 9: Assembling Objects (AO)

Time: 15 minutes; 25 questions

Directions: In this section, you will be tested on your ability to determine how an object will look when its parts are put together. For each question, select the best answer and mark the corresponding oval on your answer sheet.

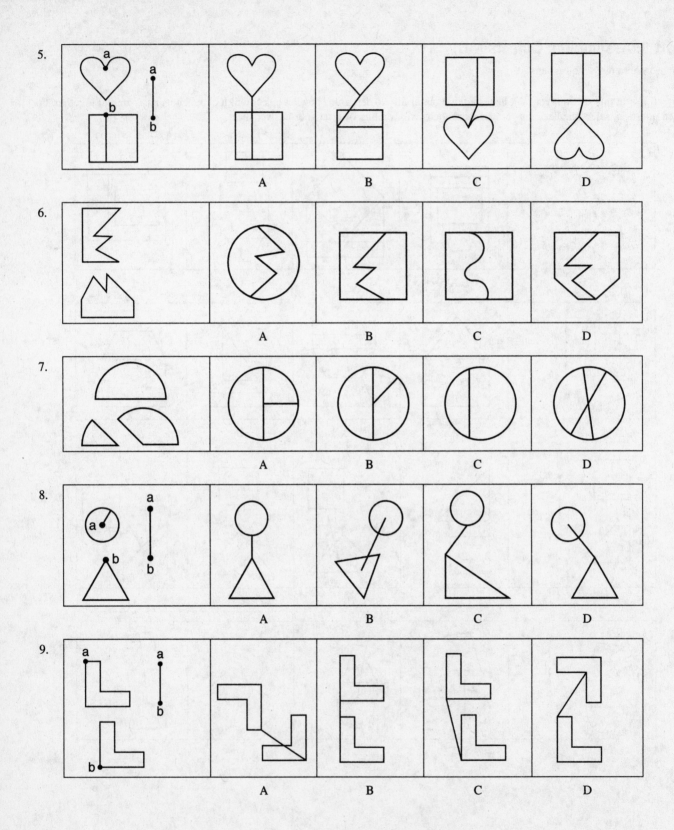

5.   A   B   C   D

6.   A   B   C   D

7.   A   B   C   D

8.   A   B   C   D

9.   A   B   C   D

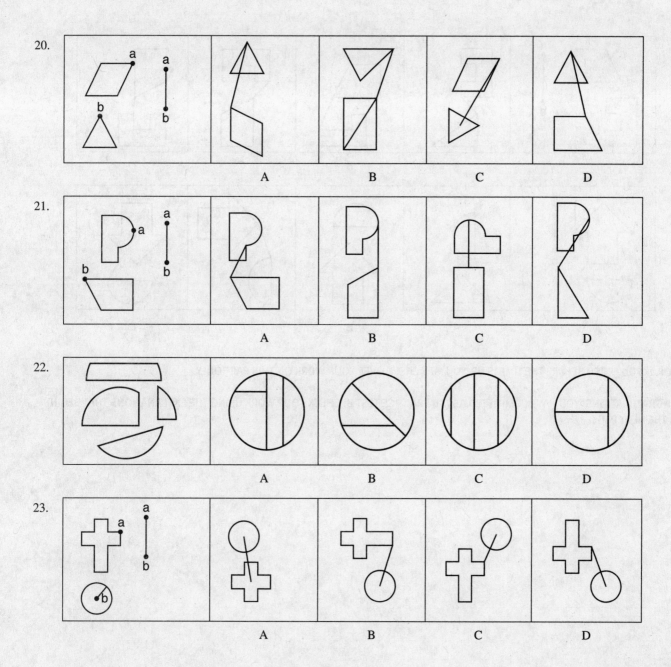

20.

    A   B   C   D

21.

    A   B   C   D

22.

    A   B   C   D

23.

    A   B   C   D

STOP. IF YOU FINISH BEFORE THE TIME IS UP, YOU MAY CHECK OVER YOUR WORK ON THIS PART ONLY.

CONGRATULATIONS! YOU HAVE COMPLETED ASVAB PRACTICE TEST B. CHECK YOUR WORK USING THE EXPLANATIONS THAT BEGIN ON THE NEXT PAGE.

ASVAB PRACTICE TEST B ANSWERS AND EXPLANATIONS

Part 1: General Science Answers and Explanations

1. **(D) saturated fats** Those wishing to reduce the bad cholesterol levels in their blood should avoid saturated fats. Sources of saturated fats include meats, shellfish, eggs, milk, and milk products.

2. **(D) 32°F** Water at sea level freezes at 32°F. This can also be expressed as 0°C and 273 K.

3. **(A) proton** Of the subatomic particles listed, the proton has the largest mass. Among subatomic particles, protons and neutrons have the most mass. Electrons, positrons, and neutrinos all have negligible masses relative to protons and neutrons.

4. **(B) an apple tree** An "autotroph" is an organism capable of synthesizing its own organic substances from inorganic compounds, as through photosynthesis. Another term for an autotroph is a producer. An apple tree is an example of an autotroph. A vulture is a type of consumer known as a scavenger, which means it feeds on dead or decaying flesh. A toadstool is a type of fungi. It feeds on and breaks down dead organic matter. A sea anemone is a consumer that feeds on small marine organisms and organic matter.

5. **(D) Precambrian eon** The Earth is approximately 4.6 billion years old, and that for most of that time, very few fossil traces were left. This is why the period from 4.6 billion years to 570 million years ago is called the Precambrian eon, meaning the period before the fossil record began.

6. **(C) Uranus** Mercury, Venus, and Mars are all smaller than Earth. Of the planets listed, only Uranus is larger than Earth.

7. **(B) meteoroids** Falling stars are meteoroids that fall into the Earth's gravitational field. They leave streaks of light, called meteors, as they are burned up in Earth's atmosphere.

8. **(B) ecology** The study of interactions between organisms and their interrelationships with the physical environment is known as *ecology*. *Cytology* is the study of cells, *physiology* is the study of processes in the organism, and *embryology* is the study of embryos and their development.

9. **(C) small intestine** The small intestine absorbs most of the nutrients in food.

10. **(D) twice a day** Tides are caused by the gravitational pull that exists between the Moon and Earth. High tides occur twice a day, when the Moon is at the points closest to and farthest from the coastline experiencing a high tide.

11. **(C) If the mass of the Earth were doubled, the gravitational force on the Earth would quadruple.** According to Newton's Law of Gravitation, if the mass of the Earth were doubled, the gravitational force on the Earth would double, not quadruple.

12. **(A) radio waves** Of the states of electromagnetic radiation listed, radio waves have the longest wavelength and lowest frequency.

13. **(D) refractive index** The speed of light can slow down, depending on the material through which the waves move. For example, light travels more slowly through water or glass than through air. The ratio by which light is slowed down is called the refractive index of that medium.

14. **(C) baking soda** A high pH indicates a substance that is basic rather than acidic. Of the food products listed, baking soda is the most basic and has the highest pH.

15. **(D) almonds** Carbohydrates include starches (potatoes and pasta) and sugars (fruits). Almonds are a type of nut and have a high fat content.

16. **(A) class** The levels of classification, from largest to smallest, are: domain, kingdom, phylum, class, order, family, genus, species. Members of a family, genus and species are all more similar than members of an order. Of the answer choices given, members of an order are only more alike than members of a class.

17. **(C) atomic number** The number of protons in the nucleus of an atom gives it its atomic number. The number of electrons can also be used to determine atomic number, but only if the atom is neutral (in a neutral atom, proton number = electron number). The atomic symbol is the letter designation of the element and is based on the element's Latin name. Atomic weight is the mass of one atom expressed in atomic mass units. Atomic radius gives the size of the atom.

18. **(A) diaphragm** The diaphragm is a system of muscles that allow the lungs to expand and contract, drawing air in and out.

19. **(B) 17 protons** The atom of an element with an atomic number of 17 must have 17 protons. The number of electrons (A), however, is only the same as the number of protons if the atom is neutral. The number of neutrons (C) is often similar to but not necessarily equal to the number of protons. For example, hydrogen often has one proton and no neutrons. And since the atomic mass (D) is contributed to by both protons and neutrons, it is almost always larger than the atomic number.

20. **(C) saprophytes** Because mushrooms absorb nutrients from decaying leaves, they are classified as saprophytes. Another term for a plant living on dead or decaying organic matter is decomposer.

21. **(A) pulmonary artery** The vessel with the least oxygenated blood is the pulmonary artery, which sends oxygen-depleted blood from the heart into the lungs to be oxygenated.

22. **(A) starch** Saliva in the mouth begins the process of breaking down starch. Fats, proteins and vitamins begin breaking down later in the digestive process.

23. **(B) Monera** The Moneran kingdom is composed of prokaryotic organisms; that is, organisms with cells that lack nuclei.

24. **(C) ion** An atom that is not electrically neutral is called an *ion*. It possesses a positive or negative charge. An *isotope* is two or more atoms of the same element that have the same atomic number but different mass number; i.e., they have the same number of protons but a different number of neutrons. A *positron* is a positively charged particle having the same mass and magnitude of charge as the electron. An *allotrope* is an element with two or more different forms; e.g., carbon is an allotrope and can exist as either graphite or diamond.

25. **(B) marble** A metamorphic rock is one that has undergone significant changes due to pressure, heat, and/or water. This results in a more compact and more highly crystalline state. Marble is an example of a metamorphic rock.

Part 2: Arithmetic Reasoning Answers and Explanations

1. **(B) 150** If a machine caps 5 bottles every 2 seconds, then it would cap 30 times as many bottles in one minute (since a minute is 60 seconds). $5 \times 30 = 150$ bottles per minute.

2. **(D) $33.80** Jonah travelled 650 miles at 25 miles per gallon. To determine how many gallons he used, divide 650 by 25. $650 \div 25 = 26$ gallons. Each gallon costs $1.30, so his cost for the trip would be $26 \times \$1.30 = \$33.80$.

3. **(B) $0.40** On problems that involve long calculations, use Backsolving. Start with either (B) or (C). Since (B), $0.40, is the easier number, start there: If there are 3.86 liters in a gallon, and a liter of gasoline costs $0.40, a gallon of gasoline costs $3.86 \times \$0.40 = \$1.544$, or roughly $1.54 a gallon, which is the correct price of a gallon.

4. **(C) 10,080** To determine the number of minutes in a week, begin with the number of minutes in an hour and work your way up from there. There are 60 minutes per hour and 24 hours per day, so there are $60 \times 24 = 1,440$ minutes per day. There are 7 days per week, so there are $1,440 \times 7 = 10,080$ minutes per week.

5. **(D) $250.00** 15% of take home pay $= \$37.50$. So,

$$0.15(x) = \$37.50. x = \frac{37.5}{0.15} = \frac{3,750}{15} = 250$$

You could also use Backsolving, starting with either (B) or (C). Trying (C) would yield:

(C) $225 \times .15 = \$33.75$, which is less than the $37.50 we are told Pat deposited. Thus, (C) is too small, and the correct answer must be (D).

6. **(C) 152** If the ratio of males to females is 3:5, then there are 8 total parts in the ratio. The total number of students must be a multiple of 8. Only choice (C), 152, is a multiple of 8. To test if a number is a multiple of 8, divide the number by 2, then by 2 again. If the result is even, the number is divisible by 8.

7. **(D) 384** A car travels 288 miles in 6 hours. Divide 288 by 6 to find the rate in miles per hour. $288 \div 6 = 48$ miles per hour. Then, 48 miles per hour multiplied by 8 hours equals 384 miles.

8. **(D) 94** If Martin's average score after 4 tests is 89, then the sum for his 4 tests would be:

$4 \times 89 = 356$.

To average 90 on 5 tests, he would have to reach a sum of:

$5 \times 90 = 450$

His score on the fifth test has to be the difference between the two sums:

$450 - 356 = 94$

9. **(A) 2019** If the first year begins with town A at 9,400 and town B at 7,600, the populations are: $9,400 - 7,600 = 1,800$ apart. Each year after 2010 beginning in 2011, the gap will close by 200. It would take 9 years for the gap to close entirely, so by 2019 the populations will be equal.

10. **(D) −50** One number is 5 times another number, and their sum is −60. You could rewrite that sentence as two equations:

$x = 5y$

$x + y = -60$

Substitute $5y$ in for x in the second equation and solve:

$5y + y = -60$

$6y = -60$

$y = -10$

If $y = -10$ and $x = 5y$:

$x = 5(-10) = -50$.

−50 is less than −10, so −50 is correct.

11. **(C) $312** There are two rates by which John gets paid: one for the first 40 cars ($6 per car) and another for all other cars after those first 40 ($6 per car plus 50% of $6, which is $6 + \$3 = \$9$ per car). Since he makes 48 cars, he gets paid 6×40 cars ($240) plus 8 extra cars at $9 per car ($72), which totals $312.

12. **(A) 8** 48 glecks at 3 glecks per fedi would equal $\frac{48}{3} = 16$ fedis. 16 fedis at 2 fedis per bora would equal $\frac{16}{2} = 8$ bora.

13. **(B) 8 p.m.** Work through the clock systematically: First reading at 12 p.m., second at 4 p.m., third at 8 p.m., fourth at midnight, fifth at 4 a.m., sixth at 8 a.m., seventh at 12 p.m., eighth at 4 p.m., ninth and final reading at 8 p.m.

14. **(B) $33\frac{1}{3}$%** If monthly tuition payments were raised from $225 to $300, use the percent increase formula to determine how much the tuition went up:

$$\text{Percent increase} = \frac{new - old}{old} = 100\%$$

$$= \frac{300 - 225}{225}$$

$$= \frac{75}{225} = \frac{75}{225} \div \frac{5}{5} = \frac{15}{45}$$

$$= \frac{15}{45} \div \frac{5}{5} = \frac{3}{9} = \frac{1}{3}$$

$$\frac{1}{3} \times 100\% = 33\frac{1}{3}\%$$

15. **(C) 2** If a truck takes 6 hours to complete a trip at 20 miles per hour, the total distance for the trip must be $6 \times 20 = 120$ miles. When travelling 120 miles at a rate of 30 miles per hour, the truck would take $\frac{120}{30} = 4$ hours. So instead of taking 6 hours, the truck would take 4 hours. That saves 2 hours.

16. **(A) 45** If a full barrel can hold 75 gallons, when it is $\frac{3}{5}$ full it will hold $\frac{3}{5}$ of 75 gallons. $\frac{3}{5} \times 75 = 3 \times 15 = 45$ gallons.

17. **(B) $27,000** A salary of $45,000 is reduced by 40%; that is the same as reducing it by $\frac{2}{5}$. You may find it easier to find $\frac{1}{5}$ first: of $45,000 is $9,000, so $\frac{2}{5}$ would be $18,000. The new salary is:

$45,000 - $18,000 = $27,000

18. **(D) 40,320** $8! = 8 \times 7 \times 6 \times 5 \times 4 \times 3 \times 2 \times 1 = 40,320$

To solve long multiplication problems without a calculator, group the numbers strategically and multiply in pieces. The calculation can become:

$$(8 \times 7) \times (6 \times 5) \times (4 \times 3) \times (2 \times 1)$$

$$= 56 \times 30 \times 12 \times 2$$

$$= 56 \times 60 \times 12$$

$$= 56 \times 720$$

$$= 40,320$$

If you are running short on time or don't feel confident with long multiplication, guess strategically using logic. 8! will be a huge number and it probably won't be a nice round number. So (D) is the best choice.

19. **(D) $390** If 15 people contribute $40 each, that would amount to $15 \times \$40 = \$600$. Thirty-five percent of the money is spent on a group gift, so the remaining 65% of the money is spent on the party. $0.65 \times \$600 = \$390$.

20. **(C) 6 hours, 42 minutes**
$\text{Average} = \frac{\text{Sum of the terms}}{\text{Number of terms}}$. In this question, an employee works for a total of 33.5 hours over 5 days. The average hours worked per day would be determined as follows:

$$\text{Average} = \frac{\text{Sum of the terms}}{\text{Number of terms}} = \frac{33.5}{5} = 6 + \frac{3.5}{5} \text{ hours}$$

All the answer choices are expressed in minutes, not hours. So you need to convert 0.7 hours into minutes. There are 60 minutes in an hour, so 0.7 hours $= 60 \times 0.7 = 42$ minutes. The average amount of time worked on a given day is 6 hours and 42 minutes.

21. **(A) 66** To find the average speed for an entire trip, divide the total distance by the total time. If a train travels 180 miles at an average speed of 60 miles per hour, that leg of the journey must have taken $\frac{180}{60} = 3 \text{ hours}$. The second leg of 150 miles at an average speed of 75 miles per hour would take $\frac{150}{75} = 2$ hours.

$$\text{Average speed} = \frac{\text{Total distance}}{\text{Total time}}$$

$$= \frac{180 + 150}{3 + 2}$$

$$= \frac{330}{5} = 66 \text{ mph.}$$

22. (C) $175.00

Try Backsolving on a question like this one. Start with choice (B). If a bicycle starts at $162 and is discounted 20%, its price would be reduced by (0.2)($162) = $32.40. The selling price would then be $129.60. This is too low. Eliminate answer choices (A) and (B). Then try answer choice (C). If a bicycle starts at $175.00 and is discounted 20%, its price would be reduced by (0.20)($175) = $35. So the new price would be $175 − $35 = $140. That's the discount price you're looking for, so it's the correct answer.

23. (B) $1,024.64

This is an addition and subtraction question. Begin by adding the deposit to the balance:

$1,162.76 + 352.68 = 1,515.44$

Then sum up the withdrawals:

$152.45 + 82.85 + 255.50 = 490.80$

Find the answer by subtracting the sum of the withdrawals from the balance:

$1,515.44 − 490.80 = 1,024.64$

24. (D) $57.38

If Harold works 4.5 hours per day for 3 days, then he works $4.5 \times 3 = 13.5$ hours at $4.25 per hour. He earns $13.5 \times \$4.25 = \$57.375$. That rounds up to $57.38.

25. (B) 0.25

To convert a fraction to a decimal, divide the denominator into the numerator. $6 \div 24 = 0.25$.

You can also reduce the fraction until it represents one you know the conversion for:

$$\frac{6}{24} \div \frac{6}{6} = \frac{1}{4} = 0.25$$

26. (B) $346

There are 100 stamps per sheet, which means that each sheet of 100 23-cent stamps would cost $23, each sheet of 37-cent stamps would cost $37, and each sheet of 60-cent stamps would cost $60. Thus, the calculations look like this:

$(4 \times \$23) + (2 \times \$37) + (3 \times \$60)$

$= \$92 + \$74 + \$180 = \$346$

27. (A) 4 hours, 15 minutes

Pacific time is three hours behind eastern time. So if a plane leaves Los Angeles at 5:30 p.m. PST, it leaves at 8:30 p.m. EST. If it arrives in New York at 12:45 a.m. EST, the total time of the flight would be 4 hours, 15 minutes.

28. (C) $160

Try Backsolving here. Start with choice (C) because you are looking for a 25% discount, which is $\frac{1}{4}$ and 160 is divisible by 4. If the original cost of the camera was $160, and it was reduced by 25% or $\frac{1}{4}$, the new cost would be:

$\$160 − 0.25(\$160)$

$= \$160 − \$40 = \$120$

That's the selling price given in the problem, so $160 is the correct original price.

29. (B) 15

A square root is a number that, when multiplied by itself, produces the given quantity. $15 \times 15 = 225$.

30. (D) 10 hours, 48 minutes

If it takes 20 minutes to type 5 pages, then it takes 4 minutes to type one page. Then the total document takes $4 \times 162 = 648$ minutes to type. 600 minutes is 10 hours, so 648 minutes is 10 hours and 48 minutes.

Part 3: Word Knowledge Answers and Explanations

1. **(B) lethargic** *Listless* means *tired, sluggish,* or *lacking energy*; thus *lethargic,* (B), is the correct answer. Word parts are not terribly helpful on this question, but you might have a sense that *listless* has a negative charge. If so, that narrows your choices down to either (B) or (D).

2. **(C) understand** Use the context of the sentence to guess the underlined word's meaning. What are great teachers able to do with complex ideas? They explain them, understand them, or simplify them. Only choice (C) reflects one of those concepts.

3. **(D) winner** Think of words that sound like *victor*. The first word that comes to mind may be *victory*, which means the act of winning or defeating others, and this fits with the sentence. A *victor* is defined as *one who defeats or vanquishes a foe*, so (D), *winner,* is the best answer.

4. **(B) relaxed** Think about what the word sounds like. Something *lacking* is *missing*. The answer missing something is (B), *relaxed*, which is the lack of stress or action. The textbook definition of lackadaisical is *lacking life, spirit, or zest*.

5. **(B) position** Mentally reread the sentence, substituting each answer choice for the underlined word. Choices (A) and (D) make no sense when you do so. Don't fall for choice (C): one might have an *idea* that more money should be spent on education, but it isn't correct usage to say that one "has an *ideal* that." In fact, *contention* is defined as a *point advanced in a debate or argument*, so the answer (B), *position* is closest in meaning to the given word.

6. **(A) notable** Break the word into parts: *news* and *worthy* are both English words, so you can guess that *newsworthy* means *interesting enough to warrant news coverage*. Answer choice (A), *notable,* is the closest in meaning.

7. **(C) irregular** Try mentally rereading the sentence and substituting each answer choice for the underlined word. It doesn't make sense to say that someone's class attendance was (A) *latent* (hidden) or (D) *common*. Class attendance could possibly be (B) *constant,* but that doesn't jibe with the phrase "if anything," which suggests that the person's class attendance is minimal or scanty. In fact, something *sporadic* is something that is *occurring occasionally*, and (C) *irregular* is the best fit.

8. **(D) possible** Remembered real-life context may be helpful here. Have you ever heard a young person described as "having a lot of potential"? That phrase is used to describe a young person who has many promising possibilities before her. Here, potential is used in its adjective form (you can tell because the answer choices are all adjectives), and as an adjective *potential* means *possible*.

9. **(B) barred** This word is made up of other English words: *black* and *list*. You can guess that being put on a black list is probably a metaphor for something fairly negative. In fact, the word *blacklisted* refers to a way of keeping out undesired people by creating a list of banned individuals. Thus, answer choice (B) is the only correct answer, as banned and *barred* are similar words.

10. **(D) overconfident** Use the context of the sentence to make a prediction. You're told that the task is a tough one, so perhaps not many people would want to volunteer for it. That suggests that *presumptuous* means something like *unrealistic*. Choice (D) *overconfident,* or too confident, is the best match.

11. **(C) souvenir** Use the context of the sentence to make a prediction. The sentence tells you that a *memento* helps you to remember something. Only choice (C) *souvenir* is something that helps you remember.

12. **(A) memory** Use the sentence's context to make a prediction. A *legacy* is something that the school president will leave behind him when he's gone. Of the choices, only (A) *memory* is something that remains behind after someone is gone.

13. **(B) danger** Use the context to make a prediction. The parents are worried, so you can infer that something bad may be coming in their children's future. Only choice (B) *danger* is sufficiently negative to fit the context.

14. **(D) honesty** There's no context, and word parts aren't going to be helpful here. Perhaps remembered real-life context could help. If you have ever heard someone referred to as a "man of integrity" or a "woman of integrity," you may remember that's a compliment. That knocks out choice (B), since *coercion* has a negative charge, and choice (C), since *togetherness* is not a trait that a single individual can have. (A family or other close-knit group might have togetherness.) That leaves only choices (A) *ability* and (D) *honesty*, and only (D) conveys the same sense of virtue as the phrase "man of integrity." In fact, *integrity* means the state of being whole or the state of being very moral or upright.

15. **(D) violation** Use the context to make a prediction. An *infraction* is something for which a person is punished, so it must be a crime or act of breaking the rules. Choice (D) *violation* is the best fit.

16. **(A) group** Think about words that sound like the underlined word: *collective* sounds like a noun or adjective form of the word *collect*. When you *collect*, you gather together things or people to form a group. That should point you to answer choice (A).

17. **(A) trick** There's no context in the question, and it would be difficult to see word parts in the word *hoax*. Perhaps remembered real-life context will help. You may have heard the word *hoax* in connection with the Loch Ness Monster, Bigfoot, UFO photos, or other fake things that people have claimed are real. In fact, a *hoax* is a trick meant to convince someone what is false is true.

18. **(C) origin** Word parts may be helpful here: the root *gen*, which relates to beginnings, also gives us *generate*. You might also have heard the word *genesis* used in real life to refer to beginnings. In fact, *genesis* means the *origin or coming into being* of something.

19. **(B) dispute** Remembered real-life context may be helpful here. The famous feud between the Hatfields and McCoys was a prolonged dispute between two families. In fact, a *feud* is defined as a *quarrel that is often prolonged*, and choice (B) fits that definition.

20. **(B) fake** There is no context in the question stem, and word parts may not be helpful if you aren't sure what *fraud* means. Remembered real-life context may be helpful. If you have heard news stories about people who have committed *tax fraud*, you know that those people lied to the government about their taxes. Thus, something *fraudulent* must have to do with lying; (B) *fake* is the best choice.

21. **(D) skilled** There's no context, and word parts may not be helpful. However, think of words that sound like *adept*. If you have ever heard someone described as *inept*, you may remember that person is ineffective or clumsy. Thus, you might guess that *adept* means the opposite. An *adept* person is someone highly skilled or well-trained.

22. **(A) passionate** The context here may be helpful: think about what words might be used to describe how supportive of a cause someone is. Only choice (A) is a word that might be used in that way. Word parts may also be helpful here. The root *ard* or *ars* relates to fire and gives us words like *arson* and *ardor*. *Ardent* is the state of being *fiery or intense in feeling*, and (A) *passionate* is the best match.

23. **(B) widespread** Use context to make a prediction: if the town was suffering, the overcrowding must have been pretty severe. Only choice (B) *widespread* suggests the same idea.

24. **(D) weak** Make a prediction based on the context. The speaker predicts that in a contest between the big dog and the fence, the big dog is going to prevail. Thus, the fence must not be very strong. Choice (D) *weak* is the best fit.

25. **(D) evil** There's no context, and word parts are unlikely to be helpful. Remembered real-life context may be helpful. If you think about where you've heard the word *sinister*, the villains in movies or comic books may come to mind. This suggests that *sinister* means *wicked* or *evil*.

26. **(C) clever** You may have heard the word *witty* used to describe people who tell good jokes. Then, ask yourself which of the answer choices would also describe good jokes. Typically, good jokes are *clever*. None of the other choices make sense.

27. **(A) clear** Make the most of context here. An account said to "open the jury's eyes" would must have clarified or illuminated a situation. Thus, the last two choices are not appropriate, as they are negative responses. Of the other two, only choice (A) fits the context of the sentence.

28. **(A) concede** There's no context, but the prefix *re-*, which means *back* or *again*, might be helpful. It's difficult to see how (B) *color* or (C) *trick* would involve doing something *back* or *again*. In fact, to *relinquish* something is to *give it up* or *give it back*, so of the answer choices, only (A), *concede* fits.

29. **(C) return** Make the most of context here: a person is most likely to hope that good times either continue or come back again. Only choice (C) *return* makes sense.

30. **(A) induce** Remembered real-life context may be helpful. You may have heard news stories in which someone "incited" others to violence. That suggests that incite means something like *cause to do*. Of the choices given, only (A) *induce* gets that meaning across.

31. **(A) enact** Use the context in the sentence to make a prediction. George's critics were paying attention to something else, so that might have been a good time for George to do whatever he thought was best. Thus, in *implementing* the strategy, George went ahead with it or set it in motion. Only answer choice (A) *enact* has that meaning.

32. **(B) question** *Query* has the same root as *question* and actually means the same thing.

33. **(B) cowardly** Make the most of context: you are told that a *timid* animal is not one you should fear. Thus, that animal is reluctant to attack you; perhaps it's likely to run away instead. In fact, *timid* means *shy or lacking in courage*. The correct answer choice is (B), *cowardly*.

34. **(C) peer** Word parts can be helpful here. *Col–* is a form of *con–*, together. A *colleague* is someone you are together in a league or group with. For example, at work, a *colleague* is a coworker. Of the choices given, only *peer* is an equivalent answer.

35. **(D) powerful** Make the most of context: an opponent who is both tough and smart would be a powerful enemy. In fact, *potent* means *having or wielding authority or influence*. Choice (D) is the best fit.

Part 4: Paragraph Comprehension Answers and Explanations

1. **(C) show that both were logical and meticulous** The question asks you to read the passage with an eye toward its use of examples. Here, the author very clearly sets up the theme that Conan Doyle's character Holmes is a logical character. To illustrate that, he brings up a recognized scientific contemporary. Choices (A) and (B) have no bearing on the paragraph. Choice (D) brings up the idea of Darwin's meticulous research abilities, but does not reference the main focus of the paragraph (Holmes). Only choice (C) includes both men.

2. **(B) based on urban structures and the environment** This Detail question asks about the specific relationship between cities and climate as illustrated in the text. The paragraph introduces its subject first, and then gives some description of the changes that might take place. The last sentence in the paragraph finally gives the information needed. Structures and man-made items affect the weather. Of the answer choices, choice (B) is the clearest paraphrase of that sentence.

3. **(B) watch news on TV** This question asks you to make a prediction based on information given in the paragraph. From the tone of the passage, you can tell that Marianne is a generally quiet woman thrust into a high-profile situation. You can make an assumption based on the tone of the piece that she is overwhelmed by the attention given to her newfound wealth. Choices (A) and (C) highlight the idea that she is a gaudy or flamboyant person, an assumption that seems all wrong given the final sentence. Choice (D) is not reflected in the passage. Only answer choice (B) is a fair assessment of Marianne's potential behavior.

4. **(D) notorious** For Vocabulary-in-Context questions, head back to the original text and find the word in question. Examine the context within which the word *infamous* is found. The group was plotting to blow up the King and the Parliament but was foiled. The gist of the paragraph is that the conspirators were up to no good, quite the opposite of heroes, choice (A). You can also use word parts: *in* means *not*, and *famous* means *well thought of*. *Infamous*, therefore, means something like *not well thought of*, or *notorious*.

5. **(A) perturbed** Take a look at the language choices used: *screamed*, *knocked*, *ran*. Now take a look at the answer choices. Choice (A) makes sense, since the action is so vivid and aggressive. Save it and check the other choices. Answer choice (B) is wrong because nothing in the passage is tender. Choice (C) has a positive connotation and Johnny is not positive in this situation. Nothing in the passage is conceited or snooty, so choice (D) is incorrect. Choice (A) is correct.

6. **(D) may be short and dynamic** Eliminate answer choices that disagree with the passage, or that may or may not be true based on the passage. Choice (A) cannot be correct because it contradicts the passage: the life cycle is a direct result of the rain levels. (B) may or may not be true: although the passage mentions "astounding" blooms, it doesn't say anything about their color. *Wildlife,* (C), isn't mentioned in the passage at all. (D) is a near-paraphrase of what the passage says about desert plant life cycles, so it is the correct answer.

7. **(C) rely on imagination and not just experience** The passage argues that many famous writers had narrow life experiences, but vivid imaginations, so look for an answer choice that makes a specific contrast between the need for imagination and experience in a writer's life. (C) makes that contrast. (A) contradicts the example of Robert Louis Stevenson, who wrote about things outside of his social scene. (B) similarly contradicts the example of Jane Austen, who did not write adventure stories. Friends and family (D) are mentioned in the passage, but not advice from friends or family.

8. **(C) talent** The passage says that Tania was a good actress and gives examples of her variety of roles, so acting *prowess* describes a quality of good actors that she possesses. (C) is a positive quality. Eliminate (B) and (D) because they are negative words. *Knowledge,* (A), is positive, but is not necessarily related to acting versatility.

9. **(B) the true beauty of coral islands is underwater** Eliminate any answer choices that do not have to be true based on the passage. The color of coral animals (A) is not mentioned in the passage at all. (B) is practically a paraphrase of sentence two, "Beneath the waves ... is a fantastic and very beautiful world," so (B) is the correct answer. (C) is contradicted by the passage when the author writes "not always as nice if seen from the land." (D) is contradicted by the last sentence, which says that vast numbers of animals—not volcanoes—form coral islands.

10. **(A) how some sought to assimilate immigrants into America** In a question about the passage as a whole, the wrong answer choices will often be either too broad or too narrow, or will mention subjects that aren't in the passage. Eliminate answer choices that don't fit the scope of the passage. (B) is incorrect because cultural contributions aren't mentioned in the passage. (C) is too broad: the passage is about groups of immigrants in a particular area and time, not the whole history of immigration. (D) is too narrow: the effect on cities is only mentioned in one sentence. (A) is the correct answer: the idea of assimilation is referred to throughout the passage.

11. **(D) preached fitting in, not standing out** The passage says that the Daughters of the American Revolution (DAR) thought that immigrants should "completely adopt American culture and customs." The rest of the paragraph about the DAR just gives examples of what they did to support that belief, so look for an answer choice that describes how they thought immigrants should conform. (D) matches that idea. Notice that, while other answer choices may or may not be true, they don't fit specifically with what the author is saying about the DAR in the passage.

12. **(A) to divert the eye from the animal's outline** In the second sentence, the passage says that an animal adapts "color, shape and behavior in order to blend into its environment." The rest of the paragraph is a list of examples about how different animals become "all but invisible" with camouflage, so look for an answer that says camouflage makes animals hard to see. (A) matches that idea. The passage says nothing about *nesting* (B) or *habitats* (C), and most of the animals mentioned are prey animals, not *predators* (D).

13. **(B) the discovery of volcanic activity on Io** The key to this question is in the first sentence: "...the biggest surprise... was the discovery...of intense volcanic activity." Choice (B), the correct answer, is a paraphrase of the sentence about surprise. Don't be distracted by the rest of the details listed in the paragraph or by the other answer choices. The key idea here is the observers' surprise.

14. **(C) early precursors to the Hula Hoop were primarily children's toys** In an "all are true EXCEPT" question, concentrate on eliminating any answer choices that are true according to the passage. Eliminate choice (A) because it is true according to the first sentence. The second sentence says that choice (B) is true, so eliminate it too. Sentence four says that adults enjoyed the early Hula Hoops, so (C) must be false. (C) is the correct answer. The last two sentences of the passage show how (D) must be true since they describe how the Hula Hoop was a hit for the "fledgling" toy company.

15. **(B) discuss the origins of the Hula Hoop** Eliminate answer choices that are too broad, too narrow, or not mentioned in the passage. (A) is too broad: the passage doesn't include any information on fads besides the Hula Hoop. (B) is the correct answer: The passage starts with the earliest origins of the hoop toy and ends up with the popularization of the Hula Hoop. (C) is too narrow: only one sentence in the passage explains how the name came about. The passage says that the Hula Hoop is popular, (D), but doesn't question why.

Part 5: Mathematics Knowledge Answers and Explanations

1. (B) $-1\frac{1}{4}$ In order to make this equation manageable, first turn the mixed number into an improper fraction, and then multiply both sides of the equation by 12 to clear the denominators:

$$\frac{3}{4}+1\frac{1}{3}=\frac{5}{6}-x$$

$$\frac{3}{4}+\frac{4}{3}=\frac{5}{6}-x$$

$$12\left(\frac{3}{4}+\frac{4}{3}\right)=12\left(\frac{5}{6}-x\right)$$

$$9+16=10-12x$$

$$12x=10-9-16$$

$$12x=-15$$

$$x=-\frac{15}{12}=-\frac{5}{4}=-1\frac{1}{4}.$$

2. (C) $12a^2 + 7a - 12$ Use FOIL:

$(3a + 4)(4a - 3)$

$(3a \times 4a) + [3a \times (-3)] + (4 \times 4a) + [4 \times (-3)]$

$= 12a^2 - 9a + 16a - 12$

$= 12a^2 + 7a - 12$

3. (D) 16 If $2m > 24$, then $m > 12$. But so are all the answer choices, so check out the other inequality. If $3m < 48$, then $m < 16$. Thus, (D), 16, is not a possible value for m.

4. (A) $11\sqrt{3}$ (D) is out because when you add square roots, you can't simply combine the sums under the radical sign, as (D) does. But what you can do is factor out perfect squares from the number under the radical signs:

$\sqrt{75} + \sqrt{108}$

$= \sqrt{25 \times 3} + \sqrt{36 \times 3}$

You can then separate the terms under the radicals because they are connected by multiplication:

$= \sqrt{25} \times \sqrt{3} + \sqrt{36} \times \sqrt{3}$

$= 5\sqrt{3} + 6\sqrt{3}$

Because the number under the radical is the same in both terms, you can add the terms together by adding the coefficients:

$5\sqrt{3} + 6\sqrt{3} = 11\sqrt{3}$

5. (B) 5 Since the lengths of each side of a square are the same, $PQ = PS$. Therefore:

$3a + 2 = 2a + 7$

$a = 5$

6. (B) 60 The three interior angles of any triangle add up to 180°, and the parts of the ratio here add up to $1 + 2 + 3 = 6$. To get the amount of one part, divide 180 by 6, which gives you 30. Now you know that the three angles have degree measures of $1 \times 30 = 30$, $2 \times 30 = 60$, and $3 \times 30 = 90$. The difference in the degree measures between the largest and the smallest angles is:

$90 - 30 = 60$

7. (A) $9 + 3\sqrt{5}$

The Pythagorean theorem states that in a right triangle, $a^2 + b^2 = c^2$, where a and b are the two perpendicular side lengths, called the legs, and c is the length of the hypotenuse. To figure out the perimeter of this triangle, first find the length of the hypotenuse using the Pythagorean theorem:

$$(3)^2 + (6)^2 = c^2$$

$$9 + 36 = c^2$$

$$45 = c^2$$

$$c = \sqrt{45} = \sqrt{9} \times \sqrt{5} = 3\sqrt{5}$$

Now add together the sides to get the perimeter:

$3 + 6 + 3\sqrt{5} = 9 + 3\sqrt{5}$

8. (D) 1 Since AE is a line segment, all the lengths are additive, so $AE = AD + DE$. The question states that $AD = 6$ and $AE = 8$. So $DE = AE - AD = 8 - 6 = 2$. The question also states that $BE = 6$. So $BD = BE - DE = 6 - 2 = 4$. The question asks for the length of BC. Since $CD = 3(BC)$, the relationship can be written like this:

$BC + 3BC = 4$

$$4BC = 4$$

$$BC = 1$$

CHAPTER 15

9. (B) 34 The central rectangle shares a side with each of the four squares, and the four squares form the legs of the four right triangles. Two of the rectangle's sides have a length of 4, so the two squares that share these sides must also have sides of length 4. The other two sides of the rectangle have a length of 3, so the other two squares, which share these sides, must also have sides of length 3. Each triangle shares a side with a small square and a side with a large square, so the legs of each triangle have lengths of 3 and 4, respectively. Since the legs are of length 3 and 4, the hypotenuse of each triangle must have a length of 5.

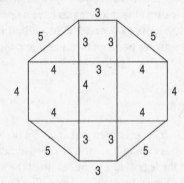

The perimeter is the sum of the hypotenuses of the triangles and a side from each square:

Perimeter = $4(5) + 2(4) + 2(3)$

$= 20 + 8 + 6$

$= 34$

10. (D) 144 If $\frac{\sqrt{n}}{3}$ is an even integer, then $\frac{\sqrt{n}}{3} = 2k$, where k is an integer because any even integer is equal to 2 multiplied by an integer. Since $\frac{\sqrt{n}}{3} = 2k$, $\sqrt{n} = 6k$. Squaring both sides of $\sqrt{n} = 6k$ gives: $(\sqrt{n})^2 = (6k)^2$, and $n = 36k^2$. So n must be a multiple of 36. Only choice (D), 144, is a multiple of 36. $144 = 4 \times 36$. Checking choice (D), $\frac{\sqrt{144}}{3} = \frac{12}{3} = 4$ and 4 is an even integer.

If all that math seems too time consuming, you could use a combination of logic and backsolving to get the correct answer. Since the problem deals with integers, then n must be a perfect square; only 81 and 144 among the answer choices are perfect squares. You could then backsolve by plugging one of those choices into the equation to determine that choice (D) 144 is correct.

11. (D) 3n − 14 This is a good opportunity to Pick Numbers. For instance, you could pick 10 for n, so that Gheri is 10 years old. In that case, Carl is 4 years old and Jean is 2 years old. Then the sum of their ages is: $10 + 4 + 2 = 16$. Now, plug 10 in for n into the answer choices, to see which gives you the target number of 16:

$3n + 4 = 3 \times 10 + 4 = 34$	Too big
$3n − 4 = 3 \times 10 − 4 = 26$	No good
$3n − 8 = 3 \times 10 − 8 = 22$	Still too big
$3n − 14 = 3 \times 10 − 14 = 16$	That's correct!

12. (C) 51 2, 37, and 67 are all prime. $51 = 3 \times 17$, so it is not prime. Knowing the *rules of divisibility* can help you when dealing with problems involving prime numbers, multiples, or factors. For instance, 51 is divisible by 3, because its digits—5 and 1—add up to 6, which is a multiple of 3.

13. (B) π The circumference of a circle $= 2\pi$ (radius), so a circle with a circumference of 2π has a radius of 1. The area of a circle $= \pi(\text{radius})^2$ so the area of a circle with a radius of 1 is $\pi(1)^2 = \pi$.

14. (D) $\frac{5}{16}$

To figure out the probability that a band member chosen at random will be a sophomore, apply the probability formula:

$$\text{Probability} = \frac{\text{Number of desired outcomes}}{\text{Number of possible outcomes}},$$

In this case:

$$\text{Probability} = \frac{\text{Number of sophomores}}{\text{Number of band members}}$$

$$= \frac{20}{13 + 20 + 16 + 15} = \frac{20}{64} = \frac{5}{16}.$$

15. (D) $\frac{5}{3}$ You could use an insight about math to solve this problem:

$a − b = −(b − a)$. So if $k − 3 = −\frac{5}{3}$, then $3 − k = −\left(−\frac{5}{3}\right) = \frac{5}{3}$.

You could also have simply done the calculations:

$k − 3 = −\frac{5}{3}$

$3k − 9 = 5$

$3k = 4$

$k = \frac{4}{3}$

Now substitute that value into the second equation:

$3 − k = 3 − \frac{4}{3} = \frac{9}{3} − \frac{4}{3} = \frac{5}{3}$

16. (A) $\frac{1}{5}$ Solve the equation $\frac{3x}{5} = 3x^2$ for x. Since $x \neq 0$, you can divide both sides by x. Then $\frac{3}{5} = 3x$. Dividing both sides by 3: $\frac{1}{5} = x$.

17. (A) $\frac{1}{3}$ You can Pick Numbers or use substitution for this problem. The best place to start Picking Numbers is with c and d. the question states that $4c = 3d$, so make $c = 3$ and $d = 4$. If $c = 3$ and $\frac{1}{2}b = c$, then $b = 6$. If $b = 6$ and $a = 2b$, then $a = 12$. Therefore, using the numbers picked: $\frac{d}{a} = \frac{4}{12} = \frac{1}{3}$.

18. (B) 72 Begin by converting the dimensions of the rectangular area to be covered to inches: 2 feet by 3 feet = 24 inches by 36 inches. 3 inches goes into 24 inches 8 times, and 4 inches go into 36 inches 9 times, so to cover the area $8 \times 9 = 72$ tiles are needed.

Alternatively, you could determine that each tile has an area of $\frac{1}{4} \times \frac{1}{3} = \frac{1}{12}$ square foot. So you need 12 tiles to cover one square foot. The area to be covered is 6 square feet, so $6 \times 12 = 72$ tiles needed.

19. (A) 6 If $\frac{7}{x} > \frac{1}{4}$, then multiply both terms by $4x$ and the result is $x < 28$. (When multiplying inequalities the sign must be flipped when multiplying by a negative number. You will remember that that means, in most cases, that you can't multiply both sides of an inequality by a variable, since you don't know whether a variable is negative or positive. However, in this case, you know from the construction of the problem that x must be positive.) Similarly, $\frac{7}{x} < \frac{1}{3}$ if, then $x > 21$. Therefore, 22, 23, 24, 25, 26, and 27 (a total of 6 numbers) are the allowable integer values of x.

20. (B) 13π The hole cover has a diameter of 14 inches, so its radius is 7 inches and its area is $\pi(7)^2 = 49\pi$ square inches. The diameter of the hole is 12 square inches, so its radius is 6 inches and its area is $\pi(6)^2 = 36\pi$ square inches. Thus, the cover is $49\pi - 36\pi = 13\pi$ square inches greater than the area of the hole.

21. (B) $\frac{3}{8}$ Some answer choices you can eliminate right away. $\frac{4}{7}$ is greater than $\frac{1}{2}$, so that's out, as is $\frac{1}{2}$. You're left with $\frac{1}{3}$, which is about 0.333, and $\frac{3}{8}$, which is 0.375 and is the closest in value to 0.40.

22. (A) $\frac{39y}{100x}$ Since the question asks for the answer in dollars, start by converting cents to dollars. There are 100 cents in a dollar, so $39\ cents = \frac{39}{100}$ dollars. Since each peach costs $\frac{39}{100}$ dollars, y peaches cost $\frac{39}{100}y$ dollars. If x oranges cost as much as y peaches, x oranges also cost $\frac{39}{100}y$ dollars or $\frac{39y}{100}$ dollars. Then one orange costs $\frac{1}{x}$ as much: $\frac{39y}{100x}$ dollars.

Alternately, this is an ideal problem to solve by Picking Numbers. Say that 5 oranges and 10 peaches cost the same; that is $x = 5$ and $y = 10$. If peaches are 39 cents each, 10 of them will cost \$3.90 and that would equal the cost of 5 oranges. That means each orange costs $\frac{\$3.90}{5}$ or \$0.78. Try the numbers in each answer choice, looking for the target number:

Choice (A): $\frac{(39)(10)}{(100)(5)} = \frac{390}{500} = \frac{39}{50} = 0.78$	This may be the answer; hold onto it for now.
Choice (B): $\frac{(39)(5)}{(100)(10)} = \frac{195}{1,000}$	Discard.
Choice (C): $\frac{3,900}{(5)(10)} = \frac{3,900}{50} = 78$	This is 78 dollars, not 78 cents, so discard.
Choice (D): $\frac{(39)(5)}{10} = \frac{195}{10} = 19.5$	Discard.

23. (C) 13 To come up with the largest number of groups, you should minimize the number of students in each group. Each group must contain at least three students, so that means you could have a total of 12 groups with 3 students in them, and one final group with 4 students in it, for a total of 13 groups.

24. (C) 8 The altitude at the base of the triangle is the same thing as the height of the triangle, and the area of a triangle $= \frac{1}{2}$(base)(height) . If the area of the triangle is 36 and its base is 9, the altitude is found as follows:

$$36 = \frac{1}{2}(9)(\text{altitude})$$

$$\text{altitude} = \frac{36}{9} \times 2 = 4 \times 2 = 8$$

25. (C) 85 Plug in -5 for x into the equation and solve:
$2(-5)^2 - 6(-5) + 5$

$= 2(25) + 30 + 5$

$= 85$

Part 6: Electronics Information Answers and Explanations

1. **(B) directly proportional** Voltage and current are directly proportional. Anytime voltage increases, current will also increase as long as the resistance remains constant, in accordance with Ohm's Law.

2. **(C) wrapping the wire around a nail** As electric current passes through a wire, a magnetic field is generated around the wire. The strength of the field at any given point at a certain distance around a straight wire will be constant for a given current value (and increasing the circumference of a non-coiled circuit will likewise have little effect). However, winding the wire into loops will cause the field to overlap and increase within the loops. Wrapping the wire in a coil around a ferrous (that is, made of iron) object like a nail, will lead to an even greater increase in the magnetic field. That's because the material's many microscopic magnets will align with and strengthen it. What about the greater wire length in answer choice (D)? Increasing the length of the wire while holding the current constant will not result in a greater field if the number of loops isn't increased. In fact, having the same number of loops spread out over a greater wire length will actually result in a smaller increase in magnetic field strength inside the loops.

3. **(D) an inductor** Inductors resist change in current, and thus act as resistors for alternating current, increasing their apparent resistance with the AC frequency. However, for a continuous direct current, an inductor is the one option listed that will offer little resistance to current flow.

4. **(A) 1** In the symbol, the number 1 indicates the base, which is the middle piece of semiconductor material inside a transistor.

5. **(B) 375 ohms** For a simple, parallel circuit with two resistors of equal value, divide the resistance by two to find the equivalent resistance. In this question, two 750 ohm resistors in a parallel circuit gives an equivalent resistance of $\frac{750 \text{ ohms}}{2} = 375$ ohms

6. **(C) self-induction** When current first flows through a coil, the magnetic field builds relatively slowly. This is because the expanding magnetic field generates a voltage in the coil that opposes the original current flow. This is known as counter-emf, and it is produced by a process known as self-induction.

7. **(C) 10 KΩ** Via Ohm's Law, $R = V/I$. But before plugging in the current, it must be converted into Amperes. 5 mA = 0.005 A. Thus $R = \frac{50V}{0.005A} = 10,000$ ohms. 10,000 ohms is the same as 10 kΩ.

8. **(C) series-parallel circuit** Resistors R2 and R3 are in parallel with each other, while R1 is in series with them both. Since this simple circuit combines series and parallel loads, it is a series-parallel circuit.

9. **(B) always decreases the effective resistance** Adding resistors in parallel always lowers the resistance, while adding resistors in series always increases it. The rule can be tested or rediscovered by making up a simple question of two resistors in parallel and calculating the effective resistance, but it's easy to remember if you just imagine more and more barriers in a row (series resistors) adding to the difficulty in moving forward, and the addition of more pathway choices (parallel resistors) making it easier by reducing crowding of electrons.

10. **(B) a free electron outside the valence shell** The crystalline structure of pure silicon is very stable. The four valence electrons in each silicon atom bond with the valence electrons in the atoms around it, so no free electrons exist to allow current flow. This can be changed by "doping" the silicon's crystal structure with phosphorus, arsenic, or antimony. Since these elements all have five electrons in their valence shell, they will bond themselves to the other silicon atoms, but leave one free electron that is able to migrate throughout the crystal. This changes the silicon crystal into an N-type material. This new material is still electrically neutral, but is able to conduct electricity due to the presence of free electrons.

11. **(A) NPN** There are two types of transistors: an NPN transistor, and a PNP transistor. An NPN transistor is made up of a thin piece of P-type material sandwiched between two pieces of N-type material. A PNP transistor is the opposite: two pieces of P-type material that have a piece of N-type material between them.

12. **(B) $\frac{1}{3}\Omega$** The reciprocals of the resistance values are $\frac{1}{2}$ and $\frac{1}{4}$. Since $\frac{1}{2}$ is equivalent to $\frac{2}{4}$, their sum can be simplified as $\frac{3}{4}$. The reciprocal is $\frac{4}{3}\Omega$, which can also be written as $1\frac{1}{3}\Omega$.

13. **(D) 6 Ω** The effective resistance is the sum of the resistances of each resistor in series, so the answer is $3 + 3 = 6\,\Omega$.

14. **(A) always increases the effective resistance** Adding a resistor when a resistor is already present, increases the effective resistance.

15. **(C) insulator** More than four electrons in the valence shell means that the element is an insulator. Insulators do not conduct electricity well, and therefore are useful for creating electrical barriers. Thus, an element with five electrons in its valence shell is an insulator.

16. **(B) coulomb** An ampere is defined as one coulomb of electrical charge flowing past a point in one second. One coulomb is the amount of charge in 6.253×10^{18} electrons. This is the same as 6,253,100,000,000,000,000 electrons. If this many electrons flow past a point in a conductor in one second, one ampere of current is flowing.

17. **(A) allow DC current to pass easily** Inductors work exactly opposite to capacitors, in the sense that they allow DC to pass easily, but resist the flow of AC. This is known as *inductive reactance,* and it will rise in direct proportion to the frequency of the current flowing through the inductor.

18. **(D) adding a resistor of 5 Ω in parallel with the original load** Only adding a resistor in parallel will decrease the overall resistance, since it allows more paths for the current to travel through. This means the answer is either (B) or (D). Answer choice (D) works, because $\frac{1}{5} + \frac{1}{5} = \frac{2}{5}$, and the reciprocal is $\frac{5}{2} = 2.5\Omega$. In contrast, answer choice (B) would result in an effective resistance of 1.6 Ω, so it does not work. You could also have solved this problem using logic. When two loads of equal resistance value are wired in parallel, their effective resistance is half of their individual resistances (likewise, with three identical resistors in parallel, their effective resistance is $\frac{1}{3}$ of their individual resistances, and with four resistors in parallel, effective resistance is decreased to $\frac{1}{4}$, et cetera). If you know this rule, (D) is the clear choice without doing any math.

19. **(B) ammeter** This is the circuit symbol for an ammeter, which is used to measure current.

20. **(C) current flow varies throughout the circuit** In a series circuit, *the current flow will be the same in all parts of the circuit.* The current that leaves the voltage source must return to the voltage source, and since there is only one path for current to follow in a series circuit, current will be the same throughout the circuit. Voltage measured across each of the components, on the other hand, may be different depending on their resistance.

Part 7: Automotive and Shop Information Answers and Explanations

1. **(A) when an air-fuel mixture explodes, rather than burns** Detonation is when an air-fuel mixture explodes, rather than burns. It can often take place when an engine's air-fuel mixture is lean.

2. **(C) secondary** The current that flows through the ignition primary winding builds a strong magnetic field that surrounds both it and the *secondary coil winding*. This is the device that creates high voltage for the spark plugs.

3. **(C) 50/50** Engine coolant is normally made up of a 50/50 mix of antifreeze and water.

4. **(C) either a ratchet or an impact wrench** The most common drive tool for sockets is the ratchet, which turns the fastener in only one direction as the handle is moved back and forth through a narrow arc. Ratchets are reversible, so they can be set to tighten or loosen a fastener. Sockets can also be used with pneumatic (compressed air) power tools, such as an air impact wrench. The air impact wrench can remove fasteners quickly by applying tremendous amounts of torque (twisting force) using a "hammering" action that vibrates fasteners loose.

5. **(D) a Crescent wrench** Automotive technicians will sometimes use a steel rule or tape measure to determine distances or the width of objects. When accuracy down to one-thousandths of an inch is required, an outside micrometer is used. The outside micrometer is made to measure the outside diameter of cylindrically shaped objects, as well as the thickness of flat objects. While a Crescent wrench can be adjusted to accommodate different widths, it is not used for measurement.

6. **(C) power stroke** The diagram indicates that the intake and exhaust valves are closed, and the piston is headed for BDC. That means that the engine is in the power stroke phase of its cycle.

7. **(D) powertrain control module** A fuel injector sprays fuel into the intake stream as it receives electrical signals from the powertrain control module (or PCM).

8. **(B) 13** Carpenters often will use a *claw hammer*, which serves a dual purpose. The hammer head has two ends: one to drive nails and the other to remove nails. Claw hammers come in a variety of sizes, and these are determined by the weight of the hammer head. A general purpose claw hammer would have a 13 oz. head.

9. **(B) start a hole for drilling** This is a center punch. Center punches are used to make small indentations that serve as starting marks for drilling operations. Making a small indentation with a center punch can help the drill bit stay on target long enough to get a hole started.

10. **(C) cylinder head.** Spark plugs are threaded into the cylinder head where the spark plug protrudes into the combustion chamber and generates the spark to initiate combustion.

11. **(A) planetary gear sets** Automatic transmissions do all of the gear selection for the driver. This is done in the transmission using hydraulics and *planetary gear sets*. The newest automatic transmissions are controlled electronically by the vehicle's powertrain control module.

12. **(A) hydraulically** Brake systems are *hydraulically operated*. A pumping piston, located in the master cylinder, is operated by the brake pedal and puts pressure on the system's brake fluid.

13. **(B)**

A hacksaw is used for cutting metals such as steel, aluminium, or copper. The blades in a hacksaw are replaceable, and it is important to choose the right blade for the material that is going to be cut.

14. **(D) wire-feed welding** MIG welding is also known as *wire-feed welding* because the electrode used for the weld process is a wire that is automatically fed from a spool.

15. **(A) carpenter's level** The carpenter's level has three level vials, which are mounted horizontally, vertically, and at a 45-degree angle. It is used in construction for checking for true vertical, true horizontal, and 45-degree angles.

16. **(D) none of the above** None of the ignition systems listed would utilize contact points. Only older cars with breaker points would have contact points.

17. **(A) a plane** When working with wood, there are many occasions when it is necessary to remove a small amount of material to make a piece fit properly or to make a surface smooth. One tool that can be used for this purpose is a *plane*.

18. **(D) pitman arm** The *pitman arm* is a short lever arm connected to the steering gear that transmits the steering force from the cross shaft to the steering linkage system. Long-short arm suspensions most commonly use linkage steering to connect the steering column to the pitman arm, center link, and idler arm.

19. **(C) emission control** The catalytic converter is responsible for converting the toxic components of engine exhaust into relatively harmless compounds such as carbon dioxide and water and is, thus, part of the emission control system.

20. **(C) wire cutter** The most common type of pliers is the *combination slip-joint*. These are adjustable at the joint of the two handles of the pliers. With two different positions to choose from, these pliers can grip objects in a wide range of sizes. Sometimes, this design also incorporates *a wire cutter* for increased versatility.

21. **(A) earlier** For higher engine speeds, the flame must be started *earlier* in order to generate the most effective downward push on the piston. This is known as *advancing* the timing.

22. **(A)**

A ball peen hammer is used for forming soft metal, peening rivet heads, and striking metal in out-of-the-way places.

23. **(D) torque converters** A common type of suspension system, long-short arm suspension systems include *ball joints*, *upper control arms,* and *lower control arms*, among other components. A (D) torque converter is part of an automatic steering system, not a suspension system.

24. **(D) cold chisel** The most common chisel is the *cold chisel*, which has a straight, sharp edge for cutting off bolt heads or separating two pieces of an assembly.

25. **(A) worn engine bearings** Of the given choices, only worn engine bearings would not be the cause of a loss of compression, as the engine bearings do not weigh in on compression issues.

Part 8: Mechanical Comprehension Answers and Explanations

1. **(D) the speed with which the surfaces are moving past each other** Kinetic friction is exhibited when surfaces/objects move past one another. The normal force, which is a factor of the weight of the object, will affect friction. (For example, move your hand across a table lightly and then again with more force; increased force leads to increased friction.) The nature and area of the surfaces in contact with each other will also affect the friction that develops between two surfaces. (For example, moving your hand across a desk with oil on it is a lot easier than with honey; also, moving one finger across a desk develops less friction than moving your entire hand.) The speed at which the surfaces move past each other however, does not impact the frictional forces (though it may generate more heat).

2. **(D) $W = F \times d$** Work is accomplished when force is applied against an object. This is summarized by the formula $W = Fd$ where F is force in newtons (N), d is distance in meters (m), and W is work in joules (J).

3. **(B) the smaller pulley turns faster** The smaller pulleys *always* turn faster than larger pulleys in a system.

4. **(A) work-energy theorem** Any work that is done to accelerate an object at rest to speed v will be converted into the kinetic energy of that object. This principle is known as the work-energy theorem.

5. **(D) 1 watt of power** Performing work at the rate of 1 joule per second is the same as expending 1 watt of power.

6. **(C) all liquids are good lubricants** There are several properties of liquids that are unchanging. First, they are effectively incompressible. Even when extremely high pressure is applied to a liquid, the volume of the liquid will decrease only a very small amount. This property makes liquids very effective for transmitting force. And the second overarching principle of hydraulics is that liquids conform themselves to the shape of their container. Whether in a pipe or a pump, liquids will always change their shape to fill the space completely. But not all liquids are by nature good lubricants.

7. **(C) The crate will not move.** The force of static friction can increase in response to an applied force, resisting movement, but only up to a maximum value. If the applied force is greater than the maximum value of static friction, the crate will move. Since the applied force is given, the maximum force of static friction is what needs to be calculated. The force of static friction has a maximum value equal to the product of the normal force and the coefficient. The coefficient is given, but the normal force is not. However, since the object is at rest on a flat, horizontal surface, the normal force will be equal and opposite to the object's weight. Therefore $F_N = 250$ N. The maximum force of static friction then is: $F_{fs} = (0.8)(250) = 200$ N.

The applied force is 200 N, but the maximum force of static friction is also 200 N. Since friction always opposes movement, it is opposite the applied force, so the net force can be calculated like this: $F_{net} = (200 \text{ N}) + (-200 \text{ N}) = 0$ N Since the net force is zero, the object will not move. Another way to put it is that the applied force is enough to take the resisting static friction to its limit, but not enough to overcome it.

8. **(B) 50 psi** Using the formula for pressure $\left(P = \frac{F}{A} \right)$, if 100 pounds of force are applied over an area of 2 square inches, then the resulting pressure is 50 pounds per square inch (psi).

9. **(D) mechanical advantage** Mechanical advantage is defined as "the advantage gained by the use of a mechanism in transmitting force." Using the proper equipment, it is possible to increase or even multiply force many times over what is initially applied.

10. **(C) fulcrum** The fulcrum is the point that the lever pivots on. The position of the fulcrum will define whether any mechanical advantage is gained. If the fulcrum is closer to the object being lifted, less effort is required to do the work.

11. **(B) $6 \frac{m}{s^2}$** Based on Newton's second law, $F = ma$, rearrange the equation for acceleration: $a = \frac{F}{m}$. Units of force must be in Newtons and mass in kg. Taking 30 N and dividing by 5 kg equals $6 \frac{m}{s^2}$.

12. **(C) the object will accelerate in the direction of the net force** According to Newton's Second Law of Motion, when a net force acts on an object, the object will accelerate in the direction of the net force. The acceleration will be less if the mass of the object is greater. (A) is not necessarily true. An object may speed up or slow down when a net force acts on it depending on the direction of the force and the object's initial motion. The cumulative force is the same as the net force, so (B) does not make much sense. As for (D), in uniform circular motion, speed (magnitude) is constant, but the direction of motion changes constantly. Thus the net force applied leads to acceleration but no change in speed.

13. **(A) clockwise** Belted pulleys, unlike meshed gears, turn in the same direction.

14. **(A) a fixed pulley** The illustration shows a fixed pulley.

15. **(C) 10 psi** The load piston has a total surface area of 10 square inches. Using the formula $P = \frac{F}{A}$, 100 pounds ÷ 10 square inches = 10 pounds per square inch (psi) of pressure that should be applied to the load piston.

16. **(C) 20 N to the left and 10 N down** Forces are vector quantities, which means they have both magnitude and direction. The 30 N and 50 N forces are acting in opposite directions on the horizontal dimension. Since 50 N > 30 N, it will dominate and the resultant is: 50 N – 30 N = 20 N in the direction of the greater force (i.e. to the left). There is nothing opposing the 10 N force, so the result is 10 N acting vertically downward.

17. **(D) 4:1** Note that in order to lift the load 1 foot, it is necessary to pull the rope a total of 4 feet. This is because each of the four rope links must shorten by 1 foot to get the lower block to move 1 foot. Neglecting friction, this gives a total mechanical advantage of 4:1, so if 4 pounds of force are required to lift a load, only 1 pound needs to be applied to the rope.

18. **(A) first-class** A child's teeter-totter is an example of a first-class lever because the fulcrum is located between the load and the applied force.

19. **(C) sliding frictional force** In the example of the hockey puck sliding along an ice surface, while ice has much less friction than most surfaces, it will still exert a sliding frictional force on the puck that eventually causes it to stop moving.

20. **(A) torque** Torque is *twisting force*. When a bolt is being tightened, torque is being applied to the bolt. For example, when tightening a fastener, if a wrench is used that is 1 foot long, and a force of 100 pounds applied to the end of the wrench in a direction perpendicular to the wrench, 100 foot-pounds (ft-lb) of torque is being applied.

21. **(B) 100 foot-pounds** When tightening a fastener, if a person uses a wrench that is 1 foot long, and applies a force of 100 pounds to the end of the wrench, 100 foot-pounds (ft-lb) of torque is being applied. Simply multiply the applied force by the length of the wrench to determine the torque.

22. **(C) 50 N** A 50 N weight will produce a 50 N force acting downward. Since the system is in equilibrium, the upward tension force must exactly balance the downward weight, which gives a Tension of 50 N acting upwards.

23. **(A) the number of pulleys used in the block and tackle** The pulleys of a block and tackle system multiply the force exerted in pulling the rope of the system by the number of pulleys in the system. Therefore, the lifting force that the pulleys exert on the object is the force exerted in pulling the rope multiplied by the number of pulleys used.

24. **(A) acceleration due to gravity** According to Newton's Gravitational Law, since gravity exerts a force on bodies that pulls them together, this force causes an acceleration due to gravity, which is represented by the symbol g.

25. **(C) the pivot point of a lever** The fulcrum is the point on which a lever pivots.

Part 9: Assembling Objects Answers and Explanations

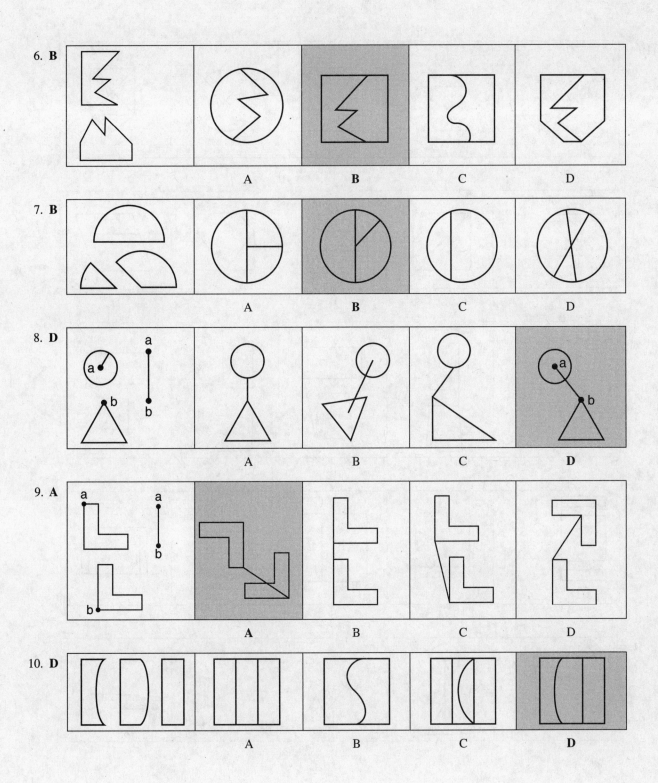

6. **B**

7. **B**

8. **D**

9. **A**

10. **D**

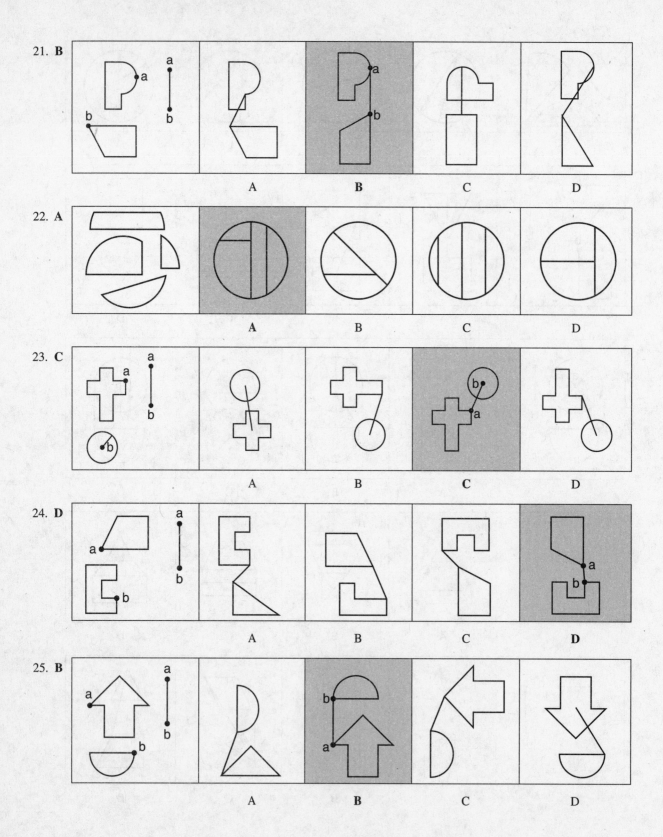

APPENDIX: WORD PARTS

This appendix contains comprehensive lists and definitions of prefixes, suffixes, and word roots, along with examples of words that contain each word part.

- Part I: prefixes
- Part II: suffixes
- Part III: word roots

If you are struggling to raise your performance on the Word Knowledge subtest, you may wish to consider making flash cards out of the word parts in this chapter, and then use them to quiz yourself as part of your ASVAB studies. In studying this word list, you will want to be familiar with the following abbreviations:

- (n) noun: a word that names a person, place, thing, or idea
- (v) verb: an action word
- (adj) adjective: a word that modifies a noun
- (adv) adverb: a word that modifies a verb, adjective, or other adverb

PART I: PREFIXES

The table below lists the most common prefixes in English, along with the meaning of each and examples.

Note: Sometimes the word parts listed below appear in the middle of words, but they appear most commonly as prefixes. Also, remember that not all words have prefixes.

Prefix	Meaning	Examples
a, an	not, without	agnostic: (n) one who believes that it cannot be known whether or not God exists; (adj) claiming no knowledge amoral: (adj) not related to morality; lacking regard for morality anomaly: (n) an irregularity anonymous: (adj) lacking a named author; having an unknown author apathy: (n) lack of feeling, interest, or emotional investment atheist: (n) one who does not believe in God atypical: (adj) not typical
ab	away from, apart from, down	abduct: (v) to take away by force abhor: (v) to hate; to detest abject: (adj) cast down; degraded abnormal: (adj) not normal; not conforming to a standard abolish: (v) to do away with, ban, or make void abstract: (v) to draw or pull away, remove; (adj) theoretical; related to ideas rather than to specific instances or objects
ad	toward, near	(Sometimes the *d* is dropped and the first letter to which *a* is prefixed is doubled.) adapt: (v) to adjust in response to new circumstances addict: (v) to cause (someone) to become dependent on a substance or activity; (n) a person who is dependent on a substance or activity address: (n) a speech; (v) to give a speech or direct a statement to adhere: (v) to stick fast; to cleave; to cling adjacent: (adj) next to, close to, or connected to adjoin: (v) to be next to, close to, or connected to admire: (v) to look up to; to look at with approval or pleasure advocate: (v) to plead for; to argue in favor of attract: (v) to draw by physical force or by an appeal to emotions or senses
ambi, amphi	both, on both sides	ambidextrous: (adj) able to use both hands equally well ambiguous: (adj) open to various interpretations amphibian: (n) an animal that lives part of its life in water and part of its life on land; a person with a twofold nature; (adj) having the traits of an amphibian
ant, ante	before	antebellum: (adj) before the war (especially the American Civil War) antecedent: (adj) existing, being, or going before antedate: (v) to precede in time anterior: (adj) placed before
anti	against	antidote: (n) a remedy intended to counteract a poison antifreeze: (n) a chemical that lowers the freezing point of a liquid such as water antiseptic: (adj) free from germs; particularly clean or neat antithetical: (adj) opposed to, contrary to

Prefix	Meaning	Examples
bi, bin	two	biennial: (adj) happening every two years bilateral: (adj) related to both sides bilingual: (adj) able to speak one's native language and another with equal facility binocular: (adj) involving two eyes bipartisan: (adj) representing two parties combination: (n) the joining of two or more things into a whole
cent	hundred	centimeter: (n) one hundredth of a meter centipede: (n) a creature with many legs century: (n) one hundred years percent: (adj) out of every hundred
circu, circum	around	circuit: (n) a path or journey around an area; a path traveled by electrical current circuitous: (adj) roundabout, indirect circumference: (n) the outer boundary of a circular area circumstances: (n) the state of affairs that exist around a particular time or person; the factors that influence a person or situation
co, col, com, con	together, completely	coerce: (v) to force (another to do an action) by using fear, authority, or violence collaborate: (v) to work with another; to cooperate collide: (v) (used of two or more objects or persons) to crash together; to make contact forcefully or violently commensurate: (adj) suitable in measure, proportionate compatible: (adj) able to exist together with someone or something else; capable of harmonious co-existence conciliate: (v) to placate; to win over connect: (v) to bind or fasten together
contra, contro, counter	against	contradict: (v) to oppose; to speak against contrary: (adj) opposed to; opposite controversy: (n) a prolonged debate or disagreement about a topic counterfeit: (adj) fake; (n) a false imitation encounter: (v) a meeting, often with an opponent
de	away, off, down, reversal	decipher: (v) to interpret; to decode; to discern a hidden meaning defame: (v) to slander; to publicly speak ill of delineate: (v) to draw the outlines of; to sketch; to describe descend: (v) to move from a higher to a lower place
deca	ten	decade: (n) ten years decathlon: (n) a sports competition composed of ten events
di, dia	in two, across, through	diagnose: (v) to determine the nature of (a sickness or problem) by examining symptoms dialogue: (n) conversation between two or more persons diameter: (n) a line going through a circle, dividing it in two dichotomy: (n) division into two parts, kinds, etc.

Prefix	Meaning	Examples
di, dis	away from, reversal, not	diffuse: (v) to pour out and spread, as in a fluid; (adj) spread out dilate: (v) to widen; to expand disperse: (v) to spread over a wide area; to drive away in various directions disseminate: (v) to scatter or spread widely; to promulgate dissuade: (v) to persuade (someone) against (a course of action); to deter; to advise against
dys	faulty, abnormal	dysfunctional: (adj) poorly functioning dyslexia: (n) an impairment of reading ability due to a neurological problem
e, ex	out of, from, former	evade: (v) to escape from; to avoid exclude: (v) to shut out; to leave out exonerate: (v) to free or declare free from blame expire: (v) to breathe one's last; to die; to reach the end of viability
em, en	inside, into	embrace: (v) to clasp in the arms; to include or contain enclose: (v) to close in on all sides
extra	outside, beyond	extract: (v) to take out; to obtain against a person's will extradite: (v) to send (a person accused of a crime) to another state or nation for trial or punishment extraordinary: (adj) beyond the ordinary; unusual extrasensory: (adj) outside the senses; coming from or pertaining to knowledge that cannot be gained through normal sense perception
fore	before	foreshadow: (v) to warn of or indicate (a future event) foresight: (n) the act of foreseeing; care for the future; prudence forestall: (v) to prevent by advance action
hemi	half	hemisphere: (n) half a sphere; half of the Earth hemiplegia: (n) paralysis of the arm, leg, and trunk on one side of the body
hetero	different, other	heterogeneous: (adj) made up of different kinds heterosexual: (adj) pertaining to different sexes; having a sexual orientation toward members of the opposite sex
homeo, homo	same, similar	homogeneous: (adj) having a uniform nature or substance homonym: (n) one of two or more words spelled and pronounced alike but different in meaning homosexual: (adj) pertaining to the same sex; having a sexual orientation toward members of the same sex
hyper	over, above, more than, excessive	hyperactive: (adj) excessively active hyperbole: (n) extreme exaggeration used to create an effect
hypo	under, beneath, less than	hypochondriac: (n) one who imagines physical ailments; one who is overly preoccupied with physical health hypocritical: (adj) pretending to have virtues or qualities one does not have hypothesis: (n) assumption subject to proof
in, im	not, without	immoral: (adj) not moral impartial: (adj) unbiased; fair inactive: (adj) not active indolence: (adj) a tendency to avoid work or exertion; laziness innocuous: (adj) harmless, inoffensive

Prefix	Meaning	Examples
in, im	inside, into	implicit: (adj) not stated; inherent incarnate: (adj) having a body or physical form indigenous: (adj) native to a place influx: (n) the pouring or flowing of one thing into another intrinsic: (adj) natural; innate
inter	between, among	interim: (n) time period between one event and another; (adj) not permanent interloper: (n) one who intrudes in the domain of others intermittent: (adj) happening on and off; not constant intersperse: (v) to scatter; to put things among other things interstate: (adj) involving two or more states
intra	inside, within	intramural: (adj) within a school; inside a city intrastate: (adj) within a state intravenous: (adj) inside the veins
macro	great, large	macroscopic: (adj) large enough to be seen without magnification macroeconomics: (n) study of the economy on a large scale
mal, male	bad, evil, wrong	maladroit: (adj) clumsy, tactless malady: (n) an illness malediction: (n) a curse malfunction: (n) the act of not working correctly; (v) to work incorrectly; to break malicious: (adj) intended to hurt someone malign: (v) to tell lies with the intent of hurting someone's reputation; to slander
med, medi	middle	immediate: (adj) nearest; having nothing in between intermediate: (adj) between the beginning and end mediate: (v) to serve as a go-between; to try to settle an argument medieval: (adj) related to the Middle Ages mediocre: (adj) of only so-so quality medium: (n) size between small and large; a substance or agency that things travel through (as, for example, light travels through air, and news is conveyed by television and newspapers)
mega, megalo	very large	megalith: (n) a very big stone megalomania: (n) a mental condition involving delusions of greatness; an obsession with achieving great things megalopolis: (n) a very large city megaphone: (n) a device for magnifying the sound of one's voice megaton: (n) explosive power equal to 1,000,000 tons of TNT
micro	very small	microbe: (n) a very small organism microcosm: (n) a small system that reflects a larger whole microorganism: (n) a very small organism microscope: (n) a device that magnifies very small things for viewing
min, mini	small	diminish: (v) to lessen diminution: (n) reduction; the act of reducing miniature: (n) a copy or model that represents something in greatly reduced size minute: (n) one-sixtieth of an hour minute: (adj) very small minutiae: (n) small or trivial details

Prefix	Meaning	Examples
mis	bad, wrong, hateful	misadventure: (n) bad luck; an unlucky accident misanthrope: (n) one who hates people or humanity misapply: (v) to use something incorrectly mischance: (n) bad luck; an unlucky accident mischief: (n) naughty or annoying behavior misconstrue: (v) to understand something incorrectly misfit: (n) somebody or something that doesn't fit in
mon, mono	one, single	monarchy: (n) rule by a single person monk: (n) a man in a religious order living apart from society monogram: (n) a design made up of letters combined into one shape monograph: (n) a scholarly paper on one topic monologue: (n) a speech or other dramatic composition recited by one person monomania: (n) an obsession with a single subject monotonous: (adj) boring; spoken using only one tone
mult	many	multiple: (adj) many; having many parts; a number containing some quantity of a smaller number without remainder multiplex: (adj) having more than one part; (n) a building with many separate units multiply: (v) to increase; to become many multitudinous: (adj) very many; containing very many; having very many forms
non	not	nonconformist: (n) one who does not conform to a church or other societal institution nonentity: (n) something that doesn't exist; something that is unimportant nonpartisan: (adj) not affiliated with a political party
nov, neo, nou	new	innovate: (v) to develop a new way of doing something neologism: (n) a newly invented word or phrase neophyte: (n) a beginner; a new convert; a new worker novice: (n) a person new to any field or activity renovate: (v) to repair something so it is like new or does not show as much wear and tear
oct	eight	octagon: (n) a shape with eight sides octogenarian: (n) a person whose age is 80–89
omni	all	omnibus: (n) an anthology of the works of one author or of writings on related subjects omnipotent: (adj) all-powerful omnipresent: (adj) being everywhere at one time omniscient: (adj) knowing everything
pan, pant	all, everyone	pandemic: (adj) widespread panoply: (n) an impressive or vast group or display panorama: (n) a view or scene that extends a long way pantheon: (n) the group made up of all the gods of a particular culture; a building that honors dead heroes

Prefix	Meaning	Examples
para	next to, beside	parable: (n) a story that teaches a lesson through allegory paragon: (n) an example of excellence to be emulated parallel: (adj) being side by side and the same distance apart at all points; having similar paths or structures paranoid: (adj) suffering from a baseless distrust of others parasite: (n) a living thing that draws its nutrients from another on which it lives; a person who lives off another without providing anything in return parody: (v) to satirize through imitation; (n) an imitative satire
pent	five	pentagon: (n) a five-sided shape pentathlon: (n) a sports competition with five events
peri	around	perimeter: (n) the distance around a shape; a border around a shape peripatetic: (adj) not stationary, moving about periscope: (n) an optical instrument used to view objects that otherwise couldn't be seen
poly	many	polyandry: (n) the practice of having multiple husbands polygamy: (n) the practice of having multiple spouses, often wives polyglot: (n) someone who speaks many languages polygon: (n) a figure with many sides polytheism: (n) belief in many gods
post	behind, after	post facto: (adv) after the fact posterior: (adj) situated at the rear posthumous: (adj) after death
pre	before, in front	precedent: (n) an act that serves as an example for subsequent situations precept: (n) a rule to govern behavior precocious: (adj) unusually advanced at a young age premonition: (n) a feeling or intuition that something is going to happen before it does
pro	in front, before, much, for	proceed: (v) to go forward profuse: (adj) occurring in large amounts; abounding; overly giving prolific: (adj) highly fruitful proselytize: (v) to convert, recruit, or attempt to convert provident: (adj) possessing foresight
prot, proto	first	protagonist: (n) the main character in a play or story protocol: (n) diplomatic etiquette; a system of proper conduct; the original record of a treaty or other negotiation prototype: (n) the first version of an invention, on which later models are based
pseud, pseudo	false	pseudonym: (n) a false name; a pen name pseudopod: (n) part of a single-celled organism that can be stuck out (like a foot) and used to move around pseudoscience: (n) false science; something believed to be based on the scientific method but actually is not

Prefix	Meaning	Examples
quad, quar, quat	four	quadrant: (n) a quarter of a circle; a 90-degree arc quadruple: (adj) four times as many quadruplets: (n) four children born in one birth quart: (n) one fourth of a gallon
quin, quint	five	quintile: (n) one-fifth quintuple: (adj) five times as many
re	back, again	recline: (v) to lean back; to lie down regain: (v) to gain again; to take back remain: (v) to stay behind; to be left; to continue to be reorganize: (v) to organize again request: (v) to ask (originally: to seek again)
retro	backward	retroactive: (adj) extending to things that happened in the past retrofit: (v) to install newer parts into an older device or structure retrograde: (adj) moving backward; appearing to move backward retrospective: (adj) looking back at the past; (n) a review of past events
se	apart, away	secede: (v) to withdraw formally from an association sedition: (n) provocation of rebellion against a government seduce: (v) to lead astray segregate: (v) to separate a larger group into two or more groups; to set an individual or subgroup apart from the larger group select: (v) to choose one thing over another separate: (v) to keep apart; to divide sequester: (v) to isolate or set apart from a larger group
semi	half	semicircle: (n) half a circle semiconscious: (adj) only partly conscious; half awake
sept	seven	septuplet: (n) one of seven children born together septennial: (adj) occurring every seven years
sex, hex	six	sextet: (n) a band with six musicians hexagon: (n) a shape with six sides
sub, sup	below, under	subliminal: (adj) existing beneath consciousness submissive: (adj) obedient; not dominant subsidiary: (adj) supplemental; secondary subterfuge: (n) a trick or stratagem used to deceive, hide something, or avoid punishment subtle: (adj) not direct; difficult to understand suppose: (v) to put down as a hypothesis; to use as the underlying basis of an argument; to assume
super, sur	over, above	superfluous: (adj) extra; more than necessary superlative: (n) the highest or best of its kind supersede: (v) to replace in power or preference by another surmount: (v) to overcome an obstacle or prevail over a problem surpass: (v) to exceed in amount or degree surveillance: (n) a watch kept over someone or something

Prefix	Meaning	Examples
sym, syn	the same, together	symbiosis: (n) the act of living together in a mutually beneficial relationship symmetry: (n) balanced proportions; having opposite parts that mirror one another sympathy: (n) the attempt to understand the feelings of others symposium: (n) a meeting at which ideas are discussed; originally: a party at which people drink together synonym: (n) a word that means the same thing as another synthesis: (n) the act of combining things to create a new whole
trans	across, beyond	transaction: (n) an exchange, especially a business deal involving buying and selling transcendent: (adj) going beyond ordinary limits transgress: (v) to disobey or violate a law; to sin transition: (n) a change from one way of being to another transparent: (adj) easy to see through; easy to perceive
un	not	unseen: (adj) not seen unusual: (adj) not usual; exceptional; strange
uni, un	one	reunion: (n) a meeting that brings people back together unanimous: (adj) in complete agreement unicorn: (n) a mythical animal with a single horn uniform: (adj) of one kind; consistent universe: (n) all things considered as one whole

PART II: SUFFIXES

As we discuss in the Word Knowledge chapter, suffixes do two things: They affect the meaning of a word, and often they also indicate the word's part of speech. The list of suffixes you see here lists the most common suffixes in English. Each is listed with the part of speech the suffix usually indicates, as well as examples demonstrating its usage.

Note: Sometimes the word parts listed below appear in the middle of words, but they appear most commonly as suffixes. Also, remember that not all words have suffixes.

Suffix	Usually indicates a(n) . . .	Meaning	Examples
a, ia	noun	state of, condition of, thing that has the quality of	insomnia: (n) condition of being unable to sleep
able, ible	adjective	capable of, worthy of	changeable: (adj) able to be changed combustible: (adj) capable of being burned; easily inflamed
age	noun	action or process, amount or rate of, place of	brokerage: (n) business of negotiating mileage: (n) number of miles orphanage: (n) place where orphans are housed
al, ial	adjective	relating to	hormonal: (adj) relating to hormones literal: (adj) relating to the usual or exact meaning of words residential: (adj) relating to a residence
an, ian	adjective or noun	adjective: relating to noun: one who relates to or is skilled at	comedian: (n) one who is funny musician: (n) one who is skilled in music reptilian: (adj) like a reptile
ance, ence, ancy, ency	noun	state of, action of	consistency: (n) state of being consistent furtherance: (n) act of furthering something
ard	noun	person who has a particular quality	coward: (n) one who is afraid, easily cowed dullard: (n) one who is dull
ary	adjective	relating to	budgetary: (adj) relating to a budget literary: (adj) relating to literature
ate	adjective, noun, or verb	adjective: having the quality of noun: one who has a quality verb: to impart or display a quality	inviolate: (adj) having not been violated renovate: (v) to make something like new again vertebrate: (n) an animal with vertebrae
cide	noun	related to killing	homicide: (n) act of murder suicide: (n) act of killing oneself insecticide: (n) product that kills insects

Suffix	Usually indicates a(n) . . .	Meaning	Examples
cracy	noun	ruling order, system of government	plutocracy: (n) rule by the wealthy class theocracy: (n) rule of God or gods
crat	noun	person who rules or has authority	plutocrat: (n) wealthy person of great influence technocrat: (n) skilled person of great influence
cy	noun	state of or quality of	bankruptcy: (n) state of being without money dormancy: (n) state of being asleep
dom	noun	state of, realm of	kingdom: (n) realm of a king wisdom: (n) state of being wise
ee	noun	person or thing that receives an action	payee: (n) one who receives payment tutee: (n) one who receives tutelage (that is, teaching)
er, or	noun	one who does	exterminator: (n) one who exterminates robber: (n) one who steals or robs
escence	noun	process of becoming or process of taking on a quality	obsolescence: (n) process of becoming obsolete or out-of-date luminescence: (n) act of emitting light
escent	adjective	having a quality, or being in the process of becoming or taking on a quality	effervescent: (adj) bubbling; lively; high-spirited luminescent: (adj) possessing the quality of emitting light
ese	adjective or noun	adjective: relating to a place or language noun: the language of a nation	Japanese: (adj) related to Japan or its language Japanese: (n) the language of Japan
esque	adjective	having or being in the style of, resembling, imitating	picturesque: (adj) resembling a painting; visually pleasing or striking statuesque: (adj) tall, shapely, and attractive, like a statue
etic	adjective	relating to, tending to, or having the quality of	apologetic: (adj) relating to apology or tending to apologize apoplectic: (adj) displaying apoplexy (extreme anger)
ette, et, let	noun	diminutive: makes small	kitchenette: (n) a small kitchen booklet: (n) a small book
ful	adjective	having the quality of	hopeful: (adj) having hope peaceful: (adj) having the quality of peace
hood	noun	state of or quality of, place with or group of people with a specific quality	brotherhood: (n) state of being brothers, or group of people who call themselves brothers neighborhood: (n) place where neighbors live

Suffix	Usually indicates a(n) . . .	Meaning	Examples
ial, ian, arian	adjective or noun	relating to or characterized by	antiquarian: (n) one who studies valuable old things centenarian: (n) one who is a hundred or more years old ceremonial: (adj) relating to ceremony disciplinarian: (n) one who is strict librarian: (n) one who works in a library vegetarian: (n) one who does not eat meat
ic, ical	adjective	relating to, having the quality of	comic: (adj) relating to comedy hypocritical: (adj) saying one thing and doing another
ify	transitive verb	to make something into something else	deify: (v) make into a god magnify: (v) make larger
ish	adjective	resembling, being related to, having the quality of	youngish: (adj) somewhat young fiendish: (adj) resembling a fiend or devil outlandish: (adj) resembling something strange or unfamiliar
ism, asm	noun	action of; state of being; state of having a quality, doctrine, or religion; bias or hatred	capitalism: (n) a belief in private ownership criticism: (n) the act of criticizing gigantism: (n) state of being abnormally large phantasm: (n) product of fantasy sexism: (n) bias against women or men
ist	noun	person who does	harpist: (n) one who plays the harp linguist: (n) one who studies language
ite	noun	person who has a trait, person who adheres to a school of thought	socialite: (n) person who is known for socializing
itis	noun	inflammation of, condition resembling a disease	arthritis: (n) disease of the joints laryngitis: (n) inflammation of the larynx
ity	noun	state of, quality of	density: (n) state of being dense; mass based on unit per volume ferocity: (n) state of being ferocious
ive	adjective or noun	adjective: having a quality of or tending to noun: (n) a person or thing with the quality of	creative: (adj) tending to create things digestive: (n) a substance that aids digestion
ize	verb (transitive or intransitive)	cause to become, treat a certain way	eulogize: (v) speak well of terrorize: (v) cause to become terrified

Suffix	Usually indicates a(n) . . .	Meaning	Examples
less	adjective	without, lacking	fearless: (adj) without fear graceless: (adj) lacking grace
logy	noun	the study of	biology: (n) study of life geology: (n) study of Earth's structure
ly	adverb	(makes a word into an adverb)	frighteningly: (adv) in a frightening manner rapidly: (adv) in a rapid manner
ment	noun	action of, state of being	contentment: (n) state of being content development: (n) action of developing something
ness	noun	state of being, condition, or quality	goodness: (n) state of being good sweetness: (n) quality of being sweet
nomy	noun	rules, system of law or order, field of study	astronomy: (n) scientific study of the universe beyond the Earth autonomy: (n) independence, self-governance
oid	adjective or noun	adjective: resembling noun: something that resembles something else	humanoid: (n) a being that resembles a human planetoid: (n) a small celestial body resembling a planet
osis	noun	act of, or disease of	hypnosis: (n) the act of hypnotizing someone psychosis: (n) disease of the mind
ous, ious	adjective	having the quality of	anxious: (adj) having anxiety poisonous: (adj) having the quality of poison
ship	noun	state of being	hardship: (n) difficult circumstances ownership: (n) the state of being the owner of something
some	adjective	having the quality of; causing a feeling or condition	fearsome: (adj) causing fear quarrelsome: (adj) tending to quarrel
tion, sion, ion	noun	act or process; result of a process; state or condition	promotion: (n) act of promoting something or someone tension: (n) state of being tense
tive	adjective	having a quality or tendency	emotive: (adj) having the quality of causing strong emotions talkative: (adj) tending to talk
tude	noun	state of being	certitude: (n) state of being certain gratitude: (n) state of being grateful
ular	adjective	of, relating to, or resembling	muscular: (adj) having well-developed muscles popular: (adj) of or relating to the people

Suffix	Usually indicates a(n) . . .	Meaning	Examples
ure, eur	noun	action of, condition of	exposure: (n) act of exposing something grandeur: (n) condition of being grand
ward	adverb	in the direction of	heavenward: (adv) toward heaven eastward: (adv) toward the east
y	adjective	having, having a quality of, or resembling	dirty: (adj) not clean; relating to dirt grouchy: (adj) resembling a grouch

PART III: WORD ROOTS

The roots below, most of which come from Greek or Latin, form the basis for many common words in English. Not all words you will see on the ASVAB are based on the word parts below. In fact, many short English words do not have Greek or Latin roots. However, knowing the word roots in this list will usually help you determine the definitions of longer words.

AC/ACR: sharp, bitter, sour
acid: (n) something that is sharp, sour, or ill-natured
acrimonious: (adj) bitter; hostile
acumen: (n) mental sharpness; quickness of wit
acute: (adj) sharp at the end; ending in a point
exacerbate: (v) to make (a problem or conflict) worse

ACT/AG: to do, to drive, to force, to lead
activate: (v) to cause something to act
agile: (adj) having good coordination and quick movements
agitate: (v) to stir up or roil

ACOU: hearing
acoustic: (adj) related to sound or hearing

AL/ALI/ALTER: other, another
alias: (n) an assumed name; another name
alibi: (n) an excuse, often that a person was at another place at the time a crime was committed
alien: (n) one born in another country; a foreigner
alter ego: (n) the second self; a substitute or deputy
alternative: (n) a possible choice
altruist: (n) someone who cares about others or gives (money or resources) in support of others

AM: love
amateur: (n) someone who does an activity for the love of it, rather than as part of her job; a hobbyist; an inexperienced person; (adj) lacking or displaying a lack of experience; non-professional
amiable: (adj) friendly, likable
amicable: (adj) characterized by exhibiting good will
amity: (n) friendship; peaceful harmony
amorous: (adj) inclined to love, esp. sexual love
enamored: (adj) inflamed with love; charmed; captivated

AMBL/AMBUL: to go, to walk
ambulance: (n) a vehicle equipped for carrying sick people (from a phrase meaning "walking hospital")
ambulatory: (adj) able to walk; having to do with walking
preamble: (n) an introductory statement (originally: to walk in front)

ANIM: of the life, mind, soul, breath
animal: (n) a living being
animosity: (n) hostility
equanimity: (n) ability to remain calm under pressure
magnanimous: (adj) generous; forgiving
unanimous: (adj) of one mind; in complete accord

ANNUI/ENNI: year
annals: (n) a log or record, often with yearly entries
anniversary: (n) yearly observance
annual: (adj) yearly
annuity: (n) periodic cash payments or receipts
perennial: (adj) lasting for an indefinite amount of time

ANTHRO/ANDR: man, human
androgynous: (adj) having both male and female traits or anatomy
android: (n) robot; mechanical man
anthropology: (n) a branch of science dealing with human origins, traits, and behavior

AQUA/AQUE: water
aquamarine: (n) a bluish-green color
aquarium: (n) a tank for keeping fish and other underwater creatures
aquatic: (adj) having to do with water
aqueduct: (n) a channel for transporting water

ARCH/ARCHI/ARCHY: chief, principal, ruler
anarchy: (n) the absence of a formal government; a state of lawlessness
archenemy: (n) chief enemy
architect: (n) the devisor, maker, or planner of anything
monarchy: (n) rule by a single person
oligarchy: (n) a state or society ruled by a select group

AUTO: self
autocrat: (n) an absolute ruler
automatic: (adj) self-moving or self-acting
autonomy: (n) independence or freedom

BEN/BENE: good
benediction: (n) act of uttering a blessing
benefit: (n) anything advantageous to a person or thing
benevolent: (adj) desiring to do good to others
benign: (adj) gracious, kindly; not harmful

BON/BOUN: good, generous
bona fide: (adj) true, authentic (literally, in good faith)
bonus: (n) something of value given beyond what is expected
bountiful: (adj) generous

BREV/BRID: short, small
abbreviate: (v) to shorten
abridge: (v) to shorten
brevity: (n) shortness
brief: (adj) short

BURS: purse, money
bursar: (n) treasurer
disburse: (v) to pay
reimburse: (v) to pay back

CANT/CENT/CHANT: to sing
accent: (n) emphasis or stress
chant: (n) a song; singing
enchant: (v) to fascinate or captivate
incantation: (n) a magical chant or spell
recant: (v) to take back something spoken or written

CAP/CIP/CEPT: to take, to get
anticipate: (v) to look forward to something; to foresee
capture: (v) to take by force
precept: (n) a rule to govern behavior
susceptible: (adj) capable of receiving, admitting, undergoing, or being affected by something

CARN: flesh
carnage: (n) slaughter, widespread killing
carnivorous: (adj) eating flesh
incarnation: (n) a being invested with a bodily form
reincarnation: (n) rebirth in a new body

CAUS/CAUT: to burn
caustic: (adj) burning or corrosive
cauterize: (v) to burn or deaden

CED/CEED/CESS: to go, to yield, to stop
accede: (v) to yield to a demand; to give in
antecedent: (adj) existing or going before
cessation: (n) the act of stopping or discontinuing (either temporarily or permanently)
concede: (v) to admit the truth of a statement (especially in a debate); to yield; to admit defeat
incessant: (adj) without stop
predecessor: (n) a person who holds an office or position prior to another person; one who comes before

CELER: speed
accelerant: (n) something used to speed up a process
accelerate: (v) to increase in speed
decelerate: (v) to decrease in speed

CENTR: center
centrist: (adj) pertaining to moderate political or social ideas; (n) a person who holds moderate views
concentrate: (v) to converge; to bring together in a central location; to focus one's attention; to intensify
concentric: (adj) (of circles or spheres) having the same center point
eccentric: (adj) off-center

CERN/CERT/CRET/CRIM/CRIT: to separate, to judge, to distinguish, to decide
ascertain: (v) to make sure of; to determine
certitude: (n) freedom from doubt
criterion: (n) a standard used in judging something
discreet: (adj) careful to keep secrets; prudent in speech; careful to avoid causing embarrassment
discrete: (adj) detached from others, separate
discriminate: (v) to distinguish between; to show preference
hypocrite: (n) someone who pretends to have beliefs or virtues he does not actually have

CHROM: color

chromatic: (adj) having to do with color

chrome: (n) a metallic element (chromium) used to make vivid colors; something plated with chromium

monochromatic: (adj) having only one color

CHRON: time

anachronism: (n) something or someone that seems to belong to a different historical time than the one it is in

chronic: (adj) constant, habitual

chronology: (n) the sequence in which events in the past occurred; a history recounted sequentially

chronometer: (n) a highly accurate clock or watch

synchronize: (v) to occur at the same time or agree in time

CIS: to cut

incision: (n) a cut, gash, or notch

incisive: (adj) penetrating, cutting

precise: (adj) definitely stated or defined

scissors: (n) cutting instrument for paper, cloth, or other material

CLA/CLO/CLU: to shut, to close

claustrophobia: (n) an abnormal fear of enclosed places

cloister: (n) enclosed courtyard; secluded place; monastery or convent

conclusive: (adj) final; closing an argument

disclose: (v) to reveal or make known

exclude: (v) to shut out from inclusion or consideration; to omit; to be incompatible with

preclude: (v) to prevent; to make impossible; to exclude

CLAIM/CLAM: to shout, to cry out

clamor: (n) a loud uproar

disclaim: (v) to claim to have no interest in; to deny; to renounce

exclaim: (v) to cry out; to say loudly or emphatically

proclaim: (v) to announce or declare in an official way

reclaim: (v) to claim or demand the return of a right or possession

CLI: to lean toward

climax: (n) the highest point; the most intense point in a story or development

decline: (v) to refuse (an offer); to withhold (from another)

disinclination: (n) aversion, distaste

recline: (v) to lean back

COGN/CONN: to know

cognition: (n) the process of knowing

incognito: (adj) with one's name or identity concealed

recognize: (v) to identify as already known

CORP/CORS: body

corporation: (n) a company legally treated as an individual

corps: (n) an organized body of troops

corpse: (n) a dead body

incorporation: (n) the act of combining into a single body; the act of forming a corporation

COSM: order, universe, world

cosmetic: (adj) improving the appearance; (n) substance used to beautify

cosmic: (adj) relating to the universe

cosmology: (n) a theory of the universe as a whole

cosmopolitan: (adj) worldly

cosmos: (n) the universe; an orderly system; order

microcosm: (n) a small system that reflects a larger whole

COUR/CUR: running, a course

concur: (v) to accord in opinion; to agree

courier: (n) a messenger

curriculum: (n) the regular course of study

cursive: (n) a fluid style of handwriting in which letters are joined

cursory: (adj) superficial (of a review of material); hasty

excursion: (n) a short journey or trip

incursion: (n) a hostile, sudden entrance into a place or group

recur: (v) to happen again

CRE/CRESC/CRET: to grow

accretion: (n) an increase by natural growth

accrue: (v) to gain by natural growth; to accumulate

creation: (n) the act of creating, inventing, or producing

increase: (v) to make greater or more in number; to grow in number or size

increment: (n) an amount added or increased; an addition; profit

CRED: to believe, to trust

credentials: (n) written proof of authority or status

credit: (n) trustworthiness

credo: (n) any formula of belief

credulous: (adj) too willing to trust in or believe

incredible: (adj) unbelievable

CRYPT: hidden

apocryphal: (adj) having questionable authenticity; possibly not genuine

crypt: (n) an underground vault or tomb

cryptology: (n) the science of interpreting secret writings, codes, ciphers, and the like

CUB/CUMB: to lie down

cubicle: (n) a small, partitioned space

incubate: (v) to cause to develop or hatch (as when hens sit on eggs); to develop or take form

incumbent: (n) a person who holds an office; (adj) holding an office or position

succumb: (v) to yield; to give way

CULP: fault, blame

culpable: (adj) blameworthy; at fault; guilty

culprit: (n) a person guilty of an offense

inculpate: (v) to accuse; to incriminate

DAC/DOC: to teach

didactic: (adj) related to instruction; prone to instruct too often

docile: (adj) tame, teachable

doctor: (n) a medical practitioner; someone with an advanced degree

doctrine: (n) principles or teachings relating to a specific principle or group

indoctrinate: (v) to teach a doctrine to a person

DELE: to erase

delete: (v) to erase; to remove

indelible: (adj) impossible to erase; lasting

DEM: people

democracy: (n) government by the people

demographics: (n) vital and social statistics of populations

epidemic: (adj) affecting a large number of people simultaneously; (n) a widespread disease or problem

DEXT: right hand, right side, deft

ambidextrous: (adj) able to use both hands (e.g., for writing)

dexterity: (n) quality of being skilled at working with one's hands

DI: day

dial: (n) a surface that displays information in a circular form (such as a clock face); a rotatable knob

diary: (n) a record of one's days

dismal: (adj) gloomy (from "bad days")

DIC/DICT/DIT: to say, to tell, to use words

dictionary: (n) a compilation of the meanings of words

interdict: (v) to forbid; to prohibit

predict: (v) to foresee; to give a forecast of

verdict: (n) a judgment or decision

dictate: (v) to give a directive; to talk while being recorded

DIGN: worth

deign: (v) to think fit or in accordance with one's dignity

dignitary: (n) a person who holds a high rank or office

dignity: (n) the state of being titled or privileged; worthiness

DOG/DOX: opinion, belief

dogma: (n) a strongly held specific belief

orthodox: (adj) holding customary or traditional beliefs

paradox: (n) a situation that seems to contradict itself

DOL: to suffer, to pain, to grieve

condolence: (n) expression of sympathy

doleful: (adj) sorrowful; mournful

dolorous: (adj) sorrowful; causing sorrow

indolence: (n) tendency to be inactive; laziness

DON/DOT/DOW: to give

anecdote: (n) a short narrative about an interesting event

antidote: (n) a remedy intended to counteract a poison

donate: (v) to give; to contribute

endow: (v) to give in a way that provides future income or future benefits

pardon: (n) forgiveness; (v) to forgive

DORM: sleep

dormant: (adj) sleeping; inactive

dormitory: (n) a place for sleeping; a residence hall

DORS: back

dorsal: (adj) having to do with the back

endorse: (v) to sign on the back; to vouch for

DUB: doubt

dubious: (adj) doubtful

indubitable: (adj) unquestionable

DUC/DUCT: to lead

abduct: (v) to lead away by force or coercion

conducive: (adj) contributive; helpful

conduct: (n) behavior; (v) to lead

induce: (v) to cause an action by influence

induct: (v) to admit to a group or position, usually with formal ceremonies

produce: (v) to make; to cause to be to bring into existence; (n) (usually used collectively) things brought into existence; agricultural products

DUR: hard, lasting

dour: (adj) sullen, gloomy, stern

durable: (adj) able to resist deterioration

duration: (n) the length of time something exists

duress: (n) compulsion by threat or force

endure: (v) to last, to sustain under pressure

EGO: self

ego: (n) oneself; the part of oneself that is self-aware

egocentric: (adj) focused on oneself

egoism/egotism: (n) selfishness; self-absorption

EQU: equal, even

adequate: (adj) equal to the requirement or occasion

equation: (n) the act of comparing two equal things; the act of equalizing

equivalent: (n) the same

iniquity: (n) injustice; act of evil

ERR: to wander

err: (v) to be mistaken; to make a mistake

errant: (adj) wandering, unsteady, deviating

erratic: (adj) deviating from the proper or usual course in conduct

error: (n) something that is incorrect or untrue; a mistake

ESCE: becoming

adolescent: (adj) between childhood and adulthood

convalescent: (adj) recovering from illness

incandescent: (adj) glowing with heat; shining

reminiscent: (adj) reminding of; suggestive of

FAB/FAM: to speak

affable: (adj) friendly; courteous

defame: (v) to slander; to publicly speak ill of

fable: (n) fictional tale, esp. legendary

famous: (adj) well known; celebrated

ineffable: (adj) inexpressible

FAC/FIC/FIG/FAIT/FEIT/FY: to do, to make

configuration: (n) manner of arrangement; shape

counterfeit: (n) imitation; forgery

deficient: (adj) incomplete or insufficient

faction: (n) a subgroup within a larger group or party; strife; dissention

factory: (n) building used for manufacturing

prolific: (adj) producing many offspring or much output

FAL: to err, to deceive

default: (v) to fail

fail: (v) to be insufficient; to be unsuccessful; to die out

fallacy: (n) a flawed argument

false: (adj) not true; erroneous; lying

infallible: (adj) incapable of being wrong or being deceived

FATU: foolish

fatuity: (n) foolishness; stupidity

fatuous: (adj) foolish; stupid

infatuated: (adj) swept up in a fit of passion, impairing one's reason

FER: to bring, to carry, to bear

confer: (v) to grant; to bestow

offer: (v) to present for acceptance, refusal, or consideration

proffer: (v) to offer

proliferate: (v) to reproduce; to produce rapidly

referendum: (n) a vote on a political question by the entire electorate; the process of referring political questions to such a vote

FERV: to boil, to bubble

effervescent: (adj) bubbling; lively; high-spirited

fervid: (adj) ardent; intense

fervor: (n) passion; zeal

FI/FID: faith, trust
affidavit: (n) written statement made under oath
confide: (v) to entrust with a secret
fidelity: (n) faithfulness; loyalty
infidel: (n) one who does not accept a particular religion

FIN: end
confine: (v) to keep or restrict within certain limits; to imprison
definitive: (adj) decisive; unconditional; final
final: (adj) at the end; coming last
infinite: (adj) boundless; endless
infinitesimal: (adj) infinitely or very small

FLAGR/FLAM: to burn
conflagration: (n) a large destructive fire
flagrant: (adj) blatant; scandalous
inflame: (v) to set on fire

FLECT/FLEX: to bend, to turn
deflect: (v) to bend; to cause to turn aside; to dissuade from a purpose
flexible: (adj) able to bend without breaking
inflect: (v) to bend; to change pitch
reflect: (v) to throw back

FLU/FLUX: to flow
confluence: (adj) merging into one
fluctuation: (n) continual change between one state and another; wavelike motion
fluid: (n) a substance that is capable of flowing freely; (adj) able to flow freely

FORT: chance
fortuitous: (adj) happening by luck
fortunate: (adj) lucky; auspicious
fortune: (n) chance or luck in human affairs

FORT: strength
forte: (n) a person's best skill or talent; strong suit
fortify: (v) to strengthen; to strengthen defenses against attack

FRA/FRAC/FRAG/FRING: to break
fractious: (adj) irritable; peevish
fracture: (n) breakage, esp. of a bone
fragment: (n) an incomplete or broken-off part
infringe: (v) to break or violate (a law, etc.)

FUG: to flee, to fly
fugitive: (adj) on the run; (n) someone who flees
refuge: (n) a haven for those fleeing
refugee: (n) a person who flees in search of safety or freedom
subterfuge: (n) a trick or stratagem used to deceive, hide something, or avoid punishment

FUM: smoke
fume: (n) smoke; (v) to emit smoke or vapors
fumigate: (v) to treat with smoke or vapors
perfume: (n) scents, from burning incense or other sources of fragrance

FUS: to pour
diffuse: (v) to spread over a wide area; to scatter; to pour out
fusillade: (n) sustained delivery of gunshots or criticism
infusion: (n) the act of introducing or pouring; the act of steeping or soaking in liquid; the resulting liquid
profuse: (adj) occurring in large amounts; abounding; overly giving
suffuse: (v) to spread over or throughout

GEN: birth, creation, race, kind
carcinogenic: (adj) producing cancer
congenital: (adj) (of a disease or defect) existing from birth
generous: (adj) giving or given freely
genetics: (n) study of heredity and variation among animals and plants
progeny: (n) offspring; descendants

GN/GNO: to know
agnostic: (n) one who believes that it cannot be known whether or not God exists
diagnose: (v) to determine the nature of (a sickness or problem) by examining symptoms
ignorant: (adj) possessing inadequate knowledge
ignore: (v) to overlook; to refuse to consider
prognosis: (v) to forecast, especially of disease

GRAD/GRESS: to step
aggressive: (adj) given to hostile acts or feelings
degrade: (v) to humiliate; to dishonor; to reduce to lower rank
digress: (v) to depart from the main subject
progress: (n) forward movement
regress: (v) to move backward; to revert to an earlier state

GRAM/GRAPH: to write, to draw

diagram: (n) a figure made by drawing lines; an illustration

epigram: (n) a short poem; a pointed statement

grammar: (n) a system of language and its rules

graph: (n) a diagram used to convey mathematical information

graphite: (n) mineral used for writing, as the "lead" in pencils

photograph: (n) a picture, originally made by exposing chemically treated film to light

GRAT: pleasing

gracious: (adj) kindly, esp. to inferiors; merciful; courteous

grateful: (adj) thankful

gratuity: (n) money given above what is due for a service or product

ingratiate: (v) to bring oneself into favor

GREG: flock

aggregate: (n) a number of things considered as a collective whole

congregate: (v) to come together in a group

gregarious: (adj) sociable; enjoying spending time with others

segregate: (v) to separate a larger group into two or more groups; to set an individual or subgroup apart from the larger group

HAP: by chance

haphazard: (adj) at random

hapless: (adj) without luck

happen: (v) to occur (originally: to occur by chance)

happy: (adj) pleased, as by good fortune

mishap: (n) an unlucky accident

perhaps: (adv) maybe; possibly

HER/HES: to stick

adherent: (adj) able to adhere; (n) believer or advocate of a particular school of thought

adhesive: (adj) sticky; coated with glue; (n) an adhesive substance

coherent: (adj) logically consistent; hanging together (as an argument)

inherent: (adj) existing as a permanent, inborn, or essential trait

HOL: whole

catholic: (adj) universal

holocaust: (n) complete destruction by fire or other means

hologram: (n) a two-dimensional picture that appears to be three-dimensional

holistic: (adj) considering something as a unified whole

ICON: image, idol

icon: (n) a symbolic, religious picture; something seen as representative of a culture or movement

iconic: (adj) representative of a culture or movement

iconology: (n) symbolism

IT/ITER: way, journey

ambition: (n) desire to achieve

itinerant: (adj) traveling

itinerary: (n) travel plans

reiterate: (v) to repeat

transit: (n) means of transportation

JECT: to throw, to throw down

abject: (adj) miserable; wretched; contemptible

conjecture: (n) the act of forming an opinion based on inadequate information; an opinion so formed

dejected: (adj) sad; depressed

eject: (v) to throw out; to expel

inject: (v) to insert into a space or body; to introduce

JOIN/JUG/JUNCT: to meet, to join

adjoin: (v) to be next to and joined with

conjugal: (adj) related to marriage

conjunction: (n) the act or instance of joining; an instance of events occurring together; a connecting word

injunction: (n) a command; a legal order

junction: (n) the act of joining; a combination; a place where multiple paths join

rejoinder: (n) a reply or retort

subjugate: (v) to make subservient; to place under a yoke

JUD: to judge

adjudicate: (v) to act as a judge

judiciary: (n) a system of courts; members of a court system

judicious: (adj) having good judgment

prejudice: (n) a previous or premature judgment; bias

JUR: law, to swear
abjure: (v) to renounce on oath
adjure: (v) to beg or command
jurist: (n) a legal expert; a judge
perjury: (n) willful lying while on oath

JUV: young
juvenile: (adj) young; immature
rejuvenate: (v) to refresh; to make young again

LANG/LING: tongue
bilingual: (adj) speaking two languages
language: (n) a system of spoken or written
   communication
linguistics: (n) the study of language

LAUD: praise, honor
applaud: (v) to give praise
laudable: (adj) praiseworthy
laudatory: (adj) expressing praise

LAV/LAU/LU: to wash
deluge: (n) a great flood of water
dilute: (v) to thin (a liquid) with water
laundry: (n) items of clothing or linens collected for
   washing; a building where clothing is washed
lavatory: (n) a room for washing (esp. hand-washing)

LEC/LEG/LEX: to read, to speak
dialect: (n) a regional variety of a language
lectern: (n) a reading desk
lecture: (n) an instructional speech
legend: (n) a story; a written explanation of a map or
   illustration
legible: (adj) readable
lexicon: (n) dictionary

LECT/LEG: to select, to choose
collect: (v) to gather; to assemble; to accumulate
eclectic: (adj) selecting ideas, etc. from various
   sources
elect: (v) to choose; to decide
predilection: (n) preference; liking
select: (v) to choose one thing over another

LEV: to lift, to rise, light (weight)
alleviate: (v) to ease or lessen (pain, discomfort, or
   problems)
levee: (n) embankment against river flooding
levitate: (v) to rise in the air or cause to rise
levity: (n) humor; frivolity; gaiety
relevant: (adj) bearing on the current situation or topic;
   pertinent
relieve: (v) to ease a person of, or separate a person
   from, a burden or problem; to take away pain or
   responsibility

LI/LIG: to tie, to bind
ally: (v) to unite; (n) one in an alliance
league: (n) an association; a group of nations, teams,
   etc. that have agreed to work for a common cause
liable: (adj) legally responsible; bound by law
liaison: (n) a connection; one who serves to connect
lien: (n) the right to hold a property due to an
   outstanding debt
ligament: (n) a band holding bones together; a bond
oblige: (v) to make a person obligated; to make
   indebted or form personal bonds by doing a favor
rely: (v) to depend upon (originally: to come together;
   to rally)

LIBER: free
deliver: (v) to set free; to save; to hand over
liberal: (adj) generous; giving away freely
liberality: (n) generosity
liberate: (v) to set free
liberty: (n) freedom

LOC/LOG/LOQU: word, speech, thought
colloquial: (adj) of ordinary or familiar conversation
dialogue: (n) conversation, esp. in a literary work
eulogy: (n) a live speech or a written piece in praise
   of a specific person, often one who has recently
   passed away
loquacious: (adj) talkative
prologue: (n) an introduction to a written work such as
   a novel or play

LUC/LUM/LUS: light (brightness)

illuminate: (v) to make bright or fill with light; to clarify an idea

illustrate: (v) to clarify an idea by providing alternate explanations, examples, or ways of expressing it

illustrious: (adj) highly distinguished

lackluster: (adj) lacking brilliance or radiance

lucid: (adj) easily understood; intelligible

luminous: (adj) bright; brilliant; glowing

translucent: (adj) having the quality of allowing light to pass through but without perfect clarity

MAG/MAJ/MAX: big, great

magnanimous: (adj) lacking in pettiness or spite; forgiving and understanding

magnate: (n) a powerful or influential person

magnify: (v) to make an image larger than the actual object

magnitude: (n) measurement, value, or strength of a quantity

maxim: (n) an accepted principle or code within a system of thought

maximum: (n) the greatest value possible for a quantity

MAN/MANU: hand

emancipate: (v) to free from bondage

manifest: (adj) apparent; evident

manual: (adj) operated by hand

manufacture: (v) to make objects by hand or using tools or machines

MAND/MEND: to command, to order, to entrust

command: (v) to order; (n) an order; control

commend: (v) to give something over to the care of another; to praise

countermand: (v) to retract an order

demand: (v) to strongly ask for; to claim; to require

mandatory: (adj) commanded; required

recommend: (v) to praise and suggest the use of; to advise

remand: (v) to send back

MIS/MIT: to send

emissary: (n) a messenger or agent sent to represent the interests of another

intermittent: (adj) operating at intervals rather than continuously

remission: (n) a lessening; a cessation; in medicine, a period when the symptoms of a disease disppear

remit: (v) to send money

transmit: (v) to cause an item to travel from its sender to a recipient

MOB/MOM/MOT/MOV: to move

automobile: (n) a motorized vehicle

demote: (v) to move downward in an organization

immovable: (adj) impossible to move

locomotion: (n) moving from place to place, or the ability to do so

mobile: (adj) movable

mobilize: (v) to make ready for movement; to assemble

moment: (n) an instant; importance

momentous: (adj) of great importance (originally: having the power to move)

momentum: (n) the force driving a moving object to keep moving; a growing force

motion: (n) movement

motive: (n) a reason for action; what moves a person to do something

motor: (n) a device that makes something move

promote: (v) to move to a higher rank in an organization

remove: (v) to take away; to move away

MON/MONIT: to remind, to warn

admonish: (v) to mildly criticize or warn against an action

monitor: (n) a person who supervises or reminds; (v) to watch over or supervise

monument: (n) a structure, such as a building, tower, or sculpture, erected as a memorial

premonition: (n) a feeling or intuition that something is going to happen before it does

remonstrate: (v) to plead, argue, or object

summon: (v) to call together

MOR/MORT: death

immortal: (adj) undying; not subject to dying

morbid: (adj) susceptible to preoccupation with unwholesome matters

MORPH: shape

amorphous: (adj) having an indefinite shape; shapeless

metamorphosis: (n) a transformation in which a person or thing completely changes form

MUT: to change

commute: (v) to substitute; to exchange; to interchange

immutable: (adj) unchangeable, invariable

mutation: (n) the process of being changed

permutation: (n) a complete change; transformation

transmute: (v) to change from one form into another

NAT/NAS/NAI/GNA: birth

cognate: (adj) related by blood; deriving from a common origin

naive: (adj) ignorant or credulous

native: (adj) indigenous or natural to a place

natural: (adj) present due to nature, not to artificial or man-made means

NAU/NAV: ship, sailor

astronaut: (n) one who travels in outer space

nauseous: (adj) causing a squeamish feeling (originally: sea-sickness)

nautical: (adj) related to sailing or sailors

naval: (adj) related to the navy

nave: (n) the main and central section of a church (resembling the shape of a ship)

navy: (n) a military force consisting of ships and sailors

NIHIL: nothing, none

annihilate: (v) wipe out; reduce to nothing

nihilism: (n) denial of all moral beliefs; denial that existence has any meaning

NOC/NOX: harm

innocent: (adj) not guilty; uncorrupted

innocuous: (adj) harmless, inoffensive

noxious: (adj) injurious or harmful to health or morals

obnoxious: (adj) highly disagreeable or offensive

NOM/NYM/NOUN/NOWN: name

acronym: (n) a word formed by the initials of other words

anonymous: (adj) lacking a named author; having an unknown author

nominal: (adj) existing in name only; negligible

nominate: (v) to suggest that someone be considered as a candidate or member

noun: (n) a word that names a person, place, or thing

renown: (n) fame; reputation

synonym: (n) a word having a meaning similar to that of another word of the same language

NULL: nothing

annul: (v) to cancel; to make into nothing

null: (adj) worth nothing; lacking; nonexistent

nullify: (v) to cancel; to make into nothing

ONER: burden

exonerate: (v) to free from blame; originally: to relieve of a burden

onerous: (adj) burdensome; difficult

onus: (n) a burden; a responsibility

PAC/PEAC: peace

appease: (v) to satisfy or pacify; to soothe

pacifier: (n) something or someone that eases anger or agitation

pacify: (v) to ease anger or agitation

pact: (n) a formal agreement, as between nations

PAR: equal

disparage: (v) to belittle; to speak disrespectfully about someone or something

disparate: (adj) dissimilar; different

par: (n) a state of equality; an average amount or trait

parity: (n) equal representation; equivalent

PAS/PAT/PATH: feeling, suffering, disease

compassion: (n) a deep feeling of sympathy for another

dispassionate: (adj) lacking personal feeling or passion

empathy: (n) the identification with the feelings or thoughts of others

impassive: (adj) showing or feeling no emotion

sociopath: (n) a person whose behavior is antisocial and who lacks a sense of moral responsibility

sympathy: (n) agreement in feeling; the attempt to share in the feelings of others

PAU/PO/POV/PU: few, little, poor
impoverish: (v) to deplete
paucity: (n) small quantity; scarcity
pauper: (n) a poor person
poverty: (n) the condition of being poor

PED: child, education
encyclopedia: (n) a collection of texts that contains a broad range or extensive detail of information
pedant: (n) one who displays learning ostentatiously
pediatrician: (n) a doctor who primarily has children as patients

PED/POD: foot
expedite: (v) to do something more quickly; to cause something to be done more quickly
impede: (v) to hinder or obstruct
pedal: (n) a platform upon which one places a foot to work an instrument
pedestrian: (n) a person who walks
podium: (n) a raised platform used by a speaker or conductor

PEL: to drive, to push
compel: (v) to force; to command
dispel: (v) to drive away; to disperse
expel: (v) to drive out; to banish; to eject
impel: (v) to set in motion, to push forward
propel: (v) to drive forward

PEN/PUN: to pay, to compensate
penal: (adj) pertaining to criminal punishment
penalty: (n) a punishment for a crime or transgression
penitent: (adj) wanting to repent or confess
punitive: (adj) having to do with punishment

PEND/PENS: to hang, to weigh, to pay
appendage: (n) a limb or other subsidiary part that diverges from the central structure
appendix: (n) additional material found at the end of a text; a small attachment to the colon in some animals
compensate: (v) to offset with something equivalent
depend: (v) to rely; to place trust in
indispensable: (adj) necessary
stipend: (n) a payment that occurs at regular intervals

PET/PIT: to go, to seek, to strive
appetite: (n) a desire for food, drink, or something else
compete: (v) to strive to outdo another
impetuous: (adj) impulsive; acting quickly without thinking
petition: (n) a formal request addressed to a position of power

PHIL: love
bibliophile: (n) one who loves or collects books
philharmonic: (n) a lover of music; (adj) devoted to music
philology: (n) the study of literary texts to establish their authenticity and determine their meaning
philosophy: (n) the study of knowledge and being; a type of knowledge

PHOB: fear
claustrophobia: (n) fear of enclosed places
hydrophobia: (n) fear of water, which is a symptom of rabies; rabies
phobia: (n) fear; an irrational fear

PHON: sound
megaphone: (n) a device for magnifying the sound of one's voice
phonetics: (n) the study of the sounds used in speech
telephone: (n) a device for transmitting sound at a distance

PHOTO: light
photograph: (n) a picture, originally made by exposing chemically treated film to light
photon: (n) a packet of electromagnetic radiation
photosynthesis: (n) the process through which plants turn light into energy

PLAC: to please
complacent: (adj) self-satisfied; unconcerned
implacable: (adj) unable to be pleased
placebo: (n) an inert substance which a patient believes to be a medicine
placid: (adj) pleasantly calm or peaceful

PLE/PLEN: to fill, full

complete: (adj) whole, entire

deplete: (v) to reduce or exhaust a supply

implement: (n) an instrument or tool; (v) to use as a tool; to put to use

plethora: (n) excess; overabundance

replete: (adj) abundant

supplement: (n) something added to remedy a shortage; (v) to add to

PON/POS/POUND: to put, to place

component: (n) a part or ingredient

expose: (v) to uncover or reveal; to put in the way of danger

expound: (v) to explain in detail

juxtapose: (v) to place next to; to contrast with

repository: (n) a place where things are kept or stored

PORT: to carry

deportment: (n) conduct, behavior

disport: (v) to amuse oneself

export: (v) to transmit out of the country

import: (v) to bring in from another country

portable: (adj) easily carried

POT: to drink

potable: (adj) drinkable; safe to drink; a drink

potion: (n) a drinkable substance, often medical, poisonous, or magical

PREHEND/PRISE: to take, to get, to seize

apprehend: (v) to take into custody

comprise: (v) to include or contain

enterprise: (n) a project or business

reprehensible: (adj) worthy of blame or disgust

reprisal: (n) act of retaliation

surprise: (v) to act in a way that produces astonishment or shock; (n) something unexpected

PRI/PRIM: first

primary: (adj) first; most important

primal: (adj) original; most important

prime: (n) first in quality; best

primeval: (adj) ancient; going back to the first age of the world

pristine: (adj) original; like new; unspoiled; pure

PROP/PROX: near

approximate: (adj) near; close to being accurate

proximate: (adj) nearby; coming just before or just after

proximity: (n) nearness; distance

PUG: to fight

pugilist: (n) a fighter or boxer

pugnacious: (v) to quarrel or fight readily

repugnant: (adj) objectionable or offensive

PUNC/PUNG/POIGN: to point, to prick, to pierce

compunction: (n) a feeling of uneasiness for doing wrong

expunge: (v) to erase, eliminate completely

poignant: (adj) heartfelt, moving, distressing, tending to stir emotions

puncture: (n) the act of piercing; (v) to pierce

pungent: (adj) caustic, sharp or biting (as a smell or idea)

PYR: fire

pyre: (n) a pile of combustible material to be set afire, often for burning a dead body

pyromania: (n) an urge to start fires

pyrotechnics: (n) fireworks

QUE/QUIS: to seek

acquire: (v) to obtain

conquest: (n) the act of gaining control by force

exquisite: (adj) of near-perfect workmanship

inquisitive: (adj) curious; hungry for knowledge

query: (n) a question; an inquiry

QUIE/QUIT: quiet, rest

acquiesce: (v) to comply; to give in

disquiet: (n) lack of calm or peace; (v) to upset or irritate

tranquil: (adj) calm, peaceful

RECT: straight, right

correct: (v) to set right

direct: (v) to guide; to put straight

erect: (adj) upright; (v) to construct

rectangle: (n) a four-sided figure in which every angle is a right angle

REG: king, rule

realm: (n) a kingdom; a domain

regal: (adj) kingly; royal

regent: (n) one who serves on behalf of a king; one who rules

regiment: (n) a military unit; (v) to subject to a rule

regular: (adj) having a structure following some rule; orderly; normally used; average

ROG: to ask

arrogant: (adj) conceited

derogatory: (adj) belittling; disparaging

interrogate: (v) to ask a series of questions of, often formally or aggressively

surrogate: (n) a person acting in place of another

SACR/SANCT: holy

sacrament: (n) a holy symbol or practice

sacred: (adj) holy

sacrifice: (n) an offering to a deity; the act of giving up something of value; (v) to give up (something of value)

sacrilege: (n) actions or words contrary to sacred practice

sanctify: (v) to make holy

sanction: (n) approval or permission from one in authority

SALV: to save

salvage: (v) to save; (n) something saved or recovered

salvation: (n) being saved

salve: (n) a substance that aids healing and is applied to the skin

savior: (n) one who saves

SAN: healthy

sane: (adj) mentally healthy

sanitarium: (n) a place of healing

sanitary: (n) promoting health; clean; sterile

SCI: to know

conscience: (n) an instinctive sense of moral right and wrong

conscious: (adj) aware; awake

omniscient: (adj) knowing everything

prescient: (adj) able to predict future events

unconscionable: (adj) very evil

SCRIBE/SCRIPT: to write

ascribe: (v) to assign, attribute, or credit to

circumscribe: (v) to encircle, either by drawing a circle around or by traveling in a circle around

conscription: (n) military draft

describe: (v) to explain or create an image with words

postscript: (n) a written addition or addendum, usually to a letter

scribble: (v) to write hastily or sloppily; (n) a hastily or sloppily done piece of writing or drawing

script: (n) handwriting

transcript: (n) a written record of oral speech

SEC/SEQU/SUE/SUI: to follow

obsequious: (adj) fawning

prosecute: (v) to seek to prove guilt by legal action

pursue: (v) to chase after

second: (adj) next after the first

sequence: (n) the order of events

suite: (n) a series; a set; originally, a train of followers

SED/SESS/SID: to sit, to settle

dissident: (adj) disagreeing with prevailing opinion or authority (literally, "sitting apart"); (n) one who disagrees with prevailing opinion or authority

preside: (v) to exercise control; to lead (as a meeting)

resident: (n) one who resides; a dweller in a place; (adj) living in a place

residual: (adj) remaining; leftover

sediment: (n) matter (usually small particles) that has settled to the bottom of a liquid or that has been deposited by a body of water

session: (n) a meeting at which people sit together in discussion

SEM: seed, to sow

disseminate: (v) to spread; to scatter around

semen: (n) seed (of male animals)

seminary: (n) a school, esp. for religious training (originally: a place for raising plants)

SEN: old

senate: (n) the highest legislative body (from "council of elders")

senile: (adj) relating to old age; experiencing memory loss or other age-related mental impairments

sire: (n) a title for a king; a father (originally: an important person; an old man)

SENS/SENT: to feel, to be aware

dissent: (v) to disagree with the prevailing opinion or majority

presentiment: (n) a foreboding; a feeling that something will occur

resent: (v) to feel displeasure

sense: (v) to become aware of through a faculty such as sight, hearing, taste, smell, touch, or intuition; (n) one of the avenues through which one perceives stimuli

sensory: (adj) related to the senses

sentiment: (n) an attitude or feeling about something

sentinel: (n) a person or thing that watches over, especially over a border

SOL: alone

desolate: (adj) deserted; laid waste; left alone; (v) to lay waste

isolate: (v) to separate from the group; to make alone or apart

soliloquy: (n) a long speech delivered by one actor

solitude: (n) the state of being alone

SOL: sun

parasol: (n) an umbrella that protects from the sun

solar: (adj) related to the sun

solstice: (n) one of two days when the sun reaches its highest point at noon and seems to stand still

SOMN: sleep

insomnia: (n) inability to sleep

somnolent: (adj) sleep-inducing; sleepy; drowsy

SOURC/SURG/SURRECT: to rise

insurgent: (adj) rising up in revolution; rushing in; (n) a person rising in revolution

insurrection: (n) armed rebellion

resurrection: (n) the act of coming back to life; the act of rising again

source: (n) where something comes from (such as spring water rising out of the ground)

surge: (v) to rise up forcefully, as ocean waves

SPEC/SPIC: to look, to see

conspicuous: (adj) easy to see or notice

perspective: (n) one's mental view of facts, ideas, and their interrelationships

retrospective: (n) a review of the past; (adj) reflecting on or reviewing the past

specious: (adj) deceptively attractive

spectrum: (n) a broad range of related things that form a continuous series

speculation: (n) the act of making guesses based on known ideas; the act of hypothesizing

SPIR: breath

aspire: (v) to desire to achieve something

expire: (v) to breathe one's last; to die; to reach the end of viability

spirit: (n) the breath of life; the soul; an incorporeal supernatural being; a lively quality; an essence

STA/STI: to stand, to be in place

constitute: (v) to make up

destitute: (adj) extremely poor

obstinate: (adj) stubborn; unwilling to change

stasis: (n) a state of inaction; a state of equilibrium

static: (adj) unmoving or in equilibrium

STRICT/STRING/STRAN: to tighten, to bind

constrain: (v) to confine; to bind within certain limits

restriction: (n) a limitation

strangle: (v) to kill by suffocation, usually by tightening a cord or one's hand around the throat

SUA: sweet, pleasing, to urge

assuage: (v) to ease, lessen, or relieve

dissuade: (v) to deter; to advise against

persuade: (v) to encourage; to convince

suave: (adj) smooth, agreeable, pleasing

SUMM: highest, total

consummate: (adj) highly qualified; complete; perfect

sum: (n) total; amount of money

summary: (n) concisely stating the total findings on a subject; comprehensive

summit: (n) highest point

TAC/TIC: to be silent

reticent: (adj) reluctant to speak

tacit: (adj) unspoken

taciturn: (adj) uncommunicative

TACT/TAG/TAM/TANG: to touch

contact: (v) to touch; to get in touch

contagious: (adj) able to spread by contact, as disease

contaminate: (v) to corrupt, taint, or otherwise damage the integrity of something by contact or mixture

intact: (adj) untouched; whole

intangible: (adj) unable to be touched; not physical or material

tactile: (adj) touchable; having to do with the sense of touch

TAIN/TEN/TENT/TIN: to hold

abstention: (n) the act of refraining voluntarily

detain: (v) to delay or restrain

pertain: (v) to be relevant to

sustenance: (n) nourishment, means of livelihood

tenable: (adj) workable, maintainable

tenacious: (adj) holding fast

tenure: (n) length of time holding a position

TEND/TENS/TENT/TENU: to stretch, to thin

contentious: (adj) quarrelsome, disagreeable, belligerent

distend: (v) to lengthen or distort by stretching

extenuating: (adj) making less serious by offering excuses

tension: (n) tautness, stress, strain

tentative: (adj) not certain, hesitant, not finalized

TEST: to bear witness

attest: (v) to bear witness

contest: (v) to dispute (from bringing a lawsuit by calling witnesses); (n) event in which people compete

detest: (v) to hate (originally: to curse something by calling upon God to witness it)

protest: (n) a dissent; a declaration of disagreement; (v) to express dissent

testament: (n) a witnessed statement of wishes to be carried out after one's death; a will

testify: (v) to bear witness

THEO: god

atheist: (adj) one who does not believe in a deity or divine system

theocracy: (n) a form of government in which a deity is recognized as the supreme ruler

theology: (n) the study of divine things and the divine faith

THERM: heat

thermal: (adj) relating to heat; retaining heat

thermometer: (n) a device for measuring temperature

thermostat: (n) a device for regulating temperature

TOR/TORQ/TORT: to twist

contort: (v) to twist; to distort

distort: (v) to pull out of shape, often by twisting; to twist or misrepresent facts

extort: (v) to get something of value by threats or force

torque: (n) twisting force; a force that creates rotation

torture: (v) to inflict pain (including by twisting instruments like the rack or wheel)

TOX: poison

intoxication: (n) the state of being poisoned; drunkenness

toxic: (adj) poisonous

toxin: (n) poisonous or harmful substance

TRACT: to drag, to pull, to draw

abstract: (v) to draw or pull away; to remove; (adj) theoretical; related to ideas rather than to specific instances or objects

attract: (v) to draw toward by force or enticement

contract: (n) a legally binding document; (v) to enter into a contract

detract: (v) to take away from, esp. a positive thing

protract: (v) to prolong; to draw out; to extend

tractor: (n) a powerful vehicle used to pull farm machinery

ULT: last, beyond

ulterior: (adj) beyond what is immediately present; future; beyond what is stated; hidden

ultimate: (adj) last; final

ultimatum: (n) final offer; final terms

ultraviolet: (adj) beyond the spectrum of visible light (on the violet end of the spectrum)

URB: city

suburb: (n) a residential area just outside a city; an outlying area of a city

urban: (adj) relating to a city

urbane: (adj) polite; refined; polished (considered characteristic of those in cities)

urbanization: (n) the process through which a place becomes more like a city

VAIL/VAL: strength, use, worth

ambivalent: (adj) caught between contradictory feelings of equal power or worth

avail: (v) to have force; to be useful; to be of value

convalescent: (adj) recovering strength; healing

equivalent: (adj) of equal worth, strength, or use

evaluate: (v) to determine the worth of

invalid: (adj) having no force or strength; void; sickly; (n) a chronically sickly person

valid: (adj) having force; legally binding; effective; useful

value: (n) worth

VEN/VENT: to come or to move toward

contravene: (v) to conflict with; to go against

convene: (v) to assemble for some public purpose

intervene: (v) to step in between parties in a dispute; to mediate

VER: truth

aver: (v) to affirm; to declare to be true

veracious: (adj) habitually truthful

verdict: (n) a judgment or decision

verity: (n) truthfulness

VERB: word

proverb: (n) an adage; a byword; a short, commonly known saying

verbatim: (adj) exactly as stated; word-for-word

verbose: (adj) wordy

verbiage: (n) excessive use of words; diction

VERS/VERT: to turn

aversion: (n) dislike

avert: (v) to turn away from

controversy: (n) a prolonged debate or disagreement over a topic

diverse: (adj) of different kinds

extrovert: (n) an outgoing person

introvert: (n) a person concerned primarily with inner thoughts and feelings

revert: (v) to return to a previous state, habit, or position

VI: life

viable: (adj) capable of living

vivacity: (adj) the quality of being lively, animated, spirited

vivid: (adj) bright or intense

VID/VIS: to see

adviser: (n) one who gives counsel

evident: (adj) plain or clear

survey: (v) to view in a general or comprehensive way; (n) a comprehensive, high-level account

video: (n) the elements of television or other media pertaining to the image

vista: (n) a view, as of a landscape

VIL: base, mean

revile: (v) to criticize with harsh language

vile: (adj) loathsome; unpleasant

vilify: (v) to slander, to defame

villain: (n) the bad person in a story

VOC/VOK: call, word

advocate: (v) to support or argue in favor of; (n) one who supports or argues in favor of

avocation: (n) something one pursues, outside one's main vocation or career

convoke: (v) to call together

equivocate: (v) to speak ambiguously; to avoid taking a position

invoke: (v) to call on for assistance (as from a deity)

vocabulary: (n) a collection of words used by a group or person

vocation: (n) occupation; calling

VOL: wish

benevolent: (adj) characterized by or expressing good wishes

malevolent: (adj) characterized by or expressing bad wishes

volition: (n) free choice; free will; act of choosing

voluntary: (adj) freely undertaken; not forced

VOLU/VOLV: to roll, to turn

convolution: (n) a twisting or folding

evolve: (v) to develop naturally; literally, to unfold or unroll

revolt: (v) to rebel; to turn against those in authority; (n) a rebellion

revolve: (v) to rotate; to turn around

voluble: (adj) easily turning; fluent; changeable

volume: (n) a book; size or dimensions (originally, of a book)

VOR: to eat

carnivorous: (adj) meat-eating

omnivorous: (adj) eating or absorbing everything

voracious: (adj) having a great appetite

Index

A

Absolute value, 131
Absolute zero scale, 247
AC. *See* Alternating current
Acceleration
    acceleration due to
        gravity, 253, 375
    mass and, 252
    newton (N), 250
    Newton's second law of
        motion, 252, 372, 375
    physics of, 249
    weight and gravity, 253,
        375
Accessories of auto
    electrical system, 321
Acetic acid, 263
Acids and bases, 264
Action and reaction, 252,
    372
Actuators of auto
    computer, 322
Acute angles
    definition, 183
    right triangles, 187
Adding numbers
    algebraic terms, 141,
        171
    commutative property,
        150
    even/odd numbers, 130
    exponents, 141
    fractions, 136
    integers, 130
    order of operations,
        148, 149
    positive/negative
        numbers, 129
    radicals, 144
Adjectives
    definition,, 75
    suffixes indicating,, 75
Adjustable joint pliers, 356
Adjustable wrenches, 346
Advancing the timing, 308
Adverbs
    definition, 518, 75
    suffixes indicating,, 75
AFQT (Armed Forces
    Qualification Test)
    math sections, 127
    score calculation, 3, 4
    use of, 2, 203

AI. *See* Automotive
    Information (AI)
AIDS (acquired
    immunodeficiency
    syndrome), 218
Air-cooled engines, 308
Air filter (automotive), 314,
    315
Air Force minimum AFQT
    score, 3
Air friction, 378
Air-fuel mixture. *See also*
    Fuel system
    combustion, 308
    diesel engines, 306
    four-stroke cycle, 305
    internal combustion
        engines, 302
    lean, 307, 308
    operating conditions,
        307
    rich, 308
Air impact wrenches, 348
Alcohol from fermentation,
    223
Algebra. *See also*
    Mathematics Knowledge
    (MK); Variables
    arithmetic versus, 169
    equations with
        variables, 173
    inequalities, 181
    terms and expressions,
        170
Alkali metals in Periodic
    Table, 261
Alkaline substances, 263,
    264
Alleles, 220
Alternating current (AC)
    alternator, 321
    capacitors, 286
    direct current (DC)
        versus, 283
    rectification, 289, 321
Alternator
    battery supporting, 321
    charging system, 321
    voltage regulator, 321
Aluminum as conductor,
    272
Alveoli, 211
American Petroleum
    Institute (API), 311

Amino acids from trypsin,
    214
Ammeter for resistance,
    285
Amperes (amps\; A);
    Amperes (amps\; A), 270
Anaphase, 223
And in probability, 162,
    163
Angles
    angle of incidence, 255
    angle of reflection, 255
    base angles, 187
    definitions of terms,
        184
    of triangle, 185, 186,
        187
    parallelograms, 188
    rectangle, 188
    transversals, 185
Animals
    cell structures, 222
Answers. *See also*
    Predicting answers;
    Process of elimination;
    Traps among answers
    changing, 6, 399
    math backsolving
        strategy, 118
Antibiotics, 218
Antifreeze in coolant, 309,
    310
Antigens and blood types,
    213
Antilock brakes (ABS), 330
Anus, 214
AO. *See* Assembling
    Objects (AO)
Aorta, 212
API rating for engine oil,
    311
AR. *See* Arithmetic
    Reasoning (AR)
Archaea, 227
Area
    parallelograms, 188
    rectangles, 188
    squares, 189
    trapezoids, 189
    triangles, 186

Arithmetic Reasoning
    (AR). *See also* Fractions;
    Mathematics Knowledge
    (MK); Percent problems;
    Rate problems; Square
    roots
    absolute value, 131
    abstract of AR, 113, 128
    arithmetic sequence,
        160
    arithmetic vs. algebra,
        169
    backsolving strategy,
        118, 126
    combination of
        strategies, 124, 126
    combined work, 156
    commutative property,
        150
    definitions of terms,
        129
    Diagnostic Test, 18, 49
    distributive property,
        149
    factorials, 146
    factors, 132
    greatest common factor
        (GCF), 134
    guessing strategically,
        123, 126
    in AFQT score, 3
    Kaplan 4-step math
        method, 115
    least common multiple
        (LCM), 135
    number properties, 131
    order of operations, 148
    perfect squares, 144
    picking numbers
        strategy, 122, 126
    practice questions, 126,
        131, 168, 497
    probability, 163
    proportions, 152, 155
    ratios, 151, 153, 155
    scientific notation, 141
    statistical terms, 159
    test coverage, 2
    word problems, 165
Arithmetic sequence, 160
Armed Forces
    Classification Test
    (AFCT), 5

Army minimum AFQT score, 3
Arteries, 212, 213
Arterioles, 213
Arthropods, 210
AS. *See* Auto and Shop Information (AS)
Assembling Objects (AO)
abstract of AO, 400
Career Exploration Program ASVAB, 5
connector-type problems, 399, 406
Diagnostic Test, 38, 62
different skill set for, 205
jigsaw-puzzle-type problems, 399, 403
Kaplan 3-step method, 401
landmarks, 401, 402, 405
practice questions, 410, 492, 512
test coverage, 2
Asteroids, 239, 240
Asthenosphere, 232
ASVAB (Armed Services Vocational Aptitude Battery). *See also* AFQT (Armed Forces Qualification Test); CAT (computer-adaptive testing); Preparation for ASVAB; Strategies; Technical subtests
coverage, 2
retaking, 4
use of, 1
versions of, 4
Atmosphere, 236
Atomic mass in Periodic Table, 261, 262
Atomic mass unit (amu), 262
Atomic number in Periodic Table, 261, 262
Atomic reactions in the Sun, 239
Atomized fuel, 307
Atoms
definition, 259
structure of, 260, 270
Atria, 212

Audible hearing range, 254
Auto and Shop Information (AS). *See also* Automotive Information (AI); Shop Information (SI)
Career Exploration Program ASVAB, 5
Diagnostic Test, 33, 59
practice questions, 509
test coverage, 2
Automatic transmission, 323, 325
Automotive Information (AI). *See also* Auto and Shop Information (AS); Chassis systems; Combustion systems; Engine systems; Maintenance of autos
abstract of AI, 302
control systems, 302, 322, 323
electrical system, 302, 321, 322
four-stroke cycle, 305
practice questions, 333
systems vs. parts, 301
Autonomic nervous system, 217
Autotrophs, 224
Averages
solving, 159
worked examples, 118, 160
Axis of Earth, 241
Axle and wheel mechanism, 394

B

Back saws, 360
Backsolving strategy
algebra, 170
arithmetic, 118, 126
Bacteria
as decomposers, 224
as domain, 227
as pathogens, 218
as prokaryotes, 221
vaccination, 218
white blood cell count, 213
Baking soda. *See* Sodium bicarbonate

Balance and cerebellum, 216
Ball joints, 326, 327
Ball-peen hammer, 340
Band saws, 362
Base angles, 187
Base (of exponent) definition, 141
Base of transistor, 291
Bases and acids, 264
Bases (trapezoids), 189
Batteries
as DC, 282, 320
electrical system of autos, 320, 321
ignition system, 316, 317
voltage, 270, 271
Bead of tire, 328
Before top dead center (BTDC), 308
Belts of tire, 328
Bile, 214
Binomials
definition, 170
multiplying, 172
Biome, 224
Biosphere, 224
Bisecting line segments, 183
Bladder, 214
Blade of steel square, 339
Bleach. *See* Sodium hypochlorite
Block and tackle, 393
Blood
blood types, 213
circulatory system flow, 212
components of, 213
pH, 264
platelets for clotting, 213
Blood pressure
blood vessel walls, 213
heart disease, 212
hypertension, 213
Body plies of tire, 328
Bolts, 350
Bone marrow, 213
Bones, 211
Boring tools, 362
Boron as conductor, 270

Bottom dead center (BDC), 304
Box-end wrenches, 346
Brain, 216
Brainstem, 216
Brake assemblies, 329
Brake booster, 330
Brake caliper, 330
Brake fluid, 329
Brake lines, 329
Brake pedal, 328, 329
Brake shoes, 329
Brake system
abstract, 302
antilock brakes (ABS), 330
components, 329
disc brakes, 329, 330
drum brakes, 329
operation, 329
power brakes, 330
Branches of service minimum scores, 3
Breast milk production. *See* Lactation
Breathing, 211, 216
Bronchi, 211
Bronchioles, 211
Bubble levels, 338
Bullseye spirit level, 338
Bypass tube (automotive), 309

C

Cables and tension, 380
Calcium
dietary, 208
Earth's mantle, 231
yellow dwarf stars, 239
Calipers, 337
Calories. *See* Kilocalories
Camera lenses, 256
Camshaft
camshaft location, 306
definition, 303
distributor, 316
oil pump, 311
Cancer, 223
Capacitance (C), 287
Capacitive reactance, 286
Capacitors, 287, 292
Capillaries
circulatory system, 213
respiratory system, 211

Carbohydrates
    digestion, 214
    nutrition, 208
Carbon cycle, 234
Carbon dioxide
    as combustion product, 265
    carbon cycle, 234
    circulatory system, 212, 213
    photosynthesis, 222
    respiratory system, 211
Carbon monoxide in car exhaust, 319
Carburetor, 314
Cardiovascular disease, 212
Career Exploration Program, 4, 5
Carnivores, 225
Carpenter's square, 339
Carrion, 224
Cartilage, 210
Castellated nuts, 349
Catalytic converter, 318, 319
CAT (computer-adaptive testing). *See also* Paper and pencil test
    Arithmetic Reasoning (AR), 113, 127
    Assembling Objects (AO), 399
    Automotive Information (AI), 301
    Diagnostic Test versus, 9
    Electronics Information (EI), 269
    General Science (GS), 207
    Mathematics Knowledge (MK), 113, 169
    paper and pencil versus, 1, 6, 399
    Paragraph Comprehension (PC), 95
    Shop Information (SI), 335
    strategies of, 7
    Word Knowledge (WK), 69

C-clamp, 358
Cell division, 223. *See also* Reproduction of cells
Cell membrane, 222, 223
Cell structure, 224
Cell theory, 221
Cellular respiration, 223
Cell wall, 222
Celsius scale, 247
Center link, 327
Center of intelligence, 216
Center punches, 343
Centimeter (cm), 246
Central nervous system, 216
Centrosomes, 222
Cerebellum, 216
Cerebrum, 216
Channellock® pliers, 356
Charge
    current, 270
    ions, 263
    magnetism and, 293
    subatomic particles, 260
Charging system of auto
    abstract, 320
    lead-acid battery, 321
    process, 321
Chassis systems
    abstract, 302
    brake system, 302, 330
    drive train system, 302, 325
    suspension and steering systems, 302, 328
    worked examples, 330
Chemistry
    acids and bases, 264
    atomic structure, 260, 270
    chemical change, 266
    compounds, 263
    Periodic Table of the Elements, 263
    physical changes, 265, 266
Chewing, 214
Childbirth, 217
Chisels, 343, 365
Chlorine (Cl)
    in sodium chloride, 263, 266
    Periodic Table, 262

Cholesterol, 208, 209, 212
Chromatids, 223
Chromosomes
    cell division, 223
    diploid vs. haploid, 219
    DNA, 220
    sex chromosomes, 220
Chuck of electric drills, 362
Circles
    worked example, 118
Circuit breakers
    auto lighting systems, 321
    electronics of, 286, 293
Circuits
    abbreviations within, 273
    components of, 275
    forward-biased, 288
    integrated circuits, 289
    open circuits, 272, 275
    parallel circuits, 278
    reverse-biased circuits, 288
    series circuits, 276
    series-parallel circuits, 280
Circular saws, 361
Circulatory system
    anatomy of, 214
    digestive system and, 212, 213, 214
Cirrus clouds, 238
Citric acid, 263
Clamps, 358
Class (classification), 227
Classification of living things, 228
Claw hammers, 341
Clotting of blood, 213
Clouds
    fronts, 237
    types of, 238
    water cycle, 234
Clutch, 323, 325
Coast Guard minimum AFQT score, 4
Coefficient of friction (μ), 376
Coefficients
    adding/subtracting like terms, 170

    adding/subtracting radicals, 144
    multiplying/dividing, 142
Coffee pH, 263
Coil-on-plug ignitions, 317
Coil wire, 316, 317
Cold as viral infection, 218
Cold chisel, 343
Cold front, 237
Collector of transistor, 291
College credit, 3
Colon, 214
Color bands on resistors, 285
Color of light, 255
Columns of Periodic Table, 261
Combination slip-joint pliers, 355
Combination wrenches, 346
Combined work, 156
Combustion chamber (automotive)
    combustion, 308, 316
    definition, 303
    diesel engines, 306
    direct injection, 314
    four-stroke cycle, 305
    ignition timing, 308
    spark plug, 316
Combustion systems
    abstract, 302
    combustion, 308, 316
    exhaust system, 302, 319
    fuel system, 302, 315
    ignition system, 302, 317
    internal combustion engines, 302
    worked examples, 320
Comets, 239, 240
Common denominator
    adding/subtracting fractions, 136
    comparing fractions, 137
Common multiple, 134
Community (ecology), 224
Commutative property, 150

Compounds
    chemistry of, 263
    definition, 260
Compression
    of gases, 265
    of liquids, 380
Compression ignition
    engines. *See* Diesel
    engines
Compression ratio in diesel
    engines, 306
Compression stroke, 304
Computer system
    (automotive)
    abstract, 302, 322
    antilock brakes (ABS),
        330
    coil-on-plug ignitions,
        317
    components, 322
    maintenance, 322
    Powertrain Control
        Module (PCM), 314,
        322, 325
    suspension and steering
        systems, 326
    worked example, 323
Concave lenses, 256
Concave mirrors, 256
Condensation in water
    cycle, 234
Conduction of heat, 257
Conductors
    as circuit requirement,
        275
    electron flow theory,
        270, 272
    gaps in, 272, 275
    of heat, 257
    resistance of, 272
    zero resistance of, 275
Conjunction examples, 75
Connecting rod
    definition, 303
    linear to rotary
        conversion, 304
Connective tissue, 210
Connector-type problems,
    399, 401, 406
Conservation of energy,
    254
Conservation of
    mechanical energy, 386

Constant-velocity (CV)
    joints, 323
Consumers (ecology), 225
Context
    in-context word
        meaning, 70, 86
    no-context word
        meaning, 69, 81
    PC vocabulary-in-
        context questions, 107
Continuously variable
    transmission (CVT), 325
Control arms (A-arms),
    326, 327
Control system of autos.
    See Computer system
    (automotive)
Convection, 257
Converging lenses, 256
Converging mirrors, 256
Convex lenses, 256
Convex mirrors, 256
Coolant, 309, 310
Coolant recovery bottle,
    309
Cooling system, 301, 310,
    314
Coordinate geometry, 198
Coordinate grid, 196
Coordinates, 196
Coping saws, 360
Copper as conductor, 272
Cordless drills, 363
Core of Earth, 232
Corrosion by acids, 263
Cotter pins, 349
Coulomb (C)
    capacitance, 287
    current, 270
Counter-emf, 293
Covalent compounds, 263
Crankshaft
    alternator, 321
    definition, 303
    firing order, 306
    ignition timing, 308
    linear to rotary
        conversion, 304
Crescent® wrenches, 346
Crosscut saws, 359
Cross-multiplying
    proportions, 152, 154
Crust of Earth, 231, 232
Crystalline structure

ionic compounds, 263
    semiconductors, 288
Cubic centimeter (cc), 246
Cumulus clouds, 238
Current (I)
    alternating (AC) vs.
        direct (DC), 283
    as electron flow, 270
    circuit breakers, 286
    conventional current,
        272
    diodes, 288
    electrical power, 281
    electromagnets, 293
    fuses, 285
    inductors, 293
    magnetism and
        electricity, 295
    Ohm's law, 275, 281
    open circuit, 275
    parallel circuits, 278
    resistance and, 271, 273
    series circuit, 276
    series-parallel circuits,
        280
    transistors, 291
    transmission of
        electricity, 294
    voltage and, 271
Currents in ocean, 257
Cycles
    carbon cycle, 234
    water cycle, 234
Cylinder head
    camshaft location, 306
    cooling system, 310
    definition, 303
    exhaust manifolds, 318
    intake manifold, 314
    spark plug, 316
    valves per cylinder, 306
    V-type cylinder
        arrangement, 305
Cylinders (automotive)
    cylinder arrangement,
        305
    definition, 303
    distributor, 316, 317
    firing order, 306
    four-stroke cycle, 304
    multiport fuel injection,
        314
    valves per, 306

Cylinders (solid geometry),
    194
Cystic fibrosis, 220
Cytokinesis, 223
Cytoplasm, 222, 223

D
DC. *See* Direct current
Decimal numbers
    dividing, 140
    fraction conversions,
        139
    scientific notation, 141
Decoding strategies
    breaking words apart,
        73
    in-context word
        meaning, 70, 86
    no-context word
        meaning, 69, 81
    positive or negative
        connotation, 80, 84
    prefixes, 75
    suffixes, 75, 76, 77
    word roots, 79
Decomposers, 224
Deficiency diseases, 208
Definitions
    angle terms, 184
    arithmetic terms, 129
    prefixes, 518, 75
    suffixes,, 77
    word roots,, 79
Degrees centigrade, 247
Denominator, common,
    136, 137
Detonation (air-fuel
    mixture), 308
Detritivores, 224
Diagnostic data link for
    autos, 322
Diagnostic Test. *See also*
    Practice questions
    Arithmetic Reasoning
        (AR), 18, 49
    as preparation for
        ASVAB, xvii, 7
    Assembling Objects
        (AO), 38, 62
    Auto and Shop
        Information (AS), 33,
        59
    Electronics Information
        (EI), 30, 57

General Science (GS), 15, 45
Mathematics Knowledge (MK), 27, 55
Mechanical Comprehension (MC), 38, 61
online resources, xvii, 9
Paragraph Comprehension (PC), 24, 53
time required for, xvii, 9
Word Knowledge (WK), 21, 51
Diagonal cutters, 356
Diaphragm, 211
Dielectric, 286
Diesel engines
  engine oil, 311
  gasoline engines versus, 306
Differential, 324
Diffusion in capillaries, 213
Digestive system
  circulatory system and, 212, 213, 214
  digestive process, 214
  epiglottis, 211
Dimensionless quantities, 375
Diodes
  electronic overview, 288
  rectification, 289, 321
  worked example, 292
Diploid, 219
Direct current (DC)
  alternating current (AC) versus, 283
  alternator, 321
  capacitors, 286
  rectification, 289, 321
Direct injection of fuel, 314
Directly proportional, 271
Disc brakes, 329, 330
Disease
  pathogens, 218
  white blood cell count, 213
Displacement
  velocity, 249
  work, 250
Distributive property, 149

Distributor
  definition, 316
  distributor cap and rotor, 316, 317
  distributorless ignition system (DIS), 317
Diverging lenses, 256
Diverging mirrors, 256
Dividing numbers
  algebraic terms, 171
  coefficients and exponents, 142
  commutative property, 150
  decimal numbers, 140
  divisibility rules, 136
  even/odd numbers, 131
  exponents with same base, 142
  fractions, 137, 138
  fractions to decimals, 139
  integers, 130
  order of operations, 148
  positive/negative numbers, 130
  prime factorization, 135
  radicals, 145
  worked example, 119
DNA (deoxyribonucleic acid)
  cell division, 223
  genes within, 220
  structure of, 220
Domain
  Archaea, 227
  Bacteria, 227
  classification system, 226, 227
  Eukaryota, 227
Dominant traits, 221
Doping of semiconductors, 288
Doppler effect, 254
Double helix, 220
Double overhead cam (DOHC), 306
Downshifting, 325
Drag, 378
Drifts (tool), 343
Drilling tools
  drill bits, 362
  electric drills, 363
  safety, 363

Drive axle, 323, 324
Drive shaft
  definition, 324
  half shaft, 323
Drive tool, 347
Drive train system
  abstract, 302, 323
  automatic transmission, 325
  components, 324
  continuously variable transmission (CVT), 325
  gear selection, 325
Drum brakes, 329
Dry sump lubrication, 312

E
Earth
  age of, 239
  as terrestrial planet, 239
  atmosphere, 236
  geologic time scale, 233
  gravitational force and, 253
  Moon, 239, 240
  orbit of, 241
  plate tectonics, 232
  rock types, 233
  size of, 239
  structure of, 231
Earth and Space Science
  carbon cycle, 234
  geology, 233
  meteorology, 239
  practice questions, 244
  solar system, 242
  water cycle, 234
Earthquakes, 232
Ecology, 226
Ecosystems
  definition, 224
  food chains/webs, 225
Egg. *See* Ovum; Zygote
EI. *See* Electronics Information (EI)
Electrical power, 281
Electrical system of auto
  abstract, 302, 320
  battery, 320, 321
  charging system, 320, 321
  lighting system, 320, 321

  starting system, 320, 321
  voltage spikes, 321
  worked example, 322
Electric-arc welding, 354
Electric drills, 363
Electric fuel pump, 314
Electric potential, 271
Electromagnetic induction, 317
Electromagnetic spectrum, 254, 255
Electromagnets, 293
Electromotive force, 271
Electronic fuel injection, 314
Electronics Information (EI). *See also* Circuits; Current (I); Resistance (R); Shells of electrons; Voltage (V)
  abstract of EI, 269
  atomic structure, 260, 270
  capacitors, 287, 292
  circuit breakers, 286, 293, 321
  conventional current, 272
  Diagnostic Test, 30, 57
  diodes, 288, 292
  electrical power, 281
  fuses, 285, 288
  gaps in conductors, 272, 275
  ground, 283, 285
  magnetism and electricity, 295
  Ohm's law, 275, 281
  opposites attract, 270, 271, 275, 288
  path of least resistance, 277, 283
  practice questions, 298, 507
  safety, 283, 286
  semiconductors, 270, 288
  symbols, 291
  test coverage, 2
  transistors, 291
  transmission of electricity, 294

units and metric system, 281
water flow analogy, 270, 272

Electrons
atomic structure, 259
flow as current, 270, 272
shells, 261, 270
valence shells, 270

Elements
definition, 259
Periodic Table, 259, 263

Emissions of carbon, 234
Emitter of transistor, 291
Emulsification of fats, 214
Endometrial lining, 217
Endoplasmic reticulum, 222
Endoskeletons, 210

Energy
cellular respiration, 223
conservation of, 254
conservation of mechanical energy, 386
from food, 208, 214, 250
heat, 258
internal combustion engines, 302
joules (J), 250
kinetic vs. potential, 254
magnetism and electricity, 294
mechanics of, 387
mitochondria, 222, 223
photosynthesis, 222
power sources, 275
torque versus, 381
work and, 251, 254
work-energy theorem, 388

Engine block
camshaft location, 306
definition, 302
water jacket, 309

Engine Control Unit (ECU). *See* Powertrain Control Module (PCM)
Engine systems, 308. *See also* Air-fuel mixture; Lubrication system

abstract, 301
camshaft location, 306
combustion, 308, 316
cooling system, 301, 310
cylinder arrangement, 305
diesel engines, 306
engine oil, 311, 312
engine theory, 301, 305
firing order, 306, 316
four-stroke cycle, 305
ignition timing, 308
valves per cylinder, 306
worked examples, 313

Engine theory, 301, 305

English to math translation
percent problems, 157
word problems, 164

Enlistment Testing Program ASVAB, 4

Enzymes
in small intestine, 214
lipase, 214
pancreatic amylase, 214
pepsin, 214
salivary amylase, 214
trypsin, 214

Epiglottis, 211

Equations
definition, 173
slope-intercept equation, 196
two equations with two variables, 179
with one variable, 175
with two variables, 176

Equilateral triangles, 187
Esophagus, 214
Ethylene glycol, 309

Eukaryota
as domain, 227

Eukaryotic cells
cell structures, 222
nucleus, 221, 227

Evaporation in water cycle, 234

Even/odd numbers
divisibility rules, 136
prime factorization, 135
properties of, 130
worked example, 131

Excretory system
anatomy of, 214

circulatory system and, 212, 213
lysosomes, 222

Exercise
heart disease, 212
hypertension, 213

Exhalation, 211, 216
Exhaust manifolds, 318, 319
Exhaust stroke, 305

Exhaust system
abstract, 302
carbon monoxide, 319
components, 318
four-stroke cycle, 305
maintenance, 319
operation, 319
rich air-fuel mixture, 308

Exhaust valves
camshaft location, 306
definition, 303
four-stroke cycle, 305
number per cylinder, 306

Exoskeletons, 210

Exponents
adding/subtracting, 141
definition, 141
dividing same base, 142
metric system prefixes, 246
negative, 142
order of operations, 148
scientific notation, 141
with exponent, 142
worked example, 143

Expressions (algebraic)
adding/subtracting, 171
definition, 170
multiplying/dividing, 171
quadratic vs. linear, 172
worked examples, 171

External snap rings, 351
External threads, 348

F

Factorials, 146
Factoring quadratic expressions
equation equals zero, 179

reverse-FOIL, 172

Factors
divisibility rules, 136
finding, 132
multiples versus, 132
prime factors, 135
reducing fractions, 136

Fahrenheit scale, 246
Falling objects, 387
Fallopian tube, 217
Fall season, 241
Family (classification), 227
Farad, 287
Farsightedness, 256

Fasteners
bolts and nuts, 350
nails, 342
rivets, 342
screws, 345

Fatigue from practice tests, 9

Fats
digestion of, 214
endoplasmic reticulum, 222
in foods, 208

Fault lines, 232

Feedback. *See also* Scores
Diagnostic Test feedback, xvii, 9
strengths and areas of opportunity, xiv

Fermentation, 223
Fetus, 217
Fiber in diet, 208
Files (tool), 365
Filler rod, 353
Finishing tools, 366
Firing order, 306, 316
First-class lever, 391
Fixed resistors, 285
Flash cards, xv, 517

Flat cylinder arrangement
camshaft location, 305
definition, 305

Flat tip screwdrivers, 345
Flu, 218
Fluid reservoir, 329

Fluids
convection, 257
drag, 378
hydraulic pressure, 381
Pascal's law, 380

Flux, 352, 353, 354

Focal point of concave mirrors, 256

FOIL (First, Outer, Inner, Last)
    factoring quadratic expressions, 172
    multiplying binomials, 172

Food. *See also* Digestive system; Nutrition and health
    epiglottis, 211

Food chains/webs, 225

Force. *See also* Mechanical advantage
    definition, 250
    electric motors, 294
    friction, 252, 378
    gears, 394
    hydraulic pressure, 381
    mass achieving acceleration, 372
    Newton's laws of motion, 252, 372
    power, 250
    pressure, 380
    tension, 380
    torque, 383
    voltage, 271
    work, 250, 388

Forward-biased circuits, 288

Fossils, 233

Four-stroke cycle, 305

Four-valve cylinder head, 306

Four-wheel drive transfer case, 324

Fractions
    adding/subtracting, 136
    averages as, 159
    commutative property, 150
    comparing, 137
    cross-multiplying, 152
    decimal conversions, 139
    distributive property, 148
    dividing, 137, 138
    multiplying, 137
    practice questions, 138
    probability as, 163

reciprocal, 137, 138
    reducing, 134, 136
    slope as, 196, 197
    square root of, 145

Framing square, 339

Frequency
    electromagnetic spectrum, 254
    sound, 254

Friction
    auto lubrication system, 301, 311
    brake shoes, 329
    drag, 378
    mechanics of, 378

Fronts (meteorology), 237

Front-wheel drive
    drive train components, 323
    rear-wheel drive versus, 323

Fuel filter, 314, 315

Fuel injector, 314

Fuel pressure regulator, 314

Fuel pump, 314

Fuel rail, 314

Fuel system. *See also* Air-fuel mixture
    abstract, 302, 314
    components, 314
    fuel injection systems, 314
    fuel injection vs. carburetor, 314
    fuels used, 302
    maintenance, 315

Fulcrum
    levers, 391
    torque, 383

Full-length practice tests
    Diagnostic Test, 9
    instructions, xviii
    online resources, xiv, xv, xviii

Fungi
    as decomposers, 224

Fuses
    auto lighting system, 321
    electronics of, 285, 288

G

G2V (yellow dwarf) stars, 239

Gametes as haploid, 219

Gamma rays, 254

Gaseous state, 265

Gasoline engines
    API quality ratings, 311
    combustion, 308, 316
    diesel versus, 306

Gastric acids, 214

GCF. *See* Greatest common factor

Gears and gear ratios, 394

GED™ test, 3

General Science (GS). *See also* Earth and Space Science; Life science; Physical Science
    abstract of GS, 207
    Diagnostic Test, 15, 45
    metric system, 248
    practice questions, 494
    test coverage, 2
    unit/symbol confusion, 251

Generators, 293, 294

Genes, 220

Genetic code, 220

Genetics, 221

Genotype, 221

Genus, 227

Geologic time scale, 233

Geology, 233

Geometry. *See also* Angles
    circles, 118
    coordinate geometry, 198
    drawings on tests, 182
    line segments, 183
    quadrilaterals, 191
    solid geometry, 195
    triangles, 188

Germanium as semiconductor, 288

Gold (Au), 262

Golgi apparatus, 222

Grams (g), 246

Gravity
    gravitational potential energy, 387
    Newton's law of universal gravitation, 253, 374
    tides, 240
    weight, 248, 250, 375

Grease gun, 328

Greatest common factor (GCF), 134

Greek and Latin word roots,, 79

Ground (electronics), 283, 285

Groups of Periodic Table, 261

GS. *See* General Science (GS)

Guessing. *See also* Process of elimination
    math strategy, 123, 126
    penalty for, 6, 9
    strategy of, 6, 9, 125

H

Hacksaws, 361

Half shaft, 323

Hammers, 342

Hand saws, 361

Haploid, 219

Header pipes, 319

Headlights, 321

Hearing range, 254

Heart, 212, 217

Heart disease, 212

Heat
    internal combustion engines, 302
    of compression, 306
    physics of, 258

Height in triangles, 186

Hemispheres of Earth, 241

Henries (H), 294

Herbivores, 225

Heredity. *See* Genetics

Herpes, 218

Hertz (Hz)
    alternating current (AC), 283
    sound frequency, 254

Heterotrophs, 225

Heterozygous alleles, 220

High school
    ASVAB via Career Exploration, 4, 5
    graduation requirement, 3

HiSET™ exam, 3

HIV (human immunodeficiency virus), 218

Hole saws, 362

Homozygous alleles, 220
Horizontally opposed
    cylinder arrangement. *See*
    Flat cylinder arrangement
Hormone prolactin, 217
Horsepower, 389
Hours (h), 246
Household wiring. *See*
    Residential wiring
Huntington's disease, 220
Hydraulics
    brake system, 329, 330
    mechanics of, 381
Hydrochloric acid, 263
Hydrogen
    hydrogen ions (H+)
        and acids, 263
    nucleus, 259
    water as H2O, 266
Hydrologic cycle, 234
Hydroxyl ions (OH−), 263
Hypertension, 213
Hypotenuse
    Pythagorean Theorem,
        188, 198
    worked example, 118,
        187

I

Idler arm, 327
Ignition coil, 317
Ignition module, 316, 317
Ignition switch, 316, 317
Ignition system
    abstract, 302, 315
    diesel engines, 306
    distributorless ignition
        system (DIS), 317
    ignition timing, 308
    primary ignition
        components, 316
    primary ignition
        operation, 317
    secondary ignition
        components, 316
    secondary ignition
        operation, 317
Immune system
    pathogens, 218
    respiratory system, 211
    vaccination, 218
    white blood cells, 213
Immunization, 218

Impact sockets, 348
Impact wrenches, 348
Implantation, 217
Inclined plane
    stationary, 390
    wedge as movable, 390
Induction, electromagnetic,
    317
Inductors, 293
Inequalities
    direction of inequality
        sign, 181
    plotting, 181
    solving, 182
Inert gases, 261
Inertia
    as property of mass, 372
    Newton's first law of
        motion, 252, 372
    Newton's second law of
        motion, 252
Infection
    bacterial pathogens, 218
    white blood cell count,
        213
Infiltration in water cycle,
    234
Inflation pressure of tires,
    328
Infrared waves, 254
Inhalation
    breathing, 211, 216
    disease transmission,
        218
Inline cylinder
    arrangement, 305
Inside calipers, 337
Insulators
    electron flow theory,
        270
    from heat, 257
Intake air filter, 314, 315
Intake manifold
    firing order
        information, 306
    fuel system, 314
    multiport fuel injection,
        314
Intake stroke, 304
Intake valves
    camshaft location, 306
    definition, 303
    four-stroke cycle, 305

multiport fuel injection,
    314
number per cylinder,
    306
Integers
    divisibility rules, 136
    factors, 132
    greatest common factor
        (GCF), 134
    least common multiple
        (LCM), 135
    multiples, 132
    perfect squares, 144
    prime factors, 135
    properties of, 130
    worked example, 131
Integrated circuits, 289
Intelligence, brain center
    of, 216
Intercourse, 217, 218
Interior lights, 321
Interjection examples, 75
Internal combustion
    engines
        combustion, 308, 316
        definition, 302
        horsepower, 389
Internal snap rings, 351
Internal threads, 348
Interphase, 223
Inversely proportional
    current and resistance,
        271
    speed and torque, 394
Involuntary actions, 216,
    217
Ionic compounds, 263
Ions
    definition, 263
    hydrogen (H+), 263
    hydroxyl (OH−), 263
Iron-deficiency anemia,
    208
Iron (Fe)
    atomic symbol, 262
    dietary, 208
    Earth's core, 232
    Earth's mantle, 231
    electromagnets, 293
    inductors, 293
    rust as chemical
        reaction, 265
    transformers, 294

yellow dwarf stars, 239
Isosceles triangles, 187

J

Jack plane, 364
Jigsaw-puzzle-type
    problems, 399, 403
Joule (J)
    electronics, 281
    physics, 250
    work and kinetic
        energy, 388
Jounced shock absorber,
    327
Jupiter (planet), 239, 240

K

Kaplan methods
    Assembling Objects
        (AO), 401
    math, 115
    Paragraph
        Comprehension (PC),
        96
    technical subtests, 205
    Word Knowledge (WK),
        72
Kelvin scale, 247
Kerf of saw, 359
Keyless chucks, 362
Kidneys, 214
Kilocalories, 250
Kilograms (kg), 246
Kilojoules (kJ), 250
Kilometer (km), 246
Kinetic energy
    definition, 254
    friction ignored, 385,
        386
    gravitational potential
        energy and, 387
    mechanics of, 385
Kinetic friction
    coefficient of friction
        (μ), 376
    definition, 375
    static versus, 376
Kingdom (classification),
    226
Kuiper Belt, 240

L

Lactation, 217

Lactic acid, 223
Landmark in Assembling Objects (AO), 401, 402, 405
Large intestine, 214, 217
Latin and Greek word roots,, 79
Law of conservation of energy, 254
Law of inertia
   Newton's first law of motion, 252, 372
   Newton's second law of motion, 252
Law of reflection, 255
Law of universal gravitation, 253, 374
Laws of motion, 252, 372
Lead-acid batteries
   electrical system of autos, 321
   sulfuric acid, 263, 321
Lean air-fuel mixture, 307, 308
Least common multiple (LCM)
   common denominator, 136
   determining, 135
Lemon juice as acid, 263
Lenses
   concave lenses, 256
   convex lenses, 256
   refraction and, 256
Levels (spirit levels), 338
Lever arm and torque, 383
Levers, 392
Life Science
   cell structure, 224
   classification of living things, 228
   ecology, 226
   genetics, 221
   human body systems, 218
   nutrition and health, 210
   pathogens, 218
   practice questions, 219, 230
Ligaments, 210
Light
   color of, 255

electromagnetic spectrum, 254
   optics, 257
   sound vs. light waves, 255
   speed of, 255
Lighting system of auto, 320, 321
Like terms, 171
Linear expressions, 172
Lineman pliers, 356
Liner of tire, 328
Lines
   angles from intersection, 183
   line segments, 183
   slope-intercept equation, 196
Linkage steering, 327
Lipase, 214
Liquid state, 265
Liter (L), 246
Lithium electron shells, 261
Lithosphere, 232
Liver
   absorbed digested substances, 214
   bile, 214
Load (electronics)
   as resistance that converts energy, 275
   auto electrical system, 321
   parallel circuits, 278
   series circuit, 276
Locking pliers, 357
Lock nuts, 349
Lubrication of chassis, 328
Lubrication system
   abstract, 301, 311
   components, 311
   engine oil, 311
   maintenance, 312
   operation, 312
   piston rings, 303
Lungs, 211, 213
Lye, 263
Lysosomes, 222

M
Macronutrients, 208
Magnesium
   dietary, 208

Earth's mantle, 231
   yellow dwarf stars, 239
Magnetic fields
   electromagnetic induction, 317
   electromagnets, 293
   inductors, 293
   transformers, 294
Magnetism
   electricity and, 295
   electromagnetic induction, 317
   physics of, 258
Magnifying glasses, 256
Maintenance of autos
   computer system, 322
   cooling system, 310
   exhaust system, 319
   fuel-injection system, 315
   lubrication system, 312
   suspension and steering systems, 328
Managing stress, xix
Mantle of Earth, 231, 232
Manual saws, 361
Manual transmission, 323
Marine Corps minimum AFQT score, 3
Mars (planet), 239, 240
Mass
   kinetic energy, 385
   matter definition, 259, 372
   mechanical devices and, 371
   metric system, 246
   momentum, 249
   Newton's law of universal gravitation, 253, 374
   Newton's second law of motion, 252, 372, 375
   subatomic particles, 259
   weight versus, 248, 374
Master cylinder, 329, 330
Mathematics Knowledge (MK). *See also* Arithmetic Reasoning (AR); Geometry
   abstract of MK, 113, 169

backsolving strategy, 118, 126
combination of strategies, 124, 126
commutative property, 150
Diagnostic Test, 27, 55
distributive property, 149
equations with variables, 173
expressions and terms, 170
guessing strategically, 123, 126
in AFQT score, 3
Kaplan 4-step math method, 115
order of operations, 148
picking numbers strategy, 122, 126
practice questions, 126, 201, 506
terms and expressions, 170
test coverage, 2
Matter
   state changes, 265
   structure of, 260
MC. *See* Mechanical Comprehension (MC)
Meaning of words. *See* Word meanings
Mean (statistical)
   arithmetic sequences, 160
   definition, 160
Measles, 218
Measurement
   electrical units, 281
   mass vs. weight, 248, 374
   metric system prefixes, 245, 281
   of bolts, 350
   Physical Science metrics, 248
   tools for, 340
Mechanical advantage
   as multiplying force, 372, 389
   block and tackle, 393

hydraulic pressure, 380
inclined planes, 390
levers, 391
wedges, 390
wheel and axle
mechanism, 394
Mechanical
Comprehension (MC).
See also Mechanical
advantage; Physics;
Torque
abstract, 371
Diagnostic Test, 38, 61
energy, 387
gravity and weight, 375
hydraulic pressure, 381
mass and force, 372
mechanics definition,
371
Newton's laws of
motion, 372, 374
practice questions, 398,
486, 511
simple machines, 394
tension, 380
test coverage, 2
work, 388
Mechanical digestion, 214
Mechanical energy
alternator, 321
internal combustion
engines, 302
mechanics of, 387
motors and generators,
294
Median
arithmetic sequences,
160
definition, 160
Medulla, 216
Meiosis, 219
Memorizing as preparation
acceleration due to
gravity, 253, 374
classic quadratics, 173,
180
classification of living
things, 227
metric system prefixes,
246
PEMDAS, 148
planets of solar system,
240

technical subtest Kaplan
method, 205
word problem formulas,
164
Mendel, Gregor, 219
Menstrual cycle, 217
Menstruation, 217
Mercury as terrestrial
planet, 239
Mesosphere, 236, 240
Metabolic energy, 208
Metals
acids corroding, 263
alkali metals, 261
as conductors of heat,
257
cores of terrestrial
planets, 232, 239
hacksaws cutting, 361
yellow dwarf stars, 239
Metaphase, 223
Meteoroids, 236, 240
Meteorology, 239
Meteors, 240
Meter (m), 245
Metric system
electrical units, 281
overview, 245
Physical Science, 248
prefixes, 245, 281
Micrometers, 337
Micronutrients, 208
Microscope lenses, 256
Microwaves, 254
Midpoint of line segments,
183
MIG (metal-inert gas)
welding, 354
Milk production. *See*
Lactation
Milligrams (mg), 246
Milliliter (mL), 246
Millimeter (mm), 246
Minerals
decomposers, 224
dietary, 208, 209
digestion, 214
Minutes (min), 246
Mirrors
concave mirrors, 256
convex mirrors, 256
law of reflection, 255
Miter boxes, 360

Miter saws, 361
Mitochondria, 222, 223
Mitosis, 223. *See also*
Reproduction of cells
MK. *See* Mathematics
Knowledge (MK)
Mnemonics. *See*
Memorizing as
preparation
Mode, 160
Molecules, 260
Moment magnitude scale,
232
Momentum, 249
Monomials
definition, 170
multiplying/dividing,
171
worked examples, 171
Monounsaturated fats, 208
Moons of terrestrial
planets, 239, 240
Motion
friction, 252, 378
linear to rotary
conversion, 304
Newton's laws of, 252,
372
physics of, 250
Motors, 293, 294
Mouth, 214
Movement and cerebellum,
216
Muffler, 318
Multiple choice strategy, 6
Multiples
common multiple, 134
factors versus, 132
least common multiple,
135
Multiplying numbers
binomials, 172
coefficients and
exponents, 142
commutative property,
150
cross-multiplying, 152
even/odd numbers, 130
exponents, 142
fractions, 137
integers, 130
monomials, 171

order of operations,
148, 149
perfect squares, 144
positive/negative
numbers, 130
powers of ten, 140
prime factorization, 135
probability of two
events, 162
radicals, 145
worked example, 149
Multiport fuel injection,
314
Muscles
cerebellum
coordination, 216
with skeletal structure,
211

N
Nails
claw hammer, 341
definition, 342
shank, 342
Nasal cavity, 211
Navy minimum AFQT
score, 3
Nearsightedness, 256
Needle nose pliers, 357
Negative/positive numbers.
See Positive/negative
numbers
Neptune as outer planet,
239
Nerve cells, 216
Nervous system, 217
Neurons, 216
Neutrons
atomic mass, 261, 262
atomic structure, 259
Newton (N), 250
Newton, Sir Isaac, 252
Newton's laws of motion,
252, 372
Nitric acid, 263
Nitrogen in troposphere,
236
Noble gases, 261
Normal force
friction, 376
weight and, 376
Nose, 211
Nouns

definition,, 75
suffixes indicating,, 75
NPN transistors, 291
N-type material
    diodes, 288
    from doping, 288
    transistors, 290
Nucleotides, 220
Nucleus of atom, 260
Nucleus of cell
    cell division, 223
    prokaryotic vs.
        eukaryotic cells, 221
Number line and
    inequalities, 181
Numbers. *See also*
    Arithmetic Reasoning
    (AR); Decimal numbers;
    Even/odd numbers;
    Factors; Fractions;
    Integers; Mathematics
    Knowledge (MK);
    Multiples; One (1);
    Positive/negative
    numbers; Prime
    numbers; Ten (10); Zero
    (0)
        arithmetic sequence,
        160
        commutative property,
        150
        distributive property,
        149
        divisibility rules, 136
        order of operations,
        148, 149
        picking numbers
            strategy, 119, 122, 126,
            170
        properties of, 131
        scientific notation, 141
Nutrition and health, 210
Nuts (fasteners), 350

O

Obtuse angles, 183
Ocean currents, 257
Odd/even numbers. *See*
    Even/odd numbers
Ohmmeter, 271, 285
Ohm's law, 275, 281
Ohms (Ω)

capacitive reactance,
    286
resistance, 272
Oil filter, 311, 312
Oil galleries, 312
Oil pan, 311, 312
Oil pickup tube and screen,
    311
Oil pump, 311, 312
Omnivores, 225
One (1)
    exponent of, 141
    in probability, 161
    picking numbers
        strategy, 119
Online resources
    computer-based tests,
        xiv, xv, xviii
    Diagnostic Test
        feedback, xvii, 9
    registration, xvii
    strengths and areas of
        opportunity, xiv
Open circuits, 272, 275
Open-end wrenches, 346
Optics, 257
Order (classification), 227
Order of operations, 148
Organelles, 222
Or in probability, 163
Outer planets, 239
Outside calipers, 337
Outside micrometers, 337
Ovaries, 217
Overhead cam (OHC), 306
Overhead valve (OHV)
    engines, 305
Oviduct, 217
Ovulation, 217
Ovum
    as gamete, 219
    reproductive system,
        217
Oxyacetylene welding, 353
Oxygen
    circulatory system, 212,
        213
    ozone layer, 236
    photosynthesis, 222
    respiratory system, 211
    troposphere, 236
    water as H2O, 266
Ozone layer, 236

P

Pancreas, 214
Paper and pencil test. *See
    also* CAT (computer-
    adaptive testing)
    Arithmetic Reasoning
        (AR), 113, 127
    Armed Forces
        Classification Test as,
        5
    Assembling Objects
        (AO), 399, 405
    Automotive
        Information (AI), 301
    CAT versus, 1, 6, 399
    Diagnostic Test as, 9
    Electronics Information
        (EI), 269
    General Science (GS),
        207
    Mathematics
        Knowledge (MK),
        113, 169
    Paragraph
        Comprehension (PC),
        95
    Shop Information (SI),
        301, 335
    Word Knowledge (WK),
        69
Parachutes and drag, 378
Paragraph Comprehension
    (PC)
    abstract, 95
    detail questions, 102
    Diagnostic Test, 24, 53
    global questions, 99
    in AFQT score, 3
    inference questions, 104
    Kaplan 4-step method,
        96
    practice questions, 112,
        502
    predicting answers, 96,
        100, 102, 105, 106
    test coverage, 2
    vocabulary-in-context
        questions, 107
Parallel circuits, 278
Parallel lines
    properties of, 185
    rhombus, 189
    trapezoids, 189

Parallelograms, 189
Parentheses in order of
    operations, 148
Parts of speech
    overview, 518, 75
    suffixes,, 76
    word roots, 79
Part to part/whole ratios,
    151
Pascal, Blaise, 380
Pascal's law, 380
Path of least resistance,
    277, 283
Pathogens, 218
PC. *See* Paragraph
    Comprehension (PC)
PEMDAS (Parentheses,
    Exponents,
    Multiplication, Division,
    Addition, Subtraction),
    148, 149
Penis, 217
Pepsin, 214
Percent problems
    English to math
        conversion, 157
    percent change, 158
    solving, 157
    worked examples, 120,
        122, 124, 159
Perfect squares
    determining, 144
    simplifying radicals, 144
Perimeter
    polygons, 186
    quadrilaterals, 188
    rectangles, 188
    rhombuses, 189
    squares, 189
    triangles, 186
Periodic Table of the
    Elements, 263
Periods in Periodic Table,
    261
Peripheral nervous system,
    216
Perpendicular lines, 183
pH, 264
Pharynx, 211
Phase transition, 265, 266
Phenotype, 221
Phillips screwdrivers, 345

Phosphorus as insulator, 270
Photosynthesis
  as energy source, 222
  producers, 224
Phyla
  classification system, 227
Physical Science. *See also* Chemistry; Physics
  mass vs. weight, 248
  measurement, 248
  practice questions, 268
  unit/symbol confusion, 251
Physics. *See also* Mechanical Comprehension (MC)
  abstract, 248
  forces and energy, 252
  heat, 258
  kinetic vs. potential energy, 254
  magnetism, 258
  motion, 250
  Newton's laws of motion, 252
  optics, 257
  sound waves, 254
Picking numbers strategy
  algebra, 170
  arithmetic, 122, 126
Pickup coil, 316
Pin punches, 343
Piston rings, 303
Pistons
  definition, 303
  four-stroke cycle, 305
  ignition timing, 308
  Top to Bottom Dead Center, 304
Pitch of sound, 254
Pitman arm, 327
Pituitary and prolactin, 217
Pivot point. *See* Fulcrum
Planes (tools), 364
Planetary gear sets, 325
Planets
  outer planets, 239
  rings of, 239
  solar system, 239
  terrestrial planets, 239
Plants

cell structures, 222
  transpiration, 234
Plasma, 213
Platelets, 213
Plates (geology), 232
Plate tectonics, 232
Pliers, 358
Pluto the non-planet, 240
Pneumatic nail gun, 342
Pneumatic power tools, 348
Pneumonia, 218
PNP transistors, 291
Poles of Earth
    axis tilt, 241
    magnetic compass, 258
Poles of magnets, 258
Polio, 218
Polygons
  quadrilaterals, 191
  triangles, 188
Polynomials, 170
Polypeptides, 214
Polyunsaturated fats, 208
Population (ecology), 224
Positive/negative numbers
  inequality sign direction, 181
  negative exponents, 142
  percent change, 157
  properties of, 130
  radical sign, 144
Potassium
  potassium hydroxide as base, 263
Potential energy
  conservation of energy and, 254
  friction ignored, 385, 386
  gravitational potential energy, 387
  inclined plane, 390
Pounds (lb) of force, 380
Pounds per square inch (psi) pressure, 380
Power
  auto drive train system, 302, 325
  electronics, 281
  hydraulic pressure, 381
  mechanics of, 389
  physics of, 251

Power brakes, 330
Powered saws, 362
Power sources
  in circuits, 275
  rectification, 289, 321
Power stroke, 304
Powertrain Control Module (PCM)
  automatic transmission, 325
  definition, 314, 322
  fuel injector, 314
Practice as strategy, xviii, 6, 9
Practice questions
  Arithmetic Reasoning (AR), 126, 131, 168, 497
  Assembling Objects (AO), 410, 492
  Auto and Shop Information (AS), 509
  Automotive Information (AI), 333
  Diagnostic Test, 9
  Earth and Space Science, 244
  Electronics Information (EI), 298, 507
  fractions, 138
  full-length online tests, xiv, xv, xviii
  full-length paper tests, 9
  General Science (GS), 494
  Life Science, 219, 230
  Mathematics Knowledge (MK), 201, 506
  math strategies, 126
  Mechanical Comprehension (MC), 398, 486, 511
  Paragraph Comprehension (PC), 112, 502
  Physical Science, 268
  Word Knowledge (WK), 93, 500
Practice tests
  Diagnostic Test, 9
  instructions, xviii

online resources, xiv, xv, xviii
Precambrian eon, 233
Precipitation
  cloud types, 238
  fronts, 237
  water cycle, 234
Predicting answers
  Paragraph Comprehension (PC), 96, 100, 102, 105, 106
  technical subtests, 205
  Work Knowledge (WK), 71, 86
Prefixes
  breaking words apart, 73
  common meanings, 518, 75
  infrared and ultraviolet, 255
  metric system, 245
Pregnancy, 217
Pre-ignition, 308
Preparation for ASVAB. *See also* Diagnostic Test; Memorizing as preparation
  final preparations, xx
  practice as strategy, xviii, 6, 9
  stress management, xix
Preposition examples, 75
Pressure
  formula for, 380
  hydraulic pressure, 381
  inflation pressure of tires, 328
  Pascal's law, 380
  voltage, 271
Pressure relief valve (automotive), 311, 312
Primary coil
  ignition system, 316, 317
  transformers, 294
Primary consumers, 225
Prime numbers
  definition, 132
  divisibility rules, 136
  prime factors, 135
  worked example, 136
Probability, 163

Process of elimination. *See also* Guessing
  as strategy, 6, 88
  Paragraph Comprehension (PC), 96, 98, 102
  technical subtests, 205
  Word Knowledge (WK), 80, 86
Producers, 224
Production Version ASVAB. *See* Enlistment Testing Program ASVAB
Products of chemical reactions, 266
Prokaryotic cells
  bacteria as, 221
  nucleus, 221
Prolactin, 217
Pronoun examples, 75
Prophase, 223
Proportions
  as comparative relationship, 152
  directly proportional, 271
  geometry problems as, 186
  inversely proportional, 271, 394
  percent problems as, 157
  rate problems as, 155
Proteins
  digestion, 214
  endoplasmic reticulum, 222
  Golgi apparatus, 222
  nutrition, 208
  ribosomes, 222
Protons
  atomic mass, 261, 262
  atomic structure, 259
P-type material
  diodes, 288
  from doping, 288
  transistors, 290
Pulleys, 393
Pulmonary artery, 212, 213
Pulmonary vein, 212, 213
Punches (tool), 343
Pythagorean Theorem

distance between points, 198
right triangles, 188

Q
Quadratic expressions
  classic quadratics, 173, 180
  definition, 172
  equaling zero, 179
  factoring, 172, 179
Quadrilaterals, 191
Questions. *See also* Practice questions; Strategies
  hard vs. easy, 5, 7
  Kaplan technical subtest strategy, 205
  PC before reading, 96
  PC detail questions, 102
  PC global questions, 99
  PC inference questions, 104
  PC vocabulary-in-context questions, 107
  skipping, 6, 7
  Word Knowledge (WK) types, 70

R
Rack and pinion steering, 327
Radial tires, 328
Radiation, 258
Radiator
  definition, 309
  operation of cooling system, 309
Radiator cap, 309, 310
Radiator hoses, 309
Radical sign
  adding/subtracting, 144
  definition, 144
  multiplying/dividing radicals, 145
  simplifying radicals, 144
  worked example, 146
Radio waves, 254
Ramp, 390
Range
  inequalities solved, 181
  statistics, 160
Rasps, 366
Ratchet, 347

Rate problems. *See also* Proportions; Ratios
  combined work, 156
  current, 270
  power as rate of work, 389
  solving, 153
  worked examples, 123, 153, 155, 156, 166
Ratios
  air-fuel mixture, 307
  as part to part/whole relationships, 151
  gear ratios, 394
  percent problems as, 157
  rate problems as, 153, 155
  stoichiometric ratio, 307
Reactants, 266
Reaction and action, 252, 372
Reactions as chemical change, 266
Reading comprehension. *See* Paragraph Comprehension (PC)
Reading glasses, 256
Rear-wheel drive
  drive train components, 324
  front-wheel drive versus, 323
Rebounded shock absorber, 327
Recessive traits, 221
Reciprocal of fractions
  dividing fractions, 137, 138
  negative exponents, 142
Recruiters
  ASVAB registration, 4
  score information, xvii
Rectangles
  quadrilaterals, 188, 189
Rectification, 289, 321
Rectifier bridge, 321
Rectum, 214
Red blood cells
  as blood component, 213
  blood types, 213

iron in diet, 208
Reducing fractions
  factor cancellation, 136
  greatest common factor for, 134
Reflection
  concave mirrors, 256
  convex mirrors, 256
  law of reflection, 255
Reflexes and spinal cord, 216
Refraction, 255
Refractive index, 255
Reluctor, 316
Reproduction of cells
  cancer, 223
  cell division, 223
  centrosomes, 222
Reproductive system, 217
Residential wiring
  as AC, 282
  as series-parallel, 280
  ground, 283
  transformers, 294
Resistance (R)
  capacitive reactance, 286
  current and, 271, 272, 273
  load as, 275
  measuring, 271, 285
  Ohm's law, 275, 281
  parallel circuits, 278
  path of least resistance, 277, 283
  resistors, 285
  series circuit, 276
  series-parallel circuits, 280
Respiration (breathing)
  carbon cycle, 234
  definition, 211
Respiration (cellular), 223
Respiratory system, 211
Retaining rings, 351
Retaking ASVAB, 4
Retarding the timing, 308
Reverse-biased circuits, 288
Reversible drills, 362
Rh factor, 213
Rhombus, 189
Ribosomes, 222
Rich air-fuel mixture, 308

Richter scale, 232
Right angles
    definition, 183
    rectangles, 188
    right triangles, 187
Right triangles
    Pythagorean Theorem,
        188, 198
    worked examples, 118,
        187
Rim of tire, 328
Rip saws, 359
Rivets, 342
Robertson screwdrivers,
    345
Rocker arm, 305
Rock types, 233
Roots of words. *See* Word
    roots
Rosin-core solder, 352
Rosin flux, 352
Rotor and distributor cap,
    316, 317
Rows of Periodic Table, 261
Rubber mallets, 341
Runoff, 234

S
SAE oil viscosity, 311
Safety
    coefficients of friction,
        375
    dull drill bits, 363
    fuses and circuit
        breakers, 286
    grounding electrical
        devices, 283
Salivary amylase, 214
Salt. *See also* Sodium
    chloride
    acid–base reactions, 263
Saprotrophs, 224
Saturated fats, 208
Saturn as outer planet, 239
Saws
    hole saws, 362
    manual/hand, 361
    powered saws, 362
Scan tool for auto
    computer system, 322
Scavengers, 224
Scientific notation, 141
Scores

CAT advantage, 6
Diagnostic Test, xvii, 9
explanation of, 4
minimum AFQT scores,
    3
recruiters for
    information, xvii
strengths and areas of
    opportunity, xiv
valid for two years, 4
Screwdrivers, 345
Screws, 345, 348
Scurvy, 208
Seasons and Earth axis, 241
Secondary coil
    ignition system, 316,
        317
    transformers, 294
Secondary consumers, 225
Second-class lever, 392
Seconds (s), 246
Sedimentary rock, 233
Self-induction, 293
Semiconductors
    doping of, 288
    electron flow theory,
        270, 288
Sensors of auto computer,
    322
Sensory nerves, 216
Sequences, 160
Series circuits, 276
Series-parallel circuits, 280
Sex chromosomes, 220
Shank of nail, 342
Shells of electrons
    columns of Periodic
        Table, 261
    electron flow theory,
        270
    rows of Periodic Table,
        261
    valence shells, 270, 288
Shock absorbers, 326, 327
Shop Information (SI). *See
    also* Auto and Shop
    Information (AS)
    abstract of SI, 335
    cutting tools, 363
    finishing tools, 366
    flux, 352, 353, 354
    gripping tools, 358
    measuring tools, 340

snap rings, 351
soldering, 353
striking tools, 344
turning tools, 351
welding, 354, 355
SI. *See* Shop Information
    (SI)
Sidewalls of tire, 328
Sign of numbers. *See*
    Positive/negative
    numbers
Silicon as semiconductor,
    270, 288
Silver (Ag)
    as conductor, 272
    atomic symbol, 262
Similar triangles, 186
Simple reflexes and spinal
    cord, 216
Single overhead cam
    (SOHC), 306
Six-point sockets, 347
Skeletal system, 211
Skipping questions, 6, 7
Sledge hammers, 342
Sleeve of micrometer, 337
Slope
    definition, 184
    formula for, 196, 197
    parallel lines, 184
    slope-intercept
        equation, 196, 197
Small intestine, 214, 217
Smallpox, 218
SmartReports™, xiv
Smoking
    cancer, 223
    heart disease, 212
Snap rings, 351
Society of Automotive
    Engineers (SAE), 311
Socket drivers, 347
Sockets, 347
Sodium bicarbonate as
    base, 263, 264
Sodium chloride (NaCl)
    as ionic compound, 263
    chemical change, 266
    dietary, 208
Sodium hydroxide as base,
    263
Sodium hypochlorite as
    base, 263, 264

Sodium (Na)
    atomic symbol, 262
    electron shells, 261
    in sodium chloride, 263,
        266
Solar system, 242
Solar wind, 240
Solder, 352
Soldering, 353
Soldering gun, 352
Soldering iron, 352
Solid geometry, 195
Solid state, 265
Solid-state devices, 289
Solutions
    acidic, 263
    covalent compounds,
        263
    ionic compounds, 263
Somatic nervous system,
    216
Sound waves, 254, 255
Spark plug
    combustion, 308, 316,
        317
    definition, 316
    diesel engines versus,
        306
    distributor, 316, 317
    distributorless ignition
        system (DIS), 317
    four-stroke cycle, 304
    ignition timing, 308
    rich air-fuel mixture,
        308
    spark plug wires, 316,
        317
Spatial relationship skills.
    See Assembling Objects
    (AO)
Species, 227
Speed reduction via gears,
    394
Sperm
    as gamete, 219
    reproductive system,
        217
Spinal cord, 216
Spindle of micrometer, 337
Spirit levels, 338
Springs (automotive), 326,
    327
Spring season, 241

Square roots
adding/subtracting
radicals, 144
definition, 144
definition of radical
sign, 144
multiplying/dividing
radicals, 145
of fractions, 145
simplifying radicals, 144
worked example, 146
Squares (geometry), 189
Staph infections, 218
Starches
as carbohydrates, 208
pancreatic amylase, 214
salivary amylase, 214
Starting system of auto
abstract, 320
battery, 320, 321
process of, 321
State changes, 265
Static friction
coefficient of friction
(μ), 376
definition, 375
kinetic versus, 376
Stationary front, 238
Statistical terms
averages, 118, 159, 160
mean, 160
median, 160
mode, 160
range, 160
Steel rules, 335
Steel squares, 339
Steering knuckle, 326
Steering linkage, 326, 327
Steering system. *See*
Suspension and steering
systems
Step-up effect, 317
Stick welding, 354
Stinger (welding), 354
Stoichiometric ratio, 307
Stomach, 214, 217
Strategies. *See also*
Decoding strategies;
Guessing; Predicting
answers; Process of
elimination
ASVAB overall, 7
flash cards, xv, 517

math backsolving, 118,
126
math combination of
approaches, 124, 126
math picking numbers,
122, 126
math practice
questions, 126
math strategic guessing,
123, 126
Paragraph
Comprehension (PC),
99, 102, 104, 106
PEMDAS (Parentheses,
Exponents,
Multiplication,
Division, Addition,
Subtraction), 148, 149
vocabulary building, 89
Stratosphere, 236
Stratus clouds, 238
Strengths and areas of
opportunity
Diagnostic Test
feedback, xvii, 9
SmartReports™, xiv
Strep throat, 218
Stress management, xix
Substitution in algebra, 177
Subtracting numbers
algebraic terms, 141,
171
commutative property,
150
even/odd numbers, 130
exponents, 141
fractions, 136
integers, 130
order of operations, 148
positive/negative
numbers, 129
radicals, 144
Suffixes
breaking words apart,
73
common meanings, 77
parts of speech by,, 75,
76
Sugars
as carbohydrates, 208
as covalent compounds,
263
pancreatic amylase, 214

photosynthesis, 222
Sulfuric acid, 263, 321
Summer, 241
Sun
age of, 239
comets, 240
Earth's orbit, 241
gravitational force and,
253
radiation of heat, 258
size of, 239
solar system, 239
ultraviolet radiation,
236
Supplementary angles, 183
Surface area
rectangular solid, 193
three-dimensional
figures, 194
Suspension and steering
systems
abstract, 302, 326
components, 326
maintenance, 328
operation, 327

T
Table salt. *See* Sodium
chloride
Table saws, 361
Table sugar. *See also* Sugars
as covalent compound,
263
Taillights, 321
Tailpipe, 318, 319
Tape measures, 335
TASC™ test, 3
Taste
acids, 263
bases, 263
Technical subtests
Assembling Objects
(AO) differing skill
set, 205
Kaplan 4-step strategy,
205
minimum standards
waiver, 3
predicting answers, 205
use of, 2, 1
Telescope lenses, 256
Telophase, 223
Temperature

convection, 257
measurement units, 247
Ten (10)
metric system prefixes,
246
powers of, 140
Tendons, 210
Tension (mechanics), 380
Terms (algebraic)
adding/subtracting, 171
definition, 170
like terms, 171
multiplying/dividing,
171
worked examples, 171
Terrestrial planets, 239
Tertiary consumers, 225
Test. *See* AFQT (Armed
Forces Qualification
Test); ASVAB (Armed
Services Vocational
Aptitude Battery);
Diagnostic Test; Practice
tests; Technical subtests
Testes, 217
Thermosphere, 236
Thermostat (automotive),
309
Thimble of micrometer,
337
Third-class levers, 392
Threaded fasteners
bolts and nuts, 350
screws, 345
thread pitch, 350
Thread pitch, 350
Throttle body injection
system (TBI), 314
Throttle body/throttle
plate, 314
Throttle pedal, 314
Tides from Moon, 240
Tie rods, 327
Time
acceleration, 249
power, 250, 389
units of measurement,
246
vector quantities, 249
velocity, 249
Time management
CAT-ASVAB strategies,
7

Diagnostic Test time required, xvii, 9
Timing chain/belt, 305
Timing of ignition, 308
Tinning (soldering), 353
Tires (automotive), 326, 328
Tongue of steel square, 339
Top carnivores, 225
Top dead center (TDC), 304, 308
Torque
  air impact wrenches, 348
  drive shaft, 324
  engine throttle, 314
  gears and, 394
  mechanics of, 383
  torque multiplication, 394
  wrench length, 346
Torque converter, 325
Torx screwdrivers, 345
Trachea, 211
Transaxle, 323
Transfer case, 324
Transformers, 293, 294
Transistors, 291
Translation of English to math
  percent problems, 157
  word problems, 164
Transmission of auto drive train
  automatic vs. manual, 323
  definition, 324
  transaxle, 323
Transmission of disease, 218
Transpiration, 234
Transversals, 185
Transverse mounted engines, 305
Trapezoids, 189
Traps among answers
  Assembling Objects (AO), 402, 405
  math questions, 114
  percent change, 157
  preparation for, 6
  rate problems, 165
Tread of tire, 328

Triangles, 118, 188
Troposphere, 236
Trypsin, 214
Tubular spirit level, 338
Tungsten (W), 262
Twelve-point sockets, 347
Two-valve cylinder head, 306

U
Ultraviolet radiation
  electromagnetic spectrum, 254
  ozone layer, 236
  welding, 354
Unified National Coarse (UNC) threads, 350
Unified National Fine (UNF) threads, 350
Universal donor, 213
Universal joints (U-joints), 324
Universal recipient, 213
Uranus as outer planet, 239
Ureters, 214
Urethra, 214
Urine, 214
Uterus, 217

V
Vaccination, 218
Vacuum
  light waves in, 255
  sound waves in, 254
Vagina, 217
Valence shells
  electron flow theory, 270
  semiconductors, 288
Valves (automotive)
  exhaust valves, 303, 305, 306
  intake valves, 303, 305, 306, 314
  number per cylinder, 306
Valves (life science)
  heart, 212
  veins, 213
Variables. *See also* Mathematics Knowledge (MK)

adding/subtracting, 141, 171
  algebra vs. arithmetic, 169
  coefficients and exponents, 142
  equation with one variable, 175
  equation with two variables, 176
  Pick Numbers strategy, 122
  two equations with two variables, 179
  worked examples, 122, 143
Variable speed drills, 362
Vector quantities
  acceleration, 249
  force, 372
  mass not, 372
  momentum, 249
  time not, 249
  velocity, 249
  weight, 374
Veins, 213
Velocity
  acceleration, 249
  as vector quantity, 249
  displacement, 249
  kinetic energy, 385
  momentum, 249
  Newton's first law of motion, 252
Venae cavae, 212
Ventricles, 212
Venus as terrestrial planet, 239
Verbs
  definition,, 75
  suffixes indicating,, 75
Vertebrate animals endoskeletons, 210
Vertex, 186
Vertical angles, 183
Vinegar as acid, 263
Viruses
  as pathogens, 218
  vaccination, 218
  white blood cell count, 213
Viscosity of engine oil, 311
Vise-Grip® pliers, 357

Vises, 358
Visible light, 254
Vitamins in diet, 208
Vocabulary. *See also* Word Knowledge (WK)
  PC vocabulary-in-context questions, 107
  vocabulary-building strategies, 89
Voltage (V)
  as electrical pressure, 271
  current and, 271
  electrical power, 281
  inductors, 293
  Ohm's law, 275, 281
  parallel circuits, 278
  series circuit, 276
  series-parallel circuits, 280
  sources, 275
  transformers, 294
  transistors, 291
  transmission of electricity, 294
  voltage drop, 276, 321
  voltage regulator, 321
  voltage spikes, 321
Voltmeter, 271
Volts (V), 271
Volume
  liquid vs. gaseous state, 265
  metric system, 246
  of cylinder, 194
  of rectangular solid, 193
Voluntary actions, 216
V-type cylinder arrangement
  camshaft location, 306
  definition, 305

W
Warm front, 237
Washers, 345
Waste. *See* Excretory system
Water
  acid–base reactions, 263
  as combustion product, 265
  as H2O, 266

boiling/freezing temperatures, 246
electron flow analogy, 270, 272
for survival, 208
large intestine, 214
pH, 263
photosynthesis, 222
water cycle, 234
Water-cooled engines, 308
Water jacket, 309
Water pump (automotive), 309, 310
Water pump pliers, 356
Watt, James, 389
Watt (W)
electronics, 281
mechanics, 389
physics, 251
Wavelength, 254
Waves
electromagnetic spectrum, 254
optics, 257
radiation, 258
sound vs. light, 255
sound waves, 254
Weather
cloud types, 238
fronts, 237
troposphere, 236
Wedge, 390
Weight
acceleration due to gravity, 253, 375
as force, 250, 372
mass versus, 248, 374
Welding, 354, 355
Welding helmets, 354
Welding rod, 354
Wet sump lubrication, 312
Wheel and axle mechanism, 394
Wheel hub, 326
White blood cells, 213
Wind
convection, 257
fronts, 237

Wingnuts, 348
Winter, 241
Wire-feed welding, 354
WK. *See* Word Knowledge (WK)
Wood chisels, 365
Wooden mallets, 341
Word Knowledge (WK)
abstract, 69
breaking words apart, 73
diagnostic test, 21, 51
flash cards, xv, 517
in AFQT score, 3
in-context word meaning, 70, 86
Kaplan 3-step method, 72
no-context word meaning, 69, 81
paper and pencil vs. CAT, 69
positive or negative connotation, 80, 84
practice questions, 93, 500
predicting answers, 71, 86
prefixes, 75
process of elimination, 80, 86
question types, 70
roots of words, 79
suffixes, 75, 76, 77
test coverage, 2
vocabulary-building strategies, 89
Word meanings
breaking words apart, 73
context for,, 70, 81, 86
prefixes, 518, 75
suffixes,, 77
word roots,, 79
Word problems
Arithmetic Reasoning (AR), 113, 165

backsolving strategy, 118
English to math translation, 164
Mathematics Knowledge (MK), 113
Word roots
breaking words apart, 73
Greek and Latin,, 79
Work
conservation of energy and, 254
mechanics of, 388
physics of, 250
torque versus, 381
work-energy theorem, 388
Wrenches
descriptions of, 346
torque and length, 382
Wrist pin, 303

X
X-rays, 254

Y
Yellow dwarf (G2V) stars, 239
y-intercept, 196, 197

Z
Zero (0)
absolute zero (0 K), 247
exponent of, 141
in probability, 161
picking numbers strategy, 119
quadratic expression equaling, 179
resistance of circuit conductors, 275
y-intercept x-coordinate, 196
Zinc in diet, 208
Zygote, 217, 219

ASVAB
Verbal Strategy Sheet
KAPLAN

The Kaplan Method for Word Knowledge

STEP 1 Identify the word's meaning, or apply decoding strategies to guess its meaning.

STEP 2 Make a prediction.

STEP 3 Look for your prediction among the answer choices, or strategically eliminate wrong answer choices.

Two Types of Word Knowledge Questions:

1) No-Context Questions:
Use decoding strategies (looking at the word's prefix, suffix, and root), remembered context, or positive and negative charge to determine the meaning of the word.

2) In-Context Questions:
Refer to the clues and keywords in the sentence to determine the meaning of the word.

Using Word Parts: Many (but not all) long words are composed of the following parts, though not every long word has all of these parts.

Prefixes are found at the beginnings of words. Examples:

contra– against (contradictory, contraindication)

micro– very small (microscope, microchip)

pre– before, in front (predetermined, preface)

Suffixes are found at the ends of words. Examples:

–ist person who does (scientist, artist)

–less without, lacking (humorless, friendless)

–ment action of, state of being (establishment, merriment)

Roots can form the bases of words. Examples:

dict to say, to tell, to use words (dictation, dictionary)

test to bear witness (attest, testify)

vi life (vivisection, vivacious)

Consult the Appendix for a comprehensive list of prefixes, suffixes, and word roots.

The key to success in Word Knowledge on the ASVAB is a strong vocabulary.

Improve your vocabulary by:

- learning common prefixes, suffixes, and word roots
- reading as many books, newspapers, magazines, and web articles as possible
- making vocabulary flashcards when you encounter words you don't know
- using the words you are learning in daily conversations and daily correspondence

---

The Kaplan Method for Paragraph Comprehension

STEP 1 Read the question stem to identify your task.

STEP 2 Read the passage strategically.

STEP 3 Make a prediction.

STEP 4 Find the correct answer.

Strategy Tip

The ASVAB Paragraph Comprehension section is an open-book test. You don't need any outside knowledge to answer these questions correctly. Always refer back to the passage and find support for the correct answer.

Global Questions: In a question that asks you to identify the main idea of a passage, separate supporting details from opinions and recommendations to determine the author's overall point.

Which of the following is the main idea of the passage?

The purpose of the passage above is to

The passage above is primarily concerned with

Common Wrong Answer Types

- deal with just one small detail of the passage
- go beyond the scope of the passage
- contradict the information presented in the passage
- distort the author's opinion by overstating it

Detail Questions: In a question that asks you to find specific information stated in the passage, do not overanalyze or read too much into the question. The correct answer to a Detail Question will almost always be a paraphrase of something found directly in the passage.

According to the author, which of the following is a type of rug found in French castles?

The second step in constructing a picket fence is to

Which of the following is cited in the passage as an advantage of a retirement account?

Common Wrong Answer Types

- paraphrase more of the passage than is necessary
- focus on the wrong detail in the passage
- distort what the passage states

Inference Questions: In a question that asks for what is implied or suggested by the statements in a passage, piece together multiple pieces of information to make an inference or deduction.

Which of the following is implied by the passage?

The author apparently feels that

It can be inferred from the passage that

Based on the passage, which of the following is most likely true of 19th century paintings?

Common Wrong Answer Types

- contradict information in the passage
- bring in outside information that is not discussed in the passage
- distort the information presented in the passage
- exaggerate the author's view

Vocabulary-in-Context Questions: In a question that asks you for the meaning of a word used in context, find a word that can replace that word without altering the meaning of the sentence.

As it used in the passage, "breakthrough" most nearly means

Which of the following is the closest in meaning to "illuminating" as it is used in the passage above?

Common Wrong Answer Types

- provide one correct definition of the word, but not the way the word is used in the passage
- sound correct in the sentence, but not the passage as a whole

---

Conclusion Keywords

These words often signal an author's main point.

thus
in sum
in conclusion
therefore
hence
so
clearly
obviously
as a result
I suggest (or propose, or believe)
it follows that

Contrast Keywords

These words can signal the author's main point, if the author is disagreeing with someone else.

but
yet
however
on the other hand
instead
on the contrary
rather
nevertheless
in contrast

Evidence Keywords

These words often signal the facts, details, or other information an author uses to support the main point.

after all
because
since
for
due to
for example
an illustration of this
this can be seen from

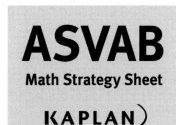

ASVAB
Math Strategy Sheet

KAPLAN

The Kaplan Method for ASVAB Math

STEP 1 Analyze the information given.
STEP 2 Identify what you are being asked for.
STEP 3 Solve strategically.
STEP 4 Confirm your answer.

Strategies for Solving Multiple-Choice Math Problems

▶ Backsolving

Use when there is an unknown in the question stem and numbers in the answer choices. Plug one of the choices into the question stem and see if the result is too large, too small, or just right. If the answer choices are arranged in numerical order, start with (B) or (C).

▶ Picking Numbers

Use when (1) there are variables in the question stem and variables in the choices or (2) there's a number (other than the answer) that the test maker doesn't provide and that would be helpful in solving the problem. Pick numbers that are permissible (allowed, given the problem) and manageable (easy to work with).

▶ Strategic Guessing Using Logic

Use when the answer choice has to have a certain property (such as being a perfect square, or being below a certain value). Eliminate answer choices that do not display that property.

Math How-Tos
Use correct order of operations:

Remember PEMDAS: Parentheses, Exponents and radicals, Multiplication and Division, Addition and Subtraction. Work from left to right.

$9 - 2 \times (5 - 3)^2 + 6 \div 3 =$
$9 - 2 \times (2)^2 + 6 \div 3 =$
$9 - 2 \times 4 + 6 \div 3 =$
$9 - 8 + 2 =$
$1 + 2 = 3$

Add or subtract fractions:

Find a common denominator. $\frac{1}{13} + \frac{1}{2} = \frac{2}{26} + \frac{13}{26} = \frac{15}{26}$

Multiply or divide fractions:

Multiply the numerators, then the denominators. To divide, invert the second fraction before multiplying. $\frac{3}{20} \times \frac{2}{5} = \frac{3 \times 2}{20 \times 5} = \frac{6}{100} = \frac{3}{50}$

$\frac{3}{20} \div \frac{2}{5} = \frac{3}{20} \times \frac{5}{2} = \frac{3 \times 5}{20 \times 2} = \frac{15}{40} = \frac{3}{8}$

Determine whether a number is divisible by another number:

Divisor	Divisibility Rule
2	All even numbers are divisible by 2.
3	Add up the individual digits of the number. If the total is divisible by 3, then the number itself is divisible by 3; for example, 243 is divisible by 3 because the sum of its digits is 2 + 4 + 3 = 9. However, 367 is not divisible by 3 because the sum of its digits is 3 + 6 + 7 = 16 and 16 is not a multiple of 3.
4	Take the last two digits and divide them by 2. If the result is even, the number is divisible by 4. If the result is odd, then the number is not divisible by 4.
5	All numbers ending in 5 or 0 are divisible by 5.
6	All *even* numbers that meet the test for divisibility by 3 are divisible by 6.
8	Divide the number by 2 twice; if the result is even, then the number is divisible by 8.
9	Add up the digits of the number; if the total is divisible by 9, then the number is divisible by 9.

Multiply or divide decimals:

To multiply decimals, multiply both numbers. Count how many digits are to the right of the decimal in both numbers and move the decimal over to the left that number of spaces in the result.
To divide decimals, move the decimal to the right in both numbers until each is a whole number.
To solve 3.11 × 2.2, multiply 311 × 22 = 6842
Then move the decimal to the left three places: 6.842
To divide 5.12 by 6.4, move the decimal in both numbers over to make 5.12 into a whole number:
5.12 ÷ 6.4 = 512 ÷ 640 = 0.8

Convert fractions to decimals or percents:

To express a fraction as a decimal, divide the numerator by the denominator. Multiply that by 100 to express as a percent. Remember these common fraction-decimal equivalencies:

$\frac{1}{2} = 0.5 = 50\%$ $\frac{1}{3} = 0.33\overline{3} = 33.\overline{3}\%$

$\frac{1}{4} = 0.25 = 25\%$ $\frac{1}{5} = 0.20 = 20\%$

$\frac{1}{8} = 0.125 = 12.5\%$ $\frac{1}{9} = 0.11\overline{1} = 11.\overline{1}\%$

$\frac{2}{3} = 0.66\overline{6} = 66.\overline{6}\%$

Perform operations with exponents:

$a^x \times a^y = a^{x+y}$
$a^x \div a^y = a^{x-y}$
$(a^x)^y = a^{xy}$
$(a^x)(b^x) = ab^x$
$a^{-x} = \frac{1}{a^x}$

When a negative number is raised to an even exponent, the result is positive. When a negative number is raised to an odd exponent, the result is negative.
When multiplying a number by a power of 10, as in scientific notation, the exponent simply represents the number of places to move the decimal. For example:
$1.75 \times 10^5 = 175,000$
$2.4 \times 10^{-4} = 0.00024$

Perform operations with radicals:

$\sqrt{a^2} = |a|$
$\sqrt{ab} = \sqrt{a} \times \sqrt{b}$
$\sqrt{\frac{a}{b}} = \frac{\sqrt{a}}{\sqrt{b}}$
$\sqrt{a+b}$ does NOT equal $\sqrt{a} + \sqrt{b}$ (and the same applies to subtraction)
$a^{\frac{1}{2}} = \sqrt{a}$

Simplify a radical:

Look for factors of the number under the radical sign that are perfect squares; then find the square root of those perfect squares. Pull those roots outside of the radical sign.

$\sqrt{200} = \sqrt{25 \times 8} = \sqrt{25 \times 4 \times 2}$
$= \sqrt{25} \times \sqrt{4} \times \sqrt{2} = 5 \times 2 \times \sqrt{2} = 10\sqrt{2}$

Calculate a factorial

Multiply the number by each positive integer smaller than that number.

$8! = 8 \times 7 \times 6 \times 5 \times 4 \times 3 \times 2 \times 1 = 40,320$

Find the prime factorization of a number:

Begin by identifying one prime factor, and then break the number down into smaller and smaller factors until only primes remain. For example, to find the prime factorization of 60:

$60 = 30 \times 2 = 15 \times 2 \times 2 = 5 \times 3 \times 2 \times 2$

Predict whether the result of a calculation will be positive or negative, even or odd:

pos + pos = pos
pos + neg = (outcome will take the sign of whichever addend has the larger absolute value)
pos × or ÷ pos = pos
pos × or ÷ neg = neg
neg × or ÷ neg = pos

odd ± odd = even
even ± even = even
even ± odd = odd
odd × odd = odd
even × even = even
even × odd = even

(There are no rules for predicting whether the result of division will be even or odd, since division does not always result in a whole number, and only whole numbers are even or odd.)

Find the mean (arithmetic average) of a set of numbers:

$\frac{sum\ of\ terms}{number\ of\ terms}$

The mean (arithmetic average) of 3, 4, 4, 6, and 8:
$\frac{3+4+4+6+8}{5} = \frac{25}{5} = 5$

Find the range of a set of numbers:

largest number − smallest number
The range of 3, 4, and 8: 8 − 3 = 5

Find the median of a set of numbers:

Find the middle number or (if the set has an even number of items) the mean of the two middle numbers.
The median of 3, 4, 4, 6, and 8: 4
The median of 3, 5, 8, and 9: $\frac{5+8}{2} = 6.5$

Find the mode of a set of numbers:

Find the number that repeats most often.
The mode of 3, 4, 4, 6, and 8: 4

Calculate probability:

number of desired possible outcomes
number of total possible outcomes

To calculate the probability that two events will occur, multiply the probabilities of each.
To calculate the probability that at least one of two independent events will occur, add the probabilities of each.

Calculate percent, whole, or part:

whole × percent (expressed as a decimal or fraction) = part
Given two parts of that equation, you can solve for the third. E.g., 18 is 60% of what number?
whole × .6 = 18
whole = 18 ÷ .6 = 30

Perform calculations involving rates:

distance = rate (that is, speed) × time
work performed = rate of work × time
Given two parts of that equation, you can solve for the third.
Given incomplete information and two journeys or work projects, set up a proportion to solve for the unknowns. For example, Joe can travel 62 miles on his bike in 5 hours. At that rate, how far could he travel in 7 hours?

$$\frac{62}{5} = \frac{x}{7}$$

Cross-multiply to solve for x.

Solve multi-part-journey problems:

total distance = average rate × total time

Multiply binomials:

Remember FOIL: first, outer, inner, last.
$(x + 3)(x - 2) = x^2 - 2x + 3x - 6 = x^2 + x - 6$

Solve a quadratic equation:

Manipulate the quadratic so that it is in the form $ax^2 + bx + c = 0$ (where a, b, and c can be positive or negative numbers). Then perform reverse-FOIL: that is, find two binomials that multiply to make the quadratic. This will usually yield two possible values for x. For example:
$$x^2 - 3x = 54$$
$$x^2 - 3x - 54 = 0$$
Find two numbers that add to −3 and multiply to −54.
$$(x - 9)(x + 6) = 0$$
$$x = 9 \text{ or } -6$$

These shortcuts may help on some quadratics:
$a^2 - b^2 = (a + b)(a - b)$
$a^2 + 2ab + b^2 = (a + b)(a + b) = (a + b)^2$
$a^2 - 2ab + b^2 = (a - b)(a - b) = (a - b)^2$

Solve a linear equation:

Isolate the variable you're solving for on one side of the equation. You may add, subtract, multiply, or divide both sides of the equation by variables or numbers, as long as you do the same thing to both sides.

Solve an inequality:

Follow the same steps as solving a linear equation, but remember these two rules:
(1) If you multiply or divide both sides of an inequality by a negative number, you must reverse the inequality sign.
(2) You cannot multiply or divide both sides of an inequality by a variable (since you do not know the sign of the variable).

Describe an angle as right, acute, obtuse, straight, or reflex:

angle measure = 90: right
angle measure < 90: acute
90 < angle measure < 180: obtuse
angle measure = 180: straight
angle measure > 180: reflex

Find angle measures, given two parallel lines and a transversal:

Corresponding angles are equal. For example, $a = e$.
Same-side interior angles are supplementary. For example, $c + f = 180$.
Opposite angles are equal, and alternate interior angles are equal. For example, $b = d = f$.
All four acute angles are equal. All four obtuse angles are equal.

Find the perimeter or area of a quadrilateral:

perimeter = 2(length) + 2(width)
area = length × width

Find the measure of an interior or exterior angle of a triangle:

The interior angles of a triangle add to 180.
An exterior angle of a triangle is equal to the sum of the two opposite interior angles.

$x + 40 + 95 = 180$
$y = 40 + 95$

Find the perimeter or area of a triangle:

perimeter: side + side + side
area: $A = \frac{1}{2} bh$, where b is the base of the triangle and h is the height (which is the perpendicular distance between the base and the vertex opposite the base)

Find the circumference (that is, perimeter) or area of a circle:

radius: half the distance across the middle of the circle
diameter: the distance across the middle of the circle, or $2r$
circumference: $C = 2\pi r$
area: $A = \pi r^2$

Use the Pythagorean theorem:

if you know the lengths of two sides of a right triangle (that is, a triangle with a 90 degree angle), you can calculate the third side.

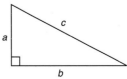

$a^2 + b^2 = c^2$
Memorize these ratios, often (but not always) displayed by the sides of right triangles:
3:4:5
5:12:13

Also, remember these proportions displayed by some right triangles:

The legs of a right triangle with angle measures 45:45:90 display this proportion: $x{:}x{:}x\sqrt{2}$

The legs of a right triangle with angle measures 30:60:90 display this proportion: $x{:}\ x\sqrt{3}{:}2x$

Use similar triangles to solve problems:

Similar triangles have the same angle measures as each other. Corresponding sides of these triangles are proportional.
$$\frac{3}{4} = \frac{x}{y} = \frac{6}{s}$$

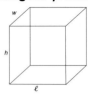

Find the volume or surface area of a cube or rectangular prism:

$V = \ell wh$
$SA = 2\ell w + 2wh + 2\ell h$

Find the volume or surface area of a cylinder:

$V = \pi r^2 h$
$SA = 2\pi r^2 + 2\pi rh$

Express the equation of a line in slope-intercept form:

$y = mx + b$, where m is the slope and b is the y-intercept

Calculate the slope of a line:

$$\text{slope} = \frac{rise}{run} \text{ or } \frac{change\ in\ y}{change\ in\ x}$$

A horizontal line has a slope of zero.
The slope of a vertical line is undefined.

Find the distance between two points on the coordinate plane:

Use the Pythagorean theorem. For example, to find the distance between points A and B below, first draw a right triangle with A and B as the two ends of the hypotenuse.

Find the distance from A to C and from B to C, and plug those distances into the Pythagorean theorem:
$$\left(\overline{AC}\right)^2 + \left(\overline{BC}\right)^2 = \left(\overline{AB}\right)^2$$
$$6^2 + 8^2 = \left(\overline{AB}\right)^2$$
$$100 = \left(\overline{AB}\right)^2$$
$$\overline{AB} = 10$$